JE

D0884610

Brooklyn College Studies on Society in Change
No. 10

Brooklyn College Studies on Society in Change

Distributed by Columbia University Press (Except No. 5)

Béla K. Király, Editor-in-Chief

1. *Tolerance and Movements of Religious Dissent in Eastern Europe.* Edited by B. K. Király. East European Monographs, 1975. Second printing, 1977.
2. *The Habsburg Empire in World War I.* Edited by R. A. Kann, B. K. Király, P. S. Fichtner. East European Monographs, 1976. Second printing, 1978.
3. *The Mutual Effects of the Islamic and the Judeo-Christian Worlds: The East European Pattern.* Edited by A. Ascher, T. Halasi-Kun, B. K. Király. Brooklyn College Press, 1979.
4. *Before Watergate: Problems of Corruption in American Society.* Edited by A. S. Eisenstadt, A. Hoogenboom, H. L. Trefousse. Brooklyn College Press, 1978.
5. *East Central European Perceptions of Early America.* Edited by B. K. Király and G. Barany. Lisse, The Netherlands: Peter de Ridder Press, 1977.
6. *The Hungarian Revolution of 1956 in Retrospect.* Edited by B. K. Király and Paul Jonas. East European Monographs, 1978.
7. Rita S. Miller. *Brooklyn, U.S.A.: Fourth Largest City in America.* Brooklyn College Press, 1979.
8. Janos Decsy. *Prime Minister Gyula Andrássy's Influence on Habsburg Foreign Policy.* East European Monographs, 1979.
9. Robert F. Horowitz. *The Great Impeacher: A Political Biography of James M. Ashley.* Brooklyn College Press, 1979.
10. *War and Society in East Central Europe during the 18th and 19th Centuries.* Vol. I. Edited by B. K. Király and Gunther E. Rothenberg. Brooklyn College Press, 1979.

War and Society in East Central Europe
Vol. I
*Special Topics and Generalizations on the
18th and 19th Centuries*

Béla K. Király and Gunther E. Rothenberg, Editors

BROOKLYN COLLEGE PRESS
DISTRIBUTED BY COLUMBIA UNIVERSITY PRESS
NEW YORK

1979

MW 9/80   13723

Table of Contents

List of Maps

Foreword

War and Society in East Central Europe during the 18th and 19th Centuries is the tenth volume published in the "Brooklyn College Studies on Society in Change" series. Five additional volumes are currently in various stages of planning and preparation. This book also introduces our new sub-series program which calls for the publication of multiple volumes dealing with the same general topic. This policy will make it possible to cover important subjects in greater depth.

The responses which the "Society in Change" series has received, both in scholarly recognition and in the level of sales, have been most gratifying. The favorable reviews encourage all those associated with the project to achieve the objective of maintaining both the quality and quantity of publications which have characterized the series to date.

A project of this nature, with many of the publications originating in broadly based conferences, is indebted for any success to more institutions and individuals than can be acknowledged here. But we do wish to acknowledge especially the participation of the Graduate School and University Center of CUNY and to express appreciation for their contributions to the series.

Finally, it is certain that the inspiration and dedication of one man—Professor Béla Király — made everything possible.

Nathan Schmukler
Dean, School of Social Science
Brooklyn College

May 1, 1979

Preface to the Series

The present volume is the first of a series which, when completed, hopes to present a comprehensive survey of the many aspects of War and Society in East Central Europe. The chapters of this and forthcoming volumes are selected from papers presented at a series of international, interdisciplinary, scholarly conferences conducted jointly by the "Brooklyn College Studies on Society in Change" and the Center for European Studies/East European Section at the Graduate School of CUNY.

These volumes deal with the peoples whose homelands lie between the Germans to the west, the Russians to the east and north, and the Mediterranean and Adriatic seas to the south. They constitute a particular civilization, an integral part of Europe, yet substantially different from the West. Within the area there are intriguing variations in language, religion, and government; so, too, are there differences in concepts of national defense, of the characters of the armed forces, and of the ways of waging war. Study of this complex subject demands a multidisciplinary approach; therefore, we have involved scholars from several disciplines, from universities and other scholarly institutions of the USA, Canada, and Western Europe, as well as the East Central European socialist countries.

Our investigation focuses on a comparative survey of military behavior and organization in these various nations and ethnic groups to see what is peculiar to them, what has been socially and culturally determined, and what in their conduct of war was due to circumstance. Besides making a historical survey, we try to define different patterns of military behavior, including the decision-making processes, the attitudes and actions of diverse social classes, and the restraints or lack of them shown in war.

We endeavor to present considerable material on the effects of social, economic, political, and technological changes, and of changes in the sciences and in international relations on the development of doctrines of national defense and practices in military organization, command, strategy, and tactics. We shall also present data on the social origins and mobility of the officer corps and the rank and file, on the differences between the officer corps of the various services, and above all, on the civil-military relationship and the origins of the East Central European brand of militarism. The studies will, we hope, result in a better understanding of the societies, governments, and politics of East Central Europe, most of whose peoples are now members of the Warsaw Treaty Organization, although one is a member of NATO and one is neutral.

Our methodology takes into account that in the last three decades the study of war and national defense systems has moved away from narrow concern with battles, campaigns, and leaders and has come to concern itself with the evolution of the entire society. In fact, the interdependence of changes in society and changes in warfare, and the proposition that military institutions closely reflect the character of the society of which they are a part have come to be accepted by historians, political scientists, sociologists, philosophers, and other students of war and national defense. Recognition of this fact constitutes one of the keystones of our approach to the subject.

Works in Western languages adequately cover the diplomatic, political, intellectual, social, and economic histories of these peoples and this area. In contrast, few substantial studies of their national defense systems have yet appeared in Western languages. Similarly, though some substantial, comprehensive accounts of the nonmilitary aspects of the history of the whole region have been published in the West, nothing has yet appeared in any Western language about the national defense systems of the area as a whole. Nor is there any study of the mutual effects of the concepts and practices of national defense in East Central Europe. Thus, this comprehensive study on War and Society in East Central Europe is a pioneering work.

The eighteenth and nineteenth centuries, the first period our efforts concentrate upon, are crucial for all these nations, for they are the era of nation-building. Many of these peoples became nation-states during the period, a development in which their armed forces played critical roles. Even in the case of the Poles, whose state was partitioned in the eighteenth century and was not to be reestablished until after the nineteenth century, insurrectionary armies played an important role in consolidating national consciousness.

The General Editors, of course, have the duty of assuring the comprehensive coverage, cohesion, internal balance, and scholarly standards of the series they have launched. They cheerfully accept this responsibility and intend this work to be neither a justification nor a condemnation of the policies, attitudes, or activities of any of the nations involved. At the same time, because so many different disciplines, languages, interpretations, and schools of thought are represented, their policy in this and in future volumes was and shall be not to interfere with the contributions of the various participants, but to present them as a sampling of the schools of thought and the standards of scholarship in the many countries to which the contributors belong.

<table>
<tr><td>December 31, 1978</td><td>Highland Lakes, New Jersey</td></tr>
<tr><td>West Lafayette, Indiana</td><td>Béla K. Király</td></tr>
<tr><td>Gunther E. Rothenberg</td><td>Brooklyn College and the</td></tr>
<tr><td>Purdue University</td><td>Graduate School of the</td></tr>
<tr><td></td><td>City University of New York</td></tr>
</table>

Acknowledgments

This volume is the product of research shared at scholarly conferences conducted in the "Program on Society in Change" at Brooklyn College and at the Center for European Studies, Graduate School of the City University of New York. No serious academic work can be done except in the proper milieu. Brooklyn College and CUNY Graduate School offered such a milieu. Many substantial as well as smaller gestures of support were extended to those who worked on this project by President John W. Kneller; Vice President and Provost Donald R. Reich; Nathan Schmukler, Dean of the School of Social Science; Ann Burton, Chairman of the Department of History at Brooklyn College; and by President Harold M. Proshansky, Vice President and Provost Hans J. Hillerbrand, and Elliot Zupnick, Director of the Center for European Studies at the Graduate School and University Center CUNY.

The research and conferences were generously funded by CUNY, the National Endowment for the Humanities, the Joint Committee on Eastern Europe of the American Council of Learned Societies and the Social Research Council, the International Research and Exchanges Board, and the Kosciuszko Foundation. The cost of printing was granted by the Brooklyn College Publications Committee, Brooklyn College Press, chaired by Edward L. Ochsenschlager, Professor and Chairman of the Department of Classics at Brooklyn College.

Fruitful exchanges of views were conducted with members of the School of Slavonic and East European Studies, University of London, Historisches Institut der Universität Wien, and the Austrian Institute at New York, among others.

Publication was furthered by the Assistant Program Director, Theodore Lauer, the staff of the Department of History, Brooklyn College, and by Graduate Fellows Jay Stone and Jon R. Jucovy. The greatest share of administrative work was done by Mrs. Gloria Feig, Secretary of the "Program on Society in Change," School of Social Science, Brooklyn College. The maps were prepared by Mrs. Ida Etelka Romann. The typing pool of Purdue University helped in the

6174

or.

typing of manuscripts. The final preparation of this volume was assisted by the careful copy-editing of Helene Zahler. It is a pleasure and privilege to express warm thanks to all those colleagues, foundations, and institutions.

Highland Lakes, March 19, 1979

Béla K. Király
Editor-in-Chief
Brooklyn College Studies on
Society in Change

EAST CENTRAL EUROPE IN 1713

0 50 100 200
Miles

KINGDOM OF SWEDEN

North Sea

KARELIA
St. Petersburg
INGRIA
Nystad
Novgorod
Narva
ESTONIA
Stockholm
LIVONIA
GOTLAND
Riga
Baltic Sea
COURLAND
LITHUANIA
RUSSIAN EMPIRE
Smolensk
Copenhagen
PRUSSIA
Danzig
Grodno
Minsk
BRANDENBURG
Hanover
Berlin
Warsaw
POLAND
Kiev
SAXONY
Lublin
Poltava
Rossbach
Dresden
SILESIA
HOLY
Prague
Cracow
Lemberg
ROMAN
BOHEMIA
MORAVIA
EMPIRE
AUSTRIA
Tisza
BAVARIA
Vienna
Danube
KINGDOM
MOLDAVIA
Sereth
BESSARABIA
Innsbruck
Salzburg
Buda
OF
TRANSYLVANIA
TYROL
Pest
HUNGARY
Milan
Trieste
Drave
Zenta
Temesvár
WALLACHIA
Black Sea
Venice
CROATIA
SLAVONIA
BANAT
①
Bucharest
REPUBLIC
①
②
Danube
TUSCANY
PAPAL
Belgrade
②①
OF VENICE
Adriatic Sea
BOSNIA
BULGARIA
Rome
STATES
SERBIA
Sofia
Constantinople
Ragusa
KINGDOM
MONTENEGRO
OTTOMAN
Naples
OF
Cetinje
EMPIRE
NAPLES
Salonika
Tyrrhenian
Sea
Aegean
Sea
Smyrna
Athens
Reggio
MOREA

i.e. roman

NOTES

① TO HABSBURGS IN 1718

② TO THE OTTOMAN EMPIRE IN 1739

Béla K. Király

War and Society in Western and East Central Europe during the Eighteenth and Nineteenth Centuries: Similarities and Contrasts

This study is part of a three-year research project, which includes the work of scholars from various countries and disciplines on special areas and periods of time. These scholars intend to complete the work by 1981. A synthesis would have been more warranted as the concluding chapter of the multivolume work we are planning than as its introduction, and indeed such an essay will close the last volume. This introduction, then, is not a final synthesis but an effort to state some questions we intend to tackle and to present some case studies and a few generalizations, samples of what we intend to do and how we are proceeding.

In considering the relationship between war and society in East Central Europe in the context of history of warfare, we confront as the first question: Why study the eighteenth and nineteenth centuries together? What common denominators distinguish these centuries from those immediately preceding and following? What makes them similar to each other? Apparently, the two centuries could not be more different. The eighteenth century saw the decline of the feudal past and was the harbinger of the liberal nineteenth-century future. The latter was so extraordinarily dynamic an age that it makes its predecessor seem static. Yet there is a common feature: the two centuries combined form a watershed between the era when infantry firepower began really to have a substantial effect on tactics — the first half of the eighteenth century — and the era when warfare's power to destroy made men wonder whether their control over this awesome power had reached its limit. The common denominator of the eighteenth and nineteenth

The author wishes to express his indebtedness to the John Simon Guggenheim Memorial Foundation for a fellowship grant which made the basic research possible, and to the National Endowment for the Humanities for a research grant which made it possible to complete the research of which this essay contains a part.

centuries, then, is the process of transformation that changed warfare from its limited eighteenth-century form to the late nineteenth-century modern form, which was the stepping stone to total war of the twentieth century. That, of course, may appear rather a vague argument for linking the two centuries into a single subject for investigation. For East Central Europe, however, the bond between the two centuries is much stronger than for Western Europe. The period as a whole is crucial for this region; it is the era of nation-building. Almost all these peoples (the national groups of the Habsburg empire being the exceptions) became nation-states between the end of the eighteenth and the end of the nineteenth century. And in this development, their armed forces played critical roles. Even in the case of the Poles, whose state was partitioned in the eighteenth century, not to be re-established until after World War I, insurrectionary armies played an exceptional role in consolidating national consciousness. From the point of view of East Central Europe, tying the two centuries together is eminently justified.

The predominant Western European armed forces in the eighteenth century were the standing armies of absolute kings. In the words of J.F.C. Fuller: ". . . the army took the form of a disciplined body of long service troops, set apart from the civil population, and rigorously restricted as to its conduct in peace and war. . . ."[1] This definition shows the potential of and the limitations on eighteenth-century standing armies. Rigorous discipline, separation from the civilian population, and numerous other restrictions imposed on the soldiery made the standing army a tool of the monarch alone. Long terms of service assured a high degree of professionalism and efficiency. But the poverty of state treasuries and the low capacity of the preindustrial manufacturing system, drastically limited both the size and the range of action of such armies. Wars waged by these armies had to be, and were, limited in goals, scope, and final effects. These wars were, in fact, the only kind compatible with the balance of power, the prevailing system of international relations. "Restricted warfare," Ferrero comments, "was one of the loftiest achievements of the eighteenth century. It belongs to a class of hot-house plants which can only thrive in an aristocratic and qualitative civilization. We are no longer capable of it. It is one of the fine things we have lost as the result of the French Revolution."[2]

Ferrero and Fuller thus rather wistfully describe the fading of the eighteenth-century society and army. The American Revolution initiated a transition in warfare by bringing back the classic concept of the citizen-soldier. This concept was expanded by the French Revolution, which first established the nation-in-arms, in which every citizen regardless of race, sex, or age had a function in the defense of the country. Modern military science, which emerged in the post-Napoleonic era, and the modern Prussian type of general staff provided the necessary theory and the institutionalized military leadership to these ever-growing masses in arms. The concomitant spread of the Industrial Revolution at last gave true meaning to the *levée en masse* introduced by the French Revolution. For only an industrialized economy could equip, supply, transport, and continuously feed a mass army from current production and so assure that the limits on its numbers, speed of movement, and range of action, would decrease. Universal obligation to military service became technologically feasible. Popularly elected constitutional governments could exact such sacrifices. (Universal military service and universal manhood suffrage have more than their initials in common.) The political and economic changes of the late eighteenth and early nineteenth centuries thus made possible the dawn of modern war in the second half of the nineteenth century; war fought by very large, highly motivated citizens' armies whose weapons, transport, and food supplies depended on mature, productive industrial economies.

The Franco-Sardinian-Austrian and the Bismarckian wars in Europe and the Civil War in America were the first wars fought under these modern conditions. The essence of two centuries of transformation in national defense and war, on the one hand, and of political, social, and economic change, on the other, is found in four basic shifts: (1) from a relatively peaceful age to an age of violence; (2) from the standing armies of eighteenth-century absolute kings to the nation-in-arms; (3) from limited to modern warfare in the late nineteenth century and to total war in the twentieth; (4) from the balance-of-power system to the twentieth-century balance of terror.

We ask now whether there is any difference between the Western and East Central European evolution of warfare, and what the differences may be? The full answer will be given only in the last volume of this series. For the time being, three samples of East Central European warfare will be presented to allow us to glance at its peculiarities and to see some similarities to and differences from their Western counterparts. These three samples describe certain features of East Central European standing armies; they show the revolutionary nature of warfare during the period and the predominance of war for liberation in both centuries. Finally, they offer a comparative analysis of the

Hungarian and Polish eighteenth-century wars of liberation, the Rákóczi Insurrection of 1703–1711 and the Kościuszko Insurrection of 1794, both of which, in various respects, embodied what might be considered characteristic East Central European forms of warfare.

From East Central European Professional Standing Armies to Nations-in-Arms

The only truly East Central European standing army at the turn of the century was the army of the Polish-Lithuanian Commonwealth. It entered the eighteenth century as a significant force, bearing the marks of the reforming zeal of John III Sobieski, the last native king of prepartition Poland (1674–96). The many reforms this soldier-king introduced into both the army of the *Korona* (Crown of Poland) and the army of the Grand Duchy of Lithuania included the transformation of infantry by increasing its fire power — through a 30 percent reduction of pikemen, with the concomitant increase of soldiers equipped with firearms. Sobieski also modernized training, improved discipline, increased tactical efficiency, and stressed cooperation in battle between the various branches of the army. Although the cavalry was still destined to launch the final blow, a massive charge against the enemy, already shaken by the infantry and artillery; nonetheless, typical, traditional Polish cavalry warfare, large-scale, rapid mobile operations behind enemy lines, was not discontinued but rather encouraged. In such operations, the infantry support that the cavalry needed in actual combat was supplied by dragoons.

Reform continued even after Sobieski's death. In 1701 the flintlock musket, complete with bayonet, was introduced; these changes, combined with up-to-date tactical doctrines and good discipline, kept the Polish standing army abreast of Western development for a while. But the remarkable performance of the Polish army in relieving Vienna from the protracted Ottoman siege, in September 1683, was in fact the swan song of that kind of Polish armed force which was a factor that European powers could disregard only at their peril. The eighteenth century witnessed the rapid decline of this force, in direct relation to the decay of the Polish state. The army's retrogression in numbers, equipment, discipline, and training gradually made it an anachronism. Even the traditional Polish cavalry lost its former prominence. In prepartition Poland, financial, political, and other domestic difficulties caused the army to reduce its effectives even beyond the official budget estimates. The Kingdom of Poland, proper, was supposed to keep only a meagre force, 8,000 strong, but it maintained only 4,700 men in the army. The Grand Duchy of Lithuania was supposed to have an army of 2,300 strong, but only 1,500 effectives served under arms[3] before the first partition of Poland.

There is no need to drag Marshal de Saxe into East Central European military history, his desire and defeated effort to become the sovereign of the Duchy of Courland, notwithstanding.[4] But among his remarkable essays on war there is a study on Poland which makes exciting and informative reading on at least two counts: It vividly indicates the Polish war potential in mid-eighteenth century — in that respect it is indeed East Central European military history. Secondly, the Marshal presents a remarkably nonapologetic recipe for the conquest of Poland. The essay is a pragmatic, professional description of how a modern army should conquer a country whose economy, transportation, and system of defense are all underdeveloped and inadequate. From these pages, Marshal de Saxe, one of the foremost captains of the age, emerges completely enmeshed in his professional calling, scrupulously sticking to his own theme, the technique of military conquest; he remains totally unaware that he is advocating an act, ruthlessly aggressive politically and bloodily destructive of an innocent population.

Polanders [he writes] "make war in such a vague and irregular manner that if an enemy makes a point of pursuing them, he will thereby be presently rendered incapable of opposing their continual inroads. It is much more prudent, therefore, not to pursue them at all, but to possess himself of certain posts upon the rivers, to fortify them, to erect barracks for his troops, and to raise contributions throughout the provinces. . . ."[5] The Poles have no artillery worth mentioning, no siege tools nor ammunition enough to challenge the strong points an occupying force might erect. Poles have only cavalry. The Poles waged unconventional warfare with customs strange to Western armies. In 1716, Saxe claims, ". . . troops which surrendered on terms were massacred, but the eighty regular horsemen, who defended themselves at Jarislaw (sic), and marched 100 leagues to Warsaw could not be defeated by the Poles and reached the capital city with only sixteen men lost. . . ."[6] In other words, disciplined, cohesive, regular professional forces were, in Saxe's view, so superior that they could match irregulars many times over their own strength.

Polish cavalry was extremely light — it could ride thirty to forty miles a day in very large bodies and fall upon the enemy before proper reconnaissance could even be completed. Polish peasants and common people in the cities readily gave their cavalry compatriots intelligence. The only counter to such a cavalry army was a system of scattered infantry strongpoints. Therefore, de Saxe recommends conquest and fortification of the northern cities — Danzig (Gdańsk), Thorn (Toruń) — as bases of operation, supplied from the sea. From there, the conqueror could gradually advance inland, building more and more fortified places. "The whole country would be so effectually covered by this disposition, that it must infallibly be reduced to the necessity of submitting patiently to the yoke...." All this, Saxe estimates, could be done by 48,000 infantry and 3,800 horse. The means of conquest should be earthworks rather than battles.[7]

Even the necessary artillery could be manufactured in the area. The Swedes would produce light pieces with carriages in great quantity and cheap; all of these could be shipped down the Vistula River to the forts. Controlling the country with the network of fortifications enables you "... to offer what terms of accommodation you please; [you] can impose your own laws, and see them carried into execution...."[8]

Marshal de Saxe's recipe for the conquest of Poland is a blueprint for war against nonregular forces. Strong points at mutually supporting distances, located at waterways, through which they could be supplied, assure the conquerer that its "yoke" will be securely imposed. This indeed was what the British tried in America, during the Revolution, and during the Boer War. It is not too much to say that Saxe's blueprint was tried by the French in Southeast Asia as well as in Algeria, and failed. In the same way, Saxe's was the basic idea behind the American "pacification" efforts that miscarried in Vietnam. What de Saxe describes as the best method of conquest was studied and faced from the other side of the hill by twentieth-century "irregulars" like Mao-Tse-tung, Ernesto Che Guevera, Vo Nguyen Giap, and others.

The destruction of Poland, however, was not achieved by the methods de Saxe recommended, but by massive conventional warfare of three great powers, against which the Poles were all but defenseless. Before the partitions, however, a remarkable revival occurred. The reforms after the first partition included the fundamental transformation and modernization of the army. The law of 1789 called for a modern force of 100,000 men. Political as well as financial difficulties, however, proved this a utopian expectation much beyond the realm of reality. The principle of voluntary enlistment, which the law envisaged, did not work; the projected effectives had to be reduced to 60,000 men. Even this number could not be secured. The Prussian type of cantonal system was therefore introduced. Every fifty farms owned by the crown and/or the clergy and every hundred farms owned by the nobility had to send one man to the new army. A modest improvement was achieved, yet the projected number of men could not be secured. Yet those who did join the army were very well trained, on the basis of up-to-date tactical doctrine. In short, the army organized after the first partition of Poland was made into a force of great combat value, albeit restricted size. This army became a nucleus, which could and indeed did expand rapidly in the initial stages of the Kościuszko Insurrection of 1794 into a force of 100,000.[9] This served as a rallying point for the more general uprising, a role quite similar to that of General Washington's Continental Army during the American Revolution.

The Poles had standing armies later, during the relatively short life of the Grand Duchy of Warsaw, and again in the Russian-controlled Kingdom of Poland, which disappeared after the November insurrection.

Another major East Central European standing army was the Hungarian portion of the Habsburg armed forces. Ever since the Ottoman onslaught in the sixteenth century, Hungary maintained a permanent military force in fortified areas which stretched from the Adriatic Sea to the Upper Tisza region.[10] These permanent forces were combined with the periodic call up of the Hungarian noble *levée* (*insurrectio*). Count Miklós Zrínyi (1620–64), prominent as a Hungarian commander and military theorist, strongly advocated a native standing army as the one sure means for liberating Hungary from Ottoman rule.[11] It was to no avail; the Habsburg dynasty prevented the creation of such force, lest an autonomous Hungarian standing army turn against the Habsburgs rather than the Turks. Hungary was liberated by standing armies in which Hungarians could and did serve as individuals, but not by a Hungarian national force.

During the Wars for Independence of Ferenc II Rákóczi (1703–1711), efforts were made to establish a permanent military force with an officers' school and a professional officer corps. But this war had only an indirect effect on future Hungarian military institutions. The war ended in the Compromise of Szatmár in 1711. The Hungarians acknowledged the Habsburg dynasty's hereditary rights in the male line. The dynasty, on the other hand, reestablished Hungary's constitutional self-government and acknowledged all the traditional privileges of the estates, including the tax-exempt status of the nobility. The dynasty's effort to tax the Hungarian nobility, as it taxed the nobility of the hereditary provinces, failed. Thus the substantial funds earmarked for military purposes which the taxation of the Hungarian nobles was expected to provide had to be supplemented from other sources. The solution was a continuation of the Szatmár Compromise. As in so many other compromises between the dynasty and the Hungarian estates, the serfs paid the bill. The dynasty persuaded the diet of 1715 to adopt a law which established the Hungarian standing army (*állandó hadsereg*). This army was to be an integral part of the Habsburg forces, maintained at Hungary's (that is, the serfs') expense. The law stated that the nobility were obliged to appear in arms, in defense of the country, and that, if necessary, the monarch would enforce the obligation. The law further stipulated that since this form of defense was insufficient, a Hungarian standing army, made up of both natives and foreigners, was to be established. Recruits and the tax (*contributio* or *subsidium*) needed to maintain them were to be voted by the estates assembled in the diet. The statute remained in force until the April laws of 1848 were promulgated. For a century and a half, this system represented three political and social realities prevailing in Hungary:

(1) Only serfs served; the taxes needed for the upkeep of the army were paid by serfs and burghers alone. The nobility's contribution to national defense, the noble *levée,* was indeed summoned occasionally, and fought with considerable effect during the Seven Years War. During the French Revolutionary and Napoleonic wars, it was called up several times, but fought only once, at the Battle of Győr on June 24, 1809. The nobles' army was smashed by Napoleon's easternmost column. There was a prolonged debate on the causes of the debacle. Some called it a shameful cowardly affair, others depicted it as the last gallant stand of the noble *levée.* Whether individual nobles in this battle were heroic or cowardly was irrelevant. The *levée* was utterly obsolete; it could not stand against the modern equipment, training, and cohesion of the masses under Napoleon's command. Never again was the *levée* called to arms.

(2) The Hungarian army (*állandó hadsereg*), an integral part of the Habsburg standing army, was as modern as any other unit of that force, but like the rest, the Hungarian army was under the exclusive authority of the monarch; the Hungarian estates had no influence over its organization, command, and/or conduct. Hence the army was less a national defense force in Hungary's service than a means to further Habsburg power within the empire and internationally.

(3) Because the diet had to vote war taxes and recruits, the nobility, the dominant factor in the diet, gained political leverage. The nobles could, and often did, refuse to vote taxes and/or recruits until the

monarch accepted their views on other matters. The Hungarian standing army thus meant burdens for the nonprivileged, political bargaining power for the privileged, and a considerable asset for the dynasty. The units of the standing army were housed in the serfs' dwellings because barrack construction, a general trend in the West, started late in Hungary and moved very slowly.

In the 1790-92 Hungarian revolt, feudal and protonationalist though it was, a grass-root tendency began to incorporate the Hungarian standing army into the Hungarian body politic. There were stirrings in Hungarian units. Officers, commissioned and noncommissioned, signed petitions demanding a Hungarian supreme command, Hungarian as the language of command, and greater advancement for native officers and noncoms.[12] This movement failed, however, when another compromise between the estates and the dynasty was reached in 1792. The ever-increasing uproar of the French Revolution hastened the closing of ranks between the dynasty and the Hungarian estates.

In the revolution of 1848-49, many Hungarian regiments of the Habsburg army sided with the revolution. Many soldiers scattered in Habsburg lands deserted their stations and came home to join the Hungarian revolutionary forces. Those stationed in Italy, however, were forced to follow Habsburg orders.

Only with the Compromise of 1867 did an autonomous Hungarian *honvéd*, a new standing army, emerge again albeit until 1908 only as an auxiliary of the imperial-royal army. Nonetheless it was the most characteristically Hungarian national armed force since 1849; it fought quite efficiently through World War I and ended as that war did.[13]

At the southern flank of East Central Europe, in the Balkans, there were no typical standing armies during the eighteenth century. Nearest, were the mercenary forces of the Danubian princes which were abolished in 1711. In the nineteenth century on the other hand (when in the north, except for the Hungarian standing army until 1849, and the Polish standing army until 1830, no such force existed before 1867), all the Balkan nations gradually established their own standing armies. These, however, were already basically different from the eighteenth-century professional armies. Born in revolutionary wars of national liberation, evolving into truly national armies, in fact into nations-in-arms, they represented to an increasing degree the Western concept of modern national defense. Article V of the Treaty of Adrianople of 1829 established the standing armies of the Danubian Principalities. The Moldavian army maintained 1,091, the Wallachian, 4,673 men under arms.[14] Article VII of the *Hatti serif* of 1830 acknowledged the existence of the Serbian national army; the London Protocol of 1830 that of the Greek national army. The Greek officers' revolt of 1843 secured a constitutional monarchy for Greece, but the military's interference in political affairs set a pattern which was followed by the officers' rebellion of October 1862. In other words, the growth of national standing armies in the Balkans was accompanied by the threat such armies often pose for civilian government: militarism and military domination.

East Central European Revolutionary Warfare: The Cycle of Wars for Liberation

The pivotal contrast between Western and East Central European warfare throughout the centuries under consideration was that, in the West, wars were limited in goal, in scope, and, concomitantly, in their results; in East Central Europe, on the other hand, wars were often ideological, more violent, with far less limited goals and more lasting results.

These tendencies, in turn, had roots in the previous centuries, when many of the wars waged in East Central Europe were between alien cultures, rather than between members of the same culture, as in the West. East Central Europe was the borderland where the Christian West fought its centuries-long struggle with the Islamic Ottoman power. Even when the great powers of the two opposite camps were at peace, a major portion of East Central Europe remained a zone of protracted, violent, unconventional small wars between people who belonged to different civilizations.

East Central Europeans fought their small wars alone and served as auxiliaries in the armies of the major powers — often on both sides — during major wars; even then, they generally carried on irregular warfare. The knowledge of, and skill in, this kind of warfare which East Central Europeans had amassed during the centuries was utilized for their own purposes first by the Ottomans, then by Habsburgs and Romanovs. Russia and Austria gradually incorporated East Central European contingents into their military establishments.

East Central Europeans in the service of the Great Powers remained most effective when they were permitted to retain their traditional command and organizational structure, their internal autonomy, and their unconventional tactics. As the two Great Powers tried first to regulate their military behavior, then to incorporate these units as the most cheaply sustained parts of their standing armies, their efficiency declined. Circumstances rather than internal strength kept the troops of the Habsburg Military Border in existence into the late nineteenth century and retained the Cossack military structure in Russia until the end of World War I.

At the opening of the period we are studying, East Central European military formations, their command structure and tactics, were quite alien to Western European military doctrine and practices. Yet it was not these military considerations that distinguished East Central European warfare from war in Western Europe, but ideology, politicosocial concepts, goals, and expectations, as well as experience and tradition. No lesser expert than Guibert reminded his Western readers that such warfare could be fought successfully only by those who had a military tradition like that of East Central Europeans. We shall deal with Guibert later; let us now turn to an earlier observer of East Central European irregular warfare, Lieutenant-General Feuquieres (1648–1711).

General Feuquieres analyzed the Hungarian insurrection of the 1670s and 1680s. That insurrection was a response to the execution of the leaders of Wesselényi *Fronde* (April 30–December 1, 1671), the occupation of Hungary by German troops, and the suppression of the Hungarian constitutional government and its replacement on February 27, 1673, by a *gubernium,* an institution of absolute rule headed by the Grand Master of the Teutonic Order, Johann Ampringen. The rapidly spreading insurrection secured French cooperation; this brought into Hungary a French-Polish force, 2,000 strong, commissioned by Louis XIV. Hence the intimate French experience with this war. The insurrection raged to nearly the end of the century; its leader since November 1, 1678, was a leading Hungarian aristocrat, Count Imre Thököly.[15]

General Feuquieres correctly recognized the precondition of this protracted insurrection as the precondition of any war of liberation: a high degree of motivation among a large number of warriors. That motivation grows out of sociopolitical doctrines, interests, and goals. Feuquieres emphasized that the Hungarians were fighting for the constitutional prerogatives of their country which the Habsburg rulers tried to suppress by "Poison, Dagger, and Murder of the [Hungarian] Grandees. . . ."[16] He asserted that "the Hungarian cause was just," for the Habsburg rulers had violated their obligations as sovereigns. These obligations include, according to Feuquieres, circumspect administration. General sedition is usually the sign of a policy which incenses large portions of the population. That is what the Habsburgs did in

Hungary, Feuquieres claims, "if the Emperor, had not distressed the Protestants and the Grandees of Hungary . . . if he had not subverted the Privileges of the whole Nation . . . this Commotion would not have been so general as it proved. . . ."[17]

Feuquieres' observations were not isolated. Guibert, as well as Duteil, Wimpfen, and the ambitious and diligent translator and interpreter of late eighteenth-century, French military works, Lieutenant-Colonel John MacDonald, also wrote about the East Central European military experience. The French officers who participated in the late seventeenth-century Hungarian insurgent wars either as combatants or as military advisors were much impressed by the performance of Hungarian light horse, and brought several *huszárokat* (*hussars*, light cavalrymen) back to France. This inspired Marshal Luxembourg to raise in 1692 the first French hussar regiment (called *mortagni*).[18] Marshal Villars then created a second, and the Elector of Bavaria presented the King of France with a third complete light horse regiment. Marshal Brissac formed the first dragoon regiment on the same pattern. The French adaptation of the Hungarian military experience was then copied all over Europe, as was natural, for the French army was considered the foremost continental armed force, and its methods were often accepted by other European armies.

Guibert describes the Hungarian light horse as basically dragoon troops. They did not wear boots or spurs. They fought as infantry, their horses tied together two by two and left behind the firing line. Guibert explains that early in the eighteenth century the Hungarian estates had made their peace with the Habsburg dynasty.[19] Thus Maria Theresa was able to incorporate into her armed forces numerous Hungarian *huszár* regiments, which, like the Croat infantry, used irregular tactics. The first Hungarian troops fighting for the dynasty appeared in Flanders during the War of the Austrian Succession. The French invaders of Bohemia, Guibert claims, were defeated primarily by Croat and Hungarian light troops.[20]

Guibert warns that it would be absurd to counter these East Central European light troops and their irregular tactics with Western light troops attempting to carry on irregular warfare which needs a tradition and long experience. Only troops who had both — the East Central Europeans — could use such tactics. The West, which lacked both experience and tradition, could not employ them. Yet, both the French and Prussian armies increased their light troops during the Seven Years War. But they did not achieve the expected success, for all their increased numbers. Guibert points out that light troops are useful in both irregular and conventional warfare. They do not depend on magazines and are extremely maneuverable, excelling in advance and as flank and rear guard as well as in reconnaissance duties. For lack of good light troops, Frederick had to employ his most trusted regular troops in such assignments.

Guibert was aware that light troops and unconventional warfare had sociopolitical prerequisites. For such warfare, he wrote, requires "a vigorous undaunted people superior to others in point of government and courage. . . ." Guibert, referring to the Hungarian example, summarizes the proper use of light troops: reconnaissance; harassing the enemy, most especially during the night. But they must also know how to fight in regular tactics; they must be picked fighters, not deserters, whom Frederick the Great pressed into his light troops. Guibert warns that the major part of a modern army must consist of regular, not irregular troops. Light troops able to use irregular tactics should be only a small portion of the army, a force 1,000 to 1,200 strong would suffice — two-thirds of them should be hussars.[21]

Lieutenant-Colonel MacDonald claimed that the future belonged to the light cavalry, which would replace heavy cavalry and be the dominant mobile service in all armies.[22] The light horse system was introduced in Britain with the establishment of the first British dragoon regiment as early as 1681.[23] In sum, then, East Central European military patterns of warfare had a considerable influence on the West during the eighteenth century.

All these late eighteenth-century military theorists were fascinated by the contrast between Western and East Central European warfare. Most of them restricted their remarks to the professional military aspects of the issue; others, like Guibert understood that political, social, and ideological factors lay at the foundation of the contrast. Indeed the typical soldiers in the standing armies of Western absolute kings had no vested interest in the war aims of their masters; hence they had small motivation to fight better. Only brutal discipline kept them in the ranks. A Western soldier could either fight the "enemy" and probably survive, or try to desert — and be killed if caught. Whether East Central Europeans fought the Ottomans or the neighboring Christian Great Powers, even when the struggle began as banditry, in the final stage, they fought for ideals. These mobilized a great portion of the population. East Central European wars were therefore more intense than balance-of-power wars in the West. In fact, a cycle of East Central European revolutionary wars commenced at the dawn of the period of our study and continued with ever-increasing intensity throughout the epoch. For the eighteenth- and nineteenth-century history of East Central Europe is the history of wars for national independence.

A typical East Central European revolutionary war opened the century: the Hungarian War for Independence — the Insurrection of Ferenc II Rákóczi (1703–1711). Another similar conflict, the Polish War for Independence (the Kościuszko Insurrection) almost closed the century. The Rákóczi war lasted as long as the American Revolution, more than eight years, Kościuszko's struggle began March 24, 1794, and ended with the capitulation of Warsaw on November 5, seven and a half months later.

Both the Polish and the Hungarian wars for independence were diametrically opposite to contemporary warfare in Western Europe. In many respects, the former resembled the American and French revolutions. So did the wars of liberation of the Balkan nations which started with the First Serbian Revolution (1804–1813). The mid-nineteenth century witnessed the revolutions of 1848–49, a series of upheavals all over East Central Europe. In the military sense, the most intense of these was Hungary's War for Independence. The army of Lajos Kossuth could be subdued only by the joint forces of the two reactionary dynasties, the Habsburgs and the Romanovs.

What began in Serbia in 1804 continued all over the Balkans through the rest of the nineteenth century. One nation after another took up arms to free itself from the Ottoman yoke. By the Act of Berlin (1878), all the Balkan nations, except Albania, were acknowledged as sovereign nation-states, although the liberation of all their national territories had to wait until the end of World War I. Meanwhile, with the Balkan wars, the cycle of wars of liberation came to a close.

This volume deals predominantly with revolutionary warfare in East Central Europe. The generalizations of this volume on this aspect of military history are nearly complete as far as the Balkans are concerned. They are less complete with respect to the northern and central zones of the area. We shall make this good in forthcoming volumes of this series. Until then, however, in order to strike a better balance, it seems necessary to present a comprehensive analysis of the eighteenth-century Polish and Hungarian wars of national liberation.

Eighteenth-Century Hungarian and
Polish Wars for Liberation

The Polish Insurrection was in an interdependent relationship with the French Revolution. The Russian empire did not participate in the conservative Great Powers' effort to defeat the French Revolution before — and anticipating — the final partition of Poland. The Prussians fought the French with decreasing interest and intensity as they shifted troops to be ready to share the booty with Russia during the second partition, and with Austria and Russia during the third. Several Polish historians assert that by this diversion of the war potentials of the Great Powers to Poland, the Poles virtually saved the French Revolution by their own sacrifice. And their claim deserves serious consideration.

The Rákóczi Insurrection, on the other hand, bore a close relationship both to the War of the Spanish Succession (1701–1715) and the Great Northern War (1700–1721). Because of the former, the Habsburg dynasty had to pull out most of its troops from Hungary and transfer them to the Italian and Western European theaters. In Transylvania alone, a substantial Habsburg garrison was kept to face the Ottoman empire. Only small garrisons were left in royal Hungary to guard certain key forts. This military vacuum gave the insurgents a chance to act. Peasant leaders, Albert Kis and Tamás Esze,[24] launched their first military action in 1697 before this evacuation and were promptly defeated. But as the Habsburg troops left the country, these same leaders felt that the time was ripe for another try. They convoked a meeting of peasant dissident leaders of the upper Tisza region. The vision of the assembled peasants was quite statesmanlike. They foresaw that achieving their goals was possible only by a nationwide armed struggle, and that required the cooperation of the nobility. For a national leader, they needed an aristocrat of the highest possible reputation and prestige. Thus, they turned to the exiled Prince Ferenc Rákóczi.[25] The meeting between the representatives of the peasant insurgents and Rákóczi took place at Brzezan in Poland where he was living in exile. An agreement was struck between them, Rákóczi accepting the leadership. The Brzezan agreement fused two movements, the nobility's resistance to the unconstitutional tyrannical rule of the Habsburg dynasty and a popular (*kuruc*) grassroots insurrection. For the first time in Hungarian history the traditions and experiences of resistance by the noble estate was joined with the popular struggle for social and economic improvement. The synthesis of the two gave the movement the broadest social foundations and was directed against Habsburg absolutism. Rákóczi's extraordinary social position, as a descendant of Transylvanian princes, Prince of the Holy Roman Empire, bearer of the Golden Fleece, the richest landlord of Hungary, tried to and indeed did bring the Hungarian struggle into the orbit of European foreign policy.[26]

The Polish War for Independence was initiated by the *szlachta,* whose status placed them at the diametrically opposite end of the social ladder from the insurgent Hungarian serfs. The chosen leader, General Tadeusz Kościuszko, exiled like Rákóczi, showed the same statesmanlike vision as the Hungarian insurgents. The Hungarian serfs did not wish to begin their armed rising without the cooperation of the nobility, Kościuszko[27] was not willing to fight for the Polish nobility alone, but he was ready to make all necessary sacrifices for the Polish nation. Consequently, he tried to, and did, draw the great masses of the peasantry into the conflict. In short then, the Rákóczi Insurrection was initiated by the nonprivileged and expanded upward to include a considerable portion of the lesser nobility and many aristocrats, the Hungarian political elite. The Kościuszko Insurrection was initiated by the *szlachta,* the Polish political elite, and expanded downward to include great masses of the nonprivileged. Opposite social evolution, notwithstanding, both these wars were, above all, wars of national liberation; the Polish from the start, the Hungarian from the time the nobility joined in.

A particular phenomenon, similar in Poland and Hungary, supplied a sizable number of trained fighters to both insurgent forces. Both countries had many unemployed trained soldiers. In Hungary, a great many soldiers who had served in the extensive fortifications were discharged when Hungary was liberated from Ottoman conquest at the end of the seventeenth century. These discharged veterans formed gangs, and like many similar bands in the Balkans, often lived by brigandage. There were fewer in the Transdanubian regions, but in the Great Hungarian Plain, between the Danube and the Tisza rivers particularly, there were many such bands. Besides the discharged soldiers, serfs who escaped their masters' lands, outcasts, enthusiastic students, even priests and former officers could be found among them. Some of these former officers, notwithstanding their nobility, saw the growing numbers of the armed bands with alarm.[28] Just as in the nineteenth-century Balkan wars of liberation, armed bands were incorporated into national armies,[20] so Rákóczi brought these Hungarian bands into his army. They contributed their warlike spirit, relentless, often cruel tactics, efficiency in using nonconventional methods — and also difficulty in imposing solid discipline.

The counterpart of these warriors in Kościuszko's forces were former members of the Polish standing army discharged after the second partition. Many in the rump army of 36,000 left in partitioned Poland could not be properly paid or supplied.[29] Hence, there were numerous deserters. The Polish unemployed soldiers' way of life was not much different from that of the Hungarian discharged veterans. They brought to Kościuszko's army the same advantages and the same problems that their Hungarian counterparts had taken into Rákóczi's army.

In numbers, serfs dominated both insurgent armies. The first fighters to join Rákóczi at the northern slopes of the Carpathians in Poland were, as he himself remembered

> . . . armed with sticks and scythe . . . there were scarcely two hundred foot, equipped with poor peasant muskets, and with them fifty horsemen came. Their leader was Tamás Esze, a peasant, my serfs from Tarpa and Albert Kis, a thief and criminal sought for his crimes. . . . The people who gathered in camps elected their own leaders. They accepted the command of swine-herds, cowboys, hair-dressers, tailors, depending on whose gallantry they estimated the highest. . . . It would have been dangerous, even impossible, to dismiss these officers, but there were none to replace them anyway.[30]

Such were the men from whom Rákóczi started to forge an army. It needed his personal attention to all details, including supplying them with their daily needs as well as introducing draconian regulations to establish discipline. The army swelled like a spring torrent and flooded central Hungary and Transylvania. The nobility escaped into forts and fortified towns, which stood like islands within an ocean of armed men. Nonetheless, very few Hungarian noblemen joined the Habsburg enemy; rather, they stayed neutral if they did not join the insurgents.

As far as Poland was concerned, facing two Great Powers' armies, its only chance was a *levée en masse,* but in the absence of substantial social reforms, that could not be achieved at the outbreak of the insurrection. A decree was issued, first by the Revolutionary Committee of Cracow, then by other municipalities and regions, which commanded that to reunify and liberate the whole of Poland all able-bodied males from eighteen to forty years of age must bear arms and start training for combat on Sundays. Every five households had to select one man, equip him with firearms, or failing firearms, with an eleven-foot pike and an axe, supply him with cash and three days' rations, and with a good peasant robe, shoes, a cap and two shirts, a blanket, and biscuits or bread for six days. All the rest of those under military obligation had to arm themselves with whatever they could, and train so that they could relieve the nation "from misery and shame."[31] From these regulations emerged the Polish territorial army, a truly revolutionary force, ready like the American militia, to fight even without regular support whenever the enemy entered their territory.

These regional, but basically identical measures were consolidated by the Polish Diet on June 6, 1794, at Warsaw, by a declaration that the army of Poland consisted of the whole population of all Polish territories. A previous regulation issued in May had divided the people into two equal portions: half to man national defense services of all kinds; half to produce the livelihood for all — a design for total mobilization. Local communities were to take age, health, and fitness into account and assign persons to the appropriate half of the nation-in-arms. The measures of the French Revolution in general and the *levée en masse* of August 23, 1793, in particular, thus had their counterparts in the Polish War for Independence.

The problem with such broad mobilization of the masses was how to keep the serfs committed to the fight. Rákóczi followed quite a different system than Kościuszko did to attain this goal. From the beginning, Rákóczi did not promise to emancipate the serfs; the early eighteenth century was far from being ripe for such a fundamental reform. Emancipation would have alienated the Hungarian nobility and thrown them into the arms of the Habsburg dynasty, a sure way to lose the war. What Rákóczi did promise — and what even the Habsburg dynasty had to grant in the compromise that ended the war — was freedom for those who joined the army for the duration. In other words, not emancipation of the serfs, which would have changed the feudal structure, but rather rewarding fighters within the feudal system by putting them on the traditional road to advancement, winning privileges by virtue of combat.

Rákóczi ennobled a good many of the leading *kuruc* warriors, but ennoblement was less common than the granting of *hajdú* liberties. This kind of freedom was first accorded by István Bocskai (1557–1606), Prince of Transylvania and Lord of royal Hungary, who fought a successful war for liberation against the Habsburg dynasty between 1604 and 1606. The main strength of his insurgent army were the *hajdúk,* a host of martial individuals, partly cattlemen, partly marauders, who fought gallantly for Bocskai and his cause. The struggle ended just as the Rákóczi Insurrection did, in one of the many compromises between the Habsburg dynasty and the Hungarian estates. This was embodied in the Treaty of Vienna of 1606 and codified by the diet of 1608.[32] The treaty guaranteed Hungary self-government, the privileges of the estates, freedom of religion, and other liberties. Bocskai repaid the services of the *hajdúk* by emancipating them from the jurisdiction of the lords, settled them on land grant cities and towns (*hajdú* towns), guaranteeing their right to landownership and personal freedom.

Precisely this Rákóczi promised to those of his soldiers who were not members of the estates, including naturally the discharged veterans. The response was great; there were enough volunteers, at least at the beginning. As the war dragged on, Rákóczi assigned quotas to the counties, a form of draft, which had to be utilized. Yet it was seldom necessary to force young men to join the flag. All these fighting men together consituted the "warrior estate"[33] (*vitézlő rend*), a new stratum in Hungarian feudal society. The warrior estate was a subterfuge for avoiding mass emancipation as well as a means of establishing a kind of citizen soldiery, the springboard of revolutionary warfare. The existence of this army was, in fact, not in the interest of the nobility. They wished the serfs to till the land rather than bear arms. Furthermore, a considerable armed force of nonnobles who entertained the traditional land hunger and desire for personal emancipation was a *de facto* threat to the *status quo*. This conflict required that Rákóczi be very tactful in order to keep the diverse elements of an insurgent army together.

Kościuszko could not offer full emancipation to the serfs of Poland, and for Rákóczi's reasons. For Rákóczi, in the early eighteenth century, total emancipation of the serfs was unthinkable. Kościuszko, two generations later, educated in France, where Enlightenment ideas blossomed, chief engineering officer of General Washington, and a brigadier of the Continental Army, had experience with a citizen army, and a free government of a free people. For him, equality of all citizens, the emancipation of the serfs, that is, seemed to be the necessary aim of a modern, enlightened society.

As supreme commander, Kościuszko clearly understood that the only way Poland could successfully challenge her enemies, the three reactionary eastern Great Powers, was by revolutionary warfare, and that such a war could be fought only by citizen-soldiers. To make citizen-soldiers of the Polish peasants, he advocated, demanded, and indeed — as dictator, actual head of the insurgent state — proclaimed at least partial emancipation of the serfs in the celebrated Manifesto of Połaniec, May 7, 1794. This document guaranteed personal freedom to all inhabitants of Poland, abolished personal service obligations, guaranteed peasants against expulsion from the land they tilled, reduced the *corvée* by twenty-five to fifty percent through the duration of the war. Government agents were to enforce these freedoms; landlords and bailiffs who violated the regulations were subject to prosecution. Thus, serfs were granted full citizenship rights but they were not emancipated economically although Kościuszko's Manifesto greatly lessened their burdens. The nobility, however, sabotaged the reforms wherever possible. Apparently, not even national independence was a high enough price for giving up part of their economic prerogatives.[34]

Rákóczi, anticipating, Kościuszko following Washington's views, was convinced that fighting an enemy's professional forces required insurgents to organize standing armies of their own so that major battles could be fought even on the enemy's conditions. Kościuszko tried to expand the Polish standing army; Rákóczi created his own. After the second partition Poland had 4 million inhabitants, 6 million having been lost to the partitioning powers. The rump Poland was supposed to have an army of 36,000, but because of immense financial difficulties, 60 percent of the men could not be paid; they lived as they could and many deserted. In contrast, the three partitioning powers had approximately a million men in arms: Russia, 400,000; Prussia, 200,000; and Austria, 300,000.[35] Early in 1794, Polish effectives numbered 26,000. They were well trained but their equipment was inferior to that of the neighboring Great Powers' armies. Yet the very existence of a Polish national standing army was an extraordinary asset for Kościuszko; the lack of one hampered Rákóczi.

Rákóczi's effort to build a regular standing army had a purely military purpose — ability to confront the Habsburg standing army and win decisive battles. As an East Central European prototype of the enlightened absolute monarch, Rákóczi also saw in that standing army-to-be the mainspring of his own government. He had immense obstacles to overcome, among them, the nobility's lack of professional military training, their eagerness to retain their political influence, and the absence of any effective means of financing the struggle.

Whereas Washington lost most of his pitched battles, Rákóczi lost them all. But he soon renewed his forces and was campaigning again. His recurring conclusion was the need for a disciplined regular army, as modern as circumstances permitted. As if we were reading one of Washington's repeated complaints to Congress, we see Rákóczi write, on January 24, 1710, after the loss of the Battle of Romhány: "I hope this battle persuaded our nation, that against the Germans we never will be able to prevail without a regular force. . . ."[36]

In developing his military theories, Rákóczi depended heavily on the work of the Hungarian military theorist Miklós Zrínyi,[37] whose *Az török áfium ellen való orvosság* appeared in 1705. Rákóczi accepted the Zrínyi thesis, that an army depends on internal discipline, good organization, purposeful leadership, a balanced proportion between the various services, and a centrally controlled logistical system, with quality stressed above quantitative growth.[38]

The organization of this standing army included varied means: many regulations were issued, some temporary, some permanent, all intended to establish order and uniformity. They dealt with defense, offense, and fortification, among other military problems. These regulations were codified by the Diet of Ónod in 1707 under the title *Regulamentum universale;*[39] this was promptly printed in Latin and Hungarian. It regulated the army's organization, the services, higher commands, logistics, pay, recruitment, the division of the state into military districts, etc. In addition Rákóczi issued edicts on morals, discipline, and the punishment of trespassers. A collection of these edicts was published in 1707.

One of Rákóczi's main concerns was the training and education of military leaders. He deplored the low level of the nobility's education. Gallantry and loyalty, he thought, were no substitute for knowledge. He created the Society of Noblemen (*Nemesi Társaság*) in order to gather young noblemen in his court where he could forge their morals, educate them, and train them to become the skilled officers he so badly needed, in order to form regular regiments. Until his own officers could be trained, like Washington, Rákóczi "imported" professional knowledge by inviting French, German, and Polish officers.[40]

The *Regulamentum universale,* then, shows Rákóczi's own views on the army: its organization, leadership, and supply, and on other aspects of national defense. The long war made it possible for him to clarify and codify the doctrines and rules of his army for the warfare it was to wage. Kościuszko's insurrection was too short-lived to disseminate its own ideas and regulations. Yet we are aware of these, for after the war, at the request of many American friends, Kościuszko published his views in *Les manoeuvres de l'artillerie montée* (1800) which goes far beyond what the title indicates to deal with strategy and tactics.[41]

For Kościuszko, the availability of well-trained officers was not a problem, but one weakness of Rákóczi's army was the lack of an adequate number of well-trained officers. The most efficient generals in his army were the former Habsburg officers, Count Antal Esterházy and Count Simon Forgách, the former a colonel and the latter, a general in the Habsburg army. Among the lesser nobles, the most professional was János Sréter, formerly an executive in mining enterprises — who, along with the Frenchman, La Motte, organized the artillery and was designated commandant of the Artillery Officers Academy. Bravest and most efficient in small warfare were Brigadiers János Bottyán[42] and László Ocskay.[43] The latter was the Hungarian Benedict Arnold; Arnold and Ocskay were identical in gallantry, professional know-how, superb tactical leadership, and treachery.

The regular troops were uniformed, paid, and equipped mostly at Rákóczi's own expense and only partially by the insurgent state. The majority of the soldiers were Hungarians, but large numbers of Ruthenians, Romanians, Slovaks, and Germans also served in the rank and file. The French and Polish experts, although a small group, contributed much to the professionalization of the regular troops. At the start of the insurrection, the total effectives amounted to approximately 70,000 men and officers. At the final stage, they decreased to 30,000. Among the twenty-six generals, eight were counts, seven barons, and ten lesser nobles. Among the brigadiers, two were non-nobles, Tamás Esze, a serf, and Orbán Czelder, a burgher. At the end of 1705, the regular army was organized into fifty-two *huszár* and thirty-one infantry regiments and six artillery companies. Most professional were the "court" regiments of Rákóczi. The first commander-in-chief of the regulars was General Simon Forgách, his successor was General Count Antal Esterházy, both former Habsburg officers. A general commissariat (*supremus bellicus commissariatus*) was responsible for the logistics; this office was headed by Count István Csáky. Health service was provided by the regimental medics. Rákóczi directed that the counties supply the army with food and fodder without payment. The main problem was transporting the collected food. Under control of the general commissariat, magazines and bakeries were built, and fortified places were established to protect the magazines. But because of the very backward transportation system, the logistics worked only if major troop concentrations did not garrison the same place long.

The main difficulty, of course, was supplying armament and ammunition. An intensive search was carried out to collect all the weapons available in the country, and to manufacture or to import arms. Major factories were founded in Besztercebánya, Kassa, and various locations in Gömör county. New iron works were built in Tiszolc. In concept and efforts, the system resembled the Reign of Terror's attempt to mobilize the preindustrial manufacturing system for the purposes of war. In France, however, an advanced mercantilist economy made it possible to produce most, if not all, the needs of the mass armies. Rákóczi, with a less developed economy, could not achieve this desired goal.

Importation was hampered by the utter lack of money. Efforts to barter cattle, wine, and copper for them did not work well. Yet some 10,000 muskets were imported during the war. Some cloth was imported from Silesia and Poland more or less on the basis of barter. The rest was produced at home or brought in by Balkan merchants, who accepted mostly copper in exchange. The troops were poorly uniformed, yet this branch of the logistic system came closest to fulfilling the army's need. It is not the low efficiency of logistics which catches one's eye, but the results Rákóczi achieved under the prevailing circumstances.[44]

Rákóczi seldom called out the *insurrectio* of the nobility (noble levy). Their frequent call up would not have been practical. It might have been an auxiliary of a standing army, as it was for the Habsburg army in the War of the Austrian Succession and, particularly, in the Seven Years War, but as a main force it was obsolete. Instead of serving, the nobles were taxed to pay for mounted substitutes, their equipment and horses. The peasantry was obliged to produce infantrymen, equipped and armed. The basis was the *porta* system, a unit of taxation based on several serf families. A *porta* had to produce ten, later four, armed infantrymen. In the initial phases of the war, volunteers were abundant; as previously stated, the more prolonged the war the more often was this obligatory enlistment used.

The Hungarians in their unconventional tactics were superior to the slow-moving, typical standing armies of the dynasty; like Washington, Rákóczi made extreme efforts, as has been shown, to create a disciplined force able to wage conventional warfare in order to be prepared for the conventional final battle with the enemy. Most of the officers, however, including Rákóczi's own right-hand man, Chief General (Marshal) Miklós Bercsényi, believed that the Hungarian forces never would adopt the "German type" of conventional warfare. The army itself resisted such a change in discipline and tactics. Bercsényi wrote to Rákóczi, "The Hungarian imbued with volunteer spirit never will adjust his behavior to monthly payment and/or regulations . . . he either pursues or runs away . . . Hungarian gallantry needs self-confidence . . ."[45]

Rákóczi's main strategical concept was identical with Washington's. He, too, looked for decisive conventional battles, to wear down, and destroy the Habsburg standing army and thus to attain independence. He readily accepted and fought six large-scale battles, and lost them all.[46] Faulty leadership, lack of discipline, subordinates' failure to understand the tactical plan, ignorance of commanders of larger units, and Rákóczi's own lack of professional military training, were the main reasons for the defeats. Lack of discipline and training often caused defeat even when the *kuruc* troops had broken the Habsburg lines; they did not know how to conclude the battle.

There were successful campaigns, however, where the purpose was not fighting major battles, but securing the cumulative effect of small encounters, in which the *kuruc* troops were superior to their enemies. The most remarkable of such campaigns was the liberation of Transdanubia by General János Bottyán which started on November 4, 1705.

Except for some retaliatory raids on the easternmost Austrian provinces, the war was waged on Hungarian soil. The population gave the insurgents much aid and information about the enemy. But raids, scorched-earth tactics, and other effects of the war gradually wearied the Hungarian people of the long war. The initial enthusiasm burned away in the flames that destroyed their homes and property.

The *kuruc* troops were, of course, most successful in small combats, and the Habsburg troops suffered most when they had to conduct long marches on Hungarian terrain, as when the imperial forces marched to Transylvania in 1705 and marched back the following year. In both cases the Hungarians refused pitched battle, but made the life of the enemy miserable by raids and ambushes, capturing foraging units and supply trains, destroying bridges, and by other unconventional methods — like those of the American militia against General John Burgoyne in 1777.

The defeat of the *kuruc* troops in the battle of Trencsén on August 3, 1708 was decisive; they never fully recuperated from their losses. Parallel political and economic difficulties made the situation desperate. The income of the insurgent state fell; the army had to be entrusted with the collection of taxes. The base of the insurrection gradually shrank back to the northeastern zones of the country where it had started. The imperial administration gradually established its rule over northern Hungary (Slovakia); Transdanubia, too, was lost. In September 1710, the last major western base, the fort of Érsekújvár, had to capitulate. A devastating plague swept over the country during these years killing approximately 10 percent of the population.[47]

Rákóczi's perseverance was the basic force which kept the war going. More than ever he looked to foreign assistance. The ever-weakening French aid seemed to be supplemented by Russian cooperation, particularly after the Battle of Poltava, July 9, 1709. Rákóczi had had a treaty with Peter the Great since September 1707. After Poltava, Rákóczi hoped to put this treaty into force. He wanted to make France change its traditional pro-Swedish policy into cooperation with Russia, but he failed. Instead, the French, in an effort to help the Swedes, recommended that the Porte declare war on Russia. Of course, the hope that the Russians could help Rákóczi against the Habsburgs was a utopian one, anyway.

Rákóczi planned a strategic withdrawal and permanent defense in the northeastern corner of Hungary, based on fortresses and fortified towns. The strategy, as well as logistical preparation for a protracted area defense, started in 1710. His goal was securing time for diplomatic negotiations. The most reliable commanders were placed over the key defense establishments. The pivotal point of the area defense was the recently modernized fort of Munkács. Indeed, this bastion surrendered only two weeks after the Szatmár Compromise gave no chance for further resistance to the commandant, István Sennyey.

At this stage of the war, the situation has been disputed.[49] Some historians, Imre Lukinich among them, claim that the imperial force faced so much hardship that a systematic offensive and sieges were beyond its potential. Field Marshal Count János Pálffy (1663–1751), the imperial commander-in-chief, was in no position to launch such an offensive. Yet, it would have been only a matter of time before the Habsburgs, after the conclusion of the War of the Spanish Succession, could have concentrated forces in Hungary to end the war by force. But that would require three or four more years of fighting.

The dynasty, however — wise for once — recognized that nobles ready for a compromise were in the majority in the *kuruc* camp. A speedy compromise seemed to offer more advantages than a protracted war, which might have alienated those nobles who were ready for a settlement in 1711. The cleverest move of the dynasty was including, as a key stipulation of the compromise, assurance of the privileges of the "warrior estate" (*vitézlő rend*). Thus, for these combatants, the backbone of Rákóczi's army, continuation of the war seemed unnecessary; they, too, were ready for compromise. So, the Treaty of Szatmár was signed on April 30, 1711, and was endorsed by the regent Empress Eleonora on behalf of her son, King Charles III, (Emperor Charles VI).

In strategy and overall military leadership, the great difference between the Rákóczi and the Kościuszko insurrections is that Rákóczi, although an accomplished statesman and political leader, was not a professional soldier; he did not have even a rudimentary education or training in military affairs. The Habsburg court first had Rákóczi educated for the Church under the supervision of Cardinal Lipót Kollonich,[50] but when Rákóczi was adamant against being a priest, he was educated to become what he was born, a grandee. Kościuszko, on the other hand, was trained in Polish and French military schools. Above all, as chief engineering officer of the Continental Army, he had long experience in actual combat in an unconventional war. In 1792, he commanded a Polish division during the short war. In 1794, he was supreme commander of the Polish army. Rákóczi's main concern was international relations and policies, the military was a poor third among his concerns. Kościuszko's main consideration was military, social reforms and policy-making came after. Kościuszko went into battle with strategical ideas he had learned and worked out. Rákóczi went to war and learned strategy "on the job."

Kościuszko was a modern military leader. He completely broke with the eighteenth-century concept of war of maneuver for maneuver's sake, and directed a real war. Anticipating Napoleon, he saw combat as intended to destroy: attack, or at least, harass the enemy incessantly until his will to fight was gone; engage part of the enemy and destroy him piece by piece. Discarding concentrated conventional cordon defense, he advocated fortifying key points and concentrating main forces, thus carrying on a dynamic rather than static defense in depth. He advocated mobility and effort to encircle the enemy, even accepting a threat to his line of communication in order to be able to conduct an indirect offensive against the enemy's vital points.[51]

Based on his American experiences and on Polish realities, Kościuszko's idea of insurgent warfare required coordination of regular and irregular forces for the greater efficiency of both, support of conventional campaigns by local insurrections to cause diversion, fighting even superior forces for the sake of causing maximum loss to the enemy.

Kościuszko's tactics advocated careful preparation, taking the chances offered by the terrain into account, use of maximum possible fire, bayonet attack, dispersion into skirmishing lines, collaboration among all branches of the service, keeping proper reserves. Partly because he was originally a military engineer, both by education and by practice under General Washington, Kościuszko probably gave more attention to defense and fortifications than he should have. That was a paradox, for in general, he advocated dynamic, mobile, offensive war.

As during 1794, the ratio of irregulars grew out of proportion,

Kościuszko introduced new tactics to meet the new circumstances. He set up three lines of battle, putting the best-trained regular soldiers into the first line; in the second (whenever possible, hidden behind hills or trees) came the insurgent troops often armed with scythes alone; in the third line, as well as at the flanks, the cavalry were deployed. Skirmishers of the American type secured flanks, rear, and the front. Although maximum fire effects were demanded, Kościuszko urged his troops to use *armes blanches,* with the greatest possible *élan.* Peasants equipped with scythes were massed in columns, just like the French revolutionary volunteers, and rushed upon those points of the enemy position already softened by the fire of the skirmishers, the first-line regulars, and the artillery. Again, Kościuszko applied his American experience by organizing sharpshooters who fired at will with considerable effect. A favorite maneuver of his foreshadowed Wellington, defense on a well-selected elevation, decimating the enemy by massive concentration of fire, then smashing the foe by a counterattack of infantry and horse.

Kościuszko's strategy and tactics both were at their zenith in the defense of Warsaw between July 13 and September 6, 1794. The joint Russian and Prussian army was 40,000 strong; Kościuszko commanded 23,000 regulars and 18,000 untrained town militia. Kościuszko carefully selected and properly fortified the key points of defense in depth, and carried out an active defense based on these strategic strong points. The enemy was harassed day and night with fire and raids. Kościuszko then instigated large-scale insurrection in the rear of the enemy. His magnificent combination of regular and irregular warfare succeeded in forcing the allies to raise the siege. Nowhere perhaps was the experience, the strategy, and tactics of the American Revolution so exactly applied as in the Polish insurrection in general and the Battle of Warsaw in particular.

Kościuszko's personal style of command borrowed much from his idol, General Washington: unflinching will to fight to the finish; careful assessment of situation and talent for fast decision; extraordinary courage; presence in the front line if and when the charisma of that presence could help morale. Like Washington, Kościuszko considered the fighting men equal fellow citizens, not just subordinates. He took great care to assure that the needs of the men in the ranks were met, emphasized constant education, training of officers and men, often addressed the soldiers and explained the particular mission and goals of individual combats, made constant effort to raise civic consciousness among his comrades-in-arms. By awakening their patriotism, he showed his trust in his men; they, in turn, trusted and loved him.[52]

As we have seen, the Hungarian war was initiated by popular forces. Its cause was massive discontent with Habsburg overtaxation, the rampages of German occupation troops, causing intolerable misery, and social and economic grievances. This popular force sought and won the leadership of Hungary's foremost exiled aristocrat, Ferenc II Rákóczi. He then persuaded a large segment of the lesser nobility and several aristocrats to join the conflict.

The Polish war was initiated by the nobility who turned to the exiled General Tadeusz Kościuszko for leadership. From the start he pledged to fight not for the nobility alone but for the nation, and gradually he did enlist widespread support from the nonprivileged.

In short, the sociopolitical evolution of the two wars for independence was diametrically opposite. The Hungarian struggle was initiated by the nonprivileged and then brought in the political elite; the Polish struggle, on the contrary, was initiated by the political elite and then drew in the nonprivileged. Yet both, as they advanced, created a national unity of a degree unprecedented in Europe outside Revolutionary France. Political and economic considerations played a great role in both wars, but the fight for national independence was the predominant factor in both, in Poland from the start, in Hungary, after the nobility joined in.

The Polish war ended in the annihilation of the Polish state. The three partitioning powers, Russia, Prussia, and Austria, pledged themselves, on January 26, 1797, never to use a title which could recall the existence of a kingdom of Poland. They believed that once and for all, Poland was extirpated from the map of Europe. Indeed, a century and a quarter had to go by before a truly independent Poland was resurrected.

The Hungarian war ended with the Treaty of Szatmár, April 30, 1711, a compromise between the Habsburg dynasty and the Hungarian estates. The compromise reestablished Hungary's self-government and the privileges of the estates; it assured freedom of conscience for Protestants; it emancipated even the nonprivileged warriors who had fought for the cause and made them free men. The Hungarian estates in return acknowledged the hereditary rights of the Habsburg dynasty, in the male line, to the Hungarian crown. The dual system, the main feature of Hungary's relationship to the hereditary provinces of the dynasty, was reinforced. Neither the compromise of 1867 nor the simultaneously established dual system was a new phenomenon in

Hungarian-Habsburg relations; they were the quintessence of that relationship — to no small degree because the Hungarians again and again were willing to fight for their rights.

This attempt to compare and contrast the insurrections of Rákóczi and Kościuszko, together with the chapters on the Habsburg empire, the frontier military systems, and the Balkan revolutions will, we hope, convey two general propositions: First, that warfare in the West interacted with warfare in East Central Europe, as did all contemporary ideological, political, economic, social and intellectual trends. The initiatives usually came from the West and spread toward the East. Nonetheless, there was a reverse trend, too; irregular warfare of light troops, as experienced in East Central Europe, affected Western concepts and practices of national defense considerably during the eighteenth century. Secondly, the character of East Central European warfare was truly revolutionary, and during both centuries it took the form of wars of liberation.

Once again, however, one should remember that this volume intends to be and indeed it is only the first step in an effort to present a comprehensive study of the interaction between East Central European society and warfare. Only after several conferences have been held and numerous volumes in this series have been published will we reach our goal: showing the interdependence of ideological, political, social, economic, and intellectual developments and the evolution of national defense and warfare in East Central Europe.

Notes

1. Major-General J.F.C. Fuller, *The Conduct of War 1789–1961: A Study of the Impact of the French, Industrial, and Russian Revolutions on War and Its Conduct* (New Brunswick, N.J., 1961), 21.

2. Guglielmo Ferrero, *Peace and War* (New York, 1933), 63–64.

3. Jan Wimmer, "L'infanterie dans l'armée polonaise aux XVe XVIII siècles," in Witold Biegański, *et al., Histoire militaire de la Pologne, problèmes choisis* (Varsovie, 1970), 92–93. (Cited as Biegański.)

4. Jon Manchip White, *Marshal of France: The Life and Times of Maurice, Comte de Saxe (1696–1750)* (Chicago, 1962), chap. IX.

5. Maurice, Count de Saxe Marshal-General of the Armies of France, *Reveries, or, Memoirs Concerning the Art of War* (Edinburgh, MDCCLIX), 134.

6. *Ibid.,* 135–36.

7. *Ibid.*, 142. De Saxe disregards the famous Polish "winged hussars," who were armored, heavy cavalry.

8. *Ibid.*, 146.

9. Wimmer, 93.

10. Detailed maps of this system may be found in Bálint Hóman and Gyula Szekfű, *Magyar történet*, 5 vols. (Budapest, 1943), III: 256, 257, 288.

11. *Ne bántsd a magyart, az török áfium ellen való orvosság avagy az töröknek magyarral való békessége ellen való antidótum,* written in 1660 or 1661, first published in 1705, and reprinted several times thereafter. References are to László Négyesy, ed., *Gróf Zrínyi Miklós válogatott munkái* (Budapest, n.d.), 293–320.

12. See Béla K. Király, *Hungary in the Late Eighteenth Century: The Decline of Enlightened Despotism* (New York, 1969), 173–95; see also, Árpád Markó, "Adalékok a magyar katonai nyelv fejlődéstörténetéhez," *Hadtörténelmi Közlemények* 7 (1959): 151–66. (Cited as *HK.*)

13. Tibor Papp, "A magyar honvédség megalakulása a kiegyezés után (1868–1890)," Part I, *HK* 14 (1967): 302–338, Part II, *HK* 14 (1967): 688–711.

14. Colonel Georghe Romanescu, "Die Einstehung der nationalen Armee und ihre Entwicklung bis zum Unabhengigkeitskrieg," Colonel Dr. Al. HG. Savu, ed., *Aus der Geschichte der Rumänischen Armee* (Bucharest, 1978), 114–16.

15. Count Imre Thököly (1657–1705), Prince of Transylvania and Upper Hungary. Allied with Turkey since 1682 and exiled there since 1699.

16. Lt. General (of the French Army) Antoine Manassés Pas, Marquis de Feuquieres [the "Wizard"], *Memoires Historical and Military,* 2 vols. (London, 1736), I: 225.

17. Feuquieres, I: 224–25.

18. A. H. Jacques, Count de Guibert, *A General Essay on Tactics with an Introductory Discourse upon the Present State of Politics and the Military Science in Europe to which is Prefixed a Plan of a Work entitled The Political and Military System of France.* [Translated from the French of M. Guibert by an Officer] (London, 1781), 300–301.

19. He, of course, refers to the Szatmár Treaty of 1711.

20. Guibert, 303.

21. *Ibid.*, 309.

22. Introduction to Chevalier Dutel, *The Formation and Maneuvers of Infantry, Calculated for the Effectual Resistance of Cavalry and for Attacking them Successfully. On New Principles of Tactics.* [Translated from the French by John MacDonald] (London, 1810), I.

23. General of Division Francis Wimpfen (de Borneborg), *The Experienced Officer; or Instructions.* [Translated from the French by John MacDonald] (London, 1804), 98.

24. Tamás Esze (1666–1708) serf, a leader of the *kuruc* insurgents, brigadier in Rákóczi's army. Albert Kis (1664–1704), serf, colonel in Rákóczi's army. Kis had long experience as a junior officer in the Thököly insurgent army. For

a few years he served in the Habsburg standing army but was discharged in 1694; thus he became one of the typical, unemployed military men, who played such an important role in Rákóczi's army.

25. Ferenc II Rákóczi of Borsi (1676–1735), Prince of Transylvania (1704–1711), ruling prince of Hungary (*vezérlő fejedelem*) (1705–1711), and Prince of the Holy Roman Empire. When his mother, Ilona Zrínyi, after successfully defending the fort of Munkács against the Habsburg besiegers for three years, fell into captivity, Rákóczi was taken to Austria and raised there by his appointed foster father Cardinal Lipót Kollonich. The owner of 1,900,000 yokes of land, Rákóczi had been since 1694, perpetual High Sheriff (*főispán*) of Sáros county, in Northern Hungary. In 1697 he refused to lead a peasant insurrection organized by Tamás Esze and Albert Kis. But in 1700, because of the increasing tyranny of the Habsburg dynasty, he turned to Louis XIV and tried to enlist the king's support for a *fronde* rather than a general insurrection in Hungary. Betrayed, arrested, Rákóczi escaped and found refuge in Poland. At the renewed invitation of the same two insurgent leaders, he now accepted the leadership he had rejected in 1697, and entered Hungary with a small band of peasant insurgents on June 6, 1703.

26. Béla Köpeczi and Ágnes R. Várkonyi, *II. Rákóczi Ferenc,* 2d enlarged ed. (Budapest, 1976), 113–14. For a rich collection of contemporary sources see Köpeczi and Várkonyi, eds., *Rákóczi tükör, naplók, jelentések, emlékiratok a szabadságharcról,* 2 vols. (Budapest, 1973). See also Köpeczi, *A Rákóczi-szabadságharc és Franciaország* (Budapest, 1966).

27. Tadeusz (also Thaddeus) Andrzej Bonaventura Kościuszko (1746–1817) came from a fairly well-to-do *szlachta* family; he was educated in the Cadet School at Warsaw and, in France, became a professional engineer officer. In 1776 he arrived in America. He helped prepare the defenses of Philadelphia, then as colonel — subsequently brigadier — served as chief engineer on General Horatio Gates's staff in the Battle of Saratoga. He constructed the fortifications of West Point; he was in 1780 chief engineering officer on General Nathanael Greene's staff. In 1789, he returned to Poland to become a major general. In the insurrection of 1792, he was divisional commander, then left Poland. In 1794, he became supreme commander of the insurgent army.

28. For the origins of these "unemployed soldiers" see László Benczédi, "Katonarétegek helyzete a török elleni háborúkban," *HK* 12 (1966): 821–29. See also Imre Bánkuti, *Rákóczi hadserege 1703–1711* (Budapest, 1976), 9–10. A collection of documents, with concise essays on the various aspects of the Hungarian insurgent army.

29. Leonard Ratajczyk, "La defense territoriale pendant l'insurrection de Kościuszko," in Biegański, 136–37.

30. *II. Rákóczi Ferenc emlékiratai* (Budapest, 1951), 38–39, 49, 48–49.

31. Ratajczyk, 140.

32. Béla K. Király, ed., *Tolerance and Movements of Religious Dissent in Eastern Europe* (Boulder, Col., 1975), 208, 210–12.

33. Ferenc Julier, *Magyar hadvezérek* (Budapest, n.d.), 283–316.

34. Ratajczyk, 130.

35. *Ibid.,* 136.

36. Letter to General Antal Esterházy. Kálmán Thaly, ed., *Archivum Rákóczianum* (Budapest, 1874), III: 10.

37. See note 11.

38. Bánkuti, 152.

39. *Regulamentum universale,* the general war regulation of the federated estates of the Kingdom of Hungary, for the military, as well as for the noble counties, the free royal towns, and all citizens. Published at Nagyszombat, 1707. Full text in Bánkuti, 181–219.

40. Bánkuti, 153.

41. Tadeusz Kościuszko, *Les manouvres de l'artillerie montée* (Paris, 1800). See also E. Tomaczak, *Taktyka artyllerii konnej wedłung regulaminu Tadeusza Kościuszko,* "Studia i materialy do historii wojskowosci," VII, Part 1 (1962): 213–41.

42. János Bottyán (1643?–1709), a lesser nobleman, cavalry officer, colonel since 1692; in 1701, he commanded his regiment at the Rhine against the French. In 1703, he was sent against the *kurucok,* but joined Rákóczi in October 1704 and was promoted brigadier. He lost an eye earlier in fighting the Turks; his soldiers fondly called him "Bottyán the Blind."

43. László Ocskay (1680–1710), son of a gentry family, officer in a hussar regiment, joined Rákóczi in 1703, rose to brigadier, in 1708 he deserted to the Habsburg army and attained the rank of colonel, captured in 1710, court-martialed and executed for treason.

44. Bánkuti, 237–38.

45. Bercsényi to Rákóczi, September 18, 1704 in Thaly, III: 124. See also Imre Bánkuti, *A kurucok első dunántúli hadjárata (1704. január-április)* (Budapest, 1975); Gyula Erdélyi, *A magyarok hadiszervezete és hadvezetési művészete ezer éven át* (Budapest, 1944), 174–208.

46. In 1704, two battles were fought at Koronco on June 13, and at Nagyszombat on December 26. In 1705, two more battles occurred at Pudmeric, August 11, and at Zsibó, November 11. In 1708 there was a battle at Trencsén on August 3; in 1710, one at Romhány on January 22. Except at Koronco Rákóczi himself commanded; on the other hand, in all but Romhány the imperial commander-in-chief directed the enemy troops. Bánkuti, 296.

47. *Ibid.,* 351.

48. B. K. Király and P. Pastor, "The Sublime Porte and Ferenc II Rákóczi's Hungary. An Episode in Islamic Christian Relations," in Abraham Ascher, Tibor Halasi-Kún, Béla Király, eds., *The Mutual Effects of the Islamic and Judeo-Christian Worlds: The East European Pattern* (New York, 1979), 129–48. See also Béla Köpeczi, ed., *A Rákóczi szabadságharc és Európa* (Budapest, 1970).

49. Mátyás Molnár, ed., *A Rákóczi-szabadságharc vitás kérdései. Tudományos emlékűlés 1976 január 29-30.* Vaja-Nyíregyháza, 1976.

50. Count Lipót Kollonich (1631–1707), Archbishop of Esztergom, Cardinal. He started his career as a soldier, fought the Turks, and was one of the main advocates of a forceful neo-Counterreformation. As chairman of the Hungarian *kamara* (central financial authority), he was the main counselor of the dynasty on Hungarian affairs. As such, he elaborated the violent reestablishment of Habsburg absolutist rule over Hungary, including colonization of Hungary by non-Hungarians to suppress Hungarian nationality.

51. Zdzisław Sulek, "Tadeusz Kościuszko — chef et reformateur social," in Biegański, 115–17.

52. Ratajczyk, in Biegański, 127–28.

I

Case Studies on the
Habsburg Empire and Poland

Robert A. Kann, Editor

EAST CENTRAL EUROPE IN 1815

Miles 0 50 100   200

KDM. OF
NORWAY AND SWEDEN ●Stockholm

North
Sea
●Göteborg

●Copenhagen

*Baltic
Sea*

St.Petersburg●

●Riga

RUSSIAN

Smolensk●

EMPIRE

Königsberg●

Vilna●

KINGDOM OF PRUSSIA

KDM. OF
POLAND
Warsaw●

●Berlin Posen●

SAXONY

Oder

Kiev●

UKRAINE

Cracow● Vistula

Lemberg●

AUSTRIAN   EMPIRE

Prague● Troppau●

BOHEMIA MORAVIA

Danube

BAVARIA

●Vienna Danube

Buda● ●Pest

KINGDOM

OF

HUNGARY

Tisza

TRANSYLVANIA
Kolozsvár●
(Cluj)

MOLDAVIA

Jassy●

BESSARABIA

Odessa●

Drave

Sereth

Milan●

Venice●

Trieste●
Fiume●

DALMATIA

MODENA

PAPAL

TUSCANY STATES

Rome●

Naples● KDM. OF

THE TWO SICILI'S

*Adriatic

Sea*

OTTOMAN

Sarajevo●

Belgrade●

●Nish

Ragusa● MONTENEGRO
Cetinje●

WALLACHIA Silistria●
Bucharest●

Vidin● Danube
Ruschuk●

●Sofia

Black

Sea

Adrianople●

Constantinople●

EMPIRE

Saloniki●

*Aegean
Sea*

Smyrna●

*Tyrrhenian

Sea*

Athens●

MOREA

Norman Davies

The Military Traditions of the Polish *Szlachta,* 1700-1864

At the end of the seventeenth century, the Polish-Lithuanian Republic was a respectable and reasonably confident military power. There was an old Polish saying: "Even if Heaven itself collapses, our hussars will hold it off on the points of their lances." As from the Great Northern War, however, disaster followed disaster. The Silent Sejm legally restricted the Republic's military establishment to a meager 24,000 men. The encroachments of powerful neighbors could not be resisted. In the three Partitions of 1772, 1793 and 1795, the Polish state was dismembered and finally annihilated. Heaven collapsed, and the hussars could not prevent it.[1]

Poland's predicament during this era of humiliation can be viewed from two aspects, the internal and the external. Each is equally important; and concentrating on internal affairs here does not intend to underrate the external pressures. Indeed, if the focus of the argument were to be the question of the decline of Poland-Lithuania and not the particular problems of "War and Society," the conclusions might well point to the decisive nature of external over internal factors.

It is also necessary to stress that Poland's military traditions cannot be arbitrarily divorced from the main principles of the "Noble Democracy" — principles which in some instances stretched back to the fourteenth and fifteenth centuries. In the Age of alleged Enlightenment, when most of Europe was paying homage to the supposed advantages of centralized state power, the dedication of the Polish nobility to such old-fashioned ideas as government by consent, the freedom of the individual, or the right of resistance, was decidedly outmoded. Yet to an American audience in particular, there is no need to apologize for the apparent paradox of serf-owning noblemen's so tenaciously clinging to individualism and democracy. After all, in this self-same period, the Founding Fathers of the American Republic, such as Jefferson and Washington, were slaveowners. They shared a great deal with their Polish counterparts not only in their political philosophy, but also in their fierce determination to defend it. The military traditions of Poland-Lithuania were designed and developed with a view to protecting the individual citizen from the abuse of governmental power — a perception which may have seemed behind the times to the eighteenth century, but which is no longer so today.

What is more, many of the fundamental principles of Polish democracy had direct military implications. The principle of *Neminem captivabimus,* for example, which guaranteed the citizen's freedom from arrest unless committed to trial, was bound to bring the interests of the royal army into conflict with those of the nobles' private regiments. Instituted in 1434, almost 250 years before the English equivalent of *habeas corpus,* it exercised a powerful influence on the development of Poland's armed forces. Similarly, the famous principle of the citizen's right of resistance, written into the constitutional articles of 1573, was bound to inhibit the growth of a standing army. In short, political concepts and military traditions were inseparably intertwined.

The *szlachta,* or "nobility" was the hereditary military estate of Polish-Lithuanian society. Its name, which came into the Polish language via the Czech, has similar etymological origins to the modern German *Schlacht* ("battle") and literally means *warrior caste.* It is important to note that the *szlachta* was not a socioeconomic class and cannot be defined by economic criteria. It included men of vast wealth and power, the so-called magnates, as well as the great mass of noble paupers, families sometimes poorer than serfs, who could function as nobles only through the patronage of the magnates. The modern fashion for translating *szlachta* as "gentry" or "lesser nobility" is clearly incorrect and leads to many misunderstandings.

The *szlachta* grew out of the earlier mediaeval knighthood, and in the course of the Jagiellonian period (1386–1572) established an impressive range of corporate legal privileges and a dominant legislative, jurisdictional, and social role. In theory, these privileges were introduced on the ground that they were matched by corresponding responsibilities for the defense of the realm. The *szlachta's* monopoly of political power was justified by the claim to a monopoly of military duties. In practice, this justification wore thin very quickly; and in the period of the Republic of Poland-Lithuania (1569–1795), the nobility made no attempt to reduce its legal privileges when its military role declined.

The Polish nobility was characterized on the one hand by exceptional size, and on the other by extreme variations of wealth. Although no census was attempted before the First Partition in 1773, there is no doubt that well over 12 percent of the population claimed noble status. In some provinces, such as Mazovia or Podlasie, there were more nobles than peasants. Nowhere else in Europe was the nobility so numerous. (In Spain, where the prolific and poverty-stricken *hidalgo* was a national joke, it never rose above 5 percent of the population. In England it stood at perhaps 2 percent, in France about 1 percent.)[2] Within the Polish nobility, the small number of powerful magnates contrasted to the vast mass of poor or landless petty nobles. Since 1600, the intermediate class of sturdy *possessionati* or "gentlemen with means" had been gradually diminished; whilst the ranks of indigent petty nobles swelled alarmingly. Over this same period, the magnatial oligarchy had taken full command of political and economic affairs, with figures like Karol Radziwiłł (1734–90) or Stanisław-Feliks Potocki (1751–1805) enjoying private incomes greater than the budget of the royal treasury. It was the most natural thing in the world that the great magnates should patronize the petty nobles, who in turn needed no encouragement to enlist in their retinues and private armies.[3]

Even so, the *szlachta* made no attempt to abolish the traditional military institution of Poland-Lithuania, the *pospolite ruszenie/motum publicum* (the *levée en masse* or "feudal host"). The host was organized on a territorial basis, with regional "standards" commanded by the royal *Wojewoda* ("Palatine") in each of the provinces. The annual parade or *okazywanie* of each standard was attended by all able-bodied noblemen of the province, who were obliged by law to present themselves fully equipped with weapons, mounts, servants, and supplies. It was put at the king's disposal for a fixed period within the campaigning season but was not normally available for service beyond the kingdom's frontiers. In the event of disorder, it could be called out by the Palatine for police duties within its own locality. The zenith of the feudal host had been reached in the second half of the fifteenth century. Its most notable achievements occurred in the victorious wars against the Teutonic Knights. Thereafter, its military value declined, and its functions were gradually taken over by a variety of new formations. But it continued to exist, if in much depleted form, right to the end of the eighteenth century. Its survival can be explained only by the nobility's disinclination to support more modern forms of a state army, and by its reluctance to arm the peasants. Kościuszko's attempt in 1794 to raise a *pospolite ruszenie* not only from the nobles but from general conscription of the male population, including the peasants, is the first sign that the noble tradition was being transformed and transcended by the new national tradition.[4]

The *szlachta*'s opposition to a standing army was nothing unusual. No European nobleman relished the proliferation of royal soldiers whose professional skills might be used against him, à la Richelieu. Yet the strength and success of the opposition in Poland-Lithuania had few parallels. As early as the sixteenth century, the spokesmen of the so-called Executionist Movement pointed out that the professional Crown Army, instituted in 1564, could never function satisfactorily so long as a large part of the Crown Lands, whose revenues were earmarked to support it, remained in the hands of noble leaseholders. The restitution of the Crown Lands was a precondition for the growth of a strong standing army. But it never happened.[5] Military finance remained under the ultimate control of the Sejm, hence of the nobility, not the king.

As from 1652, a regular system of annual military budgeting, the *komput* or "computation," removed much of the haphazard nature of the army's financial support.[6] But 1652 was also the year when the notorious *liberum veto* was first exercised.[7] The resultant disintegration of parliamentary life during the next fifty years, undermined the value of the *komput,* as of all other parliamentary institutions. By the beginning of the eighteenth century, all hope of sustaining a permanent force commensurate to the standing armies of Poland's neighbors was lost. When Augustus II (1697–1733), who was both Elector of Saxony and King of Poland-Lithuania, attempted to bring his Saxon Guard into the Republic, he provoked a major constitutional crisis. The *szlachta* would not tolerate the presence of a foreign military unit which was beyond their control. Their anxieties on this score explain the compromise worked out under Russian arbitration and confirmed at the Silent Sejm of 1717. In return for the withdrawal of the Saxon Guard, the King's opponents agreed to the permanent limitation of the standing army to the derisory establishment of 24,000 men — 18,000 for the Korona and 6,000 for the Grand Duchy. From then on, in a world where the neighboring armies of Prussia, Russia, and Austria were counted in hundreds of thousands, the Polish army exerted only a marginal influence on the political and strategic scene.[8]

Owing to the insignificance of the royal army, the ancient practice of confederation enjoyed a new lease on life. According to the terms of the Republic's constitution confirmed by the *pacta conventa* ("agreed terms") at the start of every reign, the Polish nobility had the duty to take up arms whenever it judged the laws of the Republic to be in danger. Provided that certain time-honored procedures were observed, nobles were perfectly within their rights to resist the king, or any other lawbreaker. By the same token, the king, like any other citizen, possessed the right to mobilize armed support against any group of lawless nobles. The confederation — *konfederacja* in Polish, *confederatio* in

Latin — was the means whereby this right of resistance could be legally exercised. Once a specific breach of the law had been identified, the would-be confederates convoked an assembly, stated their grievances in a formal Act of Confederation, and swore on oath to rectify the wrong by all means at their disposal. In effect, they declared war on the alleged lawbreakers, and organized a covenanted league against them. When the confederates' aims were achieved, or when they had been decisively defeated in battle, they solemnly dissolved the league and absolved themselves from their oath. But during the currency of the confederation, they were to determine their political decisions by majority vote and, in matters of military conduct, to obey the orders of their elected marshal.

In theory, the confederation was a fine example of noble democracy in action. In practice, it led to endless excesses.[9] During the eighteenth century, confederations were called on the slightest political pretext, and the formation of a confederation by one group of malcontents normally provoked the formation of a second, rival confederation by their political opponents. In the Great Northern War, for example, the Swedish-backed Confederation of Warsaw was formed to press the claims of Stanisław Leszczyński, whereas the Russian-backed Confederation of Sandomierz battled to restore the Saxon candidate, Augustus II, to his Polish throne. Similar civil wars were created by the confederations of 1733–35, 1767–68, and 1791–92.

Confederations were regularly invoked by Polish patriots in their efforts to throw off foreign, especially Russian, domination. Such indeed, were the aims of the Confederations of Tarnogród (1716), of Dzików (1734–35), of Bar (1768–72), and above all of the confederated Sejm of 1788–91. But what was sauce for the Polish goose was sauce for the Russian gander. The notorious Confederation of Targowica (1791–92) was formed for the express purpose of suppressing the Constitution of May 3 and of restoring Russian domination.[10]

In determination to preserve their individual rights, the *szlachta* often expressed unabashed contempt for those of their number who served in the royal army. In the *szlachta*'s eyes, a gentleman should live off his own. State service, except in moments of national crisis, was for poor, second-class citizens. In the eighteenth century, even officers of the Crown were sufficiently unmindful of their duty to resort to the use of *sowity* or "substitutes," usually serfs, who were paid to serve in their place.[11]

The nobility, as a corporate body, were reluctant to serve abroad. They viewed their military responsibilities as purely defensive and could not easily be persuaded to cross the frontiers of the Republic. After the wars of the Holy League 1683–99, no Polish army served abroad, although many individual noblemen were happy enough to do so. Under Frederick the Great, there were probably as many Polish noblemen engaged in the irregular units of the Prussian army, especially among the so-called *Bosniaken* ("Bosnians"), as there were at home in the army of the Republic.

The lack of a strong standing army was matched by the absence of a governmental law enforcement agency. The royal courts of Poland-Lithuania employed only one professional official, the *woźny* ("usher"), whose duties were confined to informing the interested parties of the court's proceedings. He had no means of bringing recalcitrant defendants to trial, or of executing sentence on fugitive convicts. As a result, it was usual for successful plaintiffs to be left to carry out the verdict of the courts themselves, and for unsuccessful defendants to resist with force wherever possible. Every serious litigation promised to end in a pitched battle, and many noblemen understandably thought to cut their costs by ignoring the legal process and taking up arms directly. Noblemen expected to settle their differences by the sword. Private wars and vendettas were a normal feature of provincial life. The situation described in Władysław Łoziński's study *Prawem i Lewem* (By Right or by Might, 1911) applied to the early seventeenth century;[12] but it continued right up to the Partitions. Lithuania in particular was in a state of recurrent turmoil and every political disturbance gave cover for endless feuds and domestic campaigns.

The *szlachta*'s equophilia is so well known, that it hardly needs to be emphasized. But it had important consequences. In military matters, it led to an exaggerated dependence on the cavalry arm. Even in the late eighteenth century, cavalry regiments accounted for three-quarters of the Polish army's fighting strength, whereas in the armies of neighboring countries they accounted for only about a third.[13] Cavalry tactics may have been well suited to the private wars of the nobility and to the improvised operations of confederates and insurrectionaries, but they could offer little opposition to the determined advance of a balanced professional force able to call on the interdependent services of cavalry, infantry, and artillery. If the Polish cavalry could often escape from danger by its speed and mobility, it could not stand up to the Prussians, Swedes, or Russians in set battles. Hence, the resultant pattern of warfare was eternally indecisive. Invading armies penetrated the territory of Poland-Lithuania, occupied the cities, and established fortresses with relative ease. At the same time, in the vast expanses of the Polish countryside, small detachments of scattered cavalry could keep up a seemingly endless series of ambushes, raids, and diversions. Thanks to the cavalry, the Polish *szlachta* was frequently defeated but could never be completely destroyed. Paradoxically, Poland was both indefensible, and invincible.

The *szlachta*'s obsession with cavalry was deeply rooted not only in ancient military practice, which required the knight to present himself for service with his charger, his armor, and his groom, but also in the psycho-cultural habits of self-sufficiency and individualism. The noble cavalryman-comrade who was supported in the field by the income of his own estates possessed an independence, not to say an arrogance, of outlook completely lacking in the ranks of paid soldiery. Even when the mass of the *szlachta* was no longer economically independent its members clung to the outward manifestations of their independent lifestyle with a tenacity that only increased with their poverty. It was the petty nobleman who most despised service in the infantry and who was most resistant to the drill and discipline required to create a modern standing army. Indeed, it was the *szlachta's* horror at the imposition of "alien" military ideas that ever since the reign of Ladislas IV (1632–48) had divided the line regiments of the army into two distinct formations — the *autorament cudzoziemski* ("foreign contingent") and the *autorament narodowy* ("national contingent"). The former, officered largely by Germans, contained most of the infantry and was recruited from a mixture of peasants and foreign mercenaries. The latter, composed overwhelmingly of cavalry, was the traditional resort of the noble comrades.[14] The separate corps of artillery, whose technical requirements clashed with the *szlachta's* ingrained abhorrence of crafts and industry, represented one of the few channels of military advancement for the burgher estate.[15]

The military supremacy of the *szlachta* was regularly demonstrated in the social habits of the day. Public displays of armed force were accepted as a normal part of everyday life. The nobleman always carried a saber in public. This was a legal privilege categorically denied to the other social estates. In church, the nobleman was used to stand up and unsheathe his sword during the recitation of the creed. Even indoors, and in the quiet of his own home, he felt obliged to wear at least a dagger or a short sword. Petty noblemen who could not afford a steel saber nonetheless carried a wooden sword as they worked the potato patch, as a necessary sign of their status.[16] Meetings of the Sejm and of the local dietines were surrounded by the armed retinues of the magnates. Royal elections on the Wola Field near Warsaw were conducted by up to thirty thousand noble citizens on horseback, and were usually attended by acts of violence. Recalcitrant electors, who refused to follow the verdict of the majority could usually be persuaded to change their minds by a judicious whiff of grapeshot or by a well-aimed cavalry charge. Disputed elections, as in 1704 and 1733 were the signal for civil wars. In 1764 at the last election in Poland-Lithuania when a mere score of electors were killed, the successful candidate openly rejoiced at the unexpected tranquillity of the proceedings.

Despite considerable interest in military affairs, Polish historiography has not yet done full justice to the military role of the *szlachta*. For obvious reasons, Polish military historians have been most concerned with the collapse and revival of the organs of state power. Accordingly, in eighteenth-century studies, they have concentrated their investigations on the decline of the army of the Republic in the Saxon period, or on the attempts to create a national army during the period of reform under Stanisław August. In so doing, however, they have given the impression that in the interval there was nothing much to discuss. In particular, they minimize the importance of the private armies of the magnates — the so-called *wojska nadworne* ("court forces"). Actually, private armies played a cardinal role in the social and political as well as in the military life of eighteenth-century Poland-Lithuania. Taken together, they employed far more men then did the army of the Republic, and supplied the main source of trained manpower for all the wars of the period. They were a natural magnet for the warlike masses of petty noblemen and formed the strategic base from which the magnatial oligarchy strove to perpetuate its power. Their existence presented the most important single obstacle to the resurgence of a strong central army, and hence of a strong central government. Their internecine feuds gave foreign powers a ready pretext for interference in Poland's internal affairs. It would need a Namier to unravel the intricate interconnections of magnatial patronage in the eighteenth century, but that would seem to offer the key to a full understanding not only of the relationship between Poland-Lithuania and her expanding neighbors, but also of the balance of forces in each of the decisive conflicts of the age. A detailed study of one of the great private armies of the day, such as the famous Alban Band of Karol Stanisław Radziwiłł, is much needed. Contrary to many textbooks, Poland-Lithuania was not short of soldiers. It was swarming with quarrelsome noblemen and with their arrogant retinues of heyduks and Cossacks. Yet it was paralyzed by their antagonisms and feuds. Here is a nice paradox indeed: the most militarized society in Europe was incapable of defending itself.

In conclusion, it should be said that the influence of traditional military practices on later Polish history cannot be exactly measured. But all the indications are that it was considerable. Whereas attempts to found a permanent state army in Poland have been constantly interrupted — in 1795–1807, in 1813–15, 1832–1918, and 1939–44 — the older tendency to perceive military organization as a means of resisting the state has enjoyed great continuity. The commitment to individual liberty, to self-sufficiency, to private initiative, and to the right of resistance, was no less alive after the Partitions than before them. If the noblemen of Poland-Lithuania were fiercely resolved to contest the pretensions of their own elected and democratic government, their sons and grandsons were still more determined to take up arms against the tyranny of autocratic or absolutist foreign powers. The Polish insurrectionists of the nineteenth and twentieth centuries were the heirs of the rebels, adventurers, and confederates of the old Republic. The Polish Legions of the Napoleonic Period, the cadets who launched the November Rising of 1830, and above all the guerrillas and partisans of the January Rising in 1863–64, belonged very firmly to the same spiritual community which in 150 years has not let a single generation pass without an insurrection.

Of all the oppressed nations of East Central Europe, there is no doubt that the Poles have shown the greatest willingness — and equally important, the greatest capacity — to fight for their independence. Again in the twentieth century, there is a striking sense of continuity in the aims and temper of Piłsudski's Legions, 1914–17, of the volunteers of the Polish-Soviet War, 1919–20, of the General Staff in 1939, of the Home Army in 1944, and even of Władysław Gomułka in 1956. *Polska walczy* ("Poland Fights") is a truism in Eastern Europe. For the one thing that the Poles possess in fuller measure than most of their neighbors is the awareness of a separate military tradition. It is a tradition which despises defeat and which has grown and developed in direct descent from the ideas and experiences of the Polish *szlachta* in the eighteenth century and beyond.

Notes

1. See Marian Kukiel, *Zarys historii wojskowości w Polsce,* 5th ed. (London, 1949). Other general histories include: T. Korzon, *Dzieje wojen i wojsko-*

wości w Polsce: epoka przedrozbiorowa, 3 vols. (Lwów, 1923); and *Dzieje Oręża Polskiego, do 1794 r.* vol. I, ed. E. Kozłowski, M. Wrozosek (Warsaw, 1968).

2. See Jean Meyer, "Le croissant nobiliaire," in *Noblesses et pouvoirs dans l'Europe d'Ancien Régime* (Paris, 1973).

3. On the *szlachta,* see A. Zajączkowski, "En Pologne: cadres structurels de la noblesse, 1500–1800," *Annales* 18 (1963): 88–102; A. Zajączkowski, *Hauptelemente der Adelskulter in Polen* (Marburg-Lahn, 1967); E. Starczewski, *Możnowładstwo polskie na tle dziejów,* 2 vols. (Kiev, 1916); M. Tobias, *Szlachta i możnowładstwo w dawnej Polsce* (Kraków, 1946); Maria Biernacka, *Wsie drobnoszlacheckie na Mazowszu i Podlasiu* (Wrocław, 1966).

4. J. Kowecki, *Pospolite ruszenie w insurekcji kościuszkowskiej* (Warsaw, 1964).

5. See Z. Wojciechowski, "Les débuts du programme de l'exécution des lois en Pologne au XVIème siècle," *Revue historique de droit français et étranger* 29 (1951): 173–92.

6. See Kukiel, chap. 3.

7. W. Konopczyński, *Le libérum véto* (Paris, 1930).

8. See J. Wimmer, *Wojska RP w dobie wojny północnej* (Warsaw, 1956); also Korzon, 79–120.

9. The workings of the confederations can best be followed in the introductions to the numerous published acts of confederation. Also Rembowski, *Konfederacja i rokosz* (Warsaw, 1896).

10. See Adam Wolański, *Wojna polsko-rosyjska 1792 r kampania koronna* (Kraków, 1920); Jerzy Łojek, *Upadek Konstitucji 3 ego Maja* (Wrocław, 1976); Jan Wąsicki, *Konfederacja targowicka* (Warsaw, 1952).

11. See Kukiel, chap. 5.

12. W. Łoziński, *Prawem i lewem; obyczaje na Czerwonej Rusi,* 2 vols. (Lwów, 1913).

13. See Leonard Ratajczyk, "Problems of the defence of Poland in view of the threat of loss of independence in the late eighteenth century," in *Military Technique, Policy and Strategy in History* (MON) (Warsaw, 1976), 295–346.

14. For the organization of the Foreign and National Contingents (*Autoramenty*) see Korzon, 3: 38 ff.; also M. J. Lech, "Autorament cudzoziemski wojsk Wielkiego Księstwa Litewskiego w dobie saskiej," *Studia i materiały do historii wojskowości,* t VII, cz 1 (Warsaw, 1961): 91–112.

15. See K. Górski, *Historia artylerii polskiej* (Kraków, 1902); A. Kiersnowski, *Historia rozwoju artylerii* (Toruń, 1925).

16. On the social attitudes and lifestyle of the *szlachta* see J. Bystroń, *Dzieje obyczajów w dawnej Polsce,* 2 vols. (Warsaw, 1960); W. Łoziński, *Życie polskie w dawnych wiekach* (Kraków, 1964); A. Brückner, *Dzieje kultury polskiej* (Kraków, 1931).

Charles W. Ingrao

Guerrilla Warfare in Early Modern Europe:
The *Kuruc* War (1703–1711)

The emergence of numerous revolutionary movements in the last
few decades has elicited a growing interest in, and literature on, the
phenomenon of guerrilla warfare. Although we tend to view these so-
called people's wars as a contemporary problem, the appearance of the
first *guerrilleros* in Spain in 1809 and of Clausewitz's lectures on
kleiner Krieg one year later serve as the traditional landmarks in our
periodization of guerrilla warfare. It was, after all, during the era of the
French Revolution and Napoleon that mass ideologies such as popular
sovereignty and nationalism greatly facilitated the spread of what
Walter Laqueur has termed "wars of opinion" and "liberation."[1]
    This is not to say that small war was unknown to Western man well
before the watershed dates of 1789 and 1809. Theories of guerrilla
warfare were already surfacing in the literature of the seventeenth
century, and the guerrilla prototype itself was evident as far back as
antiquity. Nevertheless prior to the last two centuries, guerrilla warfare
was generally less common and posed far less of a menace to the
internal security of European monarchy. The cultural constraints of
the feudal system and the general acceptance of dynastic legitimacy
greatly inhibited the rise of revolutionary political ideologies. When
insurrections did occur they were usually limited to one socioeconomic
class and, thus, were doomed to failure: proletarian insurrections and
peasant *jacqueries* because of a dearth of political ideology and leadership, feudal revolts because of the nobility's fear of social upheaval and
its consequent reluctance to appeal for popular support. On the rare
occasions when revolutionary movements embraced both the lower
and upper echelons of society — such as in the Dutch and Portuguese
revolts, or the English and French civil wars — they stood a much
better chance of success but were fought almost exclusively in a
conventional manner employing regular armies. Rarely was the commitment of all social classes strong enough to sustain a guerrilla war
lasting over a long period of time.[2]
    Such was the case, however, during the Rákóczi Rebellion or *Kuruc*
War (1703–1711). Though Hungary was the scene of intermittent
partisan conflicts throughout the early modern period, authorities on

guerrilla warfare have tended to overlook Hungary in general and the Rákóczi Revolt in particular.[3] Notwithstanding this neglect, the eight-year *Kuruc* War constitutes the longest self-sustained guerrilla war in early modern times, outlasting even the celebrated contest in America from its outbreak at Lexington and Concord to its conclusion at Yorktown. Like the struggle for American independence it exhibited many of the characteristics of colonial wars of liberation. Moreover, in its campaign for popular support and its struggle against the Habsburg regime in Hungary, the *kuruc* leadership employed many of the tactics familiar to today's revolutionaries.

A number of factors facilitated the outbreak of such a conflict in Hungary. For one, the kingdom had a long tradition of small war born of its partition between the Turks and Habsburgs following the Battle of Mohács (1526). For the better part of two centuries, each side had employed mobile raiding parties to harass and plunder the other's frontier districts. By the time the Habsburgs had retaken Hungary from the Turks, much of the population was already well versed in the tactics and brutality of small war. Particularly well suited were the Croatian settlers of the Austrian Military Border and the footloose herdsmen, or heyduks, whose knowledge of the terrain, superb horsemanship, and occasional banditry made them ideal candidates for guerrilla operations.

In addition the policies initiated by Emperor Leopold I in the years immediately following the reconquest had alienated virtually every segment of Hungarian society, thereby making possible a broadly based, national rebellion. To a certain extent the nation's grievances broke down along class lines. For example, townsmen and peasants suffered terribly from Leopold's simultaneous expansion of the tax base and increase of existing levies.[4] At the same time the nobility greatly resented the emperor's circumvention of its constitutional prerogative to vote and collect all extraordinary taxes.[5] In addition, however, both privileged and nonprivileged Hungarians shared to some extent a common ideological basis for revolt. In part this was provided by Leopold's persecution of the kingdom's Protestant and Greek Orthodox population. The demand for freedom of worship by persecuted religious minorities could provide a common ideological basis for a widespread revolutionary movement during the early modern period, as it did in seventeenth-century England.[6] Yet, though religious toleration was a burning issue for the victims of Leopold's religious policies, it failed to move the roughly half of the population that was Roman Catholic and generally insensitive to the grievances of the other denominations.

If there was a common element linking all segments of the revolutionary movement, it was the widespread xenophobic reaction against a regime that, by 1703 had essentially become a foreign colonial power. After Hungary's recovery from the Turks, the government in Vienna had come to treat it as little more than a strategically valuable outpost whose needs were defined in terms of the security and well-being of the *Erblände*. It was crucial to the evolution of a truly national movement that all segments of the population were in a position to witness at first hand the distinction Leopold made between his Hungarian and non-Hungarian lands and subjects, and thus were able to identify the essentially foreign and exploitative nature of the Habsburg regime. For example, with the replacement of Hungarian fiscal officials and troops by Germans, the indigenous population came to associate the hardships of increasing taxation and the excesses of local garrisons with the foreign presence.[7] Awareness of foreign exploitation intensified following the reallotment and resettlement of the Alföld by the *Commissio Neo Acquistica,* when many native peasants became enserfed by Leopold's court favorites or received as neighbors German and Serb immigrants who were readily granted the tax privileges, religious freedom, political autonomy, and land that had been denied them.[8] Peasant resentment grew further when large numbers of these Serb colonists were recruited by the army and widely used to collect the unpopular war tax, or *porció*.[9] Moreover, as Ágnes Várkonyi has demonstrated, native Hungarians may also have been alienated by the favoritism Vienna showed to Austrian merchants and garrison commanders in assisting their commercial enterprises at the expense of local peasants and nobles.[10] Of course, animosity toward the foreign regime extended beyond the reaction to tangible economic and physical hardships and also reflected the awareness, especially among the Magyar nobility, that their entire culture was viewed with open disdain by the Austrian civil and military hierarchy, a disdain which could be countered only with a humiliating emulation or a sullen hatred of all things German. Thus, though it is not fashionable to speak of "national" feeling in Europe before 1789, the xenophobic reaction brewing before the *Kuruc* War was stocked with many of the same ingredients as the modern world's national and colonial wars of liberation.[11] The peasants did not need a prior sense of nationhood but merely an awareness that Leopold's policies discriminated between them as a group and the Germans and Serbs, who both carried out, and benefited from, his decrees. Hence, even if they were not motivated by religious persecution and did not share or understand the feudal nobility's crusade for constitutional liberties, the mass of Leopold's

Hungarian subjects could fashion a crude national ideology out of a xenophobic reaction to the essentially colonial-like Austrian regime.[12]

Once the revolt had broken out, the last critical factor emerged in the leadership of Ferenc II Rákóczi. The first rising, which had occurred in the extreme northeast near Munkács, was a peasant uprising aimed as much against the local landed nobility and clergy as against royal troops and tax officials. In attacking these feudal elements, the Munkács uprising was no different from the initial guerrilla outbreak in Spain in 1809.[13] Rákóczi's contribution was to divert the initial peasant attack against the local social elite to an insurrection directed exclusively against the government. This created the possibility not only of forming a united front of all alienated social forces against the crown, but also of providing the peasant movement with elite leadership drawn from the Magyar nobility.

Of course, Rákóczi's was no mean accomplishment, especially for a revolutionary leader in early modern Europe. Though an aristocrat and one of northeast Hungary's biggest landowners, he readily appealed for support from the peasantry by promising to protect them from increased feudal dues and to exempt those who fought under his banner from all seignorial and royal taxes.[14] Though like most aristocrats, he was a devout Roman Catholic, Rákóczi also placed national unity ahead of his own denominational loyalties by embracing the cause of Hungary's religious minorities.[15] At the same time he assured the nobility that he did not intend to subvert the social order and sought their active support by demanding the restoration of the nobility's lost sovereignty.[16] Moreover, beginning with the Brezán Patent of April 1703, the kuruc leader reinforced these appeals with a broad address to the nation as a whole against the foreign regime, a call which he frequently repeated in an attempt to mold a common ideological base for his cause.[17]

The response to Rákóczi's appeal was immediate and encompassed a broad spectrum of the population. As had happened during the Thököly Uprising of 1678, first to march to the kuruc colors were the unemployed Hungarian soldiery, especially former garrison troops and heyduks, who had lost their jobs and tax privileges under the Leopoldine regime.[18] Rákóczi's support extended far beyond this element, however, to the kingdom's large serf population, which welcomed Rákóczi's promises of temporary remission from feudal dues and royal taxes and, in many cases, interpreted them as the harbinger of permanent emancipation from serfdom.[19] Meanwhile, his advocacy of religious toleration struck a responsive chord among Hungary's religious minorities and was instrumental in broadening his following among those non-Magyar nationalities with less strong resentment against Habsburg fiscal and administrative policies. Hence, most Romanians, Slovaks, and even the largely Lutheran German town populations joined the *kuruc* cause.[20] In fact, of all the non-Magyar nationalities, only the Catholic Croats and Greek Orthodox Serbs in the south and southwest remained loyal to the crown, principally because both groups enjoyed limited autonomy and social and economic privileges, and because the Serbs' religious freedom had been respected.[21] After some hesitation, the lower and middle nobility generally supported Rákóczi, as did a large number of magnates, spurred on by his constitutional demands and the promise of an independent Transylvania.[22]

To be sure, the prince's vision of a Hungary where Protestants were treated equally and where serfs gained even temporary remission from feudal servitude was not shared by most of Rákóczi's Catholic and noble supporters. Nevertheless, his program was clearly elucidated by *kuruc* propaganda and at the Hungarian malcontents' numerous conventions and, hence, served the essential function of mobilizing the Protestant and serf populations. At the same time the cooperation of the nobility was equally critical because it provided both the strong political and military leadership and the purposeful political ideology that is indispensable to the success of any revolutionary guerrilla movement.[23] True, the nobility was drawn from the same class as the Austrian ruling elite it sought to overthrow; nevertheless, as Thomas Greene has pointed out in his comparative analysis of revolutionary movements, the concurrent social status of rival revolutionary and ruling elites is as common in the nineteenth and twentieth centuries as it was in the eighteenth.[24] Nor is the remoteness of the feudal political doctrine of the Magyar nobility from popular aspirations unique either, for modern insurrections have often combined doctrinaire elites with mass movements impelled by more tangible economic and social considerations. In fact the Rákóczi Revolt lies in the mainstream of modern guerrilla wars by featuring an ideologically motivated social elite that appealed to national feeling and social millenarianism in order to utilize widespread alienation stemming from mass suffering caused by an imperialistic colonial regime.

Of course the *kuruc* did not readily win over all segments of the population. Aside from the loyalist Serbs and Croats, some of the Saxon, Romanian, and West Hungarian German peasantry remained undecided, as did many Protestants who wavered between the promises being extended to them by both sides.[25] In addition, many townsmen and nobles hesitated to join Rákóczi, fearing lest a *kuruc* victory lead to social revolution and involvement in an abortive uprising lead to proscription by the Habsburg regime. In these instances the *kuruc* proved no different from their modern counterparts by resorting to coercion. As a rule Rákóczi gave the population in newly occupied areas the choice between the benefits of joining the revolt and physical violence.[26] It did not work in some cases, as with the Serbs, who remained loyalist despite Rákóczi's personal pledge of perpetual freedom from taxation if they joined and extermination or expulsion from Hungary if they did not.[27] The *kuruc* tactics were, however, usually effective in newly liberated areas which generally did not join them until their armies actually approached but then readily did so once they had been obliged to make their sympathies known.[28] Similarly, the nobility usually adhered not only because Rákóczi managed to assuage their fears of social revolution and because they realized the insurrection would not be suppressed, but also because they were made to realize that their estates and families were at his mercy.[29]

Although the outbreak of the *Kuruc* War was the product of Hungary's unique history, Leopold's policies, and Rákóczi's broad national appeal, its immediate survival and ultimate spread were greatly facilitated by geography. Since Clausewitz, observers have stressed the importance to any guerrilla movement of a "base area" inaccessible to its enemies either because of its broken terrain or its distance from the main war zone.[30] In his discussion of the three stages of a "people's war," Mao Tse-tung emphasizes the importance to the initial phase of the conflict of the "organization, consolidation, and preservation of regional base areas situated in isolated and difficult terrain" from which partisans can later spread out in search of new converts and conquests.[31] Hungary's mountainous northeastern region, where the revolt had just broken out, provided Rákóczi with an ideal base area, as well as a further sanctuary in neighboring Poland, which periodically served as a refuge, recruiting ground, and conduit for French subsidies, supplies, and advisors. Moreover, by the summer of 1703 he was in position to break out of the northeast, occupying large areas of Transylvania and central Hungary. By the year's end, the *kuruc* army had grown to an estimated 30,000 men and had occupied, or at least infested, every part of the kingdom except the Serb areas of the south, Transdanubia, and Croatia.[32] In response to the growing *kuruc* threat Leopold transferred the crown of Saint Stephen from Pozsony (Pressburg) to Vienna, which he promptly prepared for a siege.[33]

Of course, a successful siege against so formidable a city was not possible for any guerrilla force, whatever its size. Nonetheless, the Austrians' task of reconquering and pacifying Hungary also promised to be extremely difficult, replete as it was with all the problems that face counterinsurgency operations today. Given the kingdom's great expanse and the inability to carry on reconnaissance in a hostile countryside, the Austrians found it difficult to employ conventional military strategy and battlefield tactics against the *kuruc,* who generally stuck to the hit-and-run methods of past generations, fighting only when and where they enjoyed local superiority.[34] As a result the Austrians were obliged to content themselves with garrisoning cities and fortresses, without having destroyed the *kuruc* guerrilla bands or pacified the surrounding rural areas. Meanwhile, these garrisons were themselves vulnerable to surprise attacks and sieges. During the first two years of the revolt most of the Austrian-held fortresses in Transylvania and central Hungary capitulated to prolonged blockades before the government in Vienna could either reinforce or revictual them. Moreover, the logistical difficulties involved in maintaining these garrisons were further compounded by the losses incurred in the ambushes which the *kuruc* frequently staged against the relief columns sent to their aid.

Troublesome as it was to maintain existing garrisons, it was even more difficult for the Austrians to increase the area under their control. Though their field forces could invade *kuruc*-held areas at will, logistic problems severely limited their marching radius in hostile territory. As they retreated, the *kuruc* often prepared the way for the Austrians by destroying everything that might be useful and ambushing foraging parties sent out from the main body. For example, so thoroughly did Miklós Bercsényi and Sándor Károlyi devastate the approach to Kassa in the autumn of 1706 that the officers with Field Marshal Johann Ludwig Rabutin's invading army filled their reports with incredulous accounts of the sacrifices willingly incurred by the local population.[35] When Rabutin was compelled to break off his siege of Kassa, he was obliged to conduct a nightmarish retreat to Buda during which casualties and desertions due to the lack of food, clothing, and money reduced his army to 4,000 effectives out of an original force of 12,500.[36]

Moreover, whenever the Austrians did succeed in seizing their objectives, they were further handicapped by need to garrison each new conquest, thereby placing a considerable strain on their existing manpower. Invariably the need was met by weakening their occupation forces elsewhere, thereby inviting *kuruc* strikes against skeleton garrisons in areas already pacified. Indeed, like so many counterinsurgency forces today, the Austrians found that they could not move on to new objectives without relinquishing control over areas they had just captured. Such was the lesson learned by Field Marshal Siegbert Heister during the 1704 and 1705 campaigns. After repelling Sándor Károlyi's surprise descent on the Transdanubian counties, he hurried across the Danube, where he methodically reduced the hill towns of the northwest. While he was gone, however, Károlyi's bands retook Transdanubia. Though Heister was able to recover the southwest in a lightning cavalry offensive at the beginning of 1705, he could do so only by exposing the northwestern counties, which were quickly reoccupied by Dániel Esterházy's *kuruc* forces. By spring Heister had little to show for his string of conquests. Meanwhile his own army was already unfit for further operations, having been exhausted and seriously depleted by the extraordinary labors of the past campaign.[37] Heister's failure constitutes a classic example of the futility of fighting guerrilla forces. "Butcher and bolt" and "search and destroy" are false panaceas unless they are accompanied by a permanent occupation.[38]

Of course permanent pacification required that the government recover not only the land but also the loyalty of the people. At the beginning of the revolt the Austrian military often employed violence when reoccupying territory, not only as a punitive device against traitors but also as a prophylactic measure designed to ensure future loyalty through fear. Hence, in dealing with the first outbreak in the northeast, Austrian commanders were instructed to punish whole towns if any of their inhabitants aided the rebels.[39] When the revolt spread to Transylvania, Field Marshal Rabutin employed widespread devastation and executions when recovering areas from *kuruc* control.[40] Meanwhile, the Serb and Croat irregulars commanded by Field Marshal Heister had the worst reputation for terrorism, not only because they were poorly disciplined but also because they were involved in a civil war in which both sides were seeking to earn expanded privileges from the crown — the *kuruc* by rebellion, the loyalist Slavs by service. This was especially true of the Serbs, whose status in the Alföld was not secure and who went beyond the conventional excesses of plunder, rape, arson, and murder by engaging in a lurid variety of atrocities.[41] Following the sack of Pécs (1704) one Austrian officer claimed that he had not witnessed such brutality in fifty years of service against the Turks. Indeed, the Hungarian chancery and Archbishop Primate Cardinal Pál Széchényi, as well as several Austrian field officers, vainly tried to curb the Serbs.[42] Nevertheless, at least in the early years of the revolt, the government seems to have taken the advice of Prince Eugene, whose appreciation of the Serbs' loyalty and usefulness outweighed any misgivings roused by the suffering of a rebellious nation.[43]

Of course, as in modern guerrilla wars, the government was not the only side to utilize terror both as a punitive and a coercive tactic, but was instead merely foreshadowing Napoleon's advice to General Lefèvre that "in dealing with partisans, one must behave like a partisan."[44] As we have already seen, the *kuruc* employed terror, especially against the Serbs, whose territory they frequently invaded, initially to compel their allegiance, later on to retaliate for atrocities against *kuruc* communities.[45] In addition, the Hungarian rebels sustained a massive, five-year campaign of terror against the towns and villages situated along the eastern borders of the *Erblände*. In this instance their goal was neither to coerce nor retaliate against these communities; rather it had the dual objective of helping to finance *kuruc* operations (primarily by extracting a ransom, or *Brandsteuer,* from captured towns) and of compelling the emperor to capitulate by exacting a heavy toll for the war's continuation. When the raids first began at the end of 1703, the rebels generally limited themselves to burning and looting. Although they kidnapped for ransom and killed or tortured those who offered armed resistance, the *kuruc* bands generally avoided killing innocent civilians. As the war continued, however, the raiders began torturing and murdering bystanders, including women and children.[46] Countermeasures by the local Austrian and Bohemian communities often took the form of mutilating captured *kuruc* marauders and launching equally devastating raids into Hungary.[47] Meanwhile, the provincial governments organized militia units and, in the case of Styria, established a fortified cordon across their eastern frontier for added security against rebel marauders. Yet none of these measures was completely effective against the highly mobile *kuruc* cavalry.[48]

The devastation of the *Erblände* highlighted a dilemma confronted by any government — especially a semicolonial power — engaged in fighting a guerrilla war: as the conflict drags on in unending stalemate, it becomes a war of attrition. The government must inevitably ask itself whether the heavy costs of continued operations, extended over an indefinite period of time, outweigh the economic, fiscal, and strategic advantages to be derived from carrying on the struggle. For the Habsburg monarchy the toll was indeed considerable. The exposed communities of the *Erblände* were suffering severe economic hardship. In Styria alone an estimated 1.2 million florins in losses were recorded in 1707, an amount equivalent to 8 percent of the monarchy's revenue for that year. As the *kuruc* raids continued, many homesteads were destroyed two or three times over.[49] On top of this could be added the cost of supporting large garrisons. In fact the local population complained bitterly about being subjected to the "double taxation" of the

customary *contributio* and the *quartierlast,* a burden further exacerbated by the excesses of the poorly disciplined Croatian *Grenzer* sent
by the government.[50] Moreover, as early as 1705 it was obvious that the
recovery of Hungary would require a larger army than was stationed in
the kingdom at the time. Meeting this need would drain forces and
funds from the War of the Spanish Succession currently being waged
against Louis XIV. At the very least such transfers promised to alienate Vienna's English and Dutch allies; at worst they threatened to
sacrifice the Austrian Habsburgs' stake in the huge Spanish inherit-
ance.

Given these potential sacrifices the government twice attempted to
negotiate a settlement with Rákóczi. A common trait of any revolutionary leadership, however, is its willingness to endure, to prolong a
guerrilla war rather than sacrifice its ideological and national aspirations. To the *kuruc* chieftains the demand for tangible guarantees of
the country's autonomy and the nobility's sovereignty — such as
Transylvanian independence from foreign rule — were nonnegotiable.

"I fear we have allowed ourselves to fall into a terrible labyrinth,"
exclaimed Bohemian Chancellor Count Johann Wenzel Wratislaw as
he assessed Austria's choice between a stalemate in Hungary and a far
greater fiscal and military commitment.[51] Faced with these alternatives
colonial and imperial powers have generally resolved their dilemma by
eventually — but inevitably — capitulating to the partisans' demands,
however immodest they seemed. Yet this was not the path chosen by
the new emperor, Joseph I, who succeeded his father in the spring of
1705. Though he, like his predecessors, saw and treated Hungary as an
essentially foreign appendage, he also realized that its strategic position astride the *Erblände* rendered it indispensable to the monarchy's
security. Hence, during his brief reign Joseph steadfastly rejected Rákóczi's peace terms — which would have loosened his control over the
country and detached Transylvania altogether — and resolutely pressed
on with the struggle. In so doing he clearly understood that he was
jeopardizing his war aims in the west, for his English and Dutch allies
regularly reminded him of the sacrifices he — and they — were making
in order to suppress the *kuruc* revolt.[52] Meanwhile, during the first two
years of his reign he withdrew thousands of the monarchy's best troops
from the fronts in Italy and Germany in order to bolster the Austrian
army in Hungary. By 1711 this commitment had grown to over 50,000
men from a base of about 20,000 at the time of Leopold's death.[53]

Joseph's determination to undertake the necessary sacrifices was a
major factor in determining the outcome of the *Kuruc* War. So was the

strategy he employed in meeting the challenge posed by guerrilla warfare. Upon succeeding to the throne he immediately jettisoned Heister's "butcher and bolt" tactics, which had not only failed to secure newly won territory but had also "run one army after another into the ground."[54] Heister was dismissed and his successors given both the instructions and troops necessary to proceed with the methodical reoccupation of the countryside. Of course, the government's resources were still insufficient to provide full protection from *kuruc* raids and Joseph was frequently obliged to make difficult decisions in committing the limited forces at his disposal. For example in sending a powerful army to recover Transylvania in 1705 the emperor was obliged to expose the Moravian and Lower Austrian frontiers to a series of devastating *kuruc* raids.[55] The area around Vienna itself was so unsafe that Joseph dared not visit the Favorita palace just outside the city walls without a body guard of 500 cavalry.[56] Similarly he was obliged to delay convening the Pozsony Diet in early 1708 because he could not provide protection for the delegates, and later, was unable to attend it himself for want of an adequate escort.[57] Notwithstanding these difficulties, the emperor's willingness to give priority to recovering and garrisoning the Hungarian countryside was a key factor in limiting the impact which the guerrillas' mobility had on military operations.

Concurrent with a new military strategy, the Josephine regime also made a determined effort to regain Hungary's loyalty, realizing as it did that coercion alone would never reconcile the population or create a durable peace.[58] Fortunately, Leopold's death and Heister's dismissal removed two of the biggest obstacles to regaining the nation's trust. Henceforth Joseph tried to capitalize on his own untarnished image by scrupulously obeying the kingdom's laws and seeking to redress the country's grievances against the Leopoldine regime.[59]

Although Joseph's policies were instrumental in assuring a Habsburg victory, other factors also were involved. In any guerrilla war, time is a crucial element, for only a long, drawn-out conflict permits the rebel leadership to wage a war of attrition, during which its superior dedication and will power will eventually prevail, despite the uncompromising nature of its political objectives. In this vein Vo Nguyen Giap has pointed out that revolutionary leaders must know how to prolong a war. In addition, however, Gann makes the important point that the guerrilla forces as a whole must also be willing to sustain the sacrifices concomitant with a lengthy conflict.[60] Although time was clearly Rákóczi's ally during the insurrection's early years, because it distracted Austria from its struggle against France, it became less important once the Habsburgs had secured their most critical objectives in Germany (1704), Belgium (1706), and Italy (1707). Moreover, because of conditions inherent in early modern European society and international politics, time soon turned against the *kuruc* cause.

Rákóczi's union between privileged and nonprivileged classes, Catholics and Protestants had been as crucial to *kuruc* successes as it was remarkable and unique for a premodern revolutionary movement. The coalition was, however, a fragile one. Although Hungary's marxist historians have unduly minimized the national and religious elements in Rákóczi's popular appeal, they have correctly identified underlying socioeconomic factors which impelled many peasants to take up arms. In addition, it is difficult to deny their assertion that the *kuruc* nobility's subsequent failure to address itself to the expectations of the serfs, together with Rákóczi's ruinous fiscal policies and the banditry of the *kuruc* soldiery, all helped to erode popular support.[61] When compounded by the reluctance of Hungary's Catholics to roll back the clock on a half century of religious persecution, these popular grievances placed a fatal strain on the unity of Rákóczi's national coalition.[62] Though Rákóczi may not have been personally responsible for the widening gap between his earlier promises and subsequent achievements, the *kuruc* leadership had committed the cardinal sin of losing touch with the population, and at the time that the new Habsburg regime was laboring hard to initiate a "constructive civilian program" of its own.[63] By 1707 the glamor of Rákóczi's early appeal was beginning to fade and the *kuruc* forces, which may have totaled 100,000 at their height, were suffering from both declining numbers and falling morale.[64] As he surveyed the situation, Louis XIV's representative in Hungary, Pierre Puchot, Count Desalleurs, predicted in a letter to his master that the war would be over within three years.[65]

Not only were the religious and class antagonisms of early modern society turning Rákóczi's struggle into a battle with time; so were the established conventions of contemporary international politics. From Clausewitz to Mao and Giap, the theorists of partisan warfare have generally agreed that guerrilla movements usually succeed only when assisted by conventional fighting forces.[66] These may be provided by a foreign power, as they were by the French in the American Revolution, by the English in the Spanish revolt against Napoleon, and by the North Vietnamese in the Indochinese War; or they may be raised and trained locally, as was our own Continental Army, Mao Tse-tung's

People's Liberation Army and Vo Nguyen Giap's Vietminh. Yet, Rákóczi encountered great difficulty soliciting foreign intervention, for unlike modern times when revolutionary political ideologies have been widely championed by established states and societies, in the Age of Louis XIV, revolt — even feudal revolt — was not widely sanctioned or supported by foreign powers.

Even Austria's enemies hesitated to assist Rákóczi. Though he permitted the *kuruc* to use his territory as a sanctuary, the Sultan did not recognize or significantly aid Rákóczi.[67] Although Pope Clement XI was at war with Joseph during 1708–1709, he turned a deaf ear to Rákóczi's overtures and, in fact, threatened to punish Roman Catholic clergy who participated in the insurrection.[68] True, Louis XIV did send money, supplies, advisors, and some mercenaries to Hungary during the *Kuruc* War. French support was, however, intermittent and insignificant compared with Louis XVI's expenditures on behalf of the American colonists seventy years later.[69] Moreover, though he led Rákóczi on with promises of an alliance, the Sun King never overcame his lifelong revulsion against insurgents and never seriously contemplated a lasting alliance with mutually binding obligations.[70] Though the English and Dutch could support a revolt against tyranny and religious oppression on principle — and did so by applying constant diplomatic pressure on Vienna — their alliance with the Habsburgs precluded more concrete assistance.

Of course, the 400,000 troops that Louis employed in the West did help the *kuruc* considerably by preventing the emperor from concentrating all his forces in Hungary. In this sense the French provided Rákóczi with a surrogate army, which he tried to link more firmly to Hungary's fate by concluding an alliance with Versailles. Yet, the French armies were of less value to Rákóczi after their expulsion from Germany and Italy, which enabled the emperor to transfer forces eastward. Moreover, Louis soon began to consider concluding peace with the allies. To Rákóczi, a "separate" peace between France and Austria would be disastrous: the French army would cease to fight in the West. Further, a separate peace would dash his hopes of an alliance with France that would enable him to present his demands at a general peace conference, where he was confident of receiving support from Louis XIV, as well as from Austria's own Protestant allies.

If foreign military assistance was indirect and tenuous, the possibilities of raising a strong conventional army within Hungary were even more remote. Though the *Kuruc* War had progressed rapidly through the initial and intermediate stages of guerrilla war, Rákóczi had been unable to prepare his forces satisfactorily for the classic, final phase described by Mao Tse-tung in which guerrilla operations play a subsidiary role while orthodox military units win a decision on the battlefield.[71] He had, in fact, worked hard to create such an army but had found the obstacles insurmountable. Despite efforts to establish a magazine system, Rákóczi never could adequately provide for provisioning his troops, who were obliged to suspend operations twice each year to sow and reap the harvest.[72] Barely a third of his officers and men had had any previous military experience, and most of these were heyduks and Thököly veterans who were so accustomed to guerrilla tactics that they proved intractable to reform.[73] Although there were some French and former Austrian soliders among Rákóczi's forces, they were too few and generally too mediocre to add significantly to the quality of the *kuruc* army. In fact, Count Desalleurs' arrogance and inability to speak Latin or German made it impossible for him to communicate without an interpreter — and a tactful one at that.[74] Further compounding Rákóczi's difficulties in building a formidable regular army was his own incompetence as a tactician. On each occasion that he decided to give battle to the Austrians — such as at Nagyszombat, Pudmeric, Zsibó Pass, and Romhány — he chose a hilly or heavily wooded site that seriously handicapped the all-important *kuruc* cavalry.[75]

Of course it was in the ravine at Trencsén — the one major battle Rákóczi did not intend to fight — that Hungary's fate was sealed. Having recognized his slipping support both at home and abroad, he had planned a bold thrust into the empire, hoping that he might inspire greater foreign support and return home at the head of a Franco-Bavarian army. Once committed to the operation, however, Rákóczi was unable to evade the Austrians, who had known of his intentions for several months.[76] With the defeat, the *kuruc* suffered the "single catastrophe" that Clausewitz warns can end a rebellion by destroying the people's faith in victory.[77] Though the rebels quickly returned to the guerrilla tactics that had been so successful in the past, the demoralized soldiery became increasingly restive and reluctant to fight.[78] Nor was the mood of the general population any different. When István Balogh raided the Transdanubian counties, hoping to rekindle the revolt there, he found no such inclination among the former *kuruc* communities. With his capture and beheading died the last trace of insurrection in the southwest.[79] Throughout the kingdom, towns and villages that had received the Austrians in the past with deserted streets and shuttered windows now sent delegations to pledge their allegiance to their Habsburg king.[80]

With the Peace of Szatmár, Hungary as a whole returned to its Habsburg allegiance. Rákóczi was not around to witness the end, having chosen lifelong exile instead of grudging obedience. Nor was Joseph I present to receive word of his triumph. Perhaps the last casualty in the long war of attrition between the *kuruc* and the government, he had died two weeks earlier, victim of a smallpox epidemic that had spread across the border from Hungary. Despite his death, the settlement which he had devised was destined to stand as a landmark in the history of Austro-Hungarian relations. Though it did not establish Transylvanian independence or any of the other tangible guarantees demanded by Rákóczi, it did reaffirm the sanctity of Hungary's constitutional and religious liberties. In so doing the Peace of Szatmár defied a European-wide trend by reaffirming the sovereignty of the Magyar nobility and the kingdom's autonomy within the Habsburg dominions.

There can be no question that Joseph acceded to the "Szatmár compromise" because he was determined to build a lasting peace and thus avoid the horrible cost of a second insurrection. During the past eight years he had lost perhaps half a million of his Hungarian subjects to warfare and disease. Both Hungary and the *Erblände* had suffered widespread devastation from both *kuruc* raiders and government troops. Each year the revolt had obliged Joseph to divert between a third and a half of his army and revenue from the war against Louis XIV. Meanwhile, his willingness to sacrifice his dynastic objectives in Spain had so poisoned relations with his allies that it ultimately resulted in England's fateful desertion of the Grand Alliance two years later.[81]

The wisdom of the Peace of Szatmár was to be borne out by Joseph's two immediate successors whose strict adherence to its provisions helped open a new and prosperous era in the history of Hungary. Hence, in its legacy, if not in its immediate outcome, the *Kuruc* War had reaped the fruits of a successful guerrilla struggle.

Notes

1. Walter Laqueur, *Guerrilla. A Historical and Critical Essay* (Boston, 1976), 100.
2. Regarding early writings about guerrilla tactics, cf. Walter Laqueur, "The Origins of Guerrilla Doctrine," *Journal of Contemporary History* 10 (July 1975): 3. For a historical survey of guerrilla warfare before 1809, cf.

Laqueur, *Guerrilla*; Robert B. Asprey, *War in the Shadows. The Guerrilla in History,* 2 vols. (New York, 1975); John Ellis, *Armies in Revolution* (New York, 1974) and *A Short History of Guerrilla Warfare* (New York, 1976); Lewis H. Gann, *Guerrillas in History* (Stanford, Calif., 1971); Werner Hahlweg, *Guerrilla. Krieg ohne Fronten* (Cologne, 1968).

3. Rather brief attention is given the *hajduks* by Laqueur and Rákóczi by Gann. In his most recent book, John Ellis dwells on both subjects at somewhat greater length. This treatment constitutes the exception, however. Although scholars have overlooked the *Kuruc* War as a guerrilla movement, they have far more readily enumerated several other, less extensive contemporary insurrections, among them the Catalan rebellion against the Bourbon pretender, Philip V, the counterrevolt in Castile against the Habsburg claimant Charles "III" and his Anglo-Dutch-Portuguese allies, the Tyrolean uprising of 1703, the Camisard insurrection, and the Cossack revolt against Peter the Great during the Northern War.

4. Ignác Acsády, *Magyarország története I. Lipót és I. József korában (1657-1711)* (Budapest, 1898), 536; Ágnes Várkonyi, "Hapsburg Absolutism and Serfdom in Hungary at the Turn of the XVIIth and XVIIIth Centuries," *Nouvelles études historiques* (Budapest, 1965), I: 359-60, 364-70, 385; "A jobbágyság osztályharca a Rákóczi-szabadságharc idején," *Történelmi Szemle* 7 (1964): 343.

5. Ladislas Baron Hengelmüller, *Hungary's Fight for National Existence* (London, 1913), 71-75; Theodor Mayer, *Verwaltungsreform in Ungarn nach der Türkenzeit* (Vienna, 1911), 10-11, 16-17, 24.

6. As pointed out by Ellis, *Armies in Revolution,* 22.

7. Várkonyi, "A Dunántúl felszabadítása 1705-ben," *Századok* 86 (1952): 412-13; "A Rákóczi szabadságharc kibontakozása Erdélyben," *Századok* 88 (1954): 22, 28, 36; "Absolutism and Serfdom," 356, 367, 385. Várkonyi cites the complaint of a Kecskemét peasant, "the Germans do not leave any udder of the cow unmilked," *Ibid.,* 385. The process of replacing native Hungarian with foreign garrisons began in earnest as far back as 1664, following the peace of Vasvár. Cf. László Benczédi, "A 'vitézlő rend' és ideológiája a Thököly-felkelésben," *Történelmi Szemle* 6 (1963): 35.

8. János Hornyik, "A ráczok ellenforradalma 1703-1711," *Századok* 2 (1868): 539-41; Várkonyi, "Absolutism and Serfdom," 368-69.

9. Hornyik, 540-41.

10. "Erdélyben," 26; "Absolutism and Serfdom," 377-81.

11. That national identities did exist before 1789 is amply demonstrated by Hans Kohn, *The Idea of Nationalism* (New York, 1944).

12. Although today's Hungarian marxist historians generally spurn the suggestion of a mass national ideology among the peasantry during the *Kuruc* War, this proposition is supported by Erik Molnár, "Ideológiai kérdések a feudalizmusban," *Történelmi Szemle* 9 (1961). László Benczédi and Ágnes Várkonyi do concede a national, patriotic fervor among former garrison soldiers and partisans of the Thököly uprising (1678-83), but only because of

their proximity to their noble leaders, whose ideology they adopted, and their separation from the mass of peasants. Cf. Benczédi, 37; Várkonyi, "A 'népi kurucság' ideológiája," *Történelmi Szemle* 6 (1963): 47.

13. Carl Schmitt, *Theorie des partisanen. Zwischenbemerkung zum Begriff des Politischen* (Berlin, 1963), 14.

14. Tamás Esze, *II. Rákóczi Ferenc tiszántúli hadjárata* (Budapest, 1951), 83–87, P. Z. Pach, "Le problème du rassemblement des forces nationales pendant la guerre d'indépendence de François II. Rákóczi," *Acta Historica. Academiae Scientiarum Hungaricae* 3 (1956), 100–102; Sándor Márki, *II. Rákóczi Ferencz* (Budapest, 1907–1910), I: 290, 293.

15. Regarding Rákóczi's ability to transcend his own class and religious loyalties, cf. E. Révész, *Esquisse de l'histoire de la politique religieuse hongroise entre 1705 et 1860* in *Studia Historica. Academiae Scientiarum Hungaricae* 26 (1960): 5–17; Várkonyi, "Történelmi személyiség, válság és fejlődés a XVII. századi Magyarországon," *Századok* 106 (1972).

16. Gyula Szekfű, *Magyar történet* (Budapest, 1935) IV: 288; Márki, I: 291–93. Specifically, Rákóczi sought the restoration of both the elective monarchy and the *jus resistendi,* the Magyar nobility's former right to resist any alleged violation of the kingdom's laws and constitution, as well as the restitution of an independent Transylvania as a check against royal tyranny.

17. Várkonyi, "népi kurucság," 49, 52.

18. Benczédi, 37; Acsády, 536; Várkonyi, "Dunántúl," 412–13; "Jobbágyság," 347–48.

19. Esze, 84; Várkonyi, "népi kurucság," 53–54.

20. For the effect on individual nationalities, cf. H. I. Bidermann, *Geschichte der österreichischen Gesamt-Staats-Idee, 1526–1804* (Innsbruck, 1867), II: 53, 156; I. A. Fessler, *Geschichte von Ungarn* (Leipzig, 1877), IV: 515; Acsády; Márki, I: 285, 479.

21. Kurt Wessely, "The Development of the Hungarian Military Frontier until the Middle of the Eighteenth Century," *Austrian History Yearbook* 9–10 (1973–74): 57; Hornyik, 537–39.

22. The Transylvanian nobility in particular had been alienated by the subversion of the *Diploma Leopoldinum* of 1691. Várkonyi, "Erdélyben," 32, 67.

23. Ellis, *Guerrilla Warfare,* 201; ed. and trans. Brig. Gen. S. B. Griffith, *Mao Tse Tung on Guerrilla Warfare* (New York, 1961), 43, 45; Robert Forster and Jack P. Greene, eds., *Preconditions of Revolution in Early Modern Europe* (Baltimore, 1970), 15–16.

24. *Comparative Revolutionary Movements* (Englewood Cliffs, N.J., 1974), 16–17.

25. Márki, I: 476, 490–95, 304; Fritz Posch, *Flammende Grenze. Die Steiermark in den Kuruzzenstürmen* (Vienna, 1968), 155–56, 210.

26. Várkonyi, "Dunántúl," 415; "Erdélyben," 37.

27. Hornyik, 544–45.

28. Várkonyi, "Dunántúl," 402–407; Pach, 99.

29. Pach calls these nobles "*kuruc* despite themselves,"99–102, 111; Márki, I: 285–93; Acsády, 533–34, 561; Várkonyi, "Absolutism and Serfdom," 385; "Erdélyben," 38, 42–44; "Dunántúl," 402–407; Esze, 9, 36.

30. Anatol Rapoport, *Clausewitz on War* (London, 1968), 344–45; Ellis, *Guerrilla Warfare*, 197–98.

31. Griffith, 21.

32. Stepney to Hedges, October 24, 1703, Ernő Simonyi, ed., *Angol diplomatikai iratok. II. Rákóczi Ferenc korára* (Pest, 1871–77), I.

33. Stepney to Harley, October 10, 1703, *Ibid.*

34. Árpád Markó, "II. Rákóczi Ferenc haditervei és azok kapcsolata a spanyol örökösödési háború eseményeivel," *Századok* 70 (1936): 582.

35. Hornyik, 696–97. For accounts of the rebels' destruction of the countryside caught in the path of Austrian armies during the 1705 and 1708 campaigns, cf. Hengelmüller, 256–57, 271; Meadows to Harley, December 8, 1708; Simonyi, III: 413; Fessler, V: 86.

36. Of the difference of 8,500, 2,000 had been detached earlier, thus leaving 6,500 in losses. *Feldzüge des Prinzen Eugen von Savoyen* (Vienna, 1876–92), IX: 289, 291; Fessler, V: 46–48.

37. Hengelmüller, 237.

38. Gann, 89–90.

39. Pach, 98–99. For the Croatian Ban Pálffy's defense of violence against civilians, cf. Pálffy to Forgách, March 29, 1706, Simonyi, II.

40. Várkonyi, "Erdélyben," 36–37, 39, 58, 62–63.

41. Such as roasting their victims, or stuffing their mouths with gunpowder before igniting them, or suspending women by their breasts during torture. Hornyik, 524–624, 700–701.

42. *Ibid.*, 546–48, 550–51, 613–14, 624.

43. Eugene to Joseph, March 12, 1706, *Feldzüge*, VIII, Supp., 67. Serbian privileges were, in fact, confirmed and later extended. Wessely, 62–63.

44. Schmitt, 20.

45. Hornyik, 543, 610–12, 621–23, 626–27, 694; Hengelmüller, 161; Stepney to Harley, July 1, 1705, Simonyi, II.

46. Posch, 142, 240, 290–91, 318, 321.

47. *Ibid.*, 116–21, 210; Stepney to Harley, July 22, 1705, Meadows to Harley, May 5, 1708, Simonyi, II–III.

48. Posch, 191–92, 241, 268.

49. Brigitte Holl, *Hofkammerpräsident Gundaker Thomas Graf Starhemberg und die Österreichische Finanzpolitik der Barockzeit (1703–1715)* (Vienna, 1976), 164; Posch, 265–66.

50. Posch, 265; P. Benedict Hammerl, "Die Einfälle der Kuruczen in die Gegend an der March in den Jahren 1703–1706," *Blätter des Vereins für Landeskunde von Niederösterreich* 24 (1890): 299.

51. Wratislaw to Charles, April 18, 1705, Arneth, ed., "Eigenhändige Korrespondenz des Königs Karl III. von Spanien mit dem Obersten Kanzler des Königreiches Böhmen Grafen Johann Wenzel Wratislaw," *Archiv für Kunde Österreichischer Geschichtsquellen* 16 (1856), 17.

52. Salm to Wratislaw, February 27, 1705, *Haus- Hof- und Staatsarchiv* (*HHSA*), Vienna, Staatskanzlei, Diplomatische Korrespondenz, Kleinere Betreffe 16; Charles W. Ingrao, *In Quest and Crisis: Joseph I and the Habsburg Monarchy* (West Lafayette, Ind., 1978), 127, 130, 141, 159–60.

53. *Ibid.,* 159.

54. Eugene to Joseph, May 18, 1705, to *Hofkriegsrat,* May 22, 1705, *Feldzüge,* VII, Supp. 126, 140; Wratislaw to Charles, April 18, 1.705; Arneth, "Eigenhändige," 15.

55. Rákóczi to Vetes, July 29, 1705, Joseph Fiedler, ed., *Actenstücke zur Geschichte Franz Rákóczy's und seiner Verbindung mit dem Auslande,* I *Fontes Rerum Austriacarum* IX (1855): 282, 369; Ingrao, 130; Hammerl, 290–91.

56. Béla Köpeczi, *La France et la Hongrie au début du XVIIIᵉ siècle* (Budapest, 1971), 409.

57. Ingrao, 147.

58. Stepney to Harley, February 28, 1705, Simonyi, II.

59. Ingrao, 127–29, 136, 146–48, 151–52. Joseph eventually reappointed Heister, but only because no one else was available, and after precautions had been taken to ensure both that he dealt humanely with the civilian population and followed a prearranged plan of operations devised by Prince Eugene and the *Hofkriegsrat.* Joseph's notes of August 24, 1707 Conference, *HHSA,* Staatskanzlei, Vorträge 51; Joseph to Salm, n.d. (1708), *Fürstlich Salm-Salm'sches Archiv,* Anholt, Germany, III, 59a; Eugene to Joseph, May 17, 1708, to Tiell, July 7, 1709, *Feldzüge,* X, Supp., 93–97; XI, Supp., 151.

60. Vo Nguyen Giap, *Banner of People's War, The Party's Military Line* (New York, 1970); Gann, 84.

61. Várkonyi, "Jobbágyság," 355–62, 370; Köpeczi, 221; Esze, 87; Pach, 103, 107–108, 110; F. Krones, "Zur Geschichte Ungarns im Zeitalter Franz Rákóczi's II.," *Archiv für österreichische Geschichte* 42 (1870): 290.

62. On religious discontent, cf. Márki, I: 445, 485–89, II: 367, Bidermann, II: 155.

63. On the importance to both sides of establishing or retaining close rapport with the civilian population, cf. Gann, 86–87, 90; Ellis, *Guerrilla Warfare,* 199. On Joseph's policies, cf. Ingrao, 146–48, 151–52.

64. Markó, 592; Köpeczi, 221; Várkonyi, "Jobbágyság," 371.

65. Köpeczi, 221.

66. G. Fairbairn, *Revolutionary Guerrilla Warfare* (Middlesex, 1974), 44; Giap, 82–84; Griffith, 55–57; Gann, 91, 196–97.

67. Stepney to Harley, March 24, 1706, Lawes to Lewis, May 26, 1706, Simonyi, II–III; Louis Rousseau, *Les Relations diplomatiques de la France et de la Turquie au XVIIIᵉ siècle* (Paris, 1908), I: 130–32, 136–37, 141; Kálmán Benda, "II. Rákóczi Ferenc török politikájának első évei (1702–1705)," *Történelmi Szemle* 5 (1962): 208–10.

68. Wratisław to Sinzendorf, September 14, 1709, *HSSA,* Grosse Korrespondenz, 71; Benda, "Rákóczi és a Vatikán," *Történelmi Szemle* 2 (1959); Hans Kramer, *Habsburg und Rom in den Jahren 1708–1709* (Innsbruck, 1936), 118.

69. Rákóczi to Vetes, April 29, 1708, December 8, 1709, Vetes to Rákóczi, August 15, 1709, Fiedler, I: 95, 141, 323, 336; II, *Fontes Rerum Austriacarum* XVII (1858): 452; Markó, "Les Soldats français dans la guerre d'indépendence du prince François II Rákóczi (1703–1711)," *Revue des études hongroises* (1933), 283; Köpeczi, 35–37; G. Rázsó, "La situation militaire générale et la guerre d'indépendence de Rákóczi," *Acta Historica. Academiae Scientiarum Hungaricae* 22 (1976): 317. Desalleurs estimated that the French subsidies were sufficient to maintain an army of 4,000 soldiers. Köpeczi, "La guerre d'indépendence hongroise au début du XVIIIᵉ siècle et l'Europe," *Acta Historica. Academiae Scientiarum Hungaricae* 22 (1976), 337. For French aid to the American colonies, cf. W. C. Stinchcombe, *The American Revolution and the French Alliance* (Syracuse, N.Y., 1969), 88.

70. Émile Pillias, "Louis XIV et le problème hongrois," *Nouvelle Revue de Hongrie* 54 (1936); Köpeczi, *La France.* Similarly, Protestant Sweden and Prussia declined to assist Rákóczi with more than their good offices because of their unwillingness to support rebels. Benda, *Le projet d'alliance hungaro-suédo- prussienne de 1704, Studia Historica. Academiae Scientiarum Hungaricae* 25 (1960): 22–24.

71. Griffith, 21, 57; Asprey, 388.

72. G. Perjés, "Army Provisioning, Logistics and Strategy in the Second Half of the Seventeenth Century," *Acta Historica. Academiae Scientiarum Hungaricae* 16 (1970): 25.

73. Markó, "Rákóczi Ferenc haditervei," 581–82; Hengelmüller, 227, 229.

74. Markó, "Les Soldats français," 271, 283; Várkonyi, "Dunántúl," 397.

75. Hengelmüller, 225–33, 254, 272; Fessler, IV: 583–84; *Feldzüge,* XII: 488–89.

76. Sinzendorf to Charles, June 14, 1708, *HHSA,* Grosse Korrespondenz 74a; Markó, "Rákóczi Ferenc haditervei," 575; Fessler, 85–86; A. Lefaivre, "L'Insurrection magyar sous François II Ragoczy," *Revue des questions historiques* 25 (1901): 570–71.

77. Fairbairn, 43; Asprey, 161; Gann, 84–85.

78. Wratislaw to Charles, January 15, 1709, *HHSA,* Familienkorrespondenz A 18; Sinzendorf to Kellers, April 8, 1709, *HHSA,* Grosse Korrespondenz 84d; Krones, 316, 322; Köpeczi, *La France,* 221. Regarding the renewed *kuruc* guerrilla tactics, cf. Meadows to Harley, August 8, September 8, 15, 22, 29, October 3, 1708, Simonyi, III; Fessler, V: 99, 101.

79. F. Wagner, *Historia Josephi I Caesaris* (Vienna, 1740), 400.

80. Eugene to *Hofkriegsrat,* September 19, 1708, *Feldzüge,* X, Supp.: 239; Fessler, 85–87.

81. Ingrao, 159–60, 209–13, 220, 224.

Zoltán Kramár

The Military Ethos of the Hungarian Nobility, 1700–1848

Ethos is one of those marvelously flexible Greek nouns which imply
both reality and ideal. Insofar as the term means "custom" and "usage,"
it lends itself to a rather concrete, institutional treatment. But *ethos*
may also stand for the fundamental values, the spirit and the mores of
an identifiable group. In this latter sense a more literary approach
seems to be appropriate. So far as space allows, I propose to apply
both techniques of analysis to the subject. For ready understanding of
it, however, a rough sketch of its historical context is essential. From
the Hungarians' arrival in the Carpathian basin in the late ninth
century to the Peace of Szatmár in 1711, Hungarian history had been
overwhelmingly military.[1] Indeed, it has been well said that ". . .Hun-
garian history is a continuous heroic epic."[2] Preeminently, the actors
in this centuries-long martial drama came from the nobility whose
original membership consisted of the invading Hungarian freemen, "a
class which by definition was military."[3] Indeed, as Marczali so aptly
put it: ". . . if ever there was a nobility which deserved the name of
army, such was indeed the Hungarian nobility."[4]

In time, the nobility's martial activities became anchored in law.
Specifically, in 1222, seven years after the Magna Carta, Hungary's
lesser nobility compelled their weak king, Andrew II, to sign the
Golden Bull in which, in exchange for the tax-free status of their
estates, they obligated themselves to military service whenever required.[5] In the sixteenth century the provisions of the Golden Bull were
reemphasized by the great lawyer István Werbőczi who, in his famous
Tripartitum opus iuris consuetudinarii inclyti regni Hungariae, dealt
both definitively and comprehensively with the kingdom's public and
private law.[6]

The military service of the nobility usually took the form of the noble
levy, better known as the *posse comitatus* or the *insurrectio.* If the
threat to the country was limited, the king, or in his absence, the
Palatine, could call up the *insurrectio particularis.* In the event of a
major emergency, the *insurrectio generalis* could be mobilized by
resolution of the Diet.[7]

The *insurrectio* certainly served its purpose as long as the socioeconomic conditions of late mediaeval Europe prevented potential opponents from fielding better-organized and uniformly trained and equipped armies. But as early as the fifteenth century, King Matthias Corvinus felt the need to organize a professional, standing military force. What later came to be known as his famous and much-feared Black Host, turned out to be just such an army, consisting of some 30,000 German and Czech mercenaries.[8] Upon his death, however, this formation was disbanded, and national defense once again came to be dependent upon the noble levy.

On August 29, 1526, at Mohács, Hungary fought her last battle with an army consisting entirely of the *insurrectio*. On this occasion, the king, two archbishops, and 25,000 nobles were slaughtered by the awesome hosts of Suleiman the Magnificent.[9]

During the following century and a half, when the Ottoman empire controlled two-thirds of Hungary, the nobles of "free" or "royal" Hungary continued their military activities on several fronts. Some were heavily engaged in continuous border raiding against the Turks. Many found themselves involved in a number of anti-Habsburg uprisings. Toward the end of this period there were even those who fully supported the Habsburgs against the Turks. Thus in May 1683, for instance, as Vienna, for the second time in two centuries, was about to come under Turkish guns, the Palatine, Pál Esterházy, led 6,000 nobles of the *insurrectio particularis* to join the imperial army; 12,000 more were manning frontier strongholds.[10]

One might perhaps have expected that with the liberation of Hungary, the nobility would have had the chance to turn its attention to rebuilding a cruelly ravaged land. Unfortunately, this was not yet to be. The imperial authorities chose to view the kingdom as conquered territory. As to the Hungarians, Field Marshal Count Raimondo Montecuccoli summed up the government's attitude toward them most trenchantly when he called them "'a proud, fickle and obdurate people,' who would have to be controlled with an iron rod."[11] To add further insult to injury, when it came to reapportioning the liberated lands, the Imperial Commission charged with that task submitted a plan in which it recommended that

> Germans . . . should be given preferential treatment in the new lands so that "the kingdom, or at least a large part of it, will gradually be germanized, and Hungarian blood, with its tendency to unrest and revolution, will be tempered by German, and turned thereby to a steadfast loyalty and love of their natural hereditary king."[12]

Generally speaking, governmental circles apparently thought that the

Hungarians, and especially their ruling estate, the nobility, did not carry their fair share of the war's burden. This was, at best, a badly skewed view of reality. The country itself, after all, was the battlefield with all that term implies. Its human and material losses were staggering. Furthermore, the country was expected to supply up to 70 percent of the logistical support needed by the imperial armies.[13] It is no exaggeration to say that, more than the indescribably crushing poverty of the population, it was the grossly insensitive and rapaciously hostile conduct of the imperial authorities that finally triggered Rákóczi's war for independence at the beginning of the eighteenth century.

One may state that few Hungarians, nobles, commoners, or serfs, sided with the king during the early phase of this general uprising. "Without difference of order, social class or religion, Hungary appeared to have rallied ..." to Rákóczi.[14] Alas, Prince Ferenc II Rákóczi proved to be no great military leader. When European developments finally permitted the imperial government to bring the full weight of its military forces to bear upon the insurgents, the outcome of the struggle could no longer remain in doubt. On April 30, 1711, at the town of Szatmár, a negotiated peace brought that protracted and sanguinary uprising to a conclusion. As for the Hungarian nobility and its military activities, the peace signaled the commencement of a new era.

"The chief charge brought by the Hungary of the nineteenth century against that of the eighteenth was of having allowed the national spirit to decay."[15] This charge may be substantiated by pointing to three concurrent developments during the eighteenth century. First, the higher nobility, slowly transformed itself into what may be aptly called a *supranational,* aulic *aristocracy.* As Macartney puts it: ". . . by the end of the century the magnate class was only half Hungarian."[16] Second, the lesser nobility, the gentry class, embraced a world of ideas which was strictly circumscribed by Werbőczy's *Tripartitum.*[17] In other words, it desperately held on to its privileges as an estate, leaving national interests out of sight, or at best, identifying them with those very same privileges. Third, although the very existence of the nobility's privileges developed out of, and continued to depend upon, military service, the *insurrectio* had become an anachronism as an exclusive means of national defense. Between 1708 and 1715, royal rescript after royal rescript emphasized that the kingdom could not be defended by the *insurrectio* alone, that it needed the help of the *miles extraneus* to whose upkeep the nobility had to contribute.[18] The nobles, on their part, continued to insist that although, according to the *Tripartitum,* they were duty bound personally to defend the kingdom, at the same time and for that very reason, they were specifically exempt from taxation. Thus the kingdom's defense needs — above all a modern, professional, standing army — clashed head on with the nobility's legally guaranteed privileges. Only a compromise between king and estates could lead both parties out of this impasse. At the Diet of 1715, such a compromise was found. Law VIII (1715) left the *insurrectio* intact. Hence those nobles who were subject to it remained immune from taxation. The law also recognized that the defense of the kingdom required, in addition to the *insurrectio,* the organization of a professional standing army, made up of Hungarians as well as foreigners, which Hungary would have to finance and supply.[19] Law VIII (1715) was subsequently reaffirmed by the Diets of 1723 and 1741. Unqualified operational command of the new professional army belonged to the king, who exercised it through the instrumentality of the Vienna-based *Hofkriegsrat.*[20] Officers and men were sworn to loyalty to the king-emperor and forbidden to owe allegiance to any other person or institution.[21]

Even so, the Habsburgs' chronic suspicion of everything Hungarian dogged those nobles who, seeking a professional military career, joined up.[22] The *Hofkriegsrat* had no Hungarian member. No Hungarian was placed in a leading position on the high command.[23] True, Maria Theresa had appointed János Pálffy as one of the commanding generals in Hungary. Pálffy, in turn, had a number of Hungarians on his staff.[24] But cavalry generals in operational command positions had little if any influence in the councils of the highest leadership.

This then was assuredly not the national army of which Miklós Zrínyi had dreamed during the previous century. It seems that, in exchange for continued immunity from taxation, the nobility had given up the very idea of an independent Hungarian army. Yet, those nobles — and compared to more warlike centuries, there were not that many — who served, did their duty well. Marczali quotes von Ranke as stating:

> Of old it was German soldiers who carried on the Hungarian wars, and it was said that the rivers of Hungary had been dyed with German blood, now Hungarian soldiers appeared in German wars, forming the backbone of the Imperial army. That country which had hitherto been a constant menace to the Imperial power now constituted its mainstay.[25]

All through the Seven Years War, Hungarian regiments fought steadfastly under the leadership of a number of outstanding combat commanders, men like Counts Károly Batthyány, András Hadik, and

Ferenc Nádasdy among others. Yet, even Maria Theresa never appointed a Hungarian to head a larger formation.[26] Knowledge, or at least suspicion, that they were not implicitly trusted by the high command, must have rankled with Hungary's serving nobility. At the same time, this feeling must have been blunted by the fact that the Queen's relationship with "her Hungarians" had always been characterized by cordiality and even affection. Her death changed the situation radically.

The well-intentioned but impatiently and tactlessly pushed comprehensive reforms of Joseph II almost totally alienated the Hungarian nobility from the dynasty. At the time of the hapless emperor's death, the country was not far from open rebellion. The memorable Diet of 1790 made a number of extreme demands on Leopold II, among them being one for a separate Hungarian army.[27] This time, there was at least potential muscle behind the words. Since the gentry was ready to utilize force in gaining its objectives, it prepared to marshal its military strength. It proceeded along two distinct lines. Some of the counties, traditional political strongholds of the gentry, began an inflammatory correspondence with several Hungarian regiments of the regular army. Many Hungarian officers, members of the lesser nobility themselves, responded with alacrity.[28] Six Hungarian hussar regiments: the Splényi-, Károlyi-, Pálffy-, Gyulay-, Erdődy-, and Toscana regiments joined in a written demand directed to the Diet, calling for a Hungarian army, under a Hungarian War Council, led by Hungarian noble officers.[29]

At the same time, the gentry also mobilized the *insurrectio,* thinly camouflaged under the banderial movement.[30] The *banderium* of 1790 was a unit of young nobles organized for the specific purpose of guarding the Holy Crown which Joseph II, shortly before his death, sent back from Vienna to Buda. Soon, however, as the counties set up their contingents for the national *banderium,* it became obvious that they were being organized in close imitation of the standing army. Clearly, the gentry's intention was to turn the *banderium,* properly trained and equipped, into the nucleus of an insurgent army, should the nation rise again.[31]

Although Leopold II made a number of concessions to the Diet, defense of the realm he successfully retained as a matter belonging under his exclusive jurisdiction.[32] Since at the same time, European developments once more turned favorable to the Habsburgs, the dangerously turbulent emotions in Hungary rapidly subsided. Five years later, the Diet of 1796 actually raised the strength of the Hungarian contingent of the standing army, so that throughout the period of the French Wars, twelve Hungarian infantry and twelve cavalry regiments served with the imperial forces.[33] The ranks of these Hungarian line regiments were recruited from among the serfs, but the officers came mainly from among the lesser nobility. Although not overly addicted to professional study, they were brave and rendered faithful service to the ruler. In short, until 1848, they gave the sovereign no cause for complaint. Even though Rákóczi several times called out the *insurrectio particularis,* the *insurrectio* itself, that mediaeval anachronism, lay dormant throughout much of the eighteenth century. Under modern conditions it did not, it could not contribute significantly to defense needs. Yet during the French Wars it was called up by parliamentary decision four times: in 1797, in 1800, in 1805, and in 1809. By ancient custom, the commander-in-chief was always the Palatine, who on these four occasions, was Archduke Joseph.[34]

The archduke labored mightily to transform the *insurrectio* into a modern army. Since the nobility had no previous military training, imperial officers had to be posted to these amateur formations. The acquisition of modern weaponry, however, proved to be an insoluble problem. Since the *insurrectio* could be utilized only in the immediate defense of the kingdom, armaments went first to the regular army. What was left proved to be woefully inadequate.[35] Happily, on the first three occasions the noble levy was not engaged. The *insurrectio* of 1809 was not so fortunate. On April 2, 1809, the *Hofkriegsrat* notified Archduke Joseph that it could not equip the *insurrectio.*[36] Nonetheless, the call up was obeyed. A proclamation by Napoleon, dated May 15, calling upon Hungary to shake off the foreign yoke, remained unheeded.[37] At the battle of Győr, fought on July 14, 1809, only the *insurrectio* forces of the Transdanubian counties were engaged. As individuals the nobles fought bravely, but without appropriate training, modern equipment, and professional leadership, they simply could not stand up to Napoleon's veterans.[38] The institution of the *insurrectio* remained on the statute books till 1848, but after Győr, it was never again called up.

This then had been the "reality" of the nobility's military ethos viewed in its historical setting. As is almost always the case, here, too, reality fell far short of the ideal. Yet the ideal was there, fully developed, much admired. In 1848, for a brief moment, it even had some corrective effect upon reality. Turning now to these fundamental military values of the Hungarian nobility, they can best be examined in the light of literary sources.

At the outset, some general observations are in order. The Hungarian noble saw no particular virtue in the systematic study of warfare. The testimony in this regard is unambiguous. In 1739, in his *Confessiones,* Prince Ferenc II Rákóczi had complained that his military operations suffered fatally from a lack of suitable and competent officers.[39] Just over a hundred years later, I. R. First Lieutenant János Korponay, in his *Hadi földírás* (*Military Geography*), read before the Hungarian Academy of Sciences, said, "The Hungarian solider does not like to study very much."[40] And then, of course, there is Sándor Petőfi's famous, bitter parody, *A magyar nemes* (*The Hungarian Noble*). In the fourth stanza one finds the boast:

> I do not write, I do not read
> The life of a Hungarian noble I lead!

Another observation one may make is that, much unlike their brother nobles elsewhere in Europe, the Hungarian nobles did not dislike, let alone hate, lawyers and parliamentarians.[41] They themselves were often lawyers and parliamentarians. These descendants of warrior nobles had, during the eighteenth century, became a nation of lawyers.[42] Although their estate interests were just as selfish and narrow-minded as those of any other Continental nobility, they cultivated these interests within an impeccably constitutional context. As a consequence, neither the Hungarian noble, nor his ethos, ever stood at the unqualified disposal of either a king or an ideology, be it religious or secular. Instead, the military values of the Hungarian nobility were most consistently put to the service of what they understood to be the ancient Hungarian constitution.[43] It was this uncompromising legalism, giving shape, character, and above all, purpose, to their military values, which perhaps most strikingly set the Hungarian nobles apart from their European fellows.

Turning to the nobles' military ethos, it seems reasonable to assume that an ideal value system is one which emerges from a persistent pattern of conduct on the part of a group's paradigmatic personalities. If this is true, then all the *desiderata* of such a value system are present in Hungarian history.

For centuries, the Hungarian warrior nobility had defended itself externally against foreign invaders, and internally against centralizing foreign dynasties. This double-pronged defense mission helped develop a military style which came to be characterized by hardhitting, devil-may-care, do-or-die battle centeredness. At the same time, in the truly outstanding leaders of the class, this exaggerated combativeness was rendered almost transcendent by a well-developed moral courage, with all the values that term implies. By the eighteenth century this military value system had certainly been solidly established in the consciousness of the Hungarian nobility, precisely through the known conduct of their historic heroes.

If in time, as had happened during the eighteenth century, the group's own conduct falls noticeably short of such standards, the latter may yet be regained, provided that they are kept alive in the mind and imagination of the group, in conjunction with sustained and severe self-criticism.

In the period under discussion, the foregoing conditions were also present. Throughout earlier centuries of modern European history up to the mid-1800s, the Hungarian literati, most of them nobles themselves, have been the keepers of their estate's conscience, the chief upholders of the ethos of the noble warrior.[44]

Especially in period of exhaustion, when apathy or complacency paralyzed collective action, the literati admonished, exhorted, threatened, and cajoled the "nation" to pull itself together, to arise, and to live up to the standards set for it and for all generations to come, by the great paradigmatic personalities of its past.

Regardless of period or stylistic school, these wielders of the pen, who, more often than not, had themselves been also wielders of the saber, kept stressing three simple but interrelated themes. One, the nation had been blessed in the past by more than its share of great personalities, who through wisdom, extraordinary courage, and self-sacrifice had repeatedly saved it from annihilation or, from what would have been worse, dishonor. Two, today — and *today* refers to whenever the author happened to be writing — the nation was headed down the path to perdition. Finally, that dismal destination was avoidable if the nation would only decide to follow once again in the footsteps of its heroic ancestors.

From the seventeenth century onward, the Hungarian nobility thus were continually reminded, in both prose and poetry, of their military values, not in the analyses of philosophers or social scientists, but in the lives of their national heroes and in the works of their poets. At the same time, this heroic ethos was constantly contrasted to the dismal reality of the nobility's "present" conditions, attitudes, and performances.

As illustrations of such literary prodding and self-criticism — the latter often bordering on self-flagellation — the following serve as representative samples. In the seventeenth century there was Miklós

Zrínyi, himself one of the most highly honored noble-warrior paradigms. In his *Az török áfium ellen való orvosság (Antidote to the Turkish Opium)*[45] he urged setting up a national army since, in his estimation and experience, Hungarians could rely only upon themselves. Yet his description of the contemporary nobility was devastating:

> We have fallen so far below our ancestors' standards that should our heroic forefathers return from the grave they would fail to recognize us. We have become objects of contempt before the nations, and the prey of our enemies. Why? Because of the neglect of heroic discipline, because of drunkenness, slovenliness, hatred amongst ourselves, and because of a thousand suchlike sins. . . . What we need for our own defense are arms, arms, more arms and heroic resolution. Either we defend ourselves with these or let us die like heroes, because there is no other alternative. Or should we perhaps run for it? Where to? We shall not find Hungary anywhere else, and no one is going to vacate his own country, out of friendship for us, just so that we may establish a new home in it. Our noble liberties are nowhere else to be found except in Pannonia. *Hic vobis vel vicendum vel moriendum est!*[46]

Two hundred years later, Baron József Eötvös, with scathing sarcasm, subjected the nobility to merciless ridicule. In his novel, *A falu jegyzője (The Village Notary*, 1845), he wrote: "We are an oriental people, and our ancestors came to the west only in order to find a home where the sun rises later so that they may sleep longer in the morning. It would be a great injustice to ask of us, their descendants, that we, the most noble people created by God, should view our lives as nothing but a long drawn-out drudgery."[47]

In the meantime, during the eighteenth century, while men like László Amadé, the playboy aristocrat, and József Gvadányi, Maria Theresa's retired cavalry general, sang their cheerful praises of the good and carefree military life, others continued in Zrínyi's footsteps. Dániel Berzsenyi, often referred to as the Hungarian Horace, constantly reminded the nobility of its lost ancestral virtues, most of which were military in nature. Still, his profound pessimism about his estate, momentarily turned to delight as the *insurrectio* of 1809 drew its saber against Napoleon. Prematurely he wrote:

> My nation's God still lives!
> . . . .
> And you still stand, my beloved country![48]

Ferenc Kölcsey suffered immensely because of the degraded state of the nobility. In a hymn, which later became the lyrics of the Hungarian national anthem, Kölcsey gave up on the nation's ever being able to arise by its own strength. All he could do was to beseech God that He would spare the much-tried nation further tribulation.

Ultimately, it was Mihály Vörösmarty who, after Zrínyi, put the nobility's military value system most succinctly. He accomplished that in his *Szózat*, the *Admonishment*, that veritable enchiridion of Hungarian patriotism. In it, he did not plead; he did not persuade. He commanded. The poem is studded with imperatives: "Here you must live and die!" One may have to die, but one must not break! In a poem to Ferenc Liszt, the poet asked the composer for a song to cure the soul-sick nation. The song the nation needed was to be a brain-shattering, wild, thundering, triumphal battle song, because ". . . thanks be to Heaven! Árpád's nation still has a soul."[49] And so, after almost two hundred years of literary reminders and tortured self-criticism, the nobility finally rose in 1848. Momentarily purging themselves of their parochial, meanly narrow class interests, making common cause with other progressive elements in the nation, they embraced the military ethos of Zrínyi, who had lived it, and of Vörösmarty, who had dreamed about and preached it. Thus did the ideal, for a moment of unique valor, become reality.

Notes

1. Henry Marczali, *Hungary in the Eighteenth Century* (Cambridge, 1910), 1.

2. Friedrich Tezner, *Die Wandlungen der österreichisch-ungarischen Reichsidee* (Vienna, 1905), 112, quoted in Robert A. Kann, *The Multinational Empire; Nationalism and National Reform in the Habsburg Monarchy, 1848-1918* (New York, 1964), I: 114.

3. C. A. Macartney, *Hungary: A Short History* (Chicago, 1962), 27.

4. Marczali, 7.

5. Macartney, 28-29. Also Paul Ignotus, *Hungary* (New York, 1972), 25.

6. Victor-L. Tapié, *The Rise and Fall of the Habsburg Monarchy* (New York, 1971), 28-29; Ignotus, 31.

7. Marczali, 355.

8. Tapié, 25.

9. Victor S. Mamatey, *The Rise of the Habsburg Empire, 1526-1815* (New York, 1971), 27.

10. John P. Spielman, *Leopold I of Austria* (New Brunswick, N.J., 1977), 99.

11. Gunther E. Rothenberg, *The Army of Francis Joseph* (West Lafayette, Ind., 1976), 4.

12. Spielman, 139–40.

13. Gyula Miskolczy, *A magyar nép történelme; a mohácsi vésztől az első világháborúig* (Rome, 1956), 160.

14. Tapié, 160. For the most recent works on Rákóczi, see also Béla Köpeczi and Ágnes R. Várkonyi, *II. Rákóczi Ferenc,* 2d ed. (Budapest, 1976); Imre Bánkuti, ed., *Rákóczi hadserege 1703–1711* (Budapest, 1976); Béla Köpeczi, ed., *Rákóczi szabadságharc és Európa* (Budapest, 1970); Köpeczi and Várkonyi, eds., *Rákóczi tükör, naplók, jelentések, emlékiratok a szabadságharcról* (Budapest, 1973).

15. Macartney, 110.

16. *Ibid.,* 110.

17. Erik Molnár, ed., *Magyarország története* (Budapest, 1964), 91.

18. Bálint Hóman and Gyula Szekfű, *Magyar történet* (Budapest, 1943), 4: 339. Even in peacetime, 30,000–40,000 foreign soldiers were garrisoned in Hungarian fortresses, Marczali, 318.

19. Miskolczy, 170–71.

20. For the organization and administration of the army see Béla K. Király, *Hungary in the Late Eighteenth Century; The Decline of Enlightened Despotism* (New York, 1969), 103–106.

21. Macartney, *The Habsburg Empire, 1790–1918* (London, 1968), 19.

22. This suspicion, bordering on paranoia, extended itself to the Hungarian ranks as well. Thus, purely Hungarian regiments were slow in being established. The oldest Hungarian hussar regiment, incorporated in the imperial army, dated to 1688; the second to 1696, the third to 1702. The pace picked up in 1733 when two new regiments were formed. By 1743 there were twelve Hungarian hussar regiments. Hóman and Szekfű, 4: 362–63.

23. *Ibid.,* 4: 363.

24. *Ibid.,* 4: 493. When he received news that Silesia had been invaded, it was Pálffy who ordered the *insurrectio particularis* in the Danubian counties (January 26, 1741). Counties like Pozsony, Komárom, Győr, and Pest mobilized 2,741 men. Under Hungarian leaders, such as Péter Halász and Count István Esterházy, they were to fight the Prussians in Silesia as Hungarian *Nationalhusaren.*

25. Marczali, 15, n.1.

26. Miskolczy, 184.

27. Macartney, *The Habsburg Empire,* 138.

28. Elemér Mályusz, ed., *Sándor Lipót főherceg nádor iratai, 1790–1795* (Budapest, 1926), 17.

29. Hóman and Szekfű, 5: 68–69. See also Király, 188.

30. Originally a *bandérium* was a unit of fifty warrior nobles fighting under the banner of a great noble. Most historians date the beginnings of this

institution to the Angevine dynasty of the fourteenth century. Macartney, *Hungary*, 44; Mamatey, 20. Erdélyi, on the other hand, pushes its origins back a hundred years, to the period of the Hungarian Crusade of 1217. László Erdélyi, "Bajtársi egyesületek a magyar lovagkorban," in *Emlékkönyv: dr. gróf Klebelsberg Kúnó negyedszázados kultúrpolitikai működésének emlékére* (Budapest, 1925), 252–53.

31. Király, 184–85.
32. Macartney, *The Habsburg Empire*, 140.
33. Hóman and Szekfű, 5: 199.
34. *Ibid.,* 5: 205. On Hungary's, and especially on the *insurrectio*'s role, in the Napoleonic wars, see also Marczali, *Magyarország története* (Budapest, 1898), 8: 565 ff.
35. Hóman and Szekfű, 5: 205.
36. Macartney, *The Habsburg Empire*, 188.
37. Marczali, "Magyarország története III. Károlytól a bécsi kongresszusig (1711–1815)," in Sándor Szilágyi, ed., *A magyar nemzet története* (Budapest, 1898), 8: 583. See also Király, "Napoleon's Proclamation of 1809 and its Hungarian Echo," in Stanley B. Winters and Joseph Held, eds., *Intellectual and Social Developments in the Habsburg Empire from Maria Theresa to the First World War: Essays Dedicated to Robert A. Kann* (Boulder, Col., 1975), 31–54.
38. Marczali, "Magyarország története," 586. See also Ferenc Bay, *Napoleon Magyarországon; a császár és katonái Győr városában* (Budapest, 1941); Sándor Kisfaludy, *Geschichte der Insurrection des Adels von Ungarn im Jahre 1809 und 1810* (Győr, 1931); István R. Kiss, *Az utolsó nemesi felkelés* (Budapest, 1909).
39. Julius Farkas, *Ungarns Geschichte und Kultur in Dokumenten* (Wiesbaden, 1955), 82.
40. István Nemeskürty, *"Kik érted haltak, szent Világszabadság"; A negyvennyolcas honvéd hadsereg katonaforradalmárai* (Budapest, 1977), 30.
41. Alfred Vagts, *A History of Militarism Civilian and Military* (New York, 1959), 51.
42. Marczali, *Hungary in the Eighteenth Century*, 134.
43. The Hungarian nobility's attitude toward the ruler on the one hand, and the constitution on the other, is well reflected in the paternal admonition with which the young László Szalay was sent out into the pre-March world: "... toward the Sovereign be loyal and obedient . . . but at the same time, stand steadfastly by the legally created and sanctioned constitution. . . ." Quoted in Zoltán Horváth, *Teleki László* (Budapest, 1964), 1: 118.
44. Macartney, *Hungary*, 130–31.
45. It was published several times. One useful edition, not available to this author, is *Gróf Zrínyi Miklós válogatott munkái*, ed. László Négyesy (Budapest, [1904]), 293–320.
46. Farkas, 65–66.

47. Quoted in Veremund Tóth, *A magyar irodalom története* (Buenos Aires, 1960), 326.
48. *Ibid.*, 249.
49. *Ibid.*, 311.

László Deme

The First Soldiers of the Hungarian Revolution: The National Guard in Pest in March–April, 1848

The news of the February Revolution in Paris created great expectations and political excitement in Hungary. On March 3, the leader of the liberal opposition at the Diet, Lajos Kossuth, called for abolition of serfdom and the privileges of the nobility and proposed to transform Hungary from a feudal monarchy to a modern parliamentary state. He demanded that henceforth Hungary be administered by a cabinet completely independent of the central authorities in Vienna and responsible to a popularly elected Hungarian parliament.[1]

Kossuth made these proposals at the Diet in Pozsony,[2] to an assembly composed almost exclusively of representatives of the nobility. To enlist popular support for these changes, the liberal club in Pest, the so-called Opposition Circle, decided to circulate a petition enumerating similar demands Kossuth had previously made.[3] This petition became known as the Twelve Points. It was drafted by a young Francophile lawyer-journalist, József Irinyi, who summarized the most important liberal demands for civil liberties and national independence, but also added the establishment of a national guard as Point 5 among the wishes of the nation.[4]

It appears that Irinyi's Point 5 is the first clear reference to a national guard in Hungary in 1848.[5] Although civic guards consisting of well-to-do burghers had been in existence in the bigger cities since the Napoleonic wars,[6] apart from the regular army there was no nationally organized armed force in Hungary. The radical democrat Irinyi, who was an enthusiastic admirer of everything French, was probably responsible for directing public attention to the idea of a guard in the capital.[7]

Indeed, the notion of a guard was so foreign in Hungary that before March 1848 no generally accepted term existed for it in the Hungarian language. The current *nemzetőrség* is a direct translation of the French *garde national* and it acquired its present specific meaning between March and July, 1848.[8]

Following the Viennese revolution, the Hungarian Diet in Pozsony accepted Kossuth's demands and the realization of the Twelve Points became the battle cry of a revolutionary demonstration in Pest. On March 15 a few young radical intellectuals led a large crowd demanding an end to censorship. Sándor Petőfi, already a famous poet at twenty-five, Mór Jókai, a twenty-three-year-old romantic novelist, and a twenty-two-year-old history teacher, Pál Vasvári, were the most important organizers of the group. During the demonstration, Jókai among others demanded that the "National Guard be established immediately" and added "there must be no uniforms" and "every man should be ready to defend his country."[9]

The demonstrators obtained the support of the City Council in Pest for the Twelve Points and, together with the members of the council formed a committee of public safety (rendfenntartási bizottmány) which took over the administration of the capital. Then at the head of about 20,000 demonstrators the members of the committee marched up to the palace-fortress in Buda and obtained the approval of the highest Habsburg officials in the land for the abolition of censorship. They liberated a political prisoner and also received a definite promise from the authorities that the military would not interfere in the affairs of the city.[10]

The revolutionaries correctly regarded the regular army in Hungary as an alien and hostile body. It was composed mainly of peasants from all the distant lands of the Habsburg monarchy who as a rule did not even understand Hungarian. They served under the command of cosmopolitan aristocratic officers who were faithful servants of their supreme warlord, the Habsburg emperor, and had little in common with Hungarian popular desires and aspirations.[11] Under such circumstances the committee's demand for the noninterference of the military showed real foresight, and enabled the committee to organize its own armed force.

At the first meeting, late at night on March 15, the committee decided to establish a national guard. At that time the committee was presided over by Lipót Rottenbiller, the vice-mayor of Pest and was composed of city officials, liberal nobles, and revolutionary intellectuals including Petőfi, Vasvári, and Irinyi. Consequently, the proclamation on the establishment of the guard is an interesting mixture of caution, moderation, and revolutionary mentality. Instead of a stirring manifesto, the committee stated only that the existing civic guard was to be increased by 1,500 men with the possibility of further additions later, and stressed the need to maintain "security of person and property." In a similarly moderate fashion, the committee declared: "Fellow citizens! our slogans are: long live the King, constitutional reform, liberty, equality, peace, and order."[12]

On the crucial question of eligibility for service in the guard, how-ever, the committee must have been under the sway of its radical members. Instead of following the contemporary European pattern of forming a guard out of property owners, the proclamation read as follows: "Every honest man can present himself at City Hall before the Committee and after inspection will receive arms and identification free of charge."

As identification, members of the guard were supposed to wear red, white, and green armbands and similar cockades on their hats. The same identification was to be worn by the members of the old civic guard and the new volunteers.

The early events of the revolution in Pest and especially the establish-ment of the guard show some interesting similarities with Paris of 1789. There, on July 13, 1789, revolutionary excitement led to the establish-ment of a standing committee to administer the city under an old municipal officer, the *prévot des marchands,* Jacques de Flessels, and their first move to ensure the security of the city was to enlarge the existing town guard. This enlarged town guard originally was to wear the red and blue colors of Paris.[13] Lafayette later transformed this into a national symbol by adding the white of the Bourbons, and the French National Guard he commanded served under this *tricolore.*

There can be no question that by selecting the red, white, and green in Pest the committee wished to emphasize the national rather than the municipal character of the new force. Since all the radical members of the Pest committee were enthusiastic students of the French Revolu-tion, it is likely that the French example was imitated intentionally.[14]

In many ways, however, the situation was different in Pest. The foreign soldiers of the garrison certainly could have been used against the people the same way as the German mercenaries under the Prince de Lambesc were used against the Parisians on July 12, 1789. But there was no concentration of troops around Pest and there was no assembly to dissolve. The danger of counterrevolution was imminent and real in Paris, but it was only potential in the Hungarian capital.[15]

Recruitment for the guard started immediately in the morning of March 16 in Pest; in a few days several thousand men joined in a great outburst of enthusiasm and revolutionary excitement. In the city, patriotic demonstrations, speeches, meetings, and illuminations re-placed the former passivity, and the radical organizers of the March 15 committee became popular heroes overnight. According to the reports of royal officials in Pest, "open republican tendencies" appeared,[16] and taking advantage of the abolition of censorship, the radicals established their own newspaper, the *Marczius Tizenötödike* ("March Fifteenth").[17]

When the committee established the National Guard, it called for enlistment in all the existing branches of the old municipal guard.[18] Therefore, initially the new volunteers could choose between becoming hussars, dragoons, infantrymen, grenadiers, or joining a sort of sharp-shooting unit. Apart from the division between infantry and cavalry, there is no evidence about how the equipment and training (if any) of these five units differed. One can only suspect that behind these rather grandiloquent terms there was merely the age-old desire of men to play soldier. It is unlikely that the "dragoons" were really trained to fight on horseback and on foot, or that the "grenadiers" were regarded as elite troops.

In addition to these five units a new group, the so-called "sixth unit of the Pest Guard" was formed at the Opposition Circle. It attracted university students, actors, writers, young lawyers, and other members of the radical intelligentsia.[19] This new group was referred to as the *Regiment of Equality* by the radical press.[20] Ferenc Pulszky, a popular liberal politician, was elected commander. According to Pulszky, the educated membership found it difficult to obey orders; they always argued with an ex-sergeant who tried to give them basic training and under the circumstances his efforts met with little success.[21]

On March 16 the committee made its first decisions about the organization of the guard. Five guardhouses were designated in different parts of the city, and guard members were to report for duty to the guardhouse nearest to their homes.[22] Since the committee obtained 500 guns from the army arsenals that day, it was decided to keep 100 guns at each guard station. These guns must have been intended for the new volunteers because members of the old municipal guard had their own arms. Each guard member had to return his gun to the guardhouse after completing his turn of duty. This arrangement probably made for maximum use of the available arms. It was also possible to serve with one's own gun.[23]

The guard was placed under the jurisdiction of the Committee of Public Safety and its chairman, Lipót Rottenbiller, became the commander.[24] All guard members took the following oath:

> I, as a member of the civic guard of Pest, swear by the living God that I will be faithful to the country, King, and constitution, and will always honor and obey the laws, the legal authorities and the lawful commands of my commissioned and noncommissioned civic officers; in the service of my country and my city I will not leave my flag under any circumstances; in guard duty day and night I will always behave in a manly fashion and will labor for the maintenance of public

order and security; I will give the same respect to our guard regulations as to the laws (of the country) and will follow all and will not
violate any of them. So help me God. Amen.[25]

With its emphasis on the maintenance of law and order, the oath
defined the guard primarily as an enlarged police force and this
definition probably corresponded to the desires of the well-to-do
citizens of Pest. The only sign of the ongoing revolution was that the
traditional formula "for King and for country" was reversed, and that a
reference was also made to the constitution.

The situation in the capital, however, developed in such a way that
the guard became much more than an enlarged police force. First,
sheer numbers made a difference. The *Marczius Tizenötödike* wrote
that the guard increased with remarkable speed and new units were
established every day. By March 24 the unit bearing the name of
"'Equality' became a regiment and new companies were forming continuously." The zeal of the new volunteers was such that the paper of
the radicals happily commented: "If one inspects their enthusiastic
lines one cannot doubt the future of Hungarian liberty. . . . If the enemy
against whom we are now arming ourselves will attack us, everyone
can rest assured that this unit will be the first to go to the battlefield to
defend [our] rights."[26]

Considerable variety existed among the newly formed armed groups
and some of them must have looked rather picturesque. A unit imitat-
ing the forces of Matthias Corvinus called itself the "Black Host." They
dressed in black, marched under a black flag and had a death's-head on
both their hats and their flag.[27] According to a reliable contemporary
account, this unit consisted exclusively of "young gentlemen."[28] Their
appearance must have caused some merriment in the city because the
Marczius Tizenötödike felt obliged to defend them against sarcastic
witticisms.[29]

Others wore red feathers, cockades, and armbands for identification. According to a public notice of March 20, everyone in the first
company of the Regiment of Equality wore red.[30] The color red meant
radical republican extremism in 1848 in Pest as well as in Paris.
Replacing the national tricolor with red, however, created such ad-
verse reaction in the Hungarian capital that those who wore red were
called traitors, and some of them were manhandled in the streets by
angry citizens.[31] The *Marczius Tizenötödike* understandably objected
and denounced the attackers' intolerance, but seemed to be definitely
on the defensive.

> We all know perfectly well that 10 or 12 years ago the tricolored flag
> which now flies on the royal castle and the military barracks was
> pretty much a forbidden article. Even if now the red cockade rep-
> resents a more advanced form of liberal politics, it is as unreason-
> able to oppose it as it previously had been unreasonable to consider
> wearing the *tricolore lèse-majesté*.[32]

The Committee of Public Safety issued a special communication April
9 stating that "wearing the red color in itself represents no danger" and
condemned the incident arguing that, after all, what is liberty if not the
right to do anything which does not hurt others.[33]

If most people were not willing to accept the symbol of a radical
revolution in the Hungarian capital, many enthusiastically joined to
serve under the national colors. The population of Pest was 110,516 in
1848.[34] Out of this number a little less than 5 percent of the total,
approximately 5,000, joined the guard by March 25. In addition, there
was a separate guard organization in Buda with an enlistment of
1,399.[35] Memoirs and recollections all agree that a high percentage of
the intelligentsia joined. Statistics for the enlistment of journeymen
and industrial workers are unavailable, but there is evidence that they
too must have enrolled in substantial numbers when "honesty" was the
only qualification for enlistment. Since March 18 a number of rather
cautious city burghers joined the Committee of Public Safety, the
committee resolved on that day that journeymen who were not permanent inhabitants of the city could join only if vouched for by a
guardsman of good repute. It was also specified that journeymen in the
guard had to be native-born Hungarians, which eliminated many of
the skilled workers who were Germans by birth.[36]

Similarly, restrictions were suggested in regard to Jews, many of
whom were refused the right to enlist.[37] The Jewish inhabitants of the
city identified themselves with the Hungarian national desires and
behaved as patriots. Understandably, they hoped that the liberty and
equality so loudly proclaimed in the capital would include them also.
According to an eyewitness, on March 15 during the demonstrations
"a citizen of the Hebrew faith" also made a moving speech in German:

> We have suffered a great deal for a long time . . . and were subjected
> to bloody violence and contempt. We trust in the magnaminity of the
> Hungarian nation and hope . . . that when in the whole civilized
> Europe there are movements to liberate the Israelites, our beloved
> fatherland will not forget us completely. Fraternity should be our
> slogan and we all should get rid of our centuries-old prejudices and
> become brothers.[38]

Although the speech "was received with enthusiasm by the people," a few days later Jews still suffered discrimination. Resisting anti-Semitism and enforcing equality, but also protecting the Jews from insult, the committee resolved that "Jews should report for enlistment at the unit which was forming at the Opposition Circle."[39] They were accepted in the "Regiment of Equality" without question because it primarily consisted of members of the intelligentsia and because the radicals gave them strong support. The *Marczius Tizenötödike* "could not find strong enough terms to express its indignation" over sporadic anti-Semitic behavior.[40] Vasvári and others similarly condemned it.[41] Petőfi eloquently accused the "German citizens of Pest of throwing mud at the virgin flag" of the revolution because they did not accept Jews among themselves in the National Guard and added that the cause of the anti-Semites was so shameful and unjust that it cried to heaven for punishment.[42]

Equipment was a crucial problem for the National Guard. Members of the old municipal guard had arms, but guns were needed for thousands of new volunteers. The committee took advantage of the revolutionary excitement in the city to obtain arms from the arsenals of the regular army. General Ignaz Lederer, commander of the garrison at Buda, was persuaded that "the slightest employment of the army would lead to trouble and desperate clashes," and that arming the National Guard was the only way to assure security of life and property.[43] He turned over 1,500 muskets to the Committee by March 17, but stated that no more remained in the arsenal.[44]

Apparently no one believed him. The authorities received information that the "Youth of Pest" was planning a great public meeting for March 23. It was the revolutionaries' intention to march to Buda with a large crowd and, if necessary, force the inspection of the arsenal by the people to make sure that there were really no arms for them.[45]

The search for arms is always the critical danger point in the history of revolutions. It led to large-scale violence and the destruction of the Bastille at the beginning of the Great French Revolution. As in Paris in 1789, in Pest, too, the people were motivated by enthusiasm for liberty but also by fear.[46] This fear was generated by the unsettled conditions in the city: the presence of an unusually large number of peasants and the sight of large demonstrating crowds and armed men on the streets. It is also likely that after taking a stand for freedom on March 15 the people also expected reprisals from the army and established authorities. Fear is normally followed by defensive reaction. The desire for arms could be interpreted as the manifestation of a defensive reaction, a sort of arming in self-defense.[47]

The possibility of bloodshed was certainly present in the city. Jókai recalled later that during the March days he received plans for drastic action from dubious elements with military background. It was suggested to him that at night fires were to be started at ten different points in the city and in the resulting chaos, one of the military barracks should be attacked and occupied. The cannon captured there could be used against the rest of the soldiery and other military fortified positions.[48]

Similarly, Vasvári talked about the existence of other violent schemes. Several hundred young workers suggested to him "on the first day of the revolution" that they would learn how to handle cannon in three days and would capture an important arsenal for the revolution. Other workers wanted to move violently against the guild system. Vasvári and his friends also had "two bloody plans" of their own, but wished to use them only if the reaction forced them, meaning if "Radetzky . . . moved to Hungary to continue his bloody work there" by attacking Hungarian liberty.[49] With plans like these circulating, fear and uneasiness were certainly understandable. But fear was not limited to the people. After the noisy and threatening demonstration on March 23, 1,000 more guns were turned over to the National Guard. The authorities gave in to the revolutionaries' demands because they feared large-scale violence. According to General Lederer's report, he gave the guns to the guard because he did not wish to increase distrust in the central Viennese authorities and because he wanted to avoid attack on the arsenals by the aroused masses.[50]

According to the *Marczius Tizenötödike,* at this point there were 800 rifles with the old civic guard; altogether 2,500 were obtained from the arsenals; private individuals possessed 800.[51] Thus, the guard had a total of 4,100 rifles. There is no evidence that substantially more were obtained from anywhere as long as the committee exercised authority in the capital. Since there were more volunteers than arms there was no uniform equipment, and according to contemporaries, some guardsmen did duty with rifles, others were equipped with swords and pistols.[52] Even equipping some units with lances and swords was considered. The *Marczius Tizenötödike* tersely pointed out that by itself neither the sword nor the lance was much of a weapon, but together they were truly incompatible.[53]

In advancing its own position, the radicals' newspaper defined the National Guard as "an armed force which is at the disposal of the nation at every minute," and which "in character and purpose is the opposite of the regular army. . . . The purpose of the National Guard is to defend the constitution, order, and the fatherland."

According to the *Marczius Tizenötödike,* this could be accomplished not by following Western European examples, but by using the American model: ". . . in America they know what a national guard is, what kind of arms it needs, and they know that if the Guard is well-organized it is the strongest and most irresistible army."

The article suggests that the guard be equipped with long, single-barrel, rifled guns of small caliber. The American example of target practice on squirrels is mentioned and for strategy it is suggested that the guard should not engage the enemy in the open field but fire from behind trees and other covered positions.[54]

These images unmistakably refer to the American Revolutionary War, a free people's army engaging the king's forces in a fight for freedom and independence. It is likely that many of the new volunteers in the Regiment of Equality felt closer to this characterization of the guard than to the definitions which stressed auxiliary police functions.

Equipped with a variety of weapons, the guard patrolled the streets of the capital day and night. The committee did not wish to provoke clashes with the military and even ordered guardsmen to return the salute of soldiers on duty.[55] The soldiery though was definitely put on the defensive. It was forced to accept the red, white, and green on the public buildings, including the barracks, instead of the black and yellow of the House of Austria. The regulars also retreated when the guard took determined action on matters of importance.

On March 28, late at night, it was discovered that a ship on the Danube ready to depart to the south had about 6,600 pounds of gunpowder on board. Transporting gunpowder without special precautions was highly unusual. Since ammunition was needed in the capital, a guard unit of about eighty men was dispatched to the harbor. Although informed that the powder "belonged to the Emperor," the guard unit confiscated it in the name of the Committee of Public Safety. Shortly after, a patrol of five soldiers and later a unit of about a hundred soldiers under the command of an officer were sent to the harbor, but they marched by without doing anything.[56]

The guard was able to keep the garrison in check not because it was stronger militarily, but because it had the support of the revolutionary capital. Indeed, many of the guns that came from the arsenals were outdated and "almost useless,"[57] and it is unlikely that in a showdown the untrained, poorly equipped guardsmen could have stood up to regular troops. In the March days, however, this was far from being obvious. Since the strength of the guard was not put to a test, it could be politically utilized by the Committee of Public Safety to a far greater extent than its actual military potential would have merited.

The political use of the guard centered around two issues: the committee's competition with the Diet for national leadership, and inducing Habsburg authorities to meet Hungarian national demands for greater autonomy.

Since the Diet consisted almost exclusively of members of the nobility, pressure exerted from the revolutionary capital moved the deputies to recognize the need for a thorough reform. The committee was fully aware of this. As early as March 19 a delegation was sent from Pest to Pozsony urging the Diet to legislate the demands contained in the Twelve Points.[58] On the same day when a delegation from the Diet to the committee arrived in Pest, the guard was paraded before the delegates with the obvious intent of emphasizing the strength of the committee.[59] The deputies from Pozsony were told that they were living in eventful times but they had not witnessed the greatest event, March 15 in Pest, and they were urged to enact "without delays the demands outlined in the Twelve Points."[60] Under the influence of its radical members the committee also urged the deputies to grant the "widest possible suffrage"[61] to all inhabitants of the country.

In Pozsony the principle of the freedom of press was accepted, but following the established nineteenth-century liberal pattern, it was proposed that before publication newspapers deposit 20,000 forints with the authorities as security against possible libel. This proposed restriction resulted in an angry demonstration in the capital. On the afternoon of March 21 units of the National Guard stood in arms in front of City Hall. When a new unit, "the armed youth of the university," arrived on the scene, the armed men formed a square. Some guardsmen sent for torches. The press articles were read aloud, and "amidst loud shouts of disapproval" they were publicly burnt.[62] Following the incident, the committee demanded revision of the bill by sending a special courier to Pozsony. The Diet obliged, and the required deposit was reduced by half.[63]

The Pest guard was also a forerunner of a similar force set up by the Diet on a nationwide basis and its existence was properly exploited by Kossuth at the parliamentary debate dealing with the question. Conservative deputies wanted high property qualifications for service in the National Guard because they were afraid that if the poor were armed they might turn their weapons against the estate-owning nobility.[64] Kossuth repeatedly pointed out that the guard was already an existing reality and it was not possible to take arms away from those who already possessed them.[65] The final text of the bill, interestingly, set lower property requirements for city dwellers for service in the guard than for voting.

In the countryside, however, the opposite was the case. The ownership of twice as much land was needed for becoming a guard member than for having the suffrage.[66] It is also worth noting that, whereas nobles kept their voting rights irrespective of property qualifications, for guard duty, the same criteria were used for nobles and nonnobles alike.

In regard to Hungarian national autonomy, the existence of the guard was also fully exploited. The Habsburg court agreed to an independent Hungarian Cabinet on March 17, but about ten days later the government in Vienna attempted to take back the ministries of war and finance from the Hungarians. The Diet protested, and there were demonstrations in the capital. The Committee of Public Safety issued a proclamation threatening the dynasty with war if the nation's wishes were denied.[67] Obviously, this kind of stand would have been impossible without armed force at the committee's disposal. In all likelihood such a stand was effective because, on the basis of the reports the authorities received, the guard appeared much stronger than it really was.[68] Since the dynasty was also threatened by revolutions in Vienna and Italy, it seemed safer to yield to the Hungarians and grant the contested ministries, which led to the pacification of the country under an independent responsible cabinet. The Committee of Public Safety ceased to function after April 15, and its armed force became incorporated into a National Guard which was organized all over Hungary under the direction of Prime Minister Count Lajos Batthyány. During the month of its independent existence, however, the Pest National Guard kept the king's soldiers away from the city and maintained order; this fact made the Hungarian capital the only major city in Europe in March where the revolution claimed substantial gains without bloodshed.

Notes

1. István Barta, ed., *Kossuth Lajos az utolsó rendi országgyűlésen* (Budapest, 1951), 619–28.

2. Pozsony is better known to historians by its German name *Pressburg*. Today it is called *Bratislava*. Since in 1848 this city was the constitutional

center of Hungary, it seems most appropriate to call it by its Hungarian name.

3. The two units of the Hungarian capital, Buda and Pest, had separate municipal councils in 1848. Most revolutionary events took place in the more populous urban center, Pest.

4. For the Twelve Points see further László Deme, *The Radical Left in the Hungarian Revolution of 1848* (Boulder, Col., 1976), 16–17.

5. The Liberal Party Program of 1847 does not mention a national guard. Even Kossuth's most famous speech of March 3 mentions only the need to reorganize Hungarian national defense in the following general terms: ". . . our system of national defense needs radical alteration in accordance with our national character and on the basis of the unity of interests of the different social classes of the country. . . ." Barta, 626.

6. Sándor Szilágyi, ed., *A magyar nemzet története,* 10 vols. (Budapest, 1895–98), 10: 66.

7. Irinyi wrote about the French in his travel notes in 1846: "They have glorified humanity and have done more for the cause of liberty and for the elucidation of principles and ideas than any other nation. For these reasons, I agree with Heine who says, 'Liberty is the new religion of our age . . . the chosen people of this new religion are the French'." Pál Pándi, ed., *Szöveggyűjtemény a forradalom és szabadságharc korának irodalmából* (Budapest, 1962), 315.

8. Ferenc Salamon, "A nemzeti őrseregről," *Budapesti Szemle* 64 (1890): 359–60.

9. Albert Nyári, *A magyar forradalom napjai* (Pest, 1848), 39. Eyewitness account by one of the young radicals.

10. There are countless descriptions of the events of March 15. The best contemporary accounts include the following pamphlets: Ákos Birányi, *Pesti forradalom (martius 15–19)* (Pest, 1848), 15–32. István Kléh, *A pesti forradalom története 1848-ban* (Pest, 1848), 22–29.

11. Following the old Habsburg practice of *divide et impera,* the garrison in Buda was composed mainly of Italians while many Hungarian soldiers were stationed in Italy.

12. Dénes Pap, ed., *Okmánytár Magyarország függetlenségi harczának történetéhez 1848–49,* 2 vols. (Pest, 1868–69), 1: 14–15. The proclamation was published in posters and in the newspapers.

13. J. M. Thompson, *The French Revolution* (New York, 1966), 62.

14. Petőfi wrote in his diary on March 17: "For several years the history of the French revolutions has been my almost exclusive reading, my morning and evening prayer and my daily bread. [It is] the new scripture of the world in which the second savior of mankind, Liberty, announces her teachings." Sándor Petőfi, *Összes prózai művei és levelezése* (Budapest, 1960), 402–403.

15. A participant in the March 15 demonstration described artillerymen standing with burning fuses next to their cannon: Alajos Degré, *Visszaemlékezéseim,* 2 vols. (Budapest, 1883), 2: 7. Similarly, on March 16 the royal commissioner sent to the city, Count Móric Almássy, reported to Archduke Stephen, "the soldiers in the barracks and the arsenal are ready for all even-

tualities. " He added that both he and the commander of the garrison considered the soldiers to be reliable but he "would not dare to say that in case of a clash their numbers would be sufficient." Erzsébet Andics, *A nagybirtokos arisztokrácia ellenforradalmi szerepe 1848-49-ben,* 2 vols. (Budapest, 1956–65), 2: 11. Important collection of documents.

16. Imre Deák, ed., *1848: a szabadságharc története levelekben, ahogyan a kortársak látták* (Budapest, 1942), 54. A collection of private letters and official correspondence.

17. The editor declared in the first issue that the paper's purpose was "to fight against those outworn ideas which preceded March 15." *Marczius Tizenötödike* (hereafter cited as *MT*), Mar. 19, 1848, 1.

18. Pap, 1: 15.

19. Some members of the intelligentsia preferred the old units. Albert Pálffy, editor of the *Marczius Tizenötödike,* for instance, became a "grenadier." *MT,* Mar. 19, 1848, p. 3.

20. *MT,* Mar. 24, 1848, p. 22.

21. Ferenc Pulszky, *Életem és korom,* 2 vols. (Budapest, 1884), 1: 305.

22. Kléh, 30.

23. Birányi, 39.

24. Kléh, 31.

25. *Ibid.,* 35–36.

26. *MT,* Mar. 24, 1848.

27. Birányi, 51.

28. Degré, 2: 10; according to Degré, they all behaved bravely as soldiers later in the war of independence. Some of them fought in the Hungarian army, some on the Imperial side.

29. *MT,* Mar. 29, 1848, p. 45.

30. *MT,* Apr. 6, 1848, p. 78.

31. *MT,* Apr. 1, 1848, pp. 57–58; see also Frigyes Podmaniczky, *Naplótöredékek,* 4 vols. (Budapest, 1887), 2: 240.

32. *MT,* Apr. 1, 1848, p. 58.

33. *MT,* Apr. 11, 1848, p. 94. In contemporary Paris, red was far more popular. Lamartine had to use all his eloquence to dissuade the Parisians from adopting it as the symbol of France.

34. Endre Arató, *et. al., Magyarország története, 1790-1849* (Budapest, 1961), 151. Together with the population of Buda, the suburbs, and the outskirts of the city the total was around 150,000.

35. Aladár Urbán, *A nemzetőrség és honvédség szervezése 1848 nyarán* (Budapest, 1973), 16. A thorough, detailed monograph, outstanding in every respect.

36. Birányi, 46.

37. *MT,* Mar. 19, 1848, p. 3.

38. Nyári, 52.

39. Birányi, 46.

40. *MT,* Apr. 13, 1848, p. 100.

94   WAR AND SOCIETY IN EAST CENTRAL EUROPE

41. Pál Vasvári, *Válogatott írásai* (Budapest, 1956), 292. Another participant in the March Days, Albert Nyári, also expressed strong pro-Jewish sentiments in his account of the Pest revolution. Interrupting his account of events, he included a long essay about the virtues of the "Israelites" since Roman times and declared that posterity would judge discrimination against Jews the same way as the nineteenth century judges previous persecution of the Protestants.

42. Petőfi, 410–11.

43. Count Almásy's report from Buda to Archduke Stephen on March 16. Andics, 2: 10.

44. Birányi, 36, 46. See also the general's report to Archduke Stephen in Andics, 2: 10–11.

45. *Ibid.,* 2: 37–38. Report of Count Almásy to Archduke Stephen.

46. Almásy, a reliable and acute observer, noted fear among the citizens of Pest as early as March 16. Similarly the *Marczius Tizenötödike* complained about the timidity of city merchants who immediately closed their shops when groups started to form on the streets. The paper added: "These people believe that revolution means robbing and looting. The revolution, fellow citizens, is the source of everything beautiful and good which occurred in recent times in Europe and America." (*MT,* Apr. 3, 1848, p. 66.)

47. For fear and arming in self-defense in Paris see Georges Lefebvre, *The Coming of the French Revolution* (New York, 1960), 96–101.

48. Mór Jókai, *Önmagáról* (Budapest, 1904), 112. Jókai, a romantic novelist, tended to give colorful descriptions but his reminiscences about the March Days are generally quite accurate.

49. From a speech on April 15, 1848 — Vasvári, 288–91.

50. Eure kaiserliche Hoheit sind über den dermaligen beunruhigenden Stand der Dinge in Pest zu gut unterrichtet, als daß ich mich erst darüber zu verbreiten nötig hätte. So wie ich sorgfältig bemüht bin, jeden Anlaß zu vermeiden, welcher der Bewegungs-Partei Grund zu noch grösserem Mißtrauen gegen die Regierungsgewalt in Wien geben könnte, so habe ich seither in meiner Bereitwilligkeit, der im Errichten begriffenen National-Garde Waffen zu liefern, das sicherste Mittel zu erkennen geglaubt, die aufgeregte Maße von einer offenen Empörung und von dem Vorsatze, sich des hiesigen Zeughauses mit Gewalt zu bemächtigen, abzuhalten. Andics, 2: 31–32.

51. *MT,* Mar. 23, 1848, p. 20.

52. Degré, 2: 11.

53. *MT,* Mar. 24, 1848, p. 22.

54. *MT,* Mar. 23, 1848, p. 18.

55. *MT,* Mar. 24, 1848, p. 22.

56. The editor of the *Marczius Tizenötödike* witnessed the incident and described it in detail. *MT,* Mar. 29, 1848, pp. 43–44.

57. Pulszky, 1: 300.

58. Barta, 674.

59. By March 19 the Guard already numbered some 4,000. Urbán, 15.

60. Pap, 1: 27.

61. *MT,* Mar. 27, 1848, p. 37.

62. *Ibid.,* Mar. 22, 1848, p. 16.

63. See the final text of the law: Dezső Márkus, ed., *1836–68 évi törvény-czikkek* (Budapest, 1896), 241.

64. Barta, 686.

65. *Ibid.* The Diet debated the bill establishing the Guard on March 22. By that time there also were Guard units in provincial cities but the Guard in Pest remained the most visible and strongest force.

66. City dwellers had to own real estate valued at at least 200 forints to qualify for the Guard. For suffrage, real estate worth at least 300 forints was required. For people in the countryside, possession of *one-half* of a former "serf's plot" was the minimal requirement for Guard duty; *one-fourth* of a former "serf's plot" was sufficient for voting. See Márkus, ed., *1836–68 évi törvényczikkek,* 223–24, 244–45.

67. Pap, 1: 33–34.

68. Count Almásy, for instance, reported the establishment of an artillery branch of the Guard on March 22 (Andics, 2: 35). Similarly, an English agent, Mr. Blackwell, reported from Pozsony to Viscount Ponsonby about the situation in Pest: ". . . by all that I am able to learn, they want to establish a republic, or at least 'a monarchy with republican institutions.' They are organizing a most effective National Guard with a train of artillery." *Correspondence Relative to the Affairs of Hungary 1847–49. Presented to both Houses of Parliament by Command of Her Majesty, August 15, 1850* (London, 1850), 52–53. In fact, the artillery unit in Pest never got beyond the planning stage.

Aladár Urbán

The Hungarian Army of 1848–49

A characteristic institution of the European revolutions of 1848 was the national guard. The Hungarian Revolution also established this institution which was later sanctioned by the legislature in Pozsony [Bratislava] and approved by the monarch (Statute no. 1848: 22). The officially organized National Guard was used as a police force on certain occasions. In the southern areas of the country, it was even used in the field against the Serbian insurgents. Thus, it appears that the newly created and legalized institution of the national guard was the model on which a national army could be built for war against Austria. At the outbreak of the revolution, however, the Hungarian government could use the imperial standing army only to a certain extent because a significant number of its men were not Hungarians, but Austrians, Czechs, Poles, or Italians. After the break with Vienna, important units of the imperial army — particularly the cuirassiers and light cavalry — turned against the Hungarian government.

National guard units organized on the basis of locality and hence composed of men of various ages and degrees of training, could not hold their own against the Serbian insurgents and later would have been even less able to withstand the well-trained Austrian army. The Hungarian government, however, had already learned how to organize a new military force. This was not yet directed against the Austrians; it merely increased the number of soldiers at the disposal of the Batthyány cabinet. In May 1848 the Hungarian units were set up and trained on the military model which gave rise to the *honvéd* army, and that army forced the Austrians to retreat in 1849.

Upon taking office in mid-April 1848, the Batthyány government insisted that the military forces at its disposal in Hungary were not adequate for keeping order. Hence, it asked Vienna to order Hungarian infantry and hussar units stationed abroad to return home. Since Austria was at war in Lombardy, the reply to this request was uncertain. Consequently, at the end of the month, the Hungarian cabinet began to consider organizing a military force composed of volunteers but trained on the model of the regular regiments. On May 15, when news reached the Hungarian capital that armed volunteers from neighboring Serbia had arrived at Karlóca [Sremski Karlovci] where the Serbian "National Congress" was in session and offered their help in establishing an independent province, the Batthyány government took the following steps: it ordered the fortresses in the southern part of the country to stand by for action; the border was to be strictly controlled, and no arms were to be exported to Serbia. At the same time, the government resolved to organize a military camp in the "vicinity of Szeged" and called up the previously planned volunteer battalions.

This last measure was not such a simple and self-evident decision as might be thought, particularly when we realize how hard both the Court and the new Austrian government tried to safeguard the unity of the army. Batthyány had to make a special trip to Vienna to persuade the king to issue the May decree which, in accordance with the newly ratified laws, placed the regular units of the imperial-royal army stationed in Hungary under the Hungarian minister of defense. Thus, the only legal path open to the Hungarian government was organizing the new volunteer force as part of the National Guard since that was under the authority of the government, with Prime Minister Count Lajos Batthyány as its commander-in-chief.

This explains why the summons issued on May 16 calling for three years of volunteer service discusses a "regular or mobile" National Guard, thus distinguishing the new volunteer units from the existing, lawful National Guard. Men between the ages of twenty and fifty who met the economic conditions stipulated by law could serve in the regular National Guard. The instructions on recruitment now issued specified that men between eighteen and forty who were Hungarian or who had lived at least ten years in the country might be enlisted but they imposed no property qualifications. This meant that even the poorest classes were eligible to join the newly formed volunteer units. More important — unlike the poorly equipped, poorly trained battalions of the National Guard — the volunteers were organized, equipped, and trained on the ordinary military model.

The Batthyány cabinet had to handle the new units as a "complementary part of the National Guard," first, because it had no legal right to organize a military force, having received neither royal assent nor parliamentary authorization, and second, because this was the only way to ensure that the Hungarian cabinet would have exclusive authority. Until the open break the imperial-royal regiments and military institutions were in a peculiar situation, since they were also receiving orders from the Viennese Ministry of War through its previously established military administrative apparatus. Hence, Prime Minister Batthyány, who was also commander-in-chief of the National Guard, organized the National Guard Council at the same time as he called for recruiting volunteers. This council was nominally headed by Colonel Manuel Baldacci but actually it was under the Prime Minister's direction. As subsequent events show, the Hungarian government established a new organization with functions similar to a ministry thus evading the law (Statute no. 1848: 3) approved by the responsible government.

It was to be expected that these developments would arouse opposition and suspicion in Vienna, particularly after Count Theodor Latour, who was openly hostile to the Hungarian constitutional transformation and striving for independence, became war minister. The Austrian government was indisputably suspicious: the king-emperor had fled from Vienna on May 17, and the Austrian government was also concerned about Serbian activity. For this reason, the Hungarian government's action was considered to be permissible, merely creating a defensive force against the "Serbian and Illyrian threat." The disorders around the imperial capital and the nature of the recruitment announced in Pest-Buda on May 16 obviously affected Vienna's attitude. After all, only 10,000 volunteers were to be enlisted, and only "to defend the homeland, the royal throne, and the constitution."

The prime minister immediately ordered county and municipal authorities to begin recruiting and designated twenty cities where enrollment was to be organized besides the capital. Since they wanted to give the volunteers regular military training, candidates had to be selected in accordance with the usual military requirements. Naturally, the Hungarian government disposed of the same organizations which the imperial-royal army had established earlier for this purpose. The *Werbe-Commandos,* which now took their orders from the Hungarian minister of defense, thus circumventing the *General-Commando* in Buda, examined the volunteers' fitness for service. Thus, in May and June 1848, enrollment of the volunteer *honvéd* was carried out jointly by the recently elected county and municipal officials and the old recruiting offices. Although this did not occur smoothly, the Hungarian government still considered this cooperation a success since the military corps had opposed it until mid-May. On May 15, the emergency moved the government to direct that the new units be organized. Yet it had not completed the program it had initiated. Thus, only on June 2 was the announcement published that the volunteers would be organized into ten battalions, two in the capital and the others in provincial towns. Soon afterwards, recruitment in the twin capital of Pest-Buda was halted and work began in earnest in the provincial towns. For only then did the *Werbe-Commandos* designated as recruiting offices receive exact instructions without which, understandably enough, they were unwilling to begin operations.

About this time when official recruitment began even in the provinces, the volunteer units received their name. No official decree declared that the volunteers originally designated *regular or mobile* National Guard were to be called *honvéd*. The term first appears at the end of May in documents of the National Guard Council. Soon afterward it appeared in the decrees of Prime Minister Batthyány. The term *honvéd* even appears in the press. (The word, meaning "defender of the homeland," was invented by the Hungarian language reform movement of the 1830s.) Since there was no official decision or instructions, the renaming process did not happen quickly; it was July before the term *honvéd* battalions came into general use.

Recruitment did not proceed uniformly. By June 6, 2,000 men had been recruited in the capital and within weeks two other battalions were organized in the region west of the Tisza River. In counties beyond the Danube, where four battalions had been planned, progress was slower, for the area was nearer Vienna. The results were not much better in northern Hungary where two battalions had been specified. Though the government had published its recruitment appeal in German and Slovak — northern Hungary had a large Slovak population — obviously it was the Hungarian population that was expected to provide volunteers. No recruiting stations were even designated in the southern Hungarian counties with a large Serbian population. (Since union with Transylvania had not come into force when the recruitment was announced, no *honvéd* battalions were raised there during this period.)

Summing up the partial figures on recruitment, the following results were obtained: at the beginning of July 1848, about 7,000 volunteers had enlisted for three years in the *honvéd* battalions; by the middle of August there were 9,500. It is impossible to provide detailed analysis of their age and social composition since the registers of enrollment are unavailable to researchers: after the collapse of the Hungarian fight for independence, the Austrians collected them; Hungarian officials, hearing of Austrian interest in them, hid or destroyed them. Data on some 10 percent of the entire effective force in August 1848 are available. If these are regarded as representative, we can draw the following picture of the social composition of the first ten battalions: 65.7 percent were poor peasants or landless cotters; 20.6 percent, artisans, chiefly journeymen; 10.8 percent, students or young intellectuals including men who owned land and men who did not (the latter were called *honoratiors*); and 2.9 percent were members of other strata, for example, 0.4 percent were merchants. It is worth mentioning that, based on the preceding figures, those aged eighteen to twenty-five constituted more than 80 percent of the first *honvéd* battalions.

Where did the Hungarian government get the approximately 250 officers needed to maintain discipline and effectively conduct training? The May 16 summons had called upon Hungarian officers of the regular army and other "patriots qualified to be officers" — retired officers and persons who had left the army after a few years of service — to report for duty at the National Guard Council. Since the pay offered seemed higher than in the regular army, there was no lack of volunteers. (Actually, pay was higher only for *honvéd* officers in garrison because regular army officers got a significant bonus while serving in the field.) Naturally, volunteers who had been stationed in Hungary and those who had acquaintances at the National Guard Council or the Ministry of Defense were given preference. As the summons became widely known, applications for transfer arrived from Hungarian officers stationed in various provinces of the empire. The Austrian military authorities transmitted these, albeit reluctantly. Indeed, until the fall of 1848 they even recognized the commissions of *honvéd* officers in such cases though they did everything in their power to keep them from returning home.

In addition to indisputable patriotic fervor, volunteers were further motivated when it became obvious that the Hungarian government promoted officers in the *honvéd* army to higher rank than they had held before. (Exception was made only for those recently promoted in the regular army.) Thus, majors appointed to head the ten battalions had all been captains, among them four retired officers who had returned to active service. By the end of September 1848, the Hungarian government had appointed 123 active officers and 94 persons who had received officer's training or who were retired. Former non-commissioned officers were promoted to the lowest commissioned ranks, nor is it surprising that during the first months new officers were also promoted from the rank and file. This was urged by Prime Minister Batthyány himself who had assured the large number of young intellectuals enlisting in the *honvéd* army that a certain number of positions as second lieutenant would be left open for noncommissioned *honvéd* officers who had proved their excellence during training. Thus, seventy-five men were promoted to the rank of officer in their own battalions up to September 1848.

The indisputably high proportion of intellectuals proved to be a great help in training the *honvéds*. This made it possible to begin training the battalions even though only a few officers had arrived. Batthyány ordered these officers to train educated noncommissioned officers in the morning; they then passed on their freshly acquired knowledge to the recruits in the afternoon. They encountered difficulties only with target practice since the battalions did not receive firearms — guns with bayonets — except when they were sent into the field.

Equipping the battalions did not proceed without a hitch. The stockpile in the military depot in Óbuda [Altofen] was secured by the government, but only over the opposition of the commander of the Montours-Ökonomie commission who was reluctant to hand over materiel from the "imperial stockpile." Later, boots and capes were not produced quickly enough; therefore, raw material was sent to the provinces where units were organized more slowly; there local artisans helped to make boots and uniforms. Nevertheless, some battalions had to go into the field without capes; they had not received them even by September. Some firearms were taken from the arsenal of the fort in Buda and from the artillery district of Temesvár [Timişoara]. Enough of the Belgian weapons which Batthyány's representative had bought at Lüttich in the summer were available for the volunteers.

When the Hungarian government first began recruiting the *honvéd* battalions, it planned to replace the regular army on garrison service with these units and then send the trained soldiers to fight the Serbian insurgents. The rapid spread of the Serbian insurrection and the small number of regular soldiers compelled the Batthyány government to order the poorly equipped and trained *honvéd* battalions into the field. The two battalions organized in Pest-Buda left the capital on June 24, barely three weeks after recruitment was completed. The first battalion was sent against the Croats to an army observation corps stationed along the Drava River; the second battalion was ordered to defend one of the crossing points of the Tisza River against the Serbian insurgents. The tenth battalion, recruited in Debrecen, was sent to the Banat south of the Maros River in July, and the ninth, formed in Kassa [Košice] which became famous as the "red caps," was sent to defend Weisskirchen along the Military Frontier inhabited by a mixed population of Hungarians, Germans, and Romanians. The fifth battalion, formed in Győr, and the sixth battalion, organized in Veszprém, were sent to the camp system established in the area between the Danube and Tisza rivers where, after a certain number of setbacks, the eighth from Pécs and the fourth battalion from Pozsony [Pressburg] followed them. Finally, the seventh battalion from Szombathely moved out in August, later joined the Hungarian army retreating from Jelačić's invading forces and, along with the first battalion, fought in the battle of Pákozd. This encounter which took place on September 29, 1848 stopped the Ban (governor) of Croatia whose purpose had been to occupy the capital and dissolve the Hungarian parliament and forced him to retreat toward Vienna.

This is the preliminary history of the *honvéd* army. One must add that in the summer of 1848 the government began to organize four battalions in Transylvania which had been legally united with Hungary. But by September, it had managed to form only two battalions. Since Austria was at war, the Vienna War Ministry in June advised the king to add a fourth battalion to each regiment of the regular army. The Hungarian government took this opportunity to propose that more *honvéd* battalions be formed. Archduke István, Palatine and Royal Regent, did not agree. Since his opposition probably meant that Vienna disapproved, the Hungarian government withdrew its proposal.

One may surmise from the foregoing that the organization of the *honvéd* lay within the authority of the doomed Prime Minister, Lajos Batthyány, who discharged this duty virtually as minister without portfolio.

The first ten *honvéd* battalions provided the nucleus and model for a general army, but it was not self-evident how these experiences would be put to use. Vienna later considered the organization begun in May to be a justified measure of defense but the advisors of the king-emperor would not have tolerated a significant increase in the number of *honvéd* battalions. This explains why, before August 1848 when opposition between Austria and Hungary led to open conflict, the Hungarian government was willing to organize the military force for the defense of the country within the framework of the old regular army. The left wing opposition wanted none of it; they wanted to organize the recruits exclusively into *honvéd* battalions. Finally a compromise was made: all three battalions formed from the Hungarian regiments of the imperial-royal army — to be more precise, troops from countries united under the Hungarian Crown and not always composed of Hungarians — would be filled. Furthermore, two additional companies per regiment would be organized; in hussar regiments, the available battalions were filled and a new squadron was added. Recruits left over after the battalions had been completed were grouped into new *honvéd* battalions, with Hungarian as the language of command. Dress and flags were also Hungarian. Though the proposal was a compromise, the opposition had made its point. Batthyány and his ministers knew that the bill, even in this modified form, could not get royal assent.

The just mentioned parliamentary vote occurred on August 21, three weeks before the Croatian offensive and ten days before issue of the Austrian memorandum demanding the concentration of military and financial affairs in Vienna. After General Radetzky's victories in Italy, the Vienna government's position was consolidated; the Hungarian government, beset by anti-Hungarian nationalistic movements, was forced on the defensive. If, for the time being, increasing the number of battalions was out of the question, the government could not forego enlarging the army. One of its measures to this end was gathering the *volunteer* National Guard into camps at four strategic points. Although the organization of this National Guard was begun only in the middle of August, some of its units had already fought in the battle of Pákozd. This National Guard, together with the two *honvéd* battalions, made up about 60 percent of the Hungarian army which fought the battle. Another possible method of increasing Hungarian forces was raising irregular troops; this was done in the middle of September.

Ban Jelačić led the Croatian army across the Drava River on September 11. The Batthyány government resigned the same day, ignorant that the feared Croatian attack had actually taken place. Batthyány stayed in office until the expected appointment of a new ministry, but that never occurred. For the first time since he was in office, Batthyány ordered a general levy in areas of Transdanubia threatened by the enemy. Later, having received a parliamentary mandate, he instructed the authorities to begin recruiting volunteers for the army. He made it clear that he wanted to enforce the law providing for the raising of an army although that had not received royal assent. He announced on September 18 that he wanted to recruit 42,000 men. Moreover, it soon became apparent that the recruits would be organized into *honvéd* battalions. The Prime Minister declared where the sixteen new *honvéd* battalions would be set up and saw to it that a staff of officers for the new units was commissioned.

In early October, in Vienna, Batthyány vainly tried to end the conflict. The decision had already been made to use force. The Hungarian Prime Minister resigned; the Committee of National Defense headed by Lajos Kossuth and designated by the chamber of deputies in Pest-Buda took over the government. Since the time for compromise was over, there was nothing to prevent the raising of a general *honvéd* army. This was not restricted to volunteers, for the authorities of counties and the so-called free royal boroughs were required to enlist recruits in proportion to the population, primarily among unmarried young men between the ages of nineteen and twenty-two who did not have families to support. For the most part, the authorities tried to fill the quota with volunteers enticed by bounties paid from public funds. When this was not possible, young men fit for service and not entitled to exemption had to draw lots. A man who drew the "short straw" could be released from service if he paid someone to take his place.

Thus, by the fall of 1848, for all practical purposes, the *honvéd* army had turned to a system of selective conscription. Understandably enough, this aroused opposition especially in areas heavily populated by other nationalities. The Romanians in Transylvania and the Serbs in southern Hungary were all but impossible to recruit; opposition was encountered even among the Hungarian population. One reason for this was that the term of service had been raised to four years. (The period of service in Hungary at the recruitment of 1830 was ten years; in 1840, it was eight years.) Yet these difficulties did not present serious obstacles to manning the army. In October, twelve more battalions were formed; in November eleven; in December, nine more.

Without doubt, all this bore witness to success in raising an army. One should credit not only Kossuth and the Committee of National Defense but also the efforts of district magistrates and aldermen in areas populated by Hungarians, and of deputies sent back to their electoral districts as recruiting commissioners with full powers.

The military leadership, too, adapted to the new situation. The National Guard Council which had been established to organize the *honvéd* battalions was not the only agency to carry out this task, but from December 1848 on it rallied recruits in concert with the eight *military districts*. The job of equipping them was shared by the National Guard Council and the Ministry of Defense which had progressively broken all ties with the Austrian Ministry of Defense even before the general Austrian attack. (In January 1849, the National Guard Council merged with the Ministry of Defense.)

By that time, the recruits mustered by the authorities were not assigned only to the new *honvéd* battalions but were used to fill up the battalions of the regular army under the command of the Committee of Defense. Hussar squadrons and new artillery batteries were also formed from their ranks. Kossuth's declaration of November 27 removed the formal obstacles lying in the path of this process. He announced that every unit of the army had taken an oath on the constitution, thereby wiping away every distinction between the old imperial-royal units and the new ones; henceforth every unit bore the glorious name, Hungarian *honvéd* army. This declaration proclaimed the establishment of the united *honvéd* army; this meant that, after taking the oath, units from the former regular army would use the Hungarian tricolor instead of the imperial black and yellow flags. (Of course, the black and yellow braided infantry uniforms were kept.)

The mass recruitment paved the way for the further development of the various branches of the *honvéd* army because except for a few artillery units, only infantry battalions had been formed until September 1848. The battalion was retained as the organizational unit throughout the entire war of independence. *Honvéd* regiments were not established; in fact, even the battalions of the regular army were organized into independent *honvéd* battalions in the spring of 1849. (In September 1848, the Hungarian government had twenty-one battalions of varying strength at its disposal.)

Thus, we see that sixty-two battalions had been organized at least in part by the end of 1848. Not all of these battalions, however, were formed from recruits enlisted since the end of September, because in the fall of 1848 at least eight volunteer National Guard battalions and free companies, which had engaged for a shorter term of service, were transformed into *honvéd* battalions. But even so, it was a considerable achievement to have organized about thirty battalions and have ten more undergoing training by the end of the year, the more so when we realize that organizing cavalry and artillery, too, demanded further large effective forces. Of the 65,000 to 68,000 men serving in the field at the end of 1848, 30,000 belonged to the newly established units. (This figure includes neither the National Guard, which was ordered into the field only temporarily, nor the *honvéd* battalions still being formed or trained.)

As for the cavalry, the Hungarian government did not organize new regular cavalry units in the summer of 1848. This was owing in part to lack of money and in part to negative experiences while organizing the National Horse Guard. According to the law, men required to serve in the National Guard at their place of residence could choose between serving on foot or on horseback. Since the latter choice would have obliged them to use their own horses, even people in the provinces traditionally accustomed to horses were reluctant to risk their mounts. Hence, by September 1848, only volunteer squadrons had been formed. True, the Hungarian government had a great number of the hussar regiments traditionally recruited from the population of Hungary at its disposal. In 1848, of the twelve imperial hussar regiments, four were stationed in Hungary; Vienna permitted three more to return home in exchange for other cavalry regiments; two others remained with the Austrian army fighting in Italy; men from the three other regiments, risking decimation, escaped and returned home in the fall and winter of 1848. The Committee of Defense filled these last regiments, and replaced the two which had stayed in Italy, with volunteer recruits. Five more hussar regiments were set up in the fall of 1848 including three that were first organized as free squadrons at the end of the summer. According to available data, before the recruits were used to fill up cavalry units in the fall of 1848, Kossuth and his government had sixty-five trained hussar squadrons at their disposal. Among the hussars, incidentally, the original division by regiments was retained to the end of the war of independence. A regiment was composed of eight squadrons.

Creating an artillery was, from the standpoint of army organization, the most difficult task of the Hungarian revolution because the imperial-royal army did not assign Hungarian troops to this branch of service. Of course, there were Hungarians in the Army Service Corps, which was important to the artillery. Obviously, this was one reason that the recruitment summons of May 16 announced the organization of a *battery of horse artillery*. As far as we know, three *honvéd* artillery batteries fought in the battle of Pákozd on September 29, but by that time sixteen of the artillery batteries in the imperial-royal army had been sent against the Serbian insurgents in the Bácska-Bánát region. Some of these Austrian and Czech troops later refused to obey the Hungarian government. They were disarmed and employed in making ammunition under supervision. The others accepted service and were assigned to the *honvéd* artillery. (The *honvéd* artillery, one should note, had eight cannon per battery; whereas the Austrian artillery had only six.) Some 1,800 additional recruits had been detailed to the artillery by the end of October, but it was more difficult to provide them with officers even though many noncommissioned officers of the artillery had been granted commissions. The large number of intellectuals in the infantry *honvéd* battalions made it possible for many who had volunteered for the first *honvéd* batteries — primarily engineers, surveyors, and mathematicians — to get quick promotion to commissioned rank. According to a report prepared in the middle of December 1848, thirty *honvéd* artillery batteries (about 3,200 men) had seen service on the battlefield. Nearly half of these had been recently organized. The ammunition of the *honvéd* artillery was taken from the famous *Neugebaude,* the artillery barracks in Pest.

Such was the state of the *honvéd* army created by the Hungarian Revolution at the beginning of January when the Austrian army occupied the capital. The government and the national assembly fled to Debrecen; the territory under the control of the Committee of Defense shrank to a frightening degree. Although virtually only the counties and cities beyond the Tisza River remained under the administration of the Hungarian authorities, ten infantry battalions were added to the *honvéd* army in January 1849 and the organization of engineer corps and the units of light cavalry began. In the spring of 1849, no new battalions were organized, but recruits still arriving were sent to replace the dead and wounded in existing *honvéd* battalions. Yet even so, nineteen additional battalions were organized at the end of April 1849; true, seven of these were formed from the battalions of the Székely Frontier Guard. (In Habsburg territory bordering on the Turkish empire the guards assigned to military service were under a separate administration. Only the two Székely regiments in the border guard were ethnically Hungarian.) All things considered, at the beginning of the Hungarian counterattack in early April 1849, the country's army had an infantry and cavalry about 90,000 men strong; thirty-six or thirty-eight batteries faced the enemy on the battlefield. This force did not include garrison troops and the artillery park at the fort of Komárom and Pétervárad, the new *honvéd* battalions, or the cavalry still being organized.

April 1849 produced well-known Hungarian victories: the raising of the siege of Komárom and the liberation of Pest. Continued war, however, required further development of the army and an increase in manpower. To this end, a week after the Declaration of Independence of April 14, Kossuth submitted a bill for the enlistment of 50,000 additional recruits. After the chamber of deputies ratified it, the decree for this enlistment was issued on April 29; thus, substantial effort in the counties and free royal boroughs began only in May. Although there are no detailed modern treatments concerning this period of the Hungarian fight for freedom, contemporary witnesses and documents show that the effective force of the Hungarian army grew even during May and June 1849. Organizing work antedates this time. New units, the ninety-second to the one hundred fortieth battalions, were set up but some of these were drawn, in part, from previously organized volunteer battalions; the one hundred seventh to the one hundred twenty-second battalions were organized from battalions which had not yet been numbered. Thus, it was not the effective force of the Hungarian army which grew, but merely the number of infantry units bearing *honvéd* numbers. The newly mustered recruits were organized into between eighteen and twenty battalions, whose greatest weakness was not inadequate training but lack of arms. For the manufacture of weapons could not keep up with the growth in army manpower.

The army of the Hungarian Revolution reached the peak of its strength in June 1849 before the arrival of the Russian army. As far as we know, the *complete* Hungarian army which faced the united Austrian and Russian army, including volunteers who had not enlisted for four years and newly formed pioneer formations, consisted of 164 battalions, 158 squadrons, and 450 field cannon in 56 batteries; 162,000 men altogether. All this was not enough for victory, but it was too strong a force for the Austrian army to handle on its own.

A further question remains as we reach the end of this summary: where did Kossuth and the Committee of Defense obtain the *officers and staff officers* necessary for the training and leading of the army? We may surmise: officers trained in the Austrian army who sided with, and remained loyal to, the Hungarian government in September 1848; the officers already appointed in the *honvéd* battalions; and noncommissioned officers who had distinguished themselves during the war and were quickly promoted because of the spectacular increase in the army.

A recent examination studied the composition of the upper commanding staff of the *honvéd* army down to and including the rank of major. It found that 826 officers in the Hungarian army held the rank of major or above. Of these, 116 left service and reported to the Austrians at the end of 1848 or the beginning of 1849. The decisive majority did so for political reasons. (It is worth mentioning that this did not ensure that they went unpunished.) Data on the other 710 officers show that 72.1 percent were Hungarian, 15.6 percent German, 4.4 percent Polish, and the others Serbian, Croatian, or Italian in origin. More important from the standpoint of the professional leadership of the army, of the commanding officers mentioned 62.2 percent were active or retired officers. All this helps to explain the success of the Hungarian revolutionary army which put the Austrian generals to shame in the spring of 1849.

The national composition of the aforementioned commanding officers of the Hungarian army, of course, does not reflect that of the entire effective officer force. There were few officers, for example, among Slovaks, Ruthenians, or Romanians, even in the imperial-royal army; thus only accident could have brought them into the Hungarian army. And if such officers were promoted from noncommissioned to commissioned rank in the Hungarian army of 1848–49, very few became majors, the lowest level surveyed, certainly, not enough to show up in the statistics. Only by processing the data on the several thousand individuals who attained the rank of second lieutenant, lieutenant, and captain can we learn more about the ethnic origin of officers in the Hungarian revolutionary army.

Likewise, we do not know *the composition of the rank and file* of the Hungarian revolution. We know that the first *honvéd* battalions — the first and the twelfth — organized on a volunteer basis in the summer of 1848, were almost exclusively Hungarian. In October 1848, however, local authorities were required to meet a quota of recruits, and they paid no heed to nationality. Certain representative surveys suggest that nearly half of these recruits belonged to non-Hungarian ethnic groups that lived in Hungary.

Thus, paradoxically, the *national army* fighting for an independent Hungarian state was *multinational.* Further research is needed to give a detailed picture. Then we shall know more about the "wondrous young army" which, in the words of the poet, "was born in days yet seemed as though three centuries had shaped it."

Notes

The first part of the paper is based on my research in the documents of the ministry of 1848–49. For its development, see Aladár Urbán, *A nemzetőrség és honvédség szervezése 1848 nyarán* (Budapest, 1973). For a short German summary see "Die Organisierung des Heeres der Ungarischen Revolution vom Jahre 1848. I–II." *Annales Universitatis Scientiarum Budapestinensis. Sectio Historica* 9, 12 (1967, 1972). For the relationship between the National Guard Council and the Hungarian Ministry of Defense, see Aladár Urbán, "Az 1848-as magyar hadügyminisztérium megszervezése," *Hadtörténeti Közlemények* 23 (1976): 42–71. [With a summary in German]

For the second part of the paper, the organizing activities of Kossuth and the Committee of Defense, see Lajos Kossuth, *Összes művei,* ed. István Barta (Budapest, 1952–55), XIII–XV: 13–15; J. Balázs, J. Borus, K. Nagy, *Kossuth a forradalmi honvédelem szervezője,* in *Kossuth emlékkönyv* (Budapest, 1952),

2: 287-408. A treatment of events by a participant, a valuable source even today, may be found in Rikhard Gelich, *Magyarország függetlenségi harcza 1848-49-ben,* 3 vols. (Budapest, 1882-89). For a summary of new research on the composition of the officers, see Gábor Bóna, "Az 1848-49-es szabadság-harc katonai vezetésének nemzetiségi összetételéről," *Valóság* 21 (July 1978): 80-93.

For a summary of the Hungarian revolution and war of independence see György Spira, *A magyar forradalom 1848-49-ben* (Budapest, 1959); further, see János Varga's survey in *Magyarország története,* ed. Erik Molnár, 2d ed. (Budapest, 1967), 1: 317-550.

Robert A. Kann

The Social Prestige of the Officer Corps in the
Habsburg Empire from the Eighteenth Century to 1918*

A discussion of this subject first requires clarification of the term *prestige,* by no means an unequivocal sociological concept. Older definitions tend to stress that prestige means a kind of social esteem which, in contrast to authority, cannot be rationally justified. The interests associated with prestige may lead to dangerous social conflicts as, for instance, a prestige policy in international relations. In this sense the impact of prestige is the enemy of a rational and just social order.

A specific difficulty in such an analysis of the concept is its reference not to a generally recognized system of values but to a position — and it may be added, an arbitrary position — within a specific social class system.[1] No less a scholar then Alexis de Tocqueville in *De la démocratie en Amerique* has referred to the rigid, static character of the principle of honor in an authoritarian society in contrast to honor in a democracy where it is "impossible to determine in advance for all times what honor means."[2] In its social application, honor, as discussed by Tocqueville, is only a paraphrase of social prestige in a democratic society in flux. The prestige concept in a static, authoritarian society is rigid and unadjustable. Its arbitrariness is well illustrated by reference to the statistics of suicide in the imperial and royal Habsburg army of the 1870s and 1880s. The number of suicides among young officers more than doubled within a few years after an 1875 ordinance of the Ministry of War permitted funerals with military honors for soldiers who had committed suicide. The military clergy called attention to this situation, and to remedy it, the ordinance was withdrawn in 1889. Thereafter the number of suicides rapidly fell to previous levels.[3]

H. Kluth is correct when he notes that "a man under the spell of prestige will be paralyzed in his initiative and impeded in the develop-

*I feel greatly indebted to Dr. Peter Broucek of the Kriegsarchiv in Vienna for advice on the availability of sources used in this paper.

ment of his personality."[4] This conclusion, to be sure, refers to the older irrational concept of prestige.

More recent research accordingly has attempted to separate the concept of prestige from the narrow boundaries of a rigid class structure. Prestige is still perceived as part of a hierarchical order, but the character of such order becomes variable inasmuch as society today no longer represents a closed social system. Accordingly, social prestige becomes the expression of the functional significance of a social position, above all of an important social achievement. This in turn entitles the individual to certain rights or at least chances to exercise social influence.[5] In other words, social prestige changes from a class privilege to a reward for achievement, a reward which, it may be said, is not generally, and certainly not primarily, to be measured in monetary terms.

No doubt, the social prestige of the officer class in the imperial and royal Habsburg army is predominantly of the first kind, namely, the exercise of social privileges anchored in a class system. This does not necessarily mean that it is separated from achievements, but these achievements derive their value only from service within a specific stratum of a class structure.

The key to the evolution of the officer class, its class consciousness and its prestige deriving from a profession as against dignity originating from noble origin, is to be found in institutional developments of the late sixteenth century and all during the seventeenth century. Through the better part of the sixteenth century, commanders in warfare — and this holds true for relatively major as well as mostly minor military units — were knights whose position was enhanced by their retinues. These knights were not only commanders but genuine warriors themselves; their followers pledged to them by the feudal contract actually rendered mainly auxiliary services. This system did not yet allow room for the activities of a professional officer class. The peasant wars throughout Central Europe — particularly in southern Germany, the Austrian Hereditary Alpine lands and Hungary — changed this only briefly. Although peasant revolts had a lasting albeit for some time merely intermittent effect on social conditions, they had none as far as major changes in the military hierarchy were concerned.

In this respect the religious and civil wars in the second half of the sixteenth and throughout the seventeenth century changed everything. It would go beyond the limits of our topic to discuss here how far issues of state interests and imperialist designs now became interlocked. Suffice it to state that questions of concern to far broader strata of population than heretofore were involved in warfare and that the existing military institutions could in no way cope with these interests.

The military entrepreneur system, the creation of the strange position of *Kriegsunternehmer,* was the first answer to the problem. Inadequate, indeed reprehensible as it was with respect to social justice, the system worked for well over a century with a fair degree of efficiency. The colonel in his proprietary and highly profitable position of *Regimentsinhaber* now hired the commanders of lower units irrespective of origin and social status. Thus, a professional officer class was born although the higher ranks from colonel upward were initially still reserved for the *Regimentsinhaber.*[6]

This development had manifold consequences in the Habsburg realms. Increasingly, it implied a separation between the status of nobility and that of dignity evolving from military service as officer. In this respect, to take only one outstanding example, conditions in the Habsburg armies were or rather became different from those of what soon was to be the finest army in German lands, the Prussian. There the concepts of nobleman and officer were, if not identical, at least largely overlapping in all branches of military service, including the infantry, until the Napoleonic wars of the early nineteenth century. The sovereign wore the same coat that his officers wore, more as *primus inter pares* than as supreme warlord, as was the case in other imperial and royal armed forces. This, to be sure, in no way meant any kind of democracy; it merely meant the rule of the nobility as a corporate body in Prussia's armed forces, a position reserved in the Habsburg armies not for the noble as officer but for the officer as gentleman, whether noble or not, but in any case trained in matters military.

Nobility was essential in the Habsburg armies only for command positions on the level of generals and in guard and swank cavalry regiments. But after the eighteenth century, most members of the high nobility served in such regiments mainly in the reserve. Under Maria Theresa an innovation was introduced: after thirty years of honorable service an officer could ask for and would generally be granted a raise to the lowest grade of nobility. But although nobility by letters patent to a certain degree separated the staff officer (from major upward) from the subaltern officer, it in no way approximated the social status of such an officer to that of genuine aristocracy. A patent of nobility for a staff officer merely meant that the newly ennobled gentleman belonged to a specific honorable stratum of society separated from those below, but perhaps even more from those above him.

There were other differences. The Habsburg armed forces, particularly their officer corps, were more multinational in origin than other armies of the seventeenth and eighteenth centuries. Until the nineteenth century this did not reflect only the multinational character of the Habsburg empire itself. True, Germans remained predominant among Habsburg officers born under the wings of the twin-headed eagle; they by far outnumbered Magyars and Czechs (Bohemians). But beyond the boundaries of the Eastern German Habsburg lands, scions of French, Flemish, Italian, Spanish, Swiss families — to single out only the most important groups — served in the Habsburg forces in relatively larger numbers than foreign officers did in other armies.

This, of course, was partly owing to the many noncontiguous dependencies under Habsburg rule in early modern times but partly also to the attractions of a service where command positions were not reserved for the home-grown Junker, as in Prussia. Anyway, the consequences were momentous. The Habsburg officer could not, of course, be pledged to loyalty to a single nation. Before the French Revolution of 1789 this was not common even in countries, such as France and Great Britain, where state and nation were largely identical. Yet the Habsburg officer might have been pledged to sovereign and country as was usually — though not formally — true in most foreign armed forces where the officer was meant primarily to fight for the state in the name of the supreme warlord, the king. In the Habsburg empire and its widespread, scattered territories — different in social and legal structure and interdependence with, and subordination to, the crown — the officer was pledged solely to the ruler, the emperor, a relationship that continued until 1918, as shown in the national anthem, where "Gott erhalte unsern Kaiser," with "unser Land"[7] taking only second place.

Obviously the developments traced here precede the evolution of democratic reforms in Central and Eastern Europe. It would be ahistorical to criticize the lack of influence of social factors before they were generally recognized in society outside the military system. Yet it is not superfluous to point out that the particular characteristics of the Habsburg armed forces — the multinational (or until the late nineteenth century supranational) character of the officer corps and the far larger representation of officers who were either commoners or merely ennobled for service — did little to mitigate the corps' social isolation. In fact, these devices had rather the opposite effect. The multinational, supranational, and predominantly nonaristocratic character of the officer corps accentuated its isolation from other classes and national groups. Exclusive allegiance to the sovereign further strengthened this isolation. Hence this class was and remained different from all other classes, different in ethnic and social composition and allegiance. As will be shown, this isolation continued to be the fertile ground on which a monopolistic kind of social prestige grew and prospered.

If we look at the Habsburg armed forces in the first part of the eighteenth century, that is, substantially in the pre-Maria Theresan era, the military entrepreneur system was still dominant; the colonel proprietors were genuine nobles who could proudly point to generations of noble ancestors. This gave them social prerogatives which neither commoners nor newly ennobled officers could match. When, after several generations, the distinction between the old nobility of birth and the new nobility of letters patent finally became blurred, the Habsburg empire was on its way out.

Even more difficult to match than noble ancestry was another appurtenance of the old nobility, sizable landed property. This priceless possession gave these nobles, who were strengthened in power and wealth by their feudal retinue, the chance to become regimental proprietors. By selling their services to commanders-in-chief and by selling commissions to lower officers either for cash or — in terms of power just as profitable — for allegiance, they enhanced their position further. The new officer class, whether it rose from the ranks or was hired as mercenaries, became the backbone of the military unit and then of the standing army which became necessary under the conditions of warfare that began with the War of the Spanish Succession and were almost fully developed in the War of the Austrian Succession.

As far as the army's combat ability was concerned, this did not mean a change for the worse. "In 1729, the English resident [minister] in Vienna, F. L. Saint Saphorin, reported to his government that the lower nobility [la petite noblesse] and the educated bourgeoisie [la bourgeoisie à bonne éducation] provides the Austrian army with the best officers." In addition, capable noncommissioned officers might become officers,[8] although very few of them reached a rank higher than captain. Even this limited possibility for promotion would have been inconceivable in Prussia.

Thus a class spirit was formed from below although it was also influenced from above. Here we must think of the great foreign commanders, such as Count Raimund Montecuccoli, Duke Charles of Lorraine, Margrave Louis of Baden, and above all, Prince Eugene of

Savoy who embodied the notion of the officer as the *honnête homme,* the honorable officer, who left his home country as these great generals had done.[9] To these generals without fatherland and the officer type molded by them, common allegiance to the sovereign was the bond with the armed forces, not because it stood above loyalty to country or nation in other states, but because no other loyalty existed as yet for the officer. During the course of a century this was ever more clearly beginning to change.

For the subaltern officer, however, the similarity (even if more in appearance than reality) of his allegiance relationship to that of the princely commander meant a glamorous rise in status. Yet solidarity with others of equal, almost equal, or at least obtainable rank was still more important. The low-born officer was on the march. With the gradual retreat of a now ineffective military organization in which the entrepreneur system had largely prevailed and the Estates — mostly noble Estates at that — had held the purse strings, change in the direction of a new class system was inevitable. As Allmayer-Beck so well puts it: "This new officers' corps now increasingly became the embodiment of a new bourgeois concept of achievement which by officers was often put in juxtaposition to the previous noble concept of function. Ancient nobility as sole premise for high command was no longer recognized without opposition."[10] Allmayer-Beck perceives this shift at the turn of the eighteenth century, and this is correct as far as the issue of higher command is concerned. When in 1806, Archduke Carl wrote to his brother Emperor Franz, ". . . nobility does not feel honored any longer in fulfilling its service obligations! It does not serve any longer and if it serves it does not serve well,"[11] actual changes in this direction on the lower — or perhaps more correctly on the gene-ral — level of the officer class had preceded this conclusion for some time. They were in fact fully visible in the Maria Theresan era.

The empress, as is well known, was greatly interested in matters military and only reluctantly turned these matters over to Joseph II after his installation as her co-regent. But her concern for the develop-ment of a rigid *ésprit de corps* in the officer class remained no less genuine than that of her royal counterpart, Frederick II of Prussia, even though the empress could not body forth sovereign commander-in-chief and officer all rolled into one, as Frederick did.

By now the regimental commander had replaced the regimental proprietor to a large and ever-increasing measure. Promotion within the officer corps, previously substantially a prerogative of these pro-prietors, had been gradually transferred to the Aulic Council (*Hof-*

kriegsrat) and, by 1766, to the empress herself.[12] Later, but just as surely as in France, Prussia, or Russia, the armed forces had become an instrument of the absolute state. Within this remodeled structure it became vitally necessary to tie the officer class to state power.

It has been noted that creation of the service nobility by giving retired or soon to be retired officers under Maria Theresa titles of nobility could not give them equality with nobles of ancient birth and still less with landed aristocrats. Maria Theresa tried in several ways to get around this difficulty. In 1757 the Maria Theresa Cross (*Maria Theresien Orden*) was created as the highest military decoration in the Habsburg empire. This was conferred for supreme, independent action in battle without regard to the officers' origin, rank, or religious affiliation, and made its bearers baronets. Here indeed was a distinction which could partly offset the lack of wealth and pedigree. In addition, officers in general were now admitted to Court. They became *hoffähig* and furthermore secured the privilege of hunting on cameral domains.

This latter type of advantage was, of course, of little avail. It probably counted less than the splendor of uniforms of elegant regiments and it could not offset the lack of adequate recompense for officers' services. They were notoriously poorly paid and economically worse off than under the entrepreneur system where the possibility of looting — now outlawed — had offered enticement to adventurous soldiers of fortune.

No doubt, the officer corps had become more respectable in the sense of more orderly civic conduct, but it was less romantic, less attractive to imaginative, unruly spirits resistant to discipline but potentially of outstanding bravery. Service as an officer had become a poorly paid career within a new civil service system. It had ceased to be a calling in which you staked your life on the chance of a meteorlike social rise.

One significant factor in changing society's image of the officer was the development of military science, begun under Montecuccoli in the seventeenth century, somewhat neglected under Eugene of Savoy in the early part of the eighteenth, but now taught in military schools, above all in the famous Maria Theresa Military Academy of Wiener Neustadt, founded in 1748. The drudgery involved in the curriculum of this and other military schools (such as that *an der Laimgrube* in Vienna) further scared genuine nobles away from service. They had no need to study and acquire knowledge in order to amount to something in society; they did not need to enter the army in order to get the social prestige they had in abundance. They could raise the army's prestige by joining it, but they were not keen on doing so if this involved sweat and toil. In fact, even officers of common birth began to look down on the artillery where academic training counted most and the romantic aspects of soldierly life least. The artillery became the nucleus of the commoners' share in the armed forces, commoners who were often too proud even to ask for letters patent of nobility. It is no accident that the few symptoms of a revolutionary spirit which can be found among the military of the nineteenth century can usually be found in the artillery.[13] Maria Theresa tried to make up for the genuine nobles' lack of interest in military schooling by turning the Academy into a training ground for the sons of brave officers who need not pay for their chance to earn a future meagre living in the imperial military service.[14] This new type of officer, who could be called a professional, could not match the standard of living of the civilian professional, doctor, lawyer, or engineer; yet he had lost much of the luster of the dashing daredevil officer type of old.

All things considered — the sincere efforts of the empress notwithstanding — the Maria Theresan reforms had reduced rather than strengthened the social position of the officer corps. But this very reason made it doubly necessary to cultivate and strengthen an *ésprit de corps* within the officer class itself. Concentrating on this task rather than on raising the officer's image in society, efforts were now increasingly focused on creating a caste rather than a mere class concept. And *caste* means an exclusive group with strict rejection of outsiders. This development did not, however, proceed without interruption.

It is interesting though rationally quite understandable that the first partial democratization of the Habsburg armed forces under Archduke Carl between 1806 and 1809 brought about a kind of brief revival of the nobility's role in military service. When the Archduke — far more important as military organizer than as strategist and thus the precise reverse of Eugene of Savoy — organized the militia (*Landwehr*) as a modified alternative to introducing supplementary general conscription, many aristocrats joined the colors together with their subject tenants, not unlike the mediaeval knights' retinue.

The *Landwehr,* though in changed form, remained an institution within the Habsburg military forces but the aristocracy's interest in the service beyond required legal obligations waned. The influx of the bourgeoisie into the officer corps continued, minor temporary setbacks notwithstanding. To take just one example: in 1859, only 10 percent of the general staff officers had been commoners; in 1918, their share was 75 percent. These figures include among nobles the service nobility whose members were never considered as peers by the old nobility. In fact, merger between service nobility and the nobility of ancient birth proved impossible. As Allmayer-Beck aptly puts it, "We touch . . . here upon certain social boundaries which transform the officers' corps into a social class . . . distinctly different from the aristocracy and from the big bourgeoisie. It is composed of the petty nobility, families of officers and government officials, and partly also of the petty bourgeoisie."[15]

One may add at this point that the ties of the officer corps to the aristocracy were, relatively speaking, even less remote than to the big bourgeoisie. Poor members of aristocratic families — chiefly their younger sons — formed a bridge between ancient noble and officer of common origin. Such a bond was entirely lacking with respect to the big bourgeoisie. On the other hand, the proportion of officers of petty bourgeois origin was steadily increasing, a situation that, as will be shown, became a matter of great concern to the military system in the last decades of the empire's existence.

Seemingly — but only seemingly — different are the results of the investigations of Nikolaus von Preradovich. He sees relatively very little change in the share of aristocracy and princes of the Imperial House in the high command positions of the armed forces. Yet he, too, points to the previously noted trend, in particular among top administrators and top strategists, by showing that among the twelve ministers of war from 1866 to 1918, only one belonged to the aristocracy, and among the ten chiefs of general staff during that period none was an aristocrat.[16] Yet these positions required a great deal of professional experience which princes of the blood and aristocrats were frequently neither capable of nor overly anxious to acquire.[17] As the rather liberal and certainly unorthodox Captain David Fenner von Fenneberg had noted as early as 1846, in Austria, unlike other countries, the most intelligent officers, rather than the nobility, wished to serve on the general staff.[18]

Yet, this does not contradict that in the predominantly honorary positions of commander-in-chief, members of the dynasty continued to play a predominant role until 1918.[19] Nor are Preradovich's figures — which by and large are confined to generals — sufficiently representative to draw general conclusions from them concerning the prestige of the officer class as a whole. More dubiously, in the comparative figures referring to Prussia, Preradovich sees greater consideration of the commoner and — if one wants to look at it that way — a somewhat

more democratic touch deriving from the virtual identity of the ancient
Prussian nobility, the Junkers, with the officer class. Most nobles had
been active officers in their youth. In this double capacity they had
stronger, though not necessarily more cordial, bonds in common with
society at large, especially with the rural population.[20]

Nobody has seen the consequences of this situation in regard to
social prestige more clearly than Otto Bauer, the Austrian socialist
leader who had himself been a reserve officer in the Austrian army
before and during World War I. Although one may not agree with
some of his conclusions, his observations were pungent. He relates that
during his training as an officer before the outbreak of war the chief
instructor, the so-called *Schulkommandant,* an excellent officer according to Bauer, told the new candidates:

> 'In every private first class you have to see a god whom you must obey
> blindly without blinking an eye lash.'[21] After the commander had
> ordered the noncommissioned officers to leave the room he con-
> tinued: 'The noncommissioned officers are peasants; an educated
> person has no social contact with a peasant. If I should learn that one
> of you talks to a noncommissioned officer outside of military duty,
> shakes hands with him or even joins him in the pub, he will lose
> eligibility to become an officer!'
>
> At that very moment the essence of the imperial and royal army, its
> class character, became clear to me. I saw its double hierarchy: on
> one side the military hierarchy rooted in the technical necessities of
> every army, the necessity of superiority and subordination in which
> the private first class is a god. On the other side I saw the social
> hierarchy, the class hierarchy, which distinguishes between a class of
> gentlemen and a class of workers and peasants. Nobody who wanted
> to be elevated to the class of gentlemen . . . was to have anything in
> common with them. . . . The entire structure of the old army was to
> mark this separation between the class of gentlemen and the working
> class so clearly that it sometimes appeared not as a separation of
> classes but as one of castes.[22]

The socialist Bauer noted further — in this respect not unlike the
conservative Preradovich — that the relationship of the Prussian
common soldier to his officer, who came from the Junker class with
whom he was well acquainted by tradition and experience, was closer
than that of the Austrian soldier to his officer, who usually came from
the class of petty bourgeois or *Beamter* (presumably meaning *clerk*
here). "The Austrian peasant was required to see the son of the petty
bourgeois with his sabre as an individual of exalted order. Particularly
absurd was this *Herrenmenschentum* according to rules in relationship

to the reserve officers as they existed since the 1870s."[23] One must remember from which strata of the population the bulk of the reserve officers came: minor state officials, commercial employees, grammar school teachers, etc.

One may doubt that the common soldier of the Habsburg army resented an officer from a relatively modest state in society more than he might have in Prussia where the officer of a regiment had the right to reject an officer's candidate, a rejection which in peacetime occurred regularly in the case of Jews and other socially unacceptable candidates. Whether the old feudal relationship to the Junker did not generate hatred commensurate to the contempt an Austrian private might have had for the son of a salesman as reserve officer cannot easily be verified. That the social background of the officer and reserve officer class went downward was, however, a fact having consequences fully recognized by Bauer.

Finally Bauer points to the well-known, peculiar relationship of the Habsburg officer, not to the nation, not even to king and country, but to the emperor alone. He believes that in the age of nationalism the concept of the supranational officer and soldier has become a myth. "Other officers fight for their country. The Austrian officer answers because he has taken an oath to the emperor. That is the concept of the army from a very remote past, from a feudal age. A modern army cannot be anchored in this thought."[24] Correct as this conclusion is in principle, one must remember that a powerful and in some ways noble tradition had upheld this system for a long time even in wartime. Compulsion alone cannot explain this. Quite apart from the force of tradition, it is necessary to add the simple fact that, in the mind of the soldier, and very understandably so, allegiance to the emperor implied allegiance to the country and the necessity to defend it.

The methods of defending the prestige of the officer class and with it the structure and image of an army to the liking of that class were old and forceful. After all, the preservation of the system depended on its good will. In this sense these methods were rational as long as they served their purpose. When they failed to do so because the system they served fell out of step with the time, they appeared absurd.

By and large these means to which we must now turn briefly can be divided into three principal groups. Defense of the prestige of the officer corps (a) by offensive strategy in battle, (b) by constructing and appealing to a special sense of honor of the officer, (c) by a special type of education for the officer. The second of these devices conveys at first glance a definitely antisocial impression, the third rather the reverse. Actually both are mixed bags.

As to offensive strategy, the idea has been deeply rooted in the history of warfare through the centuries that an army in battle must attack, attack, and again attack. As a leading Austrian commander, Tersztiánzky, put it in 1913, when he inspected a regiment that prepared for battle carefully, with various dodges, "What you have shown me here does not interest me at all. This slow crawling around, bending, ducking . . . I don't understand it and I don't care for it one bit. What I want to see is a regiment that shows briskly and dashingly how one can attack and fire quickly." In this sense the Austro-Hungarian armed forces attacked indeed in the fall of 1914 on the Galician battle fields, the cavalry in their blue and gold braided tunics, red pants, and shiny helmets. The result of such strategy of honor sponsored by Chief of General Staff von Conrad was that in the five months from August 1914 to the end of the year the armed forces lost 49 percent of the officer corps and 46 percent of the common soldiers.[25] The spirit that led to such tragic losses had, of course, not been alien to other armies. But they had learned the lesson that bravery is not identical with blind attack from the frightful experiences of the American Civil War, the Austro-Prussian war of 1866, the Franco-German war of 1870–71, and most recently, the Russo-Japanese war and the Balkan wars. And indeed the Austro-Hungarian forces learned that lesson after 1914. Whether the spirit of commanded self-sacrifice was used by Habsburg officers as a substitute for a spirit of nationalism as it existed in other armies is difficult to determine. In any case such a deduction cannot be lightly dismissed.

The notion that the officer has a special sense of honor different from, and above, that of the civilian, is as old as the institution of the officer corps itself. In this sense Field Marshal Prince Alfred Windischgraetz (1787–1862) certified that his bourgeois officers had done well in the face of the enemy; but he refused to make the same statement about his officers of noble origin because a nobleman's bravery should be taken for granted.[26] Implementation of that concept — often less naively than by the intellectually limited Prince Windischgraetz — occurred and occasionally still occurs in all armies with a feudal tradition and to a point even in those without it. One may note, too, that enforcement of this honor code in the Habsburg armies when its first great reorganization took place, under Maria Theresa, was never quite so brutal, never quite so permeated with absolute disdain for the civilian, including the public servant of the highest rank, as it was in the Prussia of Frederick the Great and his father Frederick William I. This may be one of the reasons — though only one — that the empress failed in her efforts to put the officer on a par with the nobleman of ancient origin.

From the foregoing it must not be concluded that the concept of the officer's honor is in itself objectionable as reactionary, utterly aggressive, and hostile to subordinates and aliens to the service. Here one must observe that the officer who indeed carries great responsibility has the obligation to be particularly honorable in his conduct, and that means to be fair, upright, and humane in relation to all those he must deal with, especially those under his command. Yet there is another aspect of honor which focuses not primarily on the officer's obligations but on his privileges. This means the honor of a specific class or in an even more restricted sense that of a caste. It is not easy to draw the line between these two concepts of honor since belief that the officer has greater responsibility to act honorably than the average man may easily lead to the further conclusion that he is also superior to others, with all the detrimental consequences of this assumption.

Still we understand what the liberal — we may well call it *positive* — concept of honor of the dedicated and fully loyal officer means when Carl Möring writes shortly before the outbreak of the revolution — incidentally in a work dedicated to Archduchess Sophie, mother of Francis Joseph — as follows:

> The Austrian army suffers from two serious organic weaknesses: a partial paralysis of the brain, the *Hofräthelei* [meaning the "influence of councillors"], and from a partial paralysis of the heart, of the free military spirit, the proud courage of a free man. Only the powerful prestige of honor can sustain the poorly paid officer from second lieutenant to general. [But where private connections, the antics of social climbers, vanity, noble origin, contempt for knowledge instead of talent dominate, how under such conditions can] honor, the most sacred value of the soldier . . . be generated, how can military honor and a sense of duty be preserved? . . . Yes, it should be repeated, the Austrian army lacks spirited intelligence among its officers, it lacks knowledge and talents within the higher ranks, it lacks character in its highest commanders.[27]

One need not agree with all the author's conclusions, but one may well agree that Möring's concept of the dedicated, loyal officer is in no way reprehensible.

A more conservative officer who had served in the Habsburg army from the revolution of 1848 to the end of the century put the problem, as he saw it, this way: "The soldier" and that means primarily the officer "must be conscious of the fact that he enters a privileged Estate with the first step he takes into the ranks of the army." Appeal to the grand tradition of old, represented and symbolized by uniforms, flags, standards, is most effective in this respect. "Consciousness of the fact that I wear the coat of those who fought so gloriously that the entire world knows it, admires me, envies me, — this gradually creates a feeling of superiority even in the most obtuse character which carries the soldier high above the others . . ."[28] These feelings are fully shared by another high officer even after the experience of two world wars. As he sees the army, the concept of knightly dignity as a special type of honor, the *Standesehre,* is prevalent. An officer's life must not be based on economic interests represented by the welfare state.

> Yes, the officer has indeed a special honor and it can be defended only if those who do not recognize it are kept out of the officers' Estate. We must insist,

> > Wer's nicht edel und nobel treibt,
> > Lieber fern vom Handwerk bleibt.[29]

Angeli and Blumenthal, the officers quoted here, both call attention to one well-known device which accentuates the isolation of the officer from society at large, namely, that officers of equal rank, even complete strangers, addressed each other socially with the familiar *Du* rather than the formal *Sie.* It may be added that the junior officer considered it a distinction if his senior called him 'thou' (*Du*), even though he was not allowed to reciprocate. Captain Fenner, on the other hand, commented as early as 1846 that the 'thou' in social life leads only to a more vulgar, if not obscene tone of conversation and he says with in many cases only limited exaggeration, "ésprit de corps means joint prejudices."[30]

In isolating the officer from others the 'thou' was certainly a relatively innocent device — comparable to the custom in other societies of addressing comparative strangers by the first name; it did not generate genuine familiarity but merely pretended to do so. In this sense pseudo familiarity may be deceptive and may help to tear down inhibitions which had better be kept under control.

In any case, more dangerous and therewith more inimical to the interests of society, including, in a way, the armed forces themselves, was the concept of a special honor which acknowledged the right of self-defense in its service. In other words, where the civilian had to turn to a court of law if he felt his honor had been violated, the officer under certain conditions was entitled to cut down the true or sometimes merely alleged trespasser on his honor with the sword. Civilians who by mere oversight encroached quite innocently on the privileges of the defender and at the same time executor of his prerogatives (for instance by colliding with him inadvertently in a crowd) could fall victim to this barbaric kind of license. Similar, often borderline, cases occurred quite frequently up to 1914. The class character of the privilege was particularly repulsive by its very limitations. It could be exercised only against those who were *satisfaktionsfähig,* i.e., those who were eligible to be challenged or to challenge to a duel. The Officer's Code of Honor tells us what this concept of *Satisfaktionsfähigkeit* means:

> Only the gentleman possesses the honor of arms (*Waffenehre*) or the honor to use arms in personal conflict. Every honorable man is a gentleman of chivalrous thought and conduct who on account of his social position (*Lebensstellung*), education, studies or birth is able and entitled to be part of society (*gute Gesellschaft*).[31]

This means that an individual with shady antecedents, in particular with a criminal record, does not possess the *Waffenehre*; but it also means just as clearly that somebody, however honorable, does not possess it if his origin, education, and social position keep him out of society. In other words, the lower strata of society are not *satisfaktionsfähig*. Within the military orbit this meant that only officers or those eligible to become officers were *satisfaktionsfähig*.

The Code provides further in Article 13 that in case of a physical insult the injured has the right to use any weapon or object at hand to chastize the attacker.

> This right to an energetic and immediate response becomes an absolute obligation if the physically insulted is an officer. Otherwise according to the views which dominate the officers' corps he would become guilty of inadequate defense of his uniform and therewith violate his honor as officer . . .[32]

This is what self-defense of honor means. Accordingly only he who by education was qualified to become an officer — at least in the reserve — was qualified to fight an officer in a duel, in other words only a gentleman was *satisfaktionsfähig*.[33] What makes this legally accepted privilege so repulsive is less its abuse, of which many examples can be found in Austrian newspapers, but the official recognition of two different kinds of honor: that of the educated or frequently pseudo-educated gentleman and that of the ordinary man. A drunken university student had to be challenged to a formal duel for the same offense for which a drunk and defenseless coachman could be cut down quite informally. Obviously the fault of such state of affairs lay far more with the system than with the individual officer who was bound to submit to it.

But in a sense the right to self-defense of honor represented only the tip of the iceberg of the duelling problem in the armed forces. The requirement to defend one's honor with sword or gun without recourse to a court of law was, in the last analysis, not only a command for the officer because he was confronted by social unequals. The tradition behind this honor system did not lack practical aspects. The soldier who had always to be ready to meet the external foe was not expected to waste his time in litigation with domestic adversaries. The commitment deriving from this necessity was quite frequently abused by German nationalists, especially students who would repeatedly and willfully challenge officers. At the turn of the nineteenth century this state of affairs led to ordinances of the War Ministry that voided the officer's obligation to accept challenges which were obvious provocations.[34]

In the last decades before the empire's dissolution, the objective of abrogating the moral compulsion to fight a duel was represented by two currents of thought with entirely different motivations. The main concern of one was that the army might lose the service of officers who had to expose themselves constantly to fights with possibly costly losses for the armed forces. The heir apparent, Archduke Francis Ferdinand sympathized with these considerations, whereas the tradition-bound old emperor who was at loggerheads with the archduke on many issues, was opposed to revisions of the duelling ritual. When the last emperor, Charles, succeeded Francis Joseph in 1916, another consideration became prevalent, namely, the religious one that duels violated the commandment to defend the sanctity of life. Accordingly in 1917 duels among officers were forbidden. The period when this prohibition — doubly reasonable in wartime — was in force in the empire was too short to measure its possibly beneficial effect. In any case the order was received with little sympathy by professional officers although the viewpoint of the by then very large number of reserve officers may have been more in line with the imperial order.[35]

Yet objection to duelling for reasons of genuine courage, namely, readiness to face the false reproach of cowardice, is much older. Captain Fenner wrote in 1846: "In my opinion the government will be forever tarnished for being incapable to protect the existence of the man who does not accept the challenge to a duel. Unfortunately I must assert categorically that the government does not have the power to defend the man who obeys its laws as well as the commandments of reason and humanitarianism." The officer who does not agree to a duel becomes a pariah.[36]

Thus, confidence in maintaining the prestige of a caste spirit was already shaken before it went out of existence some seventy years later.[37] Of all the means to protect and strengthen the prestige concept of the officer corps by appeal to a special kind of honor code, the duel had proved to be the most unjust and at the same time the most unsuitable for conveying a dignified picture of the officer to society. Its rudimentary effectiveness derived mainly from the fear it aroused among potential civilian victims of the duelling code. The assumption is not unjustified that the military authorities, intending to isolate the officer from society and its possibly dangerous influence, preferred an unpleasant image of the officer to one which might invite fraternization with other social classes.

Establishment of prestige by way of education should have reversed this course and should have brought the officer in closer touch with an enlightened citizenry. Actually the matter was more complex. In a positive sense the endeavors of Archduke Carl, the capable and upright brother of Emperor Francis I must be listed here. The Archduke's efforts to modernize the army, to humanize discipline, and to improve the educational standards of the officer corps, coincided with the Scharnhorst-Gneisenau army reforms in Prussia. They were equally well planned but less effective since the archduke was relieved from supreme command by the emperor after the war of 1809 whose outcome actually confirmed the necessity of the reforms initiated by Carl.

Subsequent advocates of reform like Captain Fenner von Fenneberg put chief emphasis on democratization. They held the view that only strongly motivated troops who represented the will of the people could be successful in war. Yet Fenner doubted that such motivation could ever be generated under a system of state absolutism. Motivation, according to Fenner, is inseparably linked to education of the officer by the officer. "The majority of officers is superior to the ordinary soldier in practical training (*materielle Bildung*) inasmuch as chiefly military craft is concerned. Yet genuine social education whose foundation is humanitarianism frequently must yield, even where it exists, to the military gospel of complete subjecton to the will of superiors and of absolute arbitrariness against subordinates." The officer is generally unpopular with the common soldier because he does not understand him. Only officers who come from the same class as the soldiers or, if they do not, who try very hard to identify with their men can be successful.[38] This is what the naturally somewhat more conservative Archduke Carl had in mind with his reforms.

So much about the positive vistas of educational reforms concerning the officer corps. Their thrust in regard to social prestige is based on the insight that a better-educated officer will not only be a better soldier but will also have a more respected position in society. Certainly this plea for better education does not seek to add to the social isolation of the officer class, but on the contrary, wants to bring officer and society closer together.

Yet another trend concerning educational reforms in the Habsburg armies moved in the opposite direction. In the last peacetime years of the empire we can observe fully conscious efforts to use education as a means of further isolating the officer from the social environment he was born into. This drive was spearheaded by General Moritz von Auffenberg (1852–1928), minister of war, 1911–12, and confidant of the heir apparent Archduke Francis Ferdinand. The beginnings of this trend are not easy to trace, but it seems fair to assume that the rigid curriculum of the military schools which stood in marked contrast to that of secondary schools for civilians contributed in no small way to this state of affairs. Obviously the officer's candidate had to master subjects which the civilian student did not need. But emphasis on semi-military subjects for juveniles between the ages of eleven and fifteen at the expense of the humanities, particularly history teaching focused almost exclusively on dynastic wars and battles, tended to increase the intellectual isolation of the future officer. Still, these were rather side effects than directly intended results of military education. In the first decade of the twentieth century, under the auspices of the heir apparent and the new Chief of the General Staff, Conrad von Hötzendorf, more attention was paid to these matters.

Auffenberg, one of the principal military advisers of the archduke, wrote two memoranda at his request on the spirit of the officer corps and ways to improve it. Auffenberg's rank and his obligation to inspect the officers' schools made the general appear particularly qualified to express an opinion on these weighty matters. His first memorandum of May 1908, shortly before the outbreak of the Bosnian annexation crisis, is titled *Über die Verfassung des Offizierskorps und die Stimmung in demselben*. After some perfunctory praise for the technical training of the officers' candidates the general comes to the core of the matter of concern to him and the archduke.

> No observer can miss the fact that recruitment of our corps of professional officers comes from increasingly lower strata of the

population. . . . Since it is absolutely beyond the power of the army administration to reverse this trend [one must ponder the consequences. They can be seen] in part clearly and directly in the military sphere, partly in the social sphere . . . [The latter in turn affects the military sphere.]

The experiences of all times and all countries teach us that outstanding efforts and an exemplary spirit of sacrifice . . . in critical situations . . . can be made only by those who according to birth and education come from the better . . . strata of the population. Extraordinary losses in battle were at all times only accepted by military units led by a homogeneous and socially well placed officers' corps with a particularly well-developed sense of honor . . . One therefore has to realize that . . . the structure of our officers' corps and probably that of the entire army cannot be expected to perform better than average. This . . . leads to very definite conclusions . . . .

The relative inferiority of the social milieu from which the majority of our officers' corps derives influences the social esteem for the officer. Time has long passed when the officer played first role in society . . . Therewith the portepée loses its recruiting power . . .

These factors . . . and the hostile atmosphere to which the officers are exposed in many parts of the empire make the officers' corps necessarily exclusive like a caste. This is no advantage for the cultural and intellectual development of the officer but it is no disadvantage in a strictly military sense either . . .

Auffenberg considers nationalist propaganda not yet to be very dangerous for the spirit of the officer corps. Socialist propaganda might become more dangerous since it is concerned with material things of interest to the officer.

Since it would be very difficult to cut off officers' contacts with their families and friends at home, exchanges should be strongly advocated [obviously meaning the transfer of officers to other parts of the country] . . . Continuous dispersal (*Durchrüttelung*) of the officers' corps where signs of too much intimacy with nationally unreliable strata of the population become apparent (Hungary, partly also Bohemia) or where the influence of socialist motives may be feared [must be brought about]. This won't help the regimental spirit. But of two evils one has to choose the lesser . . . The commanders . . . may offer another effective device to fight damaging influences. To educate, educate, educate must be their most important task. . . .

As a last device I should like to propose most strongly a thorough and not too narrow basic education for the future officer. Education frees people and also gives them necessary self-confidence. . . . There can be no doubt that a better educated man is generally held in higher esteem than a less well educated. Is it not quite natural that an officer who comes from a lowly background will loosen his relationship [with the people among whom he was brought up] more easily if he has benefitted from an education which raises him high above his milieu? I do not refer to the bonds of heart and family but to social relations since they can, under certain conditions, become dangerous to the officer's thinking and feeling.[39]

In the second Auffenberg memorandum, *Geist und innere Verfassung der Armee,* dated Sarajevo, July 1910, the general again emphasizes the great importance of the social composition and education of the officer corps. Here this clever and capable general's purpose, slightly camouflaged in the first memorandum by phrases such as education making people free and exclusivity of the officer corps not making for better cultural and intellectual development, becomes even more obvious. A superior education for the young officer is advocated

> not only for general education's sake, but to tear our officers who come largely from other [obviously meaning inferior] social strata, from the influence of their family milieu. This is best done by way of a relatively high educational standard. It dissolves some bonds, so to speak by a chemical process, that will never be ruptured mechanically. Our military schools should therefore above all bring fully educated men into the ranks of the troops. [Auffenberg elaborates further on the reasons]: . . . I believe that — in contrast to the past — none of the better educated occupational groups comes from such low strata of the population as the professional officers' corps of our army. The situation may be similar only among the rural clergy [but not quite as bad]. The roots of the officers' corps reach into the proletariat. Doubtless this represents a problem . . . All the time I find traces that overall we are confronted by socially inadequate individuals. This is confirmed by going through the records of punishment and of trials before courts of honor and criminal courts . . . Within entire military units one does not find a single elegant individual, no man of distinction . . . It may be noted also that mainly the older officers come from better strata, the younger ones . . . from the lowest. To be sure, sons of railroad watchmen, janitors of public buildings . . . grammar school teachers, petty businessmen may become good men and deserving officers . . . But service and knowledge of service regulations are by no means the only requirements that make for a good officer. If the spirit, the verve is lacking even the best knowledge of service regulations will not help him in critical situations . . .
>
> Yet, spirit and enthusiasm cannot develop if in long years of peace

and in-peace service only the sons of lower classes get together. What military school and an able and understanding commander can accomplish in years, may be destroyed by a furlough of several weeks in the narrow circles of a petty official or petty bourgeois.

After pointing to other unfavorable factors, such as the withdrawal indeed the flight of nobility from the army and the poor pay and slow advancement in service, Auffenberg notes that in no other country is the army so closely tied to the existence of the dynasty as in the Habsburg monarchy. Therefore "the officer's calling must become a magnet for the median and higher strata of society and only radical means can help toward this goal." As one of the most important means to that effect, education of the officers' candidate must be greatly improved.

> Therewith the not fully unjustified criticism could be met that the general education of the officer is [*horribile dictu*] not vastly superior to that of the grammar school teacher. But because this preliminary education [meaning that before becoming an officer's candidate] would become far more expensive, only the better social classes could compete . . . [40]

Both Auffenberg memoranda — the second actually an elaboration of the first — thus conclude that the social prestige of the officer class could only be maintained and, he hoped, strengthened if candidates from lower classes received a military and pre-military education that would separate them from their families and their general social milieu. It might be even better to curb the influx of these undesirable elements by raising the cost of military and pre-military education. Thus the social prestige of the officer class could be raised by further isolating them from the lower classes. Such isolation, to be sure, was not intended to bar contacts with the higher classes of society. Yet inasmuch as the first level of society, the aristocracy, and even the second, the high bureaucracy and the upper bourgeoisie, continued to show little inclination to commit their sons to professional military service, the desired increase of social bonds to the higher classes of society was bound to remain unachieved. The core of the Auffenberg memoranda remained the truly remarkable notion that education be used as a means of further isolating the officer from society at large.

Such plans cannot be seen as only a narrow scheme to preserve the class character of the officer corps. The problem has wider aspects, one still relevant even in contemporary democratic societies. The problem of the social prestige of the officer class cannot easily be separated from that of military discipline. The ideal that, in service, complete military discipline should prevail, but that, off duty, officer and men may have unrestricted social relations regardless of rank, is far more easily prescribed than achieved without affecting military discipline. Although we certainly cannot condone prescriptions to uphold and maintain the class character of an officer corps by various gimmicks, we cannot ignore the dilemma of maintaining military discipline.

In this sense we must recognize two facts. The social prestige and social prejudice present in the officer corps of the Habsburg armies throughout their long history existed in all contemporary armies, generally to a higher degree in the East and North, to a lesser in the West. To a large measure social prestige and prejudice operated not only to maintain a class structure for its own sake but primarily to resolve the problem of military discipline for officers and men on and off duty. We well know that the Habsburg armies' stumbling efforts to maintain discipline by developing methods to give the officer class an artificial special prestige have been only partially successful at best. We know even better that those methods have fallen increasingly, and at length completely, out of step with the spirit of our times. We may certainly doubt that contemporary nondemocratic societies have solved the problem, all the more since we cannot be absolutely convinced that the democratic ones have mastered it.

Notes

1. See *Brockhaus Enzyklopädie,* vol. 15 (Wiesbaden, 1972); H. Kluth in *Handwörterbuch der Sozialwissenschaften* (Stuttgart, 1964), 8: 534ff.

2. A. de Tocqueville, *De la democratie en Amerique,* ed. J. P. Mayer (Frankfurt, 1956), 159–72; see particularly 169, quoted in Wilhelm Korff, *Ehre, Prestige, Gewissen* (Cologne, 1966), 9. Another observer sees the basic difference between honor and prestige as the ineluctable possession of honor contrasted with the ability to buy or sell prestige. J. C. Allmayer-Beck, *Mitteilungsblatt des Vereins Alt Neustadt,* January 1978, p. 21.

3. Korff, 59. The connection between suicide rate and an honorable military funeral is suggestive although naturally not fully provable.

4. Kluth, 534–36.

5. *Ibid.,* 535f.

6. See J. C. Allmayer-Beck, "Vom letzten Ritter zum Kriegsunternehmer. Wandlungen des Heerwesens im 16. Jahrhundert," in R. Feuchtmüller, ed., *Renaissance in Österreich. Geschichte, Wissenschaft, Kunst* (Horn, 1974),

114-25; and "Die allezeit Getreuen," in H. Siegert, ed., *Adel in Österreich* (Vienna, 1971), 303-318; see also "Die Theresianische Militärakademie von ihrer Gründung bis 1918," *225 Jahre Theresianische Militärakademie* (Wiener Neustadt, 1978), 7-10. See further, Fritz Redlich, "The German Military Enterprises and Work Force," *Vierteljahrsschrift für Sozial- und Weltgeschichte,* Beiheft 47 (1964).

7. Jürg Zimmermann, "Militärverwaltung und Heeresaufbringung in Österreich bis 1806," *Handbuch zur deutschen Militärgeschichte 1648-1939* (Frankfurt, 1965), 128-30; R. A. Kann *A History of the Habsburg Empire 1526-1918* (Berkeley, 1974), 132f.

8. J. Zimmermann, 129. See also, Derek McKay, *Prince Eugene of Savoy* (London, 1977), 228.

9. Allmayer-Beck, "Die allezeit Getreuen," 310.

10. *Ibid.,* 314.

11. *Ibid.*

12. Until 1780 the co-regent Joseph II.

13. This fact was noted by Carl Möring, the brilliant high artillery officer, in *Sibyllinische Bücher aus Österreich* (Hamburg, 1848), 2: 20-26.

14. Rainer Wohlfeil, "Ritter, Söldnerheer, Offizier, Versuch eines vergleiches," *Veröffentlichungen des Institutes für geschichtliche Landeskunde der Universität Mainz* 3 (1966): 45-70; J. C. Allmayer-Beck, "Wandlungen im Heereswesen zur Zeit Maria Theresias," in *Schriften des Heeresgeschichtlichen Museums* (Vienna, 1967), 1-24, *passim.* See also Allmayer-Beck, "Die Träger der staatlichen Macht: Adel, Armee, Bürokratie," in O. Schulmeister, ed., *Spectrum Austriae* (Vienna, 1957), 257-61; and "Die Theresianische Militärakademie," 11-18; J. Zimmermann, 128-30.

15. Allmayer-Beck, 274, 272ff; and "Die allezeit Getreuen," 312ff.

16. Nikolaus von Preradovich, *Die Führungsschichten in Österreich und Preussen (1804-1909)* (Wiesbaden, 1955), 172f.

17. Allmayer-Beck, "Die allezeit Getreuen," 314; and "Wandlungen im Heerwesen zur Zeit Maria Theresias," 21f; and "Die Träger der staatlichen Macht . . . ," 261f., 272f. See also Wohlfeil, 129; and Möring, 2: 20-29.

18. Daniel Fenner von Fenneberg, *Österreich und seine Armee* (Leipzig, 1846), 140ff.; Möring, 2: 38-58.

19. For the aristocracy, this would be only partly true and not to even that degree after 1866.

20. Preradovich, 37, 43f., 69f., 71f., 172f., 176f., 182f., 185.

21. Otto Bauer, *Die Offiziere der Republik* (Vienna, 1921), 1f. Note that officer candidates were initially so-called *Einjährige Freiwillige* (volunteers for one-year's service). They had to be graduates of a secondary school with a curriculum of seven or eight years, and although they began their military service as simple privates, they had to serve only one year instead of the three required of soldiers without such secondary education. Only the *Einjährig Freiwillige* was eligible eventually to become an officer in the army reserve.

22. *Ibid.*

23. *Ibid.,* 5.

24. *Ibid.,* 8.

25. See, for instance, Peter Broucek, "Taktische Erkenntnisse aus dem russisch-japanischen Krieg und deren Beachtung in Österreich-Ungarn," *Mitteilungen des Österreichischen Staatsarchivs* 30 (1977): 191 f., 209 f., 213 f.

26. Allmayer-Beck, *Spectrum Austriae,* 254.

27. Möring, II: 5–8. The sentence first quoted is spaced out [for emphasis] in the original.

In the context of ignoring the standards of the officer's professional conduct within the frame of the honor concept so tellingly discussed by Möring, one must also consider the fear lest a judicious self-evaluation of the army's achievements undercut its prestige. Broucek calls attention to this fact often observed in military historiography. Wide recognition was given to Moltke's view that "it would be an obligation of loyalty and patriotism not to destroy the prestige which ties the victory of our army to certain personalities." This refers to Prussia. As to Austria, "that this was all the more true in case of a debacle has been proved by the defeats of 1859 and 1866. Added to this concept of preservation of prestige were certain claims based on the prohibition of truly or allegedly hurting 'the honor' of an officer and of violating the principle of comradeship." Peter Broucek, "Militärhistoriographisches Nachbeben des Feldzugsjahres 1859." (Ms., p. 35; to appear in *Mitteilungen des Österreichischen Staatsarchivs* 31–32 (1978–79).

28. Moritz von Angeli, *Aus dem Nachlass* (Vienna, 1905), 81 ff.

29. Collected writings of Colonel Johann Heinrich Blumenthal, "Die Stellung des Heeres im österreichischen Staat," *Österreichisches Kriegsarchiv,* B 1769, No. 3. On restrictions upon the admission of officers — even the liberal Captain Fenner von Fenneberg wanted to exclude foreign officers from the imperial army. Fenner, 133 f.

30. Fenner, 125 ff., 128 f.

31. Gustav Ristow, imperial and royal colonel, *Ehrenkodex,* 3d ed., Article 1. See also Franz von Bognár, *Die Regeln des Duells,* 9th ed. (Vienna, 1912), 32 f.

Webster's *Dictionary* defines a *gentleman* as "a man of good birth and social standing," obviously qualifications which a person — and this is decisive — can secure only partly by his own efforts.

32. This is the theme of Arthur Schnitzler's well-known story "Leutnant Gustl" (1900). As a consequence, Schnitzler was deprived of his officer's rank in the Army Medical Corps. See also Ferdinand v. Saar, "Leutnant Buda" (1887) concerning abuse of the duel by the ruffian type of army officer. Note that similar conditions existed in other armies. In Germany, for instance, the so-called Zaber affair of December 1913, in which the privileges just described were invoked against German civilians of French origin, turned into an international incident. It contributed to the tension which led to the outbreak of World War I.

34. Colonel J. H. Blumenthal, "Der Offizier in Staat und Gesellschaft," *Österreichisches Kriegsarchiv,* B 1769, No. 3.

35. See Moritz v. Auffenberg, Memorandum "Geist und innere Verfassung der Armee," Sarajevo, July 1910, *Österreichisches Kriegsarchiv,* Nachlass Auffenberg, 23 f., which is critical of the completely antiduelling position of the military administration.

36. Fenner v. Fenneberg, 146. On the question of duels in the army in general, see J. H. Blumenthal, "Die Frage der besonderen Ehrenauffassung des Offiziers," *Österreichisches Kriegsarchiv,* B 1769, No. 3.

37. See in this respect another work of Arthur Schnitzler, the drama *Freiwild* (1890), in which a civilian who refuses to fight an unworthy officer is consequently attacked by him and killed on a public street. Quite obviously, Saar's and Schnitzler's writings on duelling are based on personal experiences or recollections even though the topic is handled with farreaching poetic license.

38. Fenner v. Fenneberg, 48; see also 24 ff., 45 f. On the education of the officer see further Colonel Franz Brenner, "Der österreichische Offizier und seine gesellschaftliche Stellung," *Österreichisches Kriegsarchiv,* B 824 (written 1912/13); and Colonel Blumenthal, *Österreichisches Kriegsarchiv* B 1769, No. 6, on the reforms of the archduke and the educational imaprovement and indeed sometimes outstanding achievements of the officer corps in the nineteenth century. See "Kulturgeschichte der k.u.k. Armee" and "Kulturträger im österreichischen Soldatenrock, *Ibid.* On the relationship between the archduke and Emperor Francis, see Manfred Rauchensteiner, *Kaiser Franz und Erzherzog Karl. Dynastie und Heerwesen in Österreich 1796-1809* (Vienna, 1972), *passim.*

39. M. v. Auffenberg, "Über die Verfassung des Offizierskorps und die Stimmung in demselben," May 1908, *Österreichisches Kriegsarchiv,* Nachlass Auffenberg, 6-8, 10-16.

40. Auffenberg, Memorandum, "Geist und innere Verfassung der Armee," 1910, *Ibid.,* 5-12, 28-29.

Robert A. Kann

Conclusions

Of the six papers in this section, the one by Norman Davies covers the period from 1700 to 1864, those by C. W. Ingrao, László Deme, and Aladár Urbán brief phases from 1703–1711 and 1848–49, respectively. Zoltán Kramár, on the other hand, discusses the military ethos of the Hungarian nobility for the long period from 1700 to 1848, and the final paper by Robert Kann surveys the whole era from the beginning of the eighteenth century to the dissolution of the Habsburg empire.

The six papers, then, seem discordant in point of time and place covered. Yet, contrary to superficial appearance, a measure of common themes and motivations does exist in the six essays. Indeed, for all their diversity, certain common conclusions may well be drawn from them. To demonstrate this, it is neither necessary nor even advisable to abstract the specific topics of the six studies. The reader who intends to do them justice must go through each of them in full. Accordingly, the following essay will touch on only those main facets which may help us reach conclusions pertinent to all six studies.

Four main themes, besides a number of others which must be looked for in the individual essays, are obvious: the impact of the Enlightenment on the rise of the armed forces; insurrections and rebellions by peasants without formal military organizations against early regular armed forces; revolutionary military organizations against fully trained troops under absolute rule; and finally professional armed forces under the leadership of an officer class which is bound to resist social change.

Norman Davies, in his paper on the Polish *szlachta,* 1700–1864, perceives this body not as a socioeconomic class institution but as a hereditary military estate of the Polish-Lithuanian society. Within a government of nobles, it rules by unanimous consent which, by implication, should mean recognition of the freedom of the individual, a noble individual, to be sure. With his *liberum veto,* his estate claims the right of resistance to the crown.

The *szlachta* defends these rights as a body which comprises not less than about 12 percent of the population, by far the largest body of nobles in any European country, Hungary and Spain included. Its power does not derive entirely from its economic strength, since it includes many more poor than wealthy nobles. The power of the military estate is chiefly anchored in social status. The constitutional privileges claimed and largely secured by the *szlachta* make it possible to establish an army of nobles loosely organized on a territorial basis. That assures victory over the centralizing tendencies of the crown. The privileges of the *szlachta* serve the twofold purpose of fighting the creation of a standing army, which would strengthen the crown against the *szlachta* and, even more important, of preventing the arming of the peasants, which might lead to social revolution.

The members of the *szlachta* despised government service, but the *szlachta* itself was ready to make considerable sacrifices to form its own military organization which consisted chiefly of cavalry. This poorly equipped army, as Davies points out, was hardly able to defend the country; but, partly because of its mobility and partly because of the complete dispersal of its meager forces, it could not easily be destroyed. This is merely one of the many remarkably strange features of Polish institutional history from the middle of the seventeenth century to the end of the nobles' republic in the late eighteenth century. In fact, after the partitions, the spirit of this individualism survived in the Polish restoration movement of the nineteenth century.

There certainly were obvious features of a feudal tradition in this strange establishment. But just as surely, though less obviously, the institution of the *szlachta* also shows features of the Enlightenment, although of a rather confused Enlightenment. The strong feeling for individual liberty prevailing in the representative institutions of the country, as well as in a military organization which lacked the drill and regimentation of the newly rising standing armies in Western and Central Europe, speaks for this influence.

To be sure, the centralizing aspects of the political Enlightenment were very feeble in Poland well into the partition period but the numerical strength of the *szlachta* and its social composition show that one cannot speak simply of a feudal structure comparable to those existing in the East, and in the West prior to the French Revolution. The Polish military organization was an institution *sui generis,* standing between feudalism and enlightened federalism rather than absolutism, just as the Polish constitutional organization was poised between absolutism and a socially selective semidemocracy. In any case, the Enlightenment aspects of these singular institutions gradually became stronger than the feudal ones.

C. W. Ingrao's study on the *Kuruc* War (1703–1711) in Hungary as an early and striking example of guerrilla warfare focuses attention on the roots of revolutionary violence, not at the end of the Enlightenment but at its beginning. The *kuruc* risings are distinguished from large-scale revolutions like that of 1789 in France by neither lack of popular appeal nor of large-scale military action. *Kuruc* warfare drew its forces from varied groups: oppressed serfs, religious dissenters, disgruntled nobles, discharged soldiers without means of subsistence. In general, the forces of the Rákóczi Insurrection were fed by opposition to the imperial armed forces. These were perceived as agents of a foreign government and an alien sovereign who, in the name of the Counter Reformation, manhandled Hungarian liberties and completely destroyed the expectations raised by liberation from the Turkish yoke.

Yet although the consequences of the Rákóczi Insurrection were deep and widespread and its achievements embodied in the Szatmár compromise of 1711 were substantial, under existing conditions, *kuruc* warfare was still predominantly class war. It could not represent the efforts of a nation fully stratified socially as was the case in 1789 and the following years in France. Granted that Hungary at the beginning of the eighteenth century was still an agricultural nation, the concept of the nation-in-arms is not dependent on percentages of various social classes but on the image created by the presence of representatives of nobles, townships, churches, and other social bodies in addition to the great impact of the peasantry. In this sense, the Rákóczi risings resemble the peasant wars of the sixteenth century more than the revolutions from the late eighteenth century onward. This is also the main reason that the *Kuruc* War, hotly as it was fought, could never make the transition from guerrilla warfare to the concept of the nation-in-arms.

Zoltán Kramár's paper on the military ethos of the Hungarian nobility from 1700 to 1848 surveys the evolution of the Hungarian armed forces as they developed from the noble levy, the *insurrectio,* to the notion of a professional standing army. The first step in this direction — and for a brief period, a successful one — was taken under the reign of Matthias Corvinus. Continuation of his military policy was blocked by the century and a half of Turkish occupation; during that time, however, the *insurrectio* burst out of the border regions of nonoccupied Hungary to raid territory seized by the Turks. The establishment of the Hungarian military forces as a standing army of professional soldiers evolved after the ambiguous liberation of the 1860s.

But this did not spring from the national spirit, that is, as a movement of the gentry's code of chivalry into wider strata of the population. The professional army became predominantly an instrument of the Counter Reformation; it was made up largely of foreign soldiery and its leaders were almost all foreign officers who were alien if not downright hostile to the national spirit. The gradual conversion of the Hungarian high nobility into a supranational, proimperial aristocracy, a court aristocracy at that, accelerated this development.

This situation was somewhat modified by the skill and at least superficially friendly smoothness of Maria Theresa's administration, but opposition to what might be called the *imperialization* of Hungary and its military power flared up under the tempestuous centralizing regime of Emperor Joseph. Demands for a truly national army and halting attempts in this direction during the Napoleonic wars brought no tangible results. Kramár mentions the gentry's lack of interest in military science and its strange legalism opposing the military spirit before Mohács as factors contributing to the inability to create a national army.

A major break in the situation began during the early stages of the Hungarian Revolution of 1848 as sketched in László Deme's paper on the National Guard in Pest in March and April, 1848. That essay, though apparently rather limited in scope, is of great significance.

The aforementioned study by C. W. Ingrao analyzes prerevolutionary rebellion as typified by the *Kuruc* War; Deme's study analyzes postrevolutionary risings after 1789. Establishment of the National Guard in Pest in 1848 grows out of the situation Kramár noted, namely, that the professional armed forces in Hungary consisted largely of foreigners. The new National Guard, although established on narrow city grounds in March 1848, was intentionally designed on the pattern of the French National Guard of 1789 and took an oath of allegiance to country, king, and constitution — in that order. The establishment of a committee on public safety likewise followed French precedent. City residents in all walks of life, young intellectuals foremost among them, were important elements in the new National Guard. This feature, of course, was completely absent in the risings of the Rákóczi era at the beginning of the eighteenth century.

Another new factor was the property qualification demanded for admission to the National Guard by the conservatives. A compromise arranged by Kossuth lowered the property required for membership in the city National Guard below that needed for the right to vote; in rural districts, the property qualification for the suffrage was lower than for admission to the National Guard. The reason was protection of the existing rural social order, that is, of the integrity of the large estates against an influx of radicals into the National Guard. That became a nationwide force under Prime Minister Count Lajos Batthyány by mid-April 1848. In an admittedly incomplete form, the French revolutionary concept of the nation-in-arms was thus introduced in Hungary by the small-scale operations of the poorly armed guards of Pest, in March 1848.

Aladár Urbán, dealing with the Hungarian army in 1848–49, carries Deme's study further. He deals with the establishment of the so-called mobile National Guard, later converted into the *honvéds*. This *honvéd* army became a significant fighting force by December 1848 and a regular army by April of the following year. Smaller units had seen action against Serbian minorities in the summer of 1848. At the height of the War of Independence, the *honvéd* army reached a strength of more than 160,000 men, including a number of retired professional officers. Of Hungary's nationalities, only Germans were represented in substantial numbers, roughly 15 percent. Nearly 75 percent of the army was Hungarian. It is important to note this since such an ethnic distribution could be achieved only by way of a selective system and not by general conscription. Thus manpower was raised by a system of quotas required of counties and townships.

Robert Kann's essay on the social prestige of the officer class in the Habsburg empire covers the longest span of time, from the eighteenth century to 1918. It takes notice of some revolutionary changes during the period surveyed, but basically it deals with the force of tradition throughout the history of the Habsburg armed forces. This tradition is perceived as the operation of a class system anchored in the social prestige of the officers. The evolution of the standing army in the seventeenth century led, in the eighteenth, to a rather clearcut separation between prestige based on noble origin (the prerogative of higher officers) and the prestige derived from mere nobility by letters patent, in which ennoblement generally came as a routine reward for long periods of active military service. The prestige of such ennobled commoners cannot be compared to that deriving from noble ancestry as it existed, for instance, in Prussia. Nor does this new Habsburg officer class have the prestige of inherited landed wealth. In fact, except for the largely honorary positions held by commanders-in-chief — generally aristocrats, even scions of the dynasty and other princes — the Habsburg armies were led mostly by commoners whose patent of nobility carried little social weight. The aristocracy, by and large, withdrew from professional peacetime service.

Very important, too, the Habsburg empire could never become a nation-state. The officer corps was largely German, but in good part multinational. In the eighteenth century, that meant far more officers from regions west and south then east of the Austrian hereditary lands, that is, Italians, Walloons, Frenchmen, Spaniards, to a lesser extent, Hungarians and Croats, and only later, Czechs, Poles, and other Slavs. This multinational character of the Habsburg armed forces meant loyalty to the sovereign, first; to the state second; but never, of course, to a nation. In other words, for king and far less, for country. This, in turn, meant that the class character of the officer corps had to be rigidly maintained in order to assure the loyalty which was based chiefly on its members' relationship to the sovereign. It must be realized, furthermore, that even in an army based on a rigid class system — such as the Prussian, for example — there could be a social relationship between the officer, frequently a landed Junker, and the peasant soldier. Such a relationship was absent in the Habsburg forces, where officer and men not only frequently spoke different tongues but also lacked the bond of a common tie to the land.

Preserving prestige became all the more important, therefore. It could be maintained in differing ways, which could be operative at the same time: (a) in actual warfare, offensive strategy as an emanation of the spirit of valor; (b) in peacetime, appeal to a special code of honor higher than that of the civilian. In other words, *noblesse oblige,* the noblesse of the officer's uniform; (c) preservation of prestige by military education.

In the modern Habsburg armed forces not only the aristocracy but also the upper bourgeoisie increasingly withdrew from professional military service. Accordingly, the officers increasingly represented the petty bourgeoisie which was imbued with a strong and divisive sense of nationalism. Giving the officer's candidate a gentleman's education, that is, training him in such social graces as strict etiquette, dancing, fencing, horsemanship, mastery of modern languages, and so forth, was to alienate him both from his family and from the spirit of nationalism of the second half of the nineteenth and the early twentieth century. Social isolation must prevail in order to maintain an allegiance tied to the crown and not to the people.

What deductions can be drawn from these six papers beyond the mere fact that they all deal with war and society in Central and East Central Europe? Taken together, they discuss the major roots of military organization and military action in the area. Norman Davies describes the military structure within the caste system of the *szlachta.*

Its impact was, of course, far more limited than that of a military organization based on general conscription, but considerably wider than that of the late mediaeval system based on knights and their retinues. Furthermore, the emphasis on autonomous military institutions free from interference by the crown is at least tinged with enlightened ideas. The attempt to adjust the caste system to modern views is certainly a basic element in the overall theme of this volume.

Ingrao introduces the revolutionary element in the conduct of warfare by describing the *kuruc* guerrillas who fought so stubbornly in the Rákóczi Insurrection. Support of these risings was widespread among people in all walks of life, the gentry by no means excluded, yet the *kuruc* wars, as noted earlier, do not represent the concept of the nation-in-arms. Fully new, however, were the guerrilla tactics introduced by these insurrections. They recur on a large scale in early nineteenth-century Spain and in the anticolonial risings of the twentieth century in Africa, to mention only two outstanding examples.

Zoltán Kramár shows how truly outdated the so-called noble levy, or *insurrectio* was by the eighteenth century. A merely caste army lacked even the limited enlightened features of the *szlachta* army and its amazing mobility. The noble levy had no future and was swallowed by the imperial Habsburg forces in which the Magyar element played a very restricted role well into the second half of the nineteenth century.

The days of the caste army within a national frame were definitely over, but the papers on the Hungarian armed forces of 1848–49 demonstrate great progress toward the concept of the nation-in-arms in line with developments since 1789. The establishment of the Hungarian National Guard in Pest in March 1848 was particularly conspicuous in this respect although the restrictions imposed by a property qualification — to limit admission to the guard in defense of the existing social order — were, of course, incompatible with the French revolutionary tradition. In the *honvéd* army other restrictions were found necessary which impeded the establishment of a full-fledged nation-in-arms. The Hungarian nationality problem was bound to require a choice between a Hungarian-dominated army and a genuinely multinational army in line with the tradition of 1789. Hungarian nationalism, together with concern about the loyalties of other ethnic groups in Hungary, led to the adoption of a Hungarian-controlled army model by means of selective recruiting. Here we have an unanswered question: how far can a multinational state establish truly democratic armed forces?

The study by Robert Kann touches on this problem. The imperial military organization holds the middle ground between various versions of the caste army and the nation-in-arms. The Habsburg armies were not caste armies like the Hungarian forces and those of the *szlachta* in the eighteenth and early nineteenth century. Even less did they represent the nation-in-arms. They were not caste armies because they were truly multinational, commanded and held together by officers who did not represent a genuine national nobility. The officers lacked the social prestige of leaders who were the offspring of national nobilities, be they in Hungary, Prussia, or prerevolutionary France. A caste factor existed, nevertheless; but unlike the situation in the aforementioned countries, that factor did not come out of the tradition of feudalism but from a rigid separation between the officer class and other strata of society. This separation had little to do with the feudal order but rather with social isolation and contrived alienation from other classes of society.

The introduction of general conscription in the Habsburg armed forces in the nineteenth century modified this class system somewhat, since, at least in the army reserves, officers represented society at large; this factor, due above all to the influence of nationalism, increasingly loosened the officers' caste system. In contrast to the caste armies of ancient Poland and Hungary, and in a semidemocratic frame the *kuruc* guerrillas and the French revolutionary nation-in-arms, one might speak, in the Habsburg case, of a *bureaucratic* army system. Well into the second half of the nineteenth century, the factor of national diversity was basically not acknowledged, not opposed, simply ignored.

All things considered, the six papers in this section on eighteenth- and early nineteenth-century warfare represent the major issues of the evolution of militarism in the social order. The caste system, guerrilla operations as forerunner of the nation-in-arms, and finally the bureaucratic army.

In a related sense, one could also discuss war and society as a series of struggles: the institutional struggle between parliamentary institutions versus the crown (the case of the *szlachta*); people versus crown (the case of the *kuruc* wars and the National Guard and *honvéds* in Hungary); caste army versus professional army (the Hungarian noble levy); the bureaucratic professional army led by an officer class kept in isolation from, and ignorance of, social change (the case of the officers in the Habsburg imperial forces).

True, none of these types of armed forces was fully developed. All of them existed only approximately. We might call the situation one of *pragmatism versus theory* in military organization. Eventually this process was bound to lead to the triumph of social experience over military dogma.

II

Case Studies on the Balkans

Peter F. Sugar, Editor

THE BALKANS IN 1879

Danube

Tisza

Prut

Czernowitz

RUSSIA

KINGDOM OF

Budapest

Jassy

Odessa

Drave

HUNGARY

Temesvár

TRANSYLVANIA
Kolozsvár(Cluj)

Fiume

CROATIA

RUMANIA

Bucharest

Constantsa

B l a c k

BOSNIA
HERZE-
GOVINA

Belgrade

SERBIA

Danube

Varna

S e a

SANJAK OF
NOVI PAZAR

Niš

BULGARIA

Tyrnovo

A d r i a t i c   S e a

MONTE-
NEGRO

Ragusa

Sofia

EASTERN
RUMELIA

O T T O M A N

Adrianople

ITALY

Tirana

THRACE

Constantinople

MACEDONIA

Salonika

E M P I R E

Jannina

THESSALY

Aegean

Smyrna

Athens

GREECE

Sea

M e d i t e r r a n e a n

CRETE

S e a

Miles 0 50 100   200

i.e. romann

Irwin T. Sanders

Balkan Rural Societies and War

Although the Balkan countries — Albania, Bulgaria, Greece, and Yugoslavia — are very distinct national entities today, they have shared a common fate.[1] Their peninsula served as a bridge between Asia and Europe and witnessed many passing civilizations. Some parts of each country were under Ottoman rule for about five hundred years and each in its own way experienced the struggle for political independence beginning in the early part of the nineteenth century. Furthermore, they were all rural societies; the large majority of their populations were peasants or shepherds.

In order to bring the broad topic of this paper into focus, one can concentrate on the connection between nation-building and the wars in which the Balkan peoples have been engaged. But one can be even more specific and examine to what extent these wars linked the peasant populations more closely to the national society of which they were a part.

Characteristics of Balkan Rural Societies

After each country won its independence, the rural society became an identifiable part of the national whole. There are several ways to classify and describe these Balkan rural societies. One is in terms of the kind of agriculture followed, such as livestock production, with activities centered around sheep and goats. Almost from time immemorial whole ethnic groups have lived by moving flocks to mountain pastures in the summer and lowland pastures in the winter, often with habitations in both places. Most noteworthy of these are the Kutzo-Vlachs (also known as Aroumani or Macedo-Romanians), the Sarakatsani, and the Karaguni. But many Greek, Montenegrin, and Bulgarian villagers although not qualifying for the term *nomads of the Balkans* applied to the groups just mentioned, still got most of their income from livestock. Obviously, people whose lives centered around the care of animals developed a social organization somewhat different from those in settled agriculture.

Further, there were two types of settled agriculture. The first was the production of commercial crops to be sold on the world market. An early example of this is the currant (so called because it was grown and shipped from Corinth). Another is the tobacco grown in what is now northern Greece and in parts of Bulgaria and present-day Yugoslavia. Peasants depending on such crops were more vulnerable to the movement of world demand and prices than those in other types of agriculture. The second type of settled agriculture was mixed. Although crops, especially cereals, were the main source of income, some livestock was produced.

Another way of classifying the rural societies of the Balkans is by types of land ownership. In Thessaly (Greece), to mention just one area, large estates existed down to the 1920s. Here the peasants worked for a landlord, who might compensate them in kind or rent the land outright to them. In some cases and at an earlier period, a *corvée* was required, that is, the peasants on an estate had to work for the landlord so many days each year without added pay. Travelers' accounts of the Balkans give vivid pictures of the conditions of the peasants on these estates.

At the other end of the scale were the peasant proprietors. With the decline of the Ottoman empire, and during the two or three decades before liberation, Bulgarian peasants were increasingly buying their own land from departing Turks, a process which was completed with independence. After World War I, the breakup of those large estates which still existed in the Balkan countries came about through various land reform measures, thus increasing the number of independent peasant proprietors.

A third classification of Balkan rural societies is into mountain and plains villages, with their different ways of life. The mountain village figures large in glorifying the national history of each Balkan country. There the true patriot went when the plains were overrun by invading armies; it was from there that armed men (*haiduks* and *klephtes*) came to fight the Ottoman overlords; and there in the mountain village the most heroic national traits and ideals were preserved. The mountain villager was independent in spirit. He faced an economic struggle more severe than that experienced on the plains. He was the source of spiritual renewal when peaceful conditions made "the descent from the mountain" feasible. It was in the mountain village that the warrior tradition was kept alive and actively pursued. The tribal organizations in Albania and Montenegro were their own political authorities, being little beholden to outside government for help. The birth of every boy was celebrated as the "arrival of a gun," since he would add to the martial strength of the extended family unit. Blood feuds were common; a gun was an ordinary part of the male costume. From time to time, the tribes would stop fighting each other long enough to fight invading Ottoman or other forces.

The military and political structure of Western Rumeli (Greece) under the Turocracy was known as *armatolismos*.[2] This organization dates from the Byzantine empire and is one in which military and other duties were rendered in return for title to land. Although the Turks eventually occupied Western Rumeli, they did not destroy the *armatolismos*, but made treaties with the *armatoloi*, allowing them to continue their police functions while being accountable to ruling paşas.

On the eve of the Greek Revolution there were ten *armatolikia* in Western Rumeli, at the head of which was a *kapetanos*, whose first lieutenant was known as the *protopallikaro*. The next subordinates were known as *pallikaria*. These officers were usually large landowners or sheepowners and the *pallikaria* came from the small landowners. In peacetime the number in the *armatolikia* averaged from fifty to one hundred fifty, but in wartime the figure would rise to between six hundred and nine hundred. The members carried out training appropriate to their form of warfare — running and jumping, throwing rocks, scaling rocks, and shooting at a mark with their muskets.

Alongside the *armatoloi* in Western Rumeli, Macedonia, Thessaly, and Epirus there had developed groups known as *klephtes* (literally "robbers"). They were outlaws who lived partly on plunder, ravaging the property of the Turks and the Greeks who cooperated with them. Although outlaws, the *klephtes* had the blessing of the Greek church. A priest assisted at the ceremony of the initiation of a new *klephtis* and blessed the muskets. The klephtic ideal — a vague sense of patriotism and a strong religious feeling — was to supply a great moral force in Greece when the people took up arms against the Turks.

What the *klephtis* was to the Greek, the *haiduk* was to the South Slav peasants. Ruth Trouton notes:

> The best evidence that the mass of the Slav peasants sympathized with the hayduks during the last two or three centuries of Turkish rule is the peasant creation and popularization of the ballads, describing their real or imagined exploits, which form a large part of the Narodne Pesme [folk songs] ... as pictured in the Narodne Pesme the hayduks were peasants who had taken to another way of life, not

from choice but because the Turkish rulers had threatened their lives or seized their property.

. . .

Peasants sympathized with the hayduks as fellow-peasants who had been driven to a comfortless, dangerous existence through no fault of their own.[3]

. . .

After the beginning of the liberation in Serbia, that is after 1804, it was the hayduk chiefs who naturally became leaders of the peasant revolt, because of their experience in fighting the Turks. Karageorge had himself been a hayduk.[4]

Some observers of Yugoslav life relate the *haiduk* tradition more closely to the Serbs. Trouton observes that the Serbian Narodne Pesme have an epic quality like that of the Kosovo cycle and the ballads about the *haiduks*. The softer, more lyrical type of ballad, dealing mainly with peaceful peasant life, was more widespread among the Croats.

To the Serb peasant the ideal type was the "hero," however humble and laborious his own life might be. To the Croat, the ideal type was the patient peasant, a symbol of the meek, who would eventually inherit the earth when all the kings, lords and rulers had broken themselves against his massive endurance.[5]

The plains village had a different character in the public mind. It was often unhealthy, with undrained swamps contributing to malaria and other maladies. It often had a mixed population from the nationality standpoint. Lord Broughton and Lord Byron, when they visited Athens early in the nineteenth century, were surprised to learn that all the villages surrounding Athens for many miles were inhabited not by Greek-speaking but by Albanian-speaking people. Even today an antiquated Albanian is still spoken in the homes of these same villages, although the inhabitants are loyally Greek in every other respect.

The plains villages were vulnerable and must have periodically been drained of their most promising young people as well as of their food and animal supplies. When an army wanted to retaliate for some attack it had suffered, it would go to the nearest available village and destroy it as an indirect way of getting at those who had attacked them.

Before turning to the relationship of these various rural societies to war, it is necessary to call attention to many common traits of almost all Balkan peasantries despite their other differences.

The Balkan rural society was traditionally familistic. The family was the central social institution; in it people found their security. An individual's prestige was tied in with that of his family. Male supremacy was the organizing principle of family life, along with a division of labor based on sex and age. Thus there was respect for the elders, who represented the family to the outside world.

Another characteristic was attachment to the land. Even in the mountain villages there were patches of land on which the peasants grew wheat or some other cereal. In the karst region of Yugoslavia the earth was collected almost bucketful by bucketful to form a small patch, or *polje.* Pastures were a type of land very precious to the livestock producers, and the right to their use was occasionally passed on from one generation to another. On the plains, owning one's own land was a goal; to acquire additional land in the 1930s was much more important then rebuilding one's decrepit house; to pass on land as a patrimony to one's children was a sacred trust among some peasant groups.

The village often served as the peasant's social world. Not only was he physically isolated, measuring distance as he did in hours of walking time; he was also mentally isolated, for the outside world — at least in a traditional peasant setting — seemed to have little relevance to his day-to-day activities. (This was before the day of television and even before widespread use of the transistor radio.)

Life revolved around the cycle of the seasons. One took the sheep to upland pasture on St. George's Day and started them back down on St. Constantine's Day. Festivals punctuated the dull routine of village life. A wedding became a community affair, often lasting for three days. Closeness to nature was evidenced by proverbs, sayings, and ways of foretelling the weather. The behavior of animals was interpreted to mean good fortune — or death.

Religion served not only as an institution easing the passage from one life crisis to another, but under Ottoman rule it was a badge of nationality. Religion distinguished the Orthodox Serb from the Catholic Croat, the Orthodox Bulgarian from the Moslem Turk, the Uniate Romanian from the Protestant Saxon.

From the economic standpoint, the goal was self-subsistence. One did as much for oneself as one could; one bought as little as possible from outside. The traditional peasant society was not yet commercialized, with money the standard of value for all things. Such a subsistence economy required the formation of mutual aid groups to carry out tasks which no single family could do alone — e.g., to raise the roof of a new house. And experience showed that it was more pleasant to work in groups when corn needed to be hoed, potatoes to be dug, or wool to be carded, a woman's task.

Such rural societies were conservative in the true sense of that term because they did not have the economic margin for experimentation with new crops or new methods of work. If some new practice did not work out, then the family trying it would suffer, not the government agent who suggested it.

Along with all these traits went distrust of centralized government. Much of this dated from the days when peasants sought to hide from or deceive the Ottoman tax collectors; it carried over to their behavior toward their own government after independence. Even official attempts to help the peasants raise their relatively low standard of living were initially met with suspicion.

These, then, are some of the traditional characteristics which rural societies displayed. To know which ones were prominent at a given time and place calls for examination of the particular situation. Dates, too, vary for national groups according to the country's developmental progress. Although the foregoing list is not complete, the traits mentioned should suffice for the analysis of the connection between rural societies and war to which we now turn.

The background just described opens incidental avenues of inquiry that are not included in the analysis. One such lead would be the connection between the warrior tradition of many mountain villages and the militarism, which has been so characteristic of the Balkan societies in the past hundred years. A second line of inquiry would be the connection between basic social traits of the peasant populations and the level of their participation in various wars.

This paper, however, seeks only to examine the social effects of the many wars which have been waged in the Balkans. But first we must distinguish among three kinds of wars: wars of liberation or independence, regional wars of aggression or defense, and world wars.

Wars of Independence

As anyone familiar with nineteenth-century European history knows, the decline of the Ottoman empire created a vacuum into which the great European powers were only too glad to rush. These international politics need concern us here only as they call attention to the situation in Southeastern Europe and relate to the struggle of different peoples for their own national independence. Our concern is primarily with the rural population and its connection with these wars of independence.

From time to time, so-called peasant revolts had occurred in the Ottoman empire. Many of these were spontaneous risings of peasants who could no longer stand an intolerable situation and who vented their wrath in some act of violence. The Ottoman authorities were usually able to put such revolts down quickly — often with excessive force in order to teach the Christian peasants a lesson they would not forget. But other peasant revolts developed, and these had a bearing on particular movements toward independence; many of these peasant uprisings were organized, or at least fomented, by nationals who had migrated out of the Balkans and were promoting the cause of political independence, sending their agents throughout the towns and villages of the Ottoman territory to persuade local groups to take up arms. Some of these revolts will be briefly mentioned as we trace the independence movement for Serbs, Greeks, and Bulgarians.

The Serbs

Two peasant revolts played a part in gaining autonomy for Serbia.[6] The first, from 1804 to 1813, was led by George Petrović, a former peasant turned pig dealer, who came to be called Black George (Karadjordje), the founder of the Karadjordjević dynasty. Actually, "the Serbian Christians were in effect fighting to maintain the sultan's authority over the rebellious janissaries" who were creating havoc in the country, yet the Serbs were distrusted by the officials of the sultan. In 1805, Karadjordje, after consulting with a *skupština,* or assembly which had been called together after some military successes, sent the sultan proposals tantamount to local autonomy. The sultan rejected these and the Serbs converted their struggle against the janissaries into a war of independence from the sultan. After much dissension among the Serbs and some Great Power intrigues, the revolt ended unsuccessfully in October 1813. Karadjordje escaped abroad.

The second revolt was more successful. This started in 1815 and was led by Miloš Obrenović, also of peasant stock. Because of this uprising, occurring primarily in the Šumadija region south of Belgrade, the sultan granted considerable autonomy, though the area was still under Turkish sovereignty. In November 1817 the *skupština* elected Miloš hereditary prince of the country. Thus there developed a political entity which became the nucleus from which a larger Serbia grew.

The Greeks

Greeks were never in danger of losing their nationality since through their church they carried on the tradition of Byzantium. This contrasted with the lot of the Serbs and the Bulgarians who were under the clerical authority of the Greek Patriarchate in Constantinople. Despite their church, the Greeks, like the Bulgarians and Serbs, had no political area to call their own in the early nineteenth century. This was changed with a revolt which occurred in 1821 in the Peloponnesos, an event credited as the start of the Greek War of Independence. It spread to the islands (Idhra and Spetsai) and to central and northern Greece, going favorably for the insurgents until 1824, when Ibrahim Paşa, son of the governor Mehemet Ali, Paşa of Egypt, invaded the Peloponnese with an army trained by his father's European advisors. There was much dissension among the Greek leaders. After Turkey refused an armistice which Russia, France, and Great Britain had requested, Britain and France engaged the Ottoman forces in the Battle of Navarino in October 1827. Later, French forces compelled Ibrahim Paşa to evacuate the Peloponnese. The London Conference of the Allied Powers issued a protocol establishing the new state on February 3, 1832.[7] Much territory considered Greek was left outside the new state, a situation which was to be a cause of later difficulties. But an independent Greek state had been formed. It, like Serbia, faced the task of fashioning a rural population into a modern state, although the role of seamen was much greater in the Greek case.

Bulgaria

With the success of Serbia in setting up a principality, even if it was still subject to the sultan, and with the creation of an independent Greece, it was to be expected that other Balkan nationalities would also seek their own states. Yet, there were revolts that erupted as mass peasant uprisings but without proper organization or considered aims. The revolt in western Bulgaria, 1835–37, was a spontaneous reaction against the "primarily economic intolerable taxation and all manner of legalized banditry and terror on the part of the local Turks."[8] In 1841, the Niš uprising occurred in an area not yet incorporated in Serbia itself. Some uprisings, such as three emanating from Braila, Romania (1841, 1842, 1843), failed utterly. They were organized from outside.

Armed bands crossed the Danube to harass the Ottoman authorities and bring about a general uprising, but the Ottomans were informed about these in sufficient time to deal summarily with them.

The uprising which came closest to a military undertaking was that in western Bulgaria in 1850. This time the peasants were again seething with their many grievances. They had the support of Miloš of Serbia, who eventually let them down. Massacres followed and the revolt accomplished little in gaining independence. Then came the Crimean War, followed by systematic efforts by Bulgarian revolutionary leaders to organize a liberation movement.

Not until 1870 did Bulgarians get official recognition that they existed as a nationality. This came about with the sultan's firman creating an exarchate with supervision over the Slavs who were no longer subject to the Greek Patriarchate of Constantinople. The Serbs had their principality; but since the Bulgarians had none, they made much more of the church separation than did the Serbs. As a matter of fact, the exarchate proved the one entity with which the Bulgarians could identify as a separate group. Not until the end of the Russo-Turkish War of 1877–78 did Bulgaria come into existence as a political entity — which, like the other Balkan states at their beginning, covered only part of the area which their people eventually inherited. But with the adoption of the Constitution of Trnovo and the selection of Prince Alexander of Battenberg to be the ruler, Bulgaria had its own state and could begin the task of incorporating the overwhelmingly large peasant population into a new principality.

Keeping these three wars of independence in mind, we can turn to two basic questions: What new social structures came about as the result of war? What role did such social structures play in linking or articulating[9] the rural segment into the national society?

1. The creation of a state served as the political recognition of a particular nationality or nationalities. It took over the functions of the Ottoman or Austro-Hungarian empires, as the case might be, and entered upon the task of nation-building.
2. The new states assumed the form of Western constitutional democracy, with a system of political parties, election of representatives, and the like — all of which were confusing to the rural population. Eventually through peasant parties, increased social articulation occurred.
3. The modification of the agrarian structure through land reforms reduced landlords' holdings after all the wars. Land reform

led to increased peasant proprietorship and a more egalitarian class structure. (Of course, after World War II, collectivization occurred in Bulgaria, was tried and abandoned in Yugoslavia, not tried in Greece.)

4. Establishment of the armed forces into which all young males were conscripted, often for periods of eighteen to twenty-four months. Apart from its functions in time of war, the military establishment performed three tasks:

a. Served as a school for peasant youths with limited background. New skills were taught, also indoctrination into official national ideology although at times the army served as the fertile ground for alien ideology.

b. Provided a channel for upward mobility of the most talented rural youth as they were promoted into, or trained for, the officer class.

c. Nurtured a growing militarism, in the sense that the officer class had obligations only to the abstract ideal of the state, which could be invoked at will by the officer corps to rescue the fatherland.

5. The educational system tried to link rural youth to the larger society by familiarizing them with past wars — which in some textbooks are equated with national history.

Other ways in which peasants were affected might be briefly mentioned. First, obtaining independence was the precondition for any such articulation since there had to be a national state with which the rural segment could become connected. Under the Ottoman empire, the Christian *reaya* could not achieve the status of the Moslems and therefore made no claim to citizenship. Under the new national states they could.

The *peasant participation* in these wars — to the extent that this occurred — also served to make rural people feel part of the new nation. The residents of mountain villages were most likely to play a role in such wars, not only because of the warrior tradition but because they were the ones who had arms. The peasants of the plain were for the most part unarmed. Furthermore, they were most exposed to retaliation in the event the effort at independence did not succeed.

Regional Wars of Aggression-Defense

When armies move into action as they did in the regional wars of

aggression, one effect is certainly the reinforcement of national sentiment, which temporarily at least leads to greater popular solidarity. In
combat the soldier learns not only to hate the opposing nationality but
is ready to kill, even, as the record shows, with extreme cruelty. This
overflowing of national sentiments occurred in Bulgaria in 1885 with
the repulse of Serbia, which had attacked Bulgaria. Serbia did so to
forestall the establishment of a stronger Bulgaria resulting from its
annexation of Eastern Rumelia. The reverse occurred, however, at the
conclusion of the Second Balkan War in 1913 when Tsar Ferdinand
ordered Bulgarian troops to attack Serbia in hope of getting a large
slice of the territory just freed from the Ottomans in the First Balkan
War. Hatreds growing out of such encounters deepened, and certain
nationalities became, as it were, natural enemies to be put down at all
costs and on every occasion. Thus, part of every child's schooling was
the history of one's national past, the wars that had succeeded, and the
enemies who had stood in the way of success. Irredentism was thus
mixed with revenge.

The regional wars called for national mobilization of sorts. Where
such steps actually reached out to isolated villages, the people felt
drawn into the national effort.

Another result, much too important to be overlooked, was the effect
of the returned veterans from a war. Their tales of heroics or stupidities
kept the glamor of war alive before old and young alike who sat around
in the evenings listening to such accounts. Two generations or so ago,
before the advent of modern communications, storytelling was an
important means of entertainment and of socializing children. Some of
the best raconteurs gave others a vicarious experience of combat and
glorified martial exploits.

Notes

1. Romania might have been included in this group, although many Romanians prefer to think of their country as belonging to Southeastern Europe
rather than to the Balkans. Romania was not "occupied" by the Ottomans to
the same extent as the other countries of the Peninsula.

2. This section is adapted from Donna Dontas, *The Last Phase of the War
of Independence in Western Greece, 1927–1929* (Thessaloniki, 1966), 5–8.

3. Ruth Trouton, *Peasant Renaissance in Yugoslavia, 1900–1950* (London, 1952), 47.

4. *Ibid.,* 48.

5. *Ibid.,* 25.

6. H. C. Darby, *et al., A Short History of Yugoslavia from Early Times to 1966* (Cambridge, 1966), 114–18.

7. E. S. Forster, *A Short History of Modern Greece, 1921–1940* (London, 1941), 10–12.

8. Marcia Macdermott, *A History of Bulgaria, 1393–1885* (London, 1962), 170.

9. For explanation of the process of social articulation implicit in this analysis, see Irwin T. Sanders, *Rural Society* (Englewood Cliffs, N.J., 1977).

Dimitrije Djordjević

Agrarian Factors in Nineteenth-Century
Balkan Revolutions

Emancipation and modernization occurred in the Balkans in a relatively short period of time, beginning with the nineteenth century. It involved a sharp confrontation between modernization and traditionalism, between the penetrating European civilization and the Byzantine-Ottoman legacy. Development was abrupt and had markedly revolutionary features because the new had to be introduced not by reforming, but by destroying the old.

Since the overwhelming majority of the entire Balkan population were peasants, the agrarian factor was constantly present in all nineteenth-century movements. From early nineteenth-century rebellions until the wars of the twentieth century, peasants provided the manpower for all revolutions, upheavals, and military conflicts. Although the agrarian factor was omnipresent in Balkan movements, its impact changed through the century. Internal social changes produced a new, more diversified and stratified national society but the peasant stayed at the bottom. The peasant's struggle for survival, marked by a rather clear distinction between Christian serf and Moslem landlord, was replaced by a national and political struggle imbued with manifold objectives and taking complex forms. The new middle class and intelligentsia — emerging from the peasantry in a process by which the village sent its second and third generations to the city[1] — took over the national leadership.

The emancipation of the Balkans was only partially an indigenous movement and was exposed to external influences. Nationalism, to a large extent, was imported from the Balkan Diaspora and Europe.[2] It radiated from the upper social layers and filtered down to the village, transforming the peasant parochial concept of *genos* into a modern notion of *ethnos,* or nation. Furthermore, liberation of the Balkan peoples from Ottoman rule came gradually, penetrating from the periphery of the peninsula to its center. During the nineteenth century, three zones were established, stamped by specific developments: the zone of national states and the zones under Ottoman and Habsburg rule. In each, the peasant community faced a specific situation. The

Balkan state offered the peasant a framework for integration into the national economy, politics, and culture. It improved his material life but simultaneously derogated his traditional values. Change proved to be more beneficial to the city than to the rural community. Thus the old state-village and city-village confrontation was revived in another context. From century-old antipathy toward the foreign state, the peasant had to switch to a constructive acceptance of his own state.[3]

In the Balkan zone under Ottoman rule, the peasantry during the nineteenth century faced a further decline of the state administration, coupled with the unsuccessful attempts of central authorities to reorganize the economic system. An intermingling of feudal and capitalistic economies benefited urban communities but barely touched the village. Simultaneously, the neighboring liberated areas emitted a powerful attraction instigating national irredenta. This revolutionary atmosphere resulted not only in constant outbursts of peasant dissatisfaction, but also in the opposition of the conservative ruling Moslem society toward modernizing trends emanating from the central authorities.

The Balkan peasantry under Habsburg rule had to deal with a different situation. Legitimacy and a solid bureaucracy, supported by the church, prevented revolutionary outbursts, characteristic of the Ottoman Balkans. The abolition of feudal obligations in 1848, although extorted by revolution, resulted in a compromise which left the large landed estates in the hands of a foreign aristocracy. The peasantry lacked the opportunity to influence political developments, due to the absence of universal suffrage (in Austria until 1907, in Hungary till the end of the monarchy). The peasant was brushed aside in the political chess play conducted from the city.

The variety of domestic situations, combined with a number of components which influenced the peasant's development, makes it difficult to determine the effective scope of the agrarian factor in Balkan revolutions. In this study, moreover, we must eliminate the territory under Habsburg rule, which developed rather in the framework of Central European than of Balkan problems. We must also determine what caused the difference between agrarian and national movements in the Ottoman Balkans, and which characteristics would serve as a common denominator for these movements. Finally, we must see what were the specific issues which the agrarian movements expressed in opposing first the Ottoman and then their own national states.

All peasant rebellions in the Balkans were instigated and directed by a leadership which originated either among the upper layers of the rural community (representatives of the local village self-government or professional fighters and outlaws), or among educated people from developing urban centers (merchants, priests, teachers). The uneven urbanization which occurred in the nineteenth-century Balkans makes it difficult to delineate exactly the new national city from rural settlements (*palanka, varošica*) which were half-village, half-city. According to the stage of social development, the leadership either succumbed to the agrarian trends of their fellow peasants, or imposed upon them a broader approach to the general issues, agrarian as well as national-political. The predominance of the agrarian factor can be recognized in upheavals and revolts directed against *local* abuses of power, misfortunes and distresses caused by local authorities. The moment these peasant rebellions turned against the Ottoman state as such, they reflected national and political aspiration in a war for independence. The agrarian discontent was directed against the domestic landlord and feudal dues. The landlord was identified — with reason — with the representatives of the local administration. Peasant upheavals were parochial, noncoordinated, imbued with fear, and thus unsuccessful. The rural and urban elite introduced peasant upheavals into the next phase of opposition to the central state authorities, in which both factors — the agrarian and the national — were represented.

Besides the second phase of the Serbian uprising (from 1805 or 1807) and the Greek 1821 uprising, the agrarian factor dominated peasant rebellions under the Ottomans throughout the first half of the nineteenth century. Reflecting the gradual consolidation of Balkan national societies, expressed since the 1840s, the agrarian factor was increasingly subordinated to national-political objectives. In the 1860s, preparations for a general peasant uprising were inspired by tendencies to exploit the agrarian factor for national causes. Uprisings from 1875 to 1878, which spread from Hercegovina and Bulgaria to Macedonia, manifested a kind of complementary balance between the national and agrarian factors, with the accent increasingly on the former during the Eastern crisis.

The establishment and consolidation of Balkan national states in the last decades of the nineteenth century offered a different framework to peasant movements. The state had to transform the former armed rebel into a loyal subject and a disciplined soldier. The economic, as well as the political, initiative was completely transferred to city and state authorities. A century of agrarian dissension and passive, or active opposition to the new environment was necessary to integrate the peasant into his own national state. During this process the agrarian factor became an instrument in the political struggle between conservative and liberal representatives of the urban middle class and intelligentsia.

I

The agrarian factor in Balkan revolutionary movements directed against Ottoman rule resulted from the nature of Balkan village and peasant revolutionary and conservative attitudes. Opposing the Ottoman invader, the peasant locked himself into his patriarchal community protected by the rugged Balkan geography. This isolation petrified his development, but enabled his survival, preserving old and established values and peasant ethnic-national identity. Living in the past meant both surrender and militancy: it blurred reality but maintained hope. This conservatism was broken from time to time by shocks coming from outside the peasant community: by wars, trespassing armies, instigations by agents of foreign powers fighting the Ottomans, abuses of the local authorities, famines resulting from bad harvests, and epidemics. Revolutionary outbursts usually resulting from these events left a twofold impact upon the peasant. All peasant movements in the Balkans, from the sixteenth until the nineteenth century, were unsuccessful and provoked severe reprisals by the Ottoman authorities. This occurred when the peasantry supported the Austrian and Russian armies fighting the Ottomans in the wars of 1596–1606, 1686–99, 1736–39, 1768–74, and 1787–92. An imperial peace or a settlement between the powers would leave the peasant at the mercy of the ruler against whom he rebeled.

Long before developed nationalism led to conflicts between Serbia and Austria-Hungary and opposition to Russian Balkan policies, the Serbian peasant learned to mistrust any Austrian or Russian.[4] The feeling of being a mere object in the calculations of the mighty contributed to the peasant's sense of his own weakness. Centuries of rule by distant and foreign sultans overwhelmed the peasant soul. Only an emperor could deal with an emperor. Serbian rebels turned toward Russia, Austria, and Napoleon to obtain such a ruler.[5] The Greeks themselves in 1863 elected a foreign ruler. So did the Bulgarians in 1887. "No one is a prophet in his own village," is a peasant saying. The outsider was not only the arbiter in domestic issues, but corresponded to the peasant image of *the* ruler.

Frightened and isolated, suspicious but enraged, one peasant response to external pressures was banditry. This banditry was exclusively a rural movement of resistance — a reaction to local injustices and an expression of national and religious consciences, as well as brigandage. It was facilitated by the peasant tradition of keeping and hiding arms for self-defense. Much later, at the end of the nineteenth century, the rifle in the peasant home was described as "a pledge, a memory, an omen."[6] The Ottoman authorities were well aware of this threat, and from time to time, especially during crises and wars, organized extensive searches for hidden arms in peasant homes and even churches.[7] The peasant movement of *haiduks,* or *klephtes* and *morlaks* spread all over the Balkans, especially in times of war or internal disturbance in the empire. It took the form of individual bands or tribal wars or smuggling in frontier areas. These "precursors of revolution" provoked an endemic war and were treated as national heroes in popular tradition. They supplied peasant rebellions with military leadership, like Karadjordje or Stanoje Glavaš in Serbia, Kolokotrones or Botzaris in Greece, Panaiot Hitov and Filip Totiu in Bulgaria. Unlike the peasant, accustomed to fighting around and for his village, the *haiduk* bands were attached to their local area, yet capable of fighting in other regions. During the 1594 Serbian uprising in the Banat, Deli-Marko penetrated with his band into Plevna and Edirne, plundering behind the Ottoman lines.[8] The Greek *armatoli* Nikotzaras tried to join the Serbian insurgents and the Russian army by crossing the entire Balkans from Olympus to the Danube in 1807.[9] An important byproduct of this banditry was the creation of a network of peasant agents, who supplied the outlaws with food, lodging (during the winter), and information about passing caravans or anticipated Ottoman raids. Both the *haiduks* and their supporters survived Ottoman rule throughout the nineteenth century. They arose in response to national activities emanating from neighboring Balkan states and provided insurrectional intelligence and other action. The Serbian *Narodna Odbrana* ("National Defense") from 1908 and the "Black Hand" from 1911, based their anti-Austrian activity in Bosnia on the former *haiduk* and smugglers' network. The arms for the 1914 Sarajevo assassins were delivered through these channels. The work of Greek *hetereas* in Macedonia, as well as the activities of Bulgarian revolutionary committees, profited from the century-old tradition of the peasant-outlaw resistance. The IMRO bands applied the same experience of *haiduk* banditry and the work of "apostles." Interestingly, the same tradition of resistance survived Ottoman rule and expressed itself in the national Balkan state, either as an armed political opposition (*politička haidučija*) in Serbia, Greece, and Bulgaria, or as pure criminal activity. In

Eastern Serbia, on the eve of World War II, some peasants believed that there would be a bad harvest if there were no *haiduk* in the mountains.

II

Two Balkan revolutions which took place during the first decades of the nineteenth century obtained large peasant support: the Serbian uprising of 1804 and the Greek rising of 1821. Peasant involvement was caused by specific domestic and foreign developments. Both regions were located in the peripheral Balkans where foreign influences were strongest and Ottoman control weakest. Both areas enjoyed a period of economic improvement at the turn of the century, followed by a period of deterioration. The peasantry in both countries was radicalized by the eighteenth- and early nineteenth-century Austrian and Russian wars against the Ottomans.[10] The ruling Ottoman system was so debilitated by the armed rebels in both countries that it never recovered. As a result, Greece obtained independence and Serbia autonomy. Although the Serbian movement collapsed in 1813, it so radically affected the Ottoman order that it could be only superficially restored. The successes of the 1815 Serbian uprising were owing not only to the presence of the armed peasant, surviving the defeat, but also to the total collapse of the Ottoman system in the previous period. What followed was a competition between the nascent and growing Serbian national society, based on the peasant's landed property and the withering Ottoman system, deprived of social and economic roots.[11]

The peasant supplied both revolutions with manpower, and his active support determined the issues; both these facts point to the value and importance of the agrarian factor. Peasant struggles in the Balkans had one common denominator, which can be found in all movements of the sort: peasant avidity for land and resistance to feudal oppression. This leads to the question: how much did local movements mutually affect each other, as well as the peasantry in other regions of the Balkans? We know about peasant leaders originating from various parts of the Balkans who joined the common anti-Ottoman struggle.[12] What we do not know, however, because of the lack of written documents, is how much an uprising in one part of the Balkans echoed among the peasant masses of another part. A logical assumption, based on historical experience in old and modern times, would indicate that the peasantry in general was much more and much better informed about current events than one would suppose. In order to survive, the peasant developed a spontaneous underground intelligence system based on news collected from the *haiduk* (*klepht*) network, from wandering merchants, from contacts among the priesthood, from Russian agents sent to provoke unrest, and from the insurgents themselves in attempts to obtain a larger support for their own uprisings.[13] As a result of these activities, we shall see that peasant movements in the Balkans, although regional and separated, coincided, more or less, in time and were mutually influenced in adjacent and interpolated areas. The Serbian uprising affected the Serbian peasantry in neighboring Srem, Bosnia, southern Serbia, and Bulgaria. The same happened with the echo of the Greek revolution among Greeks in Epirus, Thessaly, Macedonia, and Thrace. A chain of peasant revolts occurred from the 1830s to the 1850s from Bosnia to Bulgaria. The 1875 Hercegovinian uprising stimulated the April 1876 rebellion in Bulgaria.

Peasant involvement in Balkan revolutions was determined by the level of social development. A comparison between the Serbian and Greek revolutions offers a good example of the impact of the agrarian factor in Balkan movements. Due to lesser development in Serbian society and to greater stratification in Greek society, the Serbian revolution accented the agrarian, the Greek revolution the national factor. These domestic differences, combined with the intervention or nonintervention of European powers, determined the outcome. In Serbia, radical land reform prevailed at the bottom, with a primitive military monarchy under Karadjordje, and later Miloš, on the top. In Greece, the scope of land reform was limited for the peasant and benefited the upper social strata, but the country obtained a more sophisticated form of government (first the republic, then Bavarian rule).[14]

In attempting to explain the peasant uprisings which splashed over the Balkans from the 1830s until the 1860s, modern Balkan historiography refers to the impoverishment and oppression of the peasant masses under Ottoman rule.[15] This answer seems logical, although the process was complex. First, a good number of peasant upheavals and uprisings followed an interrupted period of economic improvement, as in Serbia, Greece, and later in Bulgaria, and occurred mostly in relatively prosperous regions, plains and river valleys (such as the Sava region in Bosnia, western and Danubian Bulgaria, the Kossovo plain, etc.). Tribal movements resulting from the tribal military organization and the cattle-breeding economy (as in parts of Hercegovina, Montenegro, Albania, and Epirus) must be distinguished from agrarian movements. Second, peasant movements resulted not only from forces within the village, but also from outside agitation, either from the emancipated areas, with a nationalistic character, or developing from the bitter struggle between the conservative local Ottoman society and the reforming tendencies of the central state authorities.

Two processes were visible in the nineteenth-century Balkans: a deterioration in rural areas and an improvement in urban communities. From the 1830s, Bosnia, Macedonia, and the central Balkans witnessed an intensified process of *çiftlik* land ownership, adding new burdens to those already existing.[16] After 1826, dismissed janissaries intensified the usurpation of land.[17] Opposing reforms, some *beğs* and *captains* assumed the power of local rulers.[18] Moslem populations uprooted from the liberated areas in Serbia and Greece, and later, Bulgaria, moved toward the regions still under Ottoman rule, provoking a similar movement in the opposite direction of peasants attracted by the prospect of land ownership in emancipated areas. The period between 1831 and 1851 was marked by the military intervention of the central authorities, waging small, regional wars in Bosnia, Bulgaria, and Albania against rebellious local rulers.[19]

Parallel to the aggravation of the rural situation, the period of the *Tanzimat* reforms introduced improvements. One may argue how much improvement reached the village itself and how seriously the reforms were applied at the bottom of the social ladder, but there is a coincidence between the period of *Tanzimat* reforms and peasant movements, which stopped more or less coincident with the halt to reform, during the reign of Abdul Hamid at the end of the century. One may question how much the inviolability of life, honor, and property, as well as equality in taxation, proclaimed by the 1839 *Hatt-i-şerif* was put into practice, but one can point to some facts: for example, the urban population in Bulgaria doubled after 1839 and new settlers moved into the previously devastated areas.[20] A series of laws and decrees directed toward the modernization of the empire (penal code, 1840; laicization of schools, 1845; commercial law, 1850; reorganization of provinces, 1852, etc.) at least raised hopes among the *reaya* for improvement and encouraged their resistance to the abuses of landlords and the local administration. The system of Christian representation in local administration, introduced from 1846 through the *Meclis,* proved to be more beneficial to city people than to peasants. Prelates, corrupted by simony, *kodzabashis, chorbadzhies,* and other members of the upper layers of the urban society, often proved more oppressive to the peasant than the Ottoman ruler. But the urban development provided the village with a new leadership not recruited among those economically connected with the ruling society, but among those who found an interest in opposing it (merchants, craftsmen, and intellectuals). This segment of the urban community, developed during the *Tanzimat* era, had an interest in fighting the old Ottoman system in general, and espoused the nationalistic ideology which, besides sentimental fervor, was to procure vital changes necessary to its own progress. International troubles and wars (1828–29, 1853–56, 1875–78) and domestic crises (1831–33, 1839–41) could not but contribute to a feeling of insecurity and permanent change.

The peasant reacted to events and situations facing his community both passively and actively. His first instinct was to evacuate the imperiled area. When the Serbian uprising collapsed in 1813 more than 100,000 Serbs moved toward neighboring Austrian regions.[21] Thousands of Bulgarians crossed the Danube during the Pasvanoğlu terror, and some 130,000 peasants joined the withdrawal of Russian troops in 1830, escaping reprisals and emigrating to Wallachia and Bessarabia.[22] Following the unsuccessful uprising in the region of Niš in 1841, some 10,000 peasants rushed toward Serbia. A similar movement occurred during the 1875 Bosnian uprising when, by September, 22,000 Bosnian peasants had escaped into Austrian territory. After the 1878 Kresna uprising in western Macedonia, 25,000 peasants escaped to Bulgaria. Immigration following local crises and disturbances in neighboring Ottoman areas greatly embarrassed the governments of Balkan states and provoked financial, administrative, and other difficulties.[23]

A series of peasant uprisings erupted in the Balkans from the 1830s to the 1870s. The petitions and grievances which the peasants addressed to the central authorities and the neighboring governments of Balkan states, refer to local abuses, usurpation of land, augmentation of taxes and labor service, as well as individual insecurity (especially rape of women and children). In a typical petition, addressed from Bosnia to the Serbian government in 1848, peasants complain that they "cannot tolerate such a situation any more: we shall all rather drown in the water than to live this way."[24] Although peasant complaints reflected the miserable situation in which the peasantry found itself, and although this situation was reflected in peasant resistance, it is interesting to compare the involvement of the peasantry in uprisings with the number of those who did not participate. Some 12,000–15,000 peasants participated in the rebellion which broke out in 1833 in eastern Serbia. The 1836 Pirot uprising involved some 8,000 peasants. The first Berkovica uprising in 1836 saw 3,000 to 4,000 peasants rise;

the second in 1837, 2,000. Approximately 6,000 insurgents participated in the Niš-Leskovac uprising of 1841. The greatest Bulgarian uprising in the Vidin area, in 1850, mobilized some 10,000 to 12,000 peasants. The Albanian movements in the 1840s involved 8,000 rebels. The 1858 rebellion in northern Bosnia moved some 4,000 peasants. The famous Hercegovinian uprising in 1875, which initiated the Eastern Crisis, enrolled about 10,000 to 12,000 fighters. About 15,000 took part in the Bosnian rebellion. The 1876 April uprising in Bulgaria became better known by the number of its victims during the Ottoman reprisals (some 30,000 people) than by the number of insurgents.[25] The entire population of Bosnia and Hercegovina at that time (1879) was 1,158,164,[26] and of Bulgaria 3,155,000.[27] As Thomas Meininger states correctly, "the number and names of those Bulgarian localities which did not rebel in 1876 are just as significant as the names and number of those which did."[28] From the time of the 1814 *Filiki Etaireia,* all national Balkan anti-Ottoman activities were directed toward a general Balkan uprising which would break the backbone of Ottoman rule. Such a general uprising never occurred: the closest it came to realization was during the first phase of the Eastern Crisis in 1875–76. Instead, peasant discontent erupted in sporadic, isolated upheavals, restricted in scope, characteristic of the agrarian factor involved, as discussed at the beginning of this paper.

This does not mean that nineteenth-century Balkan history was not marked by peasant rebellions in impressive numbers, indicating an endemic state of insecurity and conflict. The 1804–1813 Serbian uprising echoed among the neighboring peasantry in the Austrian and Ottoman realms, in Srem (the Tican Rebellion, 1807), Banat (the Krušic Rebellion, 1808), Bosnia (the Jančić Rebellion, 1809), among Hercegovinian and Montenegrin tribes (Kuči, Piperi, Bíelopavlići, Klimenti), and the peasantry in southern Serbia.[29] The same echo was to be heard during the 1821–30 Greek revolution, among the Diaspora in the Ottoman empire, in northern Greece, Thessaly, Epirus, and Thrace (especially Olympus, Pelion, and the region of Thessaloníki). The period after the 1830s saw new rebellions. In Bosnia, after the abortive attempt in 1833, an uprising started in 1834 in the district of Derventa (called after its leader, the pope Jovica Rebellion).[30] Peasants attacked and burned the estates of local beğs, but were defeated by troops from the city of Banja Luka. The unrest spread toward the region of Krajina (the Mašic rebellion) but was stopped by the army. Following the Crimean War, a peasant rebellion broke out in the area of Bosanski Šamac in 1858.[31] Although acting predominantly in line with their tribal characteristics, tribes in eastern Hercegovina, Montenegro, Novi Bazar, and northern Albania constantly fought the Ottoman authorities, as well as among themselves, throughout the period between the 1830s and the 1850s. These disturbances contributed to the insurrectional atmosphere among the peasantry in the neighboring areas. At the other end of Serbia, an uprising started in 1832 in Kruševac, followed by the large Timok uprising in 1833; this resulted in the unification of these areas with the nascent Serbian state.[32] Peasant discontent and Miloš's political activities were both involved in this movement. A series of peasant uprisings erupted in the late 1830s and early 1840s in regions adjacent to Serbia's eastern and southern frontiers and western Bulgaria: in the area of Niš (1833, 1835, and 1841), the region of Pirot (1836), Belogradčik, and Berkovica (1836, 1837).[33] Peasants succeeded in besieging the fortresses of Niš and Berkovica but were crushed by troops sent from the city of Vidin. Peasant revolts broke out in 1847 in the region of Kula. They penetrated the Vidin area in 1849 and exploded into one of the largest Bulgarian uprisings in 1850. The peasants tried to seize the city of Vidin and triggered revolts in the entire region of Kula, Belogradčik, and Lom.[34] The uprising ended with the intervention of the army and heavy reprisals directed against the insurgents.[35]

The 1848 revolution in Central Europe did not penetrate the Ottoman Balkans. The revolution swept its northern confines under the Habsburgs, the Romanian Principalities, and the Ionian Islands. Although beginning in these areas as an agrarian movement directed against the landlords, the revolution switched toward national and political issues. In the second half of the nineteenth century, peasant movements became more and more "town affairs": the national factor subordinated and exploited the agrarian factor. Liberalism and romanticism in the 1860s pursued national goals. Young socialists in the 1870s united social and national factors. Revolutionary organizations were imported into the Ottoman Balkans from the neighboring Balkan states, trying to exploit peasant dissatisfaction for national purposes.[36] During the Crimean War the activity of Greek *hetereas* and bands in Thessaly and Epirus were directed from Athens. The same happened with Bulgarian activities organized within the framework of the Russian army operating in the Danubian Principalities. Rakovski and Nikola Filipov failed in attempts at a general uprising of Bulgarian peasants.[37] Trends manifested in revolutionary movements during the 1876–78 Eastern Crisis partially reflected agrarian discontent and revolutionary élan, but also showed nationalist-liberal and socialist purposes originating in the city and the neighboring Balkan states. Peasant movements, which began the crisis, were regional and poorly timed: the idea of a general peasant uprising in the Ottoman Balkans was not realized, and it was the Serbian-Montenegrin war with the Ottomans, followed by Russian intervention, that enlarged the scope and significance of the crisis. During the winter of 1875–76, the Hercegovinian uprising was limited to the south of the province. The central and northeastern parts of Bosnia did not participate in the rebellion and the movement split into guerrilla warfare conducted by former *haiduks* (Pecia Petrovic, Ostoja Kormanoš) or Serbian officers appointed by the government in Belgrade (Colonel Despotović).[38] The same happened with the April 1876 uprising in western Bulgaria, instigated by Bulgarian committees from abroad.[39] Except for the 1876 Razlog uprising in the Macedonian-Bulgarian area, the Kumanovo (1878), Kresna (1878–79), and Kičevo uprisings[40] sounded the end of the Eastern Crisis and reflected both local peasant action to end Ottoman rule, and initiatives from abroad, directed against the decisions taken at the Berlin Congress. The Albanian League of Prizrend reflected tribal Albanian-Montenegrin feuds over pastures and tribal territories. The Albanian movement turned into a conflict between tribal autonomism and a nascent nationalism directed against the central Ottoman authorities. The greatest victory of the Bulgarian peasantry was achieved during the upheaval following the 1878 Ottoman defeat by the Russian army. Peasants seized the land from the fleeing Ottoman landlord and established ownership, with all the social, political, and economic consequences for the future development of Bulgaria.[41]

The end of the Eastern Crisis in 1878 practically marked the end of larger peasant rebellions in the nineteenth century (with some exceptions, such as the 1882 anti-Austrian uprising in Bosnia and the 1903 uprising in Macedonia.) The 1909–1912 Albanian struggles were more autonomist and anticentralist than agrarian. The change resulted from the consolidation of Balkan states and national societies, an intensified economic and political interest of Europe in the Balkans, and from experience gleaned from the abortive revolution during the Eastern Crisis. The Balkans entered a period of strong nationalism in which the soldier and the diplomat achieved priority over the rebel. The Balkan rivals crisscrossed Macedonia in a bitter struggle in which the peasant became the object of nationalistic policies. There was no peasant uprising before or during the 1912 Balkan War. In this war 700,000 soldiers (mostly peasants) of the allied Balkan armies far outnumbered the few thousand peasant rebels in the previous century. The agrarian element became secondary and faced issues imposed from outside the peasant community.

III

Peasant attitudes toward the national state were determined by changes which affected all aspects of economic, social, political, and cultural life. The new state legalized results of previous revolutionary achievements (guarantee of land ownership) and began organizing the framework for further national developments.[42] Although born in war and revolutions, the Balkan state developed the conservative forms of a military monarchy with centralized political power. It was the foreigner, or the outsider from the Diaspora, who introduced the state establishment in the Balkans: the Bavarian, the Serb from southern Hungary, the imperial Russian military. Political institutions in Greece and Serbia were copied from Europe in the period of the Holy Alliance. The former cattle breeder was transformed into a tiller of the soil and the armed rebel became a subject (*podanik*) of the state. Economic liberalism introduced market competition; the state organization imposed limitations on the peasant's use of forests, pastures, and waters. Altogether the peasant again became subordinated to his own growing city and state.

Peasant traditionalism worked both ways in accepting and opposing the national state. The tradition, nourished for centuries by the church and the presence of its historical monuments (monasteries), kept alive the peasant's memory of his own state. But the same traditionalism developed attachments to established values of peasant life. Parochialism, economic self-sufficiency, refuge in the past, were challenged by innovations originating from outside which intruded into the village. The first victim of the coming epoch was the peasant *zadruga* which became an anachronism and could not respond to the new social and economic environment.

The birth of the Balkan national state was marked by a twofold struggle: the war with the Ottomans, and the conflict between the internal centralizing and decentralizing trends of the new national leadership. Wars and revolutions imposed centralization and facilitated the birth of the state. Decentralizing tendencies originated in the autonomist tradition of the Balkan village and were supported by local leaders. Although more democratic, they threatened the new state with anarchy and civil war. A clash between those approaches to the state

can be found in all the Balkan countries emancipated from the Ottomans. Karadjordje was involved in a struggle with his *voyvodas* for
supreme power. In Greece civil war began in 1822 and culminated in
the assassination of Capodistria in 1831 and the opposition to the
xenocratie. The same conflict occurred in Bulgaria during the strife
between conservatives and liberals over the 1879 Trnovo Constitution.[43] The peasant, actively or passively supporting decentralizing
trends, was the loser. The new centralized bureaucratic establishment
alienated the village from the city and the state.

Liberalism, imported from Europe into the Balkans from the 1860s
on, found instinctive support among the peasantry. Parliamentarianism in the peasant mind referred to the spirit of the *zadruga,* which
the Balkan liberals idealized in their writings.[44] A similar idealization
of the *zadruga* as a form of popular democracy could also be found in
the works of the first socialists in the Balkans (Svetozar Marković and
Hristo Botev). Both liberals and socialists reflected the peasant alienation from bureaucracy, the former in a mild, the latter in a radical
critique directed against the existing order. Yet, both were unsuccessful in penetrating the village. Inexperienced and isolated, exposed to a
centralized state machine, the peasant was much more interested in his
economic situation than his political rights. All peasant demands
addressed to Serbian national assemblies during the 1840s and 1850s
referred to freedom to use forests and communal pastures, rather than
civil rights.[45] An empty stomach took priority over a free thought.

It was the application of parliamentarianism and universal male
suffrage which secured the benefits of the peasant's numerical advantage in the policy-making process, during the last decades of the
nineteenth century. Enlargement of the electoral body introduced the
peasant into politics (Greece, 1864; Serbia, 1869; Bulgaria, 1879). A
distinct polarization between conservatives and liberals, followed by
the establishment of modern political parties and their organizations
from the 1880s on, enabled the Balkan peasant to take an active part in
politics. This process paved the way for the peasant's incorporation
into his national state. The middle-class left joined urban liberalism
with the peasant opposition to the centralized state and thus politically
mobilized the peasantry, offering new leadership. Now organized, the
peasantry responded with upheavals directed against bureaucracy and
economic burdens, and seeking decentralization and self-government.
The 1883 uprising in eastern Serbia incited by the Radicals[46] involved
12,000 to 15,000 peasants. The army crushed the uprising and a
summary court sentenced 94 insurgents to death, 640 to imprisonment.

A similar movement occurred in Bulgaria, where a 1900 protest meet-ing in Varna turned into a clash with the army in the Ruse district and resulted in 800 peasants wounded and 90 killed.[47] Violence was even more intense in Romania where local peasant upheavals at the end of the century (1885, 1889, 1894, and 1900) reached their climax in the 1907 uprising. The revolt started in northern Moldavia and spread into Wallachia. Peasants attacked landed estates and clashed with troops sent to quell the rebellion. Some 11,000 peasants were killed or wounded, provoking a shock whose consequences undermined the established order and opened issues beyond the rebellion itself.[48]

The end of the century marked a faster tempo of general economic development in the Balkans. The period witnessed a greater European interest in the region coupled with an improvement of transportation and trade. Only at the end of the century did the Balkans become an integral part of the European economic and political system. Origi-nating in the village, Balkan society in general was democratically oriented, lacking aristocracy and internal class barriers. The urban population was still attached, through direct roots and family ties, to the village. Democratic institutions were gradually introduced during the first decade of the twentieth century (Serbia from 1903, Greece from 1909; Bulgaria obtained her independence in 1908). The demo-cratic process itself enabled the integration of the peasant into his own state. In the twentieth century, the revolutionary potential of the peasantry was directed toward accomplishment of national programs with which it was hardly familiar. For the peasantry it marked both victory and defeat. The peasantry espoused the state but lost its political identity. There is a striking difference between the perform-ance of the Balkan soldier in the 1876–77 and 1897 anti-Ottoman wars and his achievements in the 1912–18 wars. The Balkan peasant, organ-ized and disciplined, integrated into his state, proved to be an excellent fighter.

IV

The peasant survived turmoil in modern Balkan history because of his vitality, stubbornness, and attachment to the soil. He supplied manpower to all Balkan movements in recent history. Although scat-tered and isolated, peasant upheavals and rebellions constantly under-mined Ottoman rule and finally paved the way for the establishment of the national state. Peasant involvement in Balkan struggles reflected problems, but did not solve them. It stressed trends, but did not formulate a definite program. The program was formulated outside the rural community, although it was based on the village. With the rise of nonvillage leadership, the peasant lost the initiative. Modernization was painful for the peasant who remained on the bottom of the social ladder. The state, originating outside the peasant community, was to impose social discipline and national programs. The rebel was to be transformed into a soldier. The process was not unusual and can be found in every peasant society developing into a modern national society throughout the world. But it also reflects the constant and ever-present agrarian factor in the ongoing changes.

Notes

1. Franz Ronnenberg, "Wandlungen der Agrargesellschaft der Südosteuropäischen Staaten," in Klaus-Detlev Grothusen, ed., *Die wirtschäftliche und soziale Entwicklung Südosteuropas im 19 und 20 Jahrhundert* (München, 1969), 48.

2. Peter Sugar, "External and Domestic Roots of Eastern European Nationalism," in Ivo Lederer and Peter Sugar, eds., *Nationalism in Eastern Europe* (Seattle, 1969), 9, 51–53. For external influences in the formation of Greek nationalism see Deno T. Geanokoplos, "The Diaspora Greeks: The Genesis of Modern Greek National Consciousness," in Nikiforos P. Diamandouros, ed., *Hellenism and the First Greek War of Liberation (1821–1830): Continuity and Change* (Thessaloniki, 1976), 59–77.

3. Dimitrije Djordjević, "The Impact of the State on Nineteenth Century Balkan Social, Economic and Political Developments," Co-rapports, *IIIᵉ Congrès international d'études du sud-est européen. Histoire C 1,* (Bucharest, 1974), 72.

4. After the Austrians' 1791 withdrawal from Serbia, the Chronicle of the Tronoša monastery states: "And so suffered and was rejected the miserable Serb who trusted the damned German." Cited in Vladimir Ćorović, *Istorija Jugoslavije* (Beograd, 1933), 402. Opposing local leaders who wanted to invite Russians to come to Serbia, Karadjordje answered: "Let us have Russians, and they will rape first my own wife." Cited in Vuk Karadžić, *Prvi i drugi srpski ustanak* (Beograd, 1947), 168.

5. Aleksa Ivić, ed., *Spisi bečkih arhiva o Prvom srpskom ustanku* (Beograd, 1933), Doc. 46, 1804, I: 117, 196.

6. Nikola Pašić, "Razoružanje narodne vojske," *Samouprava,* 1883, cited in Raša Milošević, *Timočka buna 1883 godine* (Beograd, 1923), 142–46.

7. As, for example, in Macedonia during the First Serbian Uprising. Mihailo Gavrilović, *Ispisi iz pariskih arhiva* (Beograd, 1904), Doc. 48: Report

from Thessaloniki, April 25, 1806. Also in Bosnia, during the same uprising. Keimura Seifudin Fehmi, *Prvi srpski ustanak pod Karadjordjem od 1219 do 1279 godine* (Sarajevo, 1334 [1916]), Firman to the Bosnian Valie, pp. 113-16.

8. Branislav Djurdjev, Bogo Grafenauer, Jorjo Tadić, *Istorija Naroda Jugoslavije* (Zagreb, 1959), II: 503-504. About banditry, see also Dušan Popović, *O hajducima* (Beograd, 1931); John Vasdravellis, *The Macedonians in the Revolution of 1821* (Thessaloniki, 1968); and John Petropoulos, *Politics and Statecraft in the Kingdom of Greece 1833-1843* (Princeton, 1968), 30-35; Peter Sugar, *Southeastern Europe under Ottoman Rule 1354-1804* (Seattle, 1977), 242-45; Bistra Cvetkova, *Hajdutstvoto v Blgarskite zemi prez 15-18 vek* (Sofia, 1971).

9. Michel Lascaris, "Le rôle des Grècs dans l'insurrection serbe sous Carageorge," *Les Balkans,* 1933, 9-11.

10. The best account of the Serbian Revolution in English is Michael Boro Petrovich, *A History of Modern Serbia 1804-1918* (New York, 1976), I: 27-82. An international symposium held at Stanford in 1974, *The First Serbian Revolution* (papers in press). Important for the study of the Serbian peasantry in the revolution are the *Memoirs of Prota Matija Nenadović,* ed. and trans. by Lovett P. Edwards (Oxford, 1969). Various aspects of the Greek Revolution are better represented in English: Douglas Dakin, *The Greek Struggle for Independence, 1821-1833* (Berkeley, 1973), 5-140; C. M. Woodhouse, *The Greek War of Independence,* (London, 1952); George Finley, *History of Greek Revolution* (London, 1861), 2 vols.; Richard Clogg, ed., *The Struggle for Greek Independence* (London, 1973), 1-40. For the Greek peasantry these are important: Kolokotrones, *Kleft and Warrior* (London, 1892) and *The Memoirs of General Makriyannis 1797-1864* (London, 1966).

11. Vaso Čubrilović, *Istorija političke misli u Srbiji XIX veka* (Beograd, 1958), 103-107. Khurşid Paşa, defeating the rebels, had to delay his arrival in Belgrade for a couple of weeks because of the bands of Serbian rebels that blocked the road to the capital city of the Paşalik.

12. See Notis Botzaris, *Visions balkaniques dans la préparation de la révolution grècque 1789-1821* (Paris, 1962); Vladimir Stojančević, "Prvi srpski ustanak i južnoslovenske zemlje," *Istorijski Pregled* 1 (1954): 7-16; Stojančević, "Prvi srpski ustanak prema Bugarskoj i Bugarima," *Istoriski Glasnik* 1-2 (1954): 121-45; Nikolai Todorov, *Filiki Eteria i Blgarite* (Sofia, 1965), 90-101.

13. This aspect is elaborated in detail in the paper presented at the 1974 Stanford symposium, "The Impact of the First Serbian Revolution on Balkan Peoples."

14. Dimitrije Djordjević, *Revolutions nationales des peuples balkaniques, 1804-1914* (Beograd, 1965), 54-55.

15. Hristo Hristov, "The Agrarian Problem and the National Liberation Movement in the Balkans," *Actes du premier Congrès international des études sud-est-européennes* (Sofia, 1968), IV: 65-70; Pascu Stephan *et al.,* "Mouvements paysans du centre et du sud-est de l'Europe du XV au XX siècle," *XIIe*

Congrès international des sciences historiques. Rapports (Vienna), IV: 211–35; Vladimir Stojančević, *Južnoslovenski narodi u Osmanskom carstvu od Jedrenskog mira 1829 do Pariskog kongresa 1856* (Beograd, 1971).

16. For the agrarian problem see the study by Vasilj Popović, *Agrarno pitanje u Bosni i turski neredi za vreme reformog režima Abdula Medžida 1839–1841* (Beograd, 1949).

17. In Bosnia there were only 36,000 former janissaries, 12,000 among them in the Sarajevo area.

18. Ali Paşa Rizvanbeg owned a vast part of Hercegovina. The property of Ahmed Beg included 1,300 peasant homes (families) in Bosnia. The annual income of Husein Paşa in western Bulgaria amounted to 2 million francs. Vladimir Stojančević, *Južnoslovenski narodi u Osmanskom carstvu,* 117.

19. Dragoljub Pavlović, *Pokret u Bosni i Albaniji protiv reforma Mahmuda II* (Beograd, 1923); Hamdija Kreševljaković, "Kapetanije i kapetani u Bosni i Hercegovini," *Godisnjak Istoriskog drustva Bosne i Hercegovine* 2 (1950): 89–141.

20. N. Todorov, "La genèse du capitalisme dans les provinces bulgares de l'empire ottoman au cours de la première moitié du XIX siècle," *Études historiques* (Sofia, 1960), 221–51.

21. Aleksa Ivić, "Izbeglice iz Srbije na austrijskom zemljištu godine 1813 i 1814," *Istoriski časopis* 2 (1950): 157–62. See also Vaso Čubrilović, "Politički uzroci seoba na Balkanu od 1860–1880 godine," *Glasnik geografskog društva* 16 (1930): 26–48; Slavko Gavrilović, *Prilog istoriji trgovine i migracije Balkan-Podunavlje XVIII i XIX veka* (Beograd, 1969).

22. D. Kosev, H. Hristov, D. Angelov, *Kratka istoria na Blgaria* (Sofia, 1969), 117.

23. D. Djordjević, "Prilog proučavanju migracija iz Habsburške monarhije u Srbiju 60-tih i 70-tih godina XIX veka," *Zbornik oslobodjenja gradova u Srbiji od Turaka 1862–1867,* SANU (Beograd, 1970), 321–23.

24. Vladimir Stojančević, *Južnoslovenski narodi u Osmanskom carstvu,* 227. Also Stojančević, "Cetiri pisma knezu Milošu iz 1837 i 1838 godine," *Južnoslovenski filolog* 33 (1958): 1–4.

25. It is difficult, almost impossible, to establish the exact number of insurgents in various uprisings. Stojančević offers some figures in *Južnoslovenski narodi u Osmanskom carstvu,* 138, 141, 142, 152, 246.

26. Gojko Krulj, "Gradska privreda," in *Napor Bosne i Hercegovine za oslobodjenje i ujedinjenje* (Sarajevo, 1929), 312.

27. Anastas Totev, "Characteristic Demographic Features of Bulgaria 1880–1980," in Thomas Butler, ed., *Bulgaria Past and Present* (Columbus, Ohio, 1976), 132.

28. "The Response of the Bulgarian People to the April Uprising 1876," paper presented at the 1976 annual meeting of the AAASS at St. Louis, Missouri.

29. Čubrilović, *Prvi srpski ustanak i bosanski Srbi,* 115–30; Slavko Gavrilović, "Agrarni pokreti u Sremu, Slavoniji i Moslavini pocetkom XIX

veka," *Historiski Zbornik* 1-4 (1957): 71-82; Petar Sobajić, "Udeo dinarskih plemena u Prvom srpskom ustanku," *Glasnik Etnografskog Instituta SAN* 2-3 (1957): 81-96.

30. Aleksa Ivić, *Ustanak popa Jovice Ilića (1834) i bune leskovačkih i vranjanskih Srba (1842)* (Zagreb, 1929).

31. V. N. Kondrjatjeva, "K voprosu o preoposilnah vostania 1858 g. v Bosanskoi Kraine i v Posavine," *Uc. Zapiski Instituta Savianoviedenia* 18 (1959). See also the study on Hercegovinian uprisings: Vojno-istorijski institut JNA, *Bune i ustanci u Bosni i Hercegovini u XIX veku* (Beograd, 1962), 50-55.

32. Vladimir Stojančević, *Knez Miloš i Istočna Srbija* (Beograd, 1957), 27-52.

33. Vladimir Stojančević, "Narodnooslobodilacki pokret u niškom kraju 1833 i 1834-35 godine," *Istoriski časopis* 5 (1955): 427-35.

34. Dimitur Kosev, "Vstanieto na selianite v severozapadna Blgaria i negovite pričini," *Istoričeski Pregled* 6 (1949-50): 474-92.

35. Strašimir Dimitrov, "Serbia i Krestianskoe vostanie 1850 g. vo Blgaria," *Études balkaniques* 1 (1964): 49-68.

36. I discuss the impact of the national factor in another paper in this volume.

37. Dimitur Kosev, "Otraženieto na Krimskata voina (1853-1856) v Blgaria," *Istoričeski Pregled* 3, 2 (1946-47): 183-99. For Greece, Driault Lheritier, *Histoire diplomatique de la Grece de 1821 à nos jours* (Paris, 1925), 2: 381-402.

38. The two best studies on the 1874 uprising in Bosnia and Hercegovina: Vaso Čubrilović, *Bosanski ustanak 1875-78* (Beograd, 1930); Milorad Ekmečić, *Ustanak u Bosni 1875-78* (Sarajevo, 1960). See also *Medjunarodni naučni skup povedom 100 godišnjice ustanka u Bosni i Hercegovini, drugim balkanskim zemljama i Istočnoj krizi 1875-78 godine,* Akademija nauka Bosne i Hercegovine, Posebna Izdanja knj. XXX; Sarajevo, 1977, Tom I-III.

39. S.A. Nikitin, "Revolucionarnia borba v Bolgaria v 1875-76 i Aprilskoe vostanie" in *Osvoboždenie Bolgarii od tureckog iga* (Moskva, 1953), 11-46.

40. Kiril, patriarh blgarski, *Sprotivata sreštu Berlinskia dogovor, Kresnenskoto vstanie* (Sofia, 1955); Jovan Hadži-Vasiljević, *Ustanak Srba u kumanovskoj i palanačkoj kazi u 1878 godini* (Beograd, 1906); Ivan Katardžiev, *Serskata oblast 1780-1879* (Skopje, 1961), 198-255.

41. I. Mitev, "Za agrarnia prevrat u nas izvrši se v rezultat ot osvoboditelnata voina prez 1877-1878 godine," *Istoričeski Pregled* 6 (1953): 638-56; L. Berov, "Agrarnoto dviženie v Iztočna Rumelia po vreme na osvoboždenieto," *Istoričeski Pregled* 1 (1956): 3-35.

42. Djordjević, "The Impact of the State," 72.

43. Čubrilović, *Istorija političke misli,* 77-80; Petropoulos, 120-22.

44. Gale Stokes, *Legitimacy through Liberalism. Vladimir Javanović and the Transformation of Serbian Politics* (Seattle, 1975), 40-41.

45. Jovan Miličević, "Narodne skupštine u Srbiji 1839-1845 godine," *Zbornik filozofskog fakultete* 1 (1956): 157-95.

46. Milen Nikolić, *Timočka buna 1883* (Beograd, 1954), Doc. 94, 1: 76–93.
47. *Kratka istoria na Blgaria,* 200–210.
48. G. Eidelsberg, *The Great Rumanian Peasant Revolt of 1907; Origins of a Modern Jacquerie* (Leiden, 1974); see also Henry Roberts, *Rumania: Political Problems of an Agrarian State* (New Haven, 1931) and Daniel Shirot, *Social Change in a Peripheral Society. The Creation of a Balkan Colony* (New York, 1976), 150.

Stephen Fischer-Galati

Military Factors in Balkan Revolutions

Perhaps the outstanding characteristic of Balkan revolutionary movements was their lack of success until the time, starting late in the nineteenth century, that the military prowess of the Balkan nations themselves affected the outcome of "wars of national liberation." This does not say that military factors were irrelevant in the attainment of the goals of the various revolutionary forces which manifested their discontent with conditions in the Balkans long before the nineteenth century. But realistically, whatever the power of revolutionary forces in relation to that of their adversaries, the attainment of their goals was seldom a function of military action alone. By contrast, before the nineteenth century, the frustration of the varying aspirations of the inhabitants of the Balkans was customarily achieved by military solutions imposed by the Porte. The imbalance in the relative strength of subject and ruler was historically rooted in Ottoman policies related to the bearing of arms by the peoples of the Balkans dating back to the fourteenth century.

In theory, and usually also in practice, bearing arms, except for purposes expressly authorized by the Porte, was prohibited on the assumption that it was for the Turkish armed forces to protect the security of the empire against foreign enemies. Such exceptions as were granted, most notably to the vassal states of Wallachia and Moldavia, were primarily a function of the need for auxiliary military action against foreign enemies and internal marauders who, for strategic or geographic considerations, could not be restrained by regular Ottoman forces.[1] In practice more than in theory, disarming the population was also motivated by fear of subversion, uprisings, and even revolutionary action by unruly elements whether Christian or Moslem. Whether, in fact, the Porte was apprehensive over what has been characterized as a constant state of discontent with Moslem rule by Balkan Christendom is a matter of conjecture. One may question whether, before the end of the seventeenth century, the peninsula could be rightly described as a revolutionary powder keg which required constant military surveillance. If anything, the evidence tends to refute the validity of the doctrine of permanent Ottoman alertness and favor one stressing the increased reliance of the Porte on auxiliary Christian military forces which shared the common interest of protecting the inhabitants of the Balkans against military activities by uncontrollable elements of the Ottoman army and also, it was hoped, against external "liberators" of Balkan Christendom.[2]

The growing Ottoman reliance on ostensibly trustworthy armatoles, voevods, sipahis, and other armed men, which gained momentum in the eighteenth century, proved counterproductive largely because the Porte could not exercise effective control over all armed forces, regular or auxiliary, Moslem or Christian.[3] As the Porte's influence and power declined, a military base for the conduct of subversive, and on occasion revolutionary, actions became firmly established. And that base, as well as the military skill of opposition forces, was strengthened in the eighteenth century by participation in foreign wars involving Austria and Russia and by internecine military confrontations involving rebel paşas, native military leaders, mutinous armies, and an ever-growing number of clandestinely armed Christian and Moslem peasants.

The availability of arms, whether provided by the Porte, by the Russians or by the Austrians to the inhabitants and military leaders of the Balkans, was probably more important in militarizing resistance to direct or indirect abuses attributable to Turkish rule than was allegiance to the liberation causes expounded by Austria or Russia. There was at best limited ideological motivation behind the military encounters of hostile and loyal forces in the eighteenth century, and there is little evidence to support contentions that such events as the Austrian occupation of Ottoman territories between 1718 and 1739 provided Serbian and Romanian military men with military training which could be put to good use against the Porte.[4] It is known that Austrian military discipline was unpopular and that Austrian military tactics and strategy were not necessarily suitable for the conduct of military action within the Balkans. The same may also be said of such training and strategy as the Russians made available to reluctant Moldavians and Wallachians in the eighteenth century.

Military preparedness for confrontation with either regular Turkish forces or with *dahis,* rebellious janissaries, or the retinues mustered by such men as Pasvanoğlu was at best inadequate at the end of the eighteenth century. Were it not for the exceptional circumstances created by the French Revolutionary wars, particularly after the assumption of power by Napoleon, it is doubtful that the first major Balkan revolution, the Serbian, which started in February 1804, could have succeeded as well as it did. Granted that the "people's army," consisting of *haiduks* and peasants armed chiefly with Austrian contraband arms or arms seized from the Turks, showed its prowess against superior Ottoman forces at Ivankovac, Mišar, and Deligrad, it is questionable whether continuing successes could have been recorded had it not been for the outbreak of the Russo-Turkish war in 1806 and the ensuing military support provided by the Russians.[5] In fact, as the Napoleonic campaigns gained in intensity, the Serbian revolutionaries' military successes became more and more related to Russian military action on the Danube. Clearly, after the war ended in 1812, Serbian insurrectionary forces were no match against the Turkish armies which entered Belgrade in October 1813 and ended, albeit temporarily, the revolution. Military action by *haiduks*, which continued in a desultory manner until the second insurrection broke out in April 1815, and even the original successes scored by Miloš Obrenović's forces at Rudnik, Palež, and Čačak against the Turks did show the efficacy of the Serbian contingents, but that proved ephemeral when, after the Congress of Vienna, the Turks were able to despatch armies from Bosnia and Rumelia against the insurgents. In fact, the ensuing abandonment of military action in favor of diplomatic negotiations as the basis for attaining the goals of the Serbian leadership was determined by the realization that protracted military activity against the Turks could not succeed either in the short run or in the long. Perhaps Miloš Obrenović's greatest contribution to the history of Serbia was that realization, coupled with the corollary awareness that military dependence on foreign enemies of the Porte would not lead to satisfactory solutions of Serbian problems.[6] Russian betrayal of the Serbian revolutionary forces first recorded in the Treaty of Bucharest in 1812 and Austrian policies on supplying weapons to the Serbs persuaded Miloš and his supporters that autonomy could best be gained by means other than military confrontation with the Porte. Similar conclusions were reached by anti-Ottoman forces in the Romanian provinces.

From a military standpoint, those provinces were only marginally involved in the Russo-Turkish war of 1806–1812. This was partly because the Phanariot rulers of Moldavia and Wallachia had effectively disbanded the Romanian armies throughout the eighteenth century but also because the Russians were unwilling to arm the Romanian population.[7] The Romanian contingent of *panduri* of the tsarist army did participate in the war in a limited way, and that participation was significant so far as the *panduri* were not disbanded at the end of the war. These *panduri,* perhaps 4,000 strong, were the main armed force on which Tudor Vladimirescu relied during the revolution of 1821 in Wallachia.[8] Yet, from a military standpoint, they could not provide the basis for a successful uprising against the Porte. Hence Vladimirescu claimed that his movement was directed against the Phanariotes and not the sultan in hope that the Turks would not crush the rebellion by military force. Because of his awareness that the revolution could succeed only if Russian military support were provided, he originally identified himself with the *Philike Hetairea* but promptly abandoned the Greek cause as Russian military assistance failed to materialize. Whether Vladimirescu carried on the rebellion even after it became evident that the hoped-for intervention would not occur because he assumed that disengagement from the Greek cause and the establishment of military independence from the Russians would enhance his chances of survival with a forgiving Porte is still an unresolved question. But it seems clear that Vladimirescu was definitely intent on establishing a military power base of his own with a view to ending Phanariot rule in Wallachia and to lessening Romanian dependence on Russian military assistance.[9] The termination of Phanariot rule in the Romanian provinces in 1821 reflected limited Ottoman acceptance of Vladimirescu's goals even though the Turks remained opposed to the establishment of native Romanian armies on the premise that defending the principalities against external military action was the function of the legitimate sovereign power.

In contrast to Vladimirescu, and also to Obrenović, the plotters and organizers of the Greek revolution, led by the Hetairists, based their plans of military action almost exclusively on external assistance. Elaborate schemes for securing the military cooperation of the Balkan peoples reflected a naiveté paralleled only by ignorance of the realities of Russian political conditions. The Balkan leaders, except for *haiduks, armatoles, klephtes, uskoks,* and other guerrilla-like forces, for both political and military reasons would not support Phanariot demands for cooperation unless massive Russian military support could be assured. The Greeks, of course, counted on such Russian assistance and found themselves at an enormous military disadvantage vis-à-vis the Porte when the Russians refused to intervene on behalf of the rebels. From a military standpoint, the Greek revolution was clearly less successful than patriotic historians and propagandists have had us believe.[10] Granted that Kolokotrones and the guerrilla forces were able to hold Turkish armies at bay and even record a few military victories in the early years of the revolution, the Greek armed forces, despite advantageous territorial positions and superiority in guerrilla warfare, were no match for Ibrahim Paşa even before the disaster of Missolongi. For indeed, only the belated intervention by the British and the Russians saved the Greeks from military annihilation.

The experience of the Serbian, Romanian, and Greek revolutionaries persuaded their leaders to seek, at the end of the Greek War for Independence, to set up regular armed forces. Ostensibly, the armed forces which were to be established in Serbia, the Romanian provinces, and Greece were to guarantee the security of these lands. In fact, there were other reasons, varying and often conflicting, whose common denominator was anti-Ottoman action.

The establishment of standing armies — whether through the provisions of Article V of the Treaty of Adrianople [Edirne] for the Romanian provinces, or through Article VIII of the *Hatt-i şerif* of 1830 for Serbia, or as defined by the London Protocol of 1830 for Greece — did not significantly enhance the chances for attaining the goals of the Romanian, Serbian, and Greek leaders through the use of military force.[11] For one thing, the armed forces were very small, less than 5,000 men in both Serbia and Wallachia, for instance. In Greece, the army consisted primarily of Germans brought into the country by King Otto, an action which antagonized Greek veteran officers and soldiers as well as anti-Bavarian and anti-Ottoman political megalomaniacs.[12] In Moldavia, the Russians saw to it that only a nominal military establishment was created. Nevertheless, the existence of native armies provided a base for bolstering the schemes and ambitions of anti-Turkish politicians, mostly in Wallachia and Greece, and also for influencing domestic political affairs. In fact, the Greek officers' "rebellion" of September 1843, led by colonels Kallerges and Makryiannes, proved decisive in formulating the doctrine of limited constitutional monarchy incorporated in the Constitution of 1844.[13] Military participation in Greek politics declined considerably after 1844, but the rebellion proved a prototype for similar future actions in Greece starting with the anti-Ottonian plots of 1861 and the revolt of October 1862 which led to Otto's abdication and the crowning of George I as King of the Hellenes one year later.

Nevertheless in Greece, as well as in other Balkan lands where independence had not been gained, the role of the armed forces in seeking to alter the political order by revolutionary means remained of secondary importance. The failure of the Moldavian and Wallachian revolutions of 1848 may be largely attributed to the lack of strategic and military competence shown by the leaders of those movements.[14] Similarly, the Greek military insurrection seeking the "liberation" of Epirus and Thessaly from the Turks in 1854 failed, despite the best efforts of the commander-in-chief, General Tzavelas, in the face of a Turkish ultimatum alone. Other anti-Turkish movements, such as the joint Hercegovinian-Montenegrin of 1852, involving Luca Vukalović and Prince Danilo, or the immediately preceding uprising in the Bulgarian-inhabited regions of Kula, Belogradčik, and Lom also failed because the military resources of the anti-Ottoman rebels were totally inadequate for resisting even the feeble forces that the Porte could muster in defense of its interests.[15]

In the sixties, however, a realistic concern for military preparedness and joint military action by anti-Ottoman nations and nationalities in the Balkans began to take shape with marginally successful results. The sixties do record increased size and improved quality of Serbian and Romanian armed forces and the provision of direct and indirect military assistance to anti-Ottoman forces in Bulgarian lands as well as in Bosnia and Hercegovina by Belgrade and Bucharest. The militarization of Serbia under Michael Obrenović and of Romania under Alexandru Ion Cuza was designed to protect the integrity of the vassal states pending the attainment of independence and the eventual expulsion of the Turks from the Balkans.[16] The effectiveness of military measures and contemplated political action, including the elaborate schemes devised by Prince Michael for a Balkan alliance, was adversely affected by Austrian and even Russian opposition to militarization and, perhaps as significantly, by the lack of identification by the majority of the population with the aims and policies of their rulers and military leaders. Neither could win enthusiastic mass support for political schemes which were not related to the interests of the peasantry. Serbian, Romanian, Greek, and Bulgarian peasants were only marginally concerned with wars of national liberation conceived or fomented by domestic or foreign leaders or by self-proclaimed armed revolutionaries whose roots among their own people were fragile at best. Consequently, the role played by national armies and by military legions in the attainment of revolutionary goals continued to remain of limited significance in the sixties and in the seventies, for that matter. Even in the Cretan insurrection of the late sixties, where the Greek detachments commanded by General Kallerges showed unusual prowess, the military effort was only marginally successful, as Ömer Paşa Lates was able to cope with the rebel forces in the early stages of the revolution. Whether continuing military assistance from Greece would have ensured the ultimate victory of the rebels is a hypothetical question since the Great Powers prohibited the sending of such aid in 1869. Even without such prohibition, it is doubtful that Greek military power would have been sufficient to defeat the Turkish forces.[17] But there can be no doubt about the lack of collaboration between the Bulgarian population and the raiders sent from Romania by the "Secret Supreme National Commission of Bulgarian Citizens" or by the "Bulgarian Society" or about the inefficacy of the Bulgarian raiding forces in the face of routine Ottoman military reaction.[18] True, in the seventies, the Balkan masses became more responsive to insurrectionary appeals, the efficacy of military action by revolutionary forces changed little. This was most clearly demonstrated during the initial stages of the Bosnian, Hercegovinian, and Bulgarian uprisings of 1875 and 1876.

The Hercegovinian insurrection, like the Bosnian, was militarily ineffectual against the Turks except where the terrain was propitious for protracted guerrilla warfare. The entry of Serbia and Montenegro on the side of the insurgents in June 1876 was not very helpful from a military standpoint. After a few initial successes, the Serbian armies were all but routed by the Turks and were saved from disaster only by the Russian ultimatum to Constantinople. Attempts to support the Bulgarian uprising were equally unfruitful as, for that matter, were the elaborate but unrealistic plans devised by the leaders of the Bulgarian movement. The military achievement of the Bulgarians, Serbians, Montenegrins, Bosnians, and Hercegovinians was a heavy loss of lives inflicted upon the rebels and the supporting external armies by the Turks.[19] And although less costly, the corollary military actions undertaken by Greek officers and volunteers in Epirus, Thessaly, and Crete were similarly insufficient to ensure victory against the Porte.[20] The military failures increased both the need for, and reliance on, Russian military action against the common enemy. Even then the Turkish armies were able to offer serious resistance to the Russian forces at least until 1877, when the Russians secured the participation of Serbian, Greek, Montenegrin, and above all the heretofore neutral Romanian armies.

Of the Balkan armies, the Romanian has been singled out as the one which contributed most directly to breaking the Ottoman front along the Danube and opening the road to Constantinople for the tsarist forces following the defeat of Osman Paşa at Plevna.[21] There can be little doubt that the Serbian and Greek military efforts during the Russo-Turkish phase of the conflict were not of overriding significance in ensuring the defeat of the Ottoman forces. And there is still much controversy over the significance of the Romanian military effort itself.[22] It is unlikely that the Turkish forces could have eventually defeated the Russian armies on the Danube, but it is certain that the Romanian victories accelerated the collapse of the Turkish counter-offensive. More relevant, however, is the significance of the Roma-nians' action in terms of the role ascribable to national armies in gaining national independence. The Romanian army was the first of the Balkan armies to defeat the Ottoman forces and thus fulfill the historic "liberation goals" through victory in battle. One should note that it was the self-determined necessity to gain independence by force of arms, rather than through negotiation with the Porte or through "liberation" by the Russian armies, which dictated the massive military effort undertaken by the Romanians in 1877.[23] In that respect, the importance of national armies in attaining historic national, revolu-tionary goals became recognized not only by the victorious Romanians but also by other leaders in the Balkans. After 1878 the military factor in Balkan revolutionary and liberating actions assumed an ever greater significance and with it the military leaders began to assert themselves more and more in the determination of national policies.

This trend was particularly noticeable in Serbia, Bulgaria, and Greece whose political interests dictated the actual or potential use of military force for the attainment of "liberation" goals. It was less evident in Romania since the Romanian goals were directed against one of their allies in the Triple Alliance and, as such, demanded both discretion and secrecy. In the case of the Balkan states themselves, military plans devised in Belgrade, Sofia, and Athens were often coordinated with guerrilla activities conducted by would-be "liberees" in Macedonia or assumed guerrilla forms directly organized and manned by Serbians, Bulgarians, or Greeks. Military readiness, then, enhanced the danger of continuing confrontation with Ottoman forces and, for that matter, even with the forces of other powers opposed to changing the *status quo* in the Balkans, or even among the Balkan military establishments themselves. The militarization of political ac-tion thus kept the Balkans in nearly constant turmoil until the out-break of World War I when, in theory at least, the principal revolu-tionary goal of all the nations, i.e., the attainment of national independ-ence, was finally realized. Of course, by that time, revolutionary goals had been expanded to cover territorial aggrandizement beyond the original aspirations of earlier revolutionary leaders and the revised goals were also to be attained by force of arms.

The foci of revolutionary agitation and military intervention by supporters of liberation movements in the late nineteenth and early twentieth centuries are well known. Macedonia, Thessaly and Epirus,

Crete, Albania, and Bosnia are household words to students of Balkan revolutions. We need not dwell on details. Suffice it to say that the threat of Greek military intervention solved the Epirus and Thessaly problems in 1881 when the Turks realized that the great strengthening of the Greek armed forces after the adoption of national conscription in November 1877 had best be handled through concessions.[24] Similarly, the union of Eastern Rumelia with Bulgaria was largely a function of the military efforts of the Bulgarians which rendered opposition to the coup of September 1885 unwise. There can be little doubt that the proven military might of the Bulgarian armies, which humiliated the Serbian forces later in that very year, greatly enhanced their power in Sofia and allowed for the organization of expeditionary forces designed to "liberate" Macedonia from the Turkish yoke.[25] That the Bulgarian-speaking Macedonians, even before the establishment of IMRO, had developed their own guerrilla tactics and sought liberation without annexation to Bulgaria mattered little to Bulgarian militarists and their Macedonian supporters in Bulgaria. In fact, rivalry between the "Supremists" and the IMRO so complicated the liberation issue that Colonel Yankov's and Lieutenant-Colonel Nikolov's "četa" were seeking to destroy rival "četa" loyal to the IMRO even before the premature Supremist-led uprising of 1902 and the ill-fated Ilinden revolution itself in the following year.[26] This rivalry never ceased even after Turkish forces first annihilated the rebel units in 1903, and then, after the Young Turk Revolution, the Turks sought to collaborate with the IMRO and the Macedonian population at large in a quest for reconciliation of political differences. Yet, despite futile military action by pro-Bulgarian or pro-IMRO forces, shortly after the failure of the Young Turks' program, the military commanders of Bulgarian-speaking units in Macedonia never abandoned their goals and always hoped that a final military solution could be found for disposing of Ottoman holdings in Europe. Similarly, the Greek armed forces continued to support revolutionary activities in Crete and in Macedonia and, despite their total humiliation in the resulting Greco-Turkish war of 1897, never abandoned the goal of facilitating the realization of the *Megali Idea* in their lifetime.[27] The Greek attitude was echoed among the humiliated Serbian army leaders who, after 1885, still energetically pursued the organizing of "četa" for intervention in Macedonia, not to mention the pledging of continued support for Bosnian opponents of Austrian rule despite the failure of the Hercegovinian uprising of 1882.[28]

Of perhaps comparable importance for our discussion is the rising power of, and influence exerted on, rulers by Balkan armies in the early years of the twentieth century. The assassination of Alexander Obrenović, planned and carried out by radical army officers, ushered in a period of greater commitment to seeking military solutions for outstanding political problems. It matters relatively little whether the "Unification or Death Society" was or was not an arm of the Serbian political leaders who sought the liberation and unification of all Southern Slavs under Belgrade's auspices, but it is clear that the system of Balkan alliances which led to the Balkan Wars and the final humiliation of the once redoutable Ottoman forces could not have been conceived without the express support of the armed forces. And this was true also of the relationship between King Ferdinand and Bulgaria's military leaders, in both Balkan Wars, and between King Carol of Romania and his generals after the success of the Balkan allies in the First Balkan War.[29] In Greece, the army staged the coup of 1909 which brought Venizelos to power and committed Greece to renewed action for the realization of the *Megali Idea.*[30] Even in lowly Albania, the tribal forces which had fared so badly against the Turks — at Peć in 1900, in the Kolašin Affair of 1901, at Kroya and Argircastro in 1905, in Elbassan in 1906 and 1907, and at Kossovo in 1909 — gathered effectively in 1910 in a mass movement directed against the Young Turks, whose solutions for pacification were found unsatisfactory by the variegated leadership. The revolt gained in intensity in 1912 as the Ottoman forces could not cope with Albanian insurgents when they had to face the Balkan allies in the First Balkan War. True, the Albanian leadership was divided and opportunistic and the armed forces were badly organized and chaotic, but the establishment of the Albanian state in November 1912 was attained by force of arms.[31]

Despite extravagant claims made by nationalist politicians and historians on the eve of World War I with respect to the fighting qualities and to the actual and potential strength of the armed forces of the Balkan countries — not to mention claims regarding the national enthusiasm of the peoples of the Balkans for the attainment of the ultimate political goals of the victorious forces of the Second Balkan War — the fact is the fortunes of the military leaders and of the armed forces of the Balkan states were always a function of the strength of their opponents. The Ottoman forces, at least until the beginning of the twentieth century, could readily cope with the armies of the Balkan nations unless those armies were supported by Russia or fought on the Russian side. This was true both in open battle and in guerrilla warfare. The gaining of independence and the realization of imperial dreams by

Balkan leaders could be contemplated in military terms but, with rare exceptions, could be attained only by political and diplomatic means. The commitment of the peoples of the Balkans to the attainment of their leaders' national goals grew as military action became the instrumentality of, or the prelude to, the achievement of those goals. This is not to say, however, that the masses' patriotism necessarily entailed readiness to sacrifice their lives for revolution or liberation. Rather, outrageous Turkish military responses engendered by revolutionary activities left the Balkan peasantry with few options other than to side with those who committed them to revolution and war as survival in an Ottoman system became increasingly hazardous at best and unlikely at worst. It has been argued that the armed forces of the Balkan nations provided a basis for nationalist indoctrination and for political education. This may be questionable but, be that as it may, it is remarkable that historically the political influence of the armed forces and of their leaders was much more limited in the Balkans than in comparable political systems elsewhere in the world. Army officers could, on occasion, topple an unpopular ruler and encourage political adventurism but could never assume control of the political system or set up a ruling junta. Whether the situation would have been different had the Balkan liberation movements not been controlled, directed, or supervised by the European powers is another question. It is, however, a question which, like many others related to the role of the military in Balkan revolutionary activities, deserves careful investigation by students of the problems alluded to in this essay.

Notes

1. A comprehensive discussion of Ottoman policies will be found in Peter F. Sugar, *Southeastern Europe under Ottoman Rule, 1354–1804* (Seattle, 1977) with ample bibliographic references.

2. L. S. Stavrianos, "Antecedents to the Balkan Revolutions of the Nineteenth Century," *Journal of Modern History* 29 (1957): 335–48; Stephen Fischer-Galati, "Revolutionary Activity in the Balkans from Lepanto to Kuchuk-Kainardji," *Südost-Forschungen* 21 (1962): 194–213.

3. *Ibid.* See also Ezel Kural Shaw, "The Political, Practical and Psychological Aspects of *Pax Ottomanica*," in Béla K. Király, ed., *Tolerance and Movements of Religious Dissent in Eastern Europe* (Boulder, Colo. and New York, 1975), 165–82 and Fischer-Galati, "Revolutionary Activity in the

Balkans in the Eighteenth Century," *Actes du Premier Congrès International des Études Balkaniques et Sud-Est Européennes* (Sofia, 1969), 4: 327–37.

4. Dušan J. Popović, *Srbija i Beograd od Požarevačkog do Beogradskog mira, 1718–1739* (Beograd, 1950); A. Oțetea, *et al., Istoria Rominiei* (București, 1964), 3: 433–84.

5. Essential for the study of all Balkan revolutions in the nineteenth and early twentieth centuries is Dimitrije Djordjević, *Révolutions nationales des peoples balkaniques, 1804–1914* (Belgrade, 1965). On Serbian events consult Stojan Novaković, *Vaskrs države srpske; političko-istorijska studija o Prvom srpskom ustanku, 1804–1913* (Beograd, 1904); Grgur Jakšić, *L'Europe et la résurrection de la Serbie (1804–1834)* (Paris, 1907). See also the excellent, if somewhat brief, discussion in Michael Boro Petrovich, *A History of Modern Serbia, 1804–1918* (New York, 1976), 1: 27–128 and the valuable bibliographical survey by Wayne S. Vucinich, "Marxian Interpretations of the First Serbian Revolution," *Journal of Central European Affairs* 21 (1961): 3–14.

6. *Ibid.* See also Mihailo Gavrilović, *Miloš Obrenović* (Beograd, 1908–1912), particularly vols. 1 and 2.

7. Const. C. Giurescu, *Principatele române la începutul secolului al XIX-lea* (București, 1957); Gheorghe Romanescu, "The Formation of the National Army and Its Development down to the War of Independence," in *Pages from the History of the Romanian Army* (București, 1975), 99–113.

8. The most comprehensive work on the subject remains A. Oțetea, *Tudor Vladimirescu și Mișcarea Eteristá in Țările Românești, 1821–1822* (București, 1945). On specific military aspects consult I. Neacșu, "Oastea Pandurilor Condusă de Tudor Vladimirescu în Răscoala din 1821," in *Studii și Referate Privind Istoria Rominiei* (București, 1954), 2: 1003–1043.

9. *Ibid.* See also the important, detailed study on certain military aspects of the revolution by Dan Berindei and Traian Mutașcu, *Aspecte Militare ale Răscoalei Populare din 1821* (București, 1962).

10. The best basic account of the Greek Revolution is Douglas Dakin, *The Greek Struggle for Independence, 1821–1833* (London, 1973). On military aspects consult Theodore Kolokotrones, *Memoirs from the Greek War of Independence, 1821–1833* (Chicago, 1969) and Ioannes Makriyannes, *The Memoirs of General Makriyannis* (London, 1966). Several of the studies in Nikiforos P. Diamandouros, *et. al.*, eds., *Hellenism and the First Greek War of Liberation (1821–1830): Continuity and Change* (Thessaloniki, 1976) are concerned with military problems.

11. *Ibid.* See also Romanescu, 100–101 and Petrovich, 204–209.

12. The best analysis of the first years of King Otto's reign is John A. Petropoulos, *Politics and Statecraft in the Kingdom of Greece: 1833–1843* (Princeton, 1968). See also S. Victor Papacosma, *The Military in Greek Politics: The 1909 Coup d'État* (Kent, Ohio, 1977), 1ff.

13. Petropoulos, 408ff.

14. On military aspects consult Constantin Căzănișteanu, "Probleme militare in Revoluția Română de la 1848," in N. Adăniloaie and Dan Berindei,

eds., *Revoluția de la 1848 în Țările Române* (București, 1974), 131–42. Corollary aspects may be found in other essays in the book.

15. Vladimir Ćorović, *Luka Vukalović i hercegovački ustanci od 1852–1862 godine* (Beograd, 1923); Z. Stoyanov, *Zapiski o Bolgarskikh Vosstanyakh* (Moscow, 1953). See also Marcia MacDermott, *A History of Bulgaria, 1393–1885* (New York, 1962), 169 ff.

16. Petrovich, 295 ff.; Romanescu, 101 ff.

17. The best treatment of this period in English is Donna M. Dontas, *Greece and the Great Powers, 1863–1875* (Thessaloniki, 1966). A very perceptive, if very brief, analysis of the issues may be found in Nicolas Svoronos, *Histoire de la Grèce Moderne* (Paris, 1953), 70 ff.

18. On Romanian-based Bulgarian military operations, see P. Constantinescu-Iași, *Studii Istorice Româno-Bulgare* (București, 1956). Important background material may be found in Charles Jelavich, *Tsarist Russia and Balkan Nationalism: Russian Influence in the Internal Affairs of Bulgaria and Serbia, 1876–1886* (Berkeley, 1958).

19. Vaso Čubrilović, *Bosanski ustanak 1875–1878* (Beograd, 1930); M. Radoičić, *Hercegovina, 1875–1878* (Nevesinje, 1961); Milo Vukčević, *Crna Gora i Hercegovina, uoči rata 1874–1876* (Cetinje, 1950); K. Gandev, *Aprilskoto Vŭstanie* (Sofia, 1956); David MacKenzie, *The Serbs and Russian Pan-Slavism, 1875–1878* (Ithaca, N.Y., 1967); David Harris, *Britain and the Bulgarian Horrors of 1876* (Chicago, 1939); K. Kosev, *et al., Istoriya na Aprilskoto Vŭstanie 1876* (Sofia, 1976).

20. The best analysis of Greek problems is Evangelos Kofos, *Greece and the Eastern Crisis 1875–1878* (Thessaloniki, 1975).

21. A comprehensive discussion of military issues will be found in Dan Berindei, "The Romanian War of Independence (1877–1878)," in *Pages from the History of the Romanian Army,* 133–50.

22. *Ibid.* See also General Radu Rosetti, *Partea luată de armata română în războiul din 1877–1878* (București, 1926).

23. See notes 21 and 22 and Ștefan Pascu, ed., *The Independence of Romania* (București, 1977) which offers some very provocative interpretations.

24. Svoronos, 72 ff.

25. Petrovich, 2: 428 ff.; MacDermott, 339 ff.

26. See particularly Fischer-Galați, "The Internal Macedonian Revolutionary Organization: Its Significance in 'Wars of National Liberation'," *East European Quarterly* 6 (1973): 454–72.

27. Papacosma, 12 ff.; Douglas Dakin, *The Greek Struggle in Macedonia 1897–1913* (Thessaloniki, 1966).

28. The most authoritative study on Serbian positions with respect to Macedonia is Wayne S. Vucinich, *Serbia between East and West: The Events of 1903–1908* (Stanford, 1954).

29. Hans Roger Madol, *Ferdinand of Bulgaria: The Dream of Byzantium* (London, 1933); Vasile Maciu, "The Romanian Army in the First World War

(1916–1918)," in *Pages from the History of the Romanian Army,* 151 ff.; Glenn Torrey, "Irredentism and Diplomacy: The Central Powers and Romania, August–November, 1914)," *Südost-Forschungen* 25 (1966): 285–332 offers interesting insights into Romanian military and political mentalities.

30. Papacosma, 14 ff., offers excellent insights and bibliographical references.

31. The definitive work on these problems is Stavro Skendi, *The Albanian National Awakening 1878–1912* (Princeton, 1967). See also Skendi, "Albanian Political Thought and Revolutionary Activity, 1881–1912," *Südost-Forschungen* 13 (1954): 1–40.

Dimitrije Djordjević

National Factors in Nineteenth-century Balkan Revolutions

The nineteenth century witnessed striking changes in the Balkans which transformed a remote and almost forgotten province of the Ottoman empire into ambitious national states and societies, eager to become a part of modern Europe. These striking changes resulted from both European and Balkan developments. In the Balkans they were expressed through two factors: the agrarian and the national. The first reflected the peasant's constant and stubborn endeavor to appropriate the soil he tilled.[1] The second showed newly born and aggressive national societies struggling for economic emancipation and political independence. These trends expressed the ideology of nationalism which stamped the modern history of the Balkans.

Nationalism dominated the nineteenth-century political scene of Western Europe, from where it was imported to the Balkans. The transplantation of a European ideology into Balkan society reflected similarities and differences existing between the two levels of development. Similarities evolved from the nature of nationalism as a socioeconomic and psychological phenomenon.[2] But apart from this general framework, further analysis shows distinctions resulting from the social and political structures peculiar to each region. Modern nationalism in Western Europe originated in the growth of the bourgeoisie, the rise of towns and commerce, the beginning of modern capitalism, and the secularization of culture. Nationalism, as a state of mind had to further the national community's self-interest and to respond to emotions acquired through a common past, language, and culture.[3] The roots and development of Balkan nationalism were different from the established European pattern. The same applies to European ideological influences like the Enlightenment, and later, romanticism, realism, and positivism.[4] Although chronologically separated in Europe, they intermingled as they radiated toward the Balkans. The developing Balkan national society produced a structure which was generally similar to, but not identical with, its European counterpart. Throughout the nineteenth century the Balkans lagged behind Europe in their socioeconomic evolution. This was reflected in specific adaptations and in a delay in application of European ideological influences. Unless we constantly keep these Balkan specifics in mind, we risk misunderstanding Balkan history.

Hans Kohn was correct in stating that "the new nationalism spread to Central and Eastern Europe long before a corresponding social and economic transformation."[5] It is generally accepted that modern nationalism reflected the switch from the *natural* (historic or tribal) feelings of a specific ethnic or linguistic, as well as cultural, group to the *acquired* idea of a political nation organized in a state.[6] Balkan national awareness sprouts primarily from natural, "instinctive" affiliation to the ethnic group. The Balkan peasant was isolated in his community in the eighteenth century as the European peasant had been during the Middle Ages. His security was jeopardized not by his own absolutist state, but by the foreign ruler. His ethnic or national individuality was identified with his religious or ecclesiastical affiliation. The process of modernization was conditioned by geopolitics (central versus peripheral parts of the Ottoman empire), exposure to Europe, international conflicts and wars, and cultural heritage. Centralization of political power, which in Europe worked toward national entity, had an opposite effect in the Balkans. Balkan nationalism originated in the Christian-Moslem confrontation (the ruled and the ruler), in religious unity, linguistic community among various ethnic groups, awareness of a common past and tradition, a social stratification providing group leadership, foreign intellectual stimulation and general discontent with the abuses of foreign rule. All these natural or "instinctive" ingredients can be traced in the development of modern nationalism in the Balkans. Professor Peter Sugar has tried to classify nationalism in Eastern and Southeastern Europe into four types: bourgeois nationalism among the Czechs; aristocratic nationalism in Poland and Hungary; popular, or egalitarian, nationalism among Serbs and Bulgarians; bureaucratic nationalism in Turkey, Greece, and Romania.[7] The classification is very suggestive. Indeed, it responds to social stratification in Eastern and Southeastern Europe and to the structures of the ruling social groups. But owing to the social composition of the region, it is difficult to find constant characteristics in phenomena in a process of continuous change. According to the degree of modernization in specific Balkan areas, one can see three phases in the development of popular nationalism: the transformation of "instinctive" into modern nationalism, from the late eighteenth century until approximately the 1840s; the period of "historical nationalism," from the 1840s until the 1870s, and the growth of national states with their special version of imperialism between the end of the 1870s and World War I.

The first phase was a period of transition. Social and economic confrontation took the form of a struggle between the Cross and the Crescent and was rooted in the village. The Ottoman *millet* system, in which ecclesiastical meant ethnic affiliation, stimulated religious-national polarization. This tradition was so deeply entrenched that it survived the collapse of Ottoman rule. In Bosnia, under Habsburg rule (1878–1914) *Orthodox* was synonymous with *Serbian, Catholic* with *Croatian* populations. The recognition of "Moslem nationality" in contemporary Yugoslavia reflects the religious-ecclesiastical identity inherited from history. The Macedonian nationality, recognized after World War II in Yugoslavia, had to be supported through formation of an independent Macedonian Church. The first Balkan revolutions in the nineteenth century, as well as later wars, had features of a crusade against the infidel. Vice versa, the Ottomans usually proclaimed a *Jihād* (Holy war) to crush insurgent movements. A Balkan peasant saying observes "God is a great warrior." God was later appropriated for specific national causes: "God and the Croats" (*Bog i Hrvati*), "God protects Serbia" (*Bog cuva Sirbiju*).

The second phase, historical nationalism, beginning in the 1840s, was inspired by romanticism and tended to justify and legalize revolutionary action. Earlier folk, ecclesiastical historicism was replaced by a scholarly and political revival of the past, in accordance with modern interest in the national state and society. The first reflected the peasant image of the past, preserved by rural conservatism. The second was the product of "awakeners" with definite political goals.[8] Historical accuracy was not important, but the militant message they offered to the struggle for independence was.[9] Historicism served practical purposes. The past was reinterpreted to maintain, or to destroy, the *status quo*. For the ruling Habsburg elite historicism supported aristocratic privileges obtained in the past. The new Central European middle class applied the same historical categories — in favor of supporting modern nationalism for its own benefit. In the Balkans historicism had to justify the revolutionary birth of the Balkan state, to legalize its inclusion in the European community of "historical nations," and to encourage nascent dreams of empire, challenged by domestic weakness and by the magnitude of foreign obstacles. Later, historicism also served to justify "national rights" over ethnically ambiguous and mixed territories in the central Balkans.[10]

Finally, after the 1870s, Balkan nationalism entered the third phase

in which the principle of national self-determination replaced historicism, but was accommodated to state interest. Establishment of states
introduced the political balance of power, diplomatic activity, the role
of the national army, and the necessity of political compromise, versus
total and unlimited nationalist fervor. The "haves" replaced the former
"have nots" in a risky game of domestic and foreign politics, and
produced a variety of Balkan imperialism which echoed its developed
European counterpart at the turn of the century.

The national factor was already demonstrated in Balkan revolutions
during the first decades of the nineteenth century. Naturally, the evolving character of nationalism in this period strongly reflected the structure of Balkan society in which the peasantry was predominant. The
ratio of illiteracy was overwhelming and the peasants' knowledge of
geography extremely poor. Both Serbian leaders, Karadjordje and
Miloš, were illiterate. Among twelve members of the first Serbian
government, only four knew how to read.[11] T. Kolokotrones states that
in Greece "there were men who knew no village one hour away from
their own."[12] The leaders often had to threaten the wary peasants to
make them join the revolution.[13]

Still, the national factor stamped the first nineteenth-century Balkan revolutions. Those were pregnant with all the features of nascent
nationalism and embodied religious-ecclesiastical, historical-traditional,
and modern-national components. In petitions addressed in 1804 to
the Austrian authorities, Karadjordje refers to "den ganzen *Servischen
Christen Nation*" or "Christliche Volk so sich in Servien befindet."[14]
Vladimirescu addresses his proclamations to the "Orthodox country
of Wallachia."[15] The Greek proclamation to the Hydriotes calls them
to "break the chains imposed by the barbarian Mahometans" and
urges them to "raise the Cross on Saint Sophie."[16] Ypsilanti identifies
Greece with the Balkans under the ecumenical concept of the Greek
Patriarchate.[17] A metropolite proclaimed the 1821 Greek war for
independence, and the Serbian insurgents put the cross on their flags.
Their slogan was "For the Holy Cross and Golden Liberty." The best
example of the evolving nationalism of this period would be the use of
the word *patrida,* to refer to the home town, to a specific region, and to
the fatherland. The same applies to the Greek use of *genos* and *ethnos,*
finally to be replaced with the political term, *Hellens.*[18] Plans to restore
the "Slaviano-Serbskoe Carstvo" and the Hellenistic-Balkan Republic
originated at the end of the eighteenth century.[19] The Serbian insur-

gents resorted to the coat of arms of the mediaeval Nemanyed dynasty; their government resided in Smederevo "the capital city of our Despots and Emperors" and assembled under the portrait of Tsar Dušan.[20] Ypsilanti urged a fight "between Marathon and the Thermopyles" in memory of "the Thebaian Epaminondas and the Athenian Thrasybule."[21]

Historians generally recognize the role of the national factor in the 1821 Greek revolution.[22] Although the Greek peasant was not developed byond the level of Balkan peasantry in general, the upper layers of Greek society were strong enough to define the national goal of the movement. Rigas, Korrais, Mavrocordatos, and other intellectuals espoused the ideas of the Enlightenment, the French Revolution, the freemasons, and modern nationalism. Only 0.6 percent of the membership of the Philiki Etaireia were peasants, in contrast to 53.7 percent, merchants, 13.1 percent, "free professionals," 11.7 percent, provincial notables, and 9.5 percent clergymen.[23] The national factor was demonstrated in the Proclamation of Independence, identical in the preambles of the Epidaurus (1822) and Astros (1823) Constitutions: "The Greek nation . . . declares today . . . before God and man, through its rightful representatives gathered in national assembly its political existence and independence."[24]

The national characteristics of the 1804–1813 Serbian uprising were recently questioned by some American scholars. They assume that "Serbian national consciousness had not progressed beyond the initial stage of cultural identification"[25] and that "the rebels' geopolitical objectives were provincial rather than national."[26] There is also a tendency to trace the formulation of Serbian nationalism only to the 1840s. The Serbian uprising was a *sui generis* peasant movement which started as a reaction against local abuses only to be transformed into a war for independence. It was the first to herald the new era of Balkan emancipation movements. The uprising was almost isolated internationally and relied for the most part on its own resources. The uprising lacked flamboyant appeals and proclamations. It produced a flexible and pragmatic diplomacy and strategy, which corresponded to the realities of the times and left much to be achieved.

Owing to the lack of written sources it is impossible to say how far ideas of modern nationalism penetrated the Serbian village; indeed, it is difficult to say how much the Serbian public knew about the pre-revolutionary plans to restore the Serbian state. But if we attribute a merely parochial character to the uprising, we cannot say why the uprising echoed among Serbs outside the *paşalik* of Belgrade (in

Srem, Banat, Bosnia, Montenegro, and Hercegovina); why the peasants opposed the imperial army after defeating the local Dahies; why the insurgents refused to accept the autonomy which the Ottomans offered in 1806 and chose to fight for independence; why a state establishment (although primitive) originated among the insurgents — along with many other questions of this sort. The Russian impact on Serbian events was unquestionably strong after 1807, but one cannot force the peasant to continue his fight if he does not find personal reasons for such a struggle, as was shown later by many failures of Russian agitation during the nineteenth-century wars with the Ottomans.

This does not mean that modern nationalism was already rooted among Serbian insurgents in a well-defined way. It proves only that it was present in nascent form, evolving parallel to the Serbs' successes, according to the French proverb: *l'appétit vient en mangeant*. Leopold Ranke was the first to understand the real meaning of the Serbian uprising when he called his study *Die Serbische Revolution* (1829). Yugoslav historiography is unanimous on this point.[27] Michael Petrovich, in his recently published history of Serbia, takes the 1805 clash with the imperial army as the beginning of the war for national liberation, saying this "aim was never absent."[28] Charles and Barbara Jelavich underline the 1807 rejection of Ottoman offers of autonomy as a turning point toward war for independence and attribute this shift to Russian influence.[29] Both dates, 1805 and 1807, point to the developing national factor in the Serbian revolution.

Similar ambiguities may be seen in the Romanian movement of Tudor Vladimirescu in 1821, which also reflected both agrarian and national trends. The Romanian peasant was primarily attracted by prospects of seizing the land; the boyar by eliminating Phanariot competition. Vladimirescu's policy was clearly directed toward the formation of a national government.[30] The failure of the Romanian movement was due to the domestic controversy between peasant and boyar which alienated Vladimirescu from both sides. The Romanian situation was peculiar because national emancipation did not necessarily liberate the peasant from the landlord, as it generally did in the rest of the Balkans.

Between the 1840s and the 1870s, the national factor in Balkan movements altered in scope and substance. It gradually took the initiative from agrarian trends and subordinated them to specific national policies. It echoed European influences and accentuated national dissension among Balkan peoples. From historicism, nationalism was moving toward the realization of the principle of national self-determination.

The shift resulted from the growth of national societies, from the establishment of Balkan national states, and from increased intercourse with Europe. Identical agrarian interests, manifested in the previous period, created a common denominator for the peasant struggle for land. It enabled collaboration between Serbs and Bulgarians, Greeks and Bulgarians, and Romanians with all of them.[31] The pursuit of specific national goals, and the origins of "Piedmont" ambitions in the struggle for emancipation provoked national rivalry. The state introduced its own interest which might, but did not necessarily, represent the interests of the entire *nation*. The state of "haves" moved toward the "have nots" — fellow nationals in the Ottoman empire — and had to deal with inevitable compromises resulting from the balance of power, the interference of European diplomacy in the Eastern Question, and most of all, with the risk of jeopardizing gains already won. Nationalism became an instrument in foreign as well as domestic politics during the polarization between conservatives and liberals in the 1860s, and socialists in the 1870s and the consequent struggle for power at home. Nationalism thus showed a double face. Positive, in mobilizing national resources for the struggle for emancipation; negative, in introducing national exclusiveness and mutual distrust. National messianism replaced national martyrdom. Earlier "religious" and "peasant wars" were replaced by "national war" in determining modern Balkan national frontiers.

National programs elaborated in Serbia and Greece during the early 1840s, the process of unification of Romanians, successful in the late 1850s, and the maturing of the Bulgarian "Vozraždenie" in the 1860s, reflect the new directions of the national factor in Balkan revolutions. The 1844 Serbian *Načertanie* (Draft) expressed a mixture of Pan-Serbism, historicism, and actual realities imposed on the nascent Serbian state: "Serbia must place herself in the rank of other European states . . ." and "if Serbia ponders what she is now . . . she is confronted with the fact that she is small and cannot long remain so. She has to absorb all the Serbian people around her . . ." Thus "as heirs of our illustrious forefathers [we] are doing nothing that is new other than completing their work . . . The Serbian idea and its national mission and existence will stand under the sacred law of history."[32] The same kind of "national mission" inspired the *Megali Idea* formulated in

1844, which saw the Byzantine political heritage, the cultural legacy of classical Greece, and the universal idea of Greek Orthodoxy, revived in the growing Greek national society, divided between the Diaspora and the homeland. "There are two great centers of Hellenism: Athens and Constantinople" said Joannes Kolettes, "Athens is only the capital city of the Kingdom. Constantinople is the great capital, *the City*, the joy and hope of all Hellens."[33] The Bulgarian struggle for the national church was extended to Macedonia, parallel to the emancipation of Bulgaria proper.

New tactics were employed in the development of the national factor on territory under Ottoman rule. In the previous period, nationalist movements had arisen out of local situations, now they had to be incited from "abroad," from the emancipated areas. They had to be centralized and synchronized with the policy and interests of the Balkan states. One can find these ingredients even before the 1840s, in Serbian, Greek, and Bulgarian reactions to various contemporary revolutionary movements. Leaders of unsuccessful peasant uprisings against the Ottomans found refuge, instruction, and encouragement in neighboring emancipated Balkan states.[34] In the 1850s and 1860s movements in areas under Ottoman rule were incited and directed from emancipated national centers in order to start a general Balkan uprising, to be followed by a war of Balkan states against the Ottomans. During the Crimean War (1853-55) Greek generals and army officers (Tzavellas, Velentzas, Caratassos), as well as national committees from the Ionian islands set insurrectional fires in Thessaly, Epirus, and Macedonia,[35] joining peasant discontent to the struggle for the national cause.

Just as ideas of modern nationalism first radiated into the peripheral Balkans from the more developed Balkan Diaspora in Europe, in the following period, nationalist ideas from the emancipated periphery echoed in the central Balkans. The "revolution" had to be imported from "abroad," with the national factor replacing its agrarian counterpart. This activity was channeled through national-revolutionary organizations and secret committees, which flourished from the 1840s and 1850s on, in Greece, Serbia, and Romania (including Bulgarian committees organized in neighboring Balkan states). These organizations were a Balkan counterpart of the Italian Carbonari or "Young Europe" in the period of liberalism and romanticism. From the 1850s till the 1875-78 Eastern Crisis, the Ottoman Balkans were crisscrossed by agents of nationalist propaganda. The "Serbo-Bosnian Committee" (1860), the "Serbian Committee" (1862), seconded in the late 1860s by the OMLADINA, worked in areas adjacent to Serbia.[36] Greek *heterias* (Phoenix, Phil-orthodoxe, Great Fraternity) and various Ionian, Epyrotan, and Cretan committees promoted the Greek cause in Epirus, Thessaly, and Macedonia, as well as on the Greek islands.[37] Similarly, on the Bulgarian side, secret groups and committees operated first from Serbia, then Romania (Benevolent Society, Supreme National Commission of Bulgarian Citizens, Bulgarian Community, Central Bulgarian Revolutionary Committee).[38] The same kind of activity may be found in Romania (*Dreptate Fratrie*), Montenegro (Association for Liberation and Unification of Serbs) as well as among young socialists in the 1870s (Committee for Revolution and Freedom in Novi Sad, 1872).

In spite of specific national objectives, these organizations all had the same kind of social structure, organizational scheme and procedure, and revolutionary strategy. They were purely nationalistic (with the exception of young socialist groups). Their leadership was made up of army officers and emigrants from Ottoman territories, attached to the governments of Balkan states. They relied on the work of individual "apostles" and a network of agents drawn from the upper levels of village and urban communities on Ottoman territory. Among the seventy-five agents of Serbian propaganda in the Austrian military confines in the early 1860s, for example, there were twenty-six teachers, twenty-five merchants, thirteen members of the free professions, and eleven priests. (Only one among them was a woman).[39] None of the agents was a peasant. The national leadership usually mistrusted the peasant and questioned his national consciousness and fighting ability. Preparing a Bosnian uprising, a Serbian revolutionary wrote in 1863, "it can never be launched, except through elements from abroad, as the Bosnians are neither capable nor determined to fight."[40] The agents' proclamations and appeals show a total absence of socioagrarian programs. National liberation was the only objective. The organizations were conspiratorial, hierarchical in structure. They had a special secret procedure for recruiting new members.[41] Activity concentrated on organizing "cells," schematically dividing the presumed insurgents' territory into "districts" and "zones," collecting arms and information, etc.[42] Due to their conspiratorial nature, their reliance on the upper social strata, and the Ottoman authorities' vigilance, these organizations never succeeded in penetrating deep into the village itself. Attempts at a general uprising usually failed. The organizations were more fertile in written plans and suggestions than effective in practice.

During the 1800s, nationalism in the Balkans entered a dynamic stage, stimulated by European and domestic, Balkan developments. The 1859 war for the unification of Italy, "the gun from Königrätz,"[43] seconded by the crisis and reorganization of the Habsburg monarchy, echoed from the Baltic to the Aegean Sea. A series of national uprisings broke out from Poland (1863) to Crete (1866). In the Balkans, the Romanian Principalities were finally unified (1861); the 1862 Ottoman bombardment of Belgrade almost resulted in war; the Ionian Islands were united with Greece (1864); and Montenegro waged war with the Ottomans during an entire decade (1852–62). Emigrés — national revolutionaries, scattered all over Europe after defeat in 1849 — were plotting to involve the Balkans in their specific nationalistic objectives. Giuseppe Mazzini, a national Messiah with "a head of a white Christ and the eyes of a hypnotist,"[44] and Garibaldi became idols of the Balkan liberal public. The Pan-Slavs, resurrected in 1858 after the Crimean crisis, professed the coming epoch of the Slavic race.[45] After more than a decade, 1848 liberal European ideas penetrated into the Balkans. Nationalism shifted from "archeological roots" and "collecting the dust of the ruins," to Fichte's "soul of the nation" and the principle of national self-determination.[46] Historicism became too narrow a basis for national emancipation. Serbian privileges obtained in Vojvodina from the Habsburg court in the seventeenth century could not oppose Hungarian historical rights from the tenth century. The new Yugoslav ideology did not depend on history.

From the 1860s and 70s, the national factor dominated Balkan politics. Conservatives, liberals, later the socialists — all pursued the solution of the national question, but in different contexts and with different goals. The conservatives thought to accomplish national emancipation and unification through a strong, centralized, authoritarian state able to deal with national foes. Freedom in domestic politics meant disunity and anarchy: thus, unity inside for unity abroad.[47] The liberals preached freedom as a mobilizing factor in the national struggle. National liberation equals political liberation: thus, no freedom abroad without freedom at home. The young socialists in the early 1870s worked for revolution at home and abroad. They identified national with socioeconomic emancipation; thus, national and social revolutions had to be joined. National revolutionaries of all schools clashed with their governments. Revolutionaries underestimated obstacles which blocked the road to their goals, governments overestimated them. Revolutionaries were eager to gamble; governments were hesitant in facing crises.

Balkan nationalist movements during the 1860s had three possible options: to exploit or to compromise with the European factor; to attack or to compromise with the Ottomans; or to apply a "fara de se" tactic. Projects for a Balkan federation, which blossomed in the 1860s, aimed to reconcile Balkan with European interests through formation of a Balkan buffer zone between East and West, a kind of eastern "Switzerland" in the Balkans.[48] The First Balkan Alliance of 1866–68 was based on a combination of the first and third options: protection from European interference and aggression against the Ottomans.[49] The Balkan governments tried to benefit from European disunity and rivalry over the Balkans by urging one great neighbor or another to come on their side. Domestic weakness, in conflict with growing nationalism, and nationalist rivalries over Balkan territory sparked attempts to exploit the Ottoman factor. The Serbs used the Cretan uprising to win freedom from Ottoman garrisons for their cities. The Bulgarian community in Constantinople developed "dualistic" theories and obtained the Exarchate from the Porte to the detriment of the Greek Patriarchate. Both Serbs and Bulgarians exploited the Eastern Crisis of 1897 to obtain gains in Macedonia. Fear of the Slavs, backed by Russia, pushed Greek policy toward the Ottomans. The "fara de se" tactic also found Balkan exponents. Rakovski, Levski, and Botev tried unsuccessfully to incite a revolution in Bulgaria itself.[50] Serbia and Montenegro attempted to solve the Balkan question by war in 1876. So did the Greeks in their war (1897) with the Ottomans.

The Eastern Crisis of 1875–78, which was expected to provide a definitive solution for Southeastern Europe, following Italian and German unification, proved to be a frustrated revolution. National endeavors did not provoke a general uprising nor unify particular Balkan groups. The Ottoman empire proved to be stronger than assumed by Balkan national romantics and the European factor predominated at the Berlin Congress. The outcome of the Berlin solution was to affect the national factor in the Balkans in the coming age of imperialism.

Nationalism completely dominated Balkan politics at the turn of the century. The Balkans became an integral part of Europe. The struggle between continental and maritime European powers for dominance in the eastern Mediterranean crossed into the Balkans. The growth of national societies in the Balkans nourished ambitions to complete the emancipation process initiated a century ago to the detriment of the Ottoman empire. Nationalist activities were transferred from revolution to war. The soldier and the diplomat became instruments of nationalist fervor. Revolutionary organizations still mushroomed, but as a device supporting state policies. At the beginning of the twentieth century, army budgets took up 25 percent of state incomes. National policies of all the Balkan states were directed toward the Balkan Peninsula and the surrounding seas. Romanian ambition was torn between Transylvania at the west and Bessarabia on the Black Sea shore. Serbia was split between aspirations pushing toward the Adriatic or the Aegean. Bulgaria was moving west and south: Macedonia and Thrace. Greece was torn between trends directed toward the northern Balkan hinterland and the southern Aegean islands. All states clashed over the central Balkans, in Macedonia, still under Ottoman rule.

Balkan nationalism developed a distinctive Balkan imperialism which encompassed messianism, historicism, characteristics of a religious crusade, hegemonism, and chauvinism — all parallel to the struggle for national emancipation. The trend toward economic emancipation supplemented political emancipation in the era of nascent Balkan industrialization. Pig wars (Serbia–Austria-Hungary, 1906–1911), chicken wars (Bulgaria–Austria-Hungary, 1906), boycotts of industrial goods (Ottoman–Austrian, 1908) followed the Austro–Romanian Customs War (1886–93). Societies promoting national propaganda in Macedonia used the historic names of St. Sava in Serbia, Cyril and Methodius in Bulgaria. "Revenge for Kossovo" was cited as the war aim in the Serbian war proclamation of 1912, which referred to *carsko Skoplje* ("imperial Skoplje").[51] Proclaiming Bulgaria a kingdom in 1908, Ferdinand took the title of Tsar (Emperor). In 1912, he planned to enter Constantinople to be crowned in Sancta Sophia as Simeon II.[52] Bands operating in Macedonia were equipped and directed by Balkan governments and their diplomats.

The aggressive stage into which nationalism entered in the decade preceding World War I responded to both cohesive and disruptive influences. Fear of European intervention, awareness of weakness in solving the Balkan part of the Eastern Question, and common anti-Ottoman attitudes acted as a unifying factor leading toward Balkan *rapprochement* and compromise among exaggerated nationalist aspirations. European interference had delayed solution of the Balkan problem in 1878. Russian involvement in the Far East in 1904–1905 offset the Austro-Russian Balkan stalemate; the 1908 Bosnian crisis was a dark omen for the future. Such a situation dictated a Balkan-European compromise and the formation of a united Balkan national front. Compromise may be seen in the Serbo-Bulgarian agreements of 1904–1905, in the support which the Hungarian struggle for independence obtained in the Balkans, and in the Yugoslav policy of the "new course" in the Habsburg monarchy.[53] These trends culminated in the 1912 Balkan Alliance and the successful war with the Ottomans. But parallel to cohesive factors, growing national appetites worked in the opposite directions. The slogan "all or nothing" imbued Balkan politics. The dynamic aggressiveness of young societies in full swing of development pushed nationalist fervor further. The collapse of Ottoman rule in the Balkans in 1912 removed the common opponent and opened the struggle for spoils. European rivalries, challenged by domestic changes, intensified the impact of the foreign factor in Balkan politics. On the eve of the war, the national factor in the Balkans was both triumphant and defeated: emancipation from Ottoman rule was achieved but the gunpowder of dissatisfaction was accumulated, ready to explode again in 1914.

One may take a positive or negative approach to Balkan nationalism in the nineteenth century, but one fact stands: its achievements are impressive. The modern historian deals with issues which were only dreams for the nineteenth-century Balkan generations. Difficulties imposed by the complexity of domestic emancipation, confronted with foreign obstacles, seemed insurmountable to members of the evolving national societies. Let us imagine, for a moment, an Ottoman serf closing his eyes at the beginning of the nineteenth century, living in a primitive, socially egalitarian peasant society, under foreign rule. Reopening them a century later, at the end of World War I, that serf would see developing national societies, successor national states, and the disappearance of the three empires which, for centuries, had determined his destiny.

The dramatic changes resulted from the development of nationalism in the Balkans. That tended to respond to the trends of nineteenth-century Europe, based on the principle "one nation–one state." But at the same time, it had to adapt to special Balkan situations. These were characterized by the existing gap between European and Balkan levels of social, economic, and political development which caused the Balkans to imitate Europe. Balkan problems were produced by the heritage of centuries-long mixing of population, by migrations and ethnic movements which made it almost impossible to delineate frontiers on truly national lines. Balkan events were constantly affected by European rivalries and the specific interests of European powers in the Balkan area. In practice, nationalism suffered from abuses and misinterpretations, reflecting both the positive and the negative aspects of modern nationalist aspirations, stimulated by the Mediterranean temperament. Yet for all its faults, Balkan nationalism encompassed the main trends of the century. For it condensed in itself the entire process of modernization, of the socioeconomic, political, and cultural emancipation of the Balkans.

Notes

1. The agrarian factor in Balkan revolutions is discussed in a separate paper.

2. Nationalism is carefully studied in the works of Hans Kohn, Carlton Hayes, Boyd Shafer, Louis Snyder, and Karl Deutsch. See also Gale Stokes, "Cognition and Function of Nationalism," *Journal of Interdisciplinary History* 4 (1974): 525–42; Peter F. Sugar and Ivo Lederer, eds., *Nationalism in Eastern Europe* (Seattle, 1969).

3. Kohn and Hayes, in Stokes, 525.

4. Dimitrije Djordjević, "Balkan versus European Enlightenment, Parallelism and Dissonances," *East European Quarterly* 9 (1975): 487–97.

5. Hans Kohn, *The Idea of Nationalism. A Study in Its Origins and Background,* 2d ed. (New York, 1961), 457.

6. Peter F. Sugar, "External and Domestic Roots of Eastern European Nationalism," in Sugar and Lederer, 3–9. For the formation of early nationalism, see also Emanuel Turczynski, *Konfession und Nation, zur Frühgeschichte der serbischen und rumänischen Nationsbildung* (Düsseldorf, 1976), 244–58.

7. *Ibid.,* 46–54.

8. Vuk Vinaver, "Istoriska tradicija u Prvom srpskom ustanku," *Istoriski Glasnik,* 1–2 (1954): 103.

9. Venelin's statement that the Bulgarians gave their alphabet to the Russians stimulated Bulgarian nationalism. Michael Boro Petrovich, "The Russian Image in Renaissance Bulgaria (1700–1878)," *East European Quarterly* 1 (1967): 89.

10. Dimitrije Djordjević, "Uloga istoricisma u formiranju balkanskih država XIX veka," *Zbornik Filozofskog fakulteta* 10 (1968): 309–311.

11. Vuk Karadžić, *Prvi srpski ustanak* (Beograd, 1947), 137.

12. George Frangos, "The Philiki Etaireia: A Premature National Coalition," in Richard Clogg, ed., *The Struggle for Greek Independence* (London, 1973), 90.

13. Douglas Dakin, *The Greek Struggle for Independence 1821–1833* (Berkeley, 1973), 71. See also Notis Botzaris, *Visions balkaniques dans la prépa-*

ration de la révolution grecque 1789-1821 (Genève-Paris, 1962), "appendice E-5," p. 240.

14. Aleksa Ivić, *Spisi bečkih arhiva o Prvom srpskom ustanku* (Beograd, 1935), 1 (1804), Doc. 46, p. 55, letter to Colonel Temerlin, Mar. 31, 1804; to the same, Apr. 4, 1804, Doc. 56, p. 69.

15. Botzaris, "Appendice 6, A Proclamation to the Wallachians," Mar. 20, 1821, p. 222.

16. *Ibid.,* "Appendice E-1, Proclamation to the Hydriotes," p. 236; "Proclamation to the Thessalians," E-5, p. 240.

17. *Ibid.,* "Appendice D-2, Proclamation to the Greeks in the Principalities," p. 226; "The Morea, Epirus, Thessaly, Serbia, Bulgaria, the Islands of the Archipelago, in one word all Greece . . . ," etc.

18. Frangos, 96-99. Stephen Xydis, "Modern Greek Nationalism," in Sugar and Lederer, 208-210.

19. Stevan Dimitrijević, *Stevana Stratimirovića mitropolita karlovačkog plan za oslobodjenje srpskog naroda* (Beograd, 1926); Nikola Radojčić, "Sava Tekelija," *Istoriski Časopis* 12-13 (1965): 9.

20. Vinaver, 111-18.

21. Botzaris, "Appendice D-3, Proclamation to the Greeks," p. 228. The same reference to history in the "Proclamation to Hydra," p. 238.

22. Some skepticism was evident on the regionalism and particular regional interests expressed through the revolution and civil war. See Frangos, 100.

23. *Ibid.,* 87-88. See also A. Otsetea, "L'Hetairie d'il y a cent cinquante ans," *Balkan Studies* 6 (1965): 249-64.

24. Xydis, "Modern Greek Nationalism," 234.

25. Roger Paxton, "Nationalism and Revolution: A Reexamination of the Origins of the First Serbian Insurrection 1804-1807," *East European Quarterly* 6 (1972): 337-62.

26. Lawrence Meriage, "The First Serbian Uprising (1804-1813): National Revival or a Search for Regional Security?" *Canadian Review of Studies in Nationalism* 4 (1977): 187.

27. See Vaso Čubrilović, *Istorija političke misli u Srbiji XIX veka* (Beograd, 1958), 85-90.

28. Michael Boro Petrovich, *A History of Modern Serbia* (New York, 1976) 1: 37.

29. Charles and Barbara Jelavich, *The Establishment of the Balkan National States, 1804-1920* (Seattle, 1977), 33.

30. D. Djordjević, *Révolutions nationales des peuples balkaniques, 1804-1914* (Beograd, 1965), 43; S. I. Samoilov, "Narodnoosvoboditelnoe dviženie 1821 v Valdhii," *Voprosy istorii* 10 (1955): 94-105. See also Stephen Fischer-Galati, "Rumanian Nationalism," in Sugar and Lederer, 377.

31. Djordjević, *Révolutions nationales,* 64-65.

32. The English text of "Načertanie" in Paul N. Hehn, "The Origins of Modern Pan-Serbism: The 1844 Načertanie of Ilija Garašanin," *East European Quarterly* 9 (1975): "Appendix," 158-60.

33. Xydis, 237.

34. Besides the initiatives coming from Serbia (Prince Miloš) to incite the 1833 uprising in eastern Serbia, other leaders of the movements of the 1830s and 40s found support in Serbia. The priest Jovica Ilić, after the failure of the 1834 uprising in Bosnia, left for Serbia and Russia, Aleksa Ivić, *Ustanak popa Jovice Ilića (1834) i bune leskovačkih i vranjanskih Srba (1842)* (Zagreb, 1919), 14. The priest Djordje Janković was in contact with the Serbian prince and the Russian representative in Serbia before and during the 1840 uprising in Leskovac (Vladimir Stojančević, *Južnoslovenski narodi u Osmanskom carstvu od Jedrenskog mira 1829 do Pariskog kongresa 1856* (Beograd, 1971), 159–63. The merchant Miloje Jovanović fled to Serbia after the failure of the uprising. Georgi Mamarčév cherished the same national objectives at Kopel in 1829, and Velco Atanasov in Silistria in 1835–36 (Vasil N. Zlatarski, "Blgarski vzstania i opita za vzstania do sredata na XIX vek" in *Blgaria 1000 godini (927–1927)* (Sofia, 1930), 731.

35. Djordjević, *Révolutions nationales,* 87–88.

36. Grgur Jakšić–Vojislav Vučković, *Spoljna politika Srbije za vlade kneza Mihaila. Prvi Balkanski Savez* (Beograd, 1963), 130–39.

37. John Petropoulos, *Politics and Statecraft in the Kingdom of Greece 1833–1843* (Princeton, 1968), 335–37.

38. Dimitur Kosev, "Vasil Levski and the Bucharest Bulgarian Revolutionary Committee," in Thomas Butler, ed., *Bulgaria Past and Present* (Columbus, Ohio, 1976), 54–64.

39. Vojislav Vučković, *Politička akcija Srbije u južnoslovenskim pokrajinama Habsburške monarhije 1859–1874* (Beograd, 1965), Doc. 57, pp. 101–103, List of nationalists in Croatia and the military confines, Jan. 1863.

40. *Ibid.,* Doc. 56, p. 97, Antonije Orešković's proposal of a war plan, Feb. 6, 1863.

41. Usually a solemn oath was required: "In the name of the Holy Trinity and in the name of my Fatherland, etc." See text of an oath required by a Greek secret association in D. Djordjević, "The Echo of the 1866 Cretan Uprising in Serbia," *Papers Presented at the International Symposium at Crete 1971* (Athens, 1975), 2: 101.

42. Dragoslav Stranjaković, *Politička propaganda Srbije u južnoslovenskim pokrajinama 1844–1858* (Beograd, 1936), 7–33. Vojislav Vučković, *Politička akcija Srbije,* Doc. 143, pp. 260–73, Plan to prepare an uprising in Bosnia, Beograd, March 1867.

43. Vučković, Doc. 145, p. 285, "Circulaire of the Beograd Committee."

44. As described by one of the Serbian liberals. Gale Stokes, *Legitimacy through Liberalism, Vladimir Jovanović and the Transformation of Serbian Politics* (Seattle, 1975), 62.

45. The best studies dealing with Panslavism are Michael Boro Petrovich, *The Emergence of Russian Panslavism 1850–1870* (New York, 1956); Hans Kohn, *Pan Slavism, Its History and Ideology* (New York, 1960).

46. The confidential circular of the Belgrade Central Committee for the

Unification of the South Slav states (March 1867): "The [Balkan] confederation of peoples has to be conceived on the basis of historicism, modified to the unavoidable demands of the principle of nationality. . . . One doesn't have to care for any specific historical past . . . but to recommend the act of unity of peoples . . . otherwise it would mean collecting the dust from old ruins. . . ." Vučković, Doc. 145, pp. 285–86.

47. Prince Michael of Serbia used to compare his country to a glass of clear water which one drop can pollute. The "drop" represented the liberals. Zivan Zivanovic, *Politička isorija Srbije* (Beograd, 1923), 1: 72.

48. Polith, *Die orientalische Frage und ihre organische Lösung* (Wien, 1862).

49. See texts of treaties and agreements: Jakšić-Vučković, Annexes: 471–77, 486–89, 494–504, 505–506, 510–21.

50. Marin Pundeff, "Bulgarian Nationalism," in Sugar and Lederer, 110–113, 116–17.

51. Stanoje Stanojević, *Srpsko-turski rat 1912 godina* (Beograd, 1928), 154–55.

52. Djordjević, *Izlazak Srbije na Jadransko more 1912* (Beograd, 1956), 22.

53. See Mirjana Gross, *Vladavina hrvatsko-srpske koalicije 1906–1907* (Beograd, 1960), 17–22.

Dan Berindei

The Romanian Armed Forces in the Eighteenth and Nineteenth Centuries

More than a century ago Jules Michelet stated that the peoples of Eastern Europe had played an extremely important part in the defense of Western Europe. This thought he reiterated:

> Peoples of the West who, for so long now remote from the "barba-rians" are able to devote yourselves to the arts of peace remember always, with gratitude, the eastern nations which, located at the frontiers of Europe, have saved you from the Tatar deluge, the armies of the Turks . . . do not forget what you owe Hungary, Poland, unfortunate Romania.[1] While idle Europe chattered, argued about divine grace, concerned itself with subtleties, those heroic defenders were protecting it with their spears.[2]

The Romanian lands, located at the crossroads of history, had a tumultuous past, but one must observe that at least part of their national territory retained a continuing autonomous status. While the peoples south of the Danube were conquered by the Turks and, since the fourteenth century, were transformed into *paşaliks,* while the Kingdom of Hungary was subject to Ottoman or Habsburg domination in the sixteenth century, while Poland, too, disappeared in the eighteenth century, two Romanian lands, Moldavia and Wallachia, remained autonomous. As for Transylvania, we should mention that it, too, kept its autonomy during the occupation of part of Hungary by the Turks; at least, it was able to retain its distinctive administrative character-istics within the framework of the Hungarian kingdom and, later, within that of the Habsburg empire. That the Romanians were able to retain the apparatus of a state in Wallachia and Moldavia throughout the period of direct Ottoman domination over a significant part of southeastern Europe represents an important aspect of the history of the Romanian people as well as of the history of liberation and, as such, of the essential story of the peoples of southeastern Europe. The Romanian Principalities, by their very existence, represented a center of latent resistance, an example and a base of support for the peoples subjugated by the Porte.

Evidently, Romanian feudal states had their vicissitudes. There were moments of glorious resistance. During the reign of Stephen the Great of Moldavia, for instance, or even more, during the reign of Michael the Brave of Wallachia when Michael united, albeit temporarily, all Romanian lands under his rule. But there were also periods when foreign domination threatened the very existence of the Romanian lands. This was particularly true during the eighteenth century, the period of greatest Turkish domination over Moldavia and Wallachia, when Phanariot princes replaced rulers selected from among the Romanian boyars. Intensified Ottoman domination culminated in the cession of Romanian lands to the Austrian and Russian empires, contrary to the wishes of the Romanians and to the obligations of the suzerain role[3] assumed by the Porte toward the Romanian provinces. One should note, too, that in the eighteenth century, and particularly after the defeat of Ferenc Rákóczi and the peace of 1711, the establishment of Habsburg authority in Transylvania marked a difficult moment in the history not only of the Romanians but also of the Szeklers, Magyars, and even for some Saxon inhabitants of that province.

The aggravation of Ottoman domination in Wallachia and Moldavia as well as the establishment of direct Habsburg domination in Transylvania coincided with the beginnings of the formation of the modern Romanian nation in the eighteenth century, a phenomenon which occurred also among other peoples of Central and Southeastern Europe. The desire for removal of foreign domination gained momentum as a result of the disintegration of feudal structures. Major sociopolitical currents made change inevitable at the very height of the period of foreign domination. A study of the military structures of that age must take these factors into account.

The eighteenth century marks, albeit temporarily, a period of regression in Romanian military history. But at the same time, as the century progressed, the bases of the Romanian military renaissance of the nineteenth century were laid. There was a cut in the armed forces of Moldavia and Wallachia — including a reduction in the number of native recruits — yet one cannot speak of actual suppression of military activities. Nevertheless, a regression caused in part by changes in types of armaments did in fact occur. Nicolae Iorga, referring primarily to the period following 1774, stated that the decline affected even "the size of the prince's guard contingents both with respect to native recruits and, particularly, with respect to foreign elements."[4] In this respect it is worth noting that, when a Polish diplomat arrived in 1759, the six military units sent by the Moldavian prince to Cirniceni to greet the mission had flags, trumpets, and drums. As noted by Adam Gołarlowski, secretary to the head of the mission, Józef Podoski, "these men were all simple peasants who were unarmed since it was prohibited to wear arms in times of peace."[5] Yet another Polish report, two decades later, describes the worsening of the situation in Moldavia when "the prince's militia consisted of a few dozen men without uniforms and without weapons commensurate with their duties."[6]

Nevertheless, military forces did exist in both Romanian principalities throughout the eighteenth century. Regular contingents were maintained for guarding frontiers, for exercising police functions, for performing guard duties for the prince, and for conducting ceremonies and staging parades.[7] One also needs to mention that the constant moving of Phanariot rulers from one Romanian province to the other contributed to making institutions in the Romanian provinces uniform and unified. This situation was also evident in the military sector. Iorga noted that, even before the establishment of the Phanariot regime, in other words at the very beginning of the eighteenth century, "the organization of the military forces of the two provinces was becoming . . . almost identical."[8] And these trends became more and more evident as the century went on. Although the size of the regular military forces decreased markedly during the eighteenth century, the developing strength, such as it was, of movements of popular resistance including actions by *haiduks,* armed peasants — particularly in Transylvania — in times of resistance or revolutionary movement (not to mention the formation of units of anti-Ottoman volunteers during wars involving Austria and Russia against the Porte) paved the way for the military renaissance of the nineteenth century. In this respect we must also stress the capital importance of the establishment of the corps of military frontiersmen at the borders of Transylvania and of the Banat.

Historical sources show the continuity of military life in the Romanian provinces throughout the eighteenth century although an occasional decline in the size of the armed forces is recorded during the second half of that century. In 1711, Dimitrie Cantemir, the ally of Peter the Great, did his best to raise a sizable army in a short time in Moldavia. He established thirty colonelships and called the entire population to military service. "It was then that everyone became a soldier: servants quit the boyars, farmhands left their masters, and many other simple people left their habitations, took money, and joined military units." The chronicler added that many of the new soldiers who could not obtain weapons made their own spears and mounted such horses as they could find.[9] All these men obeyed Cantemir's order. As stated in the chronicle: "everybody mount a horse and join the army."[10] However, because the armed forces of Moldavia which Prince Dimitrie Cantemir could dispose of at the time of his accession to the throne were numerically small (particularly in comparison with those that his father Constantin Cantemir had available a few decades earlier, i.e., nineteen units of 1,000 men each[11]), and because he had so short a time available for training his army, Dimitrie Cantemir's forces showed little prowess in combat. After all, the men he was able to draft were not only "military men but also shoemakers, tailors, furriers, tavern-keepers, servants of boyars,"[12] in other words, improvised soldiers without military experience.

Cantemir's contemporary, Constantin Brâncoveanu, ruler of Wallachia, had himself, because of financial exigencies, reduced the size of the irregular armed forces during the first years of the eighteenth century, which resulted in weakening the military power of that province. Nevertheless, in 1711, when Cantemir tried to rally his people against the Turks, Brâncoveanu could command a fairly significant army of greater military potential than the improvised forces of Moldavia.[14] In 1714 Brâncoveanu was removed from power. He was subsequently arrested, together with his entire family. He and his four sons were beheaded in Constantinople.

Following the brief reign of Ştefan Cantacuzino, the Phanariot regime was also established in Wallachia. The same successor of Cantemir, Nicolas Mavrocordat, became the first Phanariot ruler in Wallachia. He immediately started drastically cutting the armed forces by eliminating tax exemptions for military personnel.[15] He was to pay dearly for this action: during the Austro-Turkish war of 1716–18, an Austrian military unit removed him from his residence in Bucharest. A similar attempt directed against the Moldavian prince Michael Racovita the following year failed, as Racovita's army, supported by Tatar forces, destroyed the expeditionary force sent to Iaşi by the Austrians.[16]

During the following decades, the Moldavian and Wallachian armed forces remained smaller than they had been in the seventeenth century when the Wallachian ruler Matei Basarab was able to discourage the Porte from intervening militarily in the affairs of his province.[17] What matters, however, is that, in one way or another, the armed forces of the Romanian provinces continued to exist and, sometimes, for that matter, even registered significant improvements. This was true during the reign of Grigore Ghica who, indeed, was forced by contemporary events to reorganize and even enlarge the armed forces under his command. In 1727 the Porte ordered Ghica to ready his forces to contain a revolt by the Tatars. Ghica's army was characterized by a chronicler as "numerous and proud."[18] His infantry numbered 3,000 men; his cavalry, as many as 4,000.[19] And to these one had to add "courtiers and retinues of the great boyars."[20] The chronicle states that the princely army had twelve cannon.[21] Following the expedition against the Tatars which assisted in the defeat of the rebels, the prince disbanded his army; the chronicler adds, "He thanked all his officers and soldiers and allowed them to return to their homes."[22] A decade later, during the war between Turkey and the Austrians and Russians, Grigore Ghica again took measures to strengthen Moldavian armed might "by preparing his forces and assembling an army recruited from among foreigners and natives."[23] The Moldavian units defeated and forced the retreat of the Austrian units which had entered Moldavia.[24]

Grigore Ghica tried, at least at certain times, to strengthen the military forces of Moldavia, but it was the Mavrocordat princes — Nicholas as well as his son Constantin — who helped weaken the military strength of the Romanian Principalities. The nineteenth-century Romanian historian and patriot, Nicolae Bălcescu, rightly stated that Nicholas, from the very beginning of his reign, had weakened "the army and the militia": his son Constantin "ended altogether the traditional military organization of the country."[25]

Fiscal exigencies were the chief reason for this reform which primarily affected the territorial basis of the army. Constantin Mavrocordat retained, in 1739, a few hundred members of the old army, but added to it his personal guard of Albanians and Turks. Moreover, 1,620 members of the traditional territorial units were incorporated into the reformed armed forces, and the rest became subject to taxation.[26] One must stress, however, that weakening the armed forces did not mean their entire suppression even though the reductions were tantamount to *de facto* suppression.

The military corporations directed by leading dignitaries which were to be found in every district of Moldavia and Wallachia and which were recruited from among free peasants were reduced in size, beginning with the reigns of George Duca in Moldavia and Constantin Brâncoveanu in Wallachia. These reductions continued until they reached their height under Constantin Mavrocordat. Tax exemptions were ended; the military corporations were drastically cut in size or even altogether destroyed. However, contemporary sources — as Constantin C. Giurescu shows[27] — mention the existence of these military formations, as well as of certain categories of paid military units, throughout the eighteenth century. This demonstrates the continued existence, at least verbally, of traditional military institutions and formations.

While the armed forces of Moldavia and Wallachia were reduced in number, the Romanians of Transylvania were actively resisting the establishment of Habsburg domination. The participation of Romanian contingents, side by side with Hungarian and Slovak forces, in Rákóczi's armies was impressive. Prestigious military commanders are named in the records, as is the existence of Romanian units. We must also record the role played by the inhabitants of the Apuseni Mountains; they, along with the *haiduks,* constituted the core of the uprisings of the second half of the eighteenth century, and, particularly, one of their leaders Pintea the Brave, whose feats have become legendary.[28] These were the first military ventures of the Transylvanian Romanian masses in the eighteenth century. Important, too, was the military action of the Banat peasants who rose in 1735. The rebel army numbered 3,000 men comprising fourteen battalions. The rebels were defeated and brutally punished, but the spirit of revolt and resistance remained alive in the Banat for years to come.[29] In the spring of 1744, Romanians from southern Transylvania rose in arms against the forcible union of the Orthodox and Catholic churches.[30] For the same reasons the Romanian Orthodox masses rose again in 1760. This time the affected area was larger, and the imperial authorities, under the leadership of General Buccow, were prompted to put down the rebellion in blood.[31] These revolutionary activities excited the Romanian — and also the Hungarian and Serbian — masses and thus contributed to increase their spirit of militancy. Apparently, the establishment of border guard regiments was in fact a Habsburg attempt to channel the revolutionary energy of these peoples to its own advantage. And this presumption was substantiated by the events recorded during the peasant war of 1784.[32]

Any discussion of the military history of the Romanians for the first five and subsequent decades of the eighteenth century would be incomplete without reference to the effective participation by Romanian soldiers and officers in the armies of Charles XII of Sweden, Charles VI of Austria, Catherine II of Russia, and Frederick II of Prussia, to mention only a few.[33] One must also mention, among new military formations generic to that country, the Albanians (*Arnăuți*), recruited among populations south of the Danube for guard duty for ruling princes, who represented the principal foreign military elements in the

Romanian provinces even though they were readily assimilated into the Romanian community, and the so-called *mocani* — recruited among Transylvanian shepherds. The very existence of these units indicated the natural unity of the Romanian lands in the military field.[34] Note that soldiers frequently were called up in training camps, under the military leadership of the princes themselves, that they took part in several military engagements, and that military units were employed in the fortification of towns — albeit for the benefit of the Turks. And all these activities helped strengthen their military abilities.

During the second half of the eighteenth century, certain changes occurred with respect to the development of Romanian armed forces. The most important new factor was the establishment of Romanian border guard units in Transylvania and the Banat — the First and Second Transylvanian regiments, the Banat battalion, and the regiment of dragoons.[35] At first, because of their desire to improve their social status, Romanian peasants were anxious to join these units. The notary of Mediaş, Michael Heidendorf, remarked that "in case of need, and if allowed, probably all Romanian serfs would have become border guards."[36] But being required to leave their villages and to become Greek Catholic, and getting only relatively lower fiscal obligations, created disaffection and even led to uprisings, such as that recorded in 1763. Nevertheless, organization of the Second regiment began in 1762 and was complete by 1764, when the First regiment was also established. Moreover, border guard regiments of Szeklers were also created in 1764, as were the Szekler hussar regiment and the regiment of Romanian dragoons.[37] One must also mention the establishment, in 1768 in the Banat, of a Romanian border guard battalion which, together with Serbian units, constituted one of the elements of the Romanian-Illyrian regiment.[38] The Romanian border guards distinguished themselves during the campaigns of the late eighteenth and early nineteenth centuries.[39] Colonel Heidendorf, referring to the attitude of the soldiers of the Second regiment during the war against the Turks, stated that he was "proud to have been the commander of these brave men."[40] During the battle of Arcole, one of this regiment's battalions fought heroically in defense of the bridge of Arcole. Napoleon himself referred to it as the *infernal battalion*.[41] In any event, the establishment and existence of these Romanian units constituted the nucleus of the regular, modern, Romanian army.

In the Principalities themselves the princes of the last decades of the eighteenth century took certain steps designed to achieve the reorganization of the armed forces. Nicolae Bâlcescu did condemn the Mavrocordat princes for having limited the size of the army altogether too drastically, but he also observed that Alexandru Ypsilanti was "the only Phanariot to whom gratitude must be expressed for improvements made during his rule." For it was he who "reorganized the army in 1775 by adding other armed men to the depleted contingents."[42] Ypsilanti's forces numbered 2,180 soldiers stationed inside the province and another 3,144 soldiers led by seventy-eight captains stationed on the frontiers.[43] His Moldavian contemporary, Grigore Al. Ghica, also tried to increase the province's armed manpower[44] but was by no means as successful as Ypsilanti. Nevertheless, one reason the Porte gave for Ghica's execution in 1774 was his attempted reform of the army.

The armed forces of Wallachia reached their greatest size during the reign of Nicolae Mavrogheni, who was not a Phanariot but an islander from Paros. As dragoman of the admiral of the Ottoman fleet he secured the Wallachian throne on the eve of the Austro-Russo–Ottoman conflict of 1787–92. As the war broke out he despatched his troops to the frontiers while organizing new forces which, in due course, displayed their prowess on the battlefield. His forces numbered 10,000 combat soldiers plus another 3,000 or so in border units. According to Turkish sources his army numbered as many as 16,000 men. Contemporary records also indicate that his armies included tavernkeepers, shoemakers, and itinerant merchants. Mavrogheni was concerned with supplying his forces; his soldiers wore a variety of uniforms distinguishable by rank. All companies also carried flags. In any event, that army which operated on the side of the Turks — at one stage of the war Mavrogheni was assigned the supreme command in Wallachia — fought successfully in 1788 and 1789 not only in Wallachia but also in Moldavia and Transylvania where the presence of Mavrogheni's men excited the spirits of the Transylvanian masses, the Romanians in particular.[45]

Only a few years before the establishment of Mavrogheni's army and the extension of its military activities, the military abilities and fervor of the revolutionary masses of Transylvania were evidenced during the great peasant uprising of 1784, led by Horea, Cloşca, and Crişan. The rebels attacked not only manors but also took successful action against certain cities. The expansion of the uprising, the recorded collaboration among varying peasant detachments, the victories achieved, the rebels' ability to defeat even regular forces at Brad, Lupşa, and Remeţi, the manner in which the revolutionary armies were organized, the art of mobilizing the peasant masses[46] — all stress the significance of that historic moment which remained even during the nineteenth century "a permanent appeal to struggle."[47]

Of special interest is the development of the volunteer movement which was recorded during the wars between the Ottoman empire and Austria and Russia. The first opportunity to organize units of volunteers during the second half of the eighteenth century occurred during the Russo-Turkish war of 1768–74. Artisans, merchants, and particularly, peasants comprised the bulk of the detachments which assisted the Russian armed forces. The size of these detachments reached into the thousands.[48] It is also noteworthy that anti-Ottoman boyars suggested, in 1770, the creation of a regular army of 12,000 men in Moldavia and one of 20,000 men in Wallachia which would consist in part of volunteers.[49]

Romanian volunteers were to be found in the Russian as well as in the Austrian armies during the Russo-Austro-Turkish war of 1787–92. During the battle of Rimnic, when Suvorov scored a major victory over the Turks, the Romanian volunteers captured five Turkish flags.[50] Romanian participation in military activity on Romanian soil during the second half of the eighteenth century is part of the historic process of Romanian liberation. The Romanian fighters, chiefly drawn from the ranks of the people, realized on the battlefield that the Turks could be defeated and that it was up to the Romanians to achieve liberation. The volunteer units which participated in these wars represented the nucleus of the national army of the future. At the same time, they were a military training school for volunteers who included, among others, the so-called *panduri* (soldiers recruited primarily from among the free peasants of Little Wallachia). According to the chronicler Ilie Fotino, the *panduri* were "a kind of soldier wearing a simple peasant garb," chiefly "worthy, courageous men more used than others to wearing and manning weapons."[51] Their role was to be most striking in the early nineteenth century.

During the first decade of the century, the preliminaries of another Russo-Turkish war entailed a further change in the military organization of Wallachia. This time it was Constantin Ypsilanti who — determined to break with the Porte with a view to establishing his own rule over several countries under Ottoman control — was concerned with setting up an efficient army. First he increased the size of the princely guard by "adding a large number of Albanian and other mercenaries" and a "mob of armed, foreign, Croats." He was equally concerned with the *panduri* whom he transformed into "a special military corps which he enlarged by adding to it many poor peasants." And the chronicler concludes by stating, "in this manner the voevod Constantin Ypsilanti became the leader of a large number of armies."[52] Nevertheless, since Russia's entry into the war occurred only in the fall of 1806, Ypsilanti was removed from his throne by the Turks and had to flee Wallachia. After the Russians began military action, however, Ypsilanti returned to Bucharest and reorganized his army. According to one chronicler, even before his return he "suggested to the boyars of the [Moldavian] divan the formation of a Moldavian army of 10,000 men who would wear green uniforms and special headgear and who would be known as Macedonian dragoons."[53]

After recovering the Wallachian throne and assuming the new title of "Prince of Moldavia and of Wallachia," Ypsilanti reorganized the army by recruiting a large number of foreigners and by ordering uniforms and weapons. The military units were then sent to the front alongside units of the Russian army.[54] A decree by the tsar even authorized Ypsilanti to "establish ranks in the native army ranging from lieutenant to general," ranks which had "authority on their own . . . but at a lower level than their equivalents in the Russian army."[55] By the end of May 1807, when Ypsilanti was again forced to leave Bucharest and set up headquarters at Focşani, his army was, on his own estimate, made up as follows: 4,500 *panduri,* "Cossacks," and *Arnăuţi* at Craiova; the "Greek" legion numbering 1,500 men to which were also attached 530 "Cossacks" and 300 *panduri* and *Arnăuţi*; 500 soldiers who were with Ypsilanti in Focşani; another 800 men stationed between Buzau and Măxineni in northern Wallachia; another 1,000 odd men comprising the "national guard" of Bucharest; and, finally, 5,000 Moldavian volunteers whom the prince was obligated to maintain.[56]

Both the conclusion of the Russo-Turkish armistice at Slobozia and, even more important, the conflicts with certain Russian generals which forced Ypsilanti to leave the Principalities led to the gradual dissolution of his armies, except for the *pandur* units of Little Wallachia.[57] These units, placed under the leadership of the Russian general Isaiev, performed well during the next few years and continuously increased in numbers. At the end of 1807 there were 2,000 *panduri* in Little Wallachia; in 1810, 3,000; in the spring of 1811, more than 6,000.[58] The free peasant who became a boyar, Tudor Vladimirescu, proved to be a fine commander during the war; and because of his achievements the *panduri* regarded him as their actual leader. A contemporary characterized him as follows: "man of war, audacious, fiery, man of few words but kind and generous, of very sound judgment, and courageous."[59] In any event, during the spring of 1811, Vladimirescu appears to have commanded "more than 6,000 *panduri,*" which did not prevent his receiving permission a few months later to raise yet another battalion.[60] The *panduri* showed their prowess sufficiently to prompt Admiral Tchitchiagov, the last commander of the Russian armies in the Principalities, to suggest in 1812 the organization of a militia in Wallachia of not less than 5,000 *panduri.*[61]

The conclusion of the Peace of Bucharest in May 1812 put the *panduri* in a difficult position. Implicitly, peace meant the dissolution of many a *pandur* unit; moreover, the *panduri* feared Turkish reprisals. Nevertheless, the experience gained during the Russo-Turkish war of 1806-1812 gave the *panduri* useful military training. One should regard their participation in the war as a step toward forming the future modern Romanian army in which the *panduri* were to provide some of the strongest contingents. For Tudor Vladimirescu, too, the experience gained as the main leader of the *panduri* proved to be most valuable. During the war, Vladimirescu mastered planning, learned how to conduct military operations, both defensive and offensive, became acquainted with the art of fortification, with reconnaissance operations, the leadership of military units, and above all, learned military discipline.

The new prince, Ioan Caragea (1812-18), motivated by fiscal considerations as well as by the Porte's opposition to the maintenance of a native military force in Wallachia "destroyed the institution of the *panduri.*"[62] A contemporary observer, Dimitrie Macedonski, stated: "sold like cattle at the fair some were ashamed of having borne that name" while others died "in prisons."[63] Caragea created an atmosphere of crisis by limiting the number of *panduri,* in the spring of 1814, to 701 men, 400 of whom were obliged to serve outside Little Wallachia, and by restricting the tax exemptions heretofore granted the *panduri* to all but a few, thus making them subject to paying taxes on wine, beehives, and tobacco.[64] Together with the general dissatisfaction prevalent in Wallachia, the disaffection of the *panduri* led to their revolt at the end of 1814. The uprising lasted until February 1815 and ended with the defeat of the insurgents. In fact, this revolt should be regarded as the prelude to the revolution of 1821.

The revolutionary events of 1821 mark a turning point in the history of the Romanians. Those events began the process of forming the modern Romanian state. Its program was the foundation of that elaborated by the generation of 1848.[65] From a military standpoint, the revolution of 1821 began the reconstruction of the national and modern army, the army which was to play its part in creating the Romanian state.

The revolution, which broke out on January 30, spread rapidly because of growing popular support and also because of effective military planning. The revolution in the Romanian provinces had many elements in common with comparable actions in contemporary Italy, Spain, Portugal, as well as in Latin America. The detachments which Tudor Vladimirescu commanded as leader and initiator of the revolution consisted, particularly at the beginning of the movement, of *panduri* who had fought under his command during the war of 1806–1812. These units acted like experienced formations. Later, as the peasant masses responded to Vladimirescu's call to arms (a chronicler even noted that he "had as auxiliary soldiers the entire Romanian peasantry"[66]), they themselves became part of the *panduri,* as the *panduri* were the core of the army until the end of the revolution.

Recruitment centers and organizational headquarters were established in fortified monasteries occupied by the revolutionary forces. Garrisons were stationed in these monasteries and they also served as food, arms, and munitions depots, thus becoming centers of resistance to the enemies of the revolution. The revolutionary army, known as the *people's assembly,* was stationed in military camps first at Țînțăreni, close to the capital of Little Wallachia, then at Slatina en route to Wallachia proper where they were set up at Cotroceni near Bucharest.[67] Vladimirescu organized infantry detachments comprising regiments of 1,000 men each, subdivided into companies of 100 men each, cavalry detachments, each numbering between 50 and 200 men, and also a small artillery unit.[68] One should observe that Vladimirescu did not organize his armies into battalions, in the Russian manner of 1806–1812, as he preferred organization into regiments each of which comprised twice the manpower of a battalion.[69] The weapons consisted of swords, spears, and firearms — guns and pistols — and a few cannon as well as bludgeons and pitchforks.[70] The army was well disciplined and the peasant soldiers were subject to regular drills.

The army was established in January and grew in size during the weeks that followed. Vladimirescu assembled it near the Olt River, at Slatina, from which the "assembly of the people" moved into Wallachia proper in the direction of Bucharest. The army, on March 22, 1821, numbered 6,000 infantry and 2,000 horsemen; the number of commanders was about a hundred.[71] Vladimirescu was in charge of the march of the "assembly of the people" to the capital city of Wallachia, as the occupation of Bucharest was tantamount to giving the revolutionary forces control of the entire province. Despite bad weather and the rather flimsy quality of the military equipment of the peasant army, the march proceeded at an average speed of twenty-five kilometers per day, a normal rate of progress for marches of contemporary regular armies.[72] On April 2, 1821, Vladimirescu made his entry into Bucharest. Several days later Prince Alexandru Ypsilanti, leader of the *Hetairea,* also reached Colentina on the city's outskirts.[73]

Vladimirescu was able to conclude an agreement with some of the boyars but his alliance with the *Hetairea* did not work well. Ypsilanti withdrew to Tîrgovişte when Tsar Alexander I failed to support the liberation movements of Romanians and Greeks in the Romanian Principalities. The hetairist forces which had been assembled in Moldavia, where the leaders of the Greek liberation movement arrived from southern Russia, showed little military prowess from the very beginning of their activities. Without meaningful assistance from these forces and, particularly, from Russian contingents, the Romanian rebel forces were too weak to oppose the Ottoman armies by themselves. Consequently, concurrently with intensification of efforts to increase the number of recruits in Bucharest, to improve their armaments, and to maintain military discipline, Vladimirescu was forced to start negotiations with the representatives of the Porte.[74] Note, however, that throughout this period Vladimirescu continued to reinforce Bucharest in order to stage a resistance movement should the tsar's forces appear on behalf of the rebels after all.[75] His negotiations with the Porte proved to be disappointing, which prompted the evacuation of Bucharest.[76] Vladimirescu's army withdrew into the northern part of Little Wallachia where he intended to make a stand in the fortified monasteries of the region.

As the *Hetairea* suspected him of dealing with the Ottomans, Vladimirescu was kidnapped by order of the chief of the *Hetairea.* After a mock trial he was executed; his body was never recovered. Nevertheless, his army continued its orderly withdrawal, and upon crossing the Olt River, it proved its military prowess by defeating the Turkish forces at Drăgăşani on June 11.[77] Ten days later, however, a second battle between the hetairist army, supported by a detachment of *panduri,* proved to be disastrous.[78] The Romanian Principalities were occupied by the victorious Ottoman forces. We should add that the Romanian revolutionary army disbanded almost entirely after the battle of Drăgăşani partly because it had reached Little Wallachia, the homeland of most of the combatants, and partly because Vladimirescu was dead and Ottoman forces were so strongly present in the Romanian provinces. The *panduri* opted for cessation of hostilities until they could be resumed under more auspicious circumstances. Nevertheless, several detachments did fight on the side of the hetairists in the second battle of Drăgăşani; others continued to engage in guerrilla warfare for yet another few months.[79]

The Romanian Principalities might have been subject to Ottoman occupation, but the revolution helped convince the Porte of the necessity to end Phanariot rule in Romanian lands. Thus, in 1822, Romanian princes began to rule in Wallachia and in Moldavia. Moreover, a program of reforms was to be inaugurated. In 1829, another Russo-Turkish war, in which *panduri* units also took part, came to an end. By the Treaty of Adrianople, Ottoman suzerainty was limited by increased autonomy for the Romanian provinces, by termination of Ottoman monopoly over the distribution of the main products of Moldavia and Wallachia, and by the return of three fortified towns held by the Turks north of the Danube.[80] Thus, establishment of a modern Romanian state seemed at hand. True, as a result of the weakening of Ottoman suzerainty, intervention by the protective power, tsarist Russia, in the internal affairs of the Principalities became more acute; in fact, the Russians occupied the Romanian provinces for half a decade.[81] During this period of occupation, the Romanian boyars, under strict Russian surveillance, worked out the Organic Statutes — the fundamental laws of Moldavia and Wallachia for the next three decades of the nineteenth century. Still, the period of the Organic Statutes was one beginning of modernization although progress was limited by the maintenance of an *ancien régime*.

The modern national army was established in the two Romanian provinces at the level of development of the border guard regiments of Transylvania and the Banat which had proved their worth in the late eighteenth and early nineteenth centuries.[82] The governor of the Romanian Principalities, General Kisseleff, stated his government's objectives in 1830 as follows: "The creation of the militia marks the core of an army which, under Russia's supervision and on the basis of the Russian model, will perform well in case of war with Turkey."[83] The immediate objectives stated in the military statutes annexed to the Organic Statutes were ensuring internal order and protecting the frontiers even though, according to law, the only function envisaged was the "surveillance of the borders with respect to trading activities and quarantines."[84]

Since it was set up during a period of occupation, commanded by Russian officers, and equipped with Russian arms, the Russian government regarded the Moldavian-Wallachian militia as only an auxiliary Russian force. Nevertheless, according to Nicolae Iorga, this revived army took care of "the needs of a century past."[85] It represented the beginnings of a national army which, like the border guard regiments of Transylvania and of the Banat, was to respond to the needs of national liberation. Moreover, as many have justly observed, the militia, originally created for internal police and border guard duty, gradually became a force which comprised "almost all the armies of the period."[86] We should also add that a foreign observer thought Romanian soldiers "excellent,"[87] and that they were rapidly moving toward the level of other contemporary armies.

As far as the structure of the units of the two small armies is concerned, one should note that three mixed regiments were established in Wallachia by combining infantry battalions and cavalry squadrons, and one mixed regiment was set up in Moldavia.[88] In 1848, before the revolution, each of the Wallachian infantry regiments, which remained after a separate regiment had been drawn from the cavalry squadron in 1835,[89] was enlarged by a third battalion.[90] In 1844, the Wallachian army had 5,806 men;[91] during the early years of the period of the Organic Statutes, the Moldavian army numbered 1,554 men.[92] Regimental garrisons were established in Wallachia at Bucharest, Ploieşti, and Craiova and in Moldavia at Iaşi.[93] An artillery unit was also established in Wallachia,[94] as was a firemen's unit in Bucharest and other such units in the principal towns of Moldavia.[95] A military vessel and several gunboats represented the naval forces of the two provinces.

The soldiers and officers wore modern uniforms; oriental clothing was completely given up.[96] Russia supplied the Principalities with arms, 4,000 guns of the 1809 model.[97] In the fall of 1834, flags were assigned to every regiment.[98] Commanders were drawn from retired Russian army officers, from Romanians trained in the Russian army, and also and primarily, from young Romanians, albeit mostly of boyar origin. Originally, military ranks corresponded to civilian ranks.[99] That a fairly large number of young patriots volunteered for military service indicates the significance contemporaries attached to the military renaissance. The recruitment of military personnel did, however, encounter many difficulties, chiefly because Romanian people feared that Russia would use the Romanian armed forces abroad.[100]

Soldiers were drafted during the summer months into military camps where they performed military exercises and even maneuvers.[101]

In 1838 a school for soldiers was established in Bucharest.[102] An officers' school was established, also in Bucharest, a decade later.[103] The army also had a few young officers who had received their military education in Russia, Prussia, France, Italy, Belgium, and other countries.[104] It is also noteworthy that books on military subjects, mostly but not exclusively translations of Russian and French manuals, were published in the Romanian Principalities.[105] Nicolae Bălcescu produced two large historical studies of the armed forces of Wallachia and Moldavia which urged qualitative improvements and the development of a national army.[106]

The period of the Organic Statutes marked the beginning of the modern national army whose cadres were, however, quite small. Yet, during this very period, auxiliary military forces were also established. In this respect, historic traditions were merely being followed. The border villages provided the manpower for border guard units, each unit being the responsibility of 120 peasant families which had to support four armed men at all times, a corporal and a soldier belonging to the regular army.[107] Inside the country *dorobanţi* units were organized in Wallachia and *slujitori* units in Moldavia; these were also supported by the villagers; as auxiliaries to the local administrative units, they had to bear weapons ten days per month.[108] According to Bălcescu "the power of the state rested not with the regular army but with the national reserves,"[109] in other words, with the military ability of the entire people to take care of their country's needs.

The revolution of 1848 marked a new stage in the military history of the Romanian provinces.[110] In Moldavia, the revolution could not be carried out to its fullest extent because of the proximity to Russia. In fact, Moldavia was occupied by Russian forces at the beginning of the summer. In Wallachia, however, a revolutionary government took over for more than three months; in Transylvania, the Romanian revolution manifested itself concurrently with the Hungarian one. In Moldavia the army remained generally loyal to Prince Mihai Sturdza, considering the prevailing circumstances, and we should also note that peasant contingents, too, participated in the revolution. In Wallachia and in Transylvania, the armed forces participated fully in revolutionary activities.

The regular armed forces took part in the revolution, both regular units of the Wallachian army and the Transylvanian border guard units. The latter numbered, inclusive of reserve units, some 25,000 men.[111] These forces, according to the plans of the revolutionary leaders, were to be the main available military force which would also intervene in Wallachia to support the revolutionary regime. The provisional government also began to reshuffle the military leadership of Wallachian regiments. Through dismissals and retirements, the commander of the army and the commandants of four regiments, as well as the commander of artillery forces, were replaced.[112] On the other hand, officers true to the revolution were rapidly promoted; this transformed military cadres. Foreign specialists were recruited to assist native officers. They included such men as the Polish colonel Zablocki and the French officers Dessain, Sabattier, and Lefrançais.

Throughout the revolution, the Romanian border guards of Transylvania represented the stronghold of the Romanian National Committee.[114] This also helped to increase the military efficacy of the Romanian peasant armies. In Wallachia, too, from the very beginning of the revolution at the Islaz assembly, the presence of certain military units was evident. The outbreak of the revolution in Bucharest, a few days after the meeting of Islaz, was encouraged by the army's refusal to act against the revolutionaries. Although a few reactionary Romanian officers were able to stage counterrevolutionary actions during the first month of the revolution and even to sway, albeit temporarily, some soldiers away from the revolution, it should be said that in general the army remained faithful to the revolutionary cause. Soldiers and officers took the oath of allegiance; moreover, on the eve of the entry of Ottoman forces into Bucharest, the military units were given new flags bearing the national colors. As a matter of fact, the second infantry regiment, together with a company of the first regiment and 165 Bucharest firemen, fought against the invader in the heart of the capital on September 25, 1848. The unequal struggle — 900 Romanian soldiers and officers fought against 5,000–6,000 Turks and inflicted serious losses on the Ottoman forces — marks one of the highlights of the history of the Romanian revolution of 1848.[115]

In addition to the regular armed forces, irregular armed forces participated in the revolution. These fought well, particularly in Transylvania. In Wallachia these were the national guard and the "volunteer" units as well as units of *panduri* formed in the villages of Little Wallachia. In Transylvania they were part of the Romanian revolutionary army established by the decision of the Romanian National Committee. The Romanian revolutionary army comprised fifteen legions,[116] of which those of the Apuseni Mountains proved particularly effective in combat. The irregular units were occasionally quite large. At the beginning of September 1848, the Bucharest national guard numbered 10,375 men divided into five legions of ten battalions each.[117]

Units of the national guard in Wallachian villages consisted of hundreds of members;[118] some 20,000 peasants, who responded to the appeals of revolutionary leaders, also formed military units.[119] The armed forces commanded by Avram Iancu in the Apuseni Mountains were estimated at some 25,000 men.[120] The quality of weapons was the principal military problem during the revolution. Avram Iancu's peasant army used cannon made out of bronze, some obtained by melting down church bells, or out of wood reinforced with metal.[121] The artillery forces provided cannon to the revolutionaries in Wallachia. There was a painful lack of firearms, guns and pistols. In the spring of 1849, Avram Iancu's army had only some 1,300 guns — one for fifteen to twenty men.[122] Only 10 percent of the members of the Bucharest national guard possessed firearms.[123] Among the 30,000 fighters encamped at Riureni, in Little Wallachia, only 4,000 — mostly members of the regular army — had weapons comparable to those of contemporary armies; 8,000 were poorly armed, and nearly 20,000 peasants bore only primitive weapons.[124]

In Wallachia only the battle fought by soldiers and firemen on September 25 is worth mentioning. This, because the revolutionary general Gheorghe Magheru — on the advice of the British consul Colquhoun and particularly on the basis of his own assessment of the relative strength of his forces and those of the Russo-Turkish forces moving toward the Riureni camp — dissolved the camp on October 10. On the other hand, in Transylvania the several battles and encounters recorded over a period of months serve as evidence for the effectiveness of the Romanian armed forces. Particularly worthy of our attention are the feats of the peasant army of Avram Iancu, which repeatedly defeated expeditionary forces sent against it by the Hungarian revolutionary government and thus maintained control over the citadel in the Apuseni Mountains until the fall of 1849. The organization of that army, its discipline, that each unit had a certain position to protect and that all succeeded in doing so, not to mention its prowess despite supply problems and its battle tactics — all prove the value of the soldiers and of their commander, Avram Iancu.[125] His feats also drew praise from his enemies. At one stage, Iancu ceased hostilities against Hungarian revolutionaries whose forces had attacked his for months on end and suggested the conclusion of an alliance. Nicolae Bălcescu expressed his admiration for the leaders of the irregular Transylvanian Romanian armies. He stated that the "generals of that peasant army were priests and young graduates of schools of theology, philosophy, and law." And he added, "while they lacked knowledge of military affairs they acquired such knowledge in combat."[126] In Wallachia, General Magheru "captain-general of all irregular forces . . . and general inspector of the national guard"[127] is worthy of our attention.

The revolution was defeated throughout the Romanian lands. Repression and the establishment of counterrevolutionary regimes was the old regime's answer to the revolution. Nevertheless, its achievements could not be destroyed. Revolutionary ideology and revolutionary programs remained focal for the liberation movements of the peoples of Central and Southeastern Europe. In Transylvania, the border guard regiments were suppressed in 1851. The contemporary observer, Gheorghe Barițiu, regarded that action as a blow for "not only the armed Romanian population of the past century but also for all Romanian inhabitants of Transylvania."[128] Although the organized military force of the Romanians was thus terminated in Transylvania, in Moldavia and Wallachia, the new rulers, Barbu Știrbei and Grigore Al. Ghica, paid much attention to the army within the limits allowed by the suzerain and protecting powers. Following dismemberment of the military institutions of the revolution, the new princes reorganized, in 1850 and 1851, the territorial forces — frontier guards and *dorobanți* — on the basis of postrevolutionary laws.[129] Știrbei wanted to incorporate the territorial units into those of the permanent, regular army; in 1852, the *dorobanți* were presented with flags.[130] The two princes succeeded in increasing the number of artillery pieces.[131] In Moldavia, maneuvers were conducted for the combined armies (infantry, cavalry, and artillery).[132] The army was used, particularly in Wallachia, to construct modern roads.[133] A new vessel was added to the small Wallachian fleet.[134] Young men were sent abroad for military studies,[135] and arms and other military hardware were ordered from abroad, particularly from Belgium.[136] One should also mention the publication of books on military matters.[137]

The three successive occupations of the Romanian Principalities — Russo-Turkish, 1848–51; Russian, 1853–54; Austro-Turkish, 1854–57 — put the brakes on the development of the military institutions of Wallachia and Moldavia. Nevertheless, at the end of these difficult times, a resolution by the *ad hoc* Moldavian Assembly of November 6, 1857, is worth noting since it gives evidence that reorganization of the armed forces was one of the main aims of the Romanians on the eve of the establishment of their national state. The *ad hoc* assembly, called on the basis of the decisions of the Congress of Paris of 1856, unanimously adopted a resolution which expressed its desire to establish a "national armed force" to be "used only for the defense of their territory and of internal security." The resolution stressed that the Principalities did not and would not want to create an offensive army, which might convey the notion of their being aggressive forces; all they desired, it was stated, was to set up a military organization which would "safeguard and assure their peaceful existence." The desire that the "organization of the national military force should be incorporated into a common system of defense for both principalities" was also stressed. The resolution also envisaged the construction of fortresses whose "defense would be the exclusive right of the national army."[138] In 1858, when the guaranteeing powers had assumed the role of protection and granted the principalities a new fundamental law — while denying them unification — the permanent armies of Moldavia and Wallachia numbered 11,061 men, exclusive of the territorial forces of 14,000 men.[139]

The establishment of the modern Romanian state through the union of Moldavia and Wallachia brought with it the need for reorganization and intensive modernization of the armed forces. The attainment of independence and the consolidation of the unitary state, the ensuing goals of the nation, made military reform a highest-level priority. Prince Cuza wrote the French consul Victor Place in 1859 that he wished the Romanian army to "be ready for everything."[140] On another occasion, Cuza stated that the army had the duty to show "that there was a Romania."[141] It was the question of unification and, subsequently, of a "reorganization . . . based on a new system,"[142] a reorganization which must take into account the problems of supplies, of funding, and of training officers and soldiers. The objectives of the army were not offensive. A radical newspaper of the period stated: ". . . We are not arming ourselves to annex territories, we are arming ourselves in the manner of the Serbs, the Montenegrins, of our own ancestors, to strengthen ourselves, to gain respectability, so that foreigners will no longer be able to enter the Romanian lands as if these were lands of slavery and of dead men. . . ."[143]

The army of the years of the Organic Statutes with its small contingents and insufficient funds and weapons was to be transformed radically. Even if financial means were limited, the human resources available to the rulers of the state were quite ample. One should note that even during the Crimean War, Gheorghe Adrian, one of the revolutionaries in exile, had conceived of partisan warfare to be conducted with the assistance of "the entire nation."[144] The international situation and its limitations on political maneuvering, not to mention the financial resources of the young Romanian national state, were hardly conducive to a rapid increase in the size of the military forces, but it was still possible substantially to improve the training of a "nucleus" of a new army. Thus, in his message of December 18, 1859, Prince Cuza sought the formation of "solid cadres which, in the hour of need, will be able to accommodate all Romanians who will be destined to come to the aid of their country."[145] The mobilization of the masses also posed social and political problems on the eve of the agrarian reform, when conservative forces opposed arming the peasantry. Nevertheless, the idea of universal military service was embraced by all. Even though the ideas of the radical liberals on establishing a national guard in towns were rejected by Prince Cuza and his prime minister, Mihail Kogalniceanu, the law on the organization of the army of December 9, 1864, assured the existence of a standing army of 19,345 men. In addition, three categories of men aged between seventeen and twenty and between twenty-six and fifty could also be recruited and were subject to military training and instruction.[146] "Our army," stated Cuza in his message of December 18, 1864, "was given a new draft and organization law which is compatible with our financial resources and yet allows for improved means of defense."[147]

The unification of the two armies was a complex, multilateral process which was carried out efficiently after the double election of Prince Cuza. The greatest achievements were recorded in the summer of 1859, when the two armies were assembled at Floresti in Wallachia to provide the necessary military strength to oppose a possible intervention by Austrian or Turkish forces, and subsequently, in 1860 when a common minister of war was appointed although the two principalities had not yet unified their political and administrative institutions.[148] The modernization of the army was carried out energetically. A permanent council of military training was set up; three command posts were established in Bucharest, Iaşi, and Craiova; promotions were regulated by law and a set of regulations established procedures for calling up reserves and for enrolling volunteers into the armed forces. The *Monitorul oastei* (*The Army Monitor*), official journal of the armed forces, and the review *Rômania militară* (*Military Romania*) were the first of many periodicals concerned with military affairs. Regimental schools were also established. All these actions contributed to the "radical transformation" of which the publicist Ulysse de Marsillac spoke a few years later.[149]

The new rulers of the Romanian Principalities were also greatly concerned with creating an officer corps and with training young officers who would attain the levels of proficiency manifest in the advanced countries of Europe. The centralization of the School of Military Officers in Bucharest was decided on July 18, 1862,[150] and this decision was also to promote unification of the state's military structures. Napoleon III showed his approval of that decision by admitting a number of young Romanians to such famous French schools as Saint-Cyr, Saumur, Metz, and Brest. At the same time, young Romanian officers took part in military operations in Italy, Mexico, and Africa.[151] A French military mission was sent to Bucharest in 1860 and it helped in modernizing and training the Romanian army.[152] Purchase of weapons was speeded, but importation was made difficult by actions of the Ottoman and the Habsburg empires. The establishment of military workshops and an arsenal, importation of a projectile foundry from Belgium, and the concurrent creation of a small arms industry and a cannon foundry helped to supplement, at least in part, the limited quantities of armaments which could be imported.[153]

In any event, toward the end of Cuza's reign, Romania had a modern army which comprised seven infantry regiments, two cavalry regiments, one artillery regiment, one light infantry battalion, one battalion of engineers, and one battalion of firemen, as well as six squadrons and two companies of gendarmes, ten battalions of border guards, and thirty squadrons of *dorobanţi*.[154] Writing to Napoleon III in the fall of 1865, Cuza told him that the Romanian army had 70,000 rifled and 25,000 nonrifled guns as well as 72 rifled cannon. With respect to manpower, Cuza stated that he could count on a standing army of 20,000 men "recruited from all classes of society, well armed, well equipped, whose number could be increased to three times its size by calling the reserves;" an additional 12,000 border guards, and 8,000 *dorobanţi* rounded out these figures.[155] These were impressive statistics symptomatic of the significance of the Union of the Principalities in the military history of Romania.

In 1866, following Cuza's abdication and the designation of Charles of Hohenzollern as Prince of Romania, a change in the future status of the country appeared inevitable. That was, of course, one of the primary reasons for Romanian political leaders' choosing a foreign prince related to a ruling dynasty. They hoped that such a choice would further recognition of Romania's independence by the European powers. During the decade before the renewed Eastern crisis which was to provide a propitious scene for staging a successful war of liberation, Romanian political actions designed to increase Romania's importance as a European nation were accompanied by strengthening the armed forces on the base laid during the reign of Cuza.

In the summer of 1866, as in the summer of 1859, calling up the army was designed as warning interested parties of the Romanian rulers' intentions. On June 16, 1866, the Austrian ambassador to Constantinople stated, "We must today expect the establishment of an independent Romania." And referring also to Serbia's winning independence, he added, "We will have to deal with a series of Piedmonts on our borders."[156]

During 1867–68, the radical government of Ştefan Golescu and, later, of Nicolae Golescu paid special attention to military affairs. It was decided to admit into the officer corps any officer of Romanian origin who had served in foreign armies. A shooting society was set up; paramilitary activities were promoted; new, larger military units were established; every effort was made to modernize the army's arsenal of weapons through importing Krupp cannon, Dreyse guns from Prussia, and Peabody guns from the United States.[157] The French military mission was retained until 1868 and Prince Charles also supported a Prussian military mission.[158] The radicals also concentrated on arming militia forces and the civic guard and sought donations from the entire nation to acquire the necessary weapons.[159]

Toward the end of 1868, under pressure from Prussia and France, Charles was forced to withdraw his support of the Golescu government. After a few moderate governments took their turn in office, governmental power was assumed by the conservatives who were to retain it for half a decade. But even under these changed circumstances, military preparations continued unabated. In 1869 measures were taken to encourage noncommissioned officers to reenlist, and during the summer of that very year, Charles' order for an army call up at Furceni characterized the army as the "school of progress for the people."[160] The arrival of arms for the militias was announced in the fall.[161] The establishment in December 1871 of a higher military school, repeated military inspections by the prince himself, the creation of military decorations, and above all, the establishment during the summer of 1872 of eight *dorobanţi* and eight *călăraşi* regiments[162] bear witness to concern for consolidating the country's military forces. In the fall of 1872, 11,000 soldiers took part in maneuvers. The maneuvers took place over a period of fifteen days and over a territory over 120 square kilometers. Two years later, for the first time, foreign military observers were present at maneuvers by the Romanian armed forces.[163] The distribution of new flags, the unveiling in Bucharest of the monument honoring Michael the Brave, symbolic of the struggle for unity and independence, and the adoption of a new draft law "based on the principles of compulsory and personal military service by all able-bodied young men"[164] were important steps taken on the eve of the Eastern crisis indicating even the conservative government's commitment to awareness of the need for a new international status for the nation.

The Eastern crisis broke out in the summer of 1875 with the insurrection in Hercegovina which was soon followed by a rising in Bosnia. The Bulgarian uprising of the spring of 1876 and the war of liberation which began early in the summer in Serbia and Montenegro further aggravated the crisis in the Ottoman empire. At first, Romania decided on a policy of neutrality. That was only temporary, for it was clear that the hour of liberation was at hand. Indeed, a circular issued by Prime Minister Lascăr Catargiu at the beginning of 1876 declared that the government would not "remain an indifferent spectator" and added that the Treaty of Paris of 1856 failed to assure Romania of the status of "a strong and fully independent state."[165] Several months later the conservative government surrendered power to a transitional government; later, power reverted to the opposition on May 10, 1876.

The new cabinet issued a statement indicative of its desire to exploit the international situation in order to attain independence. "Our foreign policy," it said, "will be one of peace and will adhere strictly to international treaties which will set the political status of Romania, which will assure its independence and guarantee its neutrality."[166] Thus, the cabinet tried to establish a link between neutrality and independence even though, at the time, Romania enjoyed only autonomy. Very significant, too, was the assertion that Romania had to defend its neutrality by military means. On August 1, Minister of Foreign Affairs Mihail Kogălniceanu stated in a circular that his country was on the eve of the war of liberation. "Day by day the people are getting more agitated; one of our great political parties has already committed itself in favor of the Christians; the Romanian army, disciplined and restrained, is anxious to give battle."[167]

Nevertheless, another ten months had to go by before Romania entered the war. A small country had to take into account the international situation and the games played by the great neighboring empires; Romania could not pursue adventurous military actions and thus incur the risk of an Ottoman invasion. Therefore, while military preparedness continued — the army was in fact mobilized in the fall of 1876 — negotiations were begun with Russia for possible collaboration against the Turks since Russia was the Ottoman empire's main antagonist and Russia's entry into the war was generally expected in Europe. The negotiations begun at Livadia, in the Crimea, were concluded only on April 16, 1877, with the signing of a convention at Bucharest. The convention granted the Russian armies "the right to cross Romanian territory and to enjoy the treatment accorded to friendly armies," but Russia had to pay for the maintenance of its forces. Russia "assumed the obligation of maintaining and respecting the political rights of the Romanian state, as set by existing laws and treaties, and of maintaining and defending the present integrity of Romania."[168]

Eight days after the signing of the convention between Russia and Romania which granted Romania the status of a fully sovereign state, Russian divisions moved into Romania on their way to the Danube and the Balkans. They used the Romanian railways and carts provided by the peasantry. For the modern Romanian army this was the moment of truth. The four Romanian divisions were deployed along the Danube, and pending the arrival of the Russian armies, they ensured the safety of the advance as well as of the Romanian borders. Romania was able to mobilize some 100,000 men of whom 58,700 were combat troops. The young Romanian army also had 190 cannon.[169] The country's independence was proclaimed by parliament on May 21, 1877, but the act had to be ratified by military action, by the army's ability to defend the country and to demonstrate to Europe the strength of the new independent state. For these reasons outright military participation in the war was essential.

During the first months of hostilities the Romanian divisions had to defend the Danube. The first Russian units crossed the Danube only during the night of June 26 to 27. The Balkan campaign followed the crossing. The Romanian government's proposal to collaborate militarily with the Russians was contemptuously rejected by the tsarist government. The events of the first month of hostilities south of the Danube tended to confirm the optimism of the tsar and of his dignitaries. On July 19, however, General Krüdener's forces were readily defeated before Plevna by the forces of the able and courageous Turkish general Osman Paşa.[170] Note that at the time Plevna was a system of fortifications which Osman Paşa had rendered all but impenetrable. A second defeat suffered by General Krüdener on July 30 cost the Russians 7,000 dead or wounded[171] and placed their forces in a difficult strategic position. As a result, on July 31, Grand Duke Nicholas — supreme commander of the Russian armies — telegraphed Prince Charles: "The Turks who have concentrated their forces at Plevna are doing us harm. Please join us, stage a military demonstration and, if possible, cross the Danube which is what you want to do . . ."[172]

During the second half of July the Romanian army began crossing the Danube, coming to the aid of the Russian forces. The main military force, however, crossed the river only in August when, during the visit of Romanian Premier I. C. Brătianu to the tsar's headquarters, the details regarding military collaboration were firmly settled. The Russians acknowledged the Romanians' right to command their own army and prohibited interference by Russian generals when Romanian and Russian units were combined. Moreover, it was agreed that Prince Charles himself would assume command over all forces at Plevna, i.e., of the western Russo-Romanian army.[173]

On September 6, the Russo-Romanian army assumed a combat position at Plevna. It numbered 90,000 men of whom 38,000 were Romanians. The army had 424 cannon at its disposal.[174] On September 11, the third battle of Plevna began. The day ended without Plevna being taken. But the Romanians, despite extremely heavy losses, succeeded in conquering the Grivitsa I fortification. It was a military achievement, although Plevna itself did not fall, but it was even more a political success. The seizure of Grivitsa I demonstrated the courage of the army of the state which had proclaimed its independence a few months earlier. "Grivitsa fell under the heroic blows delivered by the Romanians," wrote the correspondent of the *Daily News*; the correspondent of the *Bund* wrote, "I never thought that an army could be that brave." The statement published in the *Neue Freie Presse* is also worthy of notice: "The support given the Russians by the Romanians is considerable and it will weigh heavily."[175] True, the Romanian armed forces were small in relation to the enormous human and material resources available to Russia. However, the Romanian army reached the battlefield at an opportune moment when the Russian army had suffered major defeats, when the transporting of fresh Russian troops was bound to be delayed, given the distances and the means of transportation involved, and when the Ottoman army was anything but defeated.

Plevna was besieged during the ensuing stage of the battle which permitted Russian reserve forces, including the imperial guard, to reach the battlefield. On December 10, 1877, after an unsuccessful attempt to raise the siege — which by now involved 125 Russian and 45 Romanian battalions, 82 Russian and 38 Romanian squadrons, 64 Russian and 19 Romanian batteries — Osman surrendered with his entire army.[176] "The brilliant victory at Plevna — Grand Duke Nicholas wrote after the event — "is to a large extent the result of the participation and heroism of the Romanian armies . . . ."[177]

During the last months of the war, while Russian forces pursued their advance toward Constantinople after the conquest of Plevna, Romanian divisions fought on the Danube and besieged the important fortress of Vidin which they occupied after the signing of the armistice by the Porte.[178]

The war of 1877–78 reflected the results of the efforts to establish a modern Romanian army. Romania's participation in the war was efficacious, and the Romanian army demonstrated, in the words of a contemporary press correspondent, that it "could be favorably compared to any other European army."[179] A new chapter was to open in the military history of the Romanian nation as the country entered into a decisive stage of its history. The growth of the armed forces became easier within the framework of the independent state but the historic roots of the development were always present, and for that reason, the study of those roots is valuable to the historian.

Notes

1. Jules Michelet, *Révolution du Danube. Madame Rosetti — 1848,* in *La Pologne martyre* (Paris, 1863), 280.

2. *Idem., Kosciuszko,* in *Ibid.,* 21–22.

3. In 1775, the Habsburg empire acquired Bukovina; in 1812, Bessarabia, namely, northern and eastern Moldavia, was given to tsarist Russia.

4. N. Iorga, *Istoria armatei românești* (Bucharest, 1930), II: 223.

5. P. P. Panaitescu, *Călători poloni în tările române* (Bucharest, 1930), 182, 201.

6. *Ibid.,* 228, 236.

7. *Istoria României* (Bucharest, 1964), III: 398.

8. Iorga, 212.

9. Pseudo-Niculae Muste, *Letopisețul Moldovei* in *Cronicele României* (Bucharest, 1874), III: 45.

10. *Ibid.*

11. C. C. Giurescu, *Istoria românilor* (Bucharest, 1946), III: 743.

12. Ion Neculce, *Letopisețul Țării Moldovei,* ed., Iorgu Iordan (Bucharest, 1955), 273.

13. Giurescu, III: 742.

14. Iorga, II: 203–204.

15. Giurescu, III: 743.

16. Iorga, II: 212–15.

17. *Istoria Țării Românești (1290–1690). Letopisețul Cantacuzinesc,* eds. C. Grecescu and Dan Simonescu (Bucharest, 1960), 108.

18. *Cronica Ghiculeştilor. Istoria Moldovei între anii 1695 şi 1754*, eds., Nestor Camariano and Ariadna Camariano-Cioran (Bucharest, 1965), 270–71.

19. *Ibid.*, 274, 275.

20. *Ibid.*

21. *Ibid.*

22. *Ibid.*, 278, 279.

23. *Ibid.*, 402, 403.

24. *Ibid.*, 404–409.

25. N. Bălcescu, *Puterea armată şi arta militară de la întemeierea principatului Valahiei pînă acum* in *Opere*, eds. G. and E. Zane (Bucharest, 1974), I: 69.

26. *Ibid.*

27. Giurescu, III: 740.

28. See Ladislau Gyémánt, *Aspecte militare ale luptei sociale şi naţionale a românilor din Transilvania în secolul al XVIII–lea şi pîna jumătate a secolului al XIX–lea* in *Oastea cea mare* (Bucharest, 1972), 57–62.

29. *Ibid.*, 62–67; see also Liviu Patachi, *Românii în răscoala lui Petru Seghedinaţ, 1735* (Bucharest, 1947).

30. Gyémánt, 67–68.

31. *Ibid.*, 68–73.

32. *Ibid.*, 73–78. On the great peasant revolt of 1784 see also Gh. Georgescu-Buzău and C. Şerban, *Răscoala de la 1784 din Transilvania de sub conducerea lui Horia, Cloşca şi Crişan* (Bucharest, 1974).

33. Bălcescu, I: 70; Anastasiu, *Oastea română de-a lungul veacurilor* (Bucharest, 1933), 560, 564, 565, 575.

34. Giurescu, III: 766.

35. See Carol Göllner, *Regimentele grănicereşti din Transilvania, 1764–1851* (Bucharest, 1973).

36. *Ibid.*, 35.

37. *Ibid.*, 48, 52.

38. *Ibid.*, 57.

39. *Ibid.*, 128 ff.

40. *Ibid.*, 129.

41. *Ibid.*, 133.

42. Bălcescu, I: 70.

43. *Ibid.*, 70–71.

44. Giurescu, III: 763; see also Sergiu Iosipescu and Victor Eskenasy, *Schiţă a structurilor militare medievale din tările române* in *File de istoria militară a poporului român* (Bucharest, 1977), IV: 57.

45. Giurescu, III: 297–303, 766; see also Ştefan Chicoş, *Cum se făcea aprovizionarea armatelor lui Mihai Viteazul, Matei Basarab şi Nicolae Mavrogheni* (Bucharest, 1939).

46. Gyémánt, 73 ff.

47. David Prodan, *Supplex Libellus Valachorum*, 2d ed. (Bucharest, 1967), 270.

48. Dan Berindei, *L'année révolutionnaire 1821 dans les Pays Roumains* (Bucharest, 1973), 35 ff.

49. *Arhiva Românească*, 2d. ed. (Jassy, 1860), 210, 211.

50. A. Vianu, *Note privitoare la participarea voluntarilor români la războiul ruso-austro-turc (1787-1792)* in *Analele Româno-Sovietice Istorie* 3 (1956): 110.

51. Ilie Fotino, *Tudor Vladimirescu și Alexandru Ipsilanti în revoluțiunea din 1821, supranumită Zavera* (Bucharest, 1874), 12, n. 1.

52. Naum Rîmniceanu, "Scrisoarea Munteanului ca răsouns la scrisoarea Moldoveanului," *Biserica Ortodoxă Română* XIII (1889-90): 260; and "Istoria Zaverei în Valahia," *Ibid.* XXIII (1899): 418.

53. Dionisie Eclisiarhul, *Cronograful Țării Românești*, ed. C. I. Nicolaescu-Plopșor (Rîmnicu Vîlcea, 1934), 137.

54. Berindei, 48-50.

55. Naum Rîmniceanu, *Cronicul protosinghelului ... de la 1768-1810*, in C. Erbiceanu, *Cronicari greci care au scris despre români în epoca fanariotă* (Bucharest, 1890), 272.

56. P. P. Panaitescu, *Corespondența lui Constantin Ipsilanti cu guvernul rusesc, 1806-1810* (Bucharest, 1933), 61.

57. Berindei, 52.

58. I. Neacșu, *Oastea pandurilor condusă de Tudor Vladimirescu în răscoala din 1821* in *Studii și referate privind istoria României* (Bucharest, 1954), 1007.

59. M. Cioranu, *Revoluția lui Tudor Vladimirescu* in N. Iorga, *Izvoare contemporane asupra mișcării lui Tudor Vladimirescu* (Bucharest, 1921), 233.

60. Berindei, 60.

61. *Documente Hurmuzaki*, new ser., II (1967): 44-45.

62. Naum Rîmniceanu, "Scrisoarea unui Moldovean către un Muntean și răspunsul Munteanului sau Frățeasca îmbrățișare," *Biserica Ortodoxă Română* XIII (1889-90): 265.

63. *Documente privind istoria României. Răscoala din 1821* (Bucharest, 1962), V: 518.

64. *Ibid.*, I: 76-77; Berindei, 68.

65. For the program see Dan Berindei, "Programul mișcării revoluționare din 1821," *Revista de Filozofie* 18 (1971), No. 6.

66. Iorga, "Un cugetător politic moldovean de la jumătatea secolului al XIX-lea. Ștefan Scarlat Dăscălescu," *Memoriile Secțiunii Istorice a Academiei Române*, ser. 3, XIII (1932): 52, 54.

67. See Berindei and Mutașu, *Aspecte militare ale mișcării revoluționare din 1821*, 2d ed. (Bucharest, 1973), 52 ff.

68. *Ibid.*, 67.

69. *Ibid.*, 67-68.

70. *Ibid.*, 67.

71. *Ibid.*, 81. On the leaders see I. Neacșu, "Lista cu numele pandurilor și

căpeteniilor lor care au participat la răscoală sub conducerea lui Tudor Vla-dimirescu," *Studii și materiale de istorie modernă* I (Bucharest, 1957).

72. Berindei and Mutașcu, 85.

73. Berindei, *L'année révolutionnaire 1821,* 192.

74. *Ibid.,* 165ff.; Berindei and Mutașcu, 89ff.

75. *Ibid.,* 107–108.

76. *Ibid.,* 135ff.

77. *Ibid.,* 163–69.

78. *Ibid.,* 174–76.

79. *Ibid.,* 177–82; Berindei, *L'année révolutionnaire,* 225–28.

80. See the terms of the treaty in D. A. Sturdza *et al., Actes et documents relatifs à l'histoire de la régénération de la Roumanie* (Bucharest, 1900), I: 321, 326–31.

81. For this period see I. C. Filitti, *Principatele Române de la 1828 la 1834. Ocupația rusească și Regulamentul Organice* (Bucharest, 1934).

82. Göllner, 127–43.

83. Alexandre Papadopol-Calimah, "Generalul Pavel Kisseleff în Moldova și Țara Românească, 1829–1834, după documente rusești," *Memoriile Sec-țiunii Istorice a Academiei Române,* ser. 2, IX (1886–87): 90.

84. *Regulamentele Organice ale Valahiei și Moldovei* (Bucharest, 1944), 133, 292.

85. *Revista Infanteriei* XXXV (1930): 1.

86. Constantin Căzănișteanu, "Cu privire la dezvoltarea armatei române moderne în perioada 1830–1859," *File din istoria militară a poporului român* (Bucharest, 1977), 4: 64.

87. Felix Colson, *De l'état présent et de l'avenir des principautés de Mol-davie et de Valachie* (Paris, 1839), 19.

88. *Regulamentele Organice,* 134–35, 139, 292, 295–96, 312–13.

89. Bălcescu, *Opere,* I: 73.

90. Gh. Romanescu *Oastea română de-a lungul veacurilor* (Bucharest, 1976), 129.

91. Bălcescu, 73.

92. Filitti, 217.

93. *Regulamentele Organice,* 139, 312.

94. Căzănișteanu, 65.

95. Romanescu, 129.

96. The future prince Alexandru D. Ghica was the first to modernize the *panduri* uniforms. See Iorga, II: 248.

97. Romanescu, 128.

98. *Ibid.,* 129.

99. For equivalents, see *Regulamentele Organice,* 144, 300. For the forma-tion of the officer corps, see Dumitru Matei, "Instruarea cadrelor de comandă și a trupelor Moldovei și ale Țării Românești în anii 1830–1848," *File din istoria militară a poporului român* (Bucharest, 1973), I: 27–48. See Ion I.

Nistor, "Organizarea oştirilor pămîntene sub regimul Regulamentului Organic," *Memoriile Secţiunii Istorice a Academiei Române,* ser. 3, XXV (1943).

100. Căzănişteanu, 76, n.53.

101. *Ibid.,* 72, 73; Matei, 35.

102. For that matter, the Moldavian soldiers received elementary training at Iaşi and at Galaţi. See Matei, 36–37.

103. *Ibid.,* 40–42.

104. *Ibid.,* 42–44; Căzănişteanu, 84–85.

105. *Ibid.,* 82.

106. Bălcescu, I: 43–78, 135–50.

107. Filitti, 291–93.

108. *Ibid.,* 292, 294.

109. Bălcescu, I: 75.

110. For the revolution of 1848, see Gh. Georgescu-Buzău, *La révolution de 1848 dans les Pays Roumains* (Bucharest, 1965); Căzănişteanu, Dan Berindei, Marin Florescu, Vasile Niculae, *Revoluţia română din 1848* (Bucharest, 1974); Berindei, *Revoluţia română din 1848* (Bucharest, 1969). See also Căzănişteanu, M. Cucu, E. Popescu, *Aspecte militare ale revoluţiei din 1848 în Ţara Românească* (Bucharest, 1968); L. Loghin and C. Ucrain, *Aspecte militare ale revoluţiei din 1848–1849 în Transilvania* (Bucharest, 1970).

111. *Gazeta Transilvaniei* (Braşov), May 27, 1848.

112. Căzănişteanu, Cucu, Popescu, 45–46.

113. *Ibid.,* 49.

114. Göllner, 147 ff.

115. Căzănişteanu, Cucu, Popescu, 101–06.

116. A village had to provide a *centurie* (100 men); ten villages constituted a *tribunat,* commanded by a *tribun;* one legion consisted of ten *tribunats.* See Loghin and Ucrain, 17.

117. Maria Totu, *Garda civică din România* (Bucharest, 1976), 39.

118. *Ibid.,* 28, 35.

119. *Ibid.,* 40.

120. Loughin and Ucrain, 20.

121. *Ibid.,* 25–26.

122. *Ibid.,* 24.

123. Căzănişteanu, Cucu, Popescu, 76.

124. *Ibid.,* 115.

125. See the extensive work by Silviu Dragomir, *Avram Iancu,* 2d ed. (Bucharest, 1968).

126. Bălcescu, *Opere* (Bucharest, 1940), I: 129.

127. *Anul 1848 în Principatele Române* (Bucharest, 1902), I: 651.

128. G. Bariţiu, *Istoria regimentului al II–lea românesc* (Braşov, 1874), 61–62.

129. Căzănişteanu, *Cu privire la dezvoltarea armatei române moderne în perioada 1830–1859,* 70.

130. *Ibid.*

131. *Ibid.,* 65–66.
132. *Ibid.,* 72.
133. *Ibid.,* 67.
134. *Ibid.,* 66.
135. *Ibid.,* 81.
136. *Ibid.,* 83.
137. *Ibid.,* 74, 82.
138. D. A. Sturdza *et al.,* *Actes et documents relatifs à l'histoire de la régénération de la Roumanie* (Bucharest, 1896), VI: 615–17.
139. Căzănişteanu, 69.
140. V. Bossy, *Agenţia diplomatică a României în Paris şi legăturile politice franco-române sub Cuza Vodă* (Bucharest, 1931), 172.
141. *Mesagii, proclamaţii, răspunsuri şi scrisori oficiale ale lui Cuza Vodă* (Bucharest, 1910), 105.
142. Cezar Bolliac, "Armarea," *Românul,* Nov. 5, 1860.
143. Radu Ionescu, "Guvernul şi armarea," *Reforma,* Aug. 13, 1860.
144. Căzănişteanu, "Războiul de partizani în gîndirea militară românească din veacul al XIX-lea," *File de istorie militară a poporului român* 2 (1974): 26–27, 28–32. For Adrian, see his *Idée răpede despre rezbelul de partizani,* ed., Major-General G. Antip (Bucharest, 1973).
145. *Mesagii, proclamaţii,* 20.
146. Maria Georgescu, "Problema cuprinderii maselor populare în sistemul de apărare a tării reflectată în programele revoluţionare, unele proiecte şi legislaţia anilor 1840–1877," *Oastea cea mare* (Bucharest, 1972), 158–59.
147. *Mesagii, proclamaţii,* 135.
148. Political and administrative unification was achieved at the beginning of 1862 when the first Romanian government, replacing the earlier, separate Wallachian and Moldavian governments, was established.
149. Ulysse de Marsillac, *Histoire de l'armée roumaine* (Bucharest, 1871), 100.
150. *Monitorul,* July 25, 1862, p. 686.
151. Marsillac, 106.
152. On the French mission, see Radu Rosetti, "Relations entre l'armée française et l'armé roumaine," in *Hommage à Monsieur de Saint-Aulaire* (Bucharest, 1930), 93–104.
153. See details in the chapter on the army in Berindei, *Epoca Unirii* (Bucharest, 1978).
154. Bossy, 384.
155. *Ibid.*
156. Paul Henry, *L'abdication du prince Cuza et l'avénement de la dynastie de Hohenzollern au trône en Roumanie* (Paris, 1930), 417.
157. Berindei, "Statul naţional român în lupta pentru independenţă," *Independenţa, lupta milenară a poporului român* (Iaşi, 1977), 40.
158. Maria Georgescu, "Politica militară a guvernării liberale din 1867–1868," *File de istorie militară,* 3 (1975): 129–31.

159. *Ibid.,* 135–36.
160. Berindei, 42.
161. *Ibid.*
162. The *dorobanţi* were infantry units; the *călăraşi,* cavalry.
163. Berindei, 42.
164. *Ibid.*
165. *Documente privind istoria României. Războiul pentru independenţă* (Bucharest, 1954), I: 65–67. For the War of Independence see *România în războiul de independentă. 1807–1878* (Bucharest, 1977); *Independenţa României,* ed. Stefan Pascu (Bucharest, 1977); and Berindei, *L'indépendance de la Roumanie. 1877* (Bucharest, 1976).
166. *Documente privind istoria României. Războiul pentru independenţă,* I: 144.
167. *Ibid.,* 293–94.
168. *Ibid.,* II: 111–12.
169. *România în războiul de independenţă. 1877–1878,* 91.
170. *Ibid.,* 146–51.
171. *Ibid.,* 153–55.
172. *Notes sur la vie du roi Charles de Roumanie par un témoin occulaire* (Bucharest, 1899), III: 119.
173. Berindei, 71–72.
174. *România în războiul de independenţă. 1877–1878,* 188–89.
175. Berindei, 77–78.
176. *Ibid.,* 81.
177. *Ibid.,* 84.
178. *România în războiul de independenţă. 1877–1878,* 303.
179. Berindei, 77.

Ilie Ceauşescu

Romania's Military Policy and the National Liberation Struggle of the Peoples of Southeast and East Central Europe (1859–75)

Although political and socioeconomic developments in the feudal period led to the dispersal and independent development of the Romanian peoples in Wallachia, Moldavia, and Transylvania, they maintained strong political, economic, cultural, and religious ties. The common struggle against the Ottomans consolidated these links and even though the first unification of Romanian lands was short-lived, lasting only one year, from 1600 to 1601, the episode served as a symbol as well as a stimulus for the struggle waged by subsequent generations. When a Romanian national identity was finally established about 1848, achieving complete national unification became the major objective of progressive social and political forces in Romanian society.

After the union of Moldavia and Wallachia in 1859 created a national state, Romanian society embarked on a new stage of developing capitalism, at the same time laying the groundwork for national unification. The new state created in 1859 was the outcome of a specific historical stage in the centuries-old process of developing a Romanian people, and it emerged as the result of struggle by Romanian social and political forces, benefiting by the favorable international situation emerging from the outcome of the Crimean War.[1] The rise of a Romanian state ran counter to the interests of the large empires which had been contending for control over the Carpatho-Danubian area. Even though only partially unified, the Romanian state further weakened foreign rule on the lower Danube, interfered with foreign domination over the peoples of Southeast and Central Europe, acted as a focal point attracting the large, native Romanian populations in the provinces outside the new national boundaries, as well as other oppressed peoples in this part of Europe.

Modernization and further centralization of the political structure after the union of the two Romanian principalities was accompanied by extensive military reforms. The concrete historical circumstances, internal as well as external, attendant on the achievement of the union, imposed certain limitations on Romanian policy, with realism and versatility becoming the guiding principles of all decision making. In the area of military policy, the major objective between 1859 and the onset of the Eastern Crisis of 1875–76 was the establishment of a centralized force, capable of contributing to the consolidation of the national state, of giving it greater weight on the international scene and of serving — in the future — as an instrument to complete national unification.

Modernization of the army, both in training troops and in procuring equipment, was undertaken while the Industrial Revolution was transforming fighting methods. The conditions imposed by both internal and international circumstances required the development of a specific Romanian military policy, taking into account viable traditions, such as the people's resistance against invasion, and reconciling these, both in organization and doctrine, with the military realities facing the nation and the then current state of the military art. The final result of the reforms and reorganizations carried out between 1859 and 1875 was a defense system in which the central role devolved on the standing army, supported, however, by a large number of other formations: territorial troops, militias, national guards, and "armed bands." This enumeration indicates that almost the entire male population of the country was involved in the national defense. The formula, the "nation in arms," was the only one capable of meeting the challenge of foreign aggression. Consistent with the demands of the times, the military organization of the newly, if only partially, unified Romanian state represented, from the historical standpoint, a revival of the mediaeval institution of the "great host," the calling to arms of the entire male population capable of rendering service.

The military program of the state was designed to shape an instrument able to achieve the goals of national policy. From the organizational point of view, during the years after the union of 1859, the Romanian army was both unified and expanded. Two additional infantry regiments and a battalion of mountain troops were formed, resulting in an establishment of seven regiments of the line with two battalions each, and one reinforced mountain battalion; fifteen battalions in all, with about 12,500 men. The cavalry also was augmented with two additional squadrons, making a total of two lancer regiments. The twenty-six cannon available at the outset of Prince Cuza's reign were organized into an artillery regiment, consisting of two foot and two mounted batteries.

At the same time, great efforts were made both to procure modern arms and equipment and to lay the foundations for a modern arms industry. The government also tried to improve, or to raise entirely new, technical units — including artillery, engineer, and signal units. Although the modest resources of the country were strained, the armed forces were equipped with modern weapons, including Peabody rifles, Krupp Model 1870/75 cannon — then considered the finest artillery pieces — and Lineman entrenching tools. Along with the process of modernizing arms and equipment, Romanian military thought developed on original lines, basing both strategy and tactics on the principles of popular participation in order to defend the recently achieved national state and to establish its complete independence.[3]

A constant concern of Romanian military leadership was becoming familiar with and utilizing the experience of more developed foreign armies. Military delegations were exchanged, officers were sent abroad to study or to act as observers, and military missions were invited to Romania. Particularly close links were established with France which sent a military mission to Romania and also supplied considerable quantities of arms. The United States also was included in these activities and Romanian officers took the opportunity to learn from the experience of the Civil War.

Considering the disproportion of military resources between the Romanian state and its huge bordering empires, regaining complete national independence — the first goal after the achievement of Union in 1859 — required working out a complex formula using political actions to counterbalance military limitations. As part of this effort, links with national and democratic movements in the neighboring empire, especially the political and military support provided for these movements, became the basis of Romanian foreign policy. A second basic trend was cooperation with the small and medium-sized states in the region — Serbia and Greece, for instance.

Relations with national liberation movements in East, Central, and Southeast Europe were determined by the existence of certain common objectives, most important, regaining independence, as well as a long-standing tradition of close collaboration in the fight against foreign invaders. During the nineteenth century this collaboration became manifest in the revolutionary events of 1821.[4] Since the early years of the century, the movement for emancipation from Ottoman domination had found one of its major manifestations in the secret *Hetaeria* organization. An end to Ottoman rule on the Balkan peninsula was envisaged as the result of a general uprising of the peoples in this area — Romanians, Serbs, Greeks, and Bulgarians. The 1821 revolution in Wallachia, led by Tudor Vladimirescu, was part of this vast liberation movement. Four decades later, when the union of Moldavia with Wallachia had been achieved, even though for the most part the objectives were identical, historical conditions had changed. Economic progress, the development of the capitalist system, the advanced stage reached in the process of forming the modern nations in East and Southeast Europe, all required new forms of collaboration in the fight against the common enemy.

Some of the great powers were reluctant to accept and even hostile to the act of Union of 1859. Accordingly, Alexandru Ioan Cuza acted energetically to defend this achievement.[5] Hence, the Romanian prince's negotiations with the Hungarian revolutionaries must be seen in the context of the Franco-Sardinian alliance against Austria. Negotiations between the Romanian government, represented by Vasile Alecsandri, and the Hungarian revolutionaries, represented by General György Klapka, a former commander in the Hungarian revolutionary army of 1849, led to the conclusion of two agreements.[6]

The first agreement provided that Prince Cuza would "permit the Hungarian revolutionaries to establish ammunition depots" in the Siret River valley, at Bacău, at Roman, or in other locations, such as Ocna and Piatra. Moreover, it was stipulated that the "Prince will ask his Majesty, the Emperor of the French, for 30,000 rifles, of which 10,000 will be placed at the disposal of the leaders of the insurrection in Hungary and Transylvania." Other stipulations concerned the supply of cannon by the Serbian government, details on Klapka's activities in Paris and London, provisions for delivery of ammunition and equipment, and the enlistment of "several engineer and artillery officers" as well as the required medical personnel. Both sides pledged to maintain constant communications, both in Romania, (where Hungarian agents were to be stationed in Bucharest, Iaşi, and Galaţi) and in Paris and Belgrade.

The second agreement opened with a statement of principles: in order for the Hungarian insurrection to succeed, "it is very important that the Hungarian, Romanian, and Serbian nationalities living in Hungary forsake any party spirit, any idea of separatism, and refrain from the acts of hostility which caused such great misfortunes in 1848 and 1849." To this end, the Hungarian patriots were to proclaim at the very outset of the fight a number of principles to be incorporated in Hungary's future constitution. These included "Equal rights, equal freedom for all the inhabitants of Hungary irrespective of race or religion; the autonomy of communes and counties; inhabitants of counties with a mixed population will agree — in friendly terms — on the official language (Hungarian, Serbian, or Romanian) to be adopted." There was to be complete independence for all religions and for public education; separate Romanian and Serbian contingents should have full equality within the army and equal opportunities for promotion at all levels. "After the war," the agreement continued, "an assembly will be convened in Transylvania to deliberate on the administrative union of this province with Hungary and should the majority decide that the old autonomous administration of Transylvania is to be reestablished, the Hungarians will not oppose it."

Because of the rapid end of the Franco-Sardinian–Austrian war — negotiations for peace began after the first Austrian defeats at Magenta and Solferino — and Austria's changed attitude, recognizing Alexandru Cuza's double election, the agreements were not implemented. Nevertheless, Romania continued to assist the Hungarian revolutionists. On February 3, 1861, Prime Minister Anastase Panu informed Cuza that he had sent 222 ducats for food for the Hungarians, who had taken refuge and set up quarters at Bacău. In view of additional and higher expenses, he asked that a credit be voted by the Assembly of Deputies.[7]

As a matter of fact, the Hungarians living abroad realized that without an understanding with the Romanians they could not achieve anything solid and lasting. On November 17, 1861, a letter appeared in the Paris newspaper *Le Siècle,* in which General István Türr — an outstanding revolutionary émigré — addressed the Hungarian community of Bucharest. Türr recognized the consolidation of "fraternal concord" between Romanians and Hungarians and the solution of the problem of the nationalities, on the broadest basis of equality, in a future Hungary freed from the Austrian yoke.[8] A week later, Baligot de Beyne, secretary to the ruling prince, wrote to Cuza that General Klapka had stated that the Hungarians would achieve nothing without the assistance of the Romanians from Transylvania; the disputes between these two peoples must come to an end.

Two replies were given to the Hungarian revolutionaries' repeated calls for collaboration. One is included in a letter sent November 27, 1861, by the old and faithful friend of the Romanians, J. A. Vaillant, to General Garibaldi, "the liberator of Italy and the veteran of the philo-Romanians," pointing out the conditions on which the Romanians consented to fraternize with the Hungarians. These conditions included universal suffrage and freedom for Transylvania and for the Banat of Timiş to merge with the United Principalities.

The second reply is synthesized in an article from *Journal de Franc-*

fort, dated December 5–7, 1861, "L'indépendance constitutionnelle de Transylvanie." This, in fact, reiterates the point of view of Al. Papiu Ilarian, a well-known Romanian revolutionist of 1848, stated in his pamphlet *Independenţa constituţională a Transilvaniei* (The Constitutional Independence of Transylvania), whose contents are faithfully rendered by its title. The Hungarian refugee Ignác Helfy likewise recognized in his journal, *L'Alleanza,* appearing in Milan, a Hungarian-Romanian-Serbian alliance based on the full equality of all inhabitants, irrespective of nationality, language, or religion.[9] The same ideas were repeated by the head of Hungarian emigration, Lajos Kossuth, in an article appearing in *L'Alleanza* May 1, 1862.[10] At the same time, Hungarian émigré agents continued their activity in the Moldavian towns. The Austrian ambassador in Constantinople demanded that the Romanian authorities ask agent Sándor Buda to stop the enlistment of "Hungarians, Poles and Transylvanians" which he was carrying on at Bacău and Bîrlad.[11]

Further meetings between representatives of the Romanian state and refugee Hungarian revolutionaries occurred in 1863. On May 19, Prime Minister Nicolae Kretzulescu cabled Cuza to inform him that General Türr — who had the official title of aide-de-camp to the king of Italy — had arrived in Bucharest, that the Italian consul had received Türr, and that the general had requested an audience. The ruling prince granted the audience May 28, 1863. Türr asked for Romanian support at the moment the Italians should attack Austria. In particular he asked for 1,000 rifles to arm Hungarian émigrés in Romania who were to undertake a diversion in Hungary where they hoped to augment their ranks. The rifles would be taken from those officially ordered in Italy by Romania for her army and which the Italian king undertook to send. Cuza replied that he would not refuse this aid, but that before giving it, he must know positively whether the Hungarians were in agreement with the Romanians beyond the Carpathians.[12] Unfortunately, Türr's proposals had no result. They failed because there was no agreement between Hungarians and Romanians in Transylvania and secondly, because at this moment Napoleon III was opposed to any action against Austria. On the contrary, he supported Austria in order to exert pressure on Russia and help the Polish insurrection.

Nonetheless, links with the Hungarian revolutionaries continued. The Romanian authorities helped to transfer arms obtained from abroad to the Hungarian fighters. Prime Minister Mihail Kogălniceanu firmly rejected repeated demands by the Austrian authorities to expel the Hungarian exiles. During discussions with the Hungarian representatives, the Romanian authorities constantly stressed the need for a future Hungarian revolutionary government to approach in a positive spirit the claims of the Romanian population in Transylvania.[13]

Determined to dominate, the Vienna Court was regarded as the common enemy of the Romanian and the Hungarian people. Hungarian progressive forces fighting for national emancipation objectively helped consolidate the Romanian unity achieved in 1859. Therefore, it was only natural that the Romanian state should support the Hungarian struggle. The presence of a majority of ethnic Romanians in Transylvania complicated relations. At the beginning of Habsburg rule in Transylvania the Vienna Court recognized the political regime which gave the Magyar nobility a leading role. Later, Charles VI, attempting to obtain recognition of the Pragmatic Sanction, confirmed the constitution and autonomy of Hungary. Discrimination against Romanians made the Magyar nobility odious to the Romanian masses as well as to the other nationalities settled in Transylvania, and the Hungarian revolution of 1848–49 did not provide an adequate solution to the national problem.

The intensification of national contradictions and the crisis triggered by the defeat of 1866 resulted in a compromise, the *Ausgleich*, between the Austrian and Hungarian ruling classes concluded in 1867. This compromise increasd the oppression of the other national groups in the Dual Monarchy and resulted in further intensification of the people's struggle for emancipation.

Under Cuza's rule, close ties were also established with the Polish emigration which was divided into two major factions, one democratic, the other led by Prince Adam Czartoryski. The incident at Constanglia in 1863 — when a unit of Polish revolutionarirs under Colonel Milkowski was disarmed — was caused by the Polish fighters' attempt to cross Romanian territory armed and as an organized unit, at a moment when the European powers, yielding to Russian pressure, had all but abandoned the Polish cause.[14]

Although Romanian public opinion, even in the ruling circles, was favorable to the Polish cause, support for the Poles could not be permitted to endanger the nation. Open assistance to the Polish insurgents, in this case permission for a major detachment to cross Romanian territory to fight the tsarist army in Podolia and Wolhynia, could have provoked immediate problems with the powerful empire. Realizing the possibility of serious consequences, Cuza, though he shared the feelings of all Romanians toward the Polish fighters, was obliged to give orders for Milkowski's unit to be stopped. Cuza's action was also justified by Milkowski's initial plan, subsequently described in his memoirs: "When I deemed it necessary to pass from Turkey through Moldavia with a strong detachment in order to help the revolution," Milkowski wrote, "it stood to reason that Moldavia would have to come temporarily under Polish rule. This conquest of Moldavia, its temporary subjection, necessary because of the general situation, became a necessary part of my plan."[15] In any case, once Milkowski was halted, the Polish internees were treated with the utmost consideration. Cuza ordered that officers be permitted to retain their swords and the detachment, interned *pro forma* at Cahul, was permitted gradually to leave for either Turkey or Austria. The inhabitants of Moldavia extended their hearty sympathy to the Poles. On July 30, 1863, Milkowski in a letter to the prefect of Covurlui, acknowledged the "generous manner" in which he and his disarmed soldiers had been treated and voiced his gratitude. Some time later, in August 1863, he himself admitted that his armed enterprise had been "an act of madness."[16] This incident, therefore, did not mar the basic friendly character of Romanian-Polish relations.

This accounts for the attitude of Władisław Czartoryski, whom the revolutionary government of Poland had, in May 1863, made its diplomatic representative to the governments of France, Great Britain, Italy, Sweden, and Turkey. In September 1863, Czartoryski — through Romania's diplomatic agent in Paris, Ioan Alexandri — expressed gratitude to Prince Cuza, "for the care manifested for our compatriots and for his [Cuza's] personal sympathies for their cause."[17] Czartoryski firmly rejected Western diplomatic rumors that Austria was to have Romania as a compensation for recognition and reestablishment of Poland's independence. On the other hand, he proposed a military alliance with Romania in the common fight of the two states for national freedom. The proposal made by Czartoryski, the official plenipotentiary of the Polish revolution, was important as clear testimony that the leadership of the Polish revolution had confidence in Romania's policy.

A consequence of these Polish propositions was Cuza's letter to Napoleon III (November 11, 1863) in which he offered the French emperor Romania's military cooperation. On the other hand, in the spring of 1864, when Austria and Russia concentrated troops along Romania's frontiers as a consequence of the intensification of revolutionary agitation, Cuza addressed a circular memorandum to the ministers of foreign affairs of France, Great Britain, Prussia, and Italy, stating the political position of Romania toward the fighters of the national and social liberation movements in Southeast and Central Europe.

> Through my efforts and my vigilance, I succeeded several times in foiling intrigues, harmful to the peace of the neighboring states. Your Excellency knows that, recently, I did not hesitate to place my duty above my feelings of humanity and, at the cost of painful sacrifices, observed the neutrality of Romanian territory and simultaneously, the autonomy and internal independence of the United Principalities. Nevertheless, the discharge of these duties to maintain order and good neighborliness, does not permit me to stay indifferent to the misery of a large number of refugees who sought shelter upon our territory because of the war or for political reasons. Our traditions of hospitality provided them with a safe refuge. I saw to their needs with all the liberality permitted by our limited resources. If this is the cause of the military preparations made by the two neighboring powers, I must state that I will not yield to such coercive measures which violate public conscience.[18]

Naturally, the closest ties developed between Romania and the movements for national emancipation south of the Danube. These links, dating back for centuries, when the Romanian countries, benefiting by a statute of autonomy even after Ottoman domination, became a land of refuge for Slavs from the south whose countries had been turned into *paşaliks*.

Romanian-Serbian ties were particularly close during this period. Their political and military collaboration was furthered by several factors: an almost identical situation with respect to the Porte; Miloš Obrenović's return to the Serbian throne early in 1859, almost at the same time Prince Alexandru I Cuza became ruler of the Romanian Principalities; the agreement on political principles between him and Prince Michael, who succeeded Miloš in 1860, and especially the traditional friendly relations between the two peoples. Their collaboration was evident in the Romanian government's facilitating the transport of arms for Serbia through its territory, the conclusion of a Romanian-Serbian treaty of alliance, and the negotiations for a military alliance.[19]

In November–December 1862 the Romanian authorities permitted a large convoy of Russian arms produced in the Tula arsenal, to move across the country from the vicinity of Bolgrad [Cetatea Albă] in Bessarabia to Craiova near Gruia on the Danube. According to Serbian sources, the convoy, more than thirty-four wagons, carried 63,000 rifles and 2,000-3,000 swords. An official of the French consulate in Bucharest estimated that shipment at about 40,000 rifles with bayonets, 10,000 carbines, and 30,000 pistols. Whatever the exact figure, it is clear that the Serbian army gained up-to-date weapons.

Cuza and the Romanian government had arranged passage for the convoy with Russia, Prince Obrenović, and the Serbian government. All necessary measures were taken for protecting the convoy. As early as the end of the summer, Romania concentrated a strong detachment of infantry, cavalry, and artillery along the Danube with orders from the general staff that if the Turks attempted to halt the convoy, they should be repelled by force if necessary. Serbia also had concentrated adequate forces at the crossing point. The Turks, for their part, had deployed 5,000 soldiers and sixteen cannon at Vidin, so that action on their part was not precluded. Ultimately, however, fearing complications, they refrained from interfering with the passage of the arms across the river.

This spectacular achievement triggered a strong international diplomatic reaction. It precipitated collective, hostile intervention by the representatives of several powers in Bucharest, but ultimately ended in a political victory for Romania and Serbia which increased the prestige of their leaders.

The Austrian and British consuls, subsequently joined by the consuls of France and Prussia, repeatedly sent notes and requests to both the prince and the government, demanding seizure of the arms and their delivery into the consuls' custody. When that brought no results, the question of the arms convoy came before the six ambassadors in Constantinople who represented the major powers guaranteeing the Balkan settlement achieved at the end of the Crimean War. The Turks twice demanded that the arms be seized, but they were rebuffed. Since protest gained them no satisfaction, they now treated the arms transport as an infringement of the instruction of the Paris Convention of August 19, 1858; in accordance with the protocols of April 13 and September 5, 1859, they demanded that a Turkish commissioner be dispatched to halt the convoy.

Austria, worried by anything that might lead to a consolidation of Serbia — which she regarded as a potential opponent — supported this point of view from the very beginning. Great Britain had also sided with the Turks. But in order actually to send the Turkish commissioner, it was absolutely necessary for all the great guaranteeing powers to agree. This was impossible. Russia, which had delivered the arms and wanted them to reach their destination as soon as possible, remained firmly opposed. On the other hand, France, whose military missions superintended the organization of the two armies, supported Romania and the Serbians; hence it did not want to have the 1859 protocols enforced. Even when the minister of foreign affairs instructed the French consul in Bucharest to cooperate with his colleagues there, the French ambassador in Constantinople, De Moustier, adopted a much more understanding attitude. Thus the proposal to send a Turkish commissioner to sequestrate the transport failed. As a matter of fact, even if the proposal had been adopted, by the time the commissioner reached Romania, he would no longer have found anything. For at the end of December 1862, the arms had been transferred to Serbian territory, at Crivina near Gruia, across the Danube.

In connection with this episode, Garašanin, the Serbian minister of foreign affairs, stated: "Although Prince Cuza merely gave permission for the arms meant for us to pass across his territory, when we were threatened by danger, he proved himself ready to help us in all respects and keep his promise even at the cost of sacrifices. . . . Consequently, we shall be proud to be the allies of a nation, whose leader knows to defend so nobly his rights against a foreign aggression."[20] On the same occasion, Prince Michael Obrenović sent Prince Cuza a sword, whose inscription concisely expressed the character of Romanian policy: *amico certo in re incerta.*[21]

The conclusion of the Romanian-Serbian treaty of alliance, in January 1868, marked an important moment in Romanian foreign policy toward the Balkan peoples in general, and the Serbs in particular. Its signing was preceded by a series of steps initiated both in Bucharest and in Belgrade.

As early as the second half of February 1866, the provisional government in Bucharest had drafted "Instructions to the Romanian Agent in Belgrade," stating the principles on which the representative there was to act. He was directed to examine attentively the political atmosphere, Prince Milan's relations with the great powers, the organization of the army, the economy, finances, and administration of Serbia, etc. Simultaneously he was to report on events in the different provinces of the Ottoman empire, and especially to learn "whether the Serbian government, as well as that of Montenegro, is really committed to the vast conspiracy which appears to surround the Ottoman empire from all directions."[22] It was also desired that the Romanian diplomat pave the way to "the beginnings of an alliance between Romania and Serbia."[23] That, as a matter of fact, was the essence of these instructions as well as the main objective of Romanian diplomatic activities in Belgrade during this period. When Prince Michael Obrenović visited Romania (April 1867), he "openly expressed, in the presence of Prince Carol, his opinion that Romania, like Serbia, was interested in severing the links of vassalage with Turkey." Toward this end, the two countries should "conclude a close alliance."[24] In turn, the ruling prince of Romania deemed "Turkish suzerainty an oppressive and humiliating" foreign domination; hence, "the states should act first along a military line." In conclusion, he stated his determination "to undertake the reorganization of his army with great energy."[25]

Although no treaty of alliance was signed during Prince Michael's visit, it evidently made a considerable contribution to bringing the two sides together. Apparently, in the summer of 1867, there was support for concluding — at some opportune moment — an inter-Balkan alliance, including Greece and Montenegro along with Romania and Serbia. A draft treaty for such an arrangement has been handed down to us. Unfortunately, no solution acceptable to all parties concerned was reached, although attempts at a multilateral *rapprochement* were not lacking. In December 1866, for instance, Prince Ypsilanti proposed an alliance between Greece and Romania. Finally, there was a major achievement, for Romania, concentrating on establishing good relations with Serbia, concluded a treaty of alliance in Bucharest on January 20, 1868.

The treaty was designed to contribute to the prosperity and the progress of both countries, taking into consideration their ancient rights and their autonomous status. It contained no military provisions, nor could it be interpreted in this light. Nevertheless, a Romanian-Serbian military alliance — secret of course — is believed to have existed at that time. This might account for the fears with which A.C. Golescu, having received intelligence from Constantinople, regarded the large concentrations of Turkish troops along the Danube in May 1868. These activities reflect the apprehension created in Constantinople by news that Romania and Serbia had signed a treaty. It was considered likely that such a military clause did exist. Together with the Porte's need to be able to intervene and, if necessary, exert control in Serbia and Montenegro, this would explain the troop concentrations. In this respect there were some indications of their "making preparations for an energetic action."[26]

In any case, Romania and Serbia had shown their willingness to cooperate, albeit along peaceful lines, though by arms if necessary. It was natural, then, for military ties of various sorts to develop and become an important component of their respective Balkan policies.

Between 1859 and 1877 there were frequent exchanges of military delegations. Thus, in August 1862, Alexandru I. Cuza sent Major H. Herkt, an artillery officer, on a secret mission to Serbia. On that occasion he gathered documentation on the development of Serbian artillery and particularly on the artillery emplacements at Kraguievatz. Further, "he had the task to investigate in detail the percussion cap factory and foundry of cannons and shells,"[27] to keep abreast of methods of arms manufacture, to see and "examine the batteries and the material which Serbia would be willing to place at the disposal of the Romanian government; to inquire as to how the conveyance of the batteries and of the material to Romania could be secured." A year later, in the autumn of 1863, the prince of Serbia sent two officers, Colonel Milivoie Petrović Blažnovat and Captain Nikifor Iovanović, to attend maneuvers of the Romanian army. These officers were also to deliver to the Romanian ruler a special rifle manufactured at the Kraguievatz arsenal. Prince Cuza received them with all honor, inviting them to a gala luncheon and offering them valuable gifts upon their departure. On October 5, 1863, the Romanian prince sent a letter to Michael Obrenović, expressing appreciation for the military delegation and for the rifle. As a gesture of reciprocity, on July 5, 1865, the manager of the Bucharest arsenal, Colonel H. Herkt, was sent to Belgrade in order to give the prince of Serbia prototypes of arms manufactured in the Bucharest arsenal. In 1874, another Romanian military delegation, including Colonel Cerchez and Captain Boldescu, was sent to Belgrade to learn about the condition of the Serbian army.[28] All these exchanges testified to an active military policy directed toward liberating the two peoples from foreign domination and helping to shake the foreign yoke from all the countries of Central and Southeast Europe.

Most sustained were Romania's relations with the Bulgarian revolutionary movement. A large number of Bulgarian committees organizing the armed struggle against the Ottoman empire benefited by the assistance provided by the Romanian authorities and carried on their activity on Romanian territory.[29] Thus G.S. Rakovski's corps of *haiduks,* which crossed the Danube in 1864, had the direct support of the Romanian ruling prince. After the dethronement of Alexandru Ioan Cuza (1866), Ottoman military intervention appeared likely, and Romanian troops occupied the line of the Danube. A detachment of Bulgarian volunteers led by Ivan Kasabov, was organized then; numerous Bulgarian, Serbian, Montenegrin, Albanian, and Greek exiles also formed volunteer units. The same year, upon the initiative of C.A. Rosetti, an 1848 revolutionary, the foundations of the *Sacred Coali-*

tion were laid. The *Sacred Coalition* provided for a military alliance between the Romanian and Bulgarian peoples, to be expanded later into a Balkan-wide alliance to fight all foreign domination. During the first years of the reign of Carol I, detachments of Bulgarian volunteers commanded by Panaiot Hitov and Philip Totio were organized on Romanian soil, whence they conducted actions against the Turks south of the Danube.[30]

The closeness of Romanian-Bulgarian relations — including tacit military as well as political assistance given by the Romanian authorities — could not remain hidden from the press or foreign diplomats. The French agent in Bucharest noted that the depots of the Romanian state stored uniforms for the Bulgarian volunteers; furthermore, they regularly received arms and ammunition from Russia, without the slightest protest from the Romanian government. The Austrian agent in Galaţi reported that the Turkish authorities in the port of Sulina had seized sixty-two casks of gunpowder belonging to the Romanian government discovered on board the Prussian ship *Morgenstein,* from Antwerp.[31]

Bucharest had become an important center of the national liberation movements of the Balkan peoples. During the early 1870s, Romania's capital sheltered the Bulgarian Revolutionary Committee which organized the struggle to liberate Bulgaria. The conference of April 1872, also attended by representatives from Bulgaria itself, debated the constitution of the insurrectionary movement, worked out a practical program of action, and elected a new central committee. On March 11–12, 1873, another meeting of the Bulgarian Revolutionary Central Commitee of Bucharest decided to send armed bands south of the Danube to discover whether conditions were suitable for a general rising.

These activities which the major Bulgarian revolutionary leaders, G.S. Rakovski, V. Levski, L. Karavelov and Hristo Botev, carried on in Bucharest, and the Bulgarian journals printed there, played a decisive role in the outbreak of the great national struggle, which precipitated the new stage of the Eastern Crisis in 1875.[32] The insurrection of Stara-Zagora and the revolt of 1876 were triggered by Bulgarian revolutionary leaders operating from Romanian territory.

Articles, notes, reviews, subscription lists, as well as direct action in support of the Bulgarians, reveal the interest and sympathy of the Romanian people in the events occurring south of the Danube and the selfless aid the Romanian people gave its neighbors. A Bucharest newspaper pointed out that during the critical years 1875–76, the Romanians gave the "Serbians and Bulgarians their own country to enjoy as if it were their own homeland."[33] This paraphrased the statement made more than a decade earlier by Gheorghi Sava Rakovski, a leader in the fight for Bulgaria's national emancipation: Romania had provided for the Bulgarian people a "free and inviolable place of refuge and the house of the Romanian villager was open to the Bulgarian with the greatest hospitality."[34]

It must be emphasized that the Bulgarian revolutionaries could not have carried on their work without the consent and the active support of the Romanian authorities. Despite repeated Turkish protests and despite pressure from various European powers opposed to the disintegration of the Ottoman empire, Romania never for a moment abandoned its policy of actively supporting the national liberation movements on the Balkan Peninsula.[35]

During the period discussed in this essay, the Romanian state promoted an active policy toward Greece, then the only Balkan state which had achieved its full independence, but which also, in collaboration with other peoples in the Balkan area and south of the Danube, sought to liberate the remainder of its territory still under Ottoman rule. Significant, too, were the Bucharest talks of 1866 and 1869 looking toward the conclusion of a treaty of alliance among Romania and Serbia and Montenegro.

Romania's military policy from 1859 to 1875 was subordinated to the fundamental objectives of the Romanian state: the consolidation of national unity and the restoration of total independence. In line with this policy, one aspect of the effort to create favorable conditions for consolidating the union and restoring independence consisted in the support given to the national liberation movements in Eastern, Central, and Southeastern Europe. Romania, indeed, became a polarizing center of the fight to shake off foreign domination by the peoples of this part of Europe. The struggle was so powerful and so feared that the two great empires with irreconcilable interests in the area, went as far as trying to cooperate in order to end the policy promoted by the governing circles in Bucharest. In 1864, there were rumors of an attempt to draft an alliance between Turkey and Russia, essentially designed to negate the policy of the Romanian ruling prince. "The main reason for the draft of this alliance consisted in the ever more marked tendency of the reigning prince [Cuza]" — as pointed out in a document drawn up by a Romanian diplomat and handed to the leaders of the Polish emigration in Paris — "not only to get rid of the suzerainty of the Sultan but also to draw after him Serbia, Montenegro, Bulgaria, and Poland."[36]

After the achievement of Union Romania supported the revolutionary movements of national liberation in Eastern and Southeastern Europe. Its policy, between 1859 and 1875, represented the continuation on a higher plane of certain aspects of collaboration, originating in the Middle Ages, in the fight against the Ottoman yoke. That Romanian external and military policy was correct and fruitful was fully confirmed by political developments in Southern and Southeastern Europe at the end of the nineteenth and the beginning of the twentieth century. The major objectives of Romanian policy — the conquest of independence and the completion of national unity — required, as an indispensable condition, the weakening or disintegration of the large neighboring empires. The Balkan peoples' struggle for liberation was a major factor in the crisis that led to the decline of the Ottoman empire. The war of 1877–78 opened the era of the formation of national states in Southeast Europe. As Ottoman power declined, the focus of the revolutionary struggle for national liberation shifted to the Austro-Hungarian monarchy, and history inscribed on its agenda the task of destroying this "prison of the peoples." The all but simultaneous collapse in 1917–18 of the Habsburg and tsarist empires was the result of long struggle for emancipation carried on by the oppressed peoples in these two empires, peoples who, as has been shown, benefited from active Romanian support. The disintegration of these empires brought about national unification for Romanians and Yugoslavs. The Czechoslovak national state was established. The Polish national state was restored. In these far-reaching changes — the results of prolonged struggles for liberation — Romania's contribution played an important part. Support for the fight to win national freedom and unity appears as a constant purpose of Romanian policy, which finds its best medium for development in today's socialist state.

Notes

1. For the general circumstances in which the union was achieved see *History of the Romanian People* (New York, 1974), 367–74.

2. The question of the union of Moldavia and Wallachia in the European context is treated by L. Boicu, *Geneza "chestiunii românești" ca problemă internațională* (Iași, 1975).

3. For the history of the Romanian army during the period, see *România, în războiul de independență, 1877–1878* (București, 1977), 55–73.

4. A. Oțetea, *Tudor Vladimirescu și revoluția din 1821* (București, 1971).

5. For the foreign policy of Al. I. Cuza, see C. C. Giurescu, *Viața și opera lui Cuza Vodă*, 2d ed. (București, 1970).

6. See L. Kossuth, *Souvenirs et écrits de mon exil. Période de la guerre d'Italie* (Paris, 1880), 236–38, and Th. Codrescu, *Uricariul* (Iași, 1889), XIII: 319–21.

7. *Arhiva Cuza*, XLVII, doc. no. 127.

8. *Ibid.*, LVIII, fascicle *Documents*, 1861.

9. *Ibid.*, LVIII, fascicle *Documents*, 1862.

10. *Ibid.*, I, f. 278–79, v.

11. *Ibid.*

12. *Ibid.*, XVI, f. 301–309.

13. Giurescu, 127–31; Dan Berindei, "Les Principautés roumaines unies et la lutte de libération nationale du sud-est de l'Europe," *Actes du premier Congrès international des études balkaniques et sud-est européenes* (cited as APCI) (Sofia, 1969), IV: 322–23; idem., "Mihail Kogălniceanu prim ministru al Moldovei și emigrația maghiară (1860–1861)," *Studii și materiale de istorie moderna*, II (1960).

14. Gh. Duzinchievici, *Cuza Vodă și revoluția polonă din 1863* (București, 1935).

15. P. P. Panaitescu, "Unirea Principatelor, Cuza Vodă și polonii," *Romanoslavica, Istorie* V (1962): 80.

16. *Arhiva Cuza*, XVII, f. 33–33.

17. Panaitescu, 81.

18. Gh. I. Brătianu, *Politica externă a lui Cuza Vodă și dezvoltarea ideii de unitate națională* (București, 1930), 133–34.

19. C. C. Giurescu, "Transitul armelor sîrbești prin România sub Cuza Vodă (1862)," *Romanoslavica* XI (1965): 33–65.

20. Berindei, 325.

21. *Ibid.*

22. N. Ciachir, C. Bușe, "Cu privire la tratatul de alianță româno-sîrb din 1868," *Revista arhivelor*, no. 1 (1966): 191–92.

23. *Ibid.*

24. *Ibid.*, 193.

25. *Memoriile regelui Carol I al României* (de un martor ocular) (București, 1887), 39–39.

26. Ciachir, Bușe, 196.

27. P. Vasiliu-Năsturel, *Istoria artileriei române* (București, 1897), 95.

28. C. Bacalbașa, *Bucureștii de altădată 1871–1884*, 2d ed. (București, 1935), I: 141.

29. Constantin Velichi, *La Roumanie et les mouvements nationaux des Balkans (1840–1877)*, APCI, 301–310; Vl. Diculescu, "Romänien und die Frage der bulgarischen Freischaren (1866–1868)," *Revue des études sud-est européennes* I (1963): 463–83.

30. Velichi, 307.
31. See Ciachir, *Războiul pentru independenţa României în contextul european* (Bucureşti, 1977), 117.
32. P. Constantinescu-Iaşi, *Studii istorice româno-bulgare* (Bucureşti, 1956).
33. *Trompeta Carpaţilor,* October 10, 1876, p. 265.
34. *Viitorul,* no. 1, March 8, 1864.
35. Velichi, 309.
36. Panaitescu, 82.

Constantin Căzănişteanu

Romanian Military Thought and Practice
in the Service of National Unity and Independence
(1821–77)

The centuries-old struggle of the Romanian people to defend and later to regain its independence and achieve national unity, generated, as early as the fourteenth and fifteenth centuries, a peculiar military organization and way of waging war, characterized, among other things, by mobilization of all able-bodied men in a popular force — the "great host."[1] This was a genuine popular effort, involving the participation, direct or indirect, of all the country's people, especially the peasantry, stripping the land along the enemy's line of advance of people and supplies, creating a situation which frequently decimated the striking power of an invader. This type of resistance, requiring both rigorous discipline and high morale among the population, was based on political awareness of the people's role in warfare and was demonstrably superior both tactically and strategically to feudal methods of war. When, toward the end of the first half of the sixteenth century, the Ottoman empire finally gained domination over the Romanian lands, this popular resistance compelled the Ottomans to concede the Romanians a measure of autonomy. In Romanian history, therefore, popular war proved to be the only effective defense against aggressors disposing of overwhelming superiority in manpower and material.

This experience was to be repeated later. It came to constitute one essential component of the organization of the nineteenth-century modern Romanian army which contributed to the achievement of the Union of Wallachia and Moldavia in 1859 and, through its participation in the war of 1877–78, achieved Romania's full independence (May 9, 1877).[2] Romanian military thought assimilated a number of elements generated by the evolution of the technical means of warfare and their influence on the development of different military doctrines. These were borrowed, of course, but they were adapted to national realities. Furthermore, the founders of Romanian military thought during those years drew on the essence of century-old experience. This autochtonous essence, with new forms emerging from the conditions of Romanian society during the second half of the nineteenth century, is the subject of the present analysis.

The unique features of Romania's modern military organization crystallized and developed in the framework of the Romanian nation's struggle for unity, independence, and sovereignty, for preserving its national being, threatened by the policies of domination or expansion of the bordering great empires — Ottoman, Austrian, and Russian. Confronted by antagonists disposing of greatly superior military means — reminiscent of the mediaeval barbarian invaders — the Romanian people, with the representatives of progressive and revolutionary circles taking the lead — found in the mediaeval traditions of popular war solutions fit to meet the new challenges, both in terms of military organization and in the modalities required to repel aggression. This was like publishing a revised and improved edition of the old mediaeval formula of popular war. In its new form, it became the "nation in arms." That concept implies organizational forms which associated the actions of the specialized military body, the army, with the participation of the entire population in the defense effort, and as a second fundamental element, it implies the need to devise a military theory based on the formula just stated.

The specific conditions developing in Romanian society at the end of the eighteenth century and the beginning of the nineteenth century — above all an acceleration of capitalist trends — made the army into a socioprofessional body which drew liberal elements from the ranks of the boyars as well as from members of the bourgeoisie who wanted to climb the social ladder. Thus, the officer corps and the army became a suitable medium for disseminating novel ideas. Without ceasing to be an instrument of the state, the army acquired a new function; it became one factor propelling the diffusion of advanced social-political thinking. To show the progressive role played by the national army it is necessary only to mention that both the great democratic revolutionary Nicolae Bălcescu and the energetic political reformer Mihail Kogălniceanu started their careers as military men.

The revolutionaries of the 1848 generation worked out in their writings, as well as during their short-lived revolutionary government, the organizational and doctrinal framework and the roles of the future national army.[3] They believed in the principle of military training for all able-bodied citizens. Beside the standing army and an expanded territorial force (the Romanian equivalent of the *Landwehr*), other groups, generally paramilitary, were to be organized to train effectives not included in the army and territorial troops, as well as men who had

left active service. In this fashion, the country's entire fighting potential would be trained to answer the call to arms. As early as 1838, the
National Party of Wallachia, led by Colonel Ion Cîmpineanu, urged
that a "national guard" should be established as well as "the standing
army" and asserted that "every Romanian able to bear arms" should be
a "warrior."[4] Nicolae Bălcescu had concluded that to conquer freedom
and national independence the Romanian people needed "to acquire
all the conditions of power" against foreign oppressors; he emphasized
the need for an adequate national army. The military potential of a
state, its combative strength, consisted — according to Bălcescu — not
so much in the active army but rather in "the national reserves," that is,
the territorial troops, the national guard, the militia, the "armed
bands," in fact, the entire people.[5]

The Romanian revolution of 1848–49 decreed the establishment,
alongside the standing army, of such paramilitary formations to defend the revolutionary regime against both internal opponents and the
counterrevolutionary foreign armies; it also provided a favorable
framework for their training and operations. The objective requirements of the development of Romanian society, as well as the close
collaboration between leaders of the revolution from the three Romanian lands during the revolution, laid the groundwork for an original
Romanian military doctrine, which synthesized specific elements in the
program of the bourgeois-democratic revolution with elements from
the Romanian soldierly tradition.

This doctrine looked to keeping the useful elements in the system of
organization of the so-called regulations army. (The army set up by the
Organic Statutes, a fundamental law, drafted during Russian occupation after the 1828–29 war, based on the program of the native boyars,
approved by the Russian Imperial Cabinet, and promulgated in Wallachia, July 1831, and in Moldavia, January 1832.) Secondly, this
doctrine stressed the absolute necessity of setting up armed popular
forces — national guards, units of *dorobanți* (foot-soldiers), and
voluntary *pandurs,* which were supposed to form a huge reserve.
Thirdly, this doctrine held it imperative to mobilize all material and
human resources when needed to repel aggressors. To summarize, the
military doctrine of the revolution of 1848 was based upon the concept
of arming the entire people for a popular war, which, conducted in the
tradition of the century-old fight against foreign aggression, would
serve — when adapted to new conditions — to further the national and
social emancipation of the Romanian people.[6]

Suppression of the revolution did not mean the end of its military doctrine. The subsequent development of the Romanian army — the general structure of the system of national defense — particularly after the Union of 1859, was actually influenced by the ideas of the 1848 revolution on the principles and paths of Romania's military organization. Between 1859 and 1877, achievements in the military field, with all the changes required by new military technology and by the development of the art of war — as well as by the limitations imposed by social-political developments — were marked by the thought and experience gained in 1848.

The fundamental principles of the newly established Romanian state dominated — as was natural — the organization of the army. In the spirit of an entire political tradition, the army was called upon to defend the nation's unity and independence.

As early as 1857, the newspaper *Secolul* (*The Century*) returned Nicolae Bălcescu's ideas to prominence, not only in meaning but also in phrasing. It declared that "an excessively numerous standing army" burdened the country's resources by diverting "a large number of hands" from agriculture; setting up a military system in which "each Romanian should be obliged to serve in the army (except the clergy)"[7] appeared both less expensive and much more efficient for the national defense. In 1861, we find the same point of view expressed by I. Missail, who proposed universal "military service for all the citizens... drilling and the drafting of the armed bands, in case of need."[8] Cezar Bolliac likewise asserted that the only way to set up the army, in keeping with the level of development of Romanian society and with its political targets, was "the general arming of the country through a standing and regular army, through the militias and the arming of the villages."[9]

Moreover, the prospect of achieving independence by force of arms led to greater support for the concept of the "armed nations," a concept gaining support even in the ranks of the Romanian army including ranking commanders. It was no accident that Major Gheorghe Adrian, who later became a general, a former fighter in Avram Iancu's host, was among the first officers who attempted to put this concept into effect. He proposed that besides the Romanian standing army, the country should rely on the militia and on "calling up the masses."[10] Similar ideas appeared in the first modern military journal, *România militară* (*Military Romania*) during its publication of a serious debate over the future shape of the Romanian army. The concept of the "armed nation" enjoyed the widest support because it appeared to be the best solution for the specific problems facing Romania, the only likely way to contribute to the defense of the country's autonomy and ultimately to achieve the desired national independence.

"To be fully independent in the exercise of her rights, a nation is entitled to a public force [an army] capable of making its nationality respected abroad . . ." wrote Captain Gheorghe Anghelescu. But, he continued, for this purpose, war must become a "concern of the entire people," animated by the lofty ideal of "preserving the independence of thought and of its institutions." Therefore, when the country was endangered, when its independence was lost or threatened, "each citizen capable of bearing arms is in duty bound to defend it and only this support of the population is likely to provide an army with the required power and moral strength."[11] At the same time, the journal pointed out the decisive role of the army in the general effort to achieve national emancipation being undertaken by the Romanian people. "Only through the army," wrote another military thinker, "do we acquire the right to rank among the other free, independent nations"; he emphasized that the "men holding in their hands the destinies of the nation deserve this honor" only on condition that "they have done their utmost in providing us with a good system of military organization, apt to secure . . . our independence from the outside."[12] The most suitable military system, both to defend the state and regain independence, was to be founded on the concept of "arming the people" and its natural corollary — popular war. For this reason, the writer claimed that each Romanian capable of bearing arms should discharge this duty, prepared if necessary to sacrifice his life on the altar of the homeland, "defense of the homeland being deemed . . . a duty allotted to each Romanian upon his birth."[13]

To develop an effective defense system a number of past solutions were drawn on — methods for mobilizing the masses, turning to account the experience of other armies (the militia), assimilation of certain creations of the bourgeois revolution (the national guard). Four successive laws for organizing the armed forces were passed in 1864, 1868, 1872, and 1874; the first two were fundamental, for they provided a military establishment based on Romanian capabilities and in keeping with her special traditions. Several categories of military training were created which were to prove their value in the war of 1877–78. In accordance with legislative stipulations, the armed forces of the country included four distinct elements: the *standing army* with its reserves; the *territorial army* — the troops of *dorobanți* (foot-soldiers) and *călărași* (cavalrymen) — with its reserve; the *militia*; *town guards* and *armed bands* in villages.[14]

The standing army with its reserve, that is the first four contingents who had been discharged after four years of compulsory military service, made up the so-called campaign army; this would be joined in succession, depending on the seriousness of the danger, by the territorial army, the militia, the town guard, and the armed bands. In time of war or during maneuvers, the territorial troops and the militias were to be incorporated into the units of the active army; the town guards and "the armed bands" were normally used in garrison service and to secure the defense of their own localities. Propitious conditions were thus created for a huge concentration of trained forces, the only viable solution to resist a much stronger aggressor. Setting up and developing elements like the territorial troops, militias, guards — including the introduction of military training in elementary education, as early as 1874,[15] prescribed earlier in the laws of 1864 and 1868 and partially achieved —translated into fact the principle of the "armed nation," inaugurated by the military policy of Prince Alexandru Ioan Cuza (1859–66) and almost reached by the eve of the War of Independence.

The system of organizing armed forces synthesized in the formula of the "armed nation" was based upon full concord between the social and economic structures of the country and its political-military objective — defense of unity and autonomy, and at the suitable moment, the conquest of full independence.

But the fight for the Romanian people's national liberation required the use of varied military means, and among these, partisan warfare had an important place.

The idea of partisan war and the concepts guiding this specific form of fighting, usually, though not exclusively, carried on by a small people attempting to achieve their independence or to resist a stronger enemy to whom they have fallen victim, originated in Romania with the thinkers of the 1848 revolution.

Even when the revolution was in its preparatory stage, the committee headed by Nicolae Bălcescu, discussing the possibility of foreign intervention to overthrow the revolutionary power, decided, as C. A. Rosetti reported, "to defend our country arms in hand against any invasion."[16] By this time, Dr. Louis Mandel had approached the leaders in Paris and asked them to send some capable, experienced officers to Wallachia where they could strengthen the defense organization.[17] Should the country be occupied, the revolutionaries decided to "withdraw to the mountains, and even if we shall be only 300 men, we will hold out against the enemy until foreign nations come to our aid, and if they will not, we shall perish arms in hand."[18]

Immediately after the abdication of the ruling prince, Gheorghe Bibescu, the leaders of the 1848 movement in Wallachia were alarmed by reports of the impending introduction of foreign troops to overthrow the revolutionary power and therefore intensified their preparations to organize resistance. In a letter sent to A. C. Golescu from Focşani on June 25, Nicolae Bălcescu said the revolutionary army might not be able to confront regular forces in case of invasion and mapped out measures to meet that contingency.[19] He suggested that the subprefects be ordered to "take the people to the mountains," and that the grain held at the port of Braila on behalf of the state be transported to the mountains "to serve us for food there." Moreover, Bălcescu recommended to the Bucharest government a Prussian artillery officer who had come from Moldavia and who appeared to be skilled in his profession and in "partisan war."[20] This recommendation shows that the founder of Romanian military historiography, the keenest mind of the Romanian revolution of 1848–49, favored real partisan warfare, involving both regular troops and the masses of the people. This idea testified to the thoroughness of Nicolae Bălcescu's preparatory work on the military aspects of, and preparation for, the insurrection of 1848. He appeared well informed about the most modern means of resistance advocated by the most authoritative contemporary military theorists and revolutionaries.

The revolutionary authorities in Wallachia seem to have adopted this point of view when on June 19, 1848, the second counterrevolutionary plot occurred in Bucharest, the members of the provisional government initially intended to organize armed resistance in the vicinity of the capital. They soon realized that the forces at their disposal were too few and too poorly equipped to be risked in battle on an open plain. The solution ultimately adopted was that suggested by Nicolae Bălcescu: withdrawal before the onslaught of the invader to make a stand in the rugged Carpathian area. Accordingly, they decided to move the standing army to the Cimpulung area where the government and all other resistance fighters also took refuge. From there "communications with Transylvania" could be more easily maintained, for Transylvania had promised to support the revolutionaries with "frontier-guard regiments."[21]

The government's purpose could not be realized. Yet there is evidence that the soldiers of the fifth and sixth companies of the First Infantry Regiment, which had accompanied the retreating members of the provisional government on their way to Transylvania, were advised to return to their villages from Oltenia and to prepare the villagers for an armed rising when the revolutionaries returned to the country.[22] Here we see attempts to organize an armed resistance, in the shape of partisan warfare. In the same spirit, Moldavian revolutionists, in a call from Cernăuţi, on July 18, 1848, stated that they held to the idea of preparing the insurgent forces for withdrawal to the mountains where they could set up a center which — "based upon the strength gathered in the country as well as, in particular, upon the forces from Transylvania and the Banat" — would be able to undertake a large number of more serious actions in concert with Wallachia.[23]

After the revolution of 1848–49 was suppressed, and especially during 1853–54, when the Romanian Principalities were again occupied, the Romanian revolutionaries intensified their fight, on the basis of "the principle of insurrection, which is the first right of an oppressed nation," to cite an 1851 statement in *Junimea română,* the Romanian *émigré* journal in Paris. This principle, the journal continued, was the most effective base for overthrowing the reactionary regime and for winning independence "because . . . a nation may use all active means to shake off its yoke."[24] Partisan war, seen as one of these means, seemed relevant once more. In a letter, probably written in the summer of 1853, Al. C. Golescu-Albu told Ştefan C. Golescu what he thought about the military organization of Romanian *émigrés,* in case a Russo-Turkish war created a favorable situation for an attempt at liberation. Regrouping the revolutionists along the Danube, calling up the people, arming them for resistance in the mountains, and finally partisan actions — constituted the four major elements in this project. Hence, just like Bălcescu in 1848, he insistently demanded that several specialists in partisan warfare should be employed to introduce the troops — which the revolutionists hoped to gather — to the secrets of waging this specific kind of struggle. "If you can gather five or six able military men, simple officers, not more than that, but proficient in guerrilla warfare," wrote Al. C. Golescu-Albu "this would be some excellent work."[25] The leaders of the emigration seem to have thought partisan war one of the methods best suited to the Romanian geographical setting, dominated by the mountainous girdle of the Carpathians, to the social and political realities of the region, as well as to the century-old military traditions of waging war against an overwhelmingly superior enemy. To quote Nicolae Bălcescu again, when "the country's army stood in hiding in the mountains, refraining from measuring its strength in general battles against the huge crowds of the enemies, being contented to harass them, to cut off their lines of communication, to take their supplies, consequently to reduce them to starvation and to oblige them to leave the country."[26] This is one explanation — and probably not the least significant — of the insistence of the revolutionaries of 1848 on learning about and assimilating this mode of armed struggle.

As a matter of fact, during the period when he wrote his letters to C. Golescu-Albu, Ştefan C. Golescu received advice from another exile, Dimitrie Brătianu, a champion of Romanian rights in faraway London. Brătianu counseled him — and the advice, obviously, was not directed to him alone — to form a committee of the revolutionaries in Paris, that should study French works "about partisan war."[27] They were supposed to select the best one and translate it or to compile from their reading "a clever anthology containing the items most easily applicable in this country." The translated book or the anthology should be "brief, easily understandable, and ready for printing."[28] These repeated suggestions were not without results. During 1853, in Brussels, Romanian *émigrés* published an anthology, *Idee răpede despre rezbelul de partizani* (*Brief Ideas on Partisan War*), followed by *Instrucţiuni asupra serviciului de campanie* (*Instructions on Campaigning*) and by *Manual de fortificaţie pasageră* (*Textbook of Temporary Fortification*) translated from the French with some adaptations, by Gheorghe Adrian, a former soldier from the Romanian Principalities. These three military manuals were not then known to the standing army of the Romanian countries — to our knowledge — nor were they subsequently used. Hence, the first manuals distributed in the Romanian Principalities are, as has been shown, due to the initiative of the revolutionary emigration of 1848. The book did not reach those concerned for some time. In April 1864, the same Al. C. Golescu-Albu insistently asked A. C. Golescu-Arapila and Ştefan C. Golescu, to request Adrian, in case "he has not yet left, to take along the best work, according to his knowledge, referring to partisan war."[29] Consequently he had not yet received the book.

Thus during 1853-54, Adrian — a professional officer, who had fought with the Motzi in the western Carpathians during the Transylvanian Revolution of 1848 — placed a military textbook including the minimal knowledge to be mastered by anyone who wished to participate and to play a leading role in such a large-scale military operation, within reach of the patriotic revolutionary exiles who held to the ideal of liberating the Romanian countries at whatever sacrifice and by any means. These men fully shared Adrian's belief that "our nation will be able to conquer its freedom only by force of arms."[30] If anyone endeavored "to assimilate at least the few rules laid down in this book," Adrian stated, "he would surely be able to be of inestimable service to his homeland in wartime."[31]

To instruct the standing army, likewise drawn into the general effort at emancipating the Romanian people, Adrian translated *Instrucţiuni asupra serviciului de campanie* (*Instructions on Campaigning*). But as the fight was supposed to have a popular and underground character from the very beginning, occurring in areas where irregulars would constitute a most precious auxiliary, Adrian introduced into his textbook two works designed to deal with the problems of such warfare: *Idee răpede despre rezbelul de partizani* (*Brief Thoughts on Partisan War*) and *Manual de fortificaţie pasageră* (*Textbook on Temporary Fortification*).

In drafting *Idee răpede despre rezbelul de Partizani* (*Brief Thoughts on Partisan War*), the first work ever to popularize this revolutionary method of national defense in Romania — as has been recently proved[32] — Adrian made use of the fifth chapter, "On Partisan War," in the French translation (1845) of Karl von Decker's *On Small War in the Spirit of Modern Strategy*. This was not a mechanical translation, but a constructive adaptation of Karl von Decker's material.[33] Adrian made valuable improvements and additions, enriched it with his own ideas making it relevant to Romanian realities, traditions, and experience derived from the struggle of our people.

Like Karl von Decker and other progressive thinkers of his time, Adrian conceived partisan units as military formations detached from the standing army, the reserves, or the territorial troops and given special assignments to carry out operations in support of the main army; for this very reason, these units did not act according to some preestablished tactical scheme but, almost always, tried to adapt themselves to the special circumstances and unforeseen factors of the moment. Therefore they were granted initiative and independence of maneuver, and their assignments might be expanded beyond the frontiers of their own country. Viewed from this angle, partisan warfare appears to some extent as a people's war, a liberation struggle with the participation of the entire nation. Taking into account the characteristics of the Romanian lands, however, and aware that, as the revolutionaries of 1848 believed, they could regain unity and independence only through a general armed uprising of the people, and therefore could wage a war of national liberation only on their own national territory, Adrian also discerned and emphasized the possibility of turning a partisan war into a war of national liberation.

Adrian could easily envision this possibility because of his experience fighting alongside the peasant soldiers of the western Carpathians. There he had seen and come to realize what people's war was like, and this gave his book its elements of originality. As General Radu Rosetti remarked: "They were also — the outcome of the experience acquired [by Adrian] alongside Avram Iancu."[34] He underscored that, if the armies of the Romanian countries were mobilized, "wherever these liberation armies arrive, the entire nation will rise to its feet in order to help them, with all its power."[35]

But the "Romanian partisans, fighting against the foreigner in the midst of compatriots, will simultaneously have the assignment to protect and facilitate by all means, the assemblies of citizens whose patriotism urges them to rise to the defense of their homeland."[36] To put it differently, they would move toward a generalized partisan war, fusing the patriotic energies of the civilian population with those of the army to achieve the common ideal of the Romanian people. Hence the role Adrian allotted to the national guard meant support for the effort of other military forces in the event of a rising of the entire nation. Moreover, he thought that the Romanians, "through their military traditions," linked with numerous "daring" battles in the past and "even more" because of their "topographic positions," were one of the "nations best adapted to partisan war."[37] This belief moved Adrian to translate *The Textbook for Temporary Fortification*, to inform those who might need to fortify themselves in the Carpathians, when mountainous terrain represented the *sine qua non* for conducting a generalized partisan war, which was conceivable only in suitable geographical settings. "There exists a form of defensive war in the mountains," Friedrich Engels wrote (in "War in the Mountains Past and Present") that "has become very famous in our times, namely the national uprising and the guerrilla war for which, in Europe at least, such a mountainous terrain constitutes an absolute necessity."[38]

In his adaptation of Karl von Decker's work, Adrian, as we have seen, pleaded for the creation of partisan troops; he relied mainly on the striking power of regular units, but under certain circumstances, he did not exclude the participation of elements from the territorial forces, the national guard and militia, and even armed intervention by the civilian population. Still, conceiving regulars as the mainstay, as he did, Adrian seems to have a limited view of the framework of partisan war.

From the same period, however, we have a project for organizing the Romanian people for resistance and the war of national liberation.

This is founded on a broader outlook in which the people — above all the peasantry — assumed the leading role. The project was worked out by Cezar Bolliac, a leader of the Romanian revolution of 1848 in Wallachia, and published in Paris as *Choix de lettres et mémoires sur la question roumaine, 1852-1856.* In this book, Bolliac, an enthusiastic advocate of arming the masses and of popular war, set forth the claims of the Romanian people. He also urged that from the military point of view, the most effective method of defense and action in support of the national ambition for unity and independence was by forming guerrilla groups capable of organizing the entire nation to wage war. He thought that the geography of Romania provided excellent conditions for organizing a solid and lasting resistance. Bolliac pointed out that the Carpathian chain, a "natural bulwark," could become "an operational center and an excellent defense line from the Bukovina down to the Iron Gate," providing an area where, what he called "resistance companies," could be established.[39] They could be set up in Oltenia, "from the Olt River up to the Carpathians," an area which, as Bolliac probably recalled, had a tradition of anti-Ottoman and revolutionary struggle. He considered Moldavia, too, and the counties of Roman, Băcău, Suceava, and Putna as suited to resistance groups.

To perform the "great patriotic feat," the liberation of the country, Bolliac stated that the people should be called to arms. In order to realize this national ideal of liberation, a step he considered absolutely necessary to fulfilling the social program of the revolutionaries of 1848, he would have gathered the entire nation under the banner of resistance, enlisted the unanimous support of the peasantry, the "firm and energetic" support of the small landowners, indeed of all strata interested in ending foreign rule, of "all members of the national party." He estimated that mobilization of the people's forces would gather "immediately around 30,000 men under the banner," most of them trained, "coming from the army."[40] At the same time, he counted on substantial support from the Romanians living in the provinces under foreign domination, especially if at least one of the great European powers should indicate understanding and active support for the Romanian cause. According to Bolliac, there were chances that many peasants would leave their homes in order "to join up with the army in the mountains, thus increasing its ranks."[41]

Monasteries were recommended as fortified places as well as places of refuge, a suggestion to be found in Adrian's book, too. Numerous in the mountainous areas and generally located in places deemed inaccessible especially at the time, the monasteries were well suited "to serve as strongholds or places of shelter in case of attack or bad weather."[42] Well-organized and led, partisan war waged by the Romanian people in the Carpathians might have become as fierce and lasting as many other guerrilla wars in Europe and Asia.

Cezar Bolliac's proposals were not fundamentally different from Adrian's and Bolliac probably was familiar with his work. Bolliac, however, examined the situation in our country more concretely; he placed greater emphasis on the mass of the people, especially the peasantry, which both in numbers and strength was supposed to constitute the major support for the resistance. At the same time, he limited the operations of partisan war to the mountainous areas which the enemy could penetrate only with the utmost difficulty and where he could not deploy his forces, whereas the local insurgents would find the Carpathians a natural fortress providing them with multiple opportunities to organize their resistance. Cezar Bolliac envisaged partisan warfare as a fight in which Romanians from all the provinces they inhabited would participate, a manifestation of the spirit of Romanian unity and of the desire for the achievement of union and national independence.

The two works referring to partisan warfare, and therefore to popular war, show that the patriotic revolutionaries of 1848 were trying to devise the most effective modes of fighting in order to win full emancipation for Romanians. And it is to their credit to have pioneered in finding military solutions adapted to the needs of the revolutionary ideology of the international proletariat and suitable for any oppressed people wanting to struggle for its national independence.

For this reason, perhaps, partisan warfare was not mentioned either in later projects for reorganizing sociopolitical structures or for military planning. Although two military works appeared — both adaptations of foreign systems, one by Captain I. Carally (1868),[43] the other by Major Alexandru Schina (1872)[44] — which include chapters dealing with small-scale war where partisan warfare might have been discussed, neither book even mentions it. In 1873, however, a translation of the French version (1845) of Karl von Decker's book on small war[45] was published at Craiova. (This translation was by Lieutenant M. I. Eustațiu of the Fourth Infantry Regiment.)

A year later, for the first time, we find in one of the few surviving examples of the curriculum of an officers' military academy, a tiny section dealing with partisan warfare. Colonel G. Slăniceanu in his *Curs de studii, Tactica și Strategica (Course of Lectures on Tactics and Strategy)*, delivered in 1874 at the Bucharest Infantry and Cavalry

School, devoted a few pages to the principles of partisan organization and warfare and its place in the spectrum of military operations.

As Slăniceanu saw it, partisans represented independent bodies without a direct link with the operational army; they acted, as a rule, behind enemy lines under the command and responsibility of "their chief." Their objectives were "to render dangerous the territory stretching between the enemy army and its operational base, to intercept any support meant for the opponent, to take all his reinforcements, arms, ammunition, food, to destroy his depots, to free the prisoners he has taken, to gain possession of his despatches, to destroy his roads, telegraphic devices, to oblige him to split up in detachments."[46]

Partisans were to be recruited from volunteers, "men from the army or from the country" with military or war experience. Their commanders were likewise to be volunteers, selected from experienced officers, endowed with courage, intelligence, and presence of mind. As they mostly acted independently, they were supposed to show more initiative and versatility in commanding the troops under their control, to avail themselves of every moment of enemy weakness, because this was the only way they could succeed when they were so generally outnumbered. Partisan action might not be decisive for the outcome of the war, but the partisan corps nevertheless had the mission — in line with the nature of their task — to dislodge important forces of the enemy, substantially diminishing his combat strength and concentration on the main axis of attack.

Although partisan formations numbering several thousand men could defeat strong opposition, in view of their specific assignments, Slăniceanu thought it more appropriate to restrict partisan groups to 200–300 men, including both infantry and cavalry. Their upkeep was easier, they were more efficient in retreating and camouflaging; they had more independence of action. In determining the proportion of infantry and cavalry in each partisan detachment, the nature of the terrain where the operation was to take place had to be taken into account. Attacks and movements were to be fast; they were supposed to march in secret, usually at night, and bivouac in forests or remote localities. The partisans were to have friendly relations with the inhabitants and to respect their possessions and customs. After each attack, the partisans were to leave the area where they had operated.

Partisan warfare did not exist for its own sake, however; its operations were "undertakings inflicting considerable damage on the enemy and bringing a considerable advantage to the army."[47] This point of view came close to that of Karl von Decker. The impact of his work

— known in Romania in Adrian's adaptation of 1853 and in the translation published only a year before Colonel Slăniceanu's lectures — appears obvious. For Slăniceanu as for Decker, partisan operations were auxiliary to the main battles; they influenced but did not decide the outcome of a war. Recruiting partisans from volunteers gave partisan activity somewhat of a broader mass basis, but this did not place it among people's wars as the Romanian revolutionaries of 1848 had envisaged.

Partisan warfare was recognized in the Romanian countries as early as the mid-nineteenth century. Military theorists regarded it as a secondary operation, one among other components of the small-scale war waged by specialized armed units recruited from the ranks of the standing, territorial, or reserve troops, a contribution to the ultimate victory in a general war. The leaders of the Romanian revolutionary movements of 1848, on the hand, envisaged partisan action as a genuine people's war of defense and national emancipation, activating all the country's human energies and material resources, in which every citizen, soldier or civilian, became a resistance fighter. The names of Nicolae Bălcescu, Avram Iancu, Cezar Bolliac, and Gheorghe Adrian are linked to the development of and the attempt to introduce this type of war into Romanian military practice.

Subsequently, military theorists of the Romanian army took over the concept of partisan war in two ways: the first borrowed from foreign military literature, the second looked to the heritage of revolutionary progressive military thought in Romania. The military theorists tended to opt for the formula of partisan warfare as an operation in small-scale war. One should emphasize that, in this sense, partisan warfare appeared as early as the eighth decade of the last century in many military school courses on tactics and strategy given for officers, commissioned and noncommissioned.

As has been shown, partisan warfare was present in nineteenth-century Romanian military thinking in both its forms. The revolutionary formula in particular — a means of engaging the characteristic loyalties of a people fighting for national freedom or against a foreign aggressor — retains to this day its relevance on many intellectual and practical levels.

During the new stage in the Eastern Crisis (1875–78), which was decisive for the recovery of Romania's independence, the major correlation between war and society was a Romanian army based on the tradition of popular war, endowed with a doctrine which blended national individuality with the principles of modern war, and designed to be instrumental in achieving unity and independence.

In the War of Independence, 1877–78, Romanian society, through the army it produced, proved that the military forms it had created for itself were in keeping with its historical evolution, with its stage of development, and with its fundamental objectives. In the perspective of the analysis attempted here, we see clearly that contemporary Romanian military doctrine based on the concept of people's war is the continuation of an autochtonous tradition deeply rooted historically in our people's struggle.

Notes

1. From the rich literature available, see Ştefan Ştefănescu, "'Oastea ţării' şi epopeea românească a secolelor XIV–XVI" in *România şi tradiţiile luptei armate a întregului popor* (Bucureşti, 1972), 25–32; Nicolae Stoicescu, "'Oastea cea mare' în Ţara Românească şi Moldova (secolele XIV–XVI" in *Oastea cea mare* (Bucureşti, 1972), 27–51; Ştefan Pascu, "'Oastea de ţară,' oaste populară în ţările române în secolele XIV–XVI" in *Armata Republicii Socialiste România. Tradiţii şi contemporaneitate* (Bucureşti, 1975), 21–32.

2. See *România în războiul de independenţă 1877–1878* (Bucureşti, 1977), 53–74.

3. Constantin Căzănişteanu, "Probleme militare în revoluţia romană de la 1848," in *Revoluţia de la 1848 în ţările române* (Bucureşti, 1974), 131–42.

4. See Cornelia Bodea, *Lupta românilor pentru unitate naţională, 1834–1849* (Bucureşti, 1967), 219.

5. N. Bălcescu, *Scrieri militare alese* (Bucureşti, 1957), 11.

6. Constantin Căzănişteanu, "Ideea înarmării poporului şi războiului popular în gîndirea românească de la mijlocul secolului al XIX-lea" in *Oastea cea mare* (Bucureşti, 1972), 99–133.

7. "O idee despre armarea ţării," *Secolul,* May 9, 1857.

8. I. Missail, "Intărirea naţională," *Revista Carpaţilor,* Mar. 15, 1861.

9. Cezar Bolliac, "Armarea," *Românul,* Oct. 6, 1861.

10. G. Adrian, *Mémoires sur l'organisation de la force armée des deux Principautés Roumains* (Bucureşti, 1858), 9.

11. Gheorghe Anghelescu, "Organizarea sistemului militar al României," *România Militară* 1 (1864): 54, 57, 58.

12. *Pagini din gîndirea militară românească, 1821–1916* (Bucureşti, 1969), 51–52.

13. *Ibid.,* 52.

14. V. Nădejde, *Centenarul renaşterii armatei române 1830–1930* (Iaşi, 1931), 155–65.

15. Corneliu Băjenaru, *Tradiția în pregătirea tineretului studios în vederea apărării patriei* (București, 1972).

16. *Documente privind anul revoluționar 1848 în Țara Românească* (București, 1962), 17.

17. *Anul 1848 în Principatele Române. Acte și documente* (București, 1902), II: 321, Dr. Louis Mandl to Nicolae Bălcescu.

18. I. Ghica, *Amintiri din pribegia după 1848* (București, 1889), 20.

19. N. Bălcescu, *Opere* (București, 1964), IV: 93.

20. *Ibid.*

21. *Anul 1848 în Principatele Române. Acte și documente*, II: 546.

22. The State Archives, Craiova, Stock of the Prefect's Office of Dolj County, file no. 1/1848, f. 484–85.

23. Quoted from Bodea, 142.

24. *Junimea română*, May 1851.

25. Gheorghe Fotino, *Din vremea renașterii naționale a Țării Românești, Boierii Golești* (București, 1939), IV: 44.

26. Paul Cornea, Mihai Zamfir, *Gîndirea românească în epoca pașoptistă* (București, 1968), 286.

27. Al. Cretzianu, *Din arhiva lui Dimitrie Brătianu* (București, 1933), 341.

28. *Ibid.*

29. Fotino, IV: 97.

30. G. Adrian, *Idee răpede despre rezbelul de partizani, urmată de Instrucțiuni asupra serviciului de campanie și de un Manual de fortificație pasageră* (Brussels, 1853), 3.

31. *Ibid.*, 8.

32. Constantin Antip, *Ideea războiului de partizani într-o lucrare românească de la mijlocul secolului al XIX-lea în România și tradițiile luptei armate a întregului popor* (București, 1972), 109–118; Idem, "Idee răpede despre rezbelul de partizani," *Magazin istoric* (June 1970): 20–24; Adrian, *Idee răpede despre rezbelul de partizani,* ed., with an introduction by Major-General Constantin Antip (București, 1973), 5–26.

33. A competent analysis of Adrian's work — the first, as a matter of fact — may be found in the Antip studies we cite.

34. R. Rosetti, "Relations entre l'armée française et l'armée roumaine" in *L'hommage à M. Le Saint Aulaire* (București, 1930), 93.

35. Adrian, 15.

36. *Ibid.*, 15–6.

37. *Ibid.*, 3.

38. K. Marx, F. Engels, *Opere* (București, 1962), 12: 116–17.

39. Cezar Bolliac, *Choix de lettres et mémoires sur la question roumaine, 1852–1856* (Paris, 1856), 27.

40. *Ibid.*

41. *Ibid.*

42. *Ibid.*

43. I. Carally, *Manualul recunoașterilor militare în ceea ce privește pe*

ofițerii și subofițerii de infanterie și artilerie (București, 1868); the fifth chapter includes *Date asupra micului rezbel sau rezbelul posturilor.*

44. Alex. Schina, *Elemente teoretice asupra serviciului în campanie pentru a servi la instrucția tinerilor ofițeri și subofițeri de cavalerie* (București, 1872).

45. Karl von Decker, *Despre micul rezbel în spiritul strategiei moderne* (Craiova, 1873).

46. Slăniceanu, *Curs de studii. Tactica și strategia* (București, 1874), 333.

47. *Ibid.,* 334-35.

Wayne S. Vucinich

Serbian Military Tradition

Throughout most of their history, the Serbs have been scattered, not united under a single rule until 1918. Each Serbian region had its own historical experience and concomitant military tradition. But although the character of the military tradition of the Serbs in a particular region reflected local conditions and needs, that tradition invariably helped inspire Serbs in adjoining areas. Local exploits became part of the common patrimony of all Serbs, largely through the traditional media of epic poetry and folklore.

The investigation of Serbian military traditions is not, however, an easy task. It is sometimes difficult to establish which military traditions are peculiarly Serbian and which are common to all South Slavs or Serbs. The first references to the military qualities of the Balkan Slavs are found in Byzantine authors.[1] Among Western observers, Raymond of Aguilars in 1096 wrote about the high military quality of the "Sclavonians"; William of Tyre, in 1168, found the Serbs a courageous and warlike people. Mediaeval South Slav writings also allude to Serbian military skills. Grigorije Camblak commends King Stefan Uroš III for his bravery in the battle with the Bulgarians at Velebužd. In his biography of Stefan Lazarević, Konstantin Filozof hails the Serbs for their heroism and military dexterity, the Priest of Duklja tells how the Serbian kings praised and rewarded loyal and brave warriors. Several mediaeval Bosnian charters tell of Croatian and Serbian individual and collective acts of bravery.

The Serbian Mediaeval Armies

In Nemanjić Serbia (c. 1217–1371), the armed forces included feudal contingents (the principal force), mercenary troops, guards, and certain special formations. The Serbs had adopted many Byzantine practices and institutions, such as the *pronoia,* feudal estates granted to the nobility in exchange for military service. The recipient of such an estate mustered a specified number of armed men on demand. The feudal army was organized by districts (*župe*), each providing a contingent whose size depended on the district's population, economic resources, and military tradition. Although the ruler was technically the supreme commander of the armed forces,[2] often he could not depend on his nobility to meet their feudal obligations, for the nobility employed its armed contingent for its own purposes and was frequently involved in dynastic conflicts and struggles for power.

The upper nobility fought on horseback; the lower, on foot. The weaponry resembled that used elsewhere in mediaeval Europe. Although the cavalry was a more effective combat force than the infantry, the latter played a more important role in Serbia than in the West. The feudal army fought only within a specified area and at its own expense. Distant expeditions were sustained by the rulers themselves. The Serbs were apparently excellent fighters in local engagements and in nearby mountains and forests, but they were not very effective when fighting far from home.[3] For example, Serbian troops performed poorly when Tsar Dušan led them into battle south of Serres. The first Serbian military encounters with the Turks, fought on foreign soil, likewise ended in disaster.[4]

Besides the "territorial" armies, mediaeval Serbian rulers employed mercenaries, their only standing army. King Milutin used eastern light horsemen — Turkopoles, Cumans, Tatars, Alans, and Ossets; Stefan Dečanski used Western mercenaries — knights and heavy cavalrymen. The mercenaries protected the rulers, but were relatively few in number and prone to mutiny.

Armed peasants guarded fortified towns, roads, and borders; monasteries used their peasants to man monastery towers. The general population was employed only in defense of its own home base, a traditional feature of tribal social organization.[5]

The Traditional Irregular Forces

The Hayduks. Throughout early Serbian history armed individuals and groups operated outside the law. The best known of these were the *hayduks* (*hajduk, hajdut*) and *uskoks,* whose activities were evoked by the oppressive nature of Ottoman rule. (*Hayduks* or their equivalents existed elsewhere in the Balkans.) *Hayduks* and *uskoks* were so much alike that the terms often were used interchangeably. The term *hayduk* appears to be of Turkish origin and its connotation has varied. In Austria and Hungary, during the sixteenth and the early seventeenth centuries, *hayduk* was applied to mercenaries guarding the borders, for guards in cities, counties (*comitatus, županija*), and on feudal estates. Certain Austrian infantry units operating in Serbia and the Banat during the Austro-Turkish war of 1716–18 were also called *hayduks,* as were similar units in Poland. But the label was most commonly used for the outlaws in the Ottoman empire who might be either bandits or fighters against Turkish feudal, national, and religious oppression. Sometimes, battles between Turks and *hayduks* were personal, stemming from personal quarrel or challenge. Many *hayduks* who began as bandits later joined popular insurrections against Ottoman rule. Sometimes they entered Austrian or Venetian service as allies and mercenaries; sometimes, when it seemed in their interest, they collaborated with the Turks.[6]

The *hayduk* bands might number from two or three men to as many as a hundred or more. The leader (*harambaša,* from Turkish *haram basi*) was usually chosen for toughness and bravery; in some instances, however, aggressive individuals imposed themselves as leaders. The *hayduks* might wear the dress of the local population, clothes captured from the Turks, or special garb of their own. Their arms were not uniform, usually including various kinds of pistols, muskets, and long knives (*handžar* [*hancer*], *jatagan* [*yatağan*], *ćorda, sabre,* swords [*mač*]), and daggers (*bodež*). The *hayduks* made up for their scanty number by skill in ambushing caravans or armed units in larger numbers during daylight attacks than at night. Booty was divided among themselves and their local accomplices (*yataks*).

Hayduk activity in the Ottoman empire increased after the end of the sixteenth century, when the Turks suffered major military setbacks, and exploitation and abuse of the Christian peasantry progressively increased. Many Christians fled to the forests and mountains and there formed *hayduk* bands. *Hayduk* activity and other banditry became so general that diplomatic missions and caravans often had to be escorted by armed guards.

Hayduks were especially numerous along important roads and in areas where the laws could not be easily enforced. Although most prevalent in the Ottoman empire, *hayduks* presented a serious problem for Austrian civil and military authorities in the eighteenth-century Vojvodina. Habsburg officials used extreme measures (hanging, shooting, impaling, dispersing the population) in order to end *hayduk* activity.[7] Some of their leaders became well known. One *hayduk,* Laza Harambaša, won the hearts of the people in Serbia and Srem, who saw him as their hero, because he took vengeance against the oppressor and helped the poor. Many prominent leaders of the First Serbian

Uprising against the Turks (1804–1812), including Karadjordje, Stanoje Glavaš, Hajduk-Veljko Petrović, and Mladen Milovanović had contact with him. For Laza Harambaša and his band crossed into Serbia and operated there.

Forests and swamps made Vojvodina natural terrain for *hayduk* activity. The large rivers and their tributaries were suitable for piracy. In the first half of the eighteenth century, public security hardly existed; no one felt safe from the *hayduks* who attacked churches, monasteries, state and local officials, and invaded villages in the daytime, striking even larger urban centers, such as Karlovci and Vršac. In Vojvodina the *hayduks* usually operated in groups of about ten to twenty, but *hayduk* bands might number as many as a hundred men. Often they could depend on local people to protect and shelter them.[8]

The *hayduks* were an important military asset to Venice in the Cretan War (1645–69). Bands from the Makarska littoral between Split and the Neretva, operated against the Turks in the Bosnian and Hercegovinian hinterland, on the Adriatic Sea, attacking shipping and coastal settlements, and on the lower reaches of the Neretva. From 1657 on, the center of *hayduk* activity shifted to the region of the Bay of Boka Kotorska; the coastal town of Perast became a staging base for many *hayduk* forays into Hercegovina.

Most *hayduks* in Boka Kotorska were refugees from the Turkish hinterland, especially Hercegovina. Turkish oppression, natural disasters such as famine, or the prevalent anarchy and personal insecurity drove people from their homes to take refuge on Venetian territory, where they joined the *hayduks* and made a living by pillaging the area in which they had formerly lived. Venice found it difficult to utilize the *hayduks* for military purposes and maintain control over them.

Most famous among the Boka *hayduks* was Bajo Pivljanin, celebrated in epic poetry, whose career spanned the Cretan and the Morean wars (1645–69, 1684–99, 1714–19). *Hayduk* activity extended over various parts of Montenegro and eastern Hercegovina. *Hayduks* raided Turkish territory, carried off whatever valuables they could find, including livestock or captives, then retreated across the border. *Hayduks* operating from Venetian bases often crossed the territory of the Republic of Dubrovnik (Ragusa) in order to reach Hercegovina and injured the citizens and property of that republic. One should note that, as an Ottoman tributary and economic rival of Venice, Dubrovnik often remained neutral in wars between Venice and Turkey.

The Serb subjects of the Ottoman empire looked upon Venice as an ally, but they resented Dubrovnik's collaboration with the Turks. Yet *hayduk* plundering expeditions spared Christians on Turkish territory no more than Muslims. During the Cretan war, the *hayduks* made handsome profits selling captives, both Muslim and Christian, to Venetian and other Italian slave buyers.

After the Cretan war what to do with the *hayduks* during peacetime became a vexing problem for Venice. The Republic tried to turn them to agriculture. The *hayduks* of Makarska and the coast were given land and settled around Klis; many of the Boka *hayduks* were transported to Istria, but a number of them did not adjust to the new environment and moved to the Austrian Frontier, or drifted back to Hercegovina and Boka. Some, like Bajo Pivljanin, reappeared as *hayduks* in the Morean war. Toward the end of that war, the Venetians again began to settle the *hayduks* on land won from the Turks and to encourage them to take up agriculture and stockherding.

Uskoks. From the beginning of the sixteenth century, in the wake of the Turkish advance, masses of Christians fled from Serbian territory to neighboring Croatia and Dalmatia, then under Austrian and Venetian rule. They were called *uskoks* (pl. *uskoci*) or *prebezi* — those who had jumped or fled across the border. (It is difficult to establish the ethnic background of the *uskoks*. They were indubitably both Croats and Serbs.) Lika, Krbava, Dalmatian Zagora, and much of Slavonia witnessed the influx of large numbers of Dinaric refugees. These refugees had resisted the Turks, knew how to fight them, and were consequently pressed into service by Venice and Austria, who even encouraged their immigration. They were organized into bands (*četas*) operating under the command of the host country or on their own.

Initially the *uskoks* or the *hayduks* (the terms sometimes are used interchangeably) were dedicated to the idea of revenge against the Turks. But they were forced to supplement the low pay they received from Austria, with plunder gained on foraging expeditions into Ottoman lands, particularly Hercegovina. The *uskoks* also attacked the Venetians, the citizens of Dubrovnik, and Dubrovnik itself. They operated on land and on sea and were particularly known for their light maneuverable craft and their seamanship. In default of pay, the *uskoks* sustained themselves entirely on piracy and plunder, at first attacking only Venetian ships and later Austrian vessels as well.

The first *uskoks* are usually linked to the group of people which, in 1530, fled from Hercegovina to Klis, whence, under command of Petar Kružić, captain of Klis, they carried out pillaging expeditions into

Turkish territory. When the Turks captured Klis in 1537, the *uskoks* moved to Senj. Here as paid soldiers (*stipendiati*) of the Austrian emperor they were integrated in what was the Austrian Military Frontier and thus became frontier guards (*krajišnici*) under the command of their own *vojvodas*. In the Senj captaincy, the *uskoks* were organized into an armed force; they garrisoned the town and fortress of Senj and held considerable power on the Adriatic Sea.

Local people often joined the *uskoks* on their raids. Thus, what began as an expedition of a few dozen men might swell with people recruited along the way, joining voluntarily or out of fear of reprisal. Like *hayduks,* they had *yataks,* allies on enemy territory, who supported them and gave them information. In some areas, the Christian population is said to have paid tribute to the *uskoks* to preserve themselves from attack.

At first Venice sympathized with *uskok* forays into Turkey, but after the conclusion of peace between Venice and Turkey in 1540, it turned against them. Disillusioned with Venice, many Venetian *uskoks* joined their fellows in Senj and swelled the ranks of the *venturini, uskoks* who lived by banditry alone, attacking Turks and Venetians alike.[9] Austria used the *uskoks* in occasional formal military operations, for example, in the siege of Klis in 1596, but more often they were free to pursue their own peculiar method of warfare. Venice repeatedly urged Austria to suppress *uskok* activities and to drive them out of Senj. For some eighty years, Venice kept the largest part of its fleet in a state of constant alert. In 1615, it even went to war with Austria over the *uskoks.* Finally, by the Treaty of Madrid (1617) Austria agreed to expel them from Senj and to destroy their boats. The *uskoks* then moved to Žumberak, Otočac, Pazin, and other communities along the Turkish border. By the end of the sixteenth century, the term *uskok* had been localized to apply to irregular armed forces operating out of Senj and Žumberak.

As the Turks pursued their aggressive actions, the Vlachs, particularly in the seventeenth century, fled from Bosnia and Hercegovina to Venetian Dalmatia, where the Venetians employed them as guards. The Venetians, who disliked the term *uskoks,* so reminiscent of their hated Senj enemies, called the new refugees *Morlacchi,* a name which the Venetians and the coastal inhabitants used for the Slav population of the hinterland. Though the term has no ethnic significance, the records on occasion speak of Orthodox *Morlacchi.* To the Turks, all such refugees were *uskoks*; and this is the term remembered in the epic songs of the South Slavs;

Morlacchi or *uskoks* were important to Venice's military system in Dalmatia; they bore the brunt of the fighting there and in the Candian (1645–69) and Morean (1684–99) wars. Their units were led by *harambašas* and *serdars,* and in some districts by captains. Some *Morlacchi* served in the Venetian army under Venetian officers; others were employed as city, village, and frontier guards. Their style of fighting resembled that of the *hayduks,* and although they fought for Venetian interests, their activities stirred their conationals and inspired the struggle for national liberation. For whatever their faults, the *uskoks* were brave and effective soldiers, and as such aroused the popular imagination and intensified resistance to foreign rule.

Epic Poetry and the Cult of Heroism. There is much truth in the contention that had the Serbs not been under Turkish rule, they would not have had the great epic poetry which chronicles historical events and sheds light on their cultural life. Experience during Turkish rule built into the mind of the patriarchal Serb, especially in the Dinaric region, the notion that heroism serves the community. This concept of heroism grew out of the necessity to struggle for survival. Peter II Petrović Njegoš, the philosopher of heroic patriarchalism, raised the cult of heroism ("the faith of Obilić") to the mystic level of religion.

Not surprisingly, patriarchal man was sometimes carried away by a sense of his own valor and importance. But although the Serbs of Montenegro were on occasion chided for heroic posturing and self-adulation, they did inspire other South Slavs. Grouped in clans and tribes, the Montenegrins were able to live in relative freedom and preserve their traditional social organization. Each such social unit functioned as a miniature state and had an armed force made up of kinsmen. At times they fought the Turks; at other times, they fought one another. The Croatian Illyrians in the first half of the nineteenth century, for example, were more inspired by Montenegrin battles with the Turks than by the Serbian Uprising (1804–1812). Montenegro was indeed a nursery of heroes and fighters, nurtured on epic poetry.

The Serbian epic poem describes the hero realistically. A hero has more than average human strength, but he is not superhuman or semidivine. The epic poems stress not the physical but the spiritual attributes of the hero, who may, for example, be frightened, but unlike the coward, conquers his fear. The aim of epic poetry was to instill the qualities of heroism, *čojstvo* (manliness), or *humanitas heroica* — as translated by Gerhard Geseman, a German ethnologist.[10] To achieve these goals, to endure pain and setbacks is the essential feature of the heroism celebrated in an epic poem.

The epic poems are built around important events and personages, real and mythical, and fall into two categories: classical[11] and imitative.[12] Best known is the Kossovo cycle. Its message is that there can be no independence and freedom without struggle and sacrifice. The Kossovo heroes consciously sacrificed themselves in the defense of independence. This led King Lazar to choose the "heavenly kingdom" instead of the "worldly kingdom."

The cycle of Marko Kraljević depicts him as a hero, symbol of resistance and an example of bravery to be emulated. Marko was raised to the legendary pedestal by that element of the Serbian population which was first to fall under the Turks and longest under their rule. That Marko collaborated with the Turks did not trouble those who sang of his activities, because whatever Marko did was for the benefit of his people. His individual acts of heroism endeared him to them. (Parallels can be found in Western Romantic heroic literature.)

The *hayduk* cycle of epic poems is the largest of the major cycles. These epic songs glorify the *hayduk* as a brave fighter against the Turks; hence many historians see *hayduk* activity as inspiring the movement for national liberation. Epic poetry did, in fact, portray the *hayduks* as the principal avengers of Kossovo. And the *hayduks* identified with the old Serbian heroic traditions. They modeled themselves on the great heroes of the past (*voyvoda* Momčilo, Marko Kraljević, Miloš Obilić, Ivan Kosančić, and Milan Toplica) and the mediaeval *bans* and *voyvodas*.[13] The epic poems describe them as fearless, prepared at any moment to sacrifice their lives. They show the innate desire of the proud patriarchal man to live free, to escape persecution and degradation, to avenge father, brother, or friend. The *hayduk* may be tough and brave, but he is also sensitive and lonely. Poems tell of their nostalgia for life among the people, for the warm hearth and the family. The best poems, perhaps, depict the heroic exploits of *hayduk* leaders, such as Starina Novak (Baba Novak), whose exploits at the end of the sixteenth century won fame throughout the Balkans, and Bajo Pivljanin.[14]

The *uskok* cycle of epic poems eulogizes the Senj, Kotar, and other *uskoks*. The best poem in this cycle is the "Death of Senjanin Ivo" — the historical Ivan Vlaković. Other popular *uskok* epics celebrate the deeds of such heroes as Stojan and Ilija Janković, and Petar and Ilija Smiljanić. The poems describe plundering expeditions into Turkish territory, battles between *uskok* and Turkish leaders, and carrying off women as trophies.

Other cycles of epic poetry that inspired later generations of Serbs are those composed by Filip Višnjić, a blind bard, on the First Serbian Uprising and the liberation of Serbia, in which (especially the "Battle of Mišar") he describes individual acts of heroism, bloody fighting, and human suffering.[15] The Montenegrin fighting in the eighteenth and nineteenth centuries, including the guerrilla activity and insurrections in Hercegovina and neighboring districts, is celebrated in many decasyllabic poems.

Serbs in Turkish Service

The case of Marko Kraljević, who served the Turks, yet remained a hero to the Serbs, was not an isolated one. The Ottomans attempted to enlist the Serbs into their service against the European Catholic states, especially during the height of the Ottoman empire. The Serbs served in auxiliary and quasi-military organizations of *martoloses, voynuks, akincis* (a light cavalry), *azaps* (guards of fortresses and towns), *csajkás* (soldiers on river flotillas), *beşlis* (a special kind of cavalry resembling *hussars*). They were military craftsmen: *ilmanji, kalmançu* (shield makers), blacksmiths, *dunjers* (woodcutters/carvers), *dungers* and *meremetcis* (builders and maintainers of fortresses), archers, *taşçi* (stonecutters), *madenci* (guardians of wines), *demisci* (blacksmiths), *doganci* and *çakirci* (falconers and hawkers), *orizars* (rice producers), and guards of bridges.[16] The Serbs also served in the Turkish army as guides (Serb.: *vodič*; Turk. sing.: *kalavuz/kalauz*) and as intelligence agents.[17] The *voynuks* and some *martoloses,* possessed landed holdings (*baština*) in lieu of pay and paid no *haraç* or other taxes. The *derbencis,* too, enjoyed tax relief as did other similar groups, including the Vlachs. Some Serbs were also members of the Turkish feudal cavalry, and as *sipahis* had their own *sipâhliks* and *timars.*

The local Serbian population guarded the roads, canyons, and mountain passes. Sometimes whole villages were made responsible for policing services of this kind. In other instances, villages supplied horses and equipment for transportation, repaired fortresses, greased boats (those doing this job were called Turk.: *katranci*), guarded ports and ferries (Turk.: *iskele;* Serb.: *skela*), pulled boats on the river, and made arrows. Every five Vlach homes in northern Serbia supplied one soldier to guard the frontier and strategic places inside the country, or to serve as a cavalryman in military campaigns. Pastoral Vlachs (many undoubtedly Serbs) with their leaders (*kahyalar*), *knezes, primićurs,* supplied the Turkish military establishment with certain kinds of food, military supplies, and troops. In exchange for military services all these groups received certain privileges.

In the fourteenth century, the Serbs provided the Turks with contingents of heavy armored cavalry. In 1390 they fought with the Turks against the Hungarians along the Danube-Sava line. Together with Marko Kraljević and the Dejanović brothers, in 1395 Stefan Lazarević participated in Sultan Bayazid's invasion of Wallachia; the following year, he fought on the Turkish side against the Christian crusading army at Nicopolis. When Tamerlane with his Mongols broke into Asia Minor, the Ottoman army sent against him included 5,000 Serbs. At the Battle of Ankara (1402), the Turks and their allies were defeated, although the Serbian armored cavalry distinguished itself. Sultan Bayazid perished at Ankara and certain Serbian groups took part in the ensuing bloody struggle over the Ottoman succession. A Serbian cavalry unit of 1,500 men served on the Turkish side during the capture of Constantinople by Muhammad the Conqueror. Between the defeat at Ankara and the fall of the Despotate of Serbia to the Turks in 1459, Serbs fought on the side of the Turks, the Hungarians, and the Germans.

The Ottoman Turks did not underestimate the military prowess of the Serbs as opponents. The fifteenth-century Turkish historian, Dursun-beg (-c. 1499), in his eyewitness account of Mehmed the Conqueror's attempt to seize Smederevo in 1454, writes that the sultan encountered a determined and justifiably renowned Serbian army.[16] He describes the Bosnians as persistent, resolute, and brave warriors, who committed suicide rather than fall into Turkish hands.

In the sixteenth century, Grand Vezier Muhammad Sokolli (Sokolović), commandant of the Turkish armed forces (himself of Serbian origin), appealed to groups of Serbs in the Serbian language, promising tax exemption in exchange for a special kind of military service.[19] The Hungarian poet Sebestyén Tinódi (c. 1505–56) tells of Serbian cooperation with the Turks and of their help in taking Temesvár (1552). Three Serbian groups in Turkish service were particularly important: the *sipâhis, voynuks,* and *martoloses,* although the national militia, founded 1793–94, was also significant.

Christian sipâhis. Early in Turkish rule, Christians were employed for a variety of military purposes. The most important Christian group was recruited through the institution of *devşirme,* converted to Islam, and trained for the janissary corps. The many Serbian children who were taken as "blood levy" and served the Ottoman state and military establishment as Muslim converts are outside the scope of this paper which is concerned primarily with the Serbs who as Christians served in the Ottoman military system. From the very beginning the Ottomans employed Christian feudal cavalry which was allowed to retain landholdings and was exempt from certain taxes in return for military service. As noted earlier, the cavalry reinforced the Ottoman armies in various campaigns and also in garrisons.[20]

Muslim *sipâhis* came from various parts of the Ottoman empire, but the Christian *sipâhis* were probably descended mostly from the Serbian nobility. According to the Ottoman *defter* of 1467-68 there were fifty-four Christian *sipâhi timars* in Serbia. These were small, however; in some instances, several *sipâhis* shared a single *timar*. The Christian *sipâhis,* like their Muslim counterparts, supplied the Ottoman state with a specified number of mounted horsemen for military purposes. The number of men (*cebelli*) to be supplied depended on the estate's revenue. In joining the Turks, however, the Serbian *sipâhis* did not gain equality with Muslims, for the leading positions in administration and army remained in Muslim hands.

As time passed, the number of Christian *sipâhis* declined as did the revenues from their *timars.* The Christian *sipâhi* feudal cavalry, like many other Christian auxiliary troops, was maintained only as long as the Ottomans could be assured of their complete allegiance. Incentives and pressures to convert to Islam and to assimilate were such that some *sipâhi* families changed faith within two generations.[21] In time many Christian formations, including the *sipâhis,* were disbanded. Their decline was caused not only by assimilation but also by administrative fiat — confiscation of the *timars* (landholdings) of Christian *sipâhis.*[22]

Voynuks. The Serbs participated in another Ottoman military formation, the *voynuks* (Turk. pl.: *voynuklar, voynugan*). The term *voynuk* is of Slavic origin, as is *baština,* which designates land held by them. The *voynuks* were apparently a pastoral military formation, of Vlach origin, and we have reason to think that the *voynuks* are of the same origin as the *martoloses*; they may well be the same formation known by many different names.[23] During the initial period of Ottoman rule there were many *voynuks* in Serbia, Bosnia, and Bulgaria. The troops were Slav, the higher commanding personnel were Muslims, and the lower-ranking commanders were Christian. Although the most investigated *voynuks* are those that operated in Bulgaria, they existed in other parts of the Ottoman empire, including the Serbian provinces. The evidence of their presence in Bosnia and Hercegovina is incontrovertible.

Ali Caus and other Turkish sources speak of two categories of *voynuks* — imperial (*voynugani hâssa*) and ordinary (*voynugani âm-*

me). The imperial *voynuks* were predominantly stablemen; others primarily served as the *sancak beys* and a few of the *sipâhi* leaders, who could not subjugate the *voynuks* nor impose *reaya* obligations on them. Sons, brothers and cousins of a *voynuk*, serving in imperial horse stables, could not be classed as *reaya*.[24] *Voynuks* were military service units on campaign and in garrison; they served as guards, took care of horses and stables, and cut hay for the military establishment. They dug trenches and worked in and around military camps. They were exempted from the tenth and poll tax or *harač* (Ar.: *harāq*), paying only the smoke tax (*dimmina*) and *fuçi baci*, although there were other arrangements dictated by local practices. In some instances the *voynuks* were paid.

As the Ottoman borders were pushed northward and Muslim exclusiveness intensified, Christian auxiliary troops began to disappear from Turkish service. The *voynuks, akinci*, and certain other auxiliary forces, except for some noncombat troops, were phased out of the Turkish forces by the seventeenth century. Unlike the *sipâhis*, their ranks were not diminished by conversion and assimilation. Since they belonged to the lower echelons of the army, they reverted from the status of *askeri* (military or ruling class) to the status of *reaya* (subjects or chattels) and were replaced by Muslim counterparts.[25]

Martoloses. Another important Christian military force in the service of the Ottoman empire were the *martoloses*, who likewise held a position midway between the *askeri* and the *reaya* and received a special tax exemption for their service. *Martoloses* were exempted from taxes (*haraç*) fully or in part and given other privileges, depending on local conditions. In some areas they even owned their *baština*, fully or partly exempted from taxes. Some leaders of the *martoloses* were granted *timars* that yielded revenue corresponding to a salary. A few received both *timars* and pay. One should add that *martoloses* were not recruited from Serbs alone; they were ethnically and religiously heterogenous. Most scholars traced the institution to its Byzantine origin. For the term *martolos* is from the Hellenized Latin word *armatolos* (*armatons*, armsbearing individual), which referred to a person who provided military service to the state.[26] The *martoloses* (*armatoloi*) were a form of militia used not only by the Byzantines, but also by the Venetians, to protect borders and other areas. The Ottoman Turks encountered the institution of the *armatoloi* (*martoloses*) during their expansion into the Balkans and integrated it into their own system between 1421 and 1438.

The *martoloses* were a separate, uniformed, hired military formation, with their own standards, organized much like the janissaries.[27] The higher officers were almost always Muslims; the lower ones, Serbs. Some functioned as infantry and cavalry troops; others, as police. *Martoloses* units participated in almost all Ottoman campaigns against Venice, Hungary, and Austria. Some also operated in the area north of the Sava and Danube. Their service was not limited in time, but depended on performance and personal interest, and on the needs of the Ottoman state. A *martolos* was appointed by an imperial *berat*.

In the fifteenth century, *martoloses* were not numerous, but in the sixteenth century we encounter them in many South Slav regions.[28] During the sixteenth and seventeenth centuries, they served as auxiliary troops along the borders of the empire in northwestern Bulgaria, northern Serbia, along the Bosnian frontier with Croatia and Dalmatia, and in Greece in the area bordering on the Venetian possessions. Others served in interior provinces as rural police protecting communications and fighting banditry, particularly in mountain areas.[29] Many Serbs served as *martoloses* and as such found their place in several epic poems.[30] The Serbian *martoloses* supplied crews for the Danubian flotilla and maintained and guarded the boats (*csajkás*). One finds them serving with the Sava and Tisza flotillas and even on seagoing vessels. They sometimes made plundering incursions into neighboring lands. Because the *martoloses* caused disorders during the Morean War and the Russo-Turkish wars of the late seventeenth and early eighteenth centuries, the Ottoman government formally abolished the institution in 1721.

The Serbian Militia. The Treaty of Svishtov [Sistova] (1791) terminating the last Austro-Turkish War (1788–91), provided that the Turks forbid the janissaries to return to Serbia; their intolerable regime had driven the Serbs to collaborate with the Austrians. The Turks also promised the Serbs amnesty and a degree of local autonomy. The janissaries, however, could not be reconciled to their expulsion from the Paşalik of Belgrade and continued, with the backing of Vidin-based Osman Pazvanoğlu, the sultan's enemy, to attack the Paşalik.

Because he found it increasingly difficult to cope with the janissaries, Hadji Mustafa, Paşa of Belgrade; requested financial aid from the Serbian local leaders (*knezes*) in order to build an army. The *knezes* instead offered him a Serbian militia under their own commanding officer, and Hadji Mustafa acquiesced. A Serbian national militia was organized with Stanko Arambašić in command.[31]

The militia was organized on a territorial basis, the village providing the basic military unit. Each village and district (*nâhiye*) was to contribute a stated number of troops. The soldiers were expected to be well equipped and armed at their own expense. The size of the militia is not known, but estimates range from 8,000 to as many as 30,000 men. The officers bore Turkish ranks: *buljabaš* (or *buljukbaš*; Turk. *bölük-başı*), commanding fifty men, *harambaša* (or *arambaša;* Turk. *harami-başı*), commanding a hundred men, and *bimbaša* (or *binbaša*; Turk. *binbaşı*), commanding a thousand men. The units of the national militia participated in several battles against the janissaries and apparently fought well, better than the sultan's own troops, perhaps, as the latter were reluctant to engage their coreligionists. During 1797 the Serbs stopped several janissary incursions. Later we find many former national militiamen fighting in Karadjordje's army.[32]

Hard-pressed after Napoleon's invasion of Europe, in 1798, the sultan was obliged to seek reconciliation with Pazvanoğlu, recognizing him as paşa and permitting the janissaries to return to the Paşalik of Belgrade. In order to establish their control over the Paşalik, the janissaries proceeded to undermine and destroy sultanic authority in Belgrade. Among other things, they murdered Hadji Mustafa Paşa, and divided the Paşalik among the *dayis,* the four janissary leaders. All privileges which the Serbs had won in the 1790s were cancelled and systematic persecution of Serbs began. The First Serbian Uprising of 1804 was a direct response to this oppressive regime.

The Serbs as Hungarian and Austrian Mercenaries: The Emergence of the Military Frontier

Serbian society experienced many changes after coming under Ottoman Turkish rule. Serbs, *inter alia,* began to enter foreign military service as mercenaries or military auxiliaries. According to one source, they preferred to be "soldiers" rather than "serfs" (*kmets*), because with arms in hand they were better able to preserve their ethnic and religious identity.[33] Serbs served as mercenaries for a number of Western states. One of their earliest employers was the Kingdom of Hungary. After the fall of Constantinople, in several military encounters, Serbs fought Turks, either alone or alongside the Hungarians. Such collaboration with the Hungarians continued after the Serbian Despotate fell to the Turks in 1459. Many Serbs emigrated to southern Hungary where another despotate was established, albeit with a vaguely defined territory. They comprised a high percentage of the men attached to the Hungarian Danube flotilla (*csajkások, čajkaš*), a force of more than 300 boats (*csajka, naszád*),[34] and of King Matthias Corvinus's Black Legion. He set up a system of frontier defense by settling thousands of Serbian refugees from the Turks, especially in Lika and Krbava. They were granted land and promised religious freedom in exchange for military service.[35] In 1471, King Matthias designated Vuk Grgurović *Rascie despotus* (Zmaj Despot, Zmaj Ognjeni Vuk); he collected an army to fight the Turks and liberate the Serbian homeland.[36]

During the sixteenth century, Serbs may be found in the military organizations of both János Zápolya and King Ferdinand, rival claimants to the Hungarian throne, as well as in Ottoman service. The Serbs changed employers as their interests dictated. They served in all three branches of service — infantry, cavalry, and the *csajkás*. At one point, the Serbian *csajkás* abandoned Zápolya and joined Ferdinand and when the latter did not pay them regularly, they threatened to plunder Buda. In 1529, the *csajkás* took themselves and their boats into Turkish service.

Serbs also played an important part in the Habsburg Military Frontier (*Militärgrenze*), a part of which (the Maritime Frontier, *Primorska Krajina / Maritima confinia*) had its origins in the fifteenth century.[37] The Slavonian (*Windische Granitz / Confinia slavonica*) and the Croatian (*Kroatische Granitz / Confinia croatica*) frontiers were organized in the sixteenth century. The Military Frontier from the Sava to the Adriatic Sea was established in 1527.[38]

On instructions from the military command in Graz, Serbs were encouraged to settle on Habsburg territory. The Croatian *ban* also supported settling Serbs on the Frontier. As early as 1529, they are mentioned in Transylvania where some were settled, received special privileges, and became both a military and a political force. Although the Hungarians resented the influx of Serbs into the lands of the Hungarian crown, the Austrians went on recruiting Serbs into their service, because Serbian refugee families were attacked by bandits. Hungarian historian Gyula Dudás (1861–1911) observed that of all the ethnic groups who lived on Hungarian territory the Serbs were most difficult to assimilate probably because, as a military element, the Serbs had a great deal of independence.[39]

During the siege of Buda in 1530, Ferdinand's army included Serbs, and the king had a high regard for them as soldiers. Serbian mercenaries led by one Tsar Jovan, won prominence at this time[40] and were known to fight "for pay."[41] As mercenaries, they served for a month (*mensionarii*), half a year, or longer periods.[42] Some were accompanied by wives and children and maintained by the communities in which they lived. So valuable were the Serbs as fighters that, in the 1550s, Austrians and Turks competed for them. In the sixteenth century, Turks, Hungarians, and Austrians employed Serbs as informers, "diplomats," interpreters (*dragomans,* Arabic, sing.: *tärgumān*), scribes, and similar assignments.[43]

In 1552 as many as 6,000 Serbian cavalrymen were in Austrian service;[44] by the end of the sixteenth century, many Serbs had won prominence as commanders and *condottieri.* They and their units, with Zsigmond Báthory, fought against the Turks. Several Serbs attained military reputations in Transylvania at the beginning of the seventeenth century. Indeed, at one time, Avram Rac commanded a force of 20,000 men.[45] A Serbian cavalry unit also served Voivode Michael of Wallachia. Serbs, led by Janos Rac and Stanim Toholjevac among others, entered into an agreement with Prince György I Rákóczi, who gave them land and privileges. In the meantime, Serbs from the Ottoman empire continued to find refuge in the Habsburg lands, and to be encouraged to settle on the Military Frontier. Among the new arrivals, in 1579, were several groups of Morlachs (probably Serbs) from Dalmatia who asked to become military colonists. Other Serbs, from Bosnia, were settled south of Varaždin.[46]

Emperor Rudolf attached special importance to Serbian support in fighting the Turks. In 1591, it was planned that Serbs and Bulgarians should rise upon the appearance of the imperial army. During the 1590s there occurred a widespread Serbian movement for liberation from the Turks.

In 1594 they rose in Transylvania and Banat. Initially they defeated the Turks, capturing many men, guns, and river vessels. But in June 1595, the Turks suppressed the insurrection and scattered the insurgents, many of whom entered Austrian military service.[47] The Austrians did capture Petrinja and settled the area around it with several thousand refugee Serbian (Vlach) families; Archduke Ferdinand II issued them the usual charter of privileges and obligations in February 1597.[48] Serbian troops also took part in the conflict between Emperor Rudolf II and King Matthias of Bohemia.[49]

In the sixteenth century, the Military Frontier was manned largely by "Vlach" (or Serbian) refugees (*prebezi* or *uskoci*) from Turkey. Because they made excellent soldiers, the Austrian military commanders and the Croat nobility facilitated their flight and settlement on the frontier where they were given land in exchange for military service. A particularly large influx and settlements of Vlachs (many from Slavonia) occurred during the Austro-Turkish War of 1593–1605. From the end of the sixteenth century on, Vlachs continued to escape from Turkey and to settle in the Austrian and Venetian frontier region, on territory abandoned by the indigenous Croat inhabitants. The term *Vlach* was often used interchangeably with *Serb* because the latter, too, were mostly a pastoral people.

The Vlachs soon came into conflict with the nobility, who tried to tax them and to reduce them to serfs with no regard for the special rights that had been granted to them. The frontiersmen[50] frequently petitioned the emperor not to sacrifice them to the Croatian nobles. After Ferdinand II issued the *Statuta Vlachorum* on October 5, 1630,[51] the first broad privileges for Vlachs (Serbs) in the Varaždin region, the Vienna Court tried to remove the Military Frontier from civil jurisdiction. The *Statuta* defined the rights and obligations of frontiersmen and provided the first formal administrative organization for the Military Frontier, which was now detached from Croatia. The administration was taken away from the *ban* (governor of Croatia) and placed under two generalcies — the *Karlstadter Generalat* for the Croatian Military Frontier and the *Warasdiner Generalat* for the Slavonian Military Frontier.[52]

The Croatian and Slavonian diets opposed the *Statuta Vlachorum*; the Croat nobility and the Church hierarchy never ceased trying to establish undisputed control over the Vlachs.[53] The struggle over control of the Military Frontier, which began in 1477, continued until the middle of the eighteenth century.[54] Who owned the land on which the Vlachs were settled was finally solved in 1754, when it was proclaimed an imperial domain. The Court backed the Vlachs whose rights were guaranteed by the *Statuta Vlachorum,* which made the Serbian Frontiersmen full-fledged citizens (*orsaške kotrigi*) with no other obligation than military service.

During the great Christian offensive after the Turks failed to take Vienna in 1683, the Serbs initially wavered, uncertain as to who would win. But as Austrian troops moved into Serbian territory, more and more Serbs joined various Austrian military formations, including the *csajkás.*[55] When Belgrade fell to Austrian troops on September 6, 1688, the Serbs of Mačva rose; from all sides their kinsmen hastened to join the imperial army, suffering heavy losses in fighting the Turks. But Austria would not allow a movement, such as that initiated by Count George Branković, who had hoped to establish an independent Serbian state with himself as its head.

Leopold tried to attract more Serbian volunteers when, in the autumn of 1688, he had to shift part of his army to the west in order to meet a French threat. In December 1688 he appealed to Serbs in Bosnia to join the Austrians, promising them freedom of religion and the privileges they had enjoyed under the Turks. A substantial number of Serbs responded to the appeal. But after the death of General Piccolomini in September 1689, the tide of war shifted in favor of the Turks.

Leopold's proclamation ("litterae invitatoriae") of April 6, 1690, appealed to Balkan Christians, including the Serbs, to rally to the Christian cause, promising to guarantee their religious freedom and national customs, and to exempt them from taxes.[57] When the Turks started their offensive in early 1690 the desperate emperor had appealed to the Serbs, but this time there was no large response and the imperial forces retreated. The Serbs then began to abandon their homes and retreat northward. Patriarch Arsenije III and about 40,000 Serbs assembled at Belgrade; from there imperial forces helped them cross into Hungary before Belgrade fell to the Turks on October 6, 1690.[58]

The emperor granted the Serbs various "privileges" which subsequently were expanded and reconfirmed. They were granted the right to settle on Habsburg lands, to manage their own religious affairs, to choose their own *vojvodas,* and certain other privileges that the Turks had allowed them. The Serbs were settled on deserted land in Hungary and Slavonia. Several hundred families were sent to the Varaždin district to reinforce the old Frontier settlements there. Many of the remaining Serbian immigrants were settled along the Danube, Tisza, and Maros (Mureş) rivers — the land conquered from the Turks![59]

The Serbs proved militarily useful to Austria but presented a difficult political problem. Their status was confused. Imperial charters usually referred to them as a *community* and a *nation,* never as a mere population. The Serbs in southern Hungary considered themselves a political people with the right to political territory and a separate government headed by a *vojvoda.* The Austrians, however, viewed them as *patrimonium domus Austriae* (the *patrimonium* of the imperial house), and the Hungarians considered the Serbs citizens of the Hungarian state (*provinciale et politicum Hungariae*).[60]

From the Serbian refugees in the 1690s, the Austrians formed a contingent of troops, about 1,000 strong, commanded by a Serb, Jovan Monasterlija, who was given the rank of *podvojvoda.* The contingent was divided into companies, each with its own bugle, drum, and flag. Soon the number of Serbian troops rose to 10,000. They distinguished themselves at Slankamen (August 21, 1691), the only battle in which they fought under their own officers and *podvojvoda*. The battle of Senta may also have been won largely because of Serbian military effort. In 1692, the War Council ordered Austrian commanders to spare German blood and use Serbs for incursions into Turkish territory.[61] Serbian units fought the Turks in crucial battles during 1697 advancing deep into Bosnia with the imperial forces. But Austria soon concluded that maintaining an autonomous Serbian armed force was not in its best interest. Consequently, some of Monasterlija's troops were transferred to the Danube *csajkás* flotilla (with headquarters at Komoran) which, in the ensuing battles, inflicted several defeats on the Turks.[62]

A number of Austrian military and political leaders praised the Serbs for their valor and noted that they were particularly good with the sword. In addition, Johann C. von Bartenstein found the Serbs to be keen and loyal, rarely if ever deserting their units. Loyalty to their group and the emperor is repeatedly emphasized. Even Jovan Tekelija, who spoke of Peter the Great as "his Orthodox Tsar," installed the Austrian two-headed eagle on the church he erected in Arad. According to Bartenstein, the Serbs were particularly effective when fighting in forests and gorges. One source tells us that they judged one another in terms of how many Turks they killed. For a Serbian Frontiersman to be wounded was like being decorated, but a man wounded in the back was called a *whore*. Taube says that the worst thing for a Serbian Frontiersman was to be left behind the front. On the negative side, Taube discovered that the Serbs were lazy; they fought not only for altruistic reasons but also for booty and recognition.[63] And they did not like to fight far from home.

By the Treaty of Karlowitz [Sremski Karlovci] (1699) the Ottoman sultan surrendered Lika, Krbava, Bačka, and parts of the Banat, Slavonia, and Srem. The newly acquired territories belonged to the emperor, who delegated their administration to the military authorities.

From 1699 to 1712 the existing Military Frontier in Croatia was extended and new Frontiers were founded from recently liberated regions of Croatia and Hungary. The old Frontiers (Slavonian, Banal, Croatian) were no longer on the immediate Austro-Turkish border. The liberated region between Kupa, Una, and Sava made possible the extension in 1703 of the Banal Frontier and the shift of the center of defense from the Kupa to the Una. The recently acquired territory between the Kupa and Una rivers was organized into a new frontier district called the *Banal Granitz* (Banska Krajina); in 1704, it was placed under the authority of the Croatian *ban*. During 1701–1702 the liberated territory along the Sava, Danube, Tisza, and Maros rivers was made part of the extended Military Frontier, and in 1701–1703, organized into the Sava, Danube, and the Tisza-Maros frontiers. In 1712, liberated Lika and Krbava were added to the Karlovac generalcy. The Frontier was extended eastward beyond the Banat. It was reorganized and expanded on several occasions and did not reach its final organizational form until the nineteenth century.[64] Many Serbs who had found asylum on Austrian territory or who had collaborated with the imperial forces were settled in the frontier region and organized into a militia (*Raitzische National Miliz*), divided into captaincies and commanded by Austrian officers. The Serbs, anxious to avoid feudal oppression, preferred to be subordinated directly to the emperor as soldiers — a preference which corresponded with imperial interests. Members of the Serbian militia tilled the land in peacetime and fought for the kaiser in war. After 1699, through a series of major reforms, the Military Frontier lost the character of a defensive system and was transformed into a source of cheap manpower for wars in various parts of Europe.[65]

Serbia's militia did not have the status of the regular Austrian army. Serbs preferred to serve in the regular army because its troops received better food, dress, and pay.[66] Members of the Serbian militia wore their own dress and carried what arms they owned. They were under the command of their own countrymen and the language of command was Serbian. Officers sometimes earned rank on the basis of the number of soldiers that they could recruit. In some instances the officer's rank might be hereditary. *Hayduk* titles were used because, upon entering Austrian service, the leaders (*harambašas*) of *hayduk* bands retained command of their units. It needed time to complete "militarization" of what once were free-lance *hayduk* bands.

At the beginning of the eighteenth century, Austria turned to the Serbs because the regular army had proved inadequate to maintain security on the border. Badenoki, Veterani, Hildburghausen, Bartenstein, and Taube all praised Serbs as fighters; they observed further that Serbian Frontier soliders would be ready for immediate action in case of war. According to Taube, they would serve as "a living wall against the Turks." The Serbs cost less to clothe than regular troops, and they were cheaper to feed because they "fasted" many days in the year. According to Austrian military observers, the Serbs were loyal, hardier and more persevering than regular troops, and especially effective when fighting in forests and canyons. Above all, Austria found them a natural ally against the Turks and the Hungarians.

The Military Frontier produced per capita the largest number of Austrian troops. During the nineteenth century, Serbs were especially numerous in the First Banija Regiment (67 percent), the Second Banija Regiment (62.2 percent), and the Lika Regiment (70 percent).[67] The Serbian soldiers (*militari* or *hayduks,* as they were also called), were under military administration and were divided into combat troops and those serving in other ways. At first they were called after the Frontier in which they served (*Karlstädter, Slavonci, Posavci, Hrvati,* etc.); later they shared the common name of Frontiersmen (Serb.: *graničari;* Ger.: *Grenzer*). At one time they were insultingly labeled the *Schismatic Rascians* (*Raci*).[68] A large body of oral and written literature, showing their lives in peace and war,[69] depicts the long history of distinguished service by Serbian and Croatian Frontiersmen.

After the Treaty of Požarevac (1718) the Maros and Tisza Frontiers lost their importance; the Vienna Court planned to demilitarize them and bring them under the civil rule of the neighboring *županijas.* In 1741, the Court finally decided to demilitarize the two Frontiers, a decision vigorously opposed by the Frontiersmen, who were given a choice of becoming *militari* in some other area or of accepting the status of *paori.* Many embittered Serbian Frontiersmen decided to emigrate to Russia, and these troops will be dealt with elsewhere in this study.

Although *graničari* continued to serve as defensive forces along the frontier with Turkey in the eighteenth century, they were also sent to fight in many parts of Europe. They took part in wars against the Turks; they also fought Austria's western and northern enemies in Italy, in Bavaria, in Bohemia, in the Rhineland, and in Silesia. Indeed, the South Slavs fought in every major war of the Habsburg empire. They participated in the Thirty Years War and in various campaigns against the French in the seventeenth century; in the Austro-Turkish wars (1683–99; 1716–18; 1737–39; 1788–91), the War of the Austrian Succession (1741–48); the Seven Years War (1756–63); the War for Bavarian Succession (1778–79); the wars against Revolutionary France (1792–1800) and Napoleon (1805–1815), the Austro-Italian wars (1848–49, 1859, 1866), and in the war against the Hungarian rebels (1848–49).

In the Austro-Turkish War of 1716–18 Serbs fought at Varaždin and in the taking of Belgrade and Temesvár [Timişoara]. One Serbian unit fought in Wallachia, and a Serbian cavalry unit distinguished itself at the capture of Belgrade. When the war ended with the Treaty of Požarevac, Serbia (*Königreich Serwien*) was left to Austria.

Part of Serbian territory was added to Banat (Temesvár); the rest became a separate administrative unit (*absolutum dominium vel peculum regium*). A military man with headquarters in Belgrade became ruler of occupied Serbia which was divided into some fifteen regions; each of those, headed by a *provizor,* was subdivided into districts (*knežine*) made up of villages. The militia, or *hayduks* (located in about ninety *hayduk* villages) were charged with keeping peace and order; they hunted bandits (also called *hayduks*) and guarded the borders. The militia was divided into companies, each under a captain. Several companies were commanded by an *oberkapetan,* who was an important military and civil official. The militia was largely recruited from Christian refugees from Turkey and organized like the troops of the Military Frontier in Croatia and Slavonia. Militiamen were responsible to their own commanders, enjoyed special privileges, and possessed their own land.

In the Austro-Turkish war of 1737-39, Serbian units led by Austrian officers proved very effective against the Turks. Thousands of Frontiersmen and Serbian militia and cavalry fought in this war and were assigned the most difficult vanguard and rear guard posts. When Austria lost the war to the Turks in 1739, the Serbian militia, together with two companies of *Klimenti* (Albanian Catholics), withdrew to Austria. The new refugees were organized into companies under Serbian and Albanian commanders and were used to guard the frontier from Zemun to Jamena.

Finally, one must add that the Serbs were taken into special military formations, such as *Freischutzenkompanie* (founded in 1748), which participated in battle only in emergencies, and *Scharfschutzen* (established in 1769), which consisted of cannoneers and marksmen, who replaced the grenadiers in the Frontier regiments.

Besides serving along the borderlands against the Ottoman empire and campaigning in Europe, Serbian *graničari* often became embroiled in the internal disturbances of the Habsburg realm, especially the Hungarian uprisings of the eighteenth and nineteenth centuries. For example, when in the summer of 1703 the Hungarians (the so-called *kurucok*), led by Ferenc II Rákóczi, rose against the Habsburgs, a group of Serbs in Baranya [Baranja], equally dissatisfied with Habsburg policies, also revolted. The movement of the Serbs in Baranya was local and poorly organized whereas Rákóczi had the support of a large segment of the Hungarian people. Most Serbs remained loyal to the emperor and were sent to fight Rákóczi, despite his appeal, on August 9, 1703, for Serbian help. A few Serbs, however, did join the Rákóczi movement, and at least one of them held a position of command. The Court recognized the help of the Serbs in putting down the Rákóczi uprising, and rewarded the commanders of the Serbian national militia and other secular and religious leaders. But some Serbian officers, like Pera Segedinac, who fought against Rákóczi, in 1735, joined a later Hungarian insurrection against the dynasty. Such behavior is the more puzzling since this time the Serbian militia again remained loyal to the emperor and fought against the insurgents.

By far the most important internal conflict in which the *graničari* were involved was the revolutionary upheaval of Hungary in 1848. The Serbs responded quickly to the French Revolution of 1848. The initial impulse of the Serbs in Vojvodina was to join the Hungarians against the Habsburg ruler. In the Vojvodina, several thousand fighters were organized on the initiative of Djordje Stratimirović, who called himself *the Supreme Leader* (*vrhovni vožd*) and *the People's General* (*narodni general*). The *Vojvodina* insurgent forces were swelled by about 12,000–15,000 volunteers from Serbia under the command of General Stefan P. Knićanin. Under Austrian General Stefan Šupljikac, who was chosen *vojvoda,* the insurgent army swelled to about 24,180 troops.[71] (Note, too, that some Serbian officers and men served on the Italian front and in the army under the command of the Croatian *Ban* Jelačić.)

The Serbs who originally sympathized with the Hungarian liberals against the Habsburgs later realized that the success of the Hungarian Revolution would be detrimental to the Serbian national cause; they abandoned the Hungarians and threw their support behind the Court. About 35,000 Frontiersmen fought on the Austrian side under Field Marshal Radetzky and General Josip Jelačić. In June 1848, the Serbian Frontiersmen in Srem and Banat and the *csajkás* of Titel joined the newly formed Serbian National Army (*Srpska narodna vojska*). In Transylvania, the First and Second Vlach regiments remained loyal to Vienna; others joined the revolution.[72]

The Freicorps. In almost every eighteenth-century war Austria formed *Freicorps* ("free units") of Serbian volunteers and sent them to far-flung fronts. An imperial permit was needed to organize such a corps. In the 1690s, Jovan Monasterlija commanded such a volunteer unit, as did many other prominent Serbian officers in Austria. Much later, the *knezes* of Banat maintained a *Freicorps.* A special type of *Freicorps* was one whose members were recruited by an individual and which bore his name. Only prosperous and prominent men, especially nobles, could assemble such a body. *Freicorps* troops had war booty as their chief reward. The first well-known *Freicorps* (sometimes called *pandurs* and *baronovci*) was that formed by Baron Trenk, to whom Maria Theresa gave a *Werbepatent* permitting him to recruit amnestied *hayduks* and other volunteers.

Trenk's Corps consisted of two companies, each commanded by a captain, and numbered between 1,000 and 2,500 men.[73] Besides the usual ranks, Trenk retained that of *harambaša*. The troops were dressed in Turkish style — as the Serbs did at that time. They were bearded and wore two knives and a carbine. The most noticeable part of their garb was the red mantle; hence they were called *Rothmantier*. The companies were subdivided into units of fifty men, led by *harambašas*; the units, into squads of ten (*desetina*) under corporals. They fought on all Austrian fronts, from Alsace to Bohemia, and were feared in the West. (At Strasbourg the French put them on exhibit for a fee.)

Among thousands of Serbian refugees on the eve of, and during, the Austro-Turkish war of 1787–91, about 18,000 volunteers served under command of Austrian officers or of prominent Serbs. The volunteers participated in two (1787, 1788) unsuccessful attempts to capture Belgrade.

Before the declaration of war on Turkey, Emperor Joseph II had ordered that a plan be drafted for setting up a *Freicorps* of Serbian volunteers. This corps was to operate as an advance guard of the Austrian army, concentrating in the area between the Morava and the Drina. Initially, the corps comprised four companies of about 120 men each, with a battery of cannon, 496 men in all. Frontier officer Mihailo Mihaljević was made captain of this *Freicorps*; its commanders at company level were Serbs from Austria and Serbia. On the emperor's orders, the battalion was to be replenished by relatives of those serving in it. The *Freicorps,* periodically reorganized, grew in numbers; sharpshooters and hussars were added. By the end of 1788, it had grown to 3,599 men; later, it rose to 5,268.[74]

Between 1788 and 1791, the Serbian volunteers did a great deal of fighting and fought well. Initially the most active among them were those led by Koča Andjelković, who originally served in Novaković's *Freicorps.* Between February and June 1788, the volunteers under Andjelković conducted successful attacks on the fortified towns of Smederevo, Jagodina, and Kragujevac *nahijas,* and against Turkish transport on the Niš-Belgrade road. These attacks were in accordance with the Austrian plan, whose purpose was to isolate and take Belgrade. Andjelković and his 509 men, largely recruited in Serbia, for a short time, held a large part of the Paşalik of Belgrade. His feats impressed the popular mind, and the areas he liberated are popularly called the *Kočina Krajina*.[75]

There were other Serbian *Freicorps* besides those of Mihaljević and Andjelković. The *Freicorps* of Jovan Brankovački began with 400 men and increased to 1,200. Marjan Jovanović commanded a *Freicorps* of some 700 men, maintained at his expense. In 1793, the so-called Burmazer *Freicorps* was organized, made up almost exclusively of Serbs.

Pandurs. Another armed formation in which Serbs served Austria, Russia, and the Turks at different times were the *pandurs* (derived from the Magyar *pandúrok*, guard).[76] *Pandurs* who might be infantry or cavalry served the Croatian and Magyar nobility as armed personal guards or escorts. They were also employed as a militia to maintain order and security in urban and village communities. In the seventeenth century, for example, the Turks stationed *pandur* units along their border with the Venetian Republic. The *pandur* assignment was to defend the border, but occasionally they crossed into Venetian territory for plunder. *Pandurs* are first mentioned in Austria during the War of the Spanish Succession (1704–1714). Trenk's Pandur Volunteer Corps (described earlier as a *Freicorps*) was notorious for bravery and brutality during the War of the Austrian Succession (1740–48).

The *pandurs* of the Habsburg empire were recruited on a voluntary basis from serfs (*kmets*) on the estates of the Slavonian and Srem feudatories, from the men of the Danube and the Sava Frontier, and from amnestied *hayduks*. The Court, the commune, or individual nobles paid the *pandurs* and provided them with clothing and arms. Volunteers were enticed by promises of booty (not including war trophies) captured on enemy territory.

In 1879, after the occupation of Bosnia and Hercegovina, Austria organized a *pandur corps* as a special gendarmerie, about 1,000 strong. The corps was drawn from local people, Serbs who had fought the Turks, been forced to flee to Montenegro, and then returned home. Austria's retention of the Ottoman land tenure system and certain other policies demoralized the *pandurs,* however, and some of their leaders (*starešina*) defected and fled back to Montenegro. Shortly after, the escaped leaders returned to Hercegovina in order to incite a rebellion. In August 1879, the *pandurs* of Nevesinje abandoned their posts and collected on the Plain of Nevesinje. On August 27, 1879, the Austro-Hungarian head of Bosnia and Hercegovina ordered them to return to their posts and threatened to court-martial those who refused. The *pandurs* responded by attacking and burning gendarmerie stations. On September 12 the first armed encounter took place between the *pandurs* and regular Austrian troops, who established order within three days.[77]

Serbs in Venetian and Neapolitan Service

From the fifteenth century on, the Venetian Republic, as we saw earlier in this essay, employed South Slavs, including Serbs from Dalmatia and other regions, in its military forces. Venice sometimes used Serbian refugees (*uskoks*) from the Ottoman empire as irregular troops in wars against the Turks.[78] In the seventeenth and eighteenth centuries, Venice included Serbs and other South Slavs in special Slavic formations.[79] Some Serbs, along with Greeks and Orthodox Albanians, had also served in companies of *stradioti* (from Byzantine *stratiotēs*), light cavalry garrisoned in several towns of Venetian Dalmatia in the sixteenth century.[80]

One finds Serbs in the Venetian armed forces until the republic's demise in 1797. Two of the four regular infantry regiments stationed on the Ionian Islands were known as *Slavonian* regiments and manned by both Orthodox Serbs and Catholic Croats. They were important enough in the garrisons of the islands to warrant a separate "Slavonian quarter" in the fortress of Corfu.[81] In his memoirs, Dositej Obradović, a notable figure in the Serbian enlightenment, tells how, while living on Corfu in the early 1790s, he enjoyed the hospitality of the officers in the Slavonian units and served them as an Orthodox chaplain.[82]

The Kingdom of Naples also had Serbs in its armed forces, chiefly in a special unit, the *Reggimento Real Macedone*.[83] This was initially organized in 1737 and at first was composed of men from the Greco-Albanian area of Chimarra. Later, recruits from other areas of the Balkans, including Serbs, were also taken into the regiment. Between 1740 and 1750 Naples recruited men from Dubrovnik and Montenegro for the regiment.[84]

In the 1760s a dispute about the South Slavic troops arose between the Neapolitan general staff and Georgios Choraphas, commander of the Macedonian regiment: should "Illyrians" (Slavs) recruited from Venetian territory, in violation of agreements (1739, 1754) between

Venice and Naples, serve in the *Reggimento Real Macedone* with "Greeks" (Greeks and Orthodox Albanians). Recruitment of South Slavs for the *Reggimento Real Macedone* continued, however — particularly among the Serbs of Montenegro, Boka Kotorska (Bocca de Cattaro), and Paštrovići — until the nineteenth century.[85]

Russia as a Factor in Serbian Military Tradition

Contacts between Russians and Serbs, sporadic since mediaeval times, became closer and more frequent after Peter the Great ascended the Russian throne. Particularly important in this connection was merchant and diplomat, Sava Vladisavljević, a secret aide to Ambassador Ukraintsev in Istanbul, who appeared at Azov in 1702, with a loaded ship, and entered Russia's service. Peter the Great's victory over the Swedes at Poltava (1709) gave the Serbs hope that with Russian help they would soon liberate their homeland, abandon Austria, and return to villages from which they had fled. On the news that Russia was preparing for war against the Turks, Jovan Tekelija and Julin Potiški, on behalf of the Serbian militia on the Maros-Tisza Frontier, petitioned Peter the Great, asking him to think of the Serbs and their hopes and to rely on their support if needed. Meantime, Vladisaljević influenced Russia to formulate and initiate a Balkan policy. Thus, when the Russo-Turkish War began in 1711, Tsar Peter the Great, at Vladisavljević's prompting, sent two Serbian officers to Montenegro with a proclamation (*gramota*) urging the Montenegrins to rise against the Turks. On the eve of the war with Turkey, March 3, 1711, Peter himself appealed to the Christian peoples of the Balkans, especially the Montenegrin Serbs, to rise against their common enemy; he repeated the appeal on March 23. The Montenegrins responded, but Russia's defeat on the Pruth in 1711 left them to fight the Turks alone; and in 1713, when the hard-pressed Montenegrins asked the tsar to save them, he could do no more than advise them to emigrate to Russia.

During the period of uncertainty, in March 1712, three Serbian colonels commanding the Serbian militia on the Tisza, Maros, and the Danube Frontiers, offered to lead 10,000 Serbian troops to help Russia fight the Turks. But hostilities with Turkey were not resumed. Instead, Russia and Turkey concluded a treaty of peace on June 24, 1713. In return for their gesture the three colonels received expensively framed portraits of Tsar Peter.[86] In 1715, he issued a proclamation expressing Russia's gratitude to the Montenegrin Serbs for the heroism they had shown in fighting for their "common religion and language." Belief in

Russia, its power, and its dedication to the Slavic and Christian cause, had a strong influence on the Serbs' political life after Peter the Great, despite occasional disappointment in "Mother" Russia.

Peter the Great was the first to encourage Serbs to move from Hungary (then under the Habsburgs) to the Ukraine. He needed Serbian military colonists to guard the Russian frontier from the Tatars and the Turks. He reasoned that if the Serbs could so loyally serve a foreign (Habsburg) emperor, one of Catholic faith beside, they would serve him even better, and certainly would be more reliable as guardians of the Russian frontier than the Cossacks and the Ukrainians.[87] Peter had heard much about the Serbs' soldierly qualities. In the Pruth campaign a small Serbian unit, led by Jovan Albanez from Podgorica, fought with great distinction. Several years later, on October 23, 1723, Peter authorized Albanez to recruit Austrian Serbs for several hussar regiments assigned to guard Russia's southern frontier at strategic points. The Serbian recruits were invited to settle in Russia with their families and were offered various benefits. Albanez recruited 459 Serbs in the first year and another 600 in the next, most from the Tisza region.

From these Serbian colonists, Empress Anna, in 1727, organized the Serbian hussar regiment and assigned a few others to various existing regiments. The Serbian regiment took part in Russia's Persian campaign of 1731. The empress also invited the Serbs in Austria to settle in Russia; Austria, although Russia's ally, tried to discourage its recruitment of Serbs. Nonetheless, a large number of Serbs did emigrate to Russia, and some achieved prominence. One attained the rank of major general. He commanded a hussar regiment and distinguished himself fighting Poles, Tatars, and Turks. Another, formerly captain of militia on the Danubian Frontier, became a brigadier of the Serbian Hussar Regiment and married into the Russian nobility.[88] Other individual officers made brilliant military careers; one, Lieutenant Peter Tekelija moved to Russia in 1748 and ended as a field marshal of the Russian army. Other Serbs also became prominent.[89]

Thousands of Serbs made their way to Russia and in 1751–52 were colonized on its southern frontiers in two settlements (*Novaia Serbiia* and *Slavianoserbiia*) modeled on the Austrian Military Frontier.[90] These Serbian colonists, under the command of Lieutenant-Colonel Jovan Horvat, Lieutenant-Colonel Jovan Šević, and Colonel Rajko Preradović, fought in various Russian military campaigns; in peacetime, they cultivated the land. A *pandur* infantry regiment, recruited among Serbian colonists in Russia, was used to garrison the fortress of Elizavetgrad [Kirovgrad] in *Novaia Serbiia.* The regiment distinguished itself in the Seven Years War; in 1764, it was reorganized into the Elisabethan Lance Regiment.[91]

As emigration declined after the middle of the eighteenth century, the Serbian armed contingents in Russia were reduced. Because of low pay, their discipline broke down, and some Serbs began to engage in plunder. Soon the Serbian colonies were abolished as separate entities and merged into the neighboring *guberniias.* Serbian regiments and officers were absorbed by the Russian regiments stationed in the vicinity. The Serbs were rapidly assimilated, but not without leaving traces in local folklore and toponymy, and in Russia's military establishment, since many of them had risen to high military rank.[92] After the large emigration of Austrian Serbs to Russia in the mid-eighteenth century, small groups of Montenegrin Serbs — whose movement was promoted by Montenegrin bishop Vasilije — emigrated to Russia, as did other Serbs from Turkey and from Venetian territory. Russian relations with Serbs outside the empire remained close throughout the eighteenth century and into the nineteenth. The Russians never hesitated to appeal to the Serbs to rise against the Turks when this served Russia's military objectives.

Thus, on January 30, 1769, a Russian proclamation appealed to Orthodox Slavs to rise against the Turks and win independence.[93] During the ensuing Russo-Turkish War (1769–75), a substantial group of Montenegrin and Dalmatian Serbs served as marines aboard the Russian fleet operating in the Mediterranean. Some Montenegrin Serbs became members of the "Western Spartan Legion" and took part in the Morean uprising and the Orlov expedition of 1770. Others were transported to the Morea by a ship belonging to Jovan Palikuća, a Serbian volunteer captain, and one-time Venetian merchant shipper.[94] Later, in 1770, these and other South Slav troops were organized into battalions of "Slaviani," numbering over 1,200.[95] The "Slaviani" together with the "Albantsi" volunteer battalions reached an overall strength of 6,413 men, and consisted of troops of several ethnic backgrounds — Greeks, Albanians, Serbs, Bulgarians and Macedonians.[96] The Serbian troops cooperated with the regular Russian naval and marine forces in amphibious operations throughout the Eastern Mediterranean between 1770 and 1774;[97] and some Serbian and other South Slavic and non-Slav troops in Russian service settled in the Crimea and took on Russian service, together with Greek and Albanian veterans, and a certain number of young Serbs were enrolled in the so-called "Cadet Corps of Foreign Co-Religionists" (*Kadetskii Korpus chuzhestrannykh edinovertsev*), founded at St. Petersburg in 1775.[98]

The last Serbian emigrés to Russia consisted of two small groups from Montenegro and Hercegovina, which arrived in Odessa in 1804 and 1815. One group of about 97 members, led by Serdar Mina Nikšić and Ovan Tjoti, arrived in 1804 and was settled in the region of Tiraspol'.[99] The last group of "Montenegrin Serbs," consisting of sixteen families (fifty persons) arrived in May 1815 and eventually settled near the former group.[100]

Close military, political, and cultural relations between various groups of Serbs and Russians continued throughout the remainder of the eighteenth century and in the nineteenth century. Nearly all Montenegrin bishops visisted Russia, and all kinds of Russian emissaries, some (Sava Marković, Marko Ivelić) military men of Serbian origin, were sent to Montenegro and Serbia. Montenegro's bishop sent two of his men to Emperor Paul to seek Russian help and protection for his country. Paul responded by approving an annual financial grant to Montenegro. At the turn of the century, at least three Serbian clerics (Archmandrite Arsenije Gaković, Bishop Jovan Jovanović, Metropolitan Stevan Stratimirović) sought Russian assistance in liberating Serbia. During the First Serbian Uprising (1804–1812), the Russians on several occasions, urged the Porte to grant the Serbs autonomy, and also sent financial aid. In 1805–1807, Russians and Montenegrins joined forces at Boka Kotorska against the French and the Turks. In June 1807 and in 1810 Russia sent troops, military technicians, and drillmasters to Serbia for joint operations against the Turks. The Serbs of Serbia again fought alongside Russian troops during the Balkan Crisis of 1876–78.

The First Uprising: A National Inspiration

No single event in modern times has given the Serbs as much inspiration as the First Serbian Uprising. A whole cycle of epic poetry deals with that struggle. Yet one should remember that during the first period of the Uprising, from 1804 to 1806, the Serbian insurgents fought as loyal subjects of the sultan; only in 1806–1813 did they become his enemies. The insurgents' success in mobilizing their fellow nationals and in organizing armed forces is most impressive. Many Serbs had gained military experience either as *hayduks*, as members of the Austrian *Freicorps* (e.g., Aleksa Nenadović, Stanko Arambašić,

Karadjordje), or as soldiers in the Turkish-sponsored Serbian national army. A few had fought in all three. The system of recruitment by village (*knežina*) and district (*nahija*) worked quite smoothly. In time Serbian military forces numbered in the thousands. Serbs from the Austrian Military Frontier (e.g., Radič Petrović, Petar Novaković-Čardaklija) and from other parts of Austria hastened to join the insurgents.[101]

The insurgent army was divided into infantry, cavalry, and artillery.[102] The cavalry was made up of men rich enough to keep one or more horsemen at their own expense. The regular soldiers paid for their own equipment and provided their own food unless operating too far from home. One must note, however, that because of difficult conditions the Serbian armed forces were constantly being reorganized. We have no reliable estimates of the size of Karadjordje's forces. Available figures are contradictory, varying from 28,000 to as high as 60,000.[103]

The main military force was a regular army made up of volunteers and called the *national army*. Other formations included *hayduk* units, *momci* — paid soldiers who served as bodyguards for Karadjordje — and *bećari,* also paid, who garrisoned fortified towns, and guarded military installations, borders, and fortifications. The Serbs fought under many banners. Some units carried banners inscribed "With God for Faith and Fatherland." Others used *hayduk* and church flags, flags with seals taken from Hristofor Zefarović's *Stematografija* (1808), or Russian flags with the slogan "Sei orel Russiiskii Zashchitaet Serbliiu."

Serbs in the Service of Romanian Princes and in the Greek Revolution

In the late eighteenth and early nineteenth centuries, a significant number of Serbs found employment in the Danubian Principalities, especially after the Serbian risings. They enlisted in companies of *arnautsi* (*arnauţi*), mercenary bodies of soldiers of Balkan origin (Christian Albanians, Bulgarians, Greeks, and Serbs). The *arnautsi* were bodyguards of the Phanariot princes (*hospodars*) of Wallachia and Moldavia.[104] Among the Serbs who served as *arnautsi* were veterans of both the First Serbian Uprising and the Russo-Turkish War of 1806–1812. Most of the leaders and their men took part in the abortive Hetairist (*Philike Hetairea*) rising in the Danubian Principalities in 1821.[105]

Serbs also fought in the Greek War of Independence. A Montenegrin Serb, Vaso Ranković (Vasos Mavrovouniotes) attained the rank of general and commanded Greek forces in east-central Greece. Before the Greek Revolution, Vaso Ranković was well known as a *hayduk* in the Balkans and Asia Minor. After the Greek Revolution, he settled in Greece and was active in Greek politics and government.[106] Another Serb prominent in the Greek Revolution was Hadji Krsto Dabović, who commanded a unit of auxiliary cavalry composed of Serbs, Bulgarians, and Macedonians.[107] Many Serbs, mostly from Boka Kotorska, distinguished themselves in the Greek naval forces and took part in several successful battles against the larger Ottoman navy.[108]

The Second Serbian Uprising and After

Serbia was granted autonomy in 1829-30; it then faced the problem of building a modern army, for its military force could no longer be modeled on that led by Karadjordje, a poorly equipped peasant insurrectionary army, organized on the basis of patriarchal discipline. The modern Serbian army evolved gradually. Initially, Prince Miloš relied on *pandurs,* who were assigned their traditional police duties, but after the Ottoman empire formally recognized Serbia's autonomy, he was given the right to organize a regular armed force. In 1837 Prince Miloš founded the Military Academy in Požarevac, but nothing like a modern army appeared in Serbia until 1861, when Prince Michael issued a decree establishing a national army and entrusted this task to a French major whom he designated as Serbia's minister of war.

This modern Serbian army, however, performed poorly in wars with the Turks (1876, 1877-78) and Bulgarians (1885). Nonetheless, the heroic military tradition was enriched by successive Serbian insurrections against the Turks in Bosnia and Hercegovina and by several Montenegrin wars with Turkey (1836, 1852-53, 1858, 1862, 1876-78). The Montenegrin liquidation of Smail-aga Čengić (1840) has a prominent place in oral and written literature and is the subject of a beautiful epic by the Croat writer, Ivan Mažuranić. The victories over the Turks at Vučji do (July 16, 1876) and Fundina (August 2, 1876) are likewise celebrated by bard and by scholar. (The author's grandfather and two uncles, incidentally, fought at Vučji do.)

By the outbreak of the Balkan Wars, Montenegro's army remained backward in terms of contemporary military science and technology, but Serbia had a modern army. The performance of the Serbian and

Montenegrin armies during the Balkan wars (1912–13) won praise from foreign military observers and aroused the national feelings of Serbs and other South Slavs still under Turkish and Austro-Hungarian rule. The heroism and perseverance of Serbian troops during World War I confirmed the long-established reputation of the Serbian fighting man. The conditioning of history has given the Serbs a spirit both militant and military.

Although modernization has tended to erode old values and old ways of fighting, the Serbs have remained first-rate soldiers. The Serbian soldier continues to come primarily from a peasant background and to consider military service a duty to his patriarchal community as well as to his country. In each of the four major wars fought in the twentieth century, the Serbian peasant-soldier demonstrated his traditional fighting qualities. His response to the outbreak of the Second World War was typical. The *Putsch* staged in Belgrade on March 27, 1941, against the government that had signed the Tripartite Pact was a patriotic gesture inspired by the notions of the "honorable death" and "heavenly kingdom" extolled in epic poetry. Because the Serbs were respected as soldiers and were the largest Yugoslav ethnic group, Germany in World War II directed its main military and political effort in Yugoslavia toward crushing them.

Although the Yugoslav army quickly collapsed under the blows of the Axis, two resistance movements appeared — the Communist Partisans and the nationalist Chetniks — the former, preponderantly, the latter, almost exclusively, Serbs. The most extensive wartime fighting and the most bitter battles were fought in the areas where the tradition of guerrilla warfare was strongest and memories of it freshest. These were the areas in which much of the patriarchal life had survived and in which epic poetry and traditional music and dance continued to inspire heroic deeds.

Notes

1. One finds such references in Procopius, Menander, John of Ephesus, Pseudo-Mauricius, Leo VI, John Cameniates, Anna Comnena, John Cantacuzenus, and Critovoulos. The author is most grateful to Dr. Gavro Škrivanić for allowing him to see portions of his manuscript on the "Organization of the Medieval Serbian, Bosnian and Dubrovnik Armies," and to Nicholas Pappas for permitting him to consult his manuscript on the "Greeks in Russian Military Service."

2. *Vojna Enciklopedija [VE]*, 2d ed. (1973), 43. (Hereafter cited as *VE.*)

3. Dušan J. Popović, *Srbi u Vojvodini* (Novi Sad, 1957) I: 98.

4. Tsar Stephen's cavalry at Demotica in 1352; King Vukašin's encounter with the Turks at Adrianople, 1371. On the mediaeval Serbian army, see St. Novaković, *Stara Srpska Vojska* (Belgrade, 1893). Nikola Stijepović, *Srpska feudalna vojska* (Belgrade, 1954).

5. P. To., "Srbija," *VE,* 2d ed. (Belgrade, 1973), 37–59.

6. On *hayduks* among the Serbs, see Dušan Popović, *O hajducima,* 2 vols. (Belgrade, 1930–31); G. Rossen, *Die Balkan Haiduken. Ein Beitrag zu intern Geschichte des Slaventhums* (Leipzig, 1878); Radovan Samardžić, *Hajdučke borbe protiv Turaka u XVI i XVII veku* (Belgrade, 1952); Samardžić, "Hajduci," *VE,* III (Belgrade, 1972): 384–86.

7. On measures used to fight the *hayduks* and their accomplices (*yataks*), see Popović, II: 230–37.

8. On famous *harambašas* and *hayduks,* see *Ibid.,* II: 230–31.

9. On the exaggerated role attached to the *uskoks,* see Bare Poparić, *Povijest senjskih Uskoka* (Zagreb, 1936); Vladimir Dvorniković, *Karakterologija Jugoslovena* ("Kosmos," 1939), 549. See *Uskoci, Enciklopedija Leksikografskog Zavoda,* VII (Zagreb, 1964): 580–81; Gligor Stanojević, *Senjski uskoci* (Belgrade, 1972).

10. Vasa Čubrilović, *Istorija političke misli u Srbiji u XIX veku* (Belgrade, 1958), 42–48.

11. These cycles tell about Marko Kraljević, the Battle of Kossovo, the Brankovići and Crnojevići, the *hayduks,* the *uskoks,* Herceg Sćepan (Stjepan Kosač), the liberation of Serbia, and the insurrections in Bosnia and Hercegovina (1875–78).

12. Dvorniković, 534. The more recent epics on the Balkan wars, the First World War, and the exploits of the Partisans and Chetniks, are imitative and lack the quality of the classical epics.

13. For details, see Dvorniković, 552, 554–55, 578–80.

14. On Starina (Baba) Novak in Romanian and Serbian traditional poetry, see Kristea Sandu-Timok, "Starina Novak u Srpskom i Rumunskom eposu," *Narodno Stvaralaštvo Folklor* XV–XVI, Nos. 57–64 (1976–77): 74–88. Vuk St. Karadžić, *Život srpskih vojvoda* (Belgrade, 1961).

15. M. Pnić Surep. *Filip Višnjić pesnik bune* (Belgrade, 1956); V. Nedić, *Filip Višnjić* (Belgrade, 1961).

16. For a discussion of the different Turkish military formations that included Serbs, see Olga Zirojević, *Tursko vojno uredjenje u Srbiji 1459–1683* (Belgrade, 1974), 158–216, an excellent study of Turkish military organization in Serbia. See also Halil Inalçik, "Ottoman Methods of Conquest," *Studia Islamica* 2 (Hague, 1954): 107–108, 114–17; Popović, I: 209–211.

17. For details, see *VE,* 2d ed. (1973), 44.

18. Gliš Elezović, "Turski izvori za istoriju Jugoslovena," *Bratstvo* XVI (1932): 91, 104, 111–14.

19. Popović, I: 168–70. On Sokolović, see Radovan Samardžić, *Mehmed Sokolović* (Belgrade, 1971).

20. On Christian *sipahis,* see Bistra Cvetkova, "Novye dannye o khristian-skikh-spakhiakh na Balkanskom poluostrove v period turestskogo gospod-stva," *Vizantiiskii Vremennik* XIII (1958): 184–97; Halil Inalçik, "Timariotes chretiens en Albanie an XV siècle," *Mitteilungen des österreichischen Staats-archivs* 4 (1951–52): 120–31. Branislav Djurdjev, "Hrišćani spahije u Severnoj Srbiji u XV veku," *Godišnjak istoriskog društva Bosne i Hercegovine* IV (1952): 165–69.

21. Inalçik, 120, 126, 130–31; Apostolos Vakalopoulos, *Historia tou Neou Hellenismou* (Thessaloniki, 1961), 211.

22. Panagiotes Aravantinos, *Chronolographia tēs Ēpirou tōn tēi ōmoron hellēnikon kai Illyrikon choron diatrechousa kata seiran ta en autais sympanta apo tou sōtērion etous mechri tou 1854* (Athens, 1856), I: 225–27; Vakalo-poulos, 30.

23. Branislav Djurdjev, "O vojnucima (sa osvrtom na razvoj turskog feu-dalizma i na pitanje turskog agaluka)," *Glasnik Zemaljskog Muzeja u Sara-jevu* II (1947): 75–138. For different views on the origin of the *voynuks,* see Ć. Truhelka, "Historička podloga agrarnog pitanja u Bosni," *Glasnik Zemalj-skog Muzeja* XXVIII (1915): 150–54. Konstantin Jireček, *Cesty po Bulharsku* (Prague, 1888), 251–54; J. Hammer, *Des osmanischen Reichs Staatsverfas-sung* (Vienna, 1815), I: 57, 407, 413–14, 432; II: 32–33, 246; St. Novaković, *Srpska baština u starijim turskim izvorima* (Belgrade, 1892), 18–20.

24. Djurdjev, 87–89, 95. The higher commanding officers of the *voynuks* were called *çeribaşi,* the *voynuk beg* (*voynuk beyi*), and the *voynuk sancak beg* (*voynuk sancagi veyi*); the lower officers were called *lagatori. Ibid.,* 101.

25. Inalçik, "Ottoman Methods of Conquest," 117.

26. Milan Vasić, *Martolozi u Jugoslovenskim zemljama pod turskom vla-davinom,* Akademija Nauka i Umjetnosti Bosne i Hercegovine, *Djela* 24 (1967): 19–25.

27. The *oda* (the smallest unit of the Ottoman paid army) consisted of five to six men. Each unit was under an *oda başi* or *boluk başi.* Two or three *odas* made a *sermaya* under the command of an *agha.* On organization and pay of *martolosi,* see Popović, I: 207–211.

28. *Ibid.,* I: 204–207. On organization, pay, and a variety of duties by *martoloses, ibid.,* I: 207–211.

29. Vasić, 25–28, 208; Iōannēs Vasdravelles, *Armatoloi kai klephtes eis tēn makedonian,* 2nd ed. Hetaireia Makedōnikon Spoudōn, *Makedonikē Biblio-thēkē* 34 (Thessaloniki, 1970): 12–13.

30. See A. Schmaus, "Die Frage einer 'Martolosen' — Epik," *Die Welt der Slawen* III-1 (Wiesbaden, 1958): 31–41. Schmaus, "Beitrage zu südslavischen Epenforschung," *Serta Monacensia* (Leiden, 1952), 150–70. V. St. Karadžić, *Srpske narodne pjesme* (Belgrade, 1954) III: 32, 54; Karadžić, (Belgrade, 1953), II: 476. V. Bogišić, *Narodne pjesme iz starijih, najviše primorskih zapisa*

(Belgrade, 1878), I: 88. G. Gesemann, *Erlangenski rukopis starih srpsko-hrvatskih narodnih pesama* (Sremski Karlovci, 1952), 283–85. Vasić, 201–207.

31. *VE*, 2d ed. (1973), 48.

32. On the Serbian national militia, see V. Čorović, *Prota Matej Nanedović, Život i Rad* (Belgrade, 1927); D. Pantelić, *Beogradski pašaluk pred Prvi srpski ustanak (1794–1804)* (Belgrade, 1949), 123–25, 147–54. Miroslav Djordjević, *Oslobodilački rat srpskih ustanika, 1804–1806* (Belgrade, 1967), 47–49. H. Sabanović, *Turski izvori o srpskoj revoluciji 1804* (Belgrade, 1956), I: 202.

33. Popović, I: 100.

34. For details on the Serbian *čajkaš* (*csajkások*), see Popović, I: 189–95.

35. Johann C. von Engel, *Staatskunde und Geschichte von Dalmatien, Croatien und Slawonien* (Halle, 1798), 298–99, 558–59; Theodor S. von Vilovsky, *Die Serben im südlichen Ungarn, im Dalmatien, Bosnien, und in der Herzegovina* (Vienna, 1884), 65–66. Gunther Erich Rothenberg, *The Austrian Military Border in Croatia, 1522–1747* (Urbana, Ill., 1960), 6.

36. *VE*, 2d ed. (1973), 45.

37. One author believes that the *uskok* type of fighting and the Military Frontier were taken over from the Turks. Nedim Filipović, "Pogled na osmanski feudalizam," *Godišnjak Istorijskog društva Bosne i Hercegovine* (Sarajevo, 1952), IV: 5–146, 70. See Dragutin Mićović, "Krajina . . . Istorijska sadržina i epska inspiracija," *Balcanica* V (1974): 412–33, 421.

38. On the organization of the Frontier (*Krajina*) at that time and the names of the captaincies (*kapetanije*), see D. Jo., "Vojna Krajina," *VE* (1975), X: 556–60.

39. Popović, I: 100.

40. On Jovan Nenad, and his *doglavnici*, see Popović, I: 133–50.

41. In 1546, the *Muster-register* lists by name several Serbian cavalry commanders; another source, dated 1551, gives the number of cavalrymen in Ferdinand's service, the names of their commanders, and the pay they received.

42. Popović, I: 168–69.

43. *Ibid.*, I: 195–200.

44. *Ibid.*, I: 170.

45. *Ibid.*, I: 180.

46. Rothenberg, 50.

47. Popović, I: 299–304.

48. Rothenberg, 59–60.

49. Popović, I: 186–88.

50. Called *Grenzer* in German and *graničari* or *krajišnici* in Serbo-Croatian. In the Vojvodina they were sometimes also called *hajduks* or *militari*.

51. M. Valentić, "Vojna Krajina," 522–28. Popović, I: 176.

52. Franz Vaniček, *Spezialgeschichte der Militärgrenze aus den Originalquellen und Quellenwerken geschöpft*, 2 vols. (Vienna, 1875), I: 86–88.

53. Jo., 557. Popović, I: 176.

54. Valentić, 525.

55. Popović, II: 88–101, 146. The Austrian *csajkás* flotilla in 1683–99, much weaker than the Turkish, was disbanded in 1741 only to be reestablished subsequently. After three attempts, the *csajkás* finally succeeded in taking Belgrade on October 7, 1788.

56. J. Radonić, *Grof Djordje Branković i njegovo creme* (Belgrade, 1911).

57. Vilovsky, 66–68.

58. Popović, I: 313–17.

59. Rothenberg, 93–94.

60. Jovan Savković, "Borba Srba Vojvodina za svoju teritorijalnu i političku samostalnost," *Zbornik Matice Srpske.* Serija društveniha nauka, No. 3 (1952), 22–51; Popović, II: 21.

61. *Ibid.,* II: 157.

62. *Ibid.,* I: 340–42.

63. *Ibid.,* II: 31–33; 157.

64. For the list of regiments, battalions, and other military formations on the Military Frontier, their headquarters and locations, see Dragoljub Joksimović, "Vojna Krajina," *VE,* X: 556–600.

65. Valentić, *EJ,* VIII (1971): 522–28.

66. On dress, military equipment, ranks, pay, organization, deployment, billeting, and provisioning of the Serbian militia, see Popović, II: 95–98.

67. Valentić, 527.

68. On inferior status of Serbian *Grenzer,* see Popović, II: 7.

69. See, for example, Miodrag Maticki, *Srpskohrvatska graničarska epika* (Belgrade, 1974). Dragutin Mičović, "Krajina — Istoriska sadržina i epska inspiracija starije srpskohrvatske i albanske narodne poezije," *Balcanica* V (1974): 412–33.

70. *VE,* 48. *Istorija naroda Jugoslavije* (Cyrillic edition), II: 1257–60, 1265. For details see *Ibid.,* II: 1257–65.

71. Popović, III: 212–27.

72. Jo., 560.

73. M. Ptč., "Panduri," *VE,* VI: 522–23. L. Ilić, *Baron Franjo Trenk i slavonski pandur* (Zagreb, 1845); F. Šišić, *Franjo barun Trenk i njegovi panduri* (Zagreb, 1900); V. Belić, "Odelo i oružje Trenkovih pandura i graničara," *Glasnik istoriskog društva u Novom Sadu* No. 27 (1937), 1–20.

74. D. M. Pavlović, *Srbija za vreme poslednjeg Austrijsko-Turskog rata (1787–1791)* (Belgrade, 1910), 62–65, 68–69, 77, 79, 83, 92.

75. Pantelić, 14–29, 42. Pavlović, 21–46.

76. In seventeenth-century Hungary, the term *pandúr* was used for irregular military formations.

77. See M. Ptč., "Panduri," 522–23. Hamdija Kpidžić, *Hercegovački ustanak 1882 godine* (Sarajevo, 1958).

78. Bare Poparić, *Povijest senjskih uskoka* (Zagreb, 1936); Gligor Stanojević, *Senjski uskoci* (Belgrade, 1973); Stanojević, "Prilozi za istoriju senjskih uskoka," *Istoriski Glasnik* No. 1–2 (1960): 111–41; Jovan Tomić, *Crtice iz istorije senjskih uskoka* (Novi Sad, 1901); Tomič, *Iz istorije senjokih uskoka*

(Novi Sad, 1901). Many others (e.g. Franjo Rački, Luka Jelić, Karlo Horvat, Vuk Vinaver) have written on the *uskoks*. Šime Ljubić and Grga Novak have edited an invaluable collection of Venetian records on the *uskoks*: see Šime Ljubić, *Commissiones et relationes Venetae*, Jugoslavenska Akademija Znansati i Umjetnosti, I (Zagreb, 1976). The work was continued by Grga Novak; the sixth volume appeared in 1970.

79. Miloš I. Milošević, "Pokušaj mletačkog osvajanja Ulcinja 1718 godine," *Godišnjak Pomorskog Muzeja u Kotoru* XX (1972): 41–46; Grga Novak, *Prošlost Dalmacije*, 2 vols. (Zagreb, 1944), I: 193–95, 208–212; II: 221–34; S. Romanin, *Storia documentata di Venezia*, 2d ed., VIII (Venice, 1915): 369–73. Gligor Stanojević, *Jugoslovenske zemlje u mletačko-turskim ratovima XVI– XVIII vijeka* (Belgrade, 1970).

80. For names of South Slav *stradioti*, see Venetian documents published in *Mnemeia Hellenikēs Historias*. Konstantinos Sathas, ed., *Documents inedits à la l'histoire de la Grèce au Moyen Âge* (Paris, 1887–90), VII: 69–73; VIII: 332– 34, 432–33; IX: 5; and Sathas, *Hellenes stratiotai en te dysei kai he anageunesis tes hellenikes taktikes* (Athens, 1885), 11–13.

81. E. Rodocanochi, *Bonaparte et les Îles Ioniennes* (Paris, 1899), 17–18. D. D. Zermpas, *Schenai kai epeisodia apo ten katochēn tēs Kerkyras hypo ton Demokratikon Gallon* (Athens, 1962), 2; senatorial decree, July 13, 1799, *General State Archives* (Athens), Vtachogiannes collection folio G36.

82. Dositej Obradović, *Dela Dositeja Obradovića* (Belgrade, 1911), 57–58.

83. On the history of the Regiment, see Vittorio Buti, "Albanesi al servizio del Regno delle Due Sicilie," *La Rasegna Italiana Politica Letteraria e Artistica*, ser. 3, LI, No. 259 (Rome, 1939): 151–57; Georgios Choraphas, *Dissertazione istorico-cronologica del Reggimento Real Macedone nella quale si tratta sua Origine, Formazione e Progressi, e delle vicissitudini, che gli sono accadute fino all' anno 1767*, 2d ed. (Bologna, 1768); Auanasio Lehasca, *Cenno storico del servigi militari prestati nel Regno Due Sicilie dai Greci, Epiroti, Albanesi e Macedoni in epoch diverse* (Corfu, 1843).

84. Choraphas, 230–32, 265–74. On Neapolitan recruitment of Montenegrins, the Venetian Slav subjects in Dalmatia, and the Ottoman Slavs, see Choraphas, 266–72. A number of troops in the *Reggimento Real Macedone* had been recruited from men who had previously served in the Austrian Military Frontier (*Militärgrenze*) and had deserted from the Austrian army that fought in Italy during the War of the Austrian Succession. Between 1744 and 1768, there were about 200 persons of this background in the regiment. See Choraphas, 216, 233, and Lehasca, 22. Gligor Stanojević and Milan Vasić, *Istorija Crne Gore*, III, pt. 1 (Titograd, 1975): 299–312, 359–60; and Gligor Stanojević, "Seoba crnogoraca u Kraljevinu Dveju Sicilija sredinom XVIII vijeka," *Glasnik Etnografskog Instituta Srpske Akademije Nauka i Umjetnosti* IX–X (1960–61): 171–77.

85. Stanojević and Vasić, 359–60; Choraphas, 201–203, 262. Lehasca, 38– 39; and Matteo Sciambra, "Prime Vicende della Communita greco-albanese di

Palermo e suci rapporti con L'Oriente bizantino," *Bolletino della Badia Greca di Grotta-ferrata,* new ser. XVI (1962): 101–102.

86. Mita Kostić, "Srpska Naselja u Rusiji: Nova Srbija i Slavenosrbija," *Srpski Etnografski Zbornik,* SKA, XIV (1923): 1–11.

87. Zaharija Orfelin, *Petar Veliki,* II (Belgrade, 1970): 335.

88. Kostić, "Srpska naselja u Srbiji," 5–135, 12–14. Nil A. Popov, "Voyennye poseleniia Serbov v Avstrii i Rossii," *Vestnik Evropy* VI (1870): 584–614.

89. Kostić, 15.

90. Mirko R. Barjaktarević, "Sudbina odseljenih Srba u Ukrajini," *Zbornik Radova SANU,* new ser., I, Etnografski institut, No. 5 (Belgrade, 1971): 139–50.

91. M. Ptč., "Panduri," 522–23.

92. Popović, II: 117–28. Kostić, 5–135. Popov, "Voennye poseleniia," 584–614. In his memoirs Simeon Stepanovich Piščević tells about the Serbian migrations to Russia, Serbian activities there, and his own role in this emigration. Piščević, *Memoari* (Belgrade, 1963). By 1862 only about 1,000 persons still declared themselves Serbs; by 1900, the Serbs are no longer mentioned in the imperial census. According to the 1926 census, 386 Serbs lived in Ukrainian villages; probably there were as many in towns. V. I. Naulko, *Geografichne Rozmishcheniia narodiv u USSR* (Kiev, 1966), 27. It may well be that the number of Serbian immigrants was not as large as originally reported. See also note 90.

93. *Sbornik imperatorskog russkago istoricheskago obshchestva* LXXXVII (St. Petersburg, 1893): 322–26.

94. C. Rulhiere, *Histoire de l'anarchie de Pologne et du démembrement de cette république* (Paris, 1807), 3: 383–84.

95. "Zhurnal Stepana Petrova syna Khmetevskogo o voennykh deistviiakh russkago flota v Archipelag i v beregov Maloi Azii v 1770–1774," *Sovremennik* 49, no. 2 (St. Petersburg, 1855): 57.

96. On the organization of the Slaviani and Albantsy battalions, see Radi Boev, "Voenno-politicheskoe sotrudnichestvo mezhdu balkanskimi narodami i Rossiei v khode Russko-Turetskoi voiny 1768–1774 godov," *Études Balkaniques* No 2 (Sofia, 1975): 123–24.

97. "Zhurnal Stepana Petrova," 75–79, 150 53, 156, 166–67. For a list of the operations in which they took part, see S. Safonov, "Ostatki grecheskikh legionov v Rossii ili nyneishnee Balaklavy. Istoricheski ocherk," *Zapiski odesskago obshchestva istorii i drevnostei* (Odessa, 1844), 1: 208.

98. Graf de Liudolf, "Pisma o Kryme," *Russkoe obozrenie* (Moscow, 1892), 2: 155–201.

99. Barjaktarević, 142.

100. Apolon Skal'kovskii, *Khronologicheskoe obozrye istorii novrosiiskogo kraia* (Odessa, 1838), 114, 163–65, 253–54.

101. *VE,* 49.

102. Terms for military ranks were partly Turkish and partly Slavic. Village units of from ten to twenty men were put under a command of *podbuljubaša* (*mali buljubaša*). The *nahija* contingent was made up of troops from several *knežinas*, organized into a number of battalions, and headed by a *bimbaša*. A *podvojvoda* (*mali vojvoda*) was in command of a battalion, *vojvoda* in command of a battalion and larger units. Other military ranks were corporal, *urednik* (*jendrik*); captain (*buljubaša*). An *urednik* commanded a unit of twenty-five; a captain commanded a company (or *escadron*). The supreme commander, Karadjordje, was called *vožd* (leader). J. Mišković, "Srpska vojska i vojevanje za vreme ustanka od 1804–1815 godine," *Glas* No. XLVII (Belgrade, 1895): 1–50. Nikola Radojčić, "Karadjordjeva vojska," *Jugoslovenska njiva* I (1925): 150–56. D. Dinić, "Srpska vojska u doba prvog ustanka," *Vojnoistoriski glasnik,* No. 5 (1953): 25–50. R. Marković, *Vojska i naoružanje Srbije kneza Miloša* (Belgrade, 1957).

103. On the insurgent army, provisions, organization, pay, etc., see *EJ,* I (1955): 405.

104. No good study of the *arnautsi* is available. Some important data can be found in the following: Nestor Camariano, "L'activité de Georges Olympios dans les principautes roumaines avant la révolution de 1821," *Revue des études Sud-Est Européenne* 2, no. 3–4 (1964): 446–53; Sava Janković, "Neki arhivski podaci o Hadži Prodanu i Stevanu Živkoviću i Vlaškoj," *Istorijski Časopis* 14–15 (1965): 361–77. Sava Iancovici, "Date noi despre Bimbasa Sava," *Studii, Revista de Istorie* 14, no. 5 (1961): 1187–1201; Idem., "Revolta unor arnauți in 1819," *Studii și Articole di istorie* 5 (1963): 447–55. One may also find some data on *arnautsi* in the Hetairist insurrections of 1821 in the Russian principalities.

105. Iancovici, 5, *Ibid.,* 449–50, 452–55; Dan Berindei, *Aspecte militare al mișcarii revoluționare din 1821,* 2d ed. (Bucharest, 1973), 35, 41, 64, 67ff., and Nikolai Totorov, B.

106. On Vaso Ranković, see Athanasios Chrysologes, *Vasos Mavrovouniōtēs* (Athens, 1876; reprint 1978); and Soutsos, 43–47.

107. On Hadži-Krsto, see Soutsos, *Hoi Philhellēnes tōn Balkanion stēn Epanastase tou Eikosiena* (Athens, 1976), 37–42.

108. At a conference on "Greco-Serbian Relations during their Wars of Liberation, 1804–1830," at Kavalla in 1976 Greek scholars Spyridon Loukatos and Emmanouēl Protopsaltēs presented papers on Serbian participants in the Greek Revolution.

Avigdor Levy

Ottoman Attitudes to the Rise of Balkan Nationalism

The rise of Serbian and Greek nationalism has been the subject of considerable, and sometimes detailed, historical research conducted from a variety of viewpoints. It is common knowledge, however, that western scholarship, while discussing apparent Ottoman policies and acts, has taken only little account of Ottoman sources and, hence, perspectives. The purpose of the present study is to fill a certain lacuna in this respect. On the basis of Ottoman sources it intends to examine, first, how the central government in Istanbul viewed the emergence of Balkan nationalism against the background of wider imperial issues; and second, how that government attempted to formulate a coherent policy toward the emerging national movements, taking into account traditional principles of government, on one hand, and contemporary political constraints, on the other.

* * *

The weakening of central authority over the provinces, the gradual breakdown of effective administration, and the continued deterioration of public security were among the salient features of general Ottoman decline. These processes underscored a growing commonality of interests between the central government in Istanbul and the taxpaying masses, especially the peasantry, in the outlying regions. Ottoman statecraft, based on mediaeval Islamic political experience, maintained that "to control the state requires a large army; to support the troops requires great wealth; to obtain this wealth the people must be prosperous."[1] Accordingly, no matter how important the contribution of other classes, the long-range prosperity of the state ultimately rested upon the economic well-being of its taxpaying subjects, the *reaya,* or protected "flocks" of the sultan. This view was expressed even more forcefully by an eighteenth-century statesman:

> A country endures not unless there be men of substance.
> But for men of substance wealth is needed.
> Wealth is produced by the subject people.
> It comes from the culture of vineyard and garden.

> Unless there be justice the subjects are restless.
> Without justice the tent becomes not a lasting home.
> Justice is basis of the order of the world. . . .
> If the gardener will not keep open his eye
> Everyone stretches out a grasping hand.[2]

Accordingly, from the latter decades of the sixteenth century down to the nineteenth, the central government consistently endeavored — although with a declining measure of success — to establish safeguards in order to protect the common population against rapacious governors, dishonest administrators, and unruly soldiers.[3] The central government, for its own practical reasons, and the population at large had a basic, mutually shared interest in the restoration of good order and just government.

This commonality of interests was nowhere more apparent than in the district of Belgrade where, during the latter part of the eighteenth century, large numbers of unruly janissaries and their followers had found refuge. In defiance of the Ottoman authorities the rebellious soldiery terrorized the Serbian peasantry, seized their land, and forced them into a state of actual serfdom. It was mainly due to janissary oppression that during the Habsburg-Ottoman war of 1788–91 large numbers of Serbs crossed the frontier and volunteered to serve under Austrian colors against the Ottoman state.[4] After the establishment of peace, the Ottoman government of Selim III, far from exacting retribution from the Serbs, resolved to conciliate them by alleviating their grievances, restoring order and security to the province, and even encouraging those who had fled to return to their homes. The new governor of Belgrade Ebubekir Paşa was specifically charged with the task of eliminating janissary power. A series of measures introduced between 1793 and 1797 — under Ebubekir and since July 1795 under another reform-minded governor Hajji Mustafa Paşa — prohibited the janissaries from holding any lands in the district of Belgrade. At the same time, Serbian self-government was expanded by granting their elders, the *knez*es, the right to assess and collect their own taxes without Ottoman interference. In addition, the governors made an intensive effort to drive out brigands and rebellious soldiers. To help maintain public order, Hajji Mustafa encouraged the *knez*es to recruit and arm their own Serbian troops as auxiliary forces.[5]

The problem of restoring order in Serbia, as well as in other Ottoman provinces, was, however, connected with wider issues of center-periphery relations. Continued Ottoman decline, and especially the disastrous wars in which the empire had become engaged in the course of the eighteenth century, permitted the emergence of a new class of provincial rulers, usually known throughout the Balkans as *ayan*s, or notables. The power base of this class was local and its ascendancy was often in defiance of the central government. In practice, the *ayan*s' attitudes toward Istanbul, subject to constant fluctuation, ranged widely from qualified cooperation through incipient defiance to outright opposition and openly declared rebellion.[6] The rule of a few powerful *ayan*s who had established some balanced relations with the central government brought temporary order and prosperity to limited areas under their control. Nevertheless, as a class, the notables endeavored to sustain a state of "modulated anarchy"[7] in order to maintain their independence of action vis-à-vis the central government. Although *ayan* rule was widespread throughout much of the Ottoman territories in the Balkan Peninsula, the centers which most directly affected the situation in Serbia were the neighboring provinces of Bosnia and Vidin, where the local notables exhibited a most stridently defiant attitude toward the central government.[8]

The ruling elite in Istanbul considered the provincial *ayan*s "the most contemptible of people, useless both for the service of the *Pâdişah* and for warfare."[9] In the official view they were *mütegallibe,* or lawless tyrants and usurpers of legitimate authority. The state counselors urged the government "to strive to do away with the oppressive power of the provincial notables and usurers over the subject population."[10] As a matter of practical policy, however, the government, owing to its weakness, had little choice but to coopt many of the *ayan*s into the provincial administrative system. It was forced to confer official appointments and legitimacy upon them, particularly during periods of crisis. At other times, however, especially when the government was under the influence of a determined leadership, attempts were made to curb and even eliminate *ayan* power. But even at these times government action was circumscribed by the opposition of various groups at the center who had a vested interest in the maintenance of the existing order. In 1785 the energetic Grand Vezir Halil Hamid Paşa launched an attempt to curb the *ayan*s, but the outbreak of war two years later canceled whatever designs the government had entertained in that respect. When peace was restored in 1792, the campaign against the provincial notables was resumed. But when the government of Selim III encountered mounting opposition from more conservative leaders, it lacked the resolve to pursue its initial successes further. Consequently, in 1797 the policy of suppressing *ayan* power was temporarily halted. In the following year, Napoleon invaded Egypt, the Ottoman empire became embroiled in a war with France, and plans to restore central authority to the provinces had to be put into abeyance indefinitely.[11]

This turn of events had immediate repercussions on the situation in Serbia. Emboldened by the reduction of government forces in the Balkans, Pasvanoğlu Mustafa, the rebellious *ayan* of Vidin and northern Bulgaria, moved to assist his allies, the mutinous janissaries, and restore their power in Belgrade. With the help of further reinforcements from rebellious elements in Bosnia, the janissaries were able, by the end of 1801, to overrun the district, kill the reform-minded governor of Belgrade Hajji Mustafa, and reinstate a reign of terror which exceeded in brutality all that had preceded it. These acts were generally recognized as the antecedents of the Serbian uprising[12] which, in its initial stage, took the form of resistance to the janissaries; then the movement expanded to oppose the local Ottoman administration; finally, by June–July 1805, it was transformed into an open revolt against the sultan's authority.

The waning of central authority in the Balkans in the wake of the war with France greatly circumscribed direct government intervention in Serbia. Nevertheless, during the first stage of the uprising, while the Serbs still professed their allegiance to the Ottoman throne, Selim III instructed loyal neighboring governors to assist the embattled Serbs with arms and materiel. Indeed, Karadjordje and his supporters received substantial aid from Ebubekir, Paşa of Niš, the Hospodar of Wallachia, Constantine Ypsilanti, and from other Ottoman governors.[13]

The consistency of the policy of conciliation toward the Serbian population was based on a traditional maxim of Ottoman statecraft, sometimes referred to as *istimâlet* — gaining good will or friendly persuasion.[14] At this point, however, it also reflected the government's growing desire to terminate the uprising peacefully and as soon as possible. For Serbian military successes during the spring and summer of 1804 and the growing strength of the movement now became a source of alarm to the Ottomans. So long as the Ottoman government was not strong enough to reassert its own authority in the province, it was contrary to its interests to see one local party — at the present stage the Serbs — assume a predominant position which could later be turned against the government itself. In addition, the Serbian movement was now becoming a rallying point for Christian sympathizers throughout the Balkans. The administrations of the Greek Hospodars of Wallachia and Moldavia were sympathetic to the movement; Christian outlaws from Montenegro, Albania, Thessaly, Macedonia, Bulgaria, and elsewhere were joining the Serbs. Above all, the situation in Serbia was threatening to become an international problem which could invite foreign intervention.[15]

In fact, a perceptible deterioration of Ottoman-Serb relations occurred in September 1804, when the Serbian leadership demanded that any political solution to the problems of Serbia should be guaranteed by a foreign power.[16] In the Ottoman view this was tantamount to inviting foreign intervention in what had been considered an internal affair between the sultan and his "flocks." It suggested an infringement on Ottoman sovereignty over territories regarded as important not only for political and military reasons, but also on moral and religious grounds. For Ottoman resolve to hold on to Serbia, or any part of the Balkans, was deeply rooted in the Islamic heritage which found it repugnant to give up to the infidel any sovereign rights over territories inhabited by Muslims. Moreover, the Ottoman sultans had long regarded their continued rule of the Balkan provinces as essential for upholding their title as *Gazi*s, or warriors of the Faith against the infidel. This title they had used to lend strength and legitimacy to their demand on the loyalties of their own Muslim subjects as well as to support their claims for supremacy in the Islamic world.[17] The Serbian demands, unwittingly perhaps, touched upon an area of great Ottoman sensitivity. From now on the Ottomans considered the Serbs as potential rebels more dangerous to Ottoman interests than the mutinous janissaries. In May 1805 an imperial order demanded that the Serbs lay down their arms and rely for their protection on the Ottoman government. Since the order was ignored, the government now considered the Serbs to be in a state of open rebellion.[18]

The unprecedented independence of the local *ayan*s, however, their reluctance to cooperate with the capital, or with each other, rendered any government-led military operation against the Serbs totally ineffective. Furthermore, the regime of Sultan Selim III, beset by mounting crises and lacking unity within its own ranks, was soon struggling for its very survival. One aspect of the government's internal weakness was its growing involvement in the political conflicts between Napoleonic France and its enemies. As a result of French pressure and enticement, the Ottoman state gradually drifted toward another war with Russia which, in fact, broke out in November 1806. Consequently, the government was now more anxious than ever before to reach a direct agreement with the Serbs. In September 1806, the sultan agreed to accept newly formulated Serbian demands granting the Serbs extensive autonomous powers without, however, foreign guarantees. The agreement was formally ratified by the government in January 1807. But the Ottoman concessions arrived too late; the Serbs had succumbed to Russian enticements urging them to opt for full independence, and consequently, in March, the Serbs rejected the agreement and the rebellion resumed with vigor.[19]

Shortly thereafter, in May, Selim III was overthrown and a period of political anarchy marked by armed coups and civil war all but immobilized the seat of government in Istanbul for almost two years. Nevertheless, even during this period of political turmoil and rapid changes of government, Ottoman attitudes regarding the Serbian uprising remained remarkably consistent. The main thrust of Ottoman policy was to localize the conflict in Serbia and disengage it from the empire's international relations by consistently offering to reach a direct and conciliatory settlement with the Serbian leadership. During 1806 and 1807 the Ottomans repeatedly rejected several Austrian and Russian proposals to alter the political status of Serbia to that of the Danubian Principalities, a change which would entail some form of international guarantees.[20] During the Ottoman-Russian armistice negotiations in August 1807, the Russians demanded that the agreement be extended to the Serbian forces. The Ottoman representatives, however, rejected this demand and refused to accord the Serbs the status of a belligerent power. They countered by arguing that "a government cannot make an armistice with its own subjects."[21] But the Russian delegates pointed out that their own troops were stationed alongside Serbian forces and continued hostilities on the Serbian front could, therefore, jeopardize the armistice. Consequently, the Ottomans were impelled to sign a separate agreement regarding Russian forces in Serbia. But this document was so carefully phrased that it avoided any mention of Serbian forces and addressed itself only to "Russian troops among the Serbs."[22] Similarly, in December 1810, Karadjordje offered Ibrahim Hilmi Paşa, the governor of Bosnia, a local truce during the winter months. Ibrahim Hilmi was inclined to accept the offer, but the Ottoman government in Istanbul ordered him to reject it on the grounds that the Serbs were "rebellious *reaya* . . . and not a state."[23]

At the same time, however, the Ottoman government repeatedly attempted to reach a separate accommodation with the Serbs. In two instances, the government enlisted the services of the Greek Orthodox Church. In November 1807, under Sultan Mustafa IV and Grand Vezir Çelebi Mustafa Paşa, the Ottoman government offered the

Serbs, through the mediation of the Greek Patriarch of Constantinople, complete amnesty and extensive autonomy.[24] These offers were repeated in October 1808 when the government in Istanbul was headed by Bayrakdar Mustafa. The mediators in this instance were the Greek bishops of Vidin and Belgrade.[25] After Bayrakdar Mustafa's fall, Sultan Mahmud II again repeated the offer in April 1809.[26] In each instance the stumbling block appeared to be the question of foreign guarantees.

Russian-Serbian military cooperation and their joint agitation among the Christian population in the Balkans strengthened Istanbul's fear of a Russian-led general Christian uprising. This fear found its expression in official Ottoman correspondence. Thus an Imperial Order issued by Mahmud II on May 27, 1809, and addressed to the Grand Vezir Yusuf Ziya Paşa called upon him, *inter alia,* to pay close attention to the state of the Christian subjects in the realm. "In the past the *reaya* knew their obligations . . . but for some time, due to outside agitation as well as the weakness of the state . . . they no longer observe their duties." The Grand Vezir was urged to put an end to this situation.[27]

When peace negotiations between the Russians and the Ottomans were resumed at the end of 1811 and again in April–May 1812, the question of Serbia once again proved a major stumbling block on the road to an agreement. The Russians repeated their demand that Serbia be granted a status similar to that of the Danubian Principalities. But the Ottoman representatives persisted in rejecting these demands.[28] Article 8 of the Peace of Bucharest (May 28, 1812) bore testimony to Ottoman tenacity in this matter. The Serbs were to be granted a general amnesty and allowed to administer their own internal affairs, but they were to surrender all forts and fortified towns to the Ottoman government. The demand for international guarantees was totally abandoned, and the treaty declared that in the matter of its relations with the Serbs "the Sublime Porte will consult none but its own sentiments of tenderness."[29]

With the conclusion of the Russian war, the pacification of Serbia became a matter of first priority in Ottoman concerns. But the government also resolved to move with caution and in line with its former policies.[30] Through June and July 1812, the Ottomans were preoccupied with the Russian evacuation, establishing government forces and central control in the evacuated territories on the heels of the withdrawing Russians. As a result, the government's position along the Danube was greatly strengthened. Meanwhile, the Ottomans informed the Serbs of the contents of Article 8 of the Treaty of Bucharest and called upon them to comply with its requirements.[31] Similarly, Ottoman field commanders were informed of the provisions of Article 8 and instructed to take over Serbian fortresses peacefully. The orders specifically underlined that a general amnesty was declared and that punitive measures against the population were not allowed.[32] It soon became apparent, however, that the Serbs were not prepared to abide by the Treaty of Bucharest and meekly surrender their positions. The government then prepared for a showdown. At the end of August the sultan appointed Ahmed Hurşid Paşa, the governor of Sofia who had commanded the main forces on the Serbian front, as grand vezir and commander-in-chief (*Ser Asker*) of the Ottoman Imperial Army in the Balkans. He was now empowered to enforce the pacification of Serbia on the basis of the Treaty of Bucharest.[33]

But, as in the past, the problem of Serbia could not be isolated from the wider issues of central control of the provinces. In fact, in the Ottoman view the insurrection in Serbia, in spite of its dangerous ramifications, was a mere symptom of a disorder whose true causes lay in the unbridled independence of the *ayan*s. If the causes of the general disorder could be eradicated, the symptoms were certain to disappear. In terms of practical policy, the Ottoman government still intended to terminate the uprising with the time-honored method of *istimâlet*. But "persuasion" also required a measure of intimidation. In short, successful pacification of Serbia could be achieved only after the neighboring provinces were brought under effective government control. Consequently, in the summer of 1812, the government reached a major policy decision — to direct all its resources to eliminating *ayan* power. As a result, the state continued to be administered on a war footing; the Grand Vezir himself took the field, as in wartime, to direct the necessary military operations.[34]

The inability of the sultans to exercise their authority over large areas of their realm could not be measured only in terms of loss of power. According to Islamic-Ottoman political concepts, the independence of local rulers posed a serious challenge to the very legitimacy of the sultan's government. By the eighteenth century, as their actual power declined, the sultans sought to strengthen their claim to absolute authority by increasingly underscoring their religious role as caliphs, or the divinely selected and inspired leaders of Islam.[35] Sari Mehmed Paşa urged the following:

> Let everyone always and with sincere heart bless and praise the Pâdişah of mankind and hold not to the contrary course, for God

who is Great in Majesty has made him Caliph. He is the shadow of
God on the face of the earth. Prayer for him is the duty of everyone.[36]

Mahmud II also resorted to the use of such religious titles as
Commander of the Faithful (*Emir ul-Mu'minin*) and Leader of the
Muslims (*Imam ul-Muslimin*).[37] From this perspective, successful and
sustained defiance of the sultan's absolute power by his Muslim subjects was obviously a more serious challenge to the legitimacy of his
government than the disobedience of his infidel "flocks." It was from
this legal perspective that the government looked at the insubordinate
*ayan*s as usurpers of legitimate authority.

Furthermore, for Sultan Mahmud, who had ascended the throne in
1808, the *ayan* challenge acquired a more immediate and personal
dimension. During the first months of his reign, for the first time in
Ottoman history, an attempt had been made to redraft the constitutional framework of the state by limiting the sultan's sovereignty and
establishing a quasi-feudal political system. The attempt was led by
Bayrakdar Mustafa, the *ayan* of Ruse who had temporarily seized the
seat of government in Istanbul. The attempt proved abortive. Within
several months the provincial forces were driven out of the capital and
Bayrakdar Mustafa himself was killed. But this adventure, during
which the sultan himself narrowly escaped death, was believed to have
made Mahmud II determined to destroy the *ayan* class at the very first
opportunity.[38]

In addition, there was the recent record of *ayan* participation in the
war effort against Russia and the Serbs. Although several important
*ayan*s responded to the sultan's declaration of a holy war with enthusiasm and large military contingents, the contribution of others was
reluctant, and some ignored it altogether. Even when the enemy threatened their immediate territorial possessions, cooperation between *ayan*
forces and government troops was minor or nonexistent. There were
even instances in which local governors conducted separate negotiations with the enemy. In 1810 Yillikoğlu Suleyman, the *ayan* of Silistra,
declared to the advancing Russians his intentions to remain neutral in
the war. He repeatedly offered to conclude a separate truce with them.
After the Russians rejected all his offers, on June 11, 1810, he surrendered Silistra without firing one shot. He and his followers were
granted safe passage and they left for the Balkan mountains.[39] The
ayan of Ruse, Boşnak Ağa who had seized power there after the demise
of Bayrakdar Mustafa, for a while heroically defended his town
against Russian attacks, but he refused to cooperate with government

troops. On September 7, 1810, he stood by while the Russians annihilated an Ottoman army which had advanced to aid Ruse. Following this Ottoman defeat, he conducted separate negotiations with the Russians and on September 27 surrendered Ruse and Giurgiu to them on condition of safe passage for himself and his men.[40] The *ayan* of Vidin, Molla Idris who had come into power in 1807 after the death of his master Pasvanağlu Osman, also refused to cooperate with government troops. His military role was essentially reduced to a passive defense of his domains against the Russians and the Serbs, while intermittently conducting separate negotiations with the enemy.[41]

In addition, several *ayan*s whose territories were removed from the main theaters of war took advantage of wartime conditions; in open defiance of the sultan's orders, they extended their possessions at the expense of weaker neighbors. Most glaring was the case of Tepedelenli Ali of Yanina who in 1809 seized the territories of Ibrahim Paşa, the *mutasarrif* of Valona. Ali was powerful and, in addition, he undertook to raise numerous troops for the war effort. So for the time being the sultan yielded and legitimized his conquests.[42]

It was against this background that one sees Sultan Mahmud anxious to terminate the war with Russia in spite of French inducements to continue. The sultan was determined to utilize the peace in order to destroy the independence of local rulers once and for all and reestablish firm central control over the provinces.[43] He, therefore, consistently promoted and surrounded himself with persons willing to carry out these politicies.

Indeed, during the summer of 1812 government troops began eliminating minor *ayan*s in various areas of Anatolia and the Balkans.[44] In October an imperial order dismissed Molla Idris from the government of Vidin. Molla Idris tried to resist, but intimidated by superior government forces, he submitted to the sultan's will and accepted his "invitation" to come and reside in Istanbul. Molla Idris was reported to be ill and in July 1813 he died at his home in the capital. His removal from Vidin marked a major victory for the government, and it cleared the way for the envelopment of Serbia and the launching of a successful campaign there.[46]

Indeed, during July 1813, three large Ottoman armies converged on Serbia from the directions of Vidin, Niš, and Bosnia. A brief campaign lasting less than three months followed. Faced with overwhelming forces, Serbian resolve had dissipated and in October the Ottomans recaptured Belgrade without a struggle. The Ottoman government celebrated the successful unfolding of their strategy with jubilant firing of cannon in Istanbul.[47]

Following his triumphant entry to Belgrade, Grand Vezir Ahmed Hurşid Paşa reintroduced a conciliatory policy toward the Serbian population. The salient aspects of this policy included a general amnesty and a call to Serbian refugees to return to their homes. Indeed, by April 1814 some 30,000 Serbs who had fled to Austria returned and many more came down from the hills where they had taken refuge. To underscore the conciliatory Ottoman attitude, the new governor of Belgrade, Üsküplü Suleyman Paşa, appointed several well-known leaders of the last uprising, including one Miloš Obrenović, to various administrative offices. By the summer of 1814 the pacification of Serbia appeared complete.[48]

Meanwhile, government operations against the *ayan*s continued unabated. A major achievement in this respect was the capture and execution, in August 1813 near Shumla, of Yillikoğlu Suleyman.[49] Emboldened by its initial successes, in 1814 and early 1815 the government sought to impose even more stringent controls. Provincial governors were repeatedly exhorted to eliminate any signs of disobedience, to impose strict disciplinary measures, and to remit taxes on time. Zealous governors quickly translated these orders into action. As proof of their dedication to the sultan's orders they sent to Istanbul, according to Ottoman practice, numerous heads of those who had been decapitated for alleged disobedience.[50] Far from enhancing public safety, these policies contributed to further deterioration of order. For when rebel *ayan*s were annihilated by government forces, many of their men escaped to the hills to engage in brigandage. The net result of these disciplinary policies, at least in the short range, was increased lawlessness throughout many of the provinces. Indeed, these measures caused growing discontent in widely flung areas, and complaints against oppressive governors began to arrive in Istanbul in increasing numbers.[51] The Ottoman historian Cevdet who is generally favorable in his assessment of Sultan Mahmud's policies, on several occasions strongly criticizes the efficacy and justice of these harsh measures.[52]

While conditions remained volatile throughout many of the empire's provinces, another factor aggravated the situation in Serbia even further. Throughout 1814 and early 1815 Üsküplü Suleyman, possibly with excessive zeal, attempted to carry out the government's new orders. Harsh measures were introduced to assure prompt collection of taxes and the maintenance of public order. The latter was particularly hard to implement since the number of outlaws in the district — both Christian and Muslim — increased so appreciably. In addition, the Ottoman authorities suspected — and with good reason — that the Serbs still entertained hopes of independence and were in contact with foreign powers, especially Austria. Consequently, Üsküplü Suleyman tried to enforce, with great severity, a government order to collect small arms from the Serbian population. This last measure appears to have revived Serbian apprehensions as well as hopes, and in April 1815 another uprising was touched off.[53] The small Ottoman garrisons were surprised and overwhelmed and the Serbs regained control over most of the district of Belgrade. In reaction, the Ottoman government immediately ordered three large Ottoman armies to converge on Serbia. But Miloš Obrenović, the leader of the uprising, contended that the rebellion was not against the sultan's government, but merely against the oppressive policies of the governor Üsküplü Suleyman. Such complaints were not unusual at that time. Moreover, with the termination of the Napoleonic wars, Ottoman apprehensions of possible European intervention were increasing once again. Consequently, the government wanted to reach a quick accommodation with the Serbs. Indeed, in November an oral agreement — subsequently approved by imperial decrees — was reached between Miloš and the new Ottoman governor of Belgrade, Maraşli Ali. The new agreement was in essence a revival of Sultan Selim's proposals of 1806 which had been rejected by the Serbs. It granted the Serbs more extensive self-government and allowed them to retain their arms.[54] In the Ottoman view, it probably seemed a price well worth paying in order to keep out European intervention as well as permit the state to continue its centralizing policies against the *ayans*.

Indeed, as of spring 1816, the government's campaign against *ayan* power entered a new phase. Although most operations took place in Anatolia,[55] the government also began to move against some of the more powerful notables in the Balkans. In March 1816, the *ayans* of Hezargrad and Didymoteichon were wiped out.[56] During 1818 several lesser *ayans* in Thrace and Thessaly were annihilated.[57] These centralizing policies, specifically those directed against the most powerful *ayan* in the Balkans, Tepedelenli Ali of Yanina, also served as background and catalyst for the Greek uprising.

By 1819, Tepedelenli Ali Paşa established himself as the effective ruler of all southern Albania and most of northern continental Greece. Ali ruled his possessions effectively, establishing order and public security on a level then rarely found in Ottoman provinces. In time of need, he could muster military forces estimated to total some 40,000 men. His strength rested on an economic base of revenues from taxation, monopolies, and his own private estates. During various periods Ali conducted relations with European powers independently of the Ottoman government.[58]

For a long time it had become apparent that the centralizing policies of Mahmud II would lead, sooner or later, to a confrontation with Ali. But Ali's reputed military strength and political influence deterred the government from taking hasty action. On his part, Ali consistently followed a conciliatory policy toward the government, ingratiating himself whenever possible by contributing sizable military contingents in wartime and performing various political services at other times. In addition, however, Ali was an old man and for some time it was expected (or rather hoped) at the sultan's court that he would die. This would have allowed the government to divide his possessions peacefully among his three sons. Similar methods had been followed upon the death of other great *ayan*s as the first step toward the total elimination of strong provincial centers of power.[59] But Ali kept on living.

Ottoman and Western historians offer numerous reasons to explain why, in 1819, Sultan Mahmud finally lost patience and decided to move against Ali. Some sources attributed this decision to Ali's very successes at that time in making inroads in northern Albania against the *ayan* of Shkodër, Buşatli Mustafa. These successes led to the coalescence in Istanbul of a powerful lobby determined to bring Ali down.[60] Be this as it may, the decision to attack Ali must have been a painful one. It was the subject of long discussions between the sultan and his confidants. Opponents of this move, headed by the *Reis ul-Küttâb,* Canib Mehmed Emin Besim Efendi, called attention to signs pointing to an incipient rebellion in the Peloponnesus and Euboea. They pointed out the dangers of immobilizing two large Ottoman armies — that of the central government and that of Tepedelenli Ali — in a conflict against each other rather than uniting them to pacify the countryside.[61]

The chief supporter of the campaign against Ali was Halet Efendi whose political career and rise to power were based on his consistent advocacy of suppressing the local notables. No doubt, as on previous instances, he merely expressed the sultan's own innermost ambitions. Consequently, at the end of 1819, it was finally decided to attack Ali. Preparations were carried out secretly during the first half of 1820; the final break came in July when Ali was officially declared a rebel.[62]

Tepedelenli Ali retaliated by calling for an uprising both in Greece and in Albania. Indeed, through most of 1820 Istanbul received a steady stream of reports of the increase of brigandage and intensified attacks on the authorities as well as isolated Muslim communities throughout Greece and in Crete.[63] Reacting more directly to Ali's call, the warlike Souliotes rose in rebellion against the sultan in December

1820. Their openly declared alliance with Ali is considered the military antecedent of the Greek uprising.[64]

Considering the events just described, it is all the more remarkable that when Istanbul was informed about the outbreak of the Greek uprising in Moldavia in March 1821, it created such a sensation that the usually reserved Ottoman historian, Cevdet, found it necessary to describe the event as follows:

> The terrible news struck the Sublime Porte as a thunderbolt. It caused the people of Istanbul to fall into a state of perplexity . . . and the ministers of state were confused as to what is to be done.[65]

The government was now confronted with the dilemmas caused by an open conflict with an ethnoreligious group whose leadership was responsible for several major areas of government administration. From almost every perspective, the Greek uprising was immediately seen as far more threatening to vital Ottoman interests than the Serbian movement could possibly have been. Of immediate concern was the problem of the large Greek population of metropolitan Istanbul and other major cities. On the one hand, it was necessary to protect the Greeks against anticipated attacks by incited Muslim mobs, which could easily deteriorate into a state of total anarchy. On the other hand there were fears of terrorist acts by members of the Philike Hetaireia society which was known to have been active among the Greeks in Istanbul. Consequently, an imperial order was issued warning against any attacks on the Greek population. At the same time intricate security measures were implemented for Istanbul and Adrianople [Edirne]. Orders were issued to register all Greek inhabitants of these two cities according to their places of domicile. A Muslim inspector was assigned to every Greek house. Nonresident Greeks were to be expelled. All resident Greeks were required to post surety and surrender all arms. Searches were conducted for ams and the guards in the Greek quarters were considerably increased.[66]

Meanwhile, the Ottoman government began urgent deliberations at several levels to evaluate the risks involved. The sultan demanded reports from everyone in authority. Still unsatisfied, at the end of March Mahmud II dismissed Grand Vezir Seyyid Ali Paşa as well as the *Sheyh ul-Islam* Hajji Halil Efendi in gestures that signified his utter dissatisfaction with the work of his government.[67]

It is, therefore, the more remarkable that, despite this great concern, the government did not direct all its resources to suppress the Greek uprising which was now gaining strength in Greece proper. The government did order some military forces to the Danubian Principalities and against the rebels in Greece.[68] In addition, it tried to enlist the official support of the Greek Orthodox Church. The Patriarch of Constantinople was prevailed upon to issue an excommunication order against the rebels, and Ottoman governors were instructed to use this measure as well as the influence of the local Church leaders to pacify the countryside.[69] Nevertheless, the government's primary military efforts continued, for almost another full year, to be directed against Ali of Yanina. Ahmed Hurşid Paşa, now commander-in-chief of the Ottoman armies operating against Ali, was credited with having perceived the potential dangers in Greece should the rebellion be allowed to continue and gain strength. He requested permission from Istanbul to direct some of his forces against the rebels in the Peloponnesus. But the government ordered him to continue the campaign against Ali. He was also informed that efforts were being made to raise new troops in Anatolia which would take the field against the Greeks.[70] This decision by the government was obviously consistent with the view that the most dangerous source of Ottoman problems in the Balkans lay in the uncontrollable power of the *ayans*.

Ali of Yanina was able to resist and engage a major Ottoman force in the Balkans until January 1822. This gave the Greek movement a measure of respite during its first and most critical year. Perhaps more significant was the contemporary assessment that the destruction of Tepedelenli Ali eliminated the only factor which could possibly have pacified the Greek countryside. Spyridon Trikoupes, a rather prominent participant in the Greek national uprising who also wrote one of the early historical studies of the movement, concluded:

> If, at this time, the Porte had deigned to employ the services of Ali Paşa, the Greek revolution would have been smothered in its infancy, because Ali had such fame, such influence, such power, such personal knowledge of both men and places, his name spread such terror over the whole of Greece, that all would have submitted, had he but moved.[71]

Since Ottoman policy in Greece eventually met with disaster, hindsight made later observers condemn it altogether. The government had obviously misjudged the course of future developments. Yet, within the context of the time, when national sentiment in the Balkans was still an unknown quantity, before Philhellenism could make an impact and while the mood of European politics was decidedly conservative, Ottoman policy in regard to the Greek uprising had its merits.

There is a striking consistency in Ottoman policy toward its Balkan Christian subject peoples during the thirty-year period 1792–1822. This consistency derived from a strong tradition of Ottoman statecraft, borne out by centuries of political experience; and sustained, perfected, and practiced as an art by successive generations of ruling elites. In addition, however, it was reconfirmed and fortified through recent successful implementation.

From the Ottoman perspective, the initial stages of the Serbian and Greek uprisings appeared to be connected with the wider issues of relations between the center and the provinces. Traditional political experience had demonstrated that popular uprisings, whether Muslim or Christian, were generally the result of misgovernment. By the end of the eighteenth century, the ruling elites at the capital increasingly identified the excessive power of local notables as the most salient feature of provincial misgovernment. Consequently, common wisdom had it that the reestablishment of central control over the provinces, desirable in itself, would also alleviate the grievances of the local population.

The Ottoman experience in Serbia during 1812–13 seemed to have justified these views. As soon as the Ottomans reestablished central authority in neighboring provinces, Serbian opposition collapsed. The Ottoman administration then attempted to follow up the military achievement with a policy of pacification based on *istimâlet*. Even when this policy miscarried and the Serbs renewed their rebellion in 1815 under more favorable international circumstances, the result was a peaceful compromise acceptable to the Ottoman government. Sultan Mahmud's court was satisfied that it had solved, with relative speed and in accordance with traditional principles of statecraft, an acute problem which had been festering for several decades.

These achievements further strengthened the resolve of the central government to eliminate the *ayan* class completely. This policy had been in effect since the end of the war with Russia in 1812; now it was carried out more intensively. Conceivably, therefore, the decision to ignore the risks in Greece and move against Ali of Yanina had its origin in the government's recent experience in the Serbian affair. Hence, even as Greek unrest developed into a full-scale popular rebellion, the government continued to press the campaign against Ali, probably assuming that with his fall the Greek uprising would collapse.

By adopting this policy, the Ottoman government showed several characteristic attitudes. First, significant political power could be ascribed only to personal or dynastic leadership. Consequently, Ali of Yanina was clearly identifiable as a political threat. But to the Ottoman elite, the Greek movement appeared an amorphous force with many chieftains. Of the two it seemed the lesser threat.

The decision to press the campaign against Ali also reflected Ottoman-Muslim prejudices. The Ottomans recognized that among their Christian subjects certain groups and individuals were notable fighters. Nevertheless, the Ottoman experience was overwhelmingly shaped by long domination over multitudes of peaceful and submissive Christian "flocks," peasants and townsmen. This strengthened the Ottoman conviction regarding the martial inferiority of the Christian population as a whole, and led to overconfidence in their own capabilities to contain the unrest.

The ruling elite in Istanbul had a good understanding of the general dynamics of government and power throughout the empire. Their failure in Greece may be attributable to lack of specific information regarding conditions there, both military and political. By the beginning of the nineteenth century Ottoman power in Greece, as in other areas in the Balkans, rested, to a large degree, on the administrative and military infrastructure of *ayan* government. The sultan's policy of indiscriminately eliminating the local notables weakened and even uprooted this order. In Greece, where local and international conditions proved favorable, this vacuum encouraged the emergence of a successful national movement.

Nevertheless, the Ottoman government was well aware that to contain the Greek rebellion effectively it had to act within the constraint of limited time. When the fighting in Greece reached a stalemate, it was obvious that the time had come for reassessing the previous course of action. Indeed, the immediate result of this reassessment was an appeal to Muhammad Ali to help suppress the Greek movement. This invitation to the ruler of Egypt, with its concomitant promises to extend his power, contradicted the established policy of suppressing *ayan* power. This reversal, however, was only temporary. The Ottomans' worst fear, European intervention in Greece, did materialize; and as a result Greece did gain its independence. When Mahmud II realized that this could not be undone, he resumed his centralizing policies.

But the successful assertion of separatist nationalism in Greece apparently had a more lasting impact on Ottoman-Muslim society than is generally recognized. That the Greek War of Liberation was contemporaneous with the beginning of an intensive process of Ottoman military and political reform, gradually accompanied by cultural and social change, may suggest the existence of a more than coincidental relation. This relation requires further study.

Notes

A note on transliteration: Ottoman-Turkish names and terms are transliterated by using present-day Turkish spelling.

1. This quotation is from *Kutadgu Bilig,* an eleventh-century work on statecraft, cited in Halil Inalcık, *The Ottoman Empire: The Classical Age, 1300-1600* (London, 1973), 66.

2. Walter Livingston Wright, Jr., *Ottoman Statecraft; The Book of Counsel for Vezirs and Governors of Sarı Mehmed Pasha, the Defterdār* (Princeton, 1935), 76.

3. On these aspects of Ottoman policy, see Halil Inalcık, "The Ottoman Decline and Its Effects upon the Reaya," in Henrik Birnbaum and Speros Vryonis, Jr., eds., *Aspects of the Balkans: Continuity and Change* (The Hague, 1972), 338-54; Halil Inalcık, "Adâletnâmeler," *Türk Tarih Belgeleri Dergisi, 1965* II (Ankara, 1967): 49-145; Yüçel Özkaya, "XVIIInci Yüzyılda çıkarılan Adalet-nâmelere göre Türkiye'nin Iç Durumu," *Belleten* XXXVIII (Ankara, 1974): 445-91.

4. Leopold Ranke, *A History of Servia and the Servian Revolution,* trans. Mrs. Alexander Kerr (London, 1847), 89-94; Harold W. V. Temperley, *History of Serbia* (London, 1917), 66-73; Michael Boro Petrovich, *A History of Modern Serbia, 1804-1918,* 2 vols. (New York and London, 1976), I: 21-23.

5. Stanford J. Shaw, *Between Old and New: The Ottoman Empire under Sultan Selim III, 1789-1807* (Cambridge, Mass., 1971), 238-41; Petrovich, I: 23-24.

6. Cf. Avdo Sućeska, "Bedeutung und Entwicklung des Begriffes Acyan im Osmanischen Reich," *Südost-Forschungen* XXV (1966): 3-26; Dennis N. Skiotis, "From Bandit to Pasha: First Steps in the Rise to Power of Ali of Tepelen, 1750-1784," *International Journal of Middle East Studies* II (1971): 219-44; Deena R. Sadat, "Rumeli Ayanlari: The Eighteenth Century," *Journal of Modern History* XLIV (1972): 346-63.

7. Sadat, 354.

8. Shaw, *Selim III,* 237-46; Ahmet Cevat Eren, *Mahmud II Zamanında Bosna-Hersek* (Istanbul, 1965), 27-34.

9. Wright, 77.

10. *Ibid.,* 73.

11. Shaw, *Selim III,* 227-46, 298-305.

12. Ahmed Cevdet, *Tarih-i Cevdet* (Istanbul, 1288/1971-72), VII: 405-407; Cevdet (1292/1875-76), IX: 147-48; Shaw, *Selim III,* 317-18; Petrovich, I: 25-32.

13. Shaw, *Selim III,* 318-19; Ranke, 134-36; Petrovich, I: 32-33.

14. Cf. Sari Mehmed Paşa's advice: "One should seek to defend the oppressed, striving and persevering to gain the hearts of the poor and to draw

down upon one's self their blessings." Wright, 116. I am indebted to Professor Halil Inalcık for calling my attention to this important, but little-observed, aspect of Ottoman statecraft.

15. Ranke, 136–37; Temperley, 184–86; Shaw, *Selim III*, 319–22.

16. Shaw, *Selim III*, 323–24; Ranke, 144–46; Petrovich, I: 33–35.

17. Cf. Paul Wittek, *The Rise of the Ottoman Empire* (London, 1938); Stanford J. Shaw, "The Ottoman View of the Balkans," in Charles and Barbara Jelavich, eds., *The Balkans in Transition* (Berkeley and Los Angeles, 1963), 56–80.

18. Shaw, *Selim III*, 324–27; Ranke, 153–57; Petrovich, I: 35–38.

19. Cevdet (1288/1871–72), VIII: 95–112, 148–50; Shaw, *Selim III*, 339–57; Petrovich, I: 39–41.

20. Cevdet, VIII: 105–106.

21. Ahmed Asım, *Tarih-i Asım*, 2 vols. (Istanbul, n.d.–1867?), II: 103–107; Cevdet, IX: 296.

22. Asım, II: 107–108 contains the Turkish version of the separate armistice agreement regarding Russian troops in Serbia. The statement that "through *the error* of the Russian representatives, the agreement totally ignored the status of the Serbs" (Petrovich, I: 56) hardly tallies with the Ottoman accounts.

23. Cevdet, IX: 235.

24. Petrovich, I: 57.

25. *Ibid.*, I: 62.

26. *Ibid.*, I: 65–66.

27. The text of this *Hatt-i Humâyun* is published in Cevdet, IX: 349–51; a translation of the decree is found in Public Record Office, London, Foreign Office papers (henceforth abbreviated as FO) 78/63, Enclosure B in Adair's no. 24, June 3, 1809. Other official documents containing similar references are Başbakanlik Arşivi, Istanbul (henceforth abbreviated as BBA), Cevdet-Hariciye, no. 2294 (3 Cemazielâhır, 1226); Asım, II: 174–75; Cevdet, IX: 351–52, 355–56.

28. Cevdet (2d ed., 1309/1891–92), X: 5, 9, 23.

29. Translated from the French text in Gabriel Noradounghian, ed., *Recueil d'actes internationaux de l'Empire Ottoman*, 4 vols. (Paris, 1897–1903), II: 86–92. The Turkish text is given in Mehmed Ataullah Şanizade, *Tarih-i Şanizade*, 4 vols. (Istanbul 1290–1291/1873–74), II: 115–28; Cevdet, X: 242–50.

30. Cevdet, X: 90, 107–108.

31. Şanizade, II: 172–75; Petrovich, I: 75–76.

32. BBA, Cevdet-Hariciye, no. 3407 (12 Receb, 1227); no. 3179 (Safer, 1228).

33. Şanizade, II: 175–79; Cevdet, X: 84.

34. Cevdet, X: 87, 116–17.

35. Cf. Halil Inalcık, "Pâdişah," *Islâm Ansiklopedisi* (1964), IX: 491–95.

36. Wright, 68.

37. Cevdet (Istanbul, 1301/1883–84), XII: 61–62.

38. Cf. Cevdet, IX: 9.

39. Eudoxiu de Hurmuzaki, ed., *Documente privitóre la istoria Românilor,* Suppl. I (Bucharest, 1889), III: 232–45; Cevdet, IX: 214–15.

40. Şanizade, I: 395–98; Cevdet, IX: 160, 224–27, 230; FO 196/1, Stratford Canning's no. 19 of Oct. 14, 1810; FO 196/1, Stratford Canning's no. 21 of Oct. 18, 1810.

41. Şanizade, II: 58–60; Cevdet, IX: 234–35; Cevdet, X: 6.

42. Şanizade, I: 175, 338–41; Cevdet, IX: 236–39.

43. Cevdet, X: 87; William Turner, *Journal of a Tour in the Levant,* 3 vols. (London, 1820), I: 68.

44. Cevdet, X: 87, 100, 116–18.

45. Cevdet, X: 86–87.

46. Şanizade, II: 200–201; Cevdet, X: 117–18.

47. Cevdet, X: 108–109; Ranke, 278–89; Petrovich, I: 79–81.

48. Cevdet, X: 109–110; Belgradî Raşid, *Vaksa-i Hayretnüma* (Istanbul, 1291/1874–75), 7–9; Ranke, 294–98; Petrovich, I: 82–84.

49. Cevdet, X: 116–18.

50. Şanizade, II: 230–31, 246–47; Cevdet, X: 146–48, 181, 186–87.

51. Cevdet, X: 181–82, 185.

52. Cevdet, X: 181, 217, 219.

53. Raşid, 9–14; Cevdet, X: 149, 189–90; Ranke, 299–308; Petrovich, I: 84–91.

54. Şanizade, II: 260–61; Raşid, 14–19; Cevdet, X: 190–91; Petrovich, I: 91–101.

55. Cevdet, X: 194, 196–98, 201–202, 209–210, 217–18.

56. Şanizade, II: 282–83; Cevdet, X: 194.

57. Cevdet, XI: 68–69.

58. Cevdet, XI: 92; M. Cavid Baysun, "Ali Paşa, Tepedelenli," *Islâm Ansiklopedisi* (1950) I: 343–46.

59. Cevdet, XI: 94–95; Turner, I: 166–69.

60. Cf. Şanizade, III: 104–109; Cevdet, XI: 92–95; George Finlay, *A History of Greece,* 7 vols. (Oxford, 1877), VI: 69–70.

61. Cevdet, XI: 91, 93, 141–44. Cf. Douglas Dakin, *The Greek Struggle for Independence, 1821–1833* (Berkeley and Los Angeles, 1973), 50–51.

62. Şanizade, III: 109–116, 120–24; Cevdet, XI: 93–101.

63. Şanizade, III: 139–144; Cevdet, XI: 101–106, 148–52; Dennis N. Skiotis, "Mountain Warriors and the Greek Revolution," in V. J. Parry and M. E. Yapp, eds., *War, Technology and Society in the Middle East* (London, 1975), 323–29.

64. Cf. Dennis N. Skiotis, "The Greek Revolution: Ali Pasha's Last Gamble," in Nikiforos P. Diamandouros, *et al.,* eds., *Hellenism and the First Greek War of Liberation (1821–1830): Continuity and Change* (Thessaloniki, 1976), 106–107.

65. Cevdet, XI: 190.

66. BBA, Cevdet-Hariciye, no. 2300 (Şaban 1236); BBA, Tevziat, Zehayir,

Esnaf ve Ihtisab Defterleri, XXIX: 1 (11 Şaban, 1236); XXIX: 1–2 (16 Şaban, 1236); Cevdet, XI: 192–95.

67. Şanizade, III: 198–99, 207–208; Cevdet, XI: 190–93, 195–96.

68. BBA, Cevdet-Hariciye, no. 3658 (Rebiülevvel 1237); Cevdet, XI: 202–203, 211–15, 218–20.

69. Cevdet, XI: 195–96.

70. Cevdet, XI: 216–17; BBA, Cevdet-Hariciye, no. 2229 (Şaban, 1236). The maintenance of the siege of Yanina in spite of the growing intensity of the Greek uprising has prompted Western historians to offer lengthy evaluations of Ahmed Hurşid's generalship. Finlay commends him for making the right military moves. The Ottoman accounts, however, appear to indicate that Ahmed Hurşid was not allowed any freedom of choice in this matter by his superiors in Istanbul. Nevertheless, Finlay's analysis contains the gist of the official Ottoman attitude. Cf. Finlay, VI: 87–90.

71. Cited in Skiotis, "Ali Pasha's Last Gamble," 97.

Peter F. Sugar

Conclusions

Readers of the preceding case studies will have learned, just as I did, much about the military and related problems in the Balkans in the two centuries dealt with here. As is true of all collective works, each author concentrated on certain aspects of the immense variety of issues and problems that beset this region in the period under survey, raising numerous questions, answering some, and ignoring others. This was unavoidable and required that the second section of this volume have a concluding chapter. The following pages attempt to discuss some, but certainly not all, of these questions, keeping in mind two major tasks: what follows must be based on the nine chapters devoted to the Balkan area and it must concentrate on the general theme of the undertaking of which it is a part — war and society.

The foregoing paragraph raises three basic questions: How do we define the Balkan area? What — for the purposes of this volume — do we consider to constitute the eighteenth and nineteenth centuries? What do we mean when we speak of *war* and of *society*?

The Balkans have been defined in various ways, often adequately, yet not suited to our purpose. If we speak of the region south of the Danube-Sava line, we split the regions inhabited by South Slavs and Romanians; if we attempt to include all these people, then we must also deal with such regions as Slovenia and Istria, territories that have little or nothing in common culturally or historically with the other lands we discuss. I believe that for the *War and Society in East Central Europe* series, and especially for the second section of the first volume, the best and most practical way to define the *Balkans* is as those areas of Europe which were either Ottoman provinces or dependencies after the conclusion of the Peace of Karlowitz [Sremski Karlovci] in 1699. The overlordship of Istanbul, complete or partial, was an overriding, if not the single most important, factor in the life of the inhabitants of the region. Further, almost all their military efforts in the roughly two hundred years after 1699 were directed against the Ottomans. These considerations give the Balkans, as defined here, both the geographic and military unity that is needed when we study the relationship between war and society.

If the definition of the Balkan region just offered be accepted, the time frame presents itself almost automatically. Armed resistance to Ottoman rule was endemic — in one form or another — although not of equal violence, extension, and frequency for centuries, but 1804 marks the beginning of the nineteenth century in this area because it was the year when the first successful revolt against the Ottomans began. The century must end with the conclusion of the second Balkan War when the Ottoman empire was pushed back beyond Turkey's present-day borders. Most of the authors dealing with the Balkans in this volume concentrate on these years, thus showing that anti-Ottomanism gives their studies a certain built-in unity. The story of the nineteenth century, as just defined, is that of the steady decline of the legal and territorial domination of the Ottomans; their retreat began with the Peace of Karlowitz. The century between the signing of this treaty and 1804 saw numerous developments without which the events of the nineteenth century could not have occurred.

The eighteenth century, 1699–1804, sketched briefly but well by Professor Levy, was the period in which the Ottomans attempted to consolidate, to make certain that the retreat sanctioned in 1699 was not followed by further similar moves, while, on the other hand, the inhabitants of the Balkans, living under the worst conditions they have known since the arrival of their overlords, were increasingly able to learn about developments in the rest of Europe and increasingly self-conscious. Hence, they prepared to take the steps that brought the further decline of Ottoman might. This definition of the eighteenth as the most miserable, crucial, preparatory century readying the Balkans for the significant events of the nineteenth is true not only for those lands directly ruled by the Ottomans, but also for the dependent principalities of Moldavia and Wallachia. There the eighteenth century began slightly later with making the first Phanariot prince, Nicolae Mavrocordat, ruler of Moldavia in 1711 and of Wallachia in 1715. Under Phanariot rule, Ottoman influence was stronger in Romanian lands than ever before. As Professor Berindei shows, this period was marked by almost complete dissolution of the principalities' military formations that had survived during the previous long centuries of Ottoman supremacy. In the Romanian lands, the eighteenth century lasted slightly longer, until the Peace of Adrianople [Edirne] in 1829 when, under Russian pressure, the Phanariot period came to an end. Although not exactly identical with the "transitional" century in the rest of the region, the dates are close enough to serve our purpose.

War is usually a term assigned to armed conflict between two or more nations. Our authors concentrated on such struggles, although not exclusively. I should like to use *war* much more broadly, to denote any armed action or conflict that either by its scope or endemic nature influenced the lives of more people than those who took active part in it. My reason for selecting such an all-encompassing definition for war is twofold: First, it includes the actions of the various irregular units, groups well defined and described by Professor Vucinich, which were constantly active in both the eighteenth and the nineteenth centuries, as well as the various nineteenth-century Bulgarian revolts and the constant struggles in Macedonia that began in the 1880s. This first reason alone would not justify so broad a use of the term, *war*, except that these volumes are devoted to the relationship between war and society. Taken in their totality, those events usually labeled *wars* — together with those I wish to include — produced almost constant armed conflict (once again referred to by Professor Levy) during so long a time that we wind up with a picture of two hundred years of endemic war in the Balkans. Obviously, uninterrupted armed conflict affected society deeply.

The word *society* brings us to the last question raised by the opening paragraph of these concluding remarks. All the chapters in this section, but especially those by Professors Sanders and Djordjević, make it clear that we deal with differing societies. The city is different from the countryside; the Greek city with its port and shipping business has little in common with such places as Iaşi or Sofia. The village high up in the mountains, basically a cluster of hamlets, is hard to equate with the village in the Sava valley of northern Bosnia. The life of the *reaya* carrying the heaviest burden that state and landlord can impose on him is much harder than that of the numerous "peasants with privileges," some of whom are also briefly described by Professor Vucinich. A fighter in a unit of the guerrilla type, locally organized, held together by the loyalty of its members to each other and their chief, is different from a soldier in a regular army, and the relationships these two types of military men have with society differ accordingly. Independence, even if only *de facto*, produces deep changes both in the military and in society at large. The social variety is so great that the number of case studies needed to deal with all of them over a period of two hundred years would fill a library rather than a book and would have to discuss such small nuances of difference that they would become confusing if not incomprehensible. Yet, if we lump all these social groups together, if we disregard these differences, if we create an image of a Balkan society inhabiting the region between the Adriatic and the Black and

Aegean seas and stretching from the Mediterranean to the shores of the Sava and the Prut, the result will have no resemblance to reality. Its interaction with the military and its activities becomes a mere figment of the imagination.

Yet the connection between war, especially as defined here, and society clearly exists, as the chapters devoted to the Balkans show. In dealing with this connection, therefore, the concluding chapter must and will go beyond what its author's colleagues have produced while keeping their important contributions in mind.

It really does not matter which part of society one looks at when asking a few fundamental questions about its relationship to war. Any type of military action will have economic consequences for non-combatants no matter where they live or how they earn a living, pleasant or miserable. The *hayduk* serving in a small unit of six men must have a motive to fight or be compelled to do so, just as a soldier in an army of many thousands. The smallest military unit, like the largest, must have a recruiting and a supply base among a civilian population that may perform these duties either willingly or because refusing would entail grave consequences. The image of the fighting man differs sharply from place to place and age to age. The folk epics are of only historical and cultural importance, but the status of the fighting man in the society in which he lives has a crucial impact on his morale, his self-esteem, and often on his performance. The factor last mentioned depends on the kind of enemy he faces and on the attitude of this enemy toward him. For the Balkan fighter it was certainly very significant that his main foe, the Ottoman, never considered him of primary importance and did not concentrate his main forces against him before the middle of the Greek War of Independence. The reasons for this Ottoman attitude are well presented by Professor Levy. Reasons like those he discusses are seldom taken into consideration by people who chronicle the action of military units, small or large.

Authors writing military history, whether treating the army of their own countries or of others in whose action the scholar became interested, never, or only very seldom, speak of the *poor military qualities* of the subjects of their studies. Almost by definition, all peoples are "heroic"; one often wonders how anybody was ever able to lose a war. Yet every war is lost by somebody and for sufficient reason. This does not mean that the victor won only by default. Who lost and why; who won and why are questions that must be asked with respect to both combatants and noncombatants.

It is, therefore, not surprising that our authors stress the military abilities of the peoples about whom they write and may neglect some other important factors. When one realizes that armed conflict of one kind or another was endemic in the Balkans for centuries, that the Habsburg military borders were organized with soldiering in mind, and gave important privileges to those enrolled, and adds that economic pursuits were limited and often interrupted by fighting, one will not be surprised that the people living in this area developed a military ethos and tradition not unlike that of the Swiss. To see such people fighting in the employ of the Russian tsar, as Professor Vucinich shows in the case of the Serbs, merely indicates the conditions in which they lived; they can be compared to the mass of Yugoslav *Gastarbeiter* in Germany today.

The questions raised and the parallels mentioned indicate that the problems that emerge when one studies war and society in the Balkans fall into a rather general pattern. What needs investigation is the element in this pattern that is typical for the region or parts of it. When quantification is possible, the task becomes relatively simple. Unfortunately, reliable figures for the Balkan states are available only for the end of what we defined as the nineteenth century. Nevertheless, it is of some interest to make some rough comparisons based on the available data with those available for one of the mightiest military powers of the present, our country, and to see what load taxpaying populations bore to maintain their armed forces.[1]

	Budgetary Deficit (percentage of governmental income)	Percentage of Expenditures for Armed Forces
USA proposed 1980 budget	5.56	23.63
1890–1913 average, Bulgaria	48.8	32–35
1890–1913 average, Greece	22.6	32–35
1890–1913 average, Serbia	8.05	32–35
1890–1913 average, Romania	4.06	32–35
1890–1913 average, four countries	23.06	32–35

The percentage of national spending on the armed forces is uniformly higher than our country's is today. That the four states devoted less of their resources to projects benefiting the population than ours does fails to tell the whole story. Although the Balkan taxpayer got a lower return in governmental services for his taxes than does the contemporary American, his tax contribution was much greater. In the proposed 1980 USA budget, 45.2 percent of government revenue is supplied by individual income tax and 3.6 percent by excise taxes. The share of the individual taxpayer, mainly in the form of excise and other indirect taxes, paid by citizens of the Balkan states was always around 70 percent of government revenues. These few figures, rough as they are, give an indication of the Balkan societies' contribution to the military.

For earlier periods, it is all but impossible to establish the connection between the financial load of maintaining the military and society at large even in the vague manner just used for the last quarter of the nineteenth century. Nevertheless, our knowledge of the history of the region permits us to draw certain conclusions. In the eighteenth century, the burden on the population of the Romanian principalities was relatively light, as far as contributions to military establishments were concerned. As Professor Berindei has shown, the armed forces of Moldavia and Wallachia were almost liquidated during the Phanariote period, and it is logical to assume that military expenditures declined accordingly.

For the rest of the Balkans, the situation is certainly different. Here we cannot speak of direct or indirect fiscal contributions to national forces in the eighteenth century because these forces did not exist. Yet we know that the eighteenth century was the most turbulent and insecure period of the long centuries of Ottoman domination. It saw the emergence of the *ayans* and their petty states within the state discussed by Professor Levy. Areas not controlled by them suffered a total breakdown of law and order and the depredations of the janissary *yamak* forces.[2] Facing the chaotic situation, the population increasingly resorted to armed resistance. In this *bellum omnia contra omnes,* all combatants, from the regular army to the irregular units of the people, exacted the needed material support from the civilian population. No figures are available, but it appears quite obvious that the society paid, mostly under duress, great amounts in both cash and supplies to support a chaotic civil conflict from which it suffered grievously in all respects, not only the material.

The two centuries under discussion also saw several international wars, beginning with the Ottoman-Venetian conflict (1714-18) and ending with the Second Balkan War (1913) fought either by the Ottomans mainly against the Habsburgs and Romanovs or, later, by the emerging Balkan states against the Ottomans or one another. In these wars and repeatedly during years of foreign occupation, the population's fiscal load was increased by the armies' living off the land and by the fees exacted for their maintenance by the occupation forces. It is, therefore, safe to assume that the direct financial burden that Balkan society had to shoulder to support armies of various kinds must have been at least as heavy during the long years for which no approximate figures can be presented as for the quarter-century closing the period under survey. If this assumption is accepted, one can conclude that, in spite of similarities to other parts of Europe, the Balkan experience, at least in these two centuries, differed from what we can observe elsewhere. Germany might have suffered as grievously during the Thirty Years War as the Balkans did in the eighteenth and nineteenth centuries, but no part of Europe was subjected to constant military action and exactions, for one reason or another, with hardly any respite for two hundred years.

War's impact on the economy affects society directly. It would be interesting and important to investigate this connection, but it would take us into an area of inquiry not touched on by the contributors to the Balkan section of this volume. It, therefore, appears to be a topic ill suited to my task, which is drawing conclusions from their essays. Suffice it to say that, contrary to logical expectations, the economies of the Balkans did develop, albeit slowly, during the eighteenth and nineteenth centuries.[3]

Much more can be said, based on the preceding chapters, about the men who fought in the various armed formations of the Balkans. Nearly all our authors stress certain facts. They seem to agree that cities suffered less from armed conflict than did the countryside and that most of those who fought in the numerous irregular forces well described by Professor Vucinich were "mountain people." If the *pandurs* of Tudor Vladimirescu mentioned by Professor Berindei came from the slopes of the Carpathians and not from the low lands of Oltenia, almost all popular units mentioned could be considered "mountain" or at least "forest" people. Professor Sanders, referring to his previous work, warns us, quite correctly, of the danger lurking in facile generalizations. The men of Maínalon (Maina) were as different from those of the Apuseni region as were those of the Šumadija from those of the Rhodope. Yet, these and the inhabitants of several other, equally specific districts regularly supplied recruits for the popular forces throughout our two centuries. In spite of Professor Sanders's warning, one may observe some general factors that explain the activities of the inhabitants of these specific, different regions.

Life is more difficult in deep forests and on high mountains than on any other terrain. People settle such regions either because there is no room for them in more hospitable surroundings or because they have found life elsewhere unsupportable. The number of those who moved to the less desirable parts of the Balkans increased substantially in the eighteenth century. Either they could not survive in the chaotic lawlessness of the times or were forced out when they opposed imperial armies, *ayans*, or janissary *yamaks*. They seldom if ever moved as individuals; they migrated as members of groups to which they were loyal. These hardy, compact, and self-reliant groups were further steeled by the difficult life in their new surroundings. It was natural for these people to defend their areas of refuge and even to descend from their hiding places in an attempt to regain some of the better lands they had been forced to give up. Furthermore, their marginal terrain made it very difficult for them to produce enough for even a scanty survival; they were often forced to seek booty in order to supplement what they had. Consequently many of them developed the often noted dual character of freedom-fighter–bandits.[4] Their way of life, glorified and justified by tradition handed down in folklore and folk epics, transformed these men into professional fighters — like the peasant-soldiers of the Habsburg Military Border — on whose activity the survival of their home communities depended. That these communities backed them and considered them heroes is self-evident. The support they received from other segments of the population is questionable. Whatever the support they enjoyed among their countrymen, the origin of these fighting men, the backbone of future, more regular armed forces, permits us to make a second general comment. Contrary to the rest of Europe, the Balkan military "class" did not originate among the nobility, but among the peasantry of "mountain" and "forest."

These tentative findings lead to other conclusions. The first of these has been noted repeatedly by the contributors to this section. The Balkan fighters performed well near their homes, but their reliability was less certain when they were asked to do battle in "foreign" lands. Considering the origin of the population of the "fighters' regions" and their motives for fighting, the reason for their behavior becomes self-evident. Equally understandably, the core of the insurgents who started the Balkan wars of liberation and independence came from the region's military "class." What remains to be investigated is their sudden willingness to fight long and well away from their home grounds.

In answering this question, it is important not to accept the explanation given by the great majority of the historians who wrote national histories in the nineteenth and twentieth centuries. Most of them explain the behavior of their countrymen by speaking of a "national rebirth." Undoubtedly during the eighteenth century, Western ideas did penetrate into the Balkans; they did influence, at least to some extent, the thinking and action of the leaders of the various wars of liberation. As a result of their convictions, national slogans appeared in their manifestos and their letters to foreign princes. The question is: Did they speak for, did they lead self-conscious nations fighting for the right of self-determination? In other terms: Can the Balkan wars of liberation be equated with those we have witnessed since World War II in the more advanced regions (India, North Africa) of the so-called Third World? Frankly, I doubt that this was the case.

Western ideas, including nationalism, cannot be understood by people who do not have at least a modicum of sophistication and education. How could the crucial Balkan military "class" living in the most inaccessible forests and mountains acquire this knowledge during the eighteenth century when illiteracy was often the rule, even among their clergymen? The answer is obvious. Therefore, at least for the mass of the fighting men, we must reject "nationalist" behavior as an explanation. We are left with several other reasons. Changed awareness among the leaders; closer cooperation between leaders of various smaller regions; intolerable conditions created by the chaos of the eighteenth century; the intoxication of the first remarkable successes and later the common danger faced by all when the Ottomans began to take the rebellions more seriously — these are some basic explanations of the phenomenon of the liberation wars. Cooperation on a larger scale, and consequently, a steady expansion of the concept and area of the "home ground" on which these men were willing to fight were not preconditions of the revolts, but their results. This is extremely significant because it allows us to make another broad statement dealing with the region as a unit. The Balkans differed markedly not only from the previously mentioned regions of today's Third World and of other parts of Europe where wars of liberation resulted from relatively widespread national self-awareness. The area also differed from some other contemporary regions of the Third World (mainly in Africa) where not even independence brought national identification. In the Balkans, the wars of independence created nations. Once again, we see a very important historical variant emerging first in our region.

In our modern world, nations strive to become states. That nations formed in struggles for their states should feel this way seems obvious. There can be no doubt that the Romanian and Bulgarian units which fought in the war of 1876–78 and all those involved in subsequent conflicts knew what they were supposed to defend or achieve. The question is to what extent was this true in the various states right after they achieved either independence or a degree of home rule that, for all practical purposes, meant independence? Acquiring national self-consciousness does not necesarily involve loyalty to the new state and an understanding of what it is. Fighting side-by-side with a brother whom one knows and whose way of thinking and living one understands is not the same thing as being loyal to a government in a faraway capital where people, whom one does not know, issue orders. It is very easy to equate a "Serbian paşa" with his Turkish predecessor. One can quite plausibly explain the poor showing of the Serbian forces in 1885, at least in part, by the average soldier's failure to understand the *raison d'état* that prompted the Belgrade government to start hostilities.

Several important factors, affecting almost every aspect of every individual's life, are involved when a territory becomes a state or quasi state. When discussing war and society, the one aspect that must be investigated is the transformation of the military establishment. Here one is concerned with more than government policy and the attempt of those in charge of the national defense to organize the military forces. In the case of Romania, General Ceauşescu and Colonel Căzănişteanu discuss these problems for our readers. They show clearly what their countrymen had in mind when charged with creating the armed forces of their homeland. What remains to be discovered — and not only in the case of Romania — is what the population at large had in mind when it was affected by these directives coming from the government and, especially, what the young man thought when he was selected to serve in his country's army. According to at least one contemporary observer, these reactions were not enthusiastic.[5]

I would be presumptuous to attempt an analysis of the questions just raised. Nevertheless, the authors of the Balkan section of this volume have established certain facts, and a few others become obvious from their presentations. A summary may show what the major issues were even if one cannot resolve them.

First, one should consider the drastic change in the military establishment that the creation of national armies involved. However small or large the preindependence fighting unit was, it consisted of people who considered it their own formation headed by their leader and containing their friends. They fought because they wanted to fight and went home when they believed that further struggle was useless. Discipline was traditional and self-evident; off duty, the men did what they wanted; fighting often had immediate material rewards, if nothing else, the arms taken from the enemy. Life in a professional, regular army is very different; in peacetime often routine and boring, anything but glamorous. The guerrilla fighter is respected at least by his own home community, but the young man in the uniform of his state might be considered simply a missing hand in the field by his rural community although the girls might admire his uniform. In short, both the fighting man and his environment had to adjust to the change in the military structure.

Another aspect of the same problem is clearly indicated by the contributions of the two Romanian officers. Manning all active units of the army of the united principalities of Moldavia and Wallachia did not require all able-bodied youths of military age. The limitations, mainly financial, that determined the size of the armed forces must have been at least as great in the other Balkan states as in Romania (whose budget was more nearly balanced than those of the other states); hence the situation must have been identical all over the region. For several reasons, too obvious to need listing, the various governments had to draft recruits from all parts of their countries, even if the majority of those taken came from the peasantry. This need to spread the burden of service required a second kind of adjustment. Certain young men in the traditional military communities might have been resentful at not being selected, but others, from communities that lacked the soldierly tradition, might have felt resentful for different reasons. Consequently, not only had the armies to weld together men willing to serve and men who resented being called up, but both types of communities, too, had to be made aware that their grievances were baseless. Those left behind, in regions with military traditions, had to be convinced that they were not rejected as inferior to those taken; men drawn from the other communities, and especially the families of the unwilling recruits, had to understand that they were not picked unjustly, capriciously, or even spitefully. The relationship between the military and society changed when the state and military structures did, and every individual, family, and community had to learn how to live with the new realities. This was no easy task, but it was accomplished.

The final question that must be answered, if possible, is: Does reviewing the chapters in this section show a characteristically Balkan development in the difficult transition from one to another type of military-society relationship? The pattern certainly differs from that of most of Europe where the general progression was from feudal armies, to professional armies (during the Renaissance or the Thirty Years War, for example), to royal armies, and finally to national armies. To some extent a similar progression occurred even in the Ottoman empire where the dominance of the quasi-feudal army of the *ğazis* and later *sipáhis* was overshadowed first by the professionals of the *devşirme*-based units, and finally by the imperial army recruited mainly among the Anatolian peasantry. Various regions of Europe did show exceptions to this pattern of change in the military, but it would be hard to find any region where the transition from the guerrilla type of folk army to the professional national army came as suddenly and drastically as in the Balkans.

Students of the Balkans have long and repeatedly contended that if developments in this area are studied in their own context without paying too much attention to apparent — often only semantic — similarities between them and those that occurred elsewhere in Europe, research will show that this southeastern corner of the continent moved from one stage of history to another in unique ways. The people of the Balkans bound by their traditions, reacting to both the requirements of the moment and the lessons learned from thinkers who lived and events that occurred elsewhere, always managed to combine these disparate elements into solutions to their own problems that reflected their own genius. Reflecting on the case studies dealing with the Balkan region, I conclude that studying the relationship between war and society confirms this flexibility of the Balkan peoples, and shows how they managed to solve problems in this vital though neglected aspect of their communal life.

Notes

1. Using numerous, mainly secondary sources, I have calculated the following figures, for which I am fully responsible.

2. For further details see Peter F. Sugar, *Southeastern Europe under Ottoman Rule, 1354–1804* (Seattle and London, 1977), chap. 11.

3. For more detailed studies of Balkan economies, see Nikolai Todorov, *Balkanskiat Grad, XV–XIX vek* (Sofia, 1972). John Lampe and Marvin R. Jackson, *Economic History of the Balkans* (Bloomington, Ind., forthcoming).

4. On the problem of the double role of the freedom fighter-bandit see Bistra Cvetkova, *Hajdutstvoto v Bulgarskite zemi prez 15/18 vek* (Sofia, 1971) and Eric Hobsbawn, *Bandits* (London, 1969).

5. Emile de Laveleye, *The Balkan Peninsula* (London, 1887).

III

Military Frontier Systems: Habsburg and Russian Models

Gunther E. Rothenberg, Editor

Gunther E. Rothenberg

The Habsburg Military Border System:
Some Reconsiderations

Historically the terms *border* or *frontier* have had several meanings, a clearly defined demarcation line defining the territories of states as well as a geographic region with fluctuating boundaries. Such a region constituted either the outer reaches of established society or a buffer zone between different civilizations, peoples, or states. Frequently buffer zones were the setting for hostile encounters, and when these were intensive and protracted, they changed the frontier society. Defense requirements became paramount with whole communities organized for fighting. When such developments became institutionalized, often with military commanders holding both civilian and military power, the region assumed a particular martial character setting it apart from its civilian hinterland: a military border.

Military border organizations developed at various times and in many places, yet they usually had certain common features. Prolonged defense of a long frontier against a determined and persistent enemy was always difficult, and into modern times it was usually beyond the resources of states to provide adequate garrisons of full-time soldiers. Settling military colonists, peasant-soldiers, who in return for land allotments and other privileges provided men for the constant small war, was a common solution. In the mid-nineteenth century an English observer described such a fully matured system. The entire southern border of the Habsburg empire, he wrote, was organized "into regiments instead of counties, so that it is one vast camp, every soldier being a peasant and every peasant a soldier."[1]

Forming a border defense with military colonists was a very ancient expedient, going back to the soldier-colonists of the late Roman Empire. The system was continued by the Byzantines and in mediaeval western Europe. It was not just a question of military efficiency, though peasant-soldiers always displayed shortcomings, lack of organization and discipline. But these were not vital considerations. Border warfare rarely involved the clash of major formations. Instead there was an unending series of incursions, raids, forays, and ambuscades, in which men defending their families and homesteads, proved formidable. The major reasons for the decline of military borders in western Europe were that peasant-soldiers conflicted with the desire of the rising feudal nobility to establish a monopoly of arms and that gradual consolidation of states eliminated border warfare.

Conditions remained less stable in eastern Europe, especially in the Pontic and Danubic region, encompassing roughly the area of the present-day Ukraine, Romania, Hungary, and Croatia, where there was a constant threat from warlike nomadic groups and where, from the end of the fourteenth century, Christian Europe was locked in a struggle against the expanding Moslem power. As the Turks consolidated their grip on the Balkans and the north shore of the Black Sea during the next century, they continued pressure against neighboring countries, and Hungary-Croatia came under frequent attack. Although a major Turkish offensive was repulsed in 1456 at Belgrade, from their Bosnian bases, Turkish raiders penetrated across the Croatian uplands into Austria and the Venetian plain. And these raids were not mere expeditions for loot and plunder, but part of an overall strategy which so weakened the victim's power and will to resist that often no formal campaign was necessary to take over the country.[2] In 1458, the Turkish menace led to the election of Matthias Corvinus, the last powerful Hungarian king, and, besides other measures, he revived the ancient practice of military colonists. With Christian Balkan refugees streaming north, Matthias established military colonies in depopulated areas of southern Croatia and Slavonia. After his death, however, the settlements disintegrated, while Hungary fell into the hands of a selfish nobility, unwilling to make a concerted effort to defend the kingdom. On August 26, 1526, the Hungarian army and state perished in the battle of Mohács.

Historical Overview of the Habsburg Military Border

The Habsburg Military Border, the *Militärgrenze*, among the strongest, most extensive, and most elaborate of these systems, came into being as a result of the destruction of the Hungarian state apparatus. Even before Mohács, Ferdinand of Austria, alarmed by the patent decline of Hungary-Croatia, and at the request of the Croatian estates, had placed small bodies of German mercenaries in certain strategic locations.[3] A few years later he settled Christian Balkan refugees — *uskoks*, Vlachs, or Rascians as they were called in contemporary documents — predominantly members of the Orthodox faith, in north-western Croatia. After his election as king of Hungary-Croatia in 1527, Ferdinand moved to systematize these arrangements and in 1535 issued the first recorded charter to these frontier fighters. In return for perpetual military service, they were granted hereditary land allot-ments. For the first twenty years they were to be free of all taxes, and thereafter they were only to pay a quitrent to the Austrian ruler. They received no pay, but were allowed to retain a share in all booty, to elect their own leaders, and to practice their own religion. Above all, they were granted special military status which removed them from the control of the local nobility.[4] Similar charters issued in 1538 and 1547 attracted additional settlers, both refugees and remnants of the indigenous Catholic population.[5]

In time, the Habsburg appointed superior officers to fill command positions and issued additional regulations. Although the population of the region was still small, perhaps no more than 20,000 in all, two distinct districts emerged. There was the region between the Adriatic coast and the Sava River, later called after the name of its major fortress, the *Karlstadt Border,* and further inland, between the Sava and the Drava there was the Wendisch, later called the *Warasdin Border.* In 1553, Ferdinand appointed Hans Ungnad, a Carniolian nobleman, as the first "Colonel of the Border" to command all forces in both districts, as well as those in a number of smaller enclaves near Agram (Zagreb) and the port of Zengg (Senj) on the Adriatic. In this territory the colonel represented both the emperor and the Austrian archduke and his authority extended not only over the *Grenzer* but over all units stationed there. In addition, he was responsible for fortifications, arsenals, and supply. The Colonel of the Border was not subject to the control of the Croat *Banus,* the country's chief executive officer, with whom he merely was instructed to cooperate on common problems.[6]

With this appointment important and permanent characteristics of the Military Border system emerged. As a zone in which appointed commanders superseded all other authorities, the Military Border became effectively separated from "civil" Croatia and, albeit in semi-nal form for the time being, entered a special administrative rela-tionship with the central Habsburg agencies. This relationship became more clearly delineated in 1556 when Ferdinand, now emperor, created a central agency for military affairs, the *Hofkriegsrat* in Vienna to which the Colonel of the Border became responsible.[7]

These developments did not go unchallenged. Repeatedly the Croatian noble estates and their assembly, the *Sabor,* as well as the Hungarian diet protested against the alienation of territory and made continual efforts to reduce the social and religious privileges of the frontiersmen, the *Grenzer.* Affairs became even more complex when, following Ferdinand's death in 1564, the Austrian lands were divided into three family lines, each maintaining its own military establishment. Inner Austria — Carniola, Carinthia, and Styria — which since its inception had supported the frontier defense arrangements, assumed primary responsibility over the Military Border in 1578 and established a separate *Hofkriegsrat* in Graz. Dual control as well as the Habsburgs' frequent preoccupation with the affairs of western Europe led to neglect of the Military Border, especially when the Turkish threat appeared to diminish. Still, though the small war on the frontier continued despite numerous treaties and local truces, the population was swelled by new immigration and internal increase. A muster roll for 1573 indicates a total of 5,913 frontier fighters.[8]

Inner Austrian control did not provide immediate improvements and the Military Border participated only marginally in the Long Turkish War, 1593–1606. Even so, new immigrants continued to arrive and were given the usual charters. After the Peace of Zsitvatorok ended hostilities, there was a relative period of quiet, though not an end to frontier raids. After the dynasty reunited early in the seventeenth century under Ferdinand II of the Styrian line, an attempt was made to consolidate the various charters into one comprehensive document, the *Statuta Valachorum* of October 1630, originally limited to the Warasdin but soon extended to the entire Croatian Military Border.[9] The document reconfirmed the military character of the region. All men between sixteen and sixty were liable to serve not only against the Turks, but against all enemies of the emperor. The statute made the *zadruga* — the large joint-family household common among the South Slavs — the basis of the social and economic organization. It, and not the individual *Grenzer,* received the land grant and was responsible for families of men on active service. Although the *zadruga* was later regarded as a confining economic institution, for the time being it provided real advantages. A single family farm might well be ruined by the death of one adult male, the *zadruga* could absorb such a loss.

The statute also clarified the chain of command. It confirmed the election of lower officers, subject to the control of superior officers, headed by colonels for the Karlstadt and the Warasdin districts, now commonly referred to as *generalcies,* and a Border commander, usually of general's rank, with headquarters at Karlstadt. The statute was thus an attempt to resolve the disputed control over the Border and to clarify its character as a *corpus separatum*. In this it was not successful. The Inner Austrians, rejecting Hungarian-Croatian claims, continued to exploit their position on the Border to the utmost; the Hungarian-Croatian nobility persisted in efforts to dismantle the entire institution. Although Vienna, well aware of the potential importance of the institution, did not comply with these demands, there was no consistent policy. *Grenzer* units continued to fight against the Turks and, designated as Croats, spread terror and fear during the Thirty Years War in central and western Europe. They participated in the repulse of the renewed Turkish offensive in 1663 and several years later sided with the dynasty against the Conspiracy of the Magnates in Croatia and Slavonia. Even so, the Habsburgs did little to halt efforts to whittle down their privileges.

As early as 1667, following complaints by Austrian officers that the elected *Grenzer* leaders acted as "if they were independent captains of the Vlachs and not subject to the orders of the Colonel Commandant," the *Statuta Valachorum* was modified and several elected offices abolished.[10] Even more serious was continued pressure to convert Orthodox *Grenzer* to Catholicism or at least to coerce them into accepting Uniate rites. From 1670 on, Jesuit missions were active in the Warasdin Generalcy, on occasion provoking severe confrontation between the *Grenzer* and the authorities.[11] Matters were exacerbated by the self-seeking role of the Inner Austrian authorities, who with the Turkish menace apparently diminished, "considered," as one imperial general put it, "the Border as a Styrian monarchy rather than an imperial confine."[12]

The *Grenzer* played an important, if auxiliary, role during the Great Turkish War, 1683–99. They contributed elements to the operations of the main army, undertook several major raids into Bosnia, and tied down a considerable number of Turkish units. There were complaints that they showed little restraint, plundering both friend and foe, though in truth they seem to have been neither better nor worse than their comrades of the line. Even more importantly, and acting largely on their own initiative, volunteer bands of *Grenzer,* driven by the need for more land, expelled the Turks from southern Croatia and settled the Like and Krbave areas. At the same time, the *Banus* liberated the eastern portion of the region between the Una and Kupa rivers with his forces. A new Border district, the Banal Border, came into existence and because the emperor required the assistance of the Croatian estates to deal with growing unrest in Hungary, he sanctioned the arrangement.[13] Overall, as the result of the war, the emperor recovered Transylvania and the whole of Hungary save the Banat of Temesvár. The recovered areas, *neo-acquisitica* as they were called, were settled in part by Orthodox Serbian refugees who had fled to southern Hungary and Slavonia after the failure of a general rising against the Turks in 1690. The next year, these new arrivals were given extensive privileges. Many of the new arrivals were settled in new military colonies along the lines of the Tisza, Maros, and Danube; others were incorporated into the Warasdin and Karlstadt generalcies.[14] Orthodox *Grenzer* came to comprise the majority in the Karlstadt Generalcy and on the Slavonian Border; they constituted more than half the population on the Banal Border and a substantial minority in the Warasdin.[15] Almost all of them looked to Karlowitz [Sremski Karlovci], where the patents issued in 1691 by Emperor Leopold I had established a Serbian patriarchate, for spiritual and, later, political guidance.

With the recovery of Hungary and the decline of the Ottoman power came a crisis on the Military Borders. The presence of ever larger numbers of Orthodox settlers, with special and far-reaching concessions, aroused the concern of the Inner Austrian as well as the Croatian and Hungarian authorities; the Catholic Church was openly hostile. Renewed attempts were made to abrogate the special rights of the Orthodox, abetted especially in the Warasdin Generalcy, by some bigoted and brutal superior officers. Accompanied by a further decline in the Inner Austrian administration, with false musters, fraud, and failure to deliver supplies common, and by renewed attempts by the Croat estates to reduce the *Grenzer* to peasant status, the situation deteriorated. The Military Border simmered with discontent, on occasion flaring into violence. Open rebellion broke out in the Warasdin Generalcy in 1695, 1719, and 1728. There were disorders in the Karlstadt Generalcy in 1702 and open mutinies in 1714, 1728, and 1735. Similar incidents occurred in the colonies in Slavonia in 1727 and along the Tisza-Maros in 1735, and there was discontent on the Banal Border.[16]

Vienna usually turned a blind eye to violations of religious rights, but the evident reduction of military potential aroused the concern of the *Hofkriegsrat*. In the first three decades of the eighteenth century various commissions inspected the Borders, deliberated, assembled stacks of documents, resolved on administrative changes, and then disbanded without much achieved. Under these circumstances the *Grenzer* contributed little either to the Turkish War of 1718 which recovered the Banat, or to the War of the Polish Succession, while in 1735, a full-scale insurrection in the Warasdin was precipitated by another attempt to force the Uniate rite on Orthodox communities.[17]

Finally, in 1737, Joseph Friedrich Duke of Hildburghausen was sent to investigate and settle the Warasdin mutiny. The duke prized the Military Border as one of the major military resources of the dynasty, "a treasure such as never could be bought and paid for with money," and proposed to transform it from a volatile frontier militia into a nation in arms — "eine paleastra militia perpetui et ferrei" — ready to serve everywhere at short notice. Recalling that in the past the Border had functioned "not only as a rampart against the Turks, but also as a restraint upon the rebellious tendencies of the Hungarian-Croatian nobility," he estimated that, properly organized, it could field over 50,000 fighting men. The greatest obstacle, he maintained, was the maladministration of the Inner Austrian estates coupled with the antiquated system of elected captains and loosely constituted war bands. All this, he argued, should be changed. The obsolete captaincies should be abolished and the *Grenzer* formed on a regular battalion pattern. Hildburghausen wished to retain the *zadruga* system which maintained the force at very little expense to the state. To avoid the system's degenerating into a mere militia, he advocated complete militarization of the zone, placing all inhabitants under a military code of exceptional severity enforced by appointed regimental officers.[18] Basically, he envisaged the Military Border as a huge barracks, a manpower reservoir for the wars of the Austrian monarchy.

The new regime, imposing heavy burdens on the *Grenzer,* was introduced in the Warasdin Generalcy in 1737, but its extension to the other districts was delayed both by the opposition of the Inner Austrians and the Croatians and by the outbreak of another Turkish war in 1737. With operations going badly, Emperor Charles VI lost interest in military reform. In any event, reorganization of the Military Border on the scale necessary to provide forces able to participate in full-scale European warfare was delayed until another conflict nearly spelled the end of the Habsburg empire.

The early setbacks of the War of the Austrian Succession forced Queen Maria Theresa to "take all measures necessary to secure and protect my realm"; and reorganization of the Military Borders formed an integral part of her military reforms. In this she was supported by her able chancellor, Count Kaunitz, who argued that the *Grenzer* potentially were "infantry of the best and most formidable kind."[19] Maria Theresa abolished the Inner Austrian *Hofkriegsrat* in October

1743 and placed the Border under the control of a *Militär-Directo-rium,* headed between 1744 and 1749, by Hildburghausen. During his term in office, the duke organized the Croatian *Grenzer* into foot and horse regiments, the former nominally comprising 4,000 men; the latter, always difficult to maintain in view of the economic constraints, had an establishment of under 800 men. Altogether, there were four regiments of foot in the Karlstadt and two in the Warasdin, though regiments were administrative bodies and field contingents were formed by battalions.[20]

While contributing annual levies to the field armies, training went on apace and a pleased Hildburghausen noted that the "Croats train so diligently that a Croatian regiment learns as much in one week as a German regiment in a whole half-year."[21] Exaggerated, no doubt, but the queen was impressed. In 1747, she ruled that in future the Croatian *Grenzer* units "shall in all matters be treated as regulars," except that, because of their "ancient habits and customs," they should always be employed as light troops.[22] The last link with Inner Austria was severed and the *Grenzer* became part of the imperial royal army. During the same period, other officers introduced reforms along simi-lar lines in the neighboring Military Border districts. In Slavonia, three regiments of foot and one of horse were organized by 1747; the same number was formed on the Banal Border in 1750. Social and economic conditions, as well as the special martial character of the region, were again spelled out in 1754 when Maria Theresa pro-mulgated a new code, the *Militär-Gränitz-Rechten.* "Because they enjoy imperial privileges," so the code read, "all able-bodied men are bound to render service and are subject to military jurisdiction." The harshest provisions of the Hildburghausen code were softened, but basic principles remained.[23] Originally intended only for the Karlstadt and Warasdin generalcies, the code was extended after the Seven Years War to other Border districts, though it was not introduced on the Transylvanian border where social conditions, especially absence of the *zadruga,* made conditions different.

The Theresan reforms, continued after 1765 by her son and co-ruler (later, Emperor Joseph II), were based on totally changed perceptions from the earlier border defense arrangements. Whereas the need to defend an exposed frontier had been the major objective in the creation of the Croatian, and to a lesser degree the Slavonian, Military Border, now the prime purpose of the system was to provide trained troops at the lowest cost to the state. In addition, the *Grenzer* took over watch and patrol along the plague cordon, a network of posts and stations controlling traffic between the Habsburg empire and the Ottoman lands where bubonic plague was still endemic.[24] Welfare of the *Grenzer* took second place to the requirements of the military establishment, and the need for additional cheap manpower led to the forced incorporation of unwilling elements into the system.

Contrary to Hildburghausen's cheerful account of how well the *Grenzer* accepted his despotic paternalism, the changes which transformed a society still retaining traces of its former status of a free frontier community of fighters into a closely regimented military system were not accepted without resistance. In 1744, 1746, 1750, and 1751 there were mutinies, culminating in the great Warasdin Revolt of 1765 which threatened to engulf Slavonia.[25] This outbreak was not, as some historians have maintained, caused by the tactless behavior of the Austrian commanding officer and the attempt to force the Warasdiner to buy new regulation uniforms. This merely triggered the events. The cause lay far deeper. The *Grenzer* resented the basic changes in their lives, the increased demands on their time, and the abolition of their own elected officers.[26] In the end, the revolt was put down by a mixture of threats and concessions, including supplementary regulations easing *corvée* obligations, subventions for uniforms, and reservation of two-thirds of all commissions in Border regiments for native-born sons, albeit with preference given to Catholics and Uniates.[27] There now arose a native officer class, normally content to remain in the lower ranks, but with some, like the Rukavina and the Jelačić families, reaching high positions, and in this group the Austrian state found its most loyal supporters.

The Warasdin revolt marked the end of the irregular frontier establishment. By and large, during the next fifty years, most officers on the Border were hardworking, honest, and efficient, although perhaps too much given to paperwork, and there was no such succession of riots and revolts as during the previous half-century. The problem of providing a sound economic base and a modest degree of prosperity, however, remained unsolved.

The crisis had been settled just in time. War with Prussia began the following year and altogether 80,000 "regulated" *Grenzer* served during the campaigns of the Seven Years War. They gained considerable fame as light troops. There existed, Count Mirabeau wrote, "no light troops who are their equals."[28] An exaggeration, to be sure, but the *Grenzer* had performed beyond expectations and Maria Theresa and her generals decided, even while the war continued, to consolidate and expand the Military Border system. In 1763 the Karlstadt and Warasdiner regiments were combined and the military boatmen on the Danube, Tisza, and Maros rivers were formed into a *csajkás* [*Tschaikisten*] battalion. The same year, work began to raise two *Grenzer* regiments in the Banat which was still garrisoned by regulars assisted by an irregular militia. After numerous changes of location, organization, and designation, two foot regiments were established there. One, the *Deutsch-Banater* Regiment, was organized around a cadre of veteran invalids from Austria augmented by a few German colonists; the other, the *Wallachisch-Illyrisches* Regiment was recruited from Serbian frontier militia and Romanian peasants. Attempts to form a Banat cavalry regiment met much difficulty and were abandoned.[29] The *Militär-Gränitz-Rechten* and its supplementary codes, including the *zadruga* organization, were introduced here, even though they had no base in the German settlers' background.

The most disputed, and in the end, largely unsuccessful step was the extension of the Military Border system into Transylvania. In this semiautonomous principality there existed a number of diverse national elements, Hungarians, Szeklers, Saxons, and Romanians. The first three were recognized "nations," enjoying certain privileges. In particular the Szeklers, essentially a Hungarian warrior tribe established in the region since the twelfth century, had always enjoyed special immunities in return for frontier watch. Though divided into distinct social classes, all Szeklers were considered free men, their special status recognized and reconfirmed by successive rulers. They took part in the Rákóczi War of Independence, however, and after the Peace of Szatmár in 1711, were disarmed, relieved of their military duties, and subjected to taxation. Even so, they enjoyed a much higher status than the Romanians, who, almost exclusively Orthodox, were merely tolerated. Except for a few Romanian noble boyars, the Romanians constituted a large mass of landless peasants, lacking rights. They retained contact with their compatriots across the Carpathians and were influenced by national Romanian ideas emerging in Moldavia and Wallachia. Neither the Szeklers nor the Romanians were eager to accept *Grenzer* status, though the latter gained some security and a higher standard of living by joining the frontier forces.[30]

The creation of the new Military Border, the final link in the system, was undertaken between 1762 and 1766, but it never became well established in Transylvania. In 1762, General Buccow, commanding general in the region, suggested that five infantry and two cavalry regiments be raised among the Szekler and Romanian population.[31]

From the outset there was no pretense that this was for frontier defense, the motive was to obtain cheap troops. The attempt ran into bitter opposition. The Romanian villages were perturbed by the high-handed attitude of the Austrian officers and feared that incorporation in the Military Border would threaten their religion. They accepted military status only after much coercion, including floggings, deportations, and executions.[32] The Szeklers erupted into open revolt, unmercifully suppressed by General Siskovics. Regular troops massacred some Szekler groups; the most notorious incident was the "disaster of Mádéfalva," where over 400 were killed.[33] A large number of recalcitrants migrated to Moldavia; the others accepted *Grenzer* status.

With resistance broken, the authorities went on to organize two foot and one mounted regiments for the Szeklers, matched by the same number for the Romanians.[34] Although officially completed by 1766, actual implementation took longer, into the 1780s. The major difficulties were procurement of land to form solid strips, never accomplished, and the transfer of populations. In contrast with the other Borders, the Transylvanian regimental territories never were completely separated from "civil" lands, and no *zadruga* organizations were formed, placing heavy burdens on single family households.[35]

With the establishment of the Transylvanian Border, the Habsburg system was completed. Altogether the Military Borders extended for over 1,000 miles, twenty to sixty miles deep, all the way from the Adriatic to the Carpathians. A census taken in 1799 indicated a population of 823,950, including 101,692 men of military age. All mounted units were disbanded in 1786 and the region now was organized into seventeen infantry regiments with a peace establishment of 54,644 soldiers; the Borders could, if required, call up almost double that number.[36] An imposing military establishment, a people under arms, it also faced problems that were to erode its capabilities. Little had been done to provide a sound economic basis, and conditions of life remained deplorable. Then, too, the French Revolution introduced a new type of warfare which challenged the special advantages of *Grenzer* light troops. Finally, revolutionary ideas, especially nationalist sentiments, penetrated even into these remote regions and compromised the special relationship between the *Grenzer* and the dynasty. In combination these developments caused the decline and eventual dissolution of the system.

Socieconomic Aspects of the Habsburg Military Border System

A basic concept of the system was that the *Grenzer* should be self-supporting, placing the least possible burden on the public finances. All economic activity was directed toward this end; all other activities were forbidden or strictly limited. Only soldiers and their families were allowed to hold land. Officers, who received pay, were permitted to own only a small kitchen garden; except for a few small trading townships, nonmilitary elements were strictly excluded. The exception, as always, was Transylvania where there was no clear division between civil and military territories.

An additional reason for the exclusively agricultural economy was the belief, perhaps reflecting the then fashionable concept of the "noble savage," that only a harsh agricultural existence would preserve martial qualities. "I encountered," Hildburghausen reported, "a martial, brave people, rough and artless sons of nature . . . perhaps poor in knowledge and understanding, but also not debilitated by refined tastes."[37] Similar comments were made by a Prussian writer. The *Grenzer* lands, he wrote, "are characterized by sandy and rather barren soil, many woods inhabited by wild beasts, a chain of mountains and climatic extremes. But these are the very conditions which harden . . . the Croats, accustom them to all of life's hardships and form them into soldiers."[38] And Joseph II, for all his "enlightened" pretensions, agreed. "Neither industry nor education," he wrote Field Marshal Hadik in 1779, "should be improved to the point that the usefulness of this nation might be impaired."[39] Altogether there is ample substantiation for the charge made by a French military observer in the 1840s that "far from seeking to elevate the condition of the inhabitants, the government fears that this might reduce their military qualities."[40]

During the early period, up to the mid-eighteenth century, this had not posed a major problem. Conditions had been harsh indeed, but life for the *Grenzer,* apart from the tribulations of constant small war, was little different from life for the rest of eastern Europe's depressed agricultural population and may have been an improvement on the conditions of the serf masses. With the steady increase in population, both by a very high birth rate and by immigration, land became scarce and as early as the 1690s, the Karlstadt Generalcy in particular, was hard pressed to support its families. Conquest of additional territories alleviated the situation only slightly.[41]

The Theresan reforms aggravated the problem. Drill, frontier watch, and obligatory labor all increased. Even in peacetime, *Grenzer* spent about half a year on these duties and this left too little time to farm. At that, many officers, enamored of the notion of Frederician drill felt that they exercised too little. "It must be decided once and for all," Lacy, then president of the *Hofkriegsrat* and first soldier of the empire, declared, "whether the *Grenzer* are to be considered regular troops or whether they are to constitute a mere militia. If they are to be regarded as regulars they must be properly trained and exercised and this will allow very little time for agriculture. On the other hand, if they are to become little more than an ill-trained militia, the entire system will no longer be a major military resource."[42] Interestingly enough, similar complaints were heard in Prussia where under the canton system, native soldiers normally were furloughed for a greater part of the year and returned to their villages. One contemporary writer on military affairs pictured these "cantonists" as "an unhappy compromise between peasant and soldier."[43]

Whatever the level of military competence, standards of life on the Borders remained poor. To be sure, they differed from command to command and from regiment to regiment. In the Warasdin, for instance, there was a modest degree of well-being, whereas in the Karlstadt Border and in Transylvania, the *Grenzer* lived continually on the brink of starvation. Their homes were cabins and shanties, "poor miserable huts like the dwellings of savages," one observer described them, "commonly lacking floors, windows, or chimneys."[44] In the center of the hovel there was a fire over which unleavened bread of millet, oats — and sometimes the seeds of wild grasses — was baked. Consumption of wine and meat was almost unknown and there were few domestic utensils, furnishings, or other property. Famines occurred with depressing regularity, primarily because the holdings were too small and all other occupations except agriculture prohibited or discouraged. As late as 1825 one Austrian official reported that over half of the households of the Croatian regiments did not own an iron plow and that crop yields were far below the norms achieved in adjoining civil Croatia.[45] At the other extreme of the Border, in Transylvania, it was much the same story. Lacking extended-family households, the burdens of service fell heavily on individuals, creating hardships and discontent. Conditions, General Vilatta reported to Vienna in 1833, were so bad that "the common man is not able to do his best for his farm, which in any case is too small, and, seeing himself and his family deeper and deeper mired in poverty and without any hope ever to escape this condition, it is not surprising that he is unhappy with the institution to which he ascribes his impoverishment."[46] With poor soil and inadequate allotments, the Transylvanian regiments could not feed their population. There were constant shortages in cereals; potato crops failed frequently; animal husbandry, a promising additional source of income, suffered from the depredations of rustlers.[47] Perhaps the greatest natural resource, both in the Croatian Border and in Transylvania were the extensive forests, but efforts at lumbering or producing charcoal failed because of the lack of freely accessible markets.

Attempts to alleviate conditions were made. Whenever possible, the *Hofkriegsrat* tried to establish magazines in the Border region to provide aid during famines, though, especially during the the long Napoleonic Wars, Austria lacked the resources to do much. Half-hearted attempts to increase trade and commerce were made by permitting restricted development of urban centers. After 1750, a number of small townships, no more than two dozen in all, were given special status as *Militär-Kommunitäten*. Their inhabitants did not have *Grenzer* status and were permitted to engage in various trades and occupations. The military authorities, however, were fearful about their potential influence on the *Grenzer* and hampered their growth by numerous regulations and restrictions.[48] In the end, these communities had little influence on the Military Border economy.

The third, and most frequently used, method to alleviate conditions was reorganization, something close to the hearts of the bureaucrats in Vienna. No less than thirty major and countless minor reorganization schemes were made in the eighteenth century. By 1765, the Austrian army, in effort to achieve greater uniformity and efficiency, had created three general inspectorates, one for the cavalry, one for the infantry, and one for the Military Borders. Although this showed the increased importance of the Military Borders in the eyes of the *Hofkriegsrat,* it produced no improvements in living standards. The failure of the Border Inspectorate General induced Emperor Joseph II to change the command and control apparatus of the Military Border. In 1784, following suggestions made by Colonel Geneyne of the *Deutsch-Banater* Regiment, and over the objections of most senior officers, he introduced the *Canton Regulativ.*[49] Its most basic innovation was the introduction of a separate civil affairs branch with specially trained administrative officers. Opposed from the start by regimental officers who resented the division of authority, the new system lasted for only fifteen years. There were not enough trained administrators, and moreover, from 1788 on, Austria was again involved in almost constant wars which prevented training additional officers. During the wars against the French Revolution and Napoleon, the *Grenzer* furnished over 100,000 men and suffered 38,000 casualties. The wars caused severe economic dislocations and hardships, but when in 1797, for instance, there was famine on the Croatian Border, the *Hofkriegsrat* declared that "in view of the military situation, economic and agricultural matters will have to wait."[50] Conditions were just as bad in Transylvania where by 1803 prices for grain and other cereals had increased several times over and famine threatened the Szekler and Romanian regiments.[51]

When the Treaty of Luneville temporarily interrupted hostilities, the Military Border system clearly was in urgent need of attention. Archduke Charles, entrusted by his imperial brother with a complete overhaul of the entire Austrian military establishment, appointed another commission to study the situation. The result was an entirely new set of basic laws; these were approved on August 7, 1807, following the disastrous campaign of 1805. The new *Grundgesetz* failed to resolve the problems. Although its preamble declared that it "provided a constitution for Our loyal *Grenzer* more in keeping with the times and their national character," it actually was little more than a well-intentioned elaboration of eighteenth-century schemes. The new code did away with some abuses in labor service, made transfer of surplus *zadruga* property easier, and replaced the cantonal officers, abolished in 1800, by administrative officers who, however, remained under the control of regimental commanders.[52]

Retention of the *zadruga* became a controversial issue as the century proceeded. On the one hand it had proven beneficial and in Transylvania, at least, there were requests that similar arrangements be introduced.[53] In Croatia, on the other hand, there was dissatisfaction with the extended family communities, and repeated petitions, some as early as 1780, urged that they be abolished. When, between 1809 and 1813, France acquired control over six regiments of the Karlstadt Border, there was a debate concerning retention of the Austrian system. Although some French officers denounced the Border system as degrading, producing a society without progress, justice, or equality, others wished to uphold it in every respect. Finally, military considerations won out. "Military Croatia," General Clarke, Napoleon's minister of war stated, "should not be regarded as just another province but as a vast military encampment; its population as an army that maintained and reinforced itself."[54] Such views outweighed reform sentiment, and Napoleon continued the system unchanged.

Thus, except for casualties suffered by the *Grenzer* regiments in the French service, the period passed without substantial economic changes, save only for a number of splendid military roads built in surprisingly short time. Even so, after the end of the Napoleonic Wars, there was increased discontent, accompanied by numerous *Grenzer* petitions to dissolve their *zadruge.* The *Hofkriegsrat,* however, regarded these communities as the foundations on which the manpower potential of the regiments rested and refused assent. Economic distress — and the penetration of nationalist ideas into the Border region — created discontent and growing resentment against the military regime. A confidential report in 1830 conceded that "general unrest and dissatisfaction were the main causes for the constant emigration and desertions into Turkish territory," and that the basic cause was the "unfortunate condition of the inhabitants, their absolute lack of any prosperity."[55] For twenty years more, the authorities fought a rearguard action, but in 1850, after the *Grenzer* had made their last, and not entirely successful effort on behalf of the dynasty, another *Grundgesetz* declared landholdings actual property and not military fiefs and lifted occupational restrictions. At the same time, however, the law retained the military service obligations for all able-bodied men and preserved the regiments as the exclusive administrative framework.[56]

But the entire Military Border institution was now in jeopardy. Militarily, it had lost most of its justification when the French Revolutionary and Napoleonic wars permanently changed the nature of warfare; politically it was undermined by the growing influence of nationalism eroding the once proverbial, though perhaps always overrated, dynastic loyalty of the *Grenzer.* Increasingly, the Border was considered an obstacle to economic development of the entire Habsburg monarchy, militarily obsolete, and perhaps unreliable. For the first time some ministers and generals in Vienna advocated its abolition.

The Military Role of the Border

Until the mid-eighteenth century the *Grenzer* had constituted a frontier militia organized into war bands under their own captains, loosely supervised by appointed officers. Never mustering over 6,000 fighters — and even this number was rarely reached — they could not form major units, and apart from a number of deep-penetration raids into Bosnia and Dalmatia, their function was to serve as a warning screen. In addition, the bands served as auxiliaries with Austrian field armies, though normally they carried on a constant small war of their own.

Since maintaining horses was expensive, the bands consisted primarily of light infantry, foot predominating over mounted troops at a ratio of twenty to one. This light infantry carried firearms, light arquebuses for the most part, replaced after the middle of the eighteenth century by primitive flintlocks, often captured from the Turks. Although until the beginning of the eighteenth century, major battles were decided by the massed push of the pike assisted only by musketry, the *Grenzer* usually preferred firearms and individual fire, though they did not hesitate to close for hand-to-hand combat using their curved sabers. Until the great wave of immigration at the end of the seventeenth century, their major weakness was numbers, enough for small war and for an occasional raid or ambush, but not enough to make a substantial contribution to campaigns in central Europe. Small numbers and inadequate equipment, one recent writer declared, made the *Grenzer* of little significance during the early period. As late as the opening decades of the eighteenth century, they were, he continued, "at best, only inadequately nourished and equipped out of public funds ... not enough money was made available to provide them with muskets."[57] Still, they sometimes could make the difference in Hungary. During the first years of the *Kuruc* war, when regular troops were engaged elsewhere, the 4,000 *Grenzer* mustered in Croatia provided nearly half of all troops fighting the insurgents.

The high point in the military history of the *Grenzer* was reached in the wars of the mid-eighteenth century. At that time, a number of factors combined to make light infantry and its auxiliary light horse more important in western European warfare. The trend towards linear formations, massed firepower, and careful set-piece battles and campaigns, with pressed armies depending on magazines and vulnerable lines of supply, provided opportunities for light troops. They were useful in screening the movement and deployment of an army and they could be used for raids against the enemy's line of communications. Regular infantry, of course, was trained to fight in close order and generally too unreliable for independent action.

The War of the Austrian Succession and the Seven Years War showed the *Grenzer* at their most effective. Still poorly organized and disciplined, the "Croats" in 1740 mustered over 45,000 men — of whom 20,000 participated in the first campaign — out of a total Austrian force of 153,000 men.[58] As significant as their numbers was the flexibility they contributed. Against the French and Prussians they were employed mainly for small war, constantly hovering in the rear and on the flanks of their armies and forcing the enemy to detach considerable forces to defend his lines of communications. Meanwhile, as Kaunitz put it, it was due to the "Croats and the hussars that the army can sleep in peace, that the regular troops are spared, and that our lands are protected from enemy raids."[59] The *Grenzer*'s style of fighting did not appeal to Frederick who held that such actions could never achieve a decision. Yet, the Croat screen repeatedly prevented him from closing with Austrian armies and finally he was forced to hastily increase his light cavalry and raise irregular "free" battalions; France followed suit. "By the time the War of Austrian Succession had been concluded," an eminent military historian observed, "light infantry, chiefly on account of the Croats and Pandours [the name for irregulars raised in Slavonia] forced themselves willy nilly into recognition."[60]

Strengthened, disciplined, and better trained, the *Grenzer* proved even more effective during the Seven Years War. This time they participated in major battles, especially in tactical situations where regular troops might have been handicapped — in woods, hills, and in villages. When on the defense, they normally took up positions enfilading the advancing Prussians and were highly effective at Lobositz, Kolin, and other battles. Their absence at Leuthen, so Delbrück speculated, may have materially contributed to Frederick's victory.[61] They continued in their classic roles, scouting and outpost duty, and provided the bulk of the mixed raiding force on Berlin in 1757. Altogether, it was only a slight exaggeration to maintain, as Mirabeau did, that "the House of Austria owes all its military fame to its Croats and hussars."[62]

Despite their proven value, for reasons perhaps more political and social than military, light troops receded into the background after the Seven Years War. Basically light troops and irregular warfare went counter to many fundamental attitudes and conventions of the age, and despite improvements, their discipline always left much to be desired. Their scattered and "disorderly" methods of fighting conflicted with the orderly and rational patterns so esteemed in this "Age of Reason." Everywhere, the Frederican system was admired and imitated and the new Austrian regulations introduced by Field Marshal Daun left little scope for small war. Even generals like Loudon, who had made his reputation leading light troops, wanted to turn them into regulars. As early as 1757 he complained that "although the Croats are essentially extremely brave people, they have so far been unable to deliver an attack in an orderly formation. Every time we attempt it, they disperse again in their old fashion."[63]

Concern with "orderly formations" and drill on the Prussian model became a preoccupation of the Austrian army after 1763, and the *Grenzer* came to be little more than cheap troops of the line drilled in linear tactics. By the French Revolution, this had not only imposed enormous additional burdens on their economy and alienated them, it had also made them less valuable soldiers. Individual *Grenzer* units would fight and die bravely enough, but they no longer were the premier light infantry of Europe and often were hard pressed by French *voltigeurs, chasseurs,* and other light troops. General Klein, who headed the Military Border section of the *Hofkriegsrat,* had to concede in 1802 that "the ancient Croats and Pandours, as late as the Seven Years War against Prussia, had constituted a much better light infantry than the present regulated and drilled *Grenzer*." Attempts to transform them into regular infantry, he concluded, were futile, not only because it was contrary to their customs and temperament, but also because they had too "little time to learn the complicated drill and evolutions." He urged that these efforts be abandoned and that they again be employed as "scouts, vedettes, and skirmishers."[64]

In the end, the reforms of Archduke Charles did return the frontiersmen to their light infantry mission. However, they never regained their former preeminence. By the end of the Napoleonic Wars all armies had developed effective light infantry and even the line had learned to skirmish and fight in open order. The last remaining advantage of the *Grenzer* was their cheapness and this was important because of the disastrous state of Austria's treasury. Even so, the attempt to keep the *Grenzer* in a mediaeval state of agricultural development could not be reconciled with changing socioeconomic and political thinking. Although efforts were made to keep them uncontaminated by modern ideas, the rising tide of nationalism could not be stopped at the boundaries of the Military Border. The fight for Serbian independence, the Illyrian movement, and the struggle for Romanian nationhood all were reflected in various degrees on the Border. For that matter, Szeklers and Hungarians in Transylvania were not unaffected by national aspirations.

During the Revolution of 1848, the Military Borders sent field battalions to serve with Radetzky in Italy, though in Transylvania, the

Szekler regiments joined the revolution, only to be opposed, after a period of initial confusion, by the Romanians. And when there was an open break between the governments in Vienna and Pest, *Ban* Jelačić mobilized second-line *Grenzer* units in Croatia-Slavonia. His advance against the Hungarian capital, however, was repulsed and this, in the words of one historian became "the turning point in the reputation of the Croatian-Slavonian troops." They had been "overrated."[65] In 1850 the Transylvanian regiments were disbanded, though the Romanians pleaded to retain their military status.[66] The remaining regiments, subject to a revised basic law, continued, but their fighting spirit was low in 1859.[67] The Military Border was no longer considered reliable and its troops were thought to be less effective than regiments of the line. In 1866, because their combat value was regarded as low and their reliability suspect, they were mobilized but saw no major action. Only the Banat units came under fire, one battalion fighting at Custozza and another at Sadowa. The following year, the Compromise with Hungary, followed by the conclusion of a Hungarian-Croatian subcompromise, and in 1868 by new military arrangements — including the introduction of compulsory and universal military service — made the Military Borders an anachronism and their dissolution inevitable.[68]

Emperor Francis Joseph agreed in principle to dismantling the system in 1869, though the opposition of traditionalist senior officers delayed implementation until 1871. Even then, it took ten years to break up the various legal, social, and economic institutions of the system. Some opposition, especially in the Banat and in Croatia, charged that the *Grenzer* had been sold out to grasping Hungarian politicians, but except for a minor revolt in Croatia, there was no armed resistance. Socioeconomic conditions, the decline in the military role of the *Grenzer,* and finally the rising tide of nationalism raising the specter of the Military Border as an armed South Slav irredenta, all had contributed to this end.

Nationalism and the Habsburg Military Border

The often repeated assertion that on the Military Border "there arose a proverbial Habsburg patriotism, perhaps the only real one which the Habsburgs were capable of fomenting in their realm," needs to be modified.[69] Originally established as a defense against Turkish raids, the Border came to be a dynastic instrument to check the restive and self-willed Hungarian-Croatian nobility, as well as a vast experiment in colonizing a partially deserted and partially reconquered region. The colonists represented a great variety of peoples, whose precise ethnic and national identification is not possible until the nineteenth century. Terms, such as *uskok, Pribeg, Wallach* or *Vlach, Rascian,* and others in numerous spellings, had no exact meaning and were used to identify refugees from the Balkans, mostly Serbs, though there also were others.[70] Most *Grenzer* were of South Slav origin, and the first reliable statistics available for the Military Border show a total of 728,173 Slavs, overwhelmingly Croat and Serb, 121,062 Romanians (Wallachians), 79,636 Hungarians and Szeklers, 9,000 Germans, 1,500 Albanians (Clementines), and 1,500 others.[71] Until the establishment of the Banat border, when Germans and Romanians first were taken into the frontier service, the *Grenzer* were almost exclusively South Slavs, with Serbs, that is adherents of the Greek Orthodox faith, predominating after the great migrations of the 1690s and the 1730s.

Although during this period there was little consciousness of the common identity and unity of the South Slavs, the Military Border, where Catholic Croats and Orthodox Serbs shared a common fate, tended to create a feeling of corporate unity, expressing itself on many occasions in united actions to resist the efforts of the Hungarian-Croatian magnates to deprive the *Grenzer* of their special status. For that matter, Austrian officers, like Hildburghausen, normally referred to the *Grenzer* as a "nation," separate from other elements in the region. Croats as well as Serbs were involved in the series of revolts and mutinies during the early half of the eighteenth century.[72]

These incidents, however, were motivated as much by socioeconomic and antifeudal sentiments as by a separate *Grenzer* nationalism. Yet, one, perhaps the most important, aspect of this unrest, did have national implications. This was religion and confrontations over religious privileges could be, and indeed were, regarded in Vienna primarily as a national issue.

For centuries the Orthodox Church, clergy, and faith had provided a rallying point against the Turks and when it was partly transplanted to the Habsburg dominions it remained, perhaps somewhat weakened, the "center of life and unchallenged leader of the community."[73] This situation represented both opportunities and danger for the Habsburgs. The privileges granted to the Orthodox attracted additional colonists and strengthened the Military Border system. Moreover, on several occasions, in the 1690s, the 1730s, and for the last time in the 1780s, the Orthodox clergy became an instrument of Habsburg expansionist policy, actively supporting Christian Balkan insurrections. The danger was that the Orthodox faith constituted a link between the

Grenzer and their kinsmen across the frontiers and that, under certain conditions, might become the focal point for anti-Habsburg sentiments. In any case, the Habsburg rulers were prone to renege on their promises when it was politically expedient, and many of them, especially Maria Theresa, never abandoned a bitter aversion against these "schismatics." When in the eighteenth century, the Habsburgs drastically reorganized the Border establishment, a severe crisis resulted. The problem of imposing regimentation was aggravated by the *rapprochement* between the dynasty and the Catholic Hungarian-Croatian magnates. As part of this accommodation, and consistent with her own feelings, Maria Theresa abetted attempts to convert the *Grenzer* to the Catholic faith, or at least to coerce them to accept Uniate rites. These violations of ancient privileges resulted in the continued series of revolts and mutinies, during which the *Grenzer* began to look toward Serbia. In 1750, for instance, the Banal Regiments sent envoys seeking aid in both Bosnia and Serbia, and a decade later, there were said to be plans to sever the Military Border from Austria and join it to a resurrected greater Serbian state.[74]

The government, of course, took countermeasures. The functions of the *Hofkommission* (later *Hofdeputation*) *in Illyricis* were expanded to include the Military Border, "especially the Warasdin and Karlstadt generalcies,"[75] and concessions were made to local sentiment. Moreover, religious-national conditions improved after Joseph II, who never shared his mother's religious bigotry, assumed a leading role in the military establishment after 1765. This did not mean that he allowed the Orthodox clergy greater scope, but there was less outright repression. Instead, Joseph took care to influence the election of the Orthodox patriarch and the Serbian national church congress which elected him. In 1769, the *Hofkriegsrat* issued instructions to General Count Hadik, serving as royal commissioner at the national congress to be held that year in Karlowitz [Karlović], to make sure that the *Grenzer* deputations consisted of "loyal, well-reputed, and reliable individuals," and to secure the election of Ivan Georgević, a Habsburg loyalist. New "Illyrian Regulations" were issued in 1770 and 1777, followed by an *Erläuterungs-Rescript* in 1779. Together, these confirmed the privileges granted to the Orthodox Church while subjecting it to government control so that only accommodating priests would hold the patriarchal office for the next seventy years.[76]

In 1787-88, just before and during the early phases of another war against Turkey, Joseph and his advisors once again hoped to raise a large-scale Balkan Christian insurrection. In the past, such attempts had often miscarried because Habsburg ties with the Catholic Church had irritated and alienated the Orthodox. This time it was hoped that the emperor's policy of religious toleration, including the Toleration Patent of 1781, and his alliance with Orthodox Russia, would make the difference. These expectations did not materialize, especially when the initial Austrian advance faltered and then turned into disaster. Even so, the national loyalty of the Orthodox Serbs seemed assured; when after Joseph's death in early 1790, his successor, Leopold II, found Hungary once again on the verge of an insurrection, he was able to use the convocation of a "Greek diet," the Serbian national church congress, at Temesvár to counterbalance Hungarian intentions.[77]

Joseph's Balkan adventure — *misadventure* would be a better name — was the last time that Austrian policy and South Slav aspirations converged. In 1804, Vienna reversed its long-standing policy of supporting Balkan Christians against Turkish rule, and despite repeated appeals, refused to aid the Serbian revolt. On the contrary, orders were issued that no support at all should be provided. It was realized that this would alienate the Serbian *Grenzer* and precautions were taken.[78] As the Serbian revolt continued, the military were concerned about the "numerous confidential reports indicating a most dangerous disposition among the non-Uniate Greeks," and more specifically about the desertions to the insurgents and the smuggling of arms and supplies across the Danube.[79] Tension came to a head in mid-1808, when there was a pro-Serb mutiny in the Banat Wallach-Illyrian Regiment. Although the affair involved but one Orthodox priest, several junior officers, and a handful of enlisted men, it confirmed Vienna's worst fears.[80] Nationalism in whatever form was considered a danger to the Habsburg empire and to the continued effectiveness of the Military Border system.

Refusal to aid the Serbs was much resented and, together with the continuing economic hardships, explains why, when in 1809 Napoleon established the Illyrian provinces, the French were well received on the Military Border.[81] But expectations that the French would help to liberate Serbia or materially improve local conditions were disappointed. Napoleon was interested above all in exploiting the human resources of the Border, and finally the restoration of Austrian rule was welcomed. Still, the experience, including the *Grenzer* service with the imperial French army, had further exposed them to nationalist ideas. The situation became even more acute when Serbia renewed her struggle against the Turks in 1815. Though Vienna closed the frontier and again tried to repress all pro-Serb propaganda on the Border, feelings ran high and a considerable number of *Grenzer* deserted to Serbia.[82] The authorities, especially Chancellor Metternich, blamed agitation on the Orthodox clergy and issued orders to limit their activities.[83]

Even so, it proved impossible to prevent the spread of nationalist ideas, especially after 1830 when Illyrian propaganda from civil Croatia began to be effective on the Border. The Illyrians resurrected the old Croatian demands for the dissolution of the Border system. In his famous *Dissertation,* Count Drašković called for the union of Dalmatia, Croatia, and Slavonia with the Slovene areas of Carinthia and Carniola and the absorption of the Military Border into this reestablished Triune Kingdom.[84] By this time, the military authorities had to contend not only with South Slav nationalism, Serb and Croat, on the Military Border, but also with the problem of the Romanian national awakening. Here, too, the Orthodox clergy formed the backbone of the movement and provided its initial inspiration. As early as 1762, General Count Hadik had warned that the religious sensibilities of the Romanians, then being recruited into the new Border regiments in the Banat and Transylvania, should be taken into account.[85] His advice, however, was not heeded and the already controversial introduction of the system was complicated by religious discrimination resulting in desertions to Moldavia and Wallachia and in incidents, in 1764 and in 1784, when Romanian *Grenzer* joined peasant uprisings. Feelings of sharing a common fate, reinforced by religious sentiment, became an important factor forging a Romanian national consciousness on both sides of the Carpathians. In 1821, when Tudor Vladimirescu raised a national and antifeudal revolt in Wallachia, the *Hofkriegsrat* warned the Transylvanian Command of the danger that "Vladimirescu would attempt to spread the spirit of disobedience and revolt into our frontier districts, and especially make an appeal to the Wallachian *Grenzer,* closely related to his followers."[86]

The new national movements aroused concern in Vienna. When General Haller reported that Illyrian propaganda, and he included Serbian as well as Croatian influences, had indeed made some progress, an imperial directive ordered that "all necessary steps be taken to keep the Border free of political intrigues." Yet the *Hofkriegsrat* believed that as long as serfdom continued in the Habsburg lands, the *Grenzer,* "grateful for their special status," would be immune to the attractions of the various parties.[87] There remained the question of how the Border would react after serfdom was abolished.

Proof of the Border's dynastic allegiance has been seen in the events of 1848: the *Grenzer* regiments provided contingents for the field army; they constituted the bulk of Croatian intervention forces against Hungary, rejected Hungarian rule in the Banat and Srem, and except for the Szeklers, rallied to the Habsburg cause in Transylvania. Yet, they were influenced as much by nationalist sentiment as by dynastic loyalty. In Croatia, *Grenzer* participating in the *Sabor* joined with the radical Illyrians to demand an end to the military regime and advocated an organic union between Croatia and the newly proclaimed autonomous Vojvodina in southern Hungary.[88] And in Transylvania, both Szekler and Wallachian *Grenzer,* now commonly titled *Romanians,* cooperated in the early months calling for an end to labor service and noble privileges. Only when the new Hungarian government in Pest-Buda demanded incorporation of the principality into a liberal but unitary state did the *Grenzer* ranks split. The Szeklers supported Pest-Buda; the Romanian regiments joined with the Romanian peasant masses to demand national status and closer ties with Wallachia and Moldavia.[89] After a confused interval, during which the imperial government first approved and later rejected the Hungarian demands, the Romanians, like the Croats and Serbs, initially took up arms to defend their national aspirations; only a shift in Vienna's position led them into the imperial camp.

Perceptive generals were only too well aware of the ultimate implications of the national movements. They were particularly concerned about fraternization between Orthodox *Grenzer* and Russian troops in Hungary and about the establishment of the Vojvodina, a polity with close ties to Serbia. In January 1850, while new arrangements for the Military Border were being discussed, General Schütte, commanding in the Banat, wrote to General Haynau, commanding in Hungary, that the South Slavs were "hiding dangerous tendencies behind an outward mask of loyalty."[90] South Slav *Grenzer* were disappointed. Though they had rendered conspicuous service, their national ambitions were suppressed. The imperial constitution handed down in March 1849 proclaimed "the Military Border and all its inhabitants an integral part of the imperial army" and the new Border code of 1850, although making minor economic concessions, was ill-received. The neoabsolutist regime would not tolerate any national movement, proven loyal or not. An example was provided in Transylvania where the Szekler units were dissolved late in

1850. The Romanian regiments pleaded to retain their military status, but they too were disbanded. General Wohlgemuth, the civil and military governor, advised Vienna that "while in 1764 it had been necessary to create a Military Border, the reasons for such a system no longer exist." On the contrary, the continued existence of the system might well be a danger for the monarchy. And in the case of the Romanians he warned that "it was not wise to provide that nation with an armed force by way of *Grenzer* regiments."[91]

Fear that the remaining Military Borders constituted a potential armed nationalist irredenta continued to disturb the military authorities. During the Austrian mobilization against Russia and Serbia in 1854, there were reports of dissension in a number of units.[92] And during the war of 1859 the *Grenzer* units did poorly in the field, while French as well as Sardinian war plans envisaged *Grenzer* uprisings in support of projected landings on the Adriatic coast.[93]

These hopes were unrealistic, though a decade of neoabsolutist rule produced fundamental changes in the political attitude of the Border. This was demonstrated in 1861 when under the provisions of the February Patent, the *Sabor* was reconvened, with *Grenzer* delegates attending for the first time. Confirming Vienna's misgivings, the *Grenzer* promptly aligned with the opposition and cast the decisive votes against Croatian participation in the *Reichsrat*.[94] Moreover, while senior officers remained loyal to the crown, the junior officers were becoming restive, and plans to purge the Border regiments misfired when several of the most active and determined men went to Serbia.

Serbia now became the focal point for nationalist activities. As early as 1845, Garašanin had developed a plan making Serbia the center of a general South Slav uprising against all foreign domination. The plan had lain dormant until 1860 when Austria's military debacle in Italy and the evident decline of the Ottoman Porte revived it. Former *Grenzer* officers, led by Antunje Orešković, established connections on the Military Border and, at long last, in the spring of 1866, it appeared that the opportune moment was at hand. Orešković had made contacts in Berlin and Florence where a variety of schemes, all counting on armed *Grenzer* support, were under consideration. In the end, however, the orderly, if unenthusiastic mobilization and departure of the field battalions removed the cadres, while Italy hesitated and Prussian interest, always lukewarm, evaporated after the decisive victory in Bohemia.[95] Even so, the very real apprehension that the *Grenzer* might provide armed backing for large South Slav uprisings influenced many senior officers and, above all, gave the new Hungarian government leverage to persuade Emperor Francis Joseph to agree to the dissolution of the Military Border system.

Epilogue

When I first began to study the history of the Military Border and of the Austrian army in general, I accepted the interpretation that, for all its shortcomings, the Military Border had been one of the most successful supranational institutions in the Habsburg empire, developing "a strong sense of corporate unity, a reputation for military qualities, and above all a strong loyalty to the imperial family."[96] At the same time, my critique of the abuses of the system, especially its economic exploitation by the Inner Austrians, aroused a strong, on occasion intemperate, reaction among local patriots. Still, as one German historian observed, it was the first attempt to deal with the Military Border system without ethnic, regional, or national chauvinism, "a final settlement with the ideological trends of the past."[97] Since then, the history of the Border has won renewed interest, not only in Austria, but also in the socialist countries, in Hungary, Yugoslavia, and Romania.[98] Socialist historians strongly condemn the paternalistic-despotic elements so much in evidence throughout the system, but they have rightfully stressed both the meagerly rewarded military achievements of the *Grenzer* and their contributions to national revivals.

The history of the Border system is complex and, only too frequently, contradictory. It reflected complex regional, military, national, and socioeconomic issues that still are not entirely resolved. Subjected to frequent attacks and internal tensions during its existence, the Habsburg Military Border system remains a hotly disputed topic for historical discussion.

Notes

1. A. A. Paton, *Highlands and Islands of the Adriatic, including Dalmatia, Croatia, and the Southern Provinces of the Austrian Empire,* 2 vols. (London, 1849), II: 107.

2. M. Braun, *Die Slawen auf dem Balkan* (Leipzig, 1941), 150.

3. G. E. Rothenberg, "The Origins of the Austrian Military Frontier in

Croatia and the Alleged Treaty of 22 December 1522," *Slavonic and East European Review* XXXVIII (1960): 493–98.

4. Edict, Vienna, June 5, 1535, in R. Lopašić, ed., *Spomenici hrvatske krajine, Monumenta spectantia historiam Slavorum Meridionalium* (Zagreb, 1889), XX: 388–89.

5. G. E. Rothenberg, *The Austrian Military Border in Croatia, 1522–1747* (Urbana, Ill., 1960), 28–32. (Cited as Rothenberg.)

6. Lopašić, 420–26.

7. Rothenberg, 35–36.

8. F. Hurter, *Geschichte Kaiser Ferdinand II und seiner Eltern,* 11 vols. (Schaffhausen, 1850–54), I: 290 n.26 provides a muster list.

9. Rothenberg, 72–75.

10. *Ibid.,* 84–85.

11. Consult J. V. Cspalovics, *Slavonien und zum Theil Croatien,* 2 vols. (Pest, 1819), II: 23–55; on the Jesuits see F. v. Krones, "Zur Geschichte des Jesuitenordens in Ungarn seit dem Linzer Frieden bis zum Ergebnisse der Ungarischen Magnatenverschwörung, 1645–1671," *Archiv für Österreichische Geschichte* LXXIX (1893): 322–24.

12. Duke Joseph Friedrich zu Sachsen-Hildburghausen in his 1737 report on the Military Border, Kriegsarchiv Wien (hereafter cited as KA), HKR Kanz.-Arch. VII: 349.

13. Rothenberg, 91–92.

14. K. Wessely, "Neuordnung der Ungarischen Grenzen nach dem grossen Türkenkrieg," in *Die k.k. Militärgrenze, Schriften des Heeresgeschichtlichen Museums in Wien* VI (1973): 36–48.

15. Rothenberg, *The Military Border in Croatia, 1740–1881* (Chicago, 1966), 12–13.

16. Among others see J. H. Schwicker, "Zur Geschichte der kirchlichen Union in der Kroatischen Militärgrenze," *Archiv für Österreichische Geschichte* LII (1875): 275–400. Cf. Rothenberg, 101–11.

17. *Ibid.,* 110–11.

18. His report with numerous enclosures, KA HKR Kanz. Arch. VII: 349. Excerpts in Lopašić, 345–76. See also his "Beytrag zur Geschichte der Warasdiner und Carlstädter Gränz Verfaszung," KA HKR Croatien, fasc. 44 encl. 38.

19. J. J. Khevenhüller-Metsch, *Aus der Zeit Maria Theresias. Tagebuch des Fürsten Johann Josef Khevenhüller-Metsch, Kaiserlichen Obersthofmeisters 1742–1777,* 8 vols. (Vienna, 1907–72), III: 231.

20. Rothenberg, *Military Border in Croatia,* 21–26.

21. Cited in C. Duffy, *The Army of Maria Theresa* (New York, 1977), 84.

22. Resolution of Apr. 23 and decree of June 23, 1747, Nr. 138 in "Kurze Übersicht sämmtlicher für die Militairgränzen erflossen Systemal-Verordnungen," KA HKR Sondersammlung 30.

23. Code discussed in Rothenberg, *Military Border in Croatia,* 25–29. Copy of the *Militär-Gränitz-Rechten Von Ihro Kaiserl. Majestät für das Carlstädter*

und Varasdiner-Generalat Vorgeschrieben im Jahr 1754 (Vienna, n.d.), no pagination, in KA, Schriftgut Militärgrenze.

24. G. E. Rothenberg, "The Austrian Sanitary Cordon and the Control of the Bubonic Plague: 1710–1871," *Journal of the History of Medicine and Allied Sciences* XXVIII (1973): 17–19.

25. Rothenberg, *Military Border in Croatia,* 30–37. Cf. B. P. Sučević, "Razvitak 'vlaskih prava' u Varaždinskom generalatu," *Historijski zbornik* VI (1953): 33–70 which places the revolt in the framework of the gradual erosion of *Grenzer* privileges caused by developing absolutism.

26. *Ibid.* Cf. the documents in KA Mem. XXIII: 191.

27. Supplementary regulations in KA HKR Kanz. Arch. VII: 307, 309.

28. H. G. Mirabeau, *Système Militaire de la Prusse* (London, 1788), 17.

29. J. Amstadt, *Die k.k. Militärgrenze 1522–1881,* 2 vols. (Würzburg, 1969), I: 168–76.

30. C. Göllner, *Die Siebenbürgische Militärgrenze* XXVIII *Buchreihe der Südostdeutschen Historischen Kommission* (Munich, 1974): 12–15; Amstadt, I: 177–79. Other accounts include J. H. Edler v. Benigni, *Pragmatische Geschichte der siebenbürgischen Militärgränze,* 2 vols. (Vienna, 1811–12); the account by L. J. Szádeczky, *A székely határőrség szervezése 1752–64-ben* (Budapest, 1908); D. Prodan, *Infiinţarea regimentelor de graniţa,* in *Istoria României* (Bucharest, 1964), 514–23. Finally, from the viewpoint of the Vienna court there is M. Bernath, "Die Errichtung der siebenbürgischen Militärgrenze und die Wiener Rumänenpolitik in der frühjosephinischen Zeit," *Südostforschungen* XIX (1960): 164–92.

31. Göllner, 19–21.

32. *Ibid.,* 28–30.

33. *Ibid.,* 31–33.

34. Amstadt, 177–86.

35. *Ibid.*

36. C. B. v. Hietzinger, *Statistik der Militärgränze des österreichischen Kaiserthums,* 3 vols. (Vienna, 1817–23), II: 330.

37. Introduction to his "Beytrag," KA HKR Croatien, fasc. 44, encl. 3.

38. J. W. Archenholtz, *Geschichte des Siebenjährigen Krieges in Deutschland,* 5th ed.; 2 pts. (Berlin, 1840), II: 226–27.

39. KA, Mem. XXIII–57.

40. M. de Terrason, "Essai sur l'organisation des Frontières Militaires et Régiments Frontières de l'Autriche," Archives de la Guerres, Vincennes, Reconnaissances militaires, Autriche, 1599.

41. Amstadt, I: 138; Rothenberg, 90–91.

42. Lacy to Joseph II, Dec. 5, 1782 and Mar. 6, 1783, KA Hof-Commission Nostitz-Rieneck IX: 9, 11.

43. G. H. v. Behrenhorst, *Betrachtungen über die Kriegskunst,* 2d ed.; 2 vols. (Leipzig, 1798), II: 210.

44. J. A. Demian, *Statistische Beschreibung der Militärgrenze,* 2 vols. (Vienna, 1806), I: 112–17.

45. "Relation des Hofr. v. Pidoll über seine i. Jahre 1825 vorgenommene Bereisung der slawonischen u. croatischen Mil. Gränze," KA HKR Kanz. Arch. VII: 369.

46. Report of Mar. 29, 1833, KA HKR 1833-139.

47. Göllner, 94-100.

48. Rothenberg, *Military Border in Croatia*, 55-57, 92-93; Demian, I: 134-55, and the report "Von den Militär-Kommunitäten," submitted to the Border Reorganization Commission, August 17, 1803, KA Schriftgut Militärgrenze, ms. vol. 35.

49. Rothenberg, *Military Border in Croatia*, 65-69, 86-87. The system was never introduced in Transylvania.

50. HKR to Karlstadt-Warasdin Command, Vienna, Apr. 13, 1797, in Državni Arhiv u Zagrebu (hereafter cited as DAZ) Zagrebačka generalkommanda, F-20.

51. Göllner, 96-98.

52. Discussed in Rothenberg, 96-101. The *Grundgesetz für die Carlstädter, Warasdiner, Banal, Slawonische, und Banatische Militär-Gränze* (Vienna, 1807), with commentary including modifications by M. Stopfer, *Erläuterungen der Grundgesetze für die Carlstadter, Warasdiner . . . Militär-Gränze* (Vienna, 1831).

53. Göllner, 90-92.

54. P. Boppe, *La Croatie Militaire 1809-1813* (Paris, 1900), 39-53.

55. "Bemerkungen über den Zustand und die Verfassung der Militär-Grenze," A. Huszar, Pressburg, Oct. 28, 1830, KA Mem. XII: 84.

56. Discussed in Rothenberg, *Military Border in Croatia*, 157-59.

57. K. Wessely, "The Development of the Hungarian Military Frontier until the Middle of the Eighteenth Century," *Austrian History Yearbook* IX-X (1973-74): 74-75.

58. Rothenberg, *Military Border in Croatia*, 18-19.

59. Khevenhüller-Metsch, IV: 251.

60. J.F.C. Fuller, *British Light Infantry in the Eighteenth Century* (London, 1925), 56-57.

61. H. Delbrück, *et al., Geschichte der Kriegskunst im Rahmen der politischen Geschichte*, 7 vols. (Berlin, 1900-37), IV: 321-23.

62. Mirabeau, 17.

63. Cited in Duffy, 86.

64. KA Schriftgut Militärgrenze Fasc. 30; KA Mem. XXIII: 42.

65. R. Kiszling, *Die Revolution im Kaisertum Österreich 1848-1849*, 2 vols. (Vienna, 1948), II: 578.

66. Göllner, 122-23. Details in J. Gürtler, "Die Auflösung der Siebenbürgischen Militärgrenze" (Dissertation, Vienna, 1947), especially pp. 54-56, 66-67.

67. Delbrück, V: 229-30, 342, 425-28. Cf. E. Ritter Bartels v. Bartberg, *Der Krieg im Jahre 1859* (Bamberg, 1894), 261.

68. G. E. Rothenberg, "Towards a National Hungarian Army: The Military Compromise of 1868 and Its Consequences," *Slavic Review* XXXI (1972): 805-16.

69. O. Jászi, *The Dissolution of the Habsburg Monarchy* (Chicago, 1929), 57. Cf. P. F. Sugar, "The Nature of Non-Germanic Societies under Habsburg Rule," *Slavic Review* XXII (1963): 21.

70. K. v. Czoernig, *Ethnographie der Österreichischen Monarchie,* 3 vols. (Vienna, 1857), II: 168 n.6.

71. Conscription and population summary, KA HKR 1815, B-2-44.

72. G. E. Rothenberg, "The Croatian Military Border and the Rise of Yugoslav Nationalism," *Slavonic and East European Review* XLIII (1964): 35-36.

73. C. Jelavich, "Some Aspects of Serbian Religious Development in the Eighteenth Century," *Church History* XXIII (1954): 144-45.

74. Rothenberg, "Rise of Yugoslav Nationalism" 35-36.

75. See statement by Count Königsepp-Erps, in *Die Geschichte der österreichischen Zentralverwaltung in der Zeit Maria Theresias,* ed. F. Walter, *Veröffentlichungen der Kommission für neuere Geschichte Österreichs,* 2d ser., XXXII (Vienna, 1939): 117-18.

76. Rothenberg, *Military Border in Croatia,* 57-60, 71.

77. *Ibid.,* 81.

78. A. Beer, *Die orientalische Politik Österreichs seit 1774* (Prague, 1883), 188-90, 196. Cf. the directive from Archduke Ludwig to all Border commands, in A. Ivić, ed., "Dokumenti o ustanku Srba pod Karadjordjem Petrovičem," *Vjesnik hrvatsko-slavonskog i dalmatinskog zemaljskog arhiva* (hereafter cited as VZA), XXI-XXII (1920), 55.

79. Rothenberg, *Military Border in Croatia,* 105-106.

80. *Ibid.,* 107.

81. *Ibid.,* 110-11.

82. *Ibid.,* 136-37.

83. G. Rolof, "Fürst Metternich über die slavische und magyarische Gefahr im Jahre 1839," *Mitteilungen des Instituts für österreichische Geschichtsforschung* LII (1938): 69-70.

84. Rothenberg, *Military Border in Croatia,* 137-40.

85. Göllner, 65-66.

86. Cited in *ibid.,* 116-17.

87. G. Miskolczy, ed., *A horvát kérdés története és irományai a rendi állam korában,* 2 vols. (Budapest, 1927-28), II: 38-43, 603-11.

88. Rothenberg, *Military Border in Croatia,* 143-50. Cf. comments and notes by W. Vucinich, "Jelačić and the Frontier in Modern History," *Austrian History Yearbook* I (1963): 68-72.

89. Göllner, 118-21.

90. G. E. Rothenberg, *The Army of Francis Joseph* (West Lafayette, Ind., 1976), 46-47.

91. KA Kriegsministerium Präsidial 1851–3771.

92. KA Schriftgut Militärgrenze, Serbisch-Banater Armee Corps, 131–34, 136–38.

93. A. Tamborra, *Cavour e i Balcani* (Turin, 1958), 21–30; Delbruck, V: 352–53.

94. V. Bogdanov, "Uloga Vojne Krajine i njenih zastupnika u hrvatskom Saboru 1861," *Zbornik Historijske Institute Jugoslavenske Akademije,* Zagreb, III (1960): 59–214.

95. H. Wendel, *Bismarck und Serbien im Jahre 1866* (Berlin, 1927), 65–68; J. A. v. Reiswitz, *Belgrad-Berlin, Berlin-Belgrad, 1866–71* (Munich, 1936), 74–77, 92–94.

96. Rothenberg, 127.

97. W. Schulze, "Die österreichische Militär Grenze," *Militärgeschichtliche Mitteilungen* IX (1971): 190–92.

98. See the extensive bibliographies by K. Wessely and G. Zivkovic, "Bibliographie zur Geschichte der k.k. Militärgrenze," in *Schriften des Heeresgeschichtlichen Museums in Wien,* VI, *Die K.K. Militärgrenze* (Vienna, 1973), 291–324 and Wessely's "Supplementärbibliographie zur österreichischen Militärgrenze," *Österreichische Osthefte* XVI (1974): 280–328. These two bibliographies provide some 1,700 entries, both old and new.

Philip Longworth

Transformations in Cossackdom 1650–1850[1]

The character of the old Cossack communities was largely determined by their marginality. Inhabiting a perilous frontier zone
between Muscovy, Poland, the Crimea, the Caucasus, and Central
Asia, their peripheral position promoted both the independent self-
reliance and the borrowings from other cultures which made their own
so distinctive. Moreover, like other free social formations which
sprang up on the fringes of great empires in the early modern period
when governmental control over peripheral areas was weak, the
Cossacks lived by war, and their social, political, and cultural
institutions were molded by the wars they fought. As such, the
Cossacks of the earlier period, like the *haiduks, uskoks*[2] and other
groups which inhabited the borderlands of East Central Europe,
exemplify the interplay between war and society in an extreme form.

During the period under review, however, the Cossacks were transformed from essentially autonomous societies into service-bearing
groups rigidly controlled by the Russian state. It is the purpose of this
essay to consider this transformation and the complex interplay of
factors which brought it about. (A companion essay, to appear in a
later volume in this series, will focus on the specifically military aspects
of Cossackdom in this period.) In doing so, however, we shall confine
attention to the Don, Iaik/Ural,[3] Terek, Zaporozhian, and Black Sea
hosts. Limitation of space does not allow us to deal with the process of
transformation in Ukrainian Cossackdom (other than its Zaporozhian component), which displayed significant divergencies from the
rest.[4]

We shall focus initially on the somewhat ambiguous relationship
between the Cossack hosts and the Russian state in the seventeenth
century. Secondly, we shall analyze the interplay between strategic,
economic, social, and political factors in the transition from independence to subservience, and examine how far the transformation resulted from the deliberate policies of the Russian government and how
far they derived from spontaneous changes within the communities
themselves. We shall then describe the new terms of military service
imposed upon the Cossacks and consider their impact on Cossack

society. Finally, we shall draw attention to the neglected aspect of cultural change, particularly, the vexatious question of the changing Cossack ethos, and discuss the process by which the old spirit of independence and rebelliousness came to be transmuted into a spirit of loyalty to the Russian state.

Although essentially independent, Cossack relations with the Muscovite state in the seventeenth century were somewhat ambiguous. Not only did the Cossacks defend their sectors of the frontier against Tatar raiders, they furnished contingents to fight for the tsar in campaigns on other fronts,[5] and Muscovite commanders came to the Don to direct joint operations against the Tatars[6] (although they were given short shrift when they interfered in the Cossacks' internal affairs). Moreover, insofar as the Cossack communities were dependent on Muscovy for supplies of grain, powder, lead, and other necessities, they could be said to have been in a client relationship to the tsar. Muscovy, however, was so often desperate for Cossack military aid that the hosts were able to negotiate the terms of their service from a position of strength. Furthermore, although the government issued instructions and permissions to the Cossack communities, and from the 1670s even administered oaths of loyalty to them, such formalities did not reflect the true nature of the relationship. The instructions were often ignored, and the oath of loyalty frequently repudiated.

For the greater part of the seventeenth century, then, the Cossack hosts were for all practical purposes independent. As a Muscovite bureaucrat and defector of that time, Grigory Kotoshikhin, wrote:

> They are allowed to live . . . in their own way, and to choose their leaders, atamans and others, from among themselves, and to judge in all matters according to their own will and not according to the Tsar's order. . . . When in Moscow or . . . [on Muscovite service], a man who commits a crime is not subjected to the Tsar's judgment and punishment, but this is arranged among themselves. And when they come to Moscow, honor is accorded them as to foreign envoys.[7]

In Kotoshikhin's day, atamans were freely elected, the democratic assembly (*krug*) was still the key decision-making body; peasant runaways reaching Cossack territory were assured of asylum, and the military services which the Cossacks provided for the Muscovite government were performed on a contractual basis, freely negotiated every year.

Two hundred years later, however, the relationship had changed radically. As the British traveler Laurence Oliphant remarked, by the middle of the nineteenth century the Don Cossacks (largest of the communities under discussion) had been

> insidiously deprived of almost every privilege which they once possessed, and from being a free republic, responsible to no-one. . . . they have sunk into the same condition of slavery as the inhabitants of the neighbouring provinces. In former days the distinction of rank was unknown — now there is a Don Cossack aristocracy; then there was a community in landed property — now the whole district has been divided into estates, and serfdom established. . . .[8]

Oliphant's reference to slavery may have been exaggerated: the Cossacks were still privileged compared with the majority of Russian subjects. Nevertheless, the general tenor of his conclusion was correct. The *krug* had long since become a powerless ceremonial assembly; atamans of the host were no longer freely elected but appointed by the emperor; the communities were administered by members of a new Cossack elite, whom the government regarded as "responsible, God-fearing and loyal"; serfdom had been introduced, and the Cossacks themselves had become liable to compulsory resettlement.

Two dates are generally regarded as turning points in the process of subjecting the free Cossacks to the will of the state: 1721, when responsibility for dealing with the Cossack hosts was transferred from the College of Foreign Affairs to the College of War; and 1775, when a separate civil authority was established on the Don to regulate its affairs in accordance with the general laws of the empire;[9] when the Zaporozhian Sich was destroyed and its lands given over to Russian serf-owners; and when the restive Iaik Cossacks were finally suppressed in the aftermath of the Pugachev revolt. However, neither of these dates can be regarded as a firm dividing line between freedom and subjection. The process by which the state harnessed the Cossacks had begun much earlier than 1721, and it was not completed until well after 1775. Furthermore, although it was undoubtedly hastened by a series of deliberate political, military and administrative actions, it was also facilitated, as we shall see, by a complex interweave of spontaneous changes within the communities themselves — changes which the Russian government encouraged and exploited, but did not create.

The state was motivated by four major considerations in seeking to control the free Cossack communities. First, it needed to stop the flow of peasant runaways to Cossack territory, where they were accorded asylum and accepted into the Cossack ranks. Second, it wished to extend serf agriculture into the northern Don and Zaporozh'e. Third, it had to guard against the possibility of Cossacks leading more peasant revolts, which had reached frightening proportions under Stepan Razin in 1670–71, Kondraty Bulavin in 1707–08, and Yemelian Pugachev in 1773–74.[10] Fourth, it wished to prevent Cossacks defecting to hostile powers, as Don Cossacks under Nekrasov had done in 1708, as many Zaporozhians had done in 1709 and the 1790s, and as a substantial number of Iaik Cossacks attempted to do after the failure of their rebellion in 1772. Furthermore, as the Russian state, having secured its borders, began to extend them, it became increasingly appreciative of the Cossacks' qualities as pioneer colonists. Hence, the punitive re-settlement of Cossacks served the dual purpose of removing dangerous elements from proximity to the restless Russian peasantry and of securing newly won territories farther afield. The deployment of Don Cossacks in the Caucasus and the settlement of ex-Zaporozhians along the River Kuban are examples of this policy in action.[11]

Governmental policy in the eighteenth century was characterized by a much more frequent use of force against the Cossacks than in the seventeenth century, when diplomacy had been the primary means of eliciting their conformity to Russian interests. This change is attributable to a progressive improvement in Russia's military capacity; further, as the Tatar menace receded and Poland declined as a great power, Russia became less dependent on Cossack cooperation in securing her southern borders against attack. Nevertheless, although brute force was used against the Cossacks on many occasions (e.g., the destructions of the Zaporozhian Sich in 1708 and 1775; the suppression of the Don and Iaik hosts in 1708 and the 1770s) methods short of war were also employed.

In particular, the state was able to procure the election of atamans friendly to its interests, to secure the deposition of those atamans elected against its wishes (as on the Don in 1718 and 1723 and the Iaik in 1738) or acting in defiance of it (as on the Don in 1772). Finally, it was able to take effective administrative action to reinforce its position, as for example, in subordinating the Ural Cossacks to the military governor of Orenburg, reforming the Don Host Chancery, and posting a Russian procurator there to supervise its activity. Nevertheless, the success of its interventions in Cossack affairs owed a great deal to transformations in the internal structures of the Cossack communities.

Paramount among these, perhaps, was an economic transformation. As the old frontier became progressively safer, a shift developed from a gathering-predatory economy based on hunting, fishing, raiding, and mercenary service, to an economy based primarily on stock raising, agriculture, and associated enterprises. Zaporozh'e, for example, developed from a grain-importing to a grain-exporting region between the 1730s and the 1770s; by 1800 the Don had become a major agricultural and cattle-rearing region; and the Ural Cossacks, who engaged in agrarian pursuits to only a very limited extent, developed a flourishing cattle- and sheep-rearing industry to supplement income from fishing. The populations of most hosts increased rapidly during the century (the Don from some 30,000 to about 300,000 inhabitants), there was a marked increase in the pace of urbanization,[12] and a concomitant expansion of commerce, including foreign trade. In sum, the Cossack regions were characterized by growing prosperity which was conducive to a new and more complaisant attitude towards domination by the state, especially on the part of the new Cossack elite.

Economic development intensified social differentiation among the Cossacks. It is significant in this connection that the increase in grain production on the Don was not attributable to the rank-and-file Cossacks (whose family farms produced only enough grain for their own consumption), but to Cossacks, usually office holders, employing runaway peasants who would once have been granted Cossack status. It was these prosperous Cossacks who produced the bulk of the grain surplus sent to the developing port of Taganrog by the early years of the nineteenth century. Not surprisingly, these richer Cossacks sought political stability; and the state went out of its way to exploit their desire. It bolstered their power at the expense of the Cossack mass, chose the new bureaucrats of the ataman's chancery from their ranks, and encouraged their social ambitions by offering them prospects of promotion and privilege within the state system.[13]

During the eighteenth century, dynasties were established within Cossackdom which had once been noted for its egalitarianism, and their official posts enabled members to misappropriate community funds and exploit communal lands and fisheries for their private use. By the end of the century, they and the officer elite (regimental commanders and above), with which they were largely coextensive, were given substantive rank in the Russian army and heritable noble status, and allowed to enserf the peasants employed on their estates. Yet in bolstering the power of these "respectable, loyal and God-fearing" groups, the state was merely hastening an existing trend within Cossack society.

It was invited to do so, of course. As I. G. Rozner has indicated, "the

Cossack elite . . . had long sought an accommodation with the autocracy." They wanted, and ultimately gained, land, rank, and parity of rights with the Russian nobility; and they actively supported the "reforming" activity of the state insofar as it coincided with their interests, for example, in denying Cossack status to the poor.[14] However, the elite felt obliged to find historical precedents to support their pretensions. Thus they invented myths about the Cossack past which were to receive wide currency in the latter part of the nineteenth century and play a part in the indoctrination of future generations of Cossacks (a subject to which we shall return later). For example, in his history of the Host published in 1814-16, Lieutenant-Colonel A. Popov, Director of Education on the Don, laid stress on the Cossacks' noble, "well-born" antecedents and traced their origins to the Kasogs, Khazars and other warlike nations of the distant past.[15] These claims, incidently, seeded the future flowering of Cossack nationalism insofar as they emphasized ethnic differences between Cossacks and Russians (ideas which seem to have influenced foreign writers on the Cossacks, such as Dr. Clarke, who knew Popov, and the French historian Lesur).[16] Moreover, as Rozner points out, such works as Popov's also contain hints that the loyalty of the elite was conditional on the autocracy's granting them substantial concessions. To this extent, then, some Cossacks still retained a lever against the state which they could use in their own interests.

Although the greater security of the borderlands benefited one stratum of Cossacks, it also brought in train a more regular form of service which placed a strain on the sometimes frail domestic economies of the rank and file. Additional obligations to maintain roads, perform escort duties, ride post, etc., and the need to equip themselves with horses and arms added to the burden (and accounts for the increasing numbers of Ural Cossacks offering themselves as substitutes to rich Cossacks who did not wish to serve). To be sure, the state allocated pay for Cossacks when on service, but it was meager and sometimes misappropriated by their officers (in 1770 some Zaporozhians mutinied for this reason). The forcible drafting of Cossacks to new frontier territories also promoted discontent (hence the Don Cossack rebellion of 1792-94),[17] as did the recurring fear of *regularization,* that is, absorption into the Russian army, with consequent loss of privileged status, increased regimentation, and a requirement to be clean-shaven which ran counter to the faith of Old Believers (a factor in successive Iaik Cossack rebellions after 1768).

However, the coincidence of major Cossack rebellions with periods of inter-state war suggests that prolonged service on a distant front may have been the most common trigger of rebellion. Cordon-line duties close to home might be compatible with normal economic pursuits; but war service, necessitating absences from home as long as four or five years, tested the viability of their family farms. Certainly, demands for military service in excess of the normal three-year tour away from home (increasingly common in the late eighteenth century) led to an increasing rate of desertion by individuals, and to mutinies by entire units (as in 1769, 1771, 1774, and the 1790s).

Nevertheless the burden of service was not reduced. As the British military observer, Sir Robert Wilson noted, the beginning of the nineteenth century saw "incipient attempts at reformation, by regimenting the Cossaques, and by the introduction of distinctive dress to each corps."[18] Furthermore, the norm of three years' service with the colors, seventeen on reserve or on local cordon-line service, plus five years with an obligation to perform local policing, transport, and other services, continued to be exceeded. According to that conscientious observer Baron Haxthausen, during the 1840s Don Cossacks were serving abroad three years out of nine and the Ural Cossacks three out of twelve. Of 12,000 Ural Cossacks liable for service in 1837 (about half the male population) only 3,300 were "inactive at home" and most of those had paid for the privilege (on the Don, membership in the Trading Company established in 1834 enabled substantial Cossacks to pursue their lucrative careers without the distraction of military service). All in all approximately 15 percent of the Cossack population was serving at any one time.[15]

By the 1840s, however, Cossacks were accepting the burden without noticeable protest. As another German traveler noted at the time, they were

> now admirably disciplined. . . . Necessary modifications and reforms
> . . . occasioned some ill-blood. But now all changes are tolerated
> without opposition and the Cossacks become inured to them.[20]

Something approaching the long-feared regularization had at last been introduced — and without calling forth major rebellions and disturbances as in the eighteenth century. Yet it was accompanied by a marked decline in the military zeal of all classes of Cossacks. Academician Pallas noticed this as early as the close of the eighteenth century. He attributed it to a moral deterioration, concluding that although the

Cossacks had

> hitherto been very useful to Russia . . . [they were] continually more
> injured in their free constitution and daily show greater aversion to
> military service; while their affluent governors live in the most volup-
> tuous indolence and immorality.[21]

This mood of sullen obedience and the new spirit of loyalist conformity
which succeeded it require further explanation than the changing
strategic, economic, social, and political circumstances already referred to. They invite investigation of cultural factors. This, however,
is a difficult area which has been little explored — hence any conclusions must be very tentative. Nevertheless, the reports of contemporary observers throw some light on the problem and suggest some
potentially fruitful avenues for future inquiry.

Relying largely on interviews he had with Cossacks in 1843, Moritz
Wagner defined three stages in the transformation of Cossack attitudes: the period in which there prevailed "the blunt old spirit" of
sturdy independence "that Peter the Great began to bridle with his iron
hand"; a transitional stage personified by the generation of Cossack
officers who had fought in the Napoleonic Wars, who disliked the
social equality and political anarchy of early Cossackdom, but still
hankered after "the freedom of the good old times"; and the new
generation of the Cossack elite, products of the cadet school and
acquainted with the fashionable world of St. Petersburg. Yet, at the
same time, Wagner was assured that although "bankruptcy and mal-
versation, gambling, champaign and adultery" might characterize the
Don capital of Novocherkassk,

> the deeper you plunge into the heart of the steppes, the more fre-
> quently you encounter a breath of the spirit of our fathers, albeit
> mixed with some roughness.[22]

Although these remarks pertain only to the Cossack elite, they are of
general relevance insofar as they suggest that locality and time have an
uneven impact on the process of cultural change.

As noted at the beginning of this essay, the Cossacks inhabited
frontier territories which were areas of exchange as well as of conflict.
Hence, although the predominant strain in Cossackdom was Russian
and Ukrainian, Tatars, Poles, Circassians, Greeks, Turks, Kalmyks,
Armenians, and others found their way into their ranks. Those Cossack settlements most exposed to the frontier were the most influenced
by their neighbors in dress, language, values, and way of life. This

diminished the cultural homogeneity of Cossackdom. It may also help to account for what Wagner's Cossack informant noted, namely, that Don Cossacks of the southern steppe tended to preserve traditional values longer than the rest. Yet, by the same token, the Cossacks of the northern Don, descended from the more recent influxes of runaways, displayed greater sympathy for the Russian peasant than did Cossacks farther south.

The uneven effects of time should also be considered. In this connection one must recognize the force of cultural inertia upon Cossack attitudes — memories of "the good old times," the strength of tradition, and the influence of folklore which transmitted knowledge from more rebellious days. But there is another, more tangible, aspect to it. In remarking that the Cossacks of his time had "nothing in common with the Russians of the present day, except the language they use,"[23] the celebrated English visitor to the Don, Dr. Clarke, draws attention to the affinities between the Cossacks he met and the Russians of earlier times, to the tendency of Russian customs to be preserved among Cossacks after they had declined in Russia proper. Old Belief (that is, schismatic Russian Orthodoxy) which was particularly strongly entrenched among the Iaik/Ural Cossacks provides one example of this phenomenon. It figured prominently in the Pugachev revolt and was a constant source of concern to the Russian government.

Although the privileged stratum of Cossackdom had lost its old ethos by the early decades of the nineteenth century, and one may suppose that their new beliefs and attitudes toward the state would in time have reached the rank and file by process of osmosis, the strength of popular Cossack attitudes and the weight of service which they had to bear were such that the Russian government could not afford to leave the matter to chance. Indeed, as early as the last quarter of the eighteenth century it had set out to restructure Cossack attitudes. As has been seen, armed force, political manipulation, and inducements all played their parts in this program. But they were accompanied by attempts to inculcate new, loyalist traditions into the consciousness of the Cossack mass.

Education was one obvious means of achieving this objective. Although the first school on the Don was not opened until 1790, thereafter development of formal education was evidently quite rapid. Dr. Heber, an Oxford don who visited Cherkassk at the end of the eighteenth century, found the level of education to be "not so low as is generally thought, and it improves daily. All the children of the officers are sent to the academy of Tcherkask and learn German, French, etc."[24] At this stage, then, formal education touched only the offspring of the elite group, some of whom were to move on to St. Petersburg or to the University of Kharkov. However, most Don Cossacks still went through life unlettered, and as late as the 1830s fewer than a thousand children, all boys, were receiving primary education at eight district and three parish schools.[25]

On the Ural matters were even worse. In the early 1820s Ural'sk boasted only one school with ten to fifteen pupils and they "very rarely attended classes." New service regulations demanding that Cossack officers be able to read and write tended to raise the level of literacy despite the poor state of formal education,[26] nevertheless until the middle of the nineteenth century, the thrust of state indoctrination through the educational system was restricted to the officer class. Hence the minds of the rank and file could be reached only through the church, through active service, and through the propaganda effect of ceremonial. Given the generally low level of literacy, state propaganda had to take visual and aural forms — and in these forms, it had to compete with a strong folk tradition which was subversive in many of its themes.[29]

Recognizing the state church to be an important instrument of ideological, and hence social and political, control, the Russian government sought every opportunity to infiltrate it into the Cossack lands. The task was not easy. Paganism had been widespread among the Cossacks of the seventeenth century. During the Razin revolt, the successful insurgents had driven priests away from captured Astrakhan, interrupted church services, and contracted marriages by dancing round a tree. Razin himself was alleged to have "cast out blasphemous words against the Saviour."[28] That the first church in the old Don capital, Cherkassk, was founded by Peter the Great also suggests that Russian Orthodoxy may have been comparatively unpopular during the early period of Cossackdom. Certainly Catherine II made a point of encouraging church-building in the Cossack territories and donated funds for the purpose. Yet, by the beginning of the nineteenth century there were only six churches in Cherkassk to serve a population of 15,000.[29]

In view of this, it may seem surprising that Vladimir Bronevsky, writing in the 1830s, should claim that "the Don Cossacks are in general devout . . . and piously observe all the rites of the Church."[30] Like so many other writers of the time he may well have identified Cossackdom as a whole with its officer elite. However that may be, it is difficult to gauge with any precision the success of the state's campaign to bring religious conformity to the Cossack lands. We know that ex-Zaporozhians settling in the northern Caucasus strongly resented the obligation to build churches which the authorities placed upon them, and that heretical Old Belief remained widespread among the Ural Host (though the associated customs of wearing beards and abstaining from tobacco did decline following the Napoleonic Wars[31] — a change which probably owed more to exposure to Western culture through war service than to governmental policy). Nevertheless it seems that by the middle of the nineteenth century religious conformity was by no means confined to the elite, and that Orthodoxy had become the dominant creed of Cossackdom.

If the Church was one medium through which a loyalist ethos could be introduced, active service was another. Yet, although discipline on active service might serve to maintain a degree of conformity tolerable to the authorities, that conformity would not necessarily be carried back to village life afterwards. As the Ural Cossack officer, A. K. Levshin, noted

> the Ural Cossack in the army is a most conscientious and honourable obeyer of any command; but how far he is from the regular soldier when he returns home.[32]

This may explain why the program of reeducation which aimed to transform the old Cossack spirit of independence and rebelliousness into an ethos of loyalty to the state placed so much emphasis on ceremonial.

The aims were to inculcate pride in service and in past military exploits in support of the regime (as in 1812); to stress the privileged status of Cossackdom in contrast to that of the empire's population as a whole; to bolster the prestige of the imperial family, and create the illusion that a special bond existed between it and the Cossacks. Thus, Cossack Guards regiments were created (the first by Catherine II after the suppression of the Pugachev revolt to honor the Don Cossacks who had remained substantially loyal in that affair); permissions were granted to name regiments after approved Cossack heroes like Yermak who possessed martial virtues without being tainted by opposition to the state. Further, charters were issued which conferred no tangible benefit whatsoever but which represented such ancient Cossack freedoms as had survived (such as nonliability to the state poll tax, entitlement to land and the right to elect village *atamans*) as privileges granted by "imperial favor"; and impressive ceremonies were arranged to proclaim them to the hosts.

Official celebrations were also staged to mark even such apparently trivial events as "the recovery of one of the Emperor's children from the small-pox inoculation."[33] In 1827 the nine-year-old Tsarevich was proclaimed *Ataman* of the Don, Ural, and Terek hosts. Ten years later, he was theatrically presented to them in person. Regimental colors were paraded and new items of Cossack regalia presented. Henceforward, an object such as the *ataman*'s mace, which once had symbolized the Cossacks' independence, was to represent their subjection. Yet it came to be regarded as a symbol of the sovereign's special favor.

The success of the indoctrination process probably owed something to factors other than discipline and propaganda. For example, the recent work of Zasedateleva on the Terek Cossacks indicates that the original small, two-generation family household gave way to the large, extended family household comprising three or four generations during the nineteenth century.[34] This transformation may have been due to the shift from a hunting and fishing economy, to an influx of new recruits who brought the custom (usually associated with agriculture) with them, or to the need to maintain the family's livelihood while the young men were absent on campaign. Whatever the reason, the new prevalence of the extended family household probably reinforced patriarchalism, and hence authoritarianism. Consequently, it may help to explain the greater stability, conformity, and obedience of nineteenth-century Cossack society. Unfortunately, however, the information currently available allows no such conclusion, however tentative, to be drawn about such possible effects on the other Cossack hosts.

Finally, attention must be drawn to early nineteenth-century writing on the Cossacks, because one can see trends there which set a pattern for popular books on the subject appearing later in the century, by which time literacy had become more widespread (although their content no doubt percolated to the lower strata of Cossackdom by word of mouth more immediately). Such writers were almost cravenly loyalist. Two examples must suffice. The Ural Cossack Levshin, for instance, praised Catherine II for her lenient treatment of the rebels after the Pugachev rising, and characterized such measures as granting official sanction in 1806 for the hiring of substitutes as imperial "condescensions."[35] The historian of the Don Cossacks, Bronevsky, was even more extreme in his conformity. He praised Catherine II's efforts

to curb ... [Cossack] disobedience and always to protect Russia from rebellions like that of Pugachev and studiously avoided any reference to the disturbances on the Don in the 1790s.[36]

Cossack historiography of the early nineteenth century, then, already contained the seeds of a new convention which propounded loyalist myths and paraded historical falsifications — a convention with which popular writing on the subject was so redolent later in the century. They set the tone for such authors as Abaza[37] who were to present Cossack history as a chronicle of endless service to the tsar, to characterize rebels, such as Razin, as aberrant felons (if they mentioned them at all), and to ignore all claims of early Cossackdom to independence. Such legends were also to help keep the once rebellious Cossacks in thrall to the state until the twentieth century.

In sum, the transformation of Cossackdom between the late seventeenth and the early nineteenth centuries involved clearly definable, if complex, political, economic, and social changes as well as important, though less well understood, cultural shifts. In part imposed or induced by action of the Russian government, and in part a product of unguided factors operating within the communities themselves: the process was gradual and cumulative rather than suddenly decisive. And at each point in the transformation, the structures of Cossackdom interacted with military factors, the strategic balance between the Cossacks and their neighbors, and with war itself. (Examination of these facets of the problem, however, must be left for another essay, scheduled to be included in the second volume of this series.)

Notes

1. These transformations have to some extent been discussed in my survey, *The Cossacks* (London, 1969; New York, 1970), chap. 6, 8, 9. See its notes and bibliography for works on the subject published before 1969. Some others, including more recent publications, are cited later.

2. See my article "The Senj Uskoks Reconsidered," *Slavonic and East European Review* (forthcoming, 1979).

3. The Iaik Cossacks were renamed in 1775 after the Pugachev Revolt.

4. Notably in size of population, comparative weakness of autonomous institutions, extent of serfdom, rate of absorption of its elite into the Russian system, and the absence of universal military service. Registration was abolished as early as 1699, although the Hetmanate was to survive until 1764. The Slobodskaia Ukraine and the Siberian Cossacks also constitute special cases which must be omitted from the present study.

5. E.g., at Smolensk in 1632, *Donskie dela* (St. Petersburg, 1898), I: 387-89.

6. A. A. Lishin, *Akty otnosiashchiesia k istorii voiska donskogo* (Novocherkassk, 1891), no. 21, 24, 25.

7. G. Kotoshikhin, *O Rossii v tsarstvovavie Alekseia Mikhailovicha* (St. Petersburg, 1906), 135.

8. Laurence Oliphant, *The Russian Shores of the Black Sea* (London, 1854), 151.

9. E.g., Vladimir Bronevsky, *Istoriia Donskago voiska* (1834), II: 126.

10. Cossack-peasant revolt is the aspect of Cossack history best covered in Soviet historiography. Virtually all the documents on the Razin revolt have been published: Ye. A. Shvetsova, *et al.,* eds., *Krest'ianskaia voina pod predvoditel'stvom Stepana Razona,* 4 vols. (Moscow, 1962-76); the Pugachev movement has been the subject of many recent publications. The latest collections of documents include Ye. I. Indova, ed., *Krest'ianskaia voina 1773-1775gg v Rossii* (Moscow, 1973), and R. V. Ovchinnikov, *et al.,* eds., *Dokumenty stavki Ye. I. Pugacheva* (Moscow, 1975). Ovchinnikov is currently engaged in preparing the complete transcripts of the interrogations of the revolt's leaders for publication. See also my articles, "The Last Great Cossack-Peasant Rising," *Journal of European Studies* III (1973): 1-35, which deals, *inter alia* with the strategic characteristics of such movements; and "Peasant Leadership and the Pugachev Revolt," *Journal of Peasant Studies* II (1975): 183-205.

11. Though there are also interesting differences between them, the methods by which Russia used Cossacks (and others) to secure its borders bears comparison with the Austrians' organization of *uskoks* and other groups for the defense of its frontiers in the same period and earlier. See Günther E. Rothenberg, *The Austrian Military Frontier in Croatia 1522-1747* (Urbana, Ill., 1960); and *The Military Border in Croatia 1740-1881* (Chicago, 1966). Whether and how far these systems served as models for each other, or evolved independently, is largely unexplored.

12. The population of the Black Sea Cossacks, founded in 1792, remained stable for thirty years (even though its chief town, Yekaterinodar, increased tenfold to 6,000 inhabitants by 1802). Dr. Lyall attributed this to the comparative lack of women. Robert Lyall, *Travels in Russia, the Krimea, the Caucasus and Georgia* (London, 1825), I: 411. But of course these Cossacks derived from Zaporozh'e, which was untypical in its long-standing tradition of bachelordom, only partially broken down in the eighteenth century.

13. This process is outlined and discussed in Bruce W. Menning, "Imperial Russia's Cossack Captains: The Emergence of a Military-Administrative Elite in the Land of the Don Cossack Host, 1708-1836" (forthcoming, in a symposium edited by W. Pintner and D. Brower).

14. I. G. Rozner, "Kazachestvo v krest'sianskoi voine pod predvoditel'-stvom Ye. I. Pugacheva," in L. V. Cherepnin, *et al.,* eds., *Kresti'ianskie voiny v*

Rossii XVII–XVIII vekov: problemy, poiski, resheniia (Moscow, 1974), 98–115.

15. A. G. Popov, *Istoriia o Donskom voiske*, 2 parts (Novocherkassk, 1814–16).

16. E. D. Clarke, *Travels in Various Countries of Europe, Asia and Africa*, I (London, 1816); C. L. Lesure, *Histoire des Kosaques*, 2 vols. (Paris, 1814).

17. See Menning, "The Case of the Reluctant Colonists: Mutiny among the Don Cossacks 1792–94 (unpublished draft, 1976).

18. Sir Robert Wilson, *Brief Remarks on the Character and Composition of the Russian Army* (London, 1810), 31.

19. Baron von Haxthausen, *The Russian Empire* (London, 1968; reprint of 1856 edition), II: 236–37, 13. For the Cossack war establishments in 1853 and 1880 see M. P. Khoroshchin, *Kazach'i voiska: opyt voenno-statisticheskogo opisaniia* (St. Petersburg, 1881), 271.

20. Dr. Moritz Wagner, *Travels in Persia, Georgia and Koordistan: with Sketches of the Cossacks and the Caucasus* (London, 1856), I: 92. For the impact of service reforms later in the century see my "The Reform of Cossack Military Service in the Reign of Alexander II" (forthcoming).

21. P. S. Pallas, *Travels through the Southern Provinces of the Russian Empire in the Years 1793 and 1794* (London, 1802), I: 469.

22. Wagner, I: 91, 62–63.

23. Clarke, I: 369.

24. Dr. Heber's manuscript journal, quoted by Clarke, I: 355.

25. Bronevsky, III: 39.

26. A. K. Levshin, *Istoricheskoe i statisticheskoe obozrenie ural'skikh kazakov* (St. Petersburg, 1823), 72.

27. See my article, "The Subversive Legend of Sten'ka Razin" in V. Strada, ed., *Russia/Rossiia*, (Turin, 1975), II: 17–40.

28. *A Relation Concerning the Particulars of the Rebellion Lately Raised in Muscovy by Stenko Razin* (London, 1672), as reprinted in A. G. Man'kov, ed., *Zapiski inostrantsev o vosstanii Stepana Razina* (Leningrad, 1968).

29. Clarke, I: 362–63.

30. Bronevsky, III: 195.

31. Levshin, 74.

32. *Ibid.*, 73.

33. Clarke, I: 350.

34. L. B. Zasedateleva, *Terskie kazaki (seredina XVI–nachalo XX v.): istoriko-etnograficheskie ocherki* (Moscow, 1974), 293–94. This is one of the very few works to pay attention to both history and ethnography.

35. Levshin, 26–29, 32.

36. See Bronevsky, II: 125, 164 ff.

37. K. K. Abaza, *Kazaki: Dontsy, Ural'tsy, Kubantsy, Tertsy* (St. Petersburg, 1890).

Robert H. McNeal

The Reform of Cossack Military Service in the Reign of Alexander II

Even elementary textbooks on Russian history summarize the reform of the system of military service carried out under war minister
Dmitrii Miliutin during the reign of Alexander II. The well-known law
of January 1, 1874, which established a "universal" military obligation,
did not, however, apply to all the *sosloviia,* or legally established
estates, of the empire. Along with some national minorities, the special
military *soslovie* of the Cossacks was not covered by the new legislation, which in its main outlines lasted as long as the empire. The
Cossacks at the end of the reign of Alexander II in 1881 numbered
about 2.5 million people, male and female, about 2 percent of the total
imperial population, a fairly small element, but one which played a
disproportionately large role in military affairs. The Cossacks provided, mainly at their own expense, about 50 percent of the cavalry of
the tsar's army in this period, not to mention some horse artillery and
relatively small numbers of infantry.[1] Considering the importance of
cavalry in the warfare of this age, its relatively high cost, compared to
infantry, and the chronically straitened budget of the empire, the
Cossacks must be considered a vital part of the population with respect
to military service, and major changes in the laws controlling this
subject must be taken into account in any well-rounded discussion of
the Miliutin reforms. This paper attempts to provide a sketch of this
topic, which is not to be found in the principal works on the Miliutin
reforms.[2]

At the opening of the reign of Alexander II, Cossack military service
was regulated by the Don Cossack *polozhenie* of 1835, which had been
adapted to other Cossack *voiska* except those of the Ural.[3] This law
required each Cossack to be available for active duty for thirty years
(twenty-five for officers); the final five were to be on "internal service,"
that is, within the territorial limits of the *voisko.* To be sure, the
domestic economy of the *voisko* could not be maintained if all eligible
Cossacks were actually kept on active duty for thirty years, nor did the
state desire so large a force of Cossacks in peacetime. Therefore, some

system of rotation was needed, so that only a minority of eligibles would be on active duty at one time. Methods for handling this problem varied considerably among the different *voiska* in 1855. Units, such as regiments, rotated on and off active service in the Don, Ural, and Black Sea *voiska,* but in the Caucasus Line, Astrakhan, Novorossiisk, Orenburg, Bashkir, Siberian Line, and Zabaikal *voiska* they remained permanently on active service. In the latter pattern, individual Cossacks from a specified district within the *voisko* were responsible for manning a given unit and rotated between active service and leave in doing so. But in the Don *voisko* the regiments themselves were completely formed and disbanded in rotation, while the individual men were rotated separately, through a duty roster in each *stanitsa* (extended village) or *okrug* (district), which spread the burden of any one regiment over the whole *voisko.* In the Black Sea *voisko,* on the other hand, units had long-term personnel complements, who lived in the same district and went on and off active service together. Finally, the Ural system resembled that of the Don: regiments as a whole were formed and disbanded during rotation, but individuals served or did not according to a traditional system, somewhat misleadingly called *hiring (naemka).* Of this complex arrangement, suffice it to say that the Ural Cossacks needed to man a regiment due to go on active duty either volunteered or drew unlucky lots. They were then compensated by those who did not choose to serve and drew lucky lots, the "hiring" fee sometimes amounting to over a hundred rubles, a very substantial sum at the time. All Cossacks on active duty received only a miserly three rubles per year from the state.[4]

Even before Dmitri Miliutin became war minister on November 9, 1861, the impulse to reform the administration of the Cossacks and their pattern of military service appeared. At the center, a major administrative change occurred on January 1, 1858, when the Department of Military Colonies of the War Ministry was replaced by the Administration of Irregular Forces. Previously no administrative center in St. Petersburg concerned itself mainly with the Cossacks. The Department of Military Colonies had been established by Alexander I to foster his pet project for this kind of military utopia, and the Cossacks were added in 1833 to the domain of this office merely as an afterthought. Several writers, especially those defending Cossack interests, have noted the similarity between the general concept of the military colonies and the Cossacks, but there were always important distinctions. To a considerable extent, the Cossacks were historically evolved societies, which the state annexed and exploited but did not maintain financially; the military colonies were wholly creatures of the state, which lavished a substantial investment on them. When the military colonies fell from official favor with the coming of the reign of Alexander II, the War Ministry focused more of its attention on the Cossacks, who formed the overwhelming majority of the *irregular* forces referred to in the name of the new office.[5]

It seems safe to say that the Administration of Irregular Forces shared the general impulse of the new era to rationalize and modernize. A complex, nonuniform system of military service, such as that described earlier, could hardly appeal to the non-Cossack professional officers and civil servants who were responsible for the Cossacks, though the particular thrust of the reforms was not at once evident. Clearly there was some disposition to think that since the existing regulations provided more than enough Cossacks the service obligation might be reduced. The coronation of the new tsar in 1856 was the occasion for the promulgation of a substantial, though hardly well-considered, reduction of the service obligations of the Don, Black Sea, and Caucasian Line *voiska*. Henceforth ordinary Cossacks were to serve for twenty-five years, of which the final three were to be on internal service. Guards regiment Cossacks had to serve only twenty years, plus two on internal service; officers were obliged to serve twenty years rather than twenty-five. Following the conclusion of the prolonged war against the Caucasus mountaineers, the obligation for military service was further reduced, in 1863–64, for the three *voisko* that had borne the burden of that campaign: the Don, Black Sea, and Caucasian Line. These Cossacks now were obliged to serve only twenty-two years, the final seven of which were to be on their home territory. This norm was extended to other *voisko* in 1866 in honor of the marriage of the heir, the "August Ataman."[6]

The initiative for a more systematic reform of Cossack military service came not from the center but from the *ataman* of the Don Cossacks (himself no Cossack), Adjutant General M. G. Khomutov, who in 1856 petitioned the war minister for a general review of the Don *polozhenie,* which he considered to be obsolescent and internally ill-coordinated.[7] The response of the center came only on October 10, 1859 (after the establishment of the Administration of Irregular Forces) and proposed to deal with *all* the *voiska* through five regional "Special Temporary Committees." These were to meet in Novocherkassk (dealing with the Don), Stavropol (Caucasian Line and Black Sea), Orenburg (Orenburg, Ural, and Bashkir), Omsk (Siberian Line and the Tobolsk infantry battalion, a separate entity which was soon abolished), and Irkutsk (Zabaikal and the separate Irkutsk and Enisei regiments). At the request of the governor-general of Orenburg and Samarra, the Orenburg and Ural committee was divided into two separate bodies. With almost frivolous optimism, these committees were ordered to complete their review of the entire body of special legislation and regulations concerning the Cossacks within a year, submitting the drafts of their proposed reformed *polozheniia* to the war ministry by January 1, 1860. When the committees failed to perform on this timetable, the deadline was extended December 4, 1862, to mid-1863 and then to January 1865.[8]

Progress was especially slow in the Caucasus, partly owing to complexities arising from the formation in 1860 of the Terek and Kuban *voiska,* replacing the former Caucasian Line and Black Sea *voiska.* Hence on October 26, 1861, the local committee was replaced by one in St. Petersburg, headed by a civil servant from the staff of the Administration of Irregular Forces.[9]

When they were first established, the special temporary committees were issued only general instructions, and no particular reformed structure was indicated.[10] But with the coming of Miliutin as war minister, things took a different turn. In general he does not seem to have held the Cossacks or their military services in high esteem. The only reference to them in his extensive diary is to an outbreak of an epidemic among their horses, which he perhaps regarded as more important than the Cossacks themselves. At the very least, he apparently believed that the defense of the empire could get along with substantially fewer Cossacks. The one result of the work of the local committees that appears to have suited the war ministry was a memo (not the final report) from the Caucasian area committee, which was received in St. Petersburg in 1861.[11] This document argued, with superficial plausibility, that the conclusion of the protracted war in the Caucasus ended the need for substantial Cossack forces on active duty there, including not only Black Sea and Caucasian Line troops but also twenty regiments from the Don. Therefore, it was contended, the time had come to reduce Cossack forces by encouraging departures from the *soslovie,* thus settling this population in "work that is more productive for the state and society." The counterargument that Cossacks were cheap troops and would be needed in large numbers was rejected on the unsupported assertion that the government really had to contribute a lot to the support of the Cossacks.

If this did not stimulate new thinking by Miliutin, it seems to have coincided with the drift of his ideas, as was soon evident. Under his aegis, in 1862, the special temporary committees received a "General Program of the Main Bases of the *Polozhenie* of the *Voiska.*" The *atamany* who chaired the local committees, to whom this document was dispatched, were instructed to release it to their committees only if they considered the plan workable in the light of local traditions. Evidently some authority in the war ministry, very likely Lieutenant General von Karlgof, who headed the Administration of Irregular Forces, doubted its acceptability, for it was indeed a radical break with tradition. According to this proposal, Cossack military service would henceforth be voluntary, and there would be free entry into, and exit from, the *soslovie*.[12]

Whether this proposal was considered by all the local committees is not clear, but they definitely did not gratify the wishes of the war minister by embodying anything like it in draft *polozheniia* that the Don, Siberian, and Zabaikal committees submitted to the war ministry in 1865 — the remaining committees evidently still failed to meet the deadline. The main point of the Don proposal was to preserve the traditional norms, while limiting the total contribution of the Don to Cossack forces to one-third of the whole. This would enable them to reduce the service of the individual because he would be required to serve fewer turns than previously, when, according to the Don spokesmen, their *voisko* did more than its share. Miliutin was not pleased by this opposition to his goals and stated in his annual secret report to the tsar that the Don draft shows "a false understanding of historic right," that no attention was given to the war ministry proposal, and that it retained "all the conditions of the former military *soslovie*, sealed off and alienated from other *sosloviia*."[13]

The upshot of this clash of opinion was that the war ministry, presumably Miliutin himself, wrote off the previous six years' work and started anew. This time the authorities in St. Petersburg sought to meet some kind of timetable and to impose their ideas about a rational order for the Cossacks by keeping the drafting committees in the capital and under the chairmanship of the head of the Administration of Irregular Forces. The regional special temporary committees were disbanded, and on October 2, 1865, a "Temporary Committee for the Review of Cossack Statutes" was established under the Administration of Irregular Forces.[14] The temporary rules established for this body specified that the separate *voiska* should be represented in the committee by "persons of Cossack ancestry who know their needs," chosen by the *atamany* of their respective *voiska*: three from the Don, one each from the Kuban, Terek, Astrakhan, Ural, Orenburg, and Siberia, and one for all the Far East. The Administration of Irregular Forces was to have an unspecified number of its staff on the committee, which was to be chaired by the head of this office, who was never a Cossack. Moreover, a chancery of the committee was established, drawn entirely from the personnel of the Administration of Irregular Forces, and it was permitted to begin work even before the arrival of the delegates from the *voiska.* This body lasted until 1872 and, for a time, was in practice a standing subdepartment of the administration, finally handing its functions over to another suboffice whose work it really duplicated.[15]

The centralist spirit of the new approach was stressed in a report from the head of the Administration of Irregular Forces to Miliutin, which he approved on October 29, 1865. The report rejected as impractical the examination of proposals from the former local committees, went on to propose that the committee first draft rules which could be uniform for all the *voiska,* and in the military sphere, set the goal of establishing uniform service obligations for all Cossacks. Although the war ministry's previous proposal of voluntary military service for Cossacks was not specifically mentioned, the report did hint that something of the sort was still favored, inasmuch as it favored the establishment for all citizens of the right of entry to, and exit from, the *soslovie.* It appears likely that the kind of reform envisaged by Miliutin was drafted by the chancery of the committee in the following year (November 1865 – November 1866). At the end of this time, the delegates from the *voiska* appeared and on November 5, 1866, Alexander II personally opened the deliberations of the committee, perhaps in an attempt to awe the delegates into cooperation.[16]

With a committee consisting of bureaucrats who were under his control and delegates largely from small *voiska* with little sense of independence, Miliutin's representative General Karlgof (chairman of the committee and head of the Administration of Irregular Forces) was able in about six months to push through a radical reform of the system of Cossack military service. At first, the committee considered simply further reducing the term of service, but this was rejected as harmful to the military readiness of the Cossacks. What was proposed was a scheme that continued the assumption that the empire would need far fewer Cossack troops than the growing population of the *voiska* could provide. It was therefore intended to divide the *soslovie* into two categories, those which would perform military service and those who would be excused. All Cossack males between the ages of nineteen and twenty-five were to have the option of volunteering for service; if this did not produce enough men to fill the units required by the war ministry, the balance would be conscripted by lot. The term of service (including rotation to leave or *l'gota* status) remained twenty-two years. One-third of the units thus raised would be on active duty at any time and two-thirds in reserve, on leave (*l'gota*). Those choosing not to serve and drawing lucky numbers would be enrolled permanently in what amounted to a new *soslovie, voiskovie grazhdaniny* (*voisko* "citizens"). They would enjoy all the nonmilitary rights of Cossacks, but, while of serving age, would pay the *voisko* an annual levy to help sustain the military operation. Their children would be liable to the same chance of military service as those of other Cossacks. Finally, Cossack officers were entirely exempt from obligatory service.[17]

Despite the dissenting votes of the Don delegates, this general plan was approved by the Military Soviet in May 1867, with the proviso that each *voisko* should prepare its own variant on the model.[18] Orenburg quickly fell into line, adopting the reformed plan of service as of July 1, 1867. Its provisions illustrated others that followed. The *voisko* agreed to provide three artillery batteries, nine infantry battalions, and fifteen cavalry regiments, of which a third would be on duty at any given moment in peacetime, the units rotating on and off active service at intervals of two and one-half years. Those not serving were to pay four roubles per year to the *voisko* and fifty-six and two-thirds kopeks (!) to the *stanitsa*.[19] Similar statutes were adopted by the Kuban and Terek (1870), Siberia (1871), Astrakhan, and Zabaikal (1872).[20]

But the big one got away from Miliutin. The Don *voisko* doggedly opposed this change in the system of military service and had the political weight (despite the presence of a non-Cossack *ataman* appointed in St. Petersburg) to frustrate the war minister. It is hard to know what popular opinion existed in this matter, but it is clear that the Don aristocrats were strongly opposed to the proposed reform and that they made their opinions heard in St. Petersburg. During the sessions of the commmittee in 1867, two of the Don delegates, Major General Ezhov and Colonel Denisov, submitted quite an eloquent memorandum of protest. They contemptuously rejected the idea of a system of "conscription" or *landwehr* or "even the system of the Ural Cossacks" (which, it will be recalled, involved selection by volunteers and by lot). Such a system would introduce "an entirely new class of *voiskovie grazhdany*, who would be close to the *podatnye sosloviia* ("taxable estates") and would divide the Cossacks into "two hostile camps." The only change needed in the system of military service, they said, was the one proposed by the Don regional committee: the introduction of a system of rotation that would place a third of the forces on active duty in peacetime. Finally, the *kazakomany* (advocates of Cossack interest) appealed to "the IMPERIAL charters and the Emperor's Word of Four Monarchs." "Any change in this tradition would be received by the Don with regret, as the destruction of the privileges accorded them and as a departure from the path which their ancestors laid out for them."[21] Unsuccessful in the committee in St. Petersburg, such resistance made itself felt within the Don administration, including its non-Cossack component, which was supposed to be drafting a law adapting the general precepts of the Miliutin-Karlgof plan to their *voisko*. The Don protest resulted in a deferral until 1871 in the implementation on the Don of the service reform of 1867.

But the most powerful allies of the Don traditionalists turned out to be the Prussians. Their victory over the French in 1870 provided Miliutin with the argument needed to push through the introduction of a universal military obligation and the creation of a large reserve army. The commission that produced this system had already opened its deliberations on January 5, 1871, and the fruit of its labor was promulgated on January 1, 1874.[22] In the new context, the previous policy on Cossack military service, still incompletely implemented, seemed obsolete. An enlarged Russian armed establishment was now envisaged, and cutbacks on Cossack forces no longer made sense, especially if a large force of trained reserves was intended. The plan advocated by the Don — universal service with two-thirds of the active-age forces in the reserve — now fit the needs of the war ministry. It was also said that the imposition of universal military service on the people at large made it unfair to envisage any plan for Cossack military service which allowed a substantial number of eligibles to avoid serving.[23] But this argument was specious, considering that not all of the non-Cossack eligibles were actually conscripted. The unlucky names were drawn by lot, as in the attempted Cossack reform. The most persuasive reason for reinstating universal military service among the Cossacks was not equity but military expediency.[24]

This led Miliutin in a letter of May 15, 1871 to inform the Don *ataman* that the system of Cossack military service was to be reviewed by a War Department Commission which was undertaking a study of the organization of the entire army. Adopting a much more conciliatory tone, Miliutin asked that the *voisko* staff, with the participation of experienced regimental and other unit commanders, should consider the problems involved and send their responses to him. Miliutin sketched the questions that needed to be resolved, such as the shortfall in filling out the wartime personnel complement of the units (here a reverse of emphasis in policy on the numbers of Cossacks needed), the shortness of the period of active service, the absence of a regular rota of service for officers, and other technical problems. But nothing that hinted at a reduction of numbers of serving Cossacks, voluntary service, and other aspects of the unfulfilled reform plan. On May 28, 1871 the completeness of the reversal at the War Ministry was made clear by a letter from the head of the Main Administration of Irregular Forces (this office having taken on a modified name in 1869), which stated that the Don did not have to adopt any particular system of military service, that the Don staff was simply being asked to consider the question "thoroughly and in detail." Although some new kind of draft (the contents are unknown to me), was sent to the St. Petersburg administration in November 1871, this was regarded as merely advisory. With authorization to rewrite the rules of military service on its own terms, the Don leadership now proceeded to produce a modified version of its traditional system, which they submitted to the war ministry at the opening of 1873. Available evidence suggests that the differences between the ministry and the Don Cossacks were still substantial, and that the tsar's personal authority was needed to settle matters. The "main principles" of the new law were approved by the tsar with considerable dispatch in February 1873, implying that the draft passed almost immediately from the Don committee to his chancery, and only then went to the main Administration of Irregular Forces for a thorough review. This took about a year, implying the existence of some difficulties in the opinion of the war ministry officials. The revised result received the tsar's approval in January 1874. Only after this second approval of the "main principles" was a detailed law drafted, receiving the tsar's assent on October 14, 1874, and final approval by the Council of State on April 15, 1875.

Not only had the Don succeeded in resisting the model of 1867, they even succeeded in having their own reformed system of military service adopted as the model for all the other *voiska* except the Ural. As early as 1873 the decision to scrap the model of 1867 for the new Don scheme had been taken in the main Administration of Irregular Forces, and in 1876 this decision was formalized by the military council.[27] The basic idea of using the Don, by far the largest *voisko,* as the pattern for the others with respect to military service had, of course, been the policy of 1835. It had been criticized by General Karlgof at the opening of the attempted reforms of the 1860s and discarded in the work of the St. Petersburg committee under his chairmanship. But by the mid-1870s the new Don system appeared to be the easiest way to satisfy both the largest Cossack *voisko* and the war ministry's new perception of its need for substantial numbers of Cossacks on active duty and in reserve. *Polozheniia* based on the Don model were issued for Orenburg (1876), Zabaikal (1878), Amur and Semirechie (1879), Siberia (1880), Astrakhan (1881), and Kuban and Terek (1882).[28]

The new system of Cossack military service (Ural excepted) rested on the principle of universal service for all nonnoble Cossacks, except those exempted for physical defects, enrollment in the clergy or as "trading Cossacks" or for certain specified calamities, such as destruction of one's household by fire. Service for the Cossack *dvorianstvo,* on the other hand, was voluntary. The Cossack's service liability began at age eighteen and lasted twenty years. The first three years consisted of the "preparatory rank," during which the Cossack received basic training on a part-time basis in his own *stanitsa.* Those pursuing formal education were permitted to finish before starting their service, skipping the "preparatory rank." Then came twelve years in the "combatant (*stroevoi*) rank." This, however, was divided into three "turns" (*ochered'*) of four years each. In peacetime only the first of these (those aged twenty-one–twenty-four) served on active duty, inside or outside the *voisko,* according to assignment. The second and third "turns" were on "leave" (*l'gota*), meaning that men were obliged to maintain their equipment and to participate in an annual training exercise of about four weeks. Members of the "second turn" were to maintain their horses as well; those in the "third turn" could acquire one when and if they were mobilized. In time of need, the "second turn" would be called up before the third, if the latter were needed.[29] After serving twelve years in the combatant rank, the Cossack entered the "reserve rank" for five years no longer with any obligation to maintain his equipment or participate in training. Even beyond this there was a rather theoretical *opolchenie* (militia), in which the Cossack was enrolled as long as he was physically able to serve. But Cossacks in this category were to be mobilized only in dire emergency.

The Ural were not included in this pattern, out of respect for their traditional pattern of "hiring" volunteers and those drawing unlucky lots. Although this system had much in common with the ill-fated reform of 1867, there were differences. Most particularly, the system of 1867 required nonserving Cossacks to make a modest contribution to the *voisko* treasury, whereas the Ural tradition required those not serving to pay a more substantial sum to those on active duty. This tradition was respected by the new *polozhenie* for the Ural *voisko,* which was adopted on March 9, 1874, while the Don model was still in process.[30] The *polozhenie* did not actually regulate the complex system of payments among the Cossacks, but it permitted this simply by omitting the prohibition of hiring which was to be found in the Don model. Those Ural Cossacks who chose or were chosen to serve had a twenty-two year obligation. The first two and the five final years were to be spent on "internal service" (within the *voisko*), and the middle fifteen years in the "combatant rank." Unlike the other *voisko* (on the new Don model), the Ural in this rank were not divided into "turns." The three regiments (plus a guards squadron and a training "hundred") which they were required to supply in peacetime were simply kept on duty, the personnel entering and leaving as their fifteen years began and ended. Units could, however, be shifted from one assignment to another, which would lead to revision of the hiring payments to attempt to give a greater reward to those on the most burdensome service.[31] The efforts of the authorities in St. Petersburg to respect the peculiar traditions of the Ural proved to be inadequate. A substantial number of Ural Cossacks, heirs of a long tradition of obstreperous activity, refused to obey the new regulations on the ground that they violated the traditional order as guaranteed by the imperial *gramoty*. This is not the place to narrate the resulting story of repression. It is sufficient to say that the authorities had their way; about 2,500 Ural Cossacks were ordered expelled from the *voisko* in the course of this achievement.[32]

In summary, reform of Cossack military service during the Miliutin era had a tortuous course. The regime changed its objectives in mid-stream, shifting from an intended drastic reduction of Cossack forces and the diminution of their peculiarly military vocation to a system aimed at maximum exploitation of the military potentialities of the *soslovie*. The pattern of service that emerged was well suited to Miliutin's general program of building a large army of trained reserves. In theory, the Cossacks were well treated since they, like most of the rest of the people, were subject to universal military obligation. Most non-Cossacks who were under this obligation did not actually serve because the state could not afford to train them; they were allowed to draw lucky numbers, to say nothing of fairly generous exemptions based on such criteria as the number of male workers in a family. Cossacks, on the other hand, nobles excepted, almost all had to serve, or in the case of the Ural, to pay a sizable contribution. This was a substantial burden, which grew less and less supportable in later years, but it appears that a substantial body of Cossack opinion, most clearly identifiable on the Don, preferred nearly universal military service to the trend of the reform of 1867; that favored voluntary service, but at the risk of merging the Cossacks with the less privileged *sosloviia,* the *podatnye.* Thus, for all the bureaucracy's vacillations and its heavy-handed enforcement of a "reform" on unwilling Ural, it emerged with a scheme of Cossack military service which was at least minimally acceptable to the Cossacks, yet satisfied the state's desire for a large force of cavalry at a bargain price.

Notes

Abbreviations:

SPRKVM — *Sbornik pravitel'stvennykh rasporiazhenii po kazachym voi-skam* (SPB, 1870–1916). Annual volumes, compiling laws and quasi laws on Cossacks, issued by the war ministry covering 1865–1915).

SVM — D. A. Skalon, ed., *Stoletie voennago ministerstva* (SPB, 1902). All citations in this paper are to vol. XI, A. I. Nikol'skii, *Glavnoe upravlenie kazach'ykh voisk.*

VOVM — *Vsepoddanneishii otchet o deistviiakh voennago ministerstva* (SPB, 1858–1912).

1. M. Khoroshkhin, *Kazach'i voiska* (SPB, 1881), 307. Also 31 percent of the horse artillery. The total Cossack force on active duty at the end of the reign of Alexander I was more than 51,000 officers and men. *VOVM,* 1881, 8.

2. Forrest A. Miller, *Dmitrii Miliutin and the Reform Era in Russia* (Nashville, Tenn., 1968); P. A. Zaionchkovskii, *Voennie reformy v 1860–1870 godov v Rossii* (Moscow, 1952).

3. There is no intelligible English equivalent of *voisko* (plural *voiska*). *Army* is misleading when applied to the smaller *voiska* and does not convey that a civilian society is also involved. *Host* is vague, probably implying some kind of vast, primitive force, which scarcely applies qualitatively or quantitatively to the Cossacks of the later empire.

4. The details may be confirmed in *Polozhenie ob upravlenie Donskago voiska* (SPB, 1835). A clear synopsis appears in M. I. Bogdanovich, *Istori-cheskii ocherk deiatel'nosti voennago upravleniia v Rossii v pervoe dvadtsati-piatiletie blagopoluchnago tsarstvovaniia gosudaria imperatora Aleksandra Nikolaevicha (1855–1880 gg.)* (SPB, 1879–80), I: 284–293.

5. Concerning the general evolution of the military colonies, see Richard E. Pipes, "The Russian Military Colonies," *Journal of Modern History,* no. 3 (1950): 205–219; Alan D. Ferguson, "The Russian Military Settlements 1825–1966," *Essays in Russian History,* eds. Alan D. Ferguson and Alfred Levin (Hamden, Conn., 1964), 109–128. The predominantly Cossack interest

of this office was indicated by the name "Main Administration of Cossack Troops," adopted in 1879.

6. Bogdanovich, I: 340–41; SPRKV, II, #109.

7. SVM, 406–407.

8. *Ibid.*, 410.

9. *Ibid.*, 411.

10. *Ibid.*, 410.

11. *Ibid.*, 464–66.

12. Bogdanovich, III: 225; Zaionchkovskii, 81.

13. Zaionchkovskii, 81. The Don proposal itself is not available to the writer, but its essential points are discussed in a slightly later letter of protest from the Don leadership to the War Ministry. SVM, 472–73.

14. SPRKV, I–II,#91.

15. SVM, 426–27.

16. VOVM, 1866.

17. SVM, 467–69.

18. *Ibid.*, 471; S. G. Svatikov, *Rossiia i Don* (Vienna, 1924), 349.

19. SPRKV, 1967, #81.

20. SVM, 469–70.

21. *Ibid.*, 472.

22. Miller, 198, 225.

23. E.g., Khoroshkhin, 248.

24. Bogdanovich, V: 197.

25. SVM, 474–75.

26. SPRKV, 1975, #32.

27. SVM, 475; SPRKV, 1976, #46.

28. SVM, 475–76, 610.

29. *Svod zakonov Rossiiskoi Imperii,* #409–503.

30. SPRKV, 1974, #18.

31. Detailed descriptions of the system of hiring may be found in Khoroshkhin, 250–52 and I. Kostenko, "Uralskoe kazach'e voisko. Istoricheskii ocherk i sistema otbyvaniia voinskoi povinosti," *Voennyi sbornik,* no. 9, 10, 11 (1978).

32. SVM, 483–93.

Gunther E. Rothenberg

Conclusions

Military frontier systems were used throughout history to provide protection for extended and exposed border regions. Such systems, whether manned by regular garrisons, specially recruited elements, or local fighting men, were designed primarily as buffer zones; in case of a major attack, they had to be supported by field armies. Prolonged conditions of danger and military control produced special institutions and lifestyles in such regions, though commonly when the threat disappeared, these institutions were dismantled and the region reverted to normal civilian control. There were, however, exceptions. Both the Habsburg Military Border and the Russian Cossack hosts continued their military roles long after the need for an active frontier defense had passed and, while retaining special characteristics, became part of the regular defense establishment of the two empires.

Except for a brief survey by Max Jähns published in 1885, there is no systematic, comprehensive, comparative treatment of these various military frontier systems.[1] Perhaps the difficulties of dealing with a subject stretching from antiquity to our own day and encompassing areas in Europe, Asia, the Americas, and the Middle East have been too formidable. Therefore even a limited comparison may be useful and this is especially true of the Habsburg and Russian military frontier systems, both long-lasting and both surviving as peculiar military institutions for many decades after their original mission had ended. Although none of the three studies presented in this section covers the entire topic, the essays do provide comparative data and reveal marked parallels, similarities, and congruences.

The origins of the Habsburg Military Border and of Cossackdom date to the end of the first quarter of the sixteenth century. At that time, the Ottoman Turks had consolidated their hold over the Balkans, overrun Hungary, and established themselves on the northern shores of the Black Sea. Along the entire line from the Adriatic to the Volga the Turks and their allies, especially the Tatars of the Crimea, were pressing against neighboring Christian polities — the Holy Roman Empire, Poland-Lithuania, and Muscovy. And although changes in the art of war, especially the rise of a powerful infantry and the general adoption of firearms, would favor the Christians over the long run, the full impact of these developments was but slowly felt in Pontic and Danubic Europe. Beset by domestic and foreign complications, the three powers were rarely able to employ their first-line troops for extended periods. Though the Ottomans had similar difficulties, their numerous irregular forces, mounted for the most part, held the upper hand in the continual small border warfare. Their raids devastated and depopulated large regions, creating almost a political, economic, and demographic vacuum.[2]

These conditions enabled small groups of hardy local survivors, joined by refugees from Turkish territory, adventurers, and runaway serfs from the Christian hinterland, to establish rough-and-ready warrior communities free from the bonds of servitude. These Cossacks, haiduks, uskoks, Pribegs, Vlachs, and others — all designations without definite ethnographic meaning at that time — lived by hunting, fishing, and marginal agriculture, and met Moslem incursions with ambush and counterraid. Neighboring Christian princes engaged these war bands to bolster their modest frontier defenses. In the west, the Austrian rulers employed such elements as early as 1522; on the southeastern marches of Poland-Lithuania, Cossack groups were utilized by 1527. These fighters were not considered peasant-soldiers, but served as freebooting auxiliaries under leaders of their choice, and their raids did not necessarily discriminate between Christians and Moslems.[3]

This initial stage was short-lived. The original war bands conformed to the *masaic* pattern of military organization — Andreski's term, coined to describe communities combining a high military participation ratio and strong group cohesion with low subordination.[4] These characteristics were useful only for small groups; continued Turkish and Tatar pressure demanded a higher degree of organization, greater numbers, and increased command and control. The Christian rulers took steps to expand the number of these useful, if occasionally embarrassing, auxiliaries by attracting new recruits and imposing controls. They issued charters and promises of rights and immunities and also appointed officers to supervise the emerging frontier systems. On the Austrian frontier the process of integrating these *Grenzer* elements into the state service was, at least in theory, accomplished by 1553, though elected officials and a degree of autonomy survived into the eighteenth century. Transforming Cossackdom was more difficult. Although by 1571 both Poland and Muscovy had established detachments of "registered" Cossacks, men who in return for small annual payments accepted a degree of discipline, major Cossack communities retained independent roles for almost two hundred years. Finally, as the first two papers in this section show, Cossacks as well as *Grenzer* were compelled to submit to a change from "essentially autonomous societies into service-bearing groups," rigidly controlled by bureaucratic officials of the absolutist Habsburg and Romanov dynasties.

The process was slow, to be sure; on occasion it faltered and even halted. Nonetheless, it was irreversible. Two major, and ultimately conflicting, developments combined to change the status of the frontiersmen. From the outset these free communities had posed a sharp challenge to the landed nobility of the hinterland who regarded them as dangerous examples for their serfs. Only the continued Turkish-Tatar threat had prevented these influential aristocrats from forcing the crown to revoke the privileges enjoyed by the *Grenzer* and Cossacks. At that, whenever the threat receded, the noble landowners had attempted outright and unwarranted encroachments, fomenting considerable resentment. The second development was the steady growth and increased sophistication of the central state apparatus of the Habsburgs and Romanovs. The ultimate objective of the absolute monarchs was curtailing aristocratic power, but this also brought the frontier communities under much tighter supervision and control.

Until about 1650 neither the Habsburg emperors nor the Russian tsars, one preoccupied with the religious struggle in Germany, the other paralyzed by the "time of troubles" in Russia, had military energy to spare for extended operations in the border regions. The irregular frontier establishment had filled this void and had achieved the imperial purpose. From about 1600 on, the irregular Christian forces had matched the Moslem irregulars and provided an effective screen against most raids. After 1650, however, the large Christian empires began to consolidate their state apparatus, a process made possible by the new standing military forces which provided the government with the power to collect taxes and so to support standing armies. The process was more advanced in the Habsburg empire than in Russia. Tempered in the crucible of the Thirty Years War, imperial forces proved capable of halting the Turkish advance and later moving on to reconquer Hungary. By the end of the century, Russia too had acquired a combat-proven regular army organized along Western lines. Increasingly, the services of the frontier fighters became dispensable. The frontiersmen now faced the choice: complete submission to the crown, retaining a highly regimented military status, or being reduced to serfdom. The process took several decades but by

1740, Professor McNeill noted "the supremacy of the bureaucratic empire over any more local form of political organization had been definitely demonstrated in Danubian and Pontic Europe."[5] *Grenzer* and Cossacks, albeit not without revolts and mutinies lasting until the turn of the century, opted for military status and became part of the regular forces of the crown though enjoying special status.

Austrian and Russian rulers valued the frontiersmen in their new roles and used them as self-sustaining instruments for expansion and as reservoirs of manpower in their wars. With the administration of these military border zones ever more bureaucratized, the inhabitants were compelled to assume heavier military and service obligations. Because of the economic burdens this placed on small households, the Russian authorities partially adopted the South Slav extended family, the *zadruga,* already the social backbone of the Military Border. This ameliorated conditions somewhat, but the new burdens and the new officials aroused resentment, and both *Grenzer* and Cossacks frequently revolted, especially when ordered on foreign service. Some of these revolts did assume large proportions, but they never had the support of entire border populations and were suppressed by regular troops.

From the mid-eighteenth century on, fighting men from the frontiers appeared on the battlefields of Central Europe, earning reputations as effective light troops. Although this record was marred by indiscipline and brutality, their performance induced successive Austrian and Russian rulers to expand the system and to create new *Grenzer* and Cossack regiments, on occasion, incorporating unwilling populations into the framework. The problems of discipline were resolved by the emergence of native officers, especially at the all-important company, squadron, or regimental level. Economic stability was sought by cameralist means, above all, by strict regulation of economic life. Basically, both governments concerned wanted to keep the frontiersmen as closed, agriculturally based warrior societies imbued with a high degree of subordination.

The results were mixed. By 1800 there were no more mutinies, but both Austria and Russia heard complaints that the imposition of discipline had ruined the natural fighting aptitudes of the frontier troops. Yet as late as 1812, one foreign observer, General Wilson, still felt that the Cossack tendencies to loot and plunder were counterproductive.[6] Even so, although the performance of these troops under the changed conditions of the French and Napoleonic wars was uneven, after 1815 both empires retained these establishments. They were valued because they provided large numbers of men at low cost and even more perhaps because the once unruly *Grenzer* and Cossacks now were considered reliable guardians of the established order. Although historically they had been turbulent, these groups developed a corporate ethos stressing their special relationship with the dynasty and their long tradition of soldiering. Reliability of these troops was enhanced because, as long as serfdom continued in Austria and Russia, military status, even with harsh discipline and economic restrictions, was preferable.

Even so, efforts to keep these establishments uncontaminated by the major political, social, and economic currents of the nineteenth century proved difficult, more in the relatively advanced Austrian empire than in Russia. As the years passed, with a rising tide of nationalism and liberalism, maintaining closed military societies became more difficult. This was recognized as early as 1847 by an Austrian military official who wrote, "the system is not well suited to highly developed countries."[7] Cossack institutions were stabilized, but the *Grenzer* regiments made their last major contributions during the 1848–49 revolutions. Thereafter, their status became more and more precarious as national and economic discontent manifested itself within the ranks. The settlement with Hungary and the introduction of general conscription in 1867 spelled the end of the institution.

By contrast, as the third essay shows, the Cossack system remained viable. Numbering about two and a half million souls, the Cossacks, until the era following the Crimean War, formed a separate military caste, differentiated from ordinary subjects of the empire by well-defined rights and duties, and maintaining, at little expense to the state, a large proportion of the mounted troops. The reforms of Alexander II relaxed many of the special regulations. Mercantile and industrial interests wanted to exploit the natural resources of the Don and Kuban Cossack regions; hence in 1867, non-Cossacks were granted permission to own land within Cossack territories. Emancipation of the serfs in 1861 and the introduction of general military service in 1870–74 further blurred the distinction between the Cossacks and the peasantry. Efforts to overhaul the Cossack system during the reign of Alexander II alternated between an initial scheme to make service voluntary and desire to retain the greatest possible number of men. The latter objective finally prevailed. Although, especially in the Don and Kuban regions, the influx of alien elements diluted Cossack society, very substantial Cossack formations continued to exist until the end of the tsarist regime.

The Cossacks — loyal to the tsar and feared for their brutality — became one of the main supports of the imperial government and were repeatedly used to suppress popular unrest and uprisings. Their loyalty to the regime was due, in part, to the reforms undertaken by Miliutin, but more importantly, loyalty rested on the government's ability to coopt important elements of Cossack society and to create a myth of Cossack history as "a chronicle of endless service to the tsar."[8] The importance of such myths and traditions should not be underrated. They were important in holding the allegiance of the *Grenzer* after 1815 and later formed the basis for the extraordinary and unexpected cohesiveness of the Austro-Hungarian army into which the Military Border was absorbed.

The case studies of the Military Border and of Cossackdom reveal marked similarities. They seem to show that it was possible to transform temporary irregular frontier defense arrangements into permanent and regular military establishments. In both instances, the transformation was violently opposed, though once accomplished, the new institutions proved amazingly viable for prolonged periods. This success appears to have been owing to the rise of groups of native officers who demonstrated that capable leadership, discipline, and indoctrination — which many would call *tradition* — could turn difficult recruits into reliable and effective troops and that these factors could maintain military cohesion for a considerable time even in face of hostile and disintegrative political and socioeconomic trends. Both institutions came to an end, of course, but only after having left a permanent imprint on the military affairs and history of East and East Central Europe.

Notes

1. Max Jähns, *Heeresverfassung und Völkerleben* (Berlin, 1885).

2. William H. McNeill, *Europe's Steppe Frontier 1500–1800* (Chicago, 1964), 22–31.

3. See for example Gunther E. Rothenberg, "Venice and the Uskoks of Senj: 1537–1618," *Journal of Modern History* 33 (1961): 148–50.

4. Stanislav Andreski, *Military Organization and Society* (Berkeley and Los Angeles, 1968), 140–41.

5. McNeill, 182.

6. Cited in Gunther E. Rothenberg, *The Art of Warfare in the Age of Napoleon* (Bloomington, Ind., 1978), 198–99.

7. Carl Freiherr Pidoll zu Quintenbach, *Einige Worte über die russische Militär-Kolonien im Vergleiche mit der k.k. österreichischen Militär-Grenze und mit allgemeinen Betrachtungen darüber* (Vienna, 1847), 66.

8. See Longworth pp. 393–407.

Bibliography

László Alföldi and George Simor

Introduction

History underlines the importance of the topics in this volume. Some nations vanished; others were born; a few were transformed, but no land of eighteenth-century East Central Europe remained unchanged.

The works listed here support and document the views of the contributors to this volume and broaden our understanding of historical developments in that area of the world.

Most of these titles were submitted by the authors of the studies published in this volume; others were searched out and added to the list. Just as the essays analyze the historical events from various, and sometimes, opposing, viewpoints, so the bibliography tries to deal with these controversial issues in an evenhanded manner.

The more than 600 titles presented here are a selected list which will be incorporated into a projected bibliographic volume to be published after the third, concluding Conference on War and Society in East Central Europe.

The works are listed by their principal author or title, according to international bibliographic standards. The romanization of names from non-Roman alphabets follows the practice of the National Union Catalog of the Library of Congress.

We wish to thank all our colleagues for their kind cooperation and to ask for their continued help in making the final bibliographic volume as comprehensive as possible, so that it will provide scholars with a valuable research tool.

I. Reference Works

Bengescu, George. *Essai d'une notice bibliographique sur la question d'Orient: Orient européen, 1821-1897*. Paris, 1897.

Berndt, Otto. *Die Zahl im Kriege: Statistische Daten aus der neueren Kriegs-geschichte in graphischer Darstellung.* Vienna, 1897.

Bodart, Gaston. *Militärhistorisches Kriegs-lexikon (1618–1905).* Vienna, 1908.

Breslau. Osteuropa-Institut. *Osteuropäische Bibliographie.* Breslau, 1921–28. 4 vols.

Byrnes, Robert F. *Bibliography of American Publications on East Central Europe, 1945–57.* Bloomington, Ind., 1959.

Carlton, Robert G., ed. *Newspapers of East Central and Southeastern Europe in the Library of Congress.* Washington, D.C., 1965.

Conover, Helen. *The Balkans: A Selected List of References.* Washington, D.C., 1943. 5 vols.

Cust, Edward. *Annals of the Wars of the Eighteenth Century.* London, 1862. 5 vols.

Dossick, Jesse J. "Doctoral Dissertations on Russia, the Soviet Union and Eastern Europe Accepted by American, Canadian and British Universities." *Slavic Review* 24 (1965): 752–61; 25 (1966): 710–17; 26 (1967): 705–712; 27 (1968): 694–704.

Hanusch, G. "Osteuropa-Dissertationen." *Jahrbücher für Geschichte Osteuropas: Neue Folge* 1, No. 4 (1953), Supplement, 1–44; 2, No. 2 (1954), Supplement, 45–72; 3, No. 1 (1955), Supplement, 74–114; 4, No. 3 (1956), 115–52; 6, No. 4 (1958), Supplement, 153–94; 8, No. 2 (1960), Supplement, 195–239.

Horecky, Paul L., ed. *Southeastern Europe: A Guide to Basic Publications.* Chicago, 1969.

————. *East Central Europe: A Guide to Basic Publications.* Chicago, 1969.

Horecky, Paul L. and Carlton, Robert G. *The USSR and Eastern Europe: Periodicals in Western Languages.* 3d ed. Washington, D.C., 1967.

Horecky, Paul L. and Kraus, David H. *East Central and Southeast Europe: A Handbook of Library and Archival Resources in North America.* Santa Barbara, 1976.

Kerner, Robert J., ed. *Slavic Europe: A Selected Bibliography in the Western European Languages, Comprising History, Languages and Literatures.* Cambridge, Mass., 1918.

Kramm, Heinrich. *Bibliographie historischer Zeitschriften, 1939–1951.* Marburg, 1954. 3. Lieferung.

Lewanski, Richard C. *A Bibliography of Slavic Dictionaries.* New York, 1959–65. 3 vols.

Munich. Südost-Institut. *Südosteuropa-Bibliographie.* Munich, 1956–

New York Public Library, Slavonic Division. *Dictionary Catalog of the New York Public Library.* Boston, 1959. 26 vols.

Niederhauser, E. "Beiträge zur Bibliographie der Geschichte der slawischen Völker in der ungarischen bürgerlichen Geschichtsschreibung." *Studia Slavica* (Budapest) 6 (1961): 457–73.

Pohler, Johann. *Bibliotheca historico-militaris: systematische Übersicht der Erscheinungen aller Sprachen auf dem Gebiet der Geschichte der Kriege und*

Kriegswissenschaft seit Erfindung der Buchdruckerkunst bis zum Schluss des Jahres 1880. Leipzig, 1887–99. Reprint, 4 vols. New York, 1961.

Ruggles, Melville, and Mostecky, Vlaclav. *Russian and East European Publications in the Libraries of the United States*. New York, 1960.

Savadjian Léon, ed. *Bibliographie balkanique*. Paris, 1931–39. 8 vols.

Strakhovsky, Leonid, ed. *A Handbook of Slavic Studies*. Cambridge, Mass., 1949.

Sztachova, Jirina. *Mid-Europe: A Selective Bibliography*. New York, 1953.

II. General Histories

Ascher, Abraham; Halasi-Kun, Tibor; and Király, Béla K. *The Mutual Effects of the Islamic and Judeo-Christian Worlds: The East European Pattern*. New York, 1979.

Braun, Maximilian. *Die Slaven auf dem Balkan*. Leipzig, 1941.

Chlebowczyk, Jósef. *Procesy narodotwórcze we wschodniej Europie Środkowej w dobie kapitalizmu (od schyłku XVIII do początkow XX w.)*. Warsaw, 1975.

Coles, Paul. *The Ottoman Impact on Europe*. New York, 1968.

Cross, Samuel H. *Slavonic Civilization through the Ages*. Cambridge, Mass., 1948.

Čubrilović, Vaso. "Politički uzroci seoba na Balkanu od 1860–1880 godine." *Glasnik Geografskog Društva* (Belgrade) 16 (1930): 26–48.

Djordjević, Dimitrije. "Uloga istoricisma u formiranju balkanskih država XIX veka." *Zbornik Filozofskog Faculteta Beograd* (Belgrade) 10 (1968): 309–326.

_____. "The Impact of the State on Nineteenth Century Balkan Social, Economic and Political Developments," *IIIe Congrès international d'études du sud-est européen histoire C 1*, pp. 69–83. Bucharest, 1974.

_____. "Balkan versus European Enlightenment, Parallelism and Dissonances." *East European Quarterly* 9 (1975): 487–97.

Dvornik, Francis. *The Slavs in European History and Civilization*. New Brunswick, N.J., 1962.

Fischer-Galati, Stephen, ed. *Man, State, and Society in East European History*. New York, 1970.

Gavrilović, Slavko. *Prilog istoriji trgovine i migracije Balkan-Podunavlje XVIII i XIX veka*. Belgrade, 1969.

Gewehr, Wesley M. *The Rise of Nationalism in the Balkans, 1800–1930*. New York, 1931.

Gibb, H.A.R., and Bowen, Harold. *Islamic Society and the West I: Islamic Society in the Eighteenth Century*. London, 1950.

Grothusen, Klaus-Detlev, ed. *Die wirtschaftliche und soziale Entwicklung Südosteuropas im 19. und 20. Jahrhundert*. Munich, 1969.

Hristov, Hristo. "The Agrarian Problem and the National Liberation Movement in the Balkans," *Actes du premier Congrès international des études sud-est-européennes,* pp. 65–70 (Sofia), 1968.

Jelavich, Charles. *Tsarist Russia and Balkan Nationalism: Russian Influence in the Internal Affairs of Bulgaria and Serbia, 1876–1886.* Berkeley, 1958.

———. *Language and Area Studies: East Central and Southeastern Europe.* Chicago, 1969.

Jelavich, Charles, and Jelavich, Barbara, eds. *The Balkans in Transition: Essays on the Development of Balkan Life and Politics since the 18th Century.* New York, 1963.

Király, Béla K. ed. *Tolerance and Movements of Religious Dissent in Eastern Europe.* Boulder, Colo., 1975.

Kohn, Hans. *Pan Slavism: Its History and Ideology.* Notre Dame, Ind., 1953.

McNeill, William H. *Europe's Steppe Frontier, 1500–1800.* Chicago, 1964.

Miller, William. *The Ottoman Empire and Its Successors, 1801–1927.* Cambridge, 1927.

Pascu, Stephan, *et al.,* "Mouvements paysans du centre et du sud-est de l'Europe du XV au XX siècle," *XXᵉ Congrès international des sciences historiques: Rapports, IV,* pp. 211–35. Vienna.

Rajić, Jovan. *Istoriia raznyh slavenskih narodov, naipače Bolgar, Horvatov i Serbov.* Vienna, 1794–95. 4 vols. and supplement.

Sanders, Irvin T. *Rural Society.* Englewood Cliffs, N.J., 1977.

Shirot, Daniel. *Social Change in a Peripheral Society: The Creation of a Balkan Colony.* New York, 1976.

Skowronek, Jerzy. *Polityka bałkańska hotelu Lambert (1833–1856).* Warsaw, 1976.

Stadtmüller, Georg. *Geschichte Südosteuropas.* Munich, 1950.

Stavrianos, Leften S. *The Balkans since 1453.* New York, 1958.

———. "Antecedents to the Balkan Revolutions of the Nineteenth Century." *Journal of Modern History* 29 (1975): 335–48.

Stojanović, Mihailo D. *The Great Powers and the Balkans, 1875–1878.* Cambridge, 1939.

Stojančević, Vladimir. *Južnoslovenski narodi u Osmanskom carstvu od Jedrenskog mira 1829 do Pariskog kongresa 1856.* Belgrade, 1971.

Sugar, Peter F. "The Southern Slav Image of Russia in the Nineteenth Century." *Journal of Central European Affairs* 21 (1961): 45–52.

Sugar Peter F., and Lederer Ivo, eds. *Nationalism in Eastern Europe.* Seattle, 1969.

Sugar, Peter F. *Southeastern Europe under Ottoman Rule, 1354–1804.* Seattle, 1977.

Sumner, B. H. *Russia and the Balkans, 1870–1880.* Oxford, 1937.

Villari, L. *The Balkan Question.* London, 1905.

Wolff, Robert Lee. *The Balkans in Our Time.* Cambridge, Mass., 1974.

Tudorov, Nikolai. *Balkanskiat grad XV–XIX vek; socialno-ikonomichesko i demografsko razvite.* Sofia, 1972.

Turczynski, Emanuel. *Konfession und Nation: Zur Frühgeschichte der serbischen und rumänischen Nationalbildung.* Düsseldorf, 1976.

III. Wars and Revolutions

A. General

Andreski, Stanislav. *Military Organization and Society.* Berkeley, 1968.

Behrenhorst, G. H. von. *Betrachtungen über die Kriegskunst.* 2d ed. Leipzig, 1978. 2 vols.

Corvisier, André. *Armées et sociétés en Europe de 1494 à 1789.* Paris, 1976.

Djordjević, Dimitrije. *Revolutions nationales des peuples balkaniques, 1804-1914.* Belgrade, 1965.

Fischer-Galati, Stephen. "Revolutionary Activity in the Balkans from Lepanto to Kuchuk-Kainardji." *Südost-Forschungen* 21 (1962): 194-213.

_____. "Revolutionary Activity in the Balkans in the Eighteenth Century," *Actes du Premier Congrès International des Études Balkaniques et Sud-Est Européennes,* Vol. 4. pp. 327-37. Sofia, 1969.

Fuller, J.F.C. *The Conduct of War, 1789-1961: A Study of the Impact of the French, Industrial, and Russian Revolutions on War and Its Conduct.* New Brunswick, N.J., 1961.

Jähns, Max. *Heeresverfassungen und Völkerleben.* Berlin, 1885.

Langer, William L. *Political and Social Upheaval, 1832-1852.* New York, 1969.

McNeill, William H. *Europe's Steppe Frontier, 1500-1800.* Chicago, 1964.

Ralston, D. B., ed. *Soldiers and States: Civil Military Relations in Modern Europe.* Boston, 1966.

Horsetzky, Adolf von. *Kriegsgeschichtliche Übersicht der wichtigsten Feldzüge seit 1792.* 7th ed. Vienna, 1913.

B. The Great Northern War, 1700-1721

Fuller, J.F.C. *A Military History of the Western World.* New York, 1954-56. 3 vols., 2: 156-86.

Hatton, Ragnhild. *Charles XII of Sweden.* London, 1968.

Potter, G. R., et al., eds. *The New Cambridge Modern History.* 14 vols. Cambridge, 1957-70, 6: 648-833.

Schuyler, Eugene. *Peter the Great, Emperor of Russia.* New York, 1884. 2 vols.

Um die polnische Krone: Sachsen und Polen während des Nordischen Krieges, 1700-1721. Berlin, 1962.

C. The Hungarian Insurrection, 1703-1711

Acsády, Ignác. *Magyarország története I. Lipót és I. József korában (1657-1711).* Budapest, 1898.

Bánkuti, Imre. *A kurucok első dunántúli hadjárata (1704 január-április).* Budapest, 1975.

_____. *Rákóczi hadserege 1703-1711.* Budapest, 1976.

Esze, Tamás. *II. Rákóczi Ferenc tiszántúli hadjárata.* Budapest, 1951.

Fiedler, Joseph, ed. *Actenstücke zur Geschichte Franz Rákóczy und seiner Verbindung mit dem Auslande aus den Papieren Ladislas Kökényesdis von Vetes . . . 1705–1715.* Fontes Rerum Austriacarum, vols. 9, 17, Vienna, 1855, 1858; *Archiv für österreichische Geschichte,* vol. 44, Vienna, 1871.

Hengelmüller von Hengevár, Ladislas. *Hungary's Fight for National Existence: or, the History of the Great Uprising Led by Francis Rákóczi II, 1703–1711.* London, 1913.

Ingrao, Charles. *In Quest and Crisis: Emperor Joseph I and the Habsburg Monarchy.* West Lafayette, Ind., 1979.

Köpeczi, Béla. *La France et la Hongrie au debut du XVIIIᵉ siècle.* Budapest, 1971.

Köpeczi, Béla, ed. *A Rákóczi-szabadságharc és Európa.* Budapest, 1970.

Köpeczi, Béla, and Várkonyi, Ágnes R. *Rákóczi tükör, naplók, jelentések, emlékiratok a szabadságharcról.* Budapest, 1973.

———— and ————. *II. Rákóczi Ferenc.* 2d enl. ed. Budapest, 1976.

Ingrao, Charles. *In Quest and Crisis: Emperor Joseph I and the Habsburg Monarchy,* West Lafayette, Ind., 1979.

Köpeczi, Béla. *La France et la Hongrie au debut du XVIIIᵉ siècle.* Budapest, 1971.

Márki, Sándor. *II. Rákóczi Ferenc.* Budapest, 1907–1910. 3 vols.

Molnár, Mátyás, ed. *A Rákóczi-szabadságharc vitás kérdései: tudományos emlékűlés, 1976 január 29–30.*

Pach, P. Z. "Le problème du rassemblement des forces nationales pendant la guerre d'indépendence de François II. Rákóczi." *Acta Historica* 3 (1956): 95–113.

II. Rákóczi Ferenc emlékiratai. Budapest, 1951.

Simonyi, Ernő, ed. *Angol diplomáciai iratok II. Rákóczi Ferencz korára.* Budapest, 1871–77. 3 vols.

Thaly, Kálmán, ed. *Archivum Rákóczianum.* Budapest, 1874.

Várkonyi, Ágnes. "A jobbágyság osztályharca a Rákóczi szabadságharc idején." *Történelmi Szemle* 7 (1964): 338–75.

D. *The War of the Austrian Succession, 1740–48*

Coxe, William. *History of the House of Austria.* 4th ed., 4 vols. London, 1895, 3: 232–480.

Dorn, Walter L. *Competition for Empire, 1740–1763.* New York, 1940.

Germany. Greater General Staff. *Die Kriege Friedrichs des Grossen.* Berlin, 1890–95. 6 vols.

Horowitz, Sidney. "Franco-Russian Relations, 1740–1746." Ph.D. dissertation, New York University, 1951.

Khevenhüller-Metsch, J. J. *Aus der Zeit Maria Theresias: Tagebuch des Fürsten Johann Josef Khevenhüller-Metsch, kaiserlicher Oberhofmeister, 1742–1777.* Vienna, 1907–1912. 8 vols.

Spannagl-Heitmar, Auguste. "Beiträge zur Geschichte des österreichischen Erbfolgekrieges." Ph.D. dissertation. University of Vienna, 1949.

E. *The Seven Years War, 1756–63*

Andreas, Willy. *Friedrich der Grosse und der siebenjährige Krieg.* Leipzig, 1940.

Entick, John. *The General History of the Late War.* 3d ed., 5 vols. London, 1766.

Germany. Greater General Staff. *Die Kriege Friedrichs des Grossen: Der Siebenjährige Krieg.* Berlin, 1901–1919. 12 vols.

Ilchester, Earl of, and Longford-Brooke, eds. and trans. *Correspondence of Catherine the Great When Grand-Duchesse with Sir Charles Hanbury-Williams and Letters from Count Poniatowski.* London, 1928.

Jomini, Henri. *Treatise on Grand Military Operations: or a Critical and Military History of the Wars of Frederick the Great.* 2 vols. with atlas. New York, 1865.

Kaplan, Herbert H. *Russia and the Outbreak of the Seven Years' War.* Berkeley, 1968.

Konopczyński, Władysław. *Polska w dobie wojny siedmioletniej.* Cracow, 1909–1911. 2 vols.

Korobkov, N. *Semiletniaia voina (deistviia rossi v 1756–1762 gg.).* Moscow, 1940.

Lloyd, Henry. *The History of the Late War in Germany between the King of Prussia, and the Empress of Germany and Her Allies.* London, 1781. 2 vols.

Ranke, Leopold von. *Der Ursprung des siebenjährigen Krieges.* Leipzig, 1871.

Tielke, J. G. *An Account of Some of the Remarkable Events of the War between the Prussians and Russians from 1756 to 1763.* London, 1787. 2 vols.

F. *Cossack Insurrections during the Eighteenth Century*

Alexander, John Thomas. *Autocratic Politics in a National Crisis: The Imperial Russian Government and Pugachev's Revolt, 1773–1775.* Bloomington, Ind., 1969.

Dimitriev-Mamonov, A. I. *Pugachevski bunt v zaurale i sibiri.* St. Petersburg, 1907.

Fenomenov, M. Y. *Razinovshchina i Pugachevshchina.* Moscow, 1923.

Firsov, N. N. *Pugachevshchina: opyt sotsiologo-psikhologicheskoi kharakteristiki.* St. Petersburg, 1907.

Gaisinovich, A. E. *La revolte de Pougatchev.* Paris, 1938.

Longworth, Philip. "The Last Great Cossack-Peasant Rising." *Journal of European Studies* No. 3 (1973): 1–35.

———. "Peasant Leadership and the Pugachev Revolt." *Journal of Peasant Studies* 2, 2 (1975): 183–205.

Marodin, V. V., ed. *Krestyanskaya voina v Rossii v 1773–1775 godakh: vosstaniye Pugacheva.* Leningrad, 1961–70. 3 vols.

Ovchinnikov, R. V., *et al.*, eds. *Dokumenty stavki ye. I. Pugacheva.* Moscow, 1975.

Tkhorzhevski, S. T. *Pugachevshchina v pomeshchichei rossi.* Moscow, 1930.

G. *The Napoleonic Wars in East Central Europe, 1792–1815*

Askenazy, Szymon. *Napoléon et la Pologne.* Paris, 1925.

Bay, Ferenc. *Napóleon Magyarországon: A császár és katonái Győr városában.* Budapest, 1941.

Boppe, A. *L'Albanie et Napoléon (1797–1814).* Paris, 1914.

Dupuy, Trevor N. *The Battle of Austerlitz.* New York, 1968.

Handelsman, M. *Napoléon et la Pologne (1806–1807).* Paris, 1909.

Kisfaludy, Sándor. *Geschichte der Insurrection des Adels von Ungarn im Jahre 1809 und 1810.* Győr, 1931.

Kiss, István. *Az utolsó nemesi felkelés.* Budapest, 1910.

Montesquio-Fezensac, R. *The Russian Campaign, 1812.* Athens, Ga., 1970.

Palmer, Alan. *Napoleon in Russia: The 1812 Campaign.* New York, 1967.

Zych, G. *Armia Kiestwa Warszawskiego, 1807–1812.* Warsaw, 1961.

H. *The First and Second Serbian Insurrections, 1804–1817*

Čubrilović, Vaso. *Prvi srpski ustanak i bosanski Srbi.* Belgrade, 1939.

Jakšić, Grgur. *L'Europe et la résurrection de la Serbie (1804–1834).* Paris, 1907.

Jelavich, Charles and Jelavich, Barbara. *The Establishment of the Balkan National States, 1804–1920.* Seattle, 1977.

Kállay, Béla von. *Geschichte des serbischen Aufstandes, 1807–1810.* Vienna, 1910.

Karadžić, Vuk. *Prvi i drugi srpski ustanak.* Belgrade, 1947.

Meriage, Lawrence. "The First Serbian Uprising (1804–1813): National Revival or a Search for Regional Security." *Canadian Review of Studies in Nationalism* 4 (1977): 187–205.

Novaković, Stojan. *Vaskrs države srpske: političko-istorijska studija o Prvom srpskom ustanku, 1804–1813.* Belgrade, 1904.

———. *Die Wiedergeburt des serbischen Staates (1804–1813).* Sarajevo, 1912.

Paxton, Roger. "Nationalism and Revolution: A Reexamination of the Origins of the First Serbian Insurrection, 1804–1807." *East European Quarterly* 6 (1972): 337–62.

Shaw, Stanford J. *Between Old and New: The Ottoman Empire under Sultan Selim III, 1789–1807.* Cambridge, Mass., 1971.

Šobajić, Petar. "Udeo dinarskih plemena u Prvom srpskom ustanku." *Glasnik Etnografskog Instituta SAN* No. 2–3 (1957): 81–96.

Stojančević, Vladimir. "Prvi srpski ustanak i južnoslovenske zemlje." *Istoriski Pregled* (Belgrade). No. 1 (1954): 7–16.

Vinaver, Vuk. "Istoriska tradicija u Prvom srpskom ustanku." *Istoriski Glasnik* (Belgrade) No. 1–2 (1954): 103–119.

Vucinich, Wayne S. "Marxian Interpretations of the First Serbian Revolution." *Journal of Central European Affairs* 21 (1961): 3–14.

I. The Greek War of Independence, 1821–31

Botzaris, Notis. *Visions balkaniques dans la préparation de la révolution grècque, 1789–1821.* Geneva, 1962.

Clogg, Richard, ed. *The Struggle for Greek Independence.* London, 1973.

Crowley, C. W. *The Question of Greek Independence.* Cambridge, 1930.

Dakin, Douglas. *British and American Philhellenes during the War of Greek Independence, 1821–1833.* Thessaloniki, 1955.

———. *The Greek Struggle for Independence, 1821–1833.* Berkeley, 1973.

Diamandouros, Nikiforos P., *et al. Hellenism and the First Greek War of Liberation, 1821–1830: Continuity and Change.* Thessaloniki, 1976.

Finlay, George. *History of the Greek Revolution.* Edinburgh, 1861.

Fischer-Galati, Stephen. "The Internal Macedonian Revolutionary Organization: Its Significance in Wars of Liberation." *East European Quarterly* 4 (1973): 454–72.

Gordon, Thomas. *History of the Greek Revolution.* Edinburgh, 1832.

Kolokotrones, Theodoros. *Memoirs from the Greek War of Independence, 1821–1833.* Chicago, 1969.

St. Clair, William. *That Greece Might Still Be Free: The Philhellens in the War of Independence.* Oxford, 1972.

Woodhouse, C. M. *The Greek War of Independence.* London, 1952.

———. *The Battle of Navarino.* London, 1965.

J. The First Polish Revolution, 1830–31

Dutkiewicz, J. *Francja a Polska w 1831 r.* Łódź, 1950.

Hordynski, Joseph. *History of the Late Polish Revolution and the Events of the Campaign.* 2d ed. Boston, 1833.

Leslie, R. F. *Polish Politics and the Revolution of November 1830.* London, 1956.

Meloch, M. *Sprawa włościańska w powstaniu listopadowym.* 2d. ed. Warsaw, 1948.

Rostworowski, M., ed. *Dyaryusz sejmu z r. 1830–1831.* Cracow, 1907–1912. 4 vols.

Tokarz, Wacław. *Wojna rosyjska 1830–1831.* Warsaw, 1930.

K. The 1848 Revolutions in East Central Europe

Adăniloaie, N., and Berindei, Dan, eds. *Revoluția de la 1848 în Țările Române.* Bucharest, 1974.

Andics, Erzsébet. *A nagybirtokos arisztokrácia ellenforradalmi szerepe 1848–49-ben.* Budapest, 1956–65. 2 vols.

Berindei, Dan. *Revoluția română din 1848.* Bucharest, 1974.

Birányi, Ákos. *Pesti forradalom (mártius 15–19).* Pest, 1848.

Campbell, John C. *French Influence and the Rise of Rumanian Nationalism: The Generation of 1848.* Cambridge, Mass., 1940.

Căzănişteanu, C.; Cucu, M.; and Popescu, E. *Aspecte militare ale revoluţiei din 1848 în Ţăra Româneasca.* Bucharest, 1968.

Deák, Imre, ed. *1848: a szabadságharc története levelekben ahogyan a kortársak látták.* Budapest, 1942.

Deme, László. *The Radical Left in the Hungarian Revolution of 1848.* Boulder, Colo., 1976.

Görgey, Arthur. *My Life and Acts in Hungary in the Years 1848 and 1849.* New York, 1852.

Gracza, György. *Az 1848-49-iki magyar szabadságharc története.* Budapest, 1894-98. 5 vols.

Gyalókay, Jenő, "A segesvári ütközet (1849 július 31)." *Hadtörténeti Közlemények* No. 3-4 (1932): 187-236.

Holák, J. *Politické snahy slovenské v rokoch 1848-1849.* Prague, 1936.

Kiszling, Rudolph. *Die Revolution im Kaisertum Österreich, 1848-1849.* Vienna, 1948. 2 vols.

Loghin, L., and Ucrain C. *Aspecte militare ale revoluţiei din 1848-1849 în Transilvania.* Bucharest, 1970.

Mierosławski, L. *Powstanie poznańskie w roku 1848.* Paris, 1852.

Nemesűrty, István. *"Kik érted haltak szent világszabadság": A negyvennyolcas honvéd hadsereg katonaforradalmárai.* Budapest, 1977.

Pap, Dénes, ed.,*Okmánytár Magyarország függetlenségi harczának történetéhez, 1848-1849.* Pest, 1868-69. 2 vols.

Pech, Stanley, Z. *The Czech Revolution of 1848.* Chapel Hill, N.C., 1969.

Pejaković, Stephan. *Actenstücke zur Geschichte des kroatisch-slavonischen Landtages und der nationalen Bewegung vom Jahre 1848.* Vienna, 1861.

Rakowski, K. *Powstanie poznańskie w 1848 r.* Lwów-Warsaw, 1914.

Rath, John R. *The Viennese Revolution of 1848.* Austin, 1957.

Tobolka, Z. *Politicé déjiny československeho národa od 1848 a po dnešni doby.* Prague, 1932-37. 5 vols.

Urbán, Aladár. *A nemzetőrség és honvédség szervezése 1848 nyarán.* Budapest, 1973.

Whitridge, Arnold. *Men in Crisis: The Revolutions of 1848.* New York, 1949.

L. The Crimean War, 1853-56

Baker, A. J. *The War Against Russia, 1854-1856.* New York, 1971.

Dubrovin, N. *Materialy dlia istorii Krymskoi voiny i oborony Sevastopolia.* St. Petersburg, 1871-74. 5 vols.

Kinglake, A. W. *The Invasion of the Crimea: Its Origin and an Account of Its Progress.* Edinburgh, 1863-87. 8 vols.

Krushchov, A. P. *Istoriia Oborony Sevastopolia.* St. Petersburg, 1889.

Pemberton, William B. *Battles of the Crimean War.* New York, 1962.

Schroeder, Paul V. *Austria, Great Britain and the Crimean War.* Ithaca, N.Y., 1972.

Seaton, Albert. *The Crimean War: A Russian Chronicle.* New York, 1977.
Todleben, E. *Défense de Sébastopol.* St. Petersburg, 1863.

M. The Second Polish Revolution, 1863-64

Feldman, J. *Bismarck a Polska.* 3d ed. Warsaw, 1966.
Gentzen, F. H. *Grosspolen im Januaraufstand: Das Grossherzogtum Posen 1858-1864.* Berlin, 1958.
Giller, A. *Historia powstania narodu polskiego 1861-1864.* Paris, 1867. 2 vols.
Halicz, E., *et al.,* eds. *Vosstanie 1863 goda. Materialy i dokumenty. Powstanie styczniowe. Materiały i dokumenty.* Moscow-Warsaw, 1961.
Kieniewicz, S. *Sprawa włośscianska w powstaniu styczniowym.* Wrocław, 1953.
Leslie, Robert F. *Reform and Insurrection in Russian Poland, 1856-1865.* London, 1963.
Zieliński, S. *Bitwy i potyczki 1863-1864.* Rapperswyl, 1913.

N. The Austro-Prussian War of 1866

Austria-Hungary. General Staff. *Österreichs Kämpfe im Jahre 1866.* Vienna, 1867-69. 5 vols.
Bonnal, H. *Sadowa: A Study.* London, 1907.
Craig, Gordon A. *The Battle of Königgrätz.* Philadelphia, 1964.
Friedjung, Heinrich. *Der Kampf um die Vorherrschaft in Deutschland.* 10th ed. Stuttgart-Berlin, 1916. 2 vols.
Germany. Greater General Staff. *Der Feldzug von 1866 in Deutschland.* Berlin, 1867.
Glünicke, G.J.R. *The Campaign in Bohemia, 1866.* London, 1907.
Groote, Wolfgang von, and Gersdorff, Ursula von, eds. *Entscheidung 1866.* Stuttgart, 1966.
Kavarik, Otmar. *Feldzeugmeister Benedek und der Krieg, 1866.* Leipzig, 1907.
Lettow-Vorbeck, Oskar von. *Geschichte des Krieges von 1866 in Deutschland.* Berlin, 1896-1902. 3 vols.
Maguire, Thomas M. *Notes on the Austro-Prussian War of 1866.* London, 1907.
Wagner, Arthur L. *The Campaign of Königgrätz: A Study of the Austro-Prussian Conflict in the Light of the American Civil War.* 2d ed., Kansas City, Mo., 1899. 2 vols.

O. The Bulgarian Uprising, 1875-76

Gladstone, W. E. *Lessons in Massacre.* London, 1877.
———. *The Bulgarian Horrors and the Questions of the East.* London, 1876.
Harris, David. *Britain and the Bulgarian Horrors of 1876.* Chicago, 1939.
Kinov, Ivan. *Vŭoruzhenata borba na bŭlgarskiia narod sreshtu osmanskoto gospodstvo.* Sofia, 1961.

Miller, William. *The Ottoman Empire and Its Successors, 1801-1927.* Cambridge, 1927.

Stoyanoff, Zachary. *Pages from the Autobiography of a Bulgarian Insurgent.* London, 1913.

Wirthwein, Walter G. *Britain and the Balkan Crisis, 1875-1878.* New York, 1935.

P. The Russo-Turkish War of 1877-78

Anderson, John H. *Russo-Turkish War 1877-78 in Europe.* London, 1910.

Fife-Cookson, John. *With the Armies of the Balkans and at Gallipoli in 1877-1878.* London, 1880.

Greene, F. V. *The Campaign in Bulgaria, 1877-1878.* London, 1903.

La Guerre d'Orient en 1877-1878: Étude stratégique et tactique des opérations des armées Russe et Turque. Paris, 1889. 4 vols.

Herbert, William V. *The Defense of Plevna, 1877.* London, 1895.

Maurice, F. *The Russo-Turkish War 1877: A Strategical Sketch.* London, 1906.

Pfeil, Richard von. *Experiences of a Prussian Officer in the Russian Service during the Turkish War of 1877-78.* London, 1893.

Trotha, Thilo von. *Tactical Studies on the Battles Around Plevna.* Kansas City, Mo., 1896.

R. Occupation of Bosnia-Hercegovina, 1878

Austria-Hungary. General Staff. *Die Okkupation der Bosnien und Herzegovina.* Vienna, 1879-80.

Čubrilović, Vaso. *Bosanski ustanak 1875-78.* Belgrade, 1930.

Ekmečić, Milorad. *Ustanak u Bosni 1875-78.* Sarajevo, 1960.

Radoičić, Mirko S. *Hercegovina, 1875-1878.* Nevesinje, 1961.

Veltze, Alois. *Unsere Truppen in Bosnien und der Herzegovina 1878. Einzeldarstellungen.* Vienna, 1907-1909. 5 vols.

Vukčević, Milo. *Crna gora i Hercegovina uoči rata, 1874-1876.* Cetinje, 1950.

S. The Bulgarian-Serbian War of 1885-86

Bilimek, H. *Der bulgarisch-serbische Krieg.* Vienna, 1886.

Cholet, C. R. de. *Étude sur le guerre bulgaro-serbe.* Paris, 1891.

Gopčević, S. *Bulgarien und Ostrumelien mit besonderer Berücksichtigung des Zeitraums von 1878-1886.* Leipzig, 1886.

Huhn, A. von. *Der Kampf der Bulgaren um Ihre Nationaleinheit.* Leipzig, 1886.

Sydačkoff, Bressnitz von. *Die Geschichte Serbiens vom Jahre 1868 bis auf den heutigen Tag unter den Königen Milan und Alexander.* Berlin, 1895-96.

Zhekov, N. T. *Bulgarskoto voinstvo, 1878-1928 g.* Sofia, 1928.

T. *The Greco-Turkish War of 1897*

Becker, G. *La guerre contemporaine dans les Balkans, 1897.* Paris, 1899.

Bigham, Clive. *With the Turkish Army in Thessaly.* London, 1897.

Dakin, Douglas. *The Greek Struggle in Macedonia, 1897-1913.* Thessaloniki, 1966.

Garibaldi, R. *La Camicia Rossa nella guèrra grèco-turca, 1897.* Roma, 1899.

Bolton, Frederica, trans. and ed. *The Greco-Turkish War of 1897* (By a German staff officer). London, 1898.

Nevinson, H. W. *Scenes in the Thirty Day War between Greece and Turkey, 1897.* London, 1898.

U. *Other Wars, Revolutions, and Armed Conflicts*

Austria-Hungary. General Staff. *Die Krieg in Schleswig und Jütland im Jahre 1864.* Vienna, 1870.

Berindei, Dan, and Mutaşcu, Traian. *Aspecte militare ale miscărrii revoluţionare din 1821.* 2d ed. Bucharest, 1973.

Căzănişteanu, Constantin, and Ionescu, Mihail T. *Războiul neatîrnâii României, 1877-1878.* Bucharest, 1977.

Ciachir, Nicolae. *Războiul pentru independenţa României în contextual european (1875-1878).* Bucharest, 1977.

Fischer, Alan W. *The Russian Annexation of the Crimea, 1772-1783.* Cambridge, 1970.

Čulinović, Ferdo. *Seljačke bune u Hrvatskoj.* Zagreb, 1951.

Dimitrov, Strashimir. "Serbia i Krestianskoe vostanie 1850 g. ve Blgaria." *Études balkaniques* (Sofia) 1 (1964): 49-68.

Fenzl, Otto. "Zustandekommen, Vorbereitung und Durchführung der Türkenkriege 1716-1718." Ph.D. dissertation, University of Vienna, 1950.

Gründorf, Wilhelm von. *Als Holstein österreichisch wurde.* Vienna, 1966.

Ivić, Aleksa. *Ustanak popa Jovice Ilića (1834) i bune leskovačkih i vranjanskih Srba (1842).* Zagreb, 1929.

Kosev, Dimitur. "Vstanieto na selianite v severozapadna Blgaria i negovite prichini." *Istoricheski Pregled* (Sofia) 4 (1949-50): 474-92.

Mauritz, Gertrude. "Der Wiener Frieden von 1735." Ph.D. dissertation, University of Vienna, 1956.

Mazour, Anatole G. *The First Russian Revolution, 1825: The Decembrist Movement, Its Origin, Development and Significance.* Stanford, 1973.

Nikolić, Milan. *Timočka buna 1883.* Belgrade, 1954. 2 vols.

Otetea, Andrei. *Tudor Vladimirescu şi Mişcarea Etristă în Ţările Româneşti, 1821-1822.* Bucharest, 1945.

Patachi, Liviu. *Românii în rascoala lui Petru Seghedinat, 1735.* Bucharest, 1947.

444 WAR AND SOCIETY IN EAST CENTRAL EUROPE

Stojančević, Vladimir. "Narodnooslobodilački pokret u niškom kraju 1833 i 1834-5 godine." *Istoriski Časopis* (Belgrade) No. 5 (1955): 427-53.

Wylly, Harold C. *The Campaign of Magenta and Solferino, 1859.* London, 1907.

Zychowski. M. *Rok 1846 w Rzeczypospolitej Krakowskieg i Galicji.* Warsaw, 1965.

IV. The Nations and Their Armed Forces

A. Albania

Chekrezi, Constantine A. *Albania, Past and Present.* New York, 1919.

Chiara, P. *L'Albania.* Palermo, 1869.

Drizari, Nelo. *Albanian-English and English-Albanian Dictionary.* 2d enl. ed., with supplement of new words. New York, 1957.

Effendi, Wassa. *La vérité sur l'Albanie et les Albanais, étude historique et critique.* Paris, 1879.

Hahn, J. G. von. *Albanesische Studien.* Vienna, 1853-54. 2 vols.

Javanović, D. K. *O Arbanasima. Istorijska studija.* Belgrade, 1880.

Lambertz, Maximilian. *Gjergj Fishta und das albanische Heldenepos.* Tirana, 1949.

Legrand, Émile. *Bibliographie albanaise: description raisonnée des ouvrages pub. en albanais ou relatifs à l'Albanie du 15. siècle à l'année 1900.* Paris, 1912.

McClellan, Woodford D. *Svetozar Marković and the Origins of Balkan Socialism.* Princeton, 1969.

Mann, Stuart E. *An Historical Albanian-English Dictionary.* London, 1948.

Matl, J. ed. "Neuer Beitrag zur inneren Geschichte Südalbaniens in den 60-er Jahren des 19. Jhs.: Bericht des k.k. Consuls in Janina de dato 24 Juni 1868." *Südost-Forschungen* 16 (1957): 435-44.

Skendi, Stavro. "Beginnings of Albanian Nationalist Trends in Culture and Education (1878-1912)." *Journal of Central European Affairs* 12 (1953): 356-67.

――――. "Beginnings of Albanian Nationalist and Autonomous League, 1878-1881." *American Slavic and East European Review* 12 (1953): 219-32.

――――. "Albanian Political Thought and Revolutionary Activity, 1881-1912," *Südost-Forschungen* 13 (1954): 159-99.

――――. *The Albanian National Awakening, 1878-1912.* Princeton, 1967.

B. Bulgaria

Atanasov, Shteriu, *et al. Bulgarskoto voenno izkustvo prez kapitalizma.* Sofia, 1959.

Black, Cyril E. *The Establishment of Constitutional Government in Bulgaria.* Princeton, 1943.

Bulgarska akademiia na naukite. *Bulgarska entsiklopediia. Kratka bulgarska entsiklopediia.* Sofia, 1963– .

Bulgarska akademiia na naukite. *Tursko-bulgarski rechnik.* Sofia, 1952.

Butler, Thomas, ed. *Bulgaria, Past and Present.* Columbus, Ohio, 1976.

Cvetkova, Bistra. *Hajdutstvoto v blgarskite zemi prez 15–18 vek.* Sofia, 1971.

Derzhavin, Nikolai S. *Istoriia Bolgarii.* Moscow, 1945–48. 4 vols.

Giginov, T. *Istoricheski razvoi na suvremenna Bulgarii.* Sofia, 1934–35. 2 vols.

Gleichen, J. *The Armies of Europe.* London, 1890. See pp. 73–81.

Jerram, Charles S. *The Armies of the World.* London, 1899, pp. 31–32.

Jireček, C. *Geschichte der Bulgaren.* Prague, 1876.

Kinov, Ivan. *Kratka istoriia na voennoto izkustvo.* Sofia, 1960. 2 vols.

Kosev, Dimitur. "Otrazenieto na Krimskata voina (1853–1856) v Blgaria." *Istoričeski Pregled* (Sofia) 3 (1946–47): 183–99.

Kosev, Dimitur; Hristov, Hristo; and Angelov, Dimitur. *Kratka istoriia na Blgaria.* Sofia, 1969.

Mach, Richard von. *Die Wehrmacht der Türkei und Bulgariens*; Die Heere und Flotten der Gegenwart, pp. 67–98. Berlin, 1905.

Madol, Hans R. *Ferdinand of Bulgaria: The Dream of Byzantium.* London, 1933.

Mitev, Iano. "Za agrarniia prevrat u nas izversil se v rezultat ot osvoboditelnata voina prez 1877–1878 godine." *Istoričeski Pregled* (Sofia) 6 (1953): 638–56.

Petrovich, Michael B. "The Russian Image in Renaissance Bulgaria (1700–1878)." *East European Quarterly* 1 (1967): 87–105.

Pundeff, Marin V. *Bulgaria: A Bibliographic Guide.* Washington, D.C., 1965.

Radev, Simeon. *Stroitelite na suvremenna Bulgariia.* Sofia, 1911. 2 vols.

Rothschild, Joseph. *The Communist Party of Bulgaria: Origins and Development, 1883–1936.* New York, 1959.

Sakazov, Ivan. *Bulgarische Wirtschaftgeschichte.* Berlin, 1929.

Stephanove, Constantine. *Complete Bulgarian-English and English-Bulgarian Dictionary.* Sofia, 1929. 2 vols.

Stoichev, Ivan K. *Stroiteli i boini vozhdove na bulgarskata voiska, 1878–1941.* Sofia, 1941.

Stoyanov, Zakhari. *Zapiski o Bolgarskikh Vosstanyakh.* Moscow, 1950.

Todorov, Nikolai. *Filiki Eteria i Blgarite.* Sofia, 1965.

Radev, Simeon. *La Macédoine et la renaissance Bulgare au XIXᵉ siècle.* Sofia, 1918.

Zlatarski, Vasil N., and Stanev, N. *Geschichte der Bulgaren.* Leipzig, 1918. 2 vols.

C. Greece

Brown, Ann D., and Jones, Helen D. *Greece: A Selected List of References.* Washington, D.C., 1943.

Dontas, Donna M. *Greece and the Great Powers, 1863-1875.* Thessaloniki, 1966.

Goudas, A. *Bioi paralleloi.* Athens, 1869-76. 8 vols.

Heurtley, W. A., *et al. A Short History of Greece from Early Times to 1964.* New York, 1965.

Gleichen, J. *The Armies of Europe.* London, 1890, pp. 73-81.

Jerram, Charles S. *The Armies of the World.* London, 1899, pp. 184-86.

Kofos, Evangelos. *Greece and the Eastern Crisis, 1875-1878.* Thessaloniki, 1975.

Kykkōtēs, Hierotheos, *English-Greek and Greek-English Dictionary.* 2d ed. London, 1947.

Kyparissiotis, Niove. *The Modern Greek Collection in the Library of the University of Cincinnati: A Catalogue.* Athens, 1960.

Makriyannes, Ioannes. *The Memoirs of General Makiyannis, 1797-1864.* Oxford, 1966.

Megalē hellēnikē encyclopaideia, 2d ed. Athens, 1959-60. 24 vols.

Petropoulos, John A. *Politics and Statecraft in the Kingdom of Greece, 1833-1843.* Princeton, 1968.

Sergeant, Lewis. *Greece in the Nineteenth Century: A Record of Hellenic Emancipation and Progress, 1821-1897.* London, 1897.

Lamouche, Leon. *Les armées de la peninsule balkanique.* Paris, 1901.

D. Habsburg Empire

1. Reference Works

a. Bibliographies

Bakó, Elemér. *Guide to Hungarian Studies.* Stanford, 1973. 2 vols.

Boehm, Eric H. *Austrian Historical Bibliography.* Santa Barbara, Calif., 1965- (annual).

Čapek, Thomas, and Čapek, Anna V. *Bohemian (Čech) Bibliography: A Finding List of Writings in English Relating to Bohemia and the Čechs.* New York, 1918.

Kosáry, Domonkos G. *Bevezetés a magyar történelem forrásaiba és irodalmába.* Budapest, 1951-58. 3 vols.

Penjanović, Djordje. *Bosansko-Hercegovačka bibliografija.* Sarajevo, 1953.

Simonič, Franc. *Slovenska bibliografija. I. del. Knjige, 1500-1900.* Ljubljana, 1903-1905.

Ujević, Mate, ed. *Bibliografija rasprava, članaka i književnih radova.* Zagreb, 1956. 6 vols.

Valentinelli, Giuseppe. *Bibliografia della Dalmazia e del Montenegro.* Zagreb, 1855.

Uhlirz, Karl. *Handbuch der Geschichte Österreichs und seiner Nachbarländer Böhmen und Ungarn.* Graz, 1927-44. 4 vols.

Várdy, Steven Béla. *Modern Hungarian Historiography.* New York, 1976.

b. Dictionaries

Bogadek, Francis A. *New English-Croatian and Croatian-English Dictionary.* 3d enl. ed., New York, 1949. 2 vols.

Kotnik, Janko. *Slovene-English Dictionary.* 4th rev. ed. Ljubljana, 1959.

Országh, László. *Angol-magyar szótár. English-Hungarian Dictionary.* Budapest, 1960.

_____. *Magyar-angol szótár. Hungarian-English Dictionary.* 2d rev. ed. Budapest, 1963.

Procházka, Jindřich. *Slovník anglicko-český a česko-anglický . . . English-Czech and Czech-English Dictionary.* 16th rev. ed. Prague, 1959.

Škerlj, Ružena. *Angleško-slovenski slovar. English-Slovene Dictionary.* 5th ed. Ljubljana, 1960.

Vilikovská, Júlia; Vilikovský, Ján; and Šimko, Ján. *Slovensko-anglicky slovník.* Bratislava, 1959.

Vilikovský, Ján. *Anglicko-slovenský slovník.* Bratislava, 1964.

c. Encyclopedias

Brockhaus Enzyklopädie in zwanzig Bänden. 17th ed., 20 vols. Wiesbaden, 1969–75.

Československá vlastivěda. Prague, 1929–36. 10 vols.

Révai nagy lexikona; az ismeretek enciklopédiája. Budapest, 1911–35. 21 vols.

Stanojević, Stanoje, ed. *Narodna enciklopedija sprsko-hrvatsko-slovenačka.* Zagreb, 1925–29.

Slovenska vlastivěda. Bratislava, 1943–48. 5 vols.

Würzbach, Constant. *Biographisches Lexikon des Kaiserthums Österreich. . .* Vienna, 1856–90. 60 vols.

2. *General Histories*

Coxe, William. *History of the House of Austria.* 4th ed., 4 vols. London, 1895.

Hurter, Friedrich, *Geschichte Kaiser Ferdinand II und seiner Eltern.* Schaffhausen, 1850–54. 11 vols.

Jászi, Oscar. *The Dissolution of the Habsburg Monarchy.* Chicago, 1929.

Kann, Robert A. *The Multinational Empire: Nationalism and National Reform in the Habsburg Monarchy, 1848–1918.* 4th rev., enl. ed. 2 vols. New York. 1977.

_____. *The Habsburg Empire: A Study in Integration and Disintegration.* 2d rev. ed. New York, 1973.

_____. *A History of the Habsburg Empire, 1526–1918.* 2d rev. ed. Berkeley, 1977.

_____. *A Study in Austrian Intellectual History: From Late Baroque to Romanticism.* 2d ed. New York, 1973.

Macartney, C.A. *The Habsburg Empire, 1790–1918.* New York, 1969.

Mamatey, Victor S. *Rise of the Habsburg Empire, 1526-1815.* New York, 1971.

May, Arthur J. *The Habsburg Monarchy, 1867-1914.* Cambridge, Mass., 1951.

Redlich, Joseph. *Das österreichische Staats- und Reichsproblem: geschichtliche Darstellung das inneren Politik der Habsburgischen Monarchie von 1848 bis zum Untergang des Reiches.* Leipzig, 1920-26. 2 vols.

Spielman, John P. *Leopold I of Austria.* New Brunswick, N.J., 1977.

Steed, H. W. *The Habsburg Monarchy.* London, 1912.

Taylor, A.J.P. *The Habsburg Monarchy, 1809-1918.* London, 1967.

Winters, Stanley B., and Held, Joseph. *Intellectual and Social Developments in the Habsburg Empire from Maria Theresa to World War I.* Boulder, Colo., 1975.

Zwitter, Fran. *Les problèmes nationaux dans la monarchie des Habsbourg.* Belgrade, 1960.

3. *Austrian Empire*

Despalatović, Elinor M. *Ljudevit Gaj and the Illyrian Movement.* Boulder, Colo., 1975.

Gruber, Dane. *Stogodišnjica Napoleonove Ilirije, 1809-1909.* Zagreb, 1910.

Holbach, Maude M. *Bosnia and Herzegovina.* London, 1910.

Kerner, Robert J. *Bohemia in the Eighteenth Century: A Study in Political Economic and Social History.* New York, 1932.

Kimball, Stanley B. *Czech Nationalism: A Study of the National Theatre Movement, 1845-1883.* Urbana, Ill., 1964.

Klaić, V. *Geschichte Bosniens.* Leipzig, 1885.

Mandić, Dominik. *Bosna i Herzegovina.* Chicago-Rim, 1960-67. 3 vols.

Novak, Grga. *Prošlost Dalmacije.* Zagreb, 1944. 2 vols.

Paton, A. A. *Highlands and Islands of the Adriatic including Dalmatia, Croatia and the Southern Provinces of the Austrian Empire.* London, 1849. 2 vols.

Pisani, Paul. *La Dalmatie de 1797 à 1815.* Paris, 1893.

Preadovich, Nikolaus von. *Die Führungsgeschichten in Österreich und Preussen, 1804-1909.* Wiesbaden, 1955.

Rogel, Carole. *The Slovenes and Yugoslavism, 1890-1914.* Boulder, Colo., 1977.

Sugar, Peter F. *Industrialization of Bosnia-Hercegovina, 1878-1918.* Seattle, 1963.

Srbik, Heinrich. *Aus Österreichs Vergangenheit.* Salzburg, 1949.

Wiskemann, Elisabeth. *Czechs and Germans: A Study of the Struggle in the Historic Provinces of Bohemia and Moravia.* 2d ed. London, 1967.

Wright, William E. *Serf, Seigneur, and Sovereign: Agrarian Reform in Eighteenth-Century Bohemia.* Minneapolis, 1966.

Zöllner, Erich, *Geschichte Österreichs.* Vienna, 1966.

4. Kingdom of Hungary

Barany, George. *Stephen Széchenyi and the Awakening of Hungarian Nationalism, 1791-1841.* Princeton, 1969.

Capek, Thomas. *The Slovaks of Hungary.* New York, 1906.

Csaplovics, Johann von. *Slavonien und zum Theil Croatien.* Pest, 1819. 2 vols.

Eperjessy, Kálmán, *A bécsi hadilevéltár magyar vonatkozású térképeinek jegyzéke.* Szeged, 1929.

Erdélyi, Gyula. *A magyarok hadiszervezete és hadvezetési művészete ezer éven át.* Budapest, 1944.

Eternovich, Francis H., and Spalatin, Christopher, eds. *Croatia: Land, People, Culture.* Toronto, 1964. 2 vols.

Gruden, Josip. *Zgodovina slovenskega naroda.* Celje, 1910.

Hidas, Peter I. *The Metamorphosis of a Social Class in Hungary during the Reign of Young Franz Joseph.* Boulder, Colo., 1977.

Hóman, Bálint, and Szekfű, Gyula. *Magyar történet.* 7th ed., 5 vols. Budapest, 1941-43.

Király. Béla K. *Hungary in the Late Eighteenth Century: The Decline of Enlightened Despotism.* New York, 1969.

Krek, M. *Les Slovènes.* Paris, 1917.

Macartney, C. A. *Hungary: A Short History.* Chicago, 1962.

Marczali, Henry. *Hungary in the Eighteenth Century.* Cambridge, 1910.

Markó, Árpád. "Adalékok a magyar katonai nyelv fejlődéstörténetéhez." *Hadtörténelmi Közlemények* 14 (1967): 302-338; 688-711.

Miskolczy, Gyula, ed. *A horvát kérdés története és irományai a rendi állam korában.* Budapest, 1927-28. 2 vols.

Oddo, Gilbert L. *Slovakia and Its People.* New York, 1960.

Papp, Tibor. "A magyar honvédség megalakulása a kiegyezés után (1868-1890)." *Hadtörténelmi Közlemények* 14 (1967): 302-338, 688-711.

Preveden, Francis R. *A History of the Croatian People.* New York, 1955.

Prijatelj, Ivan. *Slovenska kulturnopolitična in slovstvena zgodovina 1848-1895.* Ljubljana, 1955-61. 4 vols.

Šišić, Ferdo. *Hrvatska povijest.* Zagreb, 1908-1913. 3 vols.

Srkulj, Stjepan. *Hrvatska povijest u devetnaest karata.* Zagreb, 1937.

Szana, Alexander. *Die Geschichte der Slowakei.* Bratislava, 1930-31. 2 vols.

5. The Armed Forces

Austria. War Archives. *Österreichs Kriege seit 1495.* Vienna, 1878.

Allmayer-Beck, Johann Ch. "Wandlungen im Heereswesen zur Zeit Maria Theresias." *Schriften des Heeresgeschichtlichen Museums in Wien* 4 (1967): 1-24.

Panzer, Alfonz. *Unter den Fahnen: Die Völker Österreich-Ungarns in Waffen.* Vienna, 1889.

Duffy, Christopher. *The Army of Maria Theresa.* New York, 1977.

Fenner von Fenneberg, Daniel. *Österreich und seine Armee.* Leipzig, 1846.

Cook, M. S. *The Armed Strength of Austria.* London, 1874. 2 vols.

Gatti, Friedrich, *Geschichte der k.u.k. technischen Militärakademie.* Vienna, 1905.

Great Britain. War Ministry. *Accounts of the Systems of Military Education in France, Prussia, Austria, Bavaria and the United States.* London, 1870, pp. 347–97.

Heischmann, Eugen. *Die Anfänge des stehenden Heeres in Österreich.* Vienna, 1925.

Jerram, Charles S. *The Armies of the World.* London, 1899, pp. 1–25.

Lautha, Jules M. *L'état militaire des principales puissances étrangères en 1900.* Paris, 1900, pp. 155–271.

Leverson, J. J. *Handbook of the Military Forces of Austria-Hungary.* London, 1891.

McClellan, G. B. *The Armies of Europe.* Philadelphia, 1862, pp. 314–39.

McKay, Derek. *Prince Eugene of Savoy.* London, 1977.

Meynert, Hermann. *Geschichte des Kriegeswesens und der Heeresverfassung in den verschiedenen Länder der Österreichischen Monarchie.* Vienna, 1852–54. 3 vols.

———. *Das Kriegswesen der Ungarn.* Vienna, 1876.

———. *Leitfaden der Geschichte des österr.-ung. Kriegswesens.* Vienna, 1896.

Patera, Herbert. *Unter Österreichs Fahnen.* Graz, 1960.

Petrossi, Ferdinand. *Das Heerwesen des österreichischen Kaiserstaates.* Vienna, 1865. 2 vols.

Poten, B. *Geschichte des Militär-Erziehungs- und Bildungswesen in Österreich-Ungarn.* Berlin, 1893.

Regele, Oskar. *Feldzeugmeister Benedek.* Vienna, 1960.

———. *Feldmarschall Radetzky.* Vienna-Munich, 1957.

Rothenberg, Günther E. "The Habsburg Army and the Nationality Problem in the Nineteenth Century, 1815–1914." *Austrian History Yearbook* 3 (1967).

———. "Towards a National Hungarian Army: The Military Compromise of 1868 and Its Consequences." *Slavic Review* 31 (1972): 805–816.

———. *The Army of Francis Joseph.* West Lafayette, Ind., 1976.

Schmidt-Brentano, Antonio. *Die Armee in Österreich: Militär, Staat und Gesellschaft 1848–1867.* Militärgeschichtliche Studien, vol. 20. Militärgeschichtliches Forschungsamt. Boppard am Rhein, 1975.

Schmid, Hugo. *Heereswesen.* 3d ed. Vienna, 1915.

Sokol, Anthony E. *The Imperial and Royal Austro-Hungarian Navy.* Annapolis, 1968.

Teuber, Oscar, and Ottenfeld, Rudolf. *Die österreichische Armee, 1700–1867.* Vienna, 1900.

U.S. War Department. Adjutant General's Office. *Staff of Various Armies.* Washington, D.C., 1899, pp. 15–40.

Wagner, Walter. *Geschichte des k.k. Kriegsministeriums, 1848–1888.* Graz, 1966–71. 2 vols.

Wrede. Alphons von. *Geschichte der k. und k. Wehrmacht.* Vienna, 1898–1908. 5 vols.

Zimmermann, Jürg. *Militärverwaltung und Heeresaufbringung in Österreich bis 1806.* Frankfurt am Main, 1965.

6. The Military Borders

Amstadt, Jakob. *Die k.k. Militärgrenze, 1522–1881.* Würzburg, 1969. 2 vols.

Benigni, J. H. Elder von Mildenberg. *Pragmatische Geschichte der siebenbürgischen Militärgrenze.* Vienna, 1811–12. 2 vols.

Bernath, Mathias. "Die Errichtung der siebenbürgischen Militärgrenze und die Wiener Rumänenpolitik in der frühjosephinischen Zeit." *Südostforschungen* 19 (1960): 164–92.

Bogdanov, Vaso. "Uloga Vojne Krajine i njenih zastupnika u hrvatskom Saboru 1861." *Zbornik Historijskog Instituta Jugoslavenske Akademije* (Zagreb) 3 (1960): 69–214.

Boppe, P. *La Croatie Militaire, 1809–1813.* Paris, 1900.

Demian, J. A. *Statistische Beschreibung der Militär-Grenze.* Vienna, 1806–1807. 2 vols.

Fras, Franz J. *Merkwürdigkeiten oder historisch-statistisch-topographische Beschreibung der Karlstädter-Militär-Grenze.* Karlovac, 1830.

Göllner, Carol. *Regimentele grănicereşti din Transilvania, 1764–1851.* Bucharest, 1973.

_____. *Die siebenbürgische Militärgrenze.* Buchreihe der Süddeutschen Historischen Kommission, vol. 28. Munich, 1974.

Gürtler, Ilse. "Die Auflösung der siebenbürgischen Militärgrenze." Ph.D. dissertation, University of Vienna, 1947.

Hietzinger, Carl Freiherr von. *Statistik der Militärgrenze des österreichischen Kaiserthums.* Vienna, 1817–23. 3 vols.

Die k.k. Militärgrenze: Beiträge zu Ihrer Geschichte. Schriften des heeresgeschichtlichen Museums in Wien, vol. 6. Vienna, 1973.

Lopašić, Radoslav, ed. *Acta historiam confinii militaria Croatici illustrantia (Spomenici Hrvatske, Kraine).* Monumenta spectantia historiam slavorum medionalium, vol. 15–17. Zagreb, 1884–89.

Rothenberg, Gunther E. *The Austrian Military Border in Croatia, 1522–1747.* Urbana, Ill., 1960.

_____. *The Military Border in Croatia, 1740–1881.* Chicago, 1966.

_____. "The Origins of the Austrian Military Frontier in Croatia and the Alleged Treaty of 22 December 1522," *Slavonic and East European Review* 38 (1960): 493–98.

_____. "The Croatian Military Border and the Rise of Yugoslav Nationalism." *Slavonic and East European Review* 43 (1964): 35–36.

Schulze, W. "Die österreichische Militärgrenze." *Militärgeschichtliche Mitteilungen* 9 (1971): 190–92.

Schweicker, Johann H. *Geschichte der österr. Militärgrenze.* Vienna, 1883.

_____. "Zur Geschichte der kirchlichen Union in der kroatischen Militärgrenze." *Archiv für österreichische Geschichte* 52 (1975): 275–400.

Stopfer, Mathias. *Erläuterungen der Grundgesetze für die Carlstädter, Waras-diner, Banat, slavonische and banatische Militär-Grenze.* Vienna, 1831.

Sučević, Branko P. "Razvitak 'vlaških prava' u Varaždinskom generalatu." *Historijski Zbornik* 6 (1953): 35–70.

Szádeczky, Lajos J. *A székely határőrség szervezése 1752–64-ben.* Budapest, 1908.

Turković, Milan. *Geschichte der ehemaligen croatisch-slavonischen Militär-Grenze.* Sušak, 1936.

Utjesenović, Mathias O. *Die Militär-Grenze und die Verfassung; eine Studie über den Ursprung und das Wesen der Militärgrenz Institution und die Stellung derselben zur Landesverfassung.* Vienna, 1861.

Vaniček, Franz. *Specialgeschichte der Militärgrenze.* Vienna, 1915. 4 vols.

Vucinich, Wayne S. "Jelačić and the Frontier in Modern History," *Austrian History Yearbook* 1 (1963): 68–72.

Wessely, Kurt. "The Development of the Hungarian Military Frontier until the Middle of the Eighteenth Century." *Austrian History Yearbook* 9–10 (1973–1974): 74–75.

————. "Supplementarbibliographie zur österreichischen Militärgrenze." *Österreichische Osthefte* 16 (1974): 280–328.

E. Montenegro

Dragović, M. *Crnogorski mitropolit Vasilije Petrović Njegoś ili istorija Crne Gore od 1750 do 1766 godine.* Cetinje, 1884.

Gleichen, J. *The Armies of Europe.* London, 1890, pp. 73–81.

Jerram, Charles S. *The Armies of the World.* London, 1899, p. 208.

Jovanović, Jagoš. *Stvaranje crnogorske države i razvoj crnogorske national-nosti: istorija Crne Gore od početka VIII vijeka do 1918 godine.* Cetinje, 1947.

Lamouche, Leon. *Les armées de la péninsule balkanique.* Paris, 1901.

Medaković, V.M.G. *Vladika Danilo Petrović Njegoš.* Belgrade, 1896.

Popović, Dušan J. *Istorija Crne Gore.* Belgrade, 1896.

Soć, Pero D. *Cgled bibliografije o Crnoj Gori na stranim jezicima.* Belgrade, 1948.

Wilkinson, Sir J. G. *Dalmatia and Montenegro.* London, 1898. 2 vols.

F. Poland

Askenazy, Szymon. *Napoléon et la Pologne.* Paris, 1925.

Baranovič, A. I. *Magackoe xozjajstovo na Juge Volyni v XVIII v.* Moscow, 1955.

Bieganski, Witold, *et al.,* eds. *Histoire militaire de la Pologne: problèmes choisis.* Warsaw, 1970.

Biernacka, Maria. *Wsie drobnoszlacheckie na Mazowszu i Podlasiu.* Wrocław, 1966.

Brüchner, A. *Dzieje kultury polskiej.* Cracow, 1931.

Bystroń, J. *Dzieje obyczajów w dawnej Polsce.* Warsaw, 1960. 2 vols.

Estreicher, Karol J. T. *Bibliografia polska*. Cracow, 1870–1939 (1951). 34 vols.
_____. *Bibliografia polsca 19. stulecia lata 1881–1900*. Cracow, 1906–1916.
4 vols.
Fabre, Jean. *Stanislas-Auguste Poniatowski et l'Europe des lumières*. Paris, 1952.
Frankel, Henryk. *Poland: The Struggle for Power, 1772–1939*. London, 1946.
Gardner, Monica. *Kościuszko: A Biography*. 2d rev. ed. London, 1942.
Górski, K. *Historia artylerii polskiej*. Cracow, 1902.
Kaplan, Herbert H. *The First Partition of Poland*. New York, 1962.
Kiersnowski, A. *Historia rozwoju artylerii*. Toruń, 1925.
Kierst, W. *Słownik angielsko-polski i polski-angielski*. Warsaw, 1926–28.
2 vols.
Konopczyński, Władysław. *Le Liberum veto: étude sur le développement du principe majoritaire*. Paris, 1930.
_____. *Fryderyk Wielki a Polska*. Poznań, 1947.
Korzon, T. *Dzieje wojen i wojskowości w Polsce: epoka przedrozbiorowa*. Lwów, 1923. 3 vols.
Kościuszko, Tadeusz. *Les manœuvres de l'artillerie montée*. Paris, 1800.
Kuikel, Marian. *Czartoryski and European Unity, 1770–1861*. Princeton, 1955.
_____. *Zarys historji wojskwej w Polsce*. Cracow, 1929.
Lech, M. J. "Autorament cudzoziemski wojsk Wielkiego Ksiestwa Litewskiego w dobie saskiej." *Studia i Materiały do Historii Wojskowści* 7 (1961): 91–112.
Lewanski, Richard C. *Guide to Polish Libraries and Archives*. Boulder, Colo., 1974.
Lord, Robert H. *The Second Partition of Poland: A Study of Diplomatic History*. Cambridge, Mass., 1915.
_____. "The Third Partition of Poland." *The Slavic and East European Review* 3 (1925): 481–98.
Łozinski, W. *Życie polskie w dawnych wiekach*. Cracow, 1964.
Miller, I. S., *et al.*, eds. *Ocherki revolutsionnykh sviazei narodov Rossi i Polshi, 1815–1917*. Moscow, 1976.
Orgelbrand, Samuel. *S. Orgelbranda Encyklopedja powszechna z ilustracjami i mapami*. Warsaw, 1898–1912. 18 vols.
Poland. Military Historical Institute. *Military Technique Policy and Strategy in History*. Warsaw, 1976.
Ratajczyk, Leonard. "A Contribution to the Question of Enlistment and Conscription of Recruits in the Polish Lands in the 18th Century." *Studia i Materiały do Historii Wojskowości* 15 (1969): 61–72.
Reddaway, W. F., *et al. The Cambridge History of Poland: From August II to Piłsudski (1697–1935)*. Cambridge, 1950–51. 2 vols.
Rose, William J. *The Rise of Polish Democracy*. London, 1944.
Serczyk, W. A. *Gospodarstwo magnackie w województwie podolskim w drugiej połowie XVIII wieku*. Wrocław, 1965.
Starczewski, E. *Możnowładstwo polskie na tle dziejów*. Kiev, 1916. 2 vols.

Stone, Daniel. *Polish Politics and National Reform, 1775-1788.* Boulder, Colo., 1976.

Tobias, M. *Szlachta i możnowładstwo w dawnej Polsce.* Cracow, 1946.

Towarzystvo Wiedzy Wojskowej. *Encyklopedja wojskowa.* Warsaw, 1930-39. 7 vols.

Wandycz, Piotr S. *The Lands of Partitioned Poland, 1795-1919.* Seattle-London, 1974.

Wasicki, Jan. *Konfederacja targowicka.* Warsaw, 1952.

Wimmer, J. *Wojska RP w dobie wojny północnej.* Warsaw, 1956.

Wolánski, Adam. *Wojna polskorosyjska 1792 r kampania korona.* Cracow, 1920.

Zajaczkowski, A. "En Pologne: Cadres structurels de la noblesse 1500-1800." *Annales* 18 (1963): 88-102.

————. *Hauptelemente der Adelsstruktur in Polen.* Marburg-Lahn, 1967.

G. Romania

Adrian, Gheorghe. *Idee răpede despre resbelul de partizani.* Brussels, 1855.

Anastasiu, I. *Oastea română de-a lungul veacurilor.* Bucharest, 1933.

Arbore, Zamfir C. *Basarabia în secolul XIX.* Bucharest, 1898.

Berindei, Dan. *Epoca Unirii.* Bucharest, 1978.

————. *L'Union des principautés romaines.* Bucharest, 1966.

————. *Nicolae Bălcescu.* Bucharest, 1964.

Bianu, Ioan. *Catalogul manuscriptelor Românești.* Bucharest, 1907-1913. 2 vols.

Bianu, Ioan; Hodos, Nerva; and Simonescu, Dan. *Bibliografia românescă veche, 1508-1830.* Bucharest, 1903-1943. 4 vols.

Boicu, L. *Geneza "chestiunii românești" ca problemă internaționala.* Iași, 1975.

Gallwell, C. E. *The Armed Strength of Roumania.* London, 1888.

Center for Military History and Theory Studies and Research. *Pages from the History of the Romanian Army,* Bibliotheca Historica Romaniae, vol. 15. Bucharest, 1975.

Centrul de Studii și Cercetări de Istorie și Teorie Militară. *Documente privind istoria militară a poporului român, 1878-1882.* Bucharest, 1974-75. 3 vols.

Colson, Felix. *De l'état présent et de l'avenir des principautés de Moldavie et de Valachie.* Paris, 1839.

Diculescu, V. "Rumänien und die Frage der bulgarischen Freischaren (1866-1868)." *Révue des études sud-est européennes* 1 (1963): 463-83.

East, William G. *The Union of Moldavia and Wallachia, 1859.* Cambridge, 1929.

Enciclopedia româniei. Bucharest, 1938-43. 4 vols.

Fischer-Galati, Stephen A. *Rumania: A Bibliographic Guide.* Washington, D.C., 1963.

Filitti, Ioan C. *Principatele Române de la 1828 la 1834. Ocupația rusească și Regulamentul Organic.* Bucharest, 1934.

Georgescu, Vlad. *Political Ideas and the Enlightenment in the Rumanian*

Principalities, 1750-1831. Boulder, Colo., 1971.

Giurescu, Constantin C. *Principatele române le începutul secolului al XIX-lea.* Bucharest, 1957.

_____. *Vița și opera lui Cuza Vodă.* Bucharest, 1966.

Gleichen, J. *The Armies of Europe.* London, 1890, pp. 73-81.

Henry, Paul. *L'Abdication du Prince Cuza et l'avénement de la dynastie de Hohenzollern au trône en Roumanie.* Paris, 1930.

Hitchins, Keith. *The Rumanian National Movement in Transylvania, 1780-1849.* Cambridge, Mass., 1969.

_____. *Orthodoxy and Nationality: Andreiu Saguna and the Romanians of Transylvania.* Harvard Historical Series, 94. Cambridge, Mass., 1977.

Iorga, Nicolae. *Geschichte des rumänischen Volkes.* Gotha, 1905. 2 vols.

_____. *Istoria armatei românești.* Bucharest, 1930. 2 vols.

_____. *Histoire des Roumaines et de la Romanite Orientale,* 11 vols. Bucharest, 1937-45, vol. 9-11.

Jerram, Charles S. *The Armies of the World.* London, 1899, pp. 219-20.

Lamouche, Leon. *Les armées de la péninsule balkanique.* Paris, 1901.

Lauth, Jules M. *L'État militaire des principales puissances étrangères en 1900.* Paris, 1900, pp. 541-74.

Maciu, Vasile. *Mouvements nationaux et sociaux roumains au XIXieme siècle.* Bucharest, 1971.

Marsillac, Ulysse de. *Histoire de l'armée roumaine.* Bucharest, 1871.

Neculce, Ion. *Letopisetul Țării Moldovei.* Bucharest, 1955.

Nădejde, Ion. *Centenarul armetei Române.* Bucharest, 1930.

Olteanu, Constantin, and Ceausescu, Ilie. *The Rumanian Army in the War for Rumania's State Independence, 1877-1878.* New Dehli, 1977.

Otetea, Andrei, et al. *Istoria Rominiei.* Bucharest, 1964. 3 vols.

Pascu, Ștefan, ed. *The Independence of Rumania.* Bucharest, 1978.

Prokopowitsch, Erich. *Die rumänische Nationalbewegung in der Bukowina und der Dako-Romanismus.* Graz, 1965.

Riker, Thad W. *The Making of Roumania: A Study of an International Problem, 1856-1866.* London, 1931.

Roberts, Henry L. *Rumania: Political Problems of an Agrarian State.* Hamden, Ct., 1969.

Romanescu, G. *Oastea română de-a lungul veacurilor.* Bucharest, 1976.

Savu, A. H. *Aus der Geschichte der rumänischen Armee.* Bucharest, 1978.

Schellendorff, Bronsart von. *The Duties of the General Staff.* 4th ed. Translated from the German by the British War Office. London, 1905, pp. 117-22.

Schonkron, Marcel. *Rumanian-English and English-Rumanian Dictionary.* New York, 1952. 2 vols.

Seton-Watson, Robert W. *A History of the Roumanians from Roman Times to the Completion of Unity.* Cambridge, 1934.

Tóth, Zoltán. *Az erdélyi román nacionalizmus első százada 1697-1792.* Budapest, 1946.

Vasiliu-Năsturel, P. *Istoria artileriei române.* Bucharest, 1897.

H. Russia and the Ukraine

1. *Reference Works*

Andrusyshen, C. H., and Krett, J. M. *Ukrainśko-anhliiśkyi slovnyk. Ukrainian-English Dictionary.* Toronto, 1957.

Fessenko, Tatiana. *Eighteenth Century Russian Publications in the Library of Congress.* Washington, D.C., 1961.

Florinsky, Michael T. *McGraw-Hill Encyclopedia of Russia and the Soviet Union.* New York, 1961.

Horecky, Paul L. *Basic Russian Publications: An Annotated Bibliography on Russia and the Soviet Union.* Chicago, 1962.

Kubijoryc, Volodymyr, ed. *Ukraine: A Concise Encyclopedia.* Toronto, 1963. 2 vols.

Prokhorov, M., *et al.,* eds. *Great Soviet Encyclopedia.* 3d ed., translated from the Russian. New York, 1973– 19 vols.

Wedel, E., and Romanov, A. *Langenscheidt's Russian-English, English-Russian Dictionary.* 2d ed. London, 1964.

U.S. Library of Congress. Reference Department. *Russia: A Check List Preliminary to a Basic Bibliography of Materials in the Russian Languages.* Part 1–10. Washington, D.C., 1944–46.

U.S. Library of Congress. *Cyrillic Union Catalog.* New York, 1963. (Micro-opaque, 1244 cards).

Vernadsky, George, *et al.,* eds. *A Source Book for Russian History from Early Times to 1917.* New Haven, Ct., 1972. 3 vols.

2. *General Histories*

Allen, W.E.D. *The Ukraine: A History.* Cambridge, 1941.

Haxthausen, August Baron von. *The Russian Empire.* 1856. Reprint. London, 1968.

Hrushevsky, Michael. *A History of Ukraine.* New Haven, 1941.

Jewsbury, George F. *The Russian Annexation of Bessarabia, 1774–1828.* Boulder, Colo., 1976.

Petrovich, Michael M. *The Emergence of Russian Panslavism, 1850–1870.* New York, 1956.

Soloveytchik, George. *Potemkin.* New York, 1947.

Sumner, B. H. *Peter the Great and the Ottoman Empire.* Oxford, 1949.

3. *The Armed Forces*

Almedingen, E. M. *The Emperor Alexander II.* London, 1962.

Austria-Hungary. Ministry of War. *The Armed Strength of Russia.* Translated from the German by the British War Office. London, 1873.

——. *Die russische Armee im Felde.* Vienna, 1888.

Bujac, E. *L'Armée Russe: son histoire, son organisation actuelle.* Paris, 1894.

Curtis, John. *The Russian Army under Nicholas I, 1825–1855.* Durham, N.C. 1965.

Drygalski, Albert von. *Die Organisation der russischen Armee.* Leipzig, 1902.

Grierson, J. M. *Handbook of the Military Forces of Russia.* London, 1894.

Jerram, Charles S. *The Armies of the World.* London, 1899, pp. 221–72.

Lauth, Jules M. *L'État militaire des principales puissances étrangères en 1900.* Paris, 1900, 575–680.

Lyons, M. *The Russian Imperial Army: A Bibliography of Regimental and Related Works.* Stanford, 1968.

McClellan, G. B. *The Armies of Europe.* Philadelphia, 1862, pp. 85–294.

Miller, Forrestt A. *Miliutin and the Reform Era in Russia.* Nashville, Tenn., 1968.

Murray, Wolfe J. *Handbook of the Russian Army.* London, 1889.

Palmer, Alan. *Alexander I Tsar of War and Peace.* New York, 1974.

Rediger, A. *Komplektovanie i ustroystvo vooruzhennoy sili.* 2d ed. St. Petersburg, 1892–94. 2 vols.

Schellendorff, Bronsart von. *The Duties of the General Staff.* 4th ed. London, 1905, pp. 81–98.

Weil, Capitaine. *Les Forces militaires de la Russie.* Paris, 1880. 2 vols.

Wilson, Sir Robert. *Brief Remarks on the Character and Composition of the Russian Army.* London, 1810.

Windrow, Martin; Seaton, Albert; and Youens, Michael. *The Russian Army of the Napoleonic Wars.* New York, 1973.

Zaionchkovskii, Petr A. *Voennye reformy 1860–1870 godov v Rossii.* Moscow, 1952.

4. *The Cossacks*

Bogdanovich, Modest I. *Istoricheskii ocherk deitel'nosti voennago upravleniia v Rossii v pervoe dvadtsati-piatiletie blagopoluchnago tsarstvovannia gosudaria imperatora Aleksandra Nikolaevicha (1855–1880).* St. Petersburg, 1879–81. 6 vols.

Gresson, W. P. *The Cossacks: Their History and Country.* New York, 1919.

Czaplicka, M. A. *Evolution of the Cossack Communities.* London, 1918.

Erckert, R. von. *Der Ursprung der Kosaken.* Berlin, 1882.

Golobutski, V. A. *Chernomorskoye kazachestvo.* Kiev, 1956.

———. *Zaporozhskoye kazachestvo.* Kiev, 1957.

Karpov, A. B. *Uraltsy: istoricheski ocherk.* Uralsk, 1911.

Khoroshkhin, M. *Kazachi voiska: opyt' voenno-statisticheskago opisaniia.* St. Petersburg, 1881.

Levshin, A. K. *Istoricheskoe i statisticheskoe obozrenie ural'skikh kazakov.* St. Petersburg, 1823.

Lishin, A. A. *Akty otnosiashchiesia k istorii voiska donskogo.* Novocherkassk, 1891. Nos. 21, 24, 25.

Longworth, Philip. *The Cossacks: Five Centuries of Turbulent Life on the Russian Steppes.* New York, 1970.

Lyall, Robert. *Travels in Russia, the Crimea, the Caucasus and Georgia.* London, 1825.

Miller, Forrest A. *Dimitrii Miliutin and the Reform Era in Russia.* Nashville, Tenn., 1968.

Niessel, H. A. *Les Cosaques.* Paris, 1899.

Oliphant, Laurence. *The Russian Shores of the Black Sea.* 3d ed. London, 1854.

Pallas, Peter S. *Travels through the Southern Provinces of the Russian Empire in the Years 1793 and 1794.* London, 1802.

Pipes, Richard E. "The Russian Military Colonies." *Journal of Modern History* 22 (1950): 205–219.

Rozner, I. G. *Yaik pered burei.* Moscow, 1966.

Stökl, Günter. *Die Entstehung des Kossakentums.* Veröffentlichungen des Osteuropa-Instituts München, vol. 3. Munich, 1953.

Svatikov, Sergei G. *Rossiia i Don.* Vienna, 1924.

Wagner, Moritz. *Travels in Persia, Georgia and Koordistan: with Sketches of the Cossacks and the Caucasus.* London, 1856.

Zasedateleva, L. B. *Terskie kazaki (seredina XVI-nachalo XX v.): istoriko-etnograficheskie ocherki.* Moscow, 1974.

I. Serbia

Coquelle, P. *Le Royaume de Serbie.* Paris, 1894.

Čubrilović, Vaso. *Istorija političke misli u Srbij XIX veka.* Belgrade, 1958.

Djordjević, Dimitrije. "The Echo of the 1866 Cretan Uprising in Serbia," *Papers Presented at the International Symposium at Crete, 1971,* pp. 94–109. Athens, 1975.

Drvodelić, Milan. *Englesko-hrvatsko-srpski rječnik. English-Croato-Serbian Dictionary.* Zagreb, 1962.

Edwards, Lovett P., ed. *Memoirs of Prota Matija Nenadovic.* Oxford, 1969.

Gleichen, J. *The Armies of Europe.* London, 1890, pp. 73–81.

Grgur Jakšić-Vojislav Vučković. *Spoljna politika Srbije za vlade kneza Mihaila, Prvi Balkanski Savez.* Belgrade, 1963.

Hehn, Paul. "The Origins of Modern Pan-Serbism: The 1844 Nacertanie of Ilija Garasanin." *East European Quarterly* 9 (1975): 153–71.

Jovanović, Slobodan. *Sabrana dela.* Belgrade, 1932–40. 17 vols.

Jelavich, Charles. "Serbian Nationalism and the Question of Union with Croatia in the 19th Century." *Balkan Studies* (Thessaloniki) 3 (1962): 29–42.

Jerram, Charles S. *The Armies of the World.* London, 1899, pp. 273–74.

Jireček, Konstantin, and Radonić, Jovan. *Istorija Srba.* Belgrade, 1922–23. 4 vols.

Kanitz, F. *Das Königreich Serbien.* Leipzig, 1904–1909. 2 vols.

Krleža, Miroslav, chief ed. *Enciklopedija Jugoslavije.* Zagreb, 1955– 8 vols.

Lamouch, Leon. *Les Armées de la péninsule balkanique.* Paris, 1901.

MacKenzie, David. *The Serbs and Russian Pan-Slavism, 1875-1878.* Ithaca, N.Y., 1967.

Petrovich, Michael B. *A History of Modern Serbia, 1804-1918.* New York, 1976. 2 vols.

Popović, Dušan J. *Srbija i Beograd od Požarevačkog do Beogradskog mira, 1718-1739.* Belgrade, 1950.

_____. *Srbi u Vojvodini.* Novi Sad, 1957-63. 3 vols.

Ranke, Leopold von. *History of Servia.* London, 1853.

Reiswitz, J. Albert von. *Belgrad-Berlin, Berlin-Belgrad, 1866-1871.* Munich, 1936.

Šišić, Ferdinand. *Jugoslovenska misao: istorija ideje jugoslovenskog narodnog ujedinjenja i oslobodenja od, 1790-1918.* Belgrade, 1937.

Stojančević, Vladimir. *Knez Miloš i Istočna Srbija.* Belgrade, 1957.

Stokes, Gale. *Legitimacy through Liberalism, Vladimir Jovanović and the Transformation of Serbian Politics.* Seattle, 1975.

Temperley, Harold W. V. *History of Serbia.* London, 1917.

Vučković, Vojislav. *Politička akcija Srbije u južnoslovenskim pokrajinama Habsburške monarhije 1859-1874.* Belgrade, 1965.

Wedel, Hermann. *Bismarck und Serbien im Jahre, 1866.* Berlin, 1927.

Contributors

Dr. László Alföldi, Assistant Archivist, US Army Military History Institute, Carlisle Barracks, Pennsylvania. Associate Bibliographer.

Dr. Dan Berindei, Chief, Department, N. Iorga Institute of History, Bucharest, Romania.

Dr. Constantin Căzănişteanu, Colonel, and Professor of History, Military History Institute, Bucharest, Romania.

Dr. Ilie Ceauşescu, Major General and Professor of Military History, Military Academy, Bucharest, Romania.

Dr. Norman Davies, Chairman, Department of History, University of London, School of Slavonic and East European Studies.

Dr. László Deme, Professor of History, Chairman Division of Social Sciences, New College of the University of South Florida, Sarasota, Florida.

Dr. Dimitrije Djordjevic, Professor of History, University of California, Santa Barbara, California.

Dr. Stephen Fischer-Galati, Professor of History, University of Colorado, Boulder, Colorado.

Dr. Charles W. Ingrao, Assistant Professor of History, Purdue University, West Lafayette, Indiana.

Dr. Robert A. Kann, Professor Emeritus, Rutgers University, and Professor of History, University of Vienna.

Dr. Béla K. Király, Professor of History, Brooklyn College and the Graduate School, CUNY, Editor. Principal Investigator of research group funded by NEH grant.

Dr. Zoltán Kramár, Professor of History and Dean of the School of Arts and Humanities, Central Washington University, Ellensburg, Washington.

Dr. Avigdor Levy, Associate Professor of Near Eastern Studies, Philip W. Lown School of Near Eastern and Judaic Studies, Brandeis University, Massachusetts.

Dr. Philip Longworth, Tutor and Consultant in East European History, The Open University, London. Visiting Professor, McGill University, Montreal, Canada.

Dr. Robert H. McNeal, Professor of History, University of Massachusetts, Amherst.

Dr. Gunther E. Rothenberg, Professor of History, Purdue University, Co-editor. Associate Researcher of the group funded by NEH grant.

Dr. Irwin Taylor Sanders, Professor of Sociology, Boston University, Boston.

Dr. Nathan Schmukler, Professor of Economics, Dean, School of Social Science, Brooklyn College, CUNY.

Dr. George Simor, Assistant Professor of Library Science, Acquisition Librarian, Graduate School and University Center, CUNY, New York. Bibliographer.

Dr. Peter F. Sugar, Professor of History and Chairman Russia and East European Area Program, The School of International Studies, University of Washington, Seattle.

Dr. Aladár Urbán, Professor of History, Eötvös Loránd University, Budapest, Hungary.

Dr. Wayne S. Vucinich, Robert and Florence McDonnell Professor of East European History, Director Center for Russian and East European Studies, Stanford University, California.